A Gustave Flaubert Encyclopedia

A Gustave Flaubert Encyclopedia

Edited by
LAURENCE M. PORTER

Greenwood Press
Westport, Connecticut • London

Library of Congress Cataloging-in-Publication Data

A Gustave Flaubert encyclopedia / edited by Laurence M. Porter.
p. cm.
Includes bibliographical references and index.
ISBN 0–313–30744–X (alk. paper)
1. Flaubert, Gustave, 1821–1880—Encyclopedias. I. Porter, Laurence M., 1936–
PQ2249.G85 2001
843'.8—dc21 00–042223

British Library Cataloguing in Publication Data is available.

Library of Congress Catalog Card Number: 00–042223
ISBN: 0–313–30744–X

First published in 2001

Greenwood Press, 88 Post Road West, Westport, CT 06881
An imprint of Greenwood Publishing Group, Inc.
www.greenwood.com

Printed in the United States of America

The paper used in this book complies with the
Permanent Paper Standard issued by the National
Information Standards Organization (Z39.48–1984).

10 9 8 7 6 5 4 3 2 1

CONTENTS

PREFACE

The most famous novelist of nineteenth-century France, Gustave Flaubert inspired not only the realists and naturalists who followed him in France, the rest of Europe, the United Kingdom, Russia, and the Western Hemisphere, but also the experimental writers of modernism and postmodernism who followed. Like Faulkner's novels nearly a century later, Flaubert's fiction set the standard to which other writers turned to learn their craft. He lived his art like a religion. His cult of art and his unrelenting search for stylistic perfection were a model and inspiration for many later writers: Leopoldo Alas, Guy de Maupassant, Giovanni Verga, Joseph Conrad, and James Joyce, among others. Thematically, his denunciation of materialistic, corrupt society, his fascination with altered states of consciousness, his oscillation between metaphysical longings and a radical nihilism, and his deep-seated mistrust of the adequacy of words themselves continue to resonate with many of our contemporaries.

In the United States and the United Kingdom, more nineteenth-century French scholars devote themselves to Flaubert than to any other author. A recent issue of *Nineteenth-Century French Studies* (28.1–2, Fall–Winter 1999–2000), for example, reproduces the abstracts for every article published there since the journal's inception in 1972. It devotes fourteen of 169 pages (one-twelfth of the total) to Flaubert, and only eleven to Honoré de Balzac, ten each to Charles Baudelaire and Emile Zola, nine to Stendhal, seven to George Sand, and six to Victor Hugo. Flaubert's keen awareness of the subconscious and preconscious mind has made his work a fertile terrain for psychological investigation. His androgynous sensibility provides much material for feminist, gender, and queer studies; his laborious craftsmanship and multiple plans and drafts of his work provide rich material for genetic criticism—the study of how a literary work comes into being and evolves in the imagination of its author. In other words, his interests correspond with nearly all the most fashionable preoccupations of recent criticism other than postcolonial studies. *Madame Bovary* itself is a standard for programs in comparative literature and English as well as in French, and "Un cœur simple" is widely read in introductory courses in French literature.

The major issue facing any editor of an encyclopedia is choosing what to include. We have centered our contents on Flaubert's literary works, their sources, and their influence. Experienced scholars treat all his major works at some length in this volume, and our encyclopedia mentions nearly every unpublished project of his that has a title. Some of Flaubert's chief "homes and haunts" are described here, as are a few salient contemporary events. A few well-known critics are listed, and a few critical approaches are discussed. We have not, however, included an entry for every fictional character in Flaubert's works—only those that appear in several scenes or feature prominently in at least one major scene. Nor have we by any means included every writer who influenced him or whom he influenced, despite our contributors' conscientious effort to take into account the most recent discoveries of Flaubert criticism. New sources and new imitations of Flaubert appear nearly every day. English-language criticism remains unaware of the French author's impact on much literary creation in the Far East, India, and Africa. Only gradually, as critics comb through the complete works, notes, and correspondence of authors yet untranslated into English, will we come to realize the full scope of Flaubert's influence. Even major writers such as William Faulkner have not yet been fully examined for traces of Flaubert's style, motifs, and vision.

Validated by the praise of other great writers, Flaubert's correspondence has emerged as one of his masterworks, and it offers a gold mine of his judgments on many topics (for a guide, see Charles Carlut's *La Correspondance de Flaubert: Etude et répertoire critique). Madame Bovary* remains an inexhaustible source of new insights into the writer's craft, and into human nature. "Turn to the poets," said Sigmund Freud, if you wish to learn more about our hidden emotional life than psychoanalysis can teach you.

Many entries contain a parenthetical reference to the work by Flaubert in which the character or phenomenon of the title appears: (*ES*, 1845) or (*ES*) for the two versions of *L'Education sentimentale*, (*MB*) for *Madame Bovary*, (*TSA*, 1849) or (*TSA*) for the two main versions of *La Tentation de saint Antoine*, (*TC*) for *Trois Contes*. (*Sal*) for *Salammbô*, and (*BP*) for *Bouvard et Pécuchet*. In the contributors' references, *Corr.* ordinarily stands for the Conard edition of the letters (9 vols., 1926–33), and *Corr. Supp.* for the four-volume addition issued in 1954. Jean Bruneau's five-volume edition of the correspondence, which is more scholarly, accurate, and complete, but of which volume 5 has not yet appeared, is cited as "Bruneau." Because Bruneau's edition is also very expensive and available in fewer libraries than is the Conard edition—part of the long-standard edition of Flaubert's collected works—contributors have cited it less often. Initials in parentheses at the end of each article identify the contributors. Some articles are double-signed, for example, (EFG/LMP), when I have amplified the original version. A few reference sources from 1999 appear, but most of our documentation ends with 1998.

ACKNOWLEDGMENTS

We have drawn heavily on Benjamin F. Bart's monumental biography, *Flaubert*; to a lesser extent, on Enid Starkie's two volumes *Flaubert: The Making of the Master* and *Flaubert, the Master*; and, for a few additional facts, on Herbert Lottman's *Flaubert: A Biography*. Hazel Barnes's magnificent study *Sartre and Flaubert* also served us well for details about Flaubert's youth. An encyclopedia usually can have few pretensions to originality; our many sources appear in brief bibliographies following most of the entries.

A few contributors have made a vital difference to this compendium, thanks to their clusters of articles on the major works: Scott Carpenter on *L'Education sentimentale* of 1845, Mary Donaldson-Evans on film, Eugene F. Gray on *Madame Bovary*, Dorothy Kelly on critical theory, Eric Le Calvez on the manuscripts and genetic criticism, Rosemary Lloyd on *L'Education sentimentale* of 1869, E. Nicole Meyer on *Bouvard et Pécuchet* and *Dictionnaire des idées reçues*, Jean Morris on *Trois Contes*, Anne Mullen Hohl on *Salammbô*, Marshall Olds on much of the juvenilia, Allan Pasco on *La Tentation de saint Antoine*, and Lawrence Schehr on sexuality and gender. Above all, however, I am indebted to the late Benjamin F. Bart, who served for decades as my mentor in Flaubert scholarship and opened many doors. To his memory this volume is gratefully dedicated.

A

adaptations. Adaptation is a two-edged sword. It can mean either a reworking of an author's writings in another form, a form perhaps willfully or playfully unfaithful to the original, or a description of another work of art within the frame of a fiction. In the latter instance, the possibilities are many. In Proust's novels, operas, musical performances, or paintings may serve as catalysts for special moments of privileged insight; Flaubert's internal reduplications of other works of art usually serve to highlight, by contrast, the blindness of the characters experiencing these works. Just as Paolo and Francesca, in Dante's *Inferno*, fall in love while reading to each other and report "we read no more that day"—missing the warning against adultery that they soon would have happened upon—likewise Emma, watching Donizetti's opera *Lucia di Lammermoor*, adapted from a novel by Sir Walter Scott, forgets the disastrous outcome as she yearns to imitate the heroine. Pellerin's paintings described in *L'Education sentimentale* obviously represent the grotesque failure of art, rather than its apotheosis. The artistic source, in other words, undermines rather than enhances the illusions fostered by its host. (LMP)

See also Antrobus Group; film adaptations of Flaubert's works.

References:

Barillet, Pierre. *Gustave et Louise d'après les textes de Gustave Flaubert et Louise Colet.* Paris: Actes-Sud, 1991. A dramatic production at the Théâtre des Petits Mathurins.

Daniels, Graham. "Emma Bovary's Opera: Flaubert, Scott, and Donizetti." *French Studies* 32 (1978): 285–303.

Ley, Klaus. *Die Oper im Roman: Erzählkunst und Musik bei Stendhal, Balzac, und Flaubert.* Heidelberg: Winter, 1995.

Raitt, Alan. "Flaubert Off-Stage and on Stage." In Christopher Smith, ed., *Essays in Memory of Michael Parkinson and Janine Dakyns.* 107–12. Norwich: School of Modern Languages and European Studies, University of East Anglia, 1996.

Tibbetts, John, and James M. Welsh, eds. *The Encyclopedia of Novels into Film.* New York: Facts on File, 1998.
Tulard, Jean. *Guide des films.* Nouv. ed. 2 vols. Paris: Laffont, 1997.
Williams, John R. "Emma Bovary and the Bride of Lammermoor." *Nineteenth-Century French Studies* 20 (1991–92): 352–60.

adultery. Commonplace and often accepted in the milieu of artists and authors that Flaubert frequented when he was in Paris; scandalous and unthinkable in the Norman countryside where Flaubert and his mother lived; an ambiguous social symptom of the threat of woman's independence and of the contrasting reality of the sexual exploitation of women—the disruptive phenomenon of adultery is the dramatic mover of Flaubert's greatest realist novel, *Madame Bovary*, and the ironic nonevent of his second great realist novel, *L'Education sentimentale.* Both works contrast unfulfilled adulterous yearnings of and for a married woman in one relationship with their disappointing realization in other relationships. Both suggest that bourgeois romantic attempts to update the medieval aristocratic game of *l'amour courtois* (chaste devotion to an idealized lady) must inevitably conclude in adultery (or in incest, as Chateaubriand had long since pointed out in *René*, 1801).

In terms of marriage relationships, *Madame Bovary* is a triptych. Emma Bovary and the young law clerk Léon Dupuis meet over supper at an inn as she and her husband are moving into a new town. They share the vapid romantic ideals of sensibility that had become banal by their time, and they each immediately feel that the other is a kindred spirit as they exchange clichés—which they consider deeply personal—about things they have never seen. Eventually, Emma realizes that Léon has fallen in love with her. She is immensely flattered, but she restrains herself from revealing her attraction to him, while continuing to play the role of a virtuous mother and wife. The second section of the triptych begins when Léon must leave town to continue his study of law. Emma feels that she is entitled to a reward for having been so self-sacrificing. That reward soon appears in the form of the experienced, unscrupulous Rodolphe. He quickly recognizes her boredom and sexual frustration and easily seduces her. At length, her insistence that he carry her off abroad drives him away. In the third part, Emma meets a more self-assured, experienced Léon in Rouen, at the opera, and he seduces her. From then on, they meet in Rouen every week, on the pretext that Emma is taking music lessons there. But Léon's employer and his mother become concerned about his affair with a married woman. He and Emma try in vain to revive their fading passion; he resents her domination of him; and Emma's extravagant expenditures drive the Bovarys deeply into debt. When she is faced with the legal confiscation of her household furnishings, Léon is unable and unwilling to help her. Rodolphe has no money to give her either, and she commits suicide. She imagines herself as making a heroic, romantic gesture, but she dies horribly from arsenic poisoning.

The publication of *Madame Bovary* promptly provoked legal prosecution by the French government on the grounds that the work offended public morals. Although the adulteress's punishment was exemplary, the novel had vividly depicted the exhilaration of illicit sexual pleasure (without any explicit descriptions of sexual organs or acts), the temporary but blissful happiness of sexual fulfillment, and the tedium of marriage. In his depiction of Emma's growing disillusionment during her affair with Léon, Flaubert had cautiously changed the sentence "she found in *this* adultery all the platitudes of marriage" to "she found in adultery all the platitudes of marriage." He thus eliminated the suggestion that some adulteries (even the previous one, with Rodolphe) could be superior to marriage, but let stand the implication that marriage was no better than adultery for ensuring one's happiness. Emma's harrowing end, however, allowed Flaubert's defense attorney to claim successfully that a moral message was the novel's chief meaning. *L'Education sentimentale*, twelve years later, drains adultery of any mystery, romance, or excitement, leveling it to the same mediocrity as the other targets of Flaubert's bourgeois critique. It no longer has a decisive effect on the plot; all the heroes drift. In his portrait of Rosanette Bron, Flaubert also expresses some sympathy for the kept woman, raised to become a sexual object for married men. The novel's melancholic conclusion asserts that one finds greater happiness in anticipation than in fulfillment. (LMP)

References:

Bersani, Leo. "*Madame Bovary* and the Sense of Sex." In Leo Bersani, *A Future for Astyanax: Character and Desire in Literature*. Boston: Little, Brown, 1976. 89–105.

Kaplan, Louise. *Female Perversions: The Temptations of Emma Bovary*. New York: Doubleday, 1991.

LaCapra, Dominique. Madame Bovary *on Trial*. Ithaca: Cornell University Press, 1982.

Tanner, Tony. *Adultery in the Novel: Contract and Transgression*. Baltimore: Johns Hopkins University Press, 1979.

aesthetics. Two mutually incompatible sources formed the basis of Flaubert's aesthetics: Platonic idealism and epistemological skepticism. He believed that art, like a religion, demanded a continual search for stylistic perfection, as well as rigorous documentation. He believed that the author, like God, should be "everywhere perceptible in his Creation, but nowhere visible." Typically for the romantics, he held one tenet of the organic worldview, in which each part reflects the whole (as we might say today that the DNA in each cell reveals the nature of the organism to which that cell belongs). Style, he believed, generates plot, and the ideal personality type gives rise to the individualized fictional character. However, Flaubert abandoned the second tenet of the organic worldview, that every part of that world is evolving toward eventual reunification with God. (Nostalgia for this notion persists in the final version of *La Tentation de saint Antoine* in 1874 as a holdover from the first version, written in 1848–49.)

A corollary of such skepticism is that a perfect, totalizing understanding of the world has become impossible. Thus Flaubert looks past modernism to postmodernism. In his fictions, he continually describes impairments to vision and laments the inadequacy of language for communication to underline his protagonists' limited ability to understand their world and each other. The artist's irresolvable problem, then, is to express a direct relationship between the perceiving subject and its objects. *Bouvard et Pécuchet*, Flaubert's final, unfinished work, dramatizes the frustrated search for knowledge and the resulting fragmentation that transforms the text into a sardonic mosaic of clichés. (LMP)

References:

Bart, Benjamin F. "Flaubert's Concept of the Novel." *PMLA* 80.1 (1965): 84–89.

Culler, Jonathan. *Flaubert: The Uses of Uncertainty*. London: Elek, 1974.

Debray-Genette, Raymonde. "Flaubert: Science et écriture." *Littérature* 15 (1974): 41–51.

Derrida, Jacques. "An Idea of Flaubert's 'Plato Letter.' " *MLN* 99.4 (1984): 748–68.

Gray, Eugene F. "Flaubert's Esthetics and the Problem of Knowledge." *Nineteenth-Century French Studies* 4 (1976): 295–302.

Prendergast, Christopher. "Flaubert: Quotation, Stupidity, and the Cretan Liar Paradox." *French Studies* 35 (1981): 261–77.

White, Hayden. "The Problem of Style in Realistic Representation: Marx and Flaubert." In Berel Lang, ed., *The Concept of Style*. Philadelphia: University of Pennsylvania Press, 1979. 213–29.

"Agonies: Pensées sceptiques" (1838). "Agonies: Pensées sceptiques" is one of Flaubert's early tales, dedicated to his friend Alfred Le Poittevin, as was *La Tentation de saint Antoine*. The short piece resembles a cross between Ecclesiastes and Etienne de Senancour's *Obermann*, written by a young Flaubert in search of shock value. It includes a priest who displays the incomprehension of Bournisien in *Madame Bovary*, as well as several mentions of Satan and a vignette about a man whom tigers kill (and whose blood they drink) in the desert, a scene that some think a precursor of *La Tentation*. (AHP)

Reference:

Bruneau, Jean. *Les Débuts littéraires de Gustave Flaubert, 1831–1845*. Paris: Colin, 1962.

Alas, Leopoldo Clarín (pseud. "Clarín," 1852–1901). A professor of Roman law at the University of Oviedo, Leopoldo Clarín Alas supplemented his meager income by his writing as a witty, sarcastic literary critic in the national press. His masterpiece, *La Regenta*, was published in two volumes in 1884–85. By that time, his irreverent reviews of other authors had made him many enemies, and his satire of Oviedo in the novel, combined with frankly sexual scenes and disrespect for religion, relegated his work to obscurity for eighty years. In his 3,300 pages of literary criticism, he mentions Flaubert more often than any other author; he was vehemently accused of plagiarizing *Madame Bovary* in *La Re-*

genta. Ana Ozores, the heroine of the latter, is bored, stranded in a narrow-minded bourgeois community, trapped with a ridiculous husband (Victor Quintanar), and coveted by a superficially elegant seducer (Alvaro Mesía).

Alas's psychological insights are subtle and profound. Like Flaubert, he is keenly aware of the enduring impress of childhood experience, and of the inner life of fantasies and dreams. He refines the representation of such insights by adopting the *estilo latente* (*style indirect libre*; see "free indirect style") much practiced by Flaubert, but which Alas sometimes inserts within quotation marks to represent a character's statements of her "identity theme" or central self-concept. As Helmut Hatzfeld explains, Alas consciously imitates many of Flaubert's stylistic devices: nominal style; the personification of feelings, thoughts, ideas, and inanimate objects; ternary rhythm (extended beyond Flaubert's use of the device in series of adjectives and verbal phrases to series of nouns and infinitives); reduplication for emotional emphasis; the sarcastic use of italics; impressionistic notation (particularly, in Alas, of an approaching source of noise); and the invocation of fatality.

Alas knew all Flaubert's major works. In the story "Doña Berta," the title character, like the servant Félicité of "Un cœur simple," is a naïve, isolated woman. Bonifacio Reyes, the hero of *Su único hijo* (1891), like the eponymous characters in Flaubert's *Bouvard et Pécuchet*, is a copy clerk, but he aspires to be a novelist rather than a savant. This novel, moreover, begins by evoking "Emma, a spoiled only daughter," in a broad allusion to *Madame Bovary*. Critics have also found echoes of *Salammbô, L'Education sentimentale*, and *La Tentation de saint Antoine* in Alas's fictional works. (LMP)

References:

Alas, Leopoldo. *La Regenta*. Trans. John Rutherford. Athens: University of Georgia Press, 1984. "Introduction," 7–17.

Clavería, Carlos. "Flaubert y *La Regenta*." In Carlos Clavería, *Cinco estudios de literatura espanola moderna*. Salamanca: Colegio Trilinguë, 1945. 1–28.

Hatzfeld, Helmut. "La Imitación estilística de *Madame Bovary* (1857) en *La Regenta* (1884)." *Thesaurus: Boletín del Instituto Caro y Cuervo* 32 (1977): 40–53.

Lafitte, Gaston. "*Madame Bovary* y *La Regenta*." *Bulletin Hispanique* 45–46 (1943–44): 157–63.

Melón Ruiz de Gordejuela, Santiago. "Clarín y el Bovarysmo." *Archivum* 2.1 (1952): 69–87.

Préneron Vinche, Paula. Madame Bovary, La Regenta: *Parodia y contraste*. Murcia: Universidad de Murcia, 1996.

Sánchez, Elizabeth D. "Beyond the Realist Paradigm: Subversive Stratagems in *La Regenta* and *Madame Bovary*." In Noel Valis, ed., *"Malevolent Insemination" and Other Essays on Clarín*. Ann Arbor: Department of Romance Languages, University of Michigan, 1990. 101–116.

Alexandria (*TSA*). Alexandria was the Hellenic capital of Egypt, notable for its library and its two harbors, which made it, on the one hand, a center for trade between the Mediterranean and the East and, on the other, a place where Greek, Roman, Jewish, and Egyptian cultures coexisted and to some degree combined in various philosophies and theologies. In the first of the novel's seven sections (1874 version), Anthony travels there to seek martyrdom. His journey is in vain, because the persecution of the Christians has ceased a mere three days before his arrival. He later daydreams of a comfortable secular existence there. On another occasion, enthusiastic crowds welcome him to Alexandria as a miracle worker. (AHP/LMP)

Allen, Woody (1935–). "The Kugelmass Episode" is a prize-winning, much-anthologized short story by Woody Allen, originally published in the *New Yorker* in 1977. A middle-aged humanities professor seeking a romantic affair finds a magician who transports him to the pages of *Madame Bovary* and brings Emma to New York for trysts at the Plaza Hotel. Like Léon and Rodolphe, Kugelmass gets more than he bargained for: consternated readers of the novel wonder why "a bald Jew is kissing Madame Bovary" (46); and Kugelmass fears for his marriage and his job. He wants to send her back, but the magic transporter box seems to have broken down. Jonathan Culler cites Kugelmass as the ultimate postmodern reader, one who has become an active participant in, even a creator of, the text. (CR)

References:

Allen, Woody. "The Kugelmass Episode." In Woody Allen, *Side Effects*. New York: Random House, 1980. 41–55.

Culler, Jonathan. "The Uses of *Madame Bovary*." In Naomi Schor and Henry F. Majewski, eds., *Flaubert and Postmodernism*. Lincoln: University of Nebraska Press, 1984. 1–12.

Robinson, Douglas. "Kugelmass, Translator: Some Thoughts on Translation and Its Teaching." In Peter Bush and Kirsten Malmkjaer, eds., *Rimbaud's Rainbow: Literary Translation in Higher Education*. Amsterdam: Benjamins, 1998.

Ammonaria (*TSA*). Ammonaria was a girl who was the childhood companion of the future Saint Anthony. When an old monk took him away from his family, she ran after his camel. Because, as a hermit, Anthony has had little contact with other women, he reverts to memories of Ammonaria or of legendary women to nourish his sexual fantasies. (LMP)

anatomy. "Anatomy" is the term introduced by Northrop Frye to describe an encyclopedia literary mode distinct from comedy, tragedy, romance, or irony and that had previously been overlooked or forgotten: the Menippean satire. Traceable from Lucian through Rabelais, Swift, and Voltaire's *Candide*, the anatomy finds its classical realization in Richard Burton's *The Anatomy of Melancholy* (meaning mental disorders). "Flaubert's encyclopedic approach to the construction of *Bouvard et Pécuchet* is quite understandable if we explain it as marking an affinity with the Menippean tradition," Frye observes (311). James Joyce's *Ulysses* marks the culmination of the genre.

In practice, it is difficult to tease apart the satiric and encyclopedic strains in an anatomy, and their proportions vary from one example to the next. But Flaubert's compendium of different branches of human knowledge in *Bouvard et Pécuchet*, pursuing which leads the heroes either to contradictions among authorities or to unsolvable difficulties in implementing their advice, amounts to a satire of all our human hopes for certitude. The heroes cannot even be sure of how the world will end, with a bang (a geological cataclysm) or a whimper (entropy death). With this novel, Flaubert expands to the dimensions of an entire work a satire of knowledge that, in recent times, is more commonly found in isolated episodes within a work, such as the heaping of precious objects in the antique dealer's shop in part 1 of Balzac's *La Peau de chagrin* or the "Autodidacte's" project to read an entire library in alphabetical order in Sartre's *La Nausée*. Recent critics frequently dwell on Flaubert's encyclopedism. (LMP)

Reference:

Frye, Northrop. *Anatomy of Criticism*. Princeton: Princeton University Press, 1957. 308–26.

androgyny. Masculine in appearance and basically heterosexual in his sexual activity, Gustave Flaubert nevertheless remains one of the most powerful androgynous writers in French literature. All recall his most famous, probably apocryphal statement, "Madame Bovary, c'est moi, d'après moi" (I am Madame Bovary; she's based on me). Putting aside the possible ambiguity deriving from the confusion between title character and the book itself, we find a close identification of Flaubert with his heroine. Flaubert marks her with a strong erotic relation to the dominant culture of white male heterosexuality, to which he himself belongs. Much has been made of the irony of the depiction of the character, the distance between the writer and his figure. At the same time, the fascination operated on her is his as well: he is as taken with the dominance of phallocentric ideology as is his character, and her exultant "J'ai un amant" (I have a lover) is his also. Flaubert identifies with his willful women characters, not only Emma, but also Salammbô and even Félicité, as well as with his weak, unmacho masculine ones: Frédéric, Bouvard, and Pécuchet, but also his Saint Julien who has become an anchorite and his Saint Antoine who falls prey to visions. All these male characters enact what would classically be considered feminine behavior: more acted upon than agent, more victim than dominator, more sterile (Bouvard and Pécuchet) than productive. It is a measure of Flaubert's androgynous spirit that he has captured such figures in his narratives. (LRS)

See also feminist and gender studies; queer studies.

References:

Buisine, A., ed. *Emma Bovary*. Paris: Editions Autrement, 1977.
Czyba, L. *Mythes et idéologie de la femme dans les romans de Flaubert*. Lyon: Presses Universitaires de Lyon, 1983.
Kelly, Dorothy. *Fictional Genders: Role and Representation in Nineteenth-Century French Narrative*. Lincoln: Nebraska University Press, 1989.
Leclerc, Yves. *La Spirale et le Monument: Essai sur Bouvard et Pécuchet de Gustave Flaubert*. Paris: Centre de Documentation Universitaire, 1988.
Orr, Mary. *Flaubert: Writing the Masculine*. Oxford: Oxford University Press, 2000.
Tricotel, C. *Comme deux troubadours: Histoire de l'amitié Flaubert/Sand*. Paris: Centre de Documentation Universitaire, 1978.
Williams, D. A. "Gender Stereotypes in *Madame Bovary*." *Forum for Modern Language Studies* 28.2 (1992): 130–39.

Anthony, Saint (historical figure). Born around 251 and said to have died in 356, Saint Anthony early withdrew from society to the solitude of the Thebaid. For the first fifteen years, he was reportedly tempted by what are generally taken to be hallucinations engendered by fasting and lack of sleep. A strong believer in the Trinity, he was an important supporter of Athanasius. His biographers Athanasius, Jerome, and Jacobus da Voragine, author of the *Golden Legend*, agree that he successfully repulsed the temptations. Other novice hermits joined with him, and he eventually founded several of the world's earliest monasteries. Around the year 312, he went to a cave on Mount Kolzim, near the northwest corner of the Red Sea, where he lived as a hermit until his death. A classic example of the "desert fathers," who sought God through the intellectual and physical self-discipline of a life of prayer and meditation, austerity, and manual work, he significantly influenced both cenobitic and eremitic life through his teaching and writing. (AHP)

See also Thebaid.

References:

Attwater, Donald. *The Penguin Dictionary of Saints*. Harmondsworth: Penguin, 1965.
Louis Réau. *Iconographie de l'art chrétien*. Tome 3, *Iconographie des saints*. Paris: Presses Universitaires de France, 1958. 1:101–15.

Antoine, Saint (*TSA*, all versions). Saint Antoine completely dominates all the versions of Flaubert's *Tentation de saint Antoine*. Flaubert portrays the period of the saint's life when he had retired from active polemics with the various heretics of the early Christian period to pray, meditate, and purify himself in the desert. Later, he was to return to civilization, to found and lead monastic communities. Throughout the novel, we see the saint alone outside his cave on a cliff overlooking the Nile River. The only furnishings are a mat, a pitcher of water, and a large cross set at the edge of the cliff. Every other setting that appears in the novel, and every one of the hundreds of characters who appear singly, in groups, or in processions come from the saint's memories, readings, or imaginings. Every word they speak derives from the same sources. Alternatively, we may appropriately choose to believe that all the other characters are hallucinations and dreams sent by the devil or the devil himself in disguise, or both. Flaubert leaves the question open. In terms of narrative theory, the *Tentation* represents an early (1849), extended example of *monologue intérieur*, framed with what are, in effect, brief, schematic stage directions. In traditional literary histories, Edouard Dujardin (1861–1949, in *Les Lauriers sont coupés*, 1888) and James Joyce are erroneously credited with the creation of this form of discourse (e.g., by Kearns 263).

Flaubert confessed that he had thought of castrating himself when he was nineteen, and that for two years around that time, he had not touched a woman: "There comes a moment when you need to make yourself suffer, to loathe your flesh, to throw mud in its face because it seems so frightful to you. Without my love of form, I might perhaps have been a great mystic" (Letter to Louise Colet, December 27, 1852. *Corr.* 6:392). Dissatisfied with the incoherence of the 1849 version of the *Tentation* and with the weakness of the saint's personality there, Flaubert worked toward solving both these problems together in the radically condensed 1856 version, by presenting Anthony's visions as deriving from childhood memories, more recent memories, and the day residue (the experiences and impressions of the previous day). By inaccurately depicting his protagonist as literate, Flaubert opens a rich additional source of hallucinations in letters and in sacred texts. His poignant early scene in which Antoine is carried away from a weeping mother, reproachful sister, and desperate playmate, although not historical—Antoine remained in his native village for several years after his parents' death—dramatizes a crisis of separation and individuation in adolescence.

Responding, in 1866, to a detailed questionnaire from the philosopher Hippolyte Taine (1828–93), who was investigating the creative imagination, Flaubert was further stimulated to link Saint Antoine's hallucinations to his personal experiences as he prepared the final version of the *Tentation* (for a detailed analysis, see Porter 52–67). Antoine's fantasies of power and revenge in Part II derive from memories of three letters sent him by the Emperor Constantine, and from his humiliation in theological debate at the Nicean Council. His loneliness makes him miss his favorite disciple, Hilarion, preparing the events of Part III. The hallucination of the assembly of heretics in Part IV comes from memories of heretics preaching in Alexandria when Antoine visited there. The procession of the pagan gods in Part V recalls Antoine's memories of wall paintings in the temple of Heliopolis, and of the idols carried by the barbarians who had come to negotiate a treaty with Constantine. The devil's skeptical arguments against the existence of a personal god, in Part VI, are taken from the pre-Socratic philosophers Antoine had heard speaking. The monstrous mural paintings that Antoine had seen at Belus, and a mosaic at Carthage, prepare the visions of the Sphinx and Chimera, and of the monsters, in Part VII. There too, memories of

Antoine's mother and of his childhood playmate Ammonaria develop into quasi-explicit sources for his fantasies of lust and death, the twofold identity of the devil. Hunger, thirst, and sexual deprivation in the present moment of narration make Antoine susceptible, throughout the work, to the temptations of greed and lust. Flaubert also focused more closely on Antoine's subjectivity by eliminating words that betrayed the structuring hand of the author: "then, suddenly," and so forth. Illustrious critics such as Michel Butor, Jonathan Culler, Michel Foucault, and Paul Valéry complain of the saint's weakness and passivity in part because they do not realize that Flaubert considers temptation to consist in one's own psychic projections onto one's surroundings. The devil, in particular, embodies Antoine's lust for knowledge and his proud thrust toward self-sufficiency, which clash with his yearning to submit to God. Moreover, it is Antoine's ambivalence that paralyzes him as he grapples with the challenges of the eighth and final stage of maturation as characterized by Erik Erikson: to achieve integrity versus self-contempt.

Flaubert had a lifelong fascination with sainthood: for him, the saint who chooses the unending martyrdom of an ascetic, lonely life was analogous to the dedicated artist, who likewise must struggle with doubt and despair. One may identify three phases in the evolution of Flaubert's depiction of the saint. First, Flaubert's youthful tale of the desert hermit Smarh, tempted by the devil (April 1839), depends heavily on a literary model, Goethe's *Faust*, which had only recently been completed and translated into French. Second, Flaubert combines his keen psychoanalytic insights with his fervent interest in history, making Saint Antoine the center of consciousness in an encyclopedic survey of the heresies of the early fourth century A.D., when Christianity was gradually becoming established as the official religion of the Roman Empire (the Emperor Constantine was converted around 323 A.D.). The figure of Saint Antoine was to fascinate Flaubert for a quarter of a century, from 1848 through 1874. Finally, Flaubert maintains his interest in history but achieves a broader capacity for creating saintly characters who are less like himself, and more varied, in the *Trois Contes* (1875–77): the contemporary, illiterate servant Félicité, the legendary Saint Julian the Hospitator, and Saint John the Baptist (Iaokanaan). Flaubert humorously identified himself with the saint and martyr (ca. 155) Polycarp, Bishop of Smyrna, who decried the corruption of his age, and each year from 1877 on he gathered with his friends for a banquet that celebrated his role as a pessimistic secular prophet. (LMP)

See also Anthony, Saint (historical figure); Polycarp, Saint; "Smarh"; *Tentation de saint Antoine*.

References:

Bart, Benjamin F. "Psyche into Myth: Humanity and Animality in Flaubert's *Saint-Julien.*" *Kentucky Romance Quarterly* 20 (1973): 317–42.

Erikson, Erik H. *Identity and the Life Cycle: Selected Papers*. New York: International Universities Press, 1959.

Foucault, Michel. "Un 'Fantastique' de bibliothèque." *Cahiers Renaud-Barrault* 59 (March 1967): 2–33.

Kearns, James. "Dujardin, Edouard (1861–1949)." In Peter France, ed., *The New Oxford Companion to Literature in French.* Oxford: Clarendon Press, 1995. 263.

Levin, Harry. "Flaubert: Portrait of the Artist as a Saint." *Kenyon Review* 10 (1948): 28–29, 43.

Lombard, Alfred. *Flaubert et saint Antoine*. Paris: Attinger, 1934.

Porter, Laurence M. "Projection as Ego-Defense: Flaubert's *Tentation de saint Antoine*." In Laurence M. Porter, *The Literary Dream in French Romanticism: A Psychoanalytic Interpretation.* Detroit: Wayne State University Press, 1979. 47–67.

Reik, Theodor. *Flaubert und seine* Versuchung des heiligen Antonius: *Ein Beitrag zur Künstlerpsychologie*. Minden: Bruns, 1912.

Antrobus Group. The Antrobus Group, starring Sandra Laub, performed "Wild Desires," an adaptation of *Madame Bovary*, at the Kraine Theater in New York in January 1993. John Simon called the play "a gross travesty wherein Sandra Laub, an actress of no talent and less charm, presumes to turn Flaubert's masterwork into a cross between story theater and children's theater." The "dialogue made you retch." There was "a paltry set with pitiful costumes—foul French," and ludicrous mime and sound effects. (LMP)

Reference:

Simon, John. "Theater. 'Dat Ole Sea and Other Davils.' " *New York* 26.4 (January 25, 1993): 69–70.

Anubis (*TSA*). Anubis, the jackal-headed Egyptian god of the dead, appears frequently in *La Tentation de saint Antoine*. Earlier, the god's name had been chosen as the title of a work Flaubert planned on a woman who mistakenly thought that she was making love to a god, and who would thus illustrate the motif of linking the religious and the terrestrial. (AHP)

Reference:

Bruneau, Jean. *Les Débuts littéraires de Gustave Flaubert, 1831–1845.* Paris: Colin, 1962.

Apollonius of Tyana (*TSA*, all versions). Apollonius of Tyana was a thaumaturge of the first century A.D., so famous that some considered him on a par with Christ. He appears as the last, supreme temptation to heresy in Part III of the 1874 *Tentation de saint Antoine*, in which the episode devoted to him occupies one-eighth of the entire novel. Haughty, compelling, and charismatic, tall, grave, and handsome as the Christ, he appears with his companion Damis, just after Simon the magician and his companion Ennoia have disappeared. He offers to reveal supreme wisdom to Antoine, which the saint accepts to hear on condition that it may aid in his salvation. Rather boastfully, Apollonius relates his prophecies and prodigious adventures. He and his companion have seen luxurious royal palaces and weird monsters, while he cured physical and mental illnesses. At first Antoine is astonished; then he realizes that the stories he is hearing can only gratify his curiosity while distracting him from his worship of the one true God. He tries repeatedly to dismiss his visitors, but in vain; they may be demonic apparitions, he believes, but he has no holy water to sprinkle on them. As Apollonius's harangue continues, and as he reveals parallels between his own life and the life of Christ, Antoine is sorely tempted to accompany him and Damis. The saint appeals to Christ to rescue him from temptation, but Apollonius offers to make Jesus appear to speak with them. When Antoine refuses, Apollonius declares "Leave-him alone, Damis! Like a brute beast, he believes in the reality of things [of the phenomenal world]. He is too terrified by the Gods to understand them; and he demotes his to the level of a jealous king!" (160). Apollonius then steps off the edge of the cliff, remains suspended in mid-air, and then, taking Damis by the hand, slowly rises with him toward "the world of Ideas, filled with the Word!" (160). Left alone, Antoine admits that he has been dazzled and charmed, and that Apollonius tempted him more than all hell put together. Because Antoine is more strongly attracted to the male thaumaturge than to the Queen of Sheba, one could see reflections of Flaubert's strong homosocial bias—and, possibly, of latent homosexuality—in this episode. His memories of images of the gods he has seen then reappear as vivid hallucinations in the next section.

The frame of the 1849 version is strikingly different. Damis is haughty; he asks for food and drink and is dissatisfied with Antoine's tainted water and stale bread. He scorns Antoine for being so ignorant that he knows nothing of Damis's famous master. And at the end, Apollonius is quite intemperate: he says not only that he can summon Christ, but that Christ will bow down to worship him and curse God the Father. When Antoine refuses to accept Apollonius's invitations, the thaumaturge loses his temper and threatens the terrified saint with Hell. Then the heretics reappear, together with the Seven Deadly Sins and the Three Theological Virtues (the sins and virtues are not personified in the 1874 version). Apollonius disappears unnoticed; the Virtues comfort Antoine; and the Devil, enraged, appears to reprimand the Sins for having failed to entrap Antoine. The central speeches by Apollonius are rather similar to those of the final version, however, suggesting that they represent constants in Flaubert's theological imagination. (AHP/LMP)

References:

Carlut, Charles, comp. *La Correspondance de Flaubert: Etude et répertoire critique.* Columbus: Ohio State University Press, 1968. 667–87.

Flaubert, Gustave. *La Tentation de saint Antoine* (1874). Ed. Edouard Maynial. Paris: Garnier, 1968. 131–60.

———. *La Tentation de saint Antoine* (1849). In Gustave Flaubert, *Œuvres complètes.* 28 vols. Paris: Conard, 1910–54. 17 (1924): 282–312.

Jung, Carl Gustav. *Psychological Types or the Psychology of Individuation.* London: Kegan Paul, 1946. 18–33, 70–75.

Seznec, Jean. *Nouvelles Etudes sur* La Tentation de saint Antoine. London: Warburg Institute, 1949. 47–58.

Arius and Arianism (*TSA*, 1856, 1874). Born about 256, Arius became a powerful preacher and the founder of a cult that was attacked by Athanasius, Saint Anthony's biographer, and declared a heresy by the Council of Nicaea. Arius and his followers believed that the Father alone was God, and that the Son was not of the same substance as the Father—nor did he possess the Father's power or his other divine qualities. Because Jesus was begotten by the Father, he was a creature who could not know the Father perfectly.

Arius pronounces only one sentence, lost among the shouts of a mixture of historical heretics and allegorical personifications of heresy, in the 1856 version of *La Tentation de saint Antoine*. He again makes only a cameo appearance in the 1874 version of *La Tentation de saint Antoine* (93–94), as part of a chorus of heretics all vying for attention. Too frenetic to be taken seriously, as before they have little effect on the saint other than to daze and repel him. Flaubert, however, achieves a virtuoso performance in condensing Arius's arguments to half a page, supporting them with several examples from Scripture. Arius thus illustrates a typical accretion of erudition that always tempted Flaubert, and that managed to insinuate itself in the 1874 *Tentation* despite the author's severe abridgement of that text in general. (AHP/LMP)

References:

Dowley, Tim, ed. *Eerdman's Handbook to the History of Christianity*, s.v. "Arius." Grand Rapids, MI: Eerdmans, 1977.

Flaubert, Gustave. *La Tentation de saint Antoine* (1874). Ed. Edouard Maynial. Paris: Garnier, 1968.

———. *La Tentation de saint Antoine*. In Gustave Flaubert, *Œuvres complètes*. 28 vols. Paris: Conard, 1910–54. 17 (1856): 518.

Arnoux, Jacques (*ES*). Father figure and image of a potential future Frédéric, Jacques Arnoux offers above all an ironic commentary on the romantic image of the world of art. The novel charts his progress downhill through compromise, corruption, and bankruptcy and, in so doing, reveals the seamy underside of the art business. When Frédéric first meets him, on the boat leaving Paris for Nogent, he is a robust forty-year-old, republican in his sympathies, familiar with the life of theaters and restaurants, and the owner of an art shop and a periodical oxymoronically entitled *L'Art industriel*. The novel charts Arnoux's descent through various aspects of commercial art, from his disastrous acquisition of a ceramics factory to the selling of religious artifacts. The concept of art moves therefore from that of beauty through utility to the frankly tawdry as Arnoux himself sinks from a comfortable middle-class existence through an increasingly uncertain life to little more than genteel poverty. His dubious speculative ventures rapidly involve Frédéric and typify the intermingling of the emotional and financial in his sentimental education. Arnoux also provides Frédéric with a potential model in his relations with women, especially in his endless infidelities. For these he attempts to make amends by giving presents, a reduction of human to commercial values that is typical of him and of his generation. Indeed, Arnoux's relations with society in general are based on frequently murky considerations, tax evasion, cheating, and other minor infractions that border on turpitude and that Frédéric lacks the moral courage to condemn. What is remarkable in Flaubert's achievement is his ability to show both the sleaziness of Arnoux's behavior and the strong seductive charm he exercises not just over the women in the novel but also over Frédéric. (RL)

Reference:

Paulson, William. *Sentimental Education: The Complexity of Disenchantment.* New York: Twayne, 1992.

Arnoux, Marie (*ES*). Between Frédéric's initial sighting of Mme Marie Arnoux on the boat and their final meeting, the story of their relationship masterfully combines the most banal of contemporary clichés and the bittersweet sense of something that could, after all, be unique. In part a product of Frédéric's reading and his limited vision of the world, the Mme Arnoux/Frédéric conjunction is always largely imaginary, her motives always potentially questionable, her feelings constantly concealed from us by a series of narrative strategies that remain always outside her thoughts. When Frédéric first sets eyes on her, she combines the great romantic clichés, contrasting exotic promise with maternal devotion, fair hair with dark eyes, and images of escape through her presence on the boat with images of inaccessibility through her marriage with Arnoux. Yet when she first comes to visit him alone, it is for the most banal and pragmatic of reasons, the need to borrow money. If later they are able to confide their feelings in each other, it is only because of their tacit agreement that they cannot belong to each other. Because Flaubert presents most of these conversations to us indirectly, summarizing or alluding to the shared confessions and emotions, the rare moments when he does convey their exchange directly make it seem particularly hackneyed: "Often the one who was listening would say: 'I, too' and the other in turn would respond: 'I, too.' " Her promise to meet Frédéric remains unfulfilled because of her child's sudden illness, which she sees as a warning from Providence. In this episode, Flaubert borrows with what might seem particular cynicism from Stendhal's *Le Rouge et le Noir*. It is as though what matters is the impossibility of the relationship and the hackneyed nature of everything associated with it, rather than any sense of promise of possibility, however remote. When they meet again, because Mme Arnoux's hair has turned gray and Frédéric is now middle-aged, her summary of their relationship—"we will have greatly loved each other"—is impossible to construe with any certainty: is it driven by mockery, cynicism, or sincerity? Frédéric, feeling that she may at last have come to offer herself, is now overwhelmed with some inexpressible repulsion, as though she were inviting him to commit an incestuous act. (RL)

References:

Baker, Deborah Lesko. "*L'Education sentimentale*: Figural Dimensions of Madame Arnoux." *Symposium* 44.1 (1990): 3–13.

Bem, Jeanne. "La Nausée de Flaubert." In Jeanne Bem, *Clefs pour* L'Education sentimentale. Paris: Place, 1981. 9–40.

Zaragoza, Georges. "Le Coffret de Madame Arnoux; ou, L'Achèvement d'une éducation." *Revue d'histoire littéraire de la France* 89 (1989): 674–88.

art. Art was a dominant force in Flaubert's life and thought—the plastic arts, the concept of art as style, and art as vocation. He was interested in painting and sculpture: he visited museums in Paris and on his travels in France, Italy, and the Middle East; his notebooks and correspondence contain notes and comments on artworks. Pieter Breughel's *Temptation of Saint Anthony*, which Flaubert saw in 1845 at the Balbi Palace in Genoa, gave him the idea for a play that eventually developed into this own work of that title. In Paris, he frequented the art studio of James Pradier; there he met Victor Hugo and Louise Colet. Artists and discussions of art figure prominently in *L'Education sentimentale*.

Yet Flaubert was always adamantly opposed to illustrations for his literary works. This apparent contradiction can be explained by his concept of pure art and his association of art with style, from which it follows that one art cannot be translated into another. For Flaubert, writing was a long, sometimes agonizingly slow, quest for perfection in style. His correspondence is filled with descriptions of his efforts to polish his prose, to eliminate repetition or assonance, to find *le mot juste*. He wrote to Mme Roger des Genettes, "Je crois que personne n'aime plus l'Art, l'Art en soi. Où sont-ils ceux qui trouvent du plaisir à déguster une belle phrase?" (I believe that no one loves art any more, art in itself. Where are those who find pleasure in savoring a beautiful sentence?) (May 27, 1878; Flaubert, Sel. Masson 707).

In privileging style, Flaubert greatly influenced the development of modernism, in which a central concern is the surface of the artwork rather than its subject. For him, the goals of writing were aesthetic, not entertainment or promoting social or philosophical ideas. Art's morality lay in its beauty. Thus the title of Arnoux's journal in *L'Education sentimentale, L'Art industriel*, represents a contradiction in terms and the antithesis of Flaubert's ideal. On the other hand, Victor Brombert notes that Flaubert's correspondence also emphasizes the importance of the subject; and even as he sought to find language that might best express reality, he was haunted by its inadequacy.

Whatever Flaubert's doubts, the quest for perfection through art became his main purpose in life. He found reality around him intolerable; it was mediocre, filled with stupidity (*bêtise*). He wrote to Mlle Leroyer de Chantepie, "De sorte que, *pour ne pas vivre*, je me plonge dans l'Art, en désespéré; je me grise avec de l'encre comme d'autres avec du vin" (Therefore, *in order not to live,* I plunge into Art like a desperate man; I get drunk on ink as others do on wine) (December 18, 1859, Bruneau 3:65; emphasis in original). Art became even more than a means of escape; Flaubert devoted himself to "a religion of art" (Bart 337). The only respite, indeed, the only redemption, was in art, which came to supplant reality, to replace the artist's own life. He expressed this idea in a phrase that became so famous that even Sherlock Holmes quotes it (in "The Red-headed League"): "L'homme n'est rien, l'œuvre tout" (Man is nothing, the work is all) (to George Sand, December 1875, Bruneau 4:1000). (CR)

References:

Bart, Benjamin. *Flaubert,* Syracuse: Syracuse University Press, 1967.

Brombert, Victor. "Flaubert and the Status of the Subject." In Naomi Schor and Henry F. Majewski, eds., *Flaubert and Postmodernism.* Lincoln: University of Nebraska Press, 1984. 100–115.

Flaubert, Gustave. *Correspondance.* Ed. Jean Bruneau. [5] vols. Paris: Gallimard, 1973–[1998].

———. *Correspondence.* Sel. Bernard Masson. Paris: Gallimard, 1998.

Art et progrès. During the fall term in 1834, probably under the indulgent direction of a new teacher of composition, Henry Gourgaud-Dugazon, Flaubert began to compose his own literary journal, *Art et progrès,* in study hall. Only volume 2 survives. It contains the "Voyage en enfer," modeled on such satiric works as Alain-René Lesage's *Le Diable boîteux* (1707, revised 1736). It "borrows the first two cantos of Byron's semiautobiographical *Childe Harold's Pilgrimage* (1812), and is indebted to Edgar Quinet's *Ahasvérus* (1833), whose hero thirsted for knowledge" (Griffin, ed., xiii). Satan takes the author on a tour of this world, and after forcing him to witness manifold cruelties and injustices, the devil reveals that this world itself is Hell. A second piece relates conventional adolescent sexual fantasies. (LMP)

References:

Flaubert, Gustave. "A Trip to Hell." In Robert Griffin, ed., *Early Writings. Gustave Flaubert.* Lincoln: University of Nebraska Press, 1991. 1–2.

Lottman, Herbert. *Flaubert: A Biography.* New York: Fromm, 1990. 18–22.

Athanasius (*TSA,* 1874). Athanasius, Saint Anthony's biographer, was a great theologian of the fourth century (ca. 295–372 A.D.), a bishop of the church of Alexandria, a member of the Council of Nicaea (325), and one of the four Fathers of the Greek church. He was important in defining the Christian doctrine of the Trinity, in which one single God is said to be manifested in three distinct persons: Father, Son, and Holy Spirit. He was exiled five times because of his fierce opposition to the Arians (followers of Arius), who believed that Jesus did not come in the flesh, and that only the spirit has importance. The real Saint

Anthony was a friend and supporter of the embattled Athanasius, whereas Flaubert's fictional saint Antoine envies him. (AHP)

References:

Attwater, Donald. *The Penguin Dictionary of Saints*. Harmondsworth: Penguin, 1965.
Réau, Louis. *Iconographie de l'art chrétien*. Tome 3, *Iconographie des saints*. Paris: Presses Universitaires de France, 1958. 1:101–15.

attudinal dynamics. In narrative text, "attitude" is one of the elements ("sublimina") establishing overall textual effect, while never actually being in focus. Readers' responses are partly determined by attitudinal markers they unconsciously privilege. In *L'Education sentimentale*, the opening chapter oscillates between two attitudinal viewpoints: Frédéric's optimistic, naïve mentality is offset by indicators of a more banal reality. For example, when Frédéric first sees Mme Arnoux, his bedazzled perspective is privileged. An analysis of the description of Mme Arnoux, however, reveals a more unromantic portrait. The contrast between the description and Frédéric's reaction allows the reader both to approve and to question Frédéric's inspiration. (LK)

Reference:

Hayman, David. "Attitudinal Dynamics in Narrative: Flaubert, Lawrence, Joyce." *Journal of Modern Literature* 19.2 (1995): 201–14.

Aubain, Madame (*TC*). In "Un cœur simple," the first tale of *Trois Contes*, Madame Aubain is a widow whose loyal, hardworking servant Félicité is the envy of the other middle-class women in Pont-L'Evêque. The secondary character Madame Aubain provides a counterpoint to Félicité, the protagonist, whose "simple heart" contrasts with her mistress's aloof, unresponsive one. The *beau garçon* Madame Aubain married had died young, leaving her with two small children, Paul and Virginie (a sarcastic allusion to the title characters of Jacques-Henri Bernardin de Saint-Pierre's saccharine preromantic novel), and with an accumulation of debts that forced her to settle in an old family residence replete with reminders of more prosperous times. Typically for Flaubert, *Madame* (the italics represent Flaubert's sarcastic reference to Madame Aubain's insistence on Félicité's addressing her in the third person—a mark of distinction; compare Emma and her maid in *Madame Bovary*) is characterized as much through descriptions of her possessions as through her actions. The musty house, the old piano, the barometer, the clock, and the furnishings mark both her social class and her economic decline. Madame Aubain's cold character emerges notably in her discouraging any display of affection by Félicité. The social distance between master and servant is carefully enforced by Madame Aubain and is erased only momentarily by their sorrowful embrace after the loss of Virginie. In contrast with Félicité, who asserts herself rarely and speaks little, Madame Aubain exerts a measure of control over her experience through her more directive speech. Careful bourgeois rituals of linguistic evasion regarding subjects such as sex, parting, and death mark her discourse, as if by speaking around them, she can control or deny their effect on her existence (Killick 310). Whereas Madame Aubain differs from Félicité in the affective, social, and economic domains, both women are profoundly affected by the absence of a desired Other—*Monsieur* (the honorific title that Madame Aubain insists be used to refer to her late husband) and then Virginie for Madame Aubain and Théodore, her nephew Victor, and Virginie for Félicité. Madame Aubain's emotional deprivation, along with her attempts to control events and emotions through her rigidly codified bourgeois language and behavior, defines her character, supporting the notion that the name "Aubain" is an ironic masculinization of the word *aubaine*, which translates as "windfall" or "godsend." (JM)

Reference:

Killick, Rachel. " 'The Power and the Glory'? Discourses of Authority and Tricks of Speech in *Trois Contes." Modern Language Review* 88.2 (1993): 307–20.

Auden, W[ystan] H[ugh] (1907–73). W. H. Auden was an English (later American citizen) poet, critic, and playwright. Initially, Flaubert appears to have served as a role model for the young Auden, who admired the asceticism of the novelist's literary vocation. During Auden's socially committed left-wing period in the 1930s, however, he became critical of Flaubert's aesthetic withdrawal. As Auden's views shifted during World War II owing to an increasing preoccupation with Christianity, works such as *New Year Letter* and *The Quest* (both 1941) suggest that Flaubert once again came to represent for Auden an artist-hero whose detachment and self-abnegation in art were worthy of emulation. (AA)

References:

Emig, Rainer. *W. H. Auden*. Basingstoke: Macmillan, 1999.

Fuller, John. " 'The Hero': Auden and Flaubert." In Kathleen Buchnell and Nicholas Jenkins, eds. *W. H. Auden. "The Map of All My Youth": Early Works, Friends, and Influences*. Oxford: Clarendon Press, 1990.

Augier, Emile (1820–89). While Flaubert was traveling on the Nile in 1850, he received a complimentary copy of Emile Augier's play *Gabrielle* (1849), which depicts a simpleminded husband whose wife, a romantic, is bored and dissatisfied with him. At the end, she realizes that a devoted, hardworking husband is a prize, and she gladly resumes the role of a dutiful wife. *Madame Bovary* may in part be a more profound, pessimistic reworking of this story, with the upbeat ending reduced to one admission by the dying heroine to her husband: "Tu es bon, toi" (You're a kind person). (LMP)

References:

Ambrière, Francis. "Augier et son théâtre." *Annales. Economies, sociétés, civilisations* 230 (1969): 32–49.

Gaillard de Champris, Henry. *Emile Augier et la comédie sociale*. Paris: Grasset, 1910.

autobiographical elements. The presence of an author's lived experience, transposed and reattributed, pervades fictional works. For example, the details of Charles Bovary's one truly successful medical treatment (other than avoiding harmful interventions), setting his future father-in-law's broken leg—an act that determines his unhappy destiny—probably derive in part from Flaubert's similar treatment of one of his hired crewmen on the Nile in 1850. The early tale *Novembre* is considered by some Flaubert's only truly autobiographical work, transcribing his youthful infatuation with Elisa Schlésinger. Both versions of *L'Education sentimentale* also show parallels with the author's life. The only specific date given in the first version is December 12, 1845, which happens to be Flaubert's twenty-fourth birthday. In that work, the writer-hero Jules shares Flaubert's androgynous sensibility and thoughts of suicide. In the later version, Frédéric's study of law in Paris—first he fails, then passes an examination—corresponds to Flaubert's (although Charles Bovary's initial dissipation as a student on his own for the first time, his mishaps with his medical exams, and the reactions of his family may transpose the author's personal memories as well). Critics often find traces of autobiography in motifs that appear in more than one work, such as the distaste for agricultural fairs displayed by the anonymous narrator of *Madame Bovary* and then attributed to Frédéric in *L'Education sentimentale* of 1869, when he loses votes by disdaining to appeal for votes at such a fair. The motif of a youthful visit to a house of prostitution is also often assumed by critics to derive from the writer's life. The theory of reference, of correspondences between details of fictional works and their possible autobiographical or historical sources, remains to be developed, perhaps along the lines suggested by Anna Whiteside and Michael Issacharoff. (LMP)

References:

Brombert, Victor. *Flaubert par lui-même*. Paris: Seuil, 1971.

Ginsburg, Michal Peled. "La Tentation du biographe." *Revue des lettres modernes* 1165–72 (1994): 21–42.

Riffaterre, Michael. *Fictional Truth*. New York: Johns Hopkins University Press, 1990.

Shroder, Maurice Z. "Gustave Flaubert: The Artist as Raging Saint." In Maurice Z. Shroder, *Icarus: The Image of the Artist in French Romanticism*. Cambridge, MA: Harvard University Press, 1961. 151–80.

Steegmuller, Francis. *Flaubert and* Madame Bovary: *A Double Portrait*. Rev. ed. New York: Farrar, 1968.

Whiteside, Anna, and Michael Issacharoff, eds. *On Referring in Literature*. Bloomington: Indiana University Press, 1987.

l'Aveugle (*MB*). L'Aveugle is the blind beggar who haunts the road Emma Bovary must take to meet her lover Léon in Rouen. He tries to cling to the side of the stagecoach to ask for alms, and the driver dislodges him by striking him with his whip. The pharmacist Homais, who illegally practices medicine, tries to obtain free publicity by offering the blind man a free medicinal ointment; when the treatment fails to restore his sight, and the blind man repeatedly denounces this failure in public, Homais manages to have him committed to an asylum by representing him as a public menace in a series of false articles in the local newspaper. Before this happens, however, the blind beggar is coincidentally present outside Emma's window as she dies. The ribald song he sings then sums up her past hopes for happiness and sexual fulfillment, contrasted with the hideous reality of physical deterioration they share at that moment. She reacts by crying out in horror. He seems to symbolize both human illusions and their ironic refutation through suffering and death: his blindness may have resulted from tertiary syphillis. (LMP)

Reference:

Donaldson-Evans, Mary. "A Pox on Love: Diagnosing *Madame Bovary*'s Blind Beggar." *Symposium* 44.1 (1990): 15–27.

Azorín (José Martínez Ruiz, 1873–1967). In *Diario de un enfermo*, the Spanish author Azorín twice cites Flaubert's *Bouvard et Pécuchet*, and in a serialized version of the *Diario*, he says that "I would like to write the novel of indeterminacy: a novel without space, time, or characters" (Risco 270). This is Flaubert's "book about nothing," a phrase that recurs in Azorín's *Capricho* (1943). The fictive author Victor Albert in *El Enfermo* (1943) tells his wife how much influence Flaubert has exercised on him in every way. "In my youth, intoxicated with Flaubert, I sallied forth impetuously to seek objects; in my old age, weary of color and line, I incline to ideal syntheses," but he still needs to know how to balance them with the real (Azorín 6:627–28). (LMP)

References:

Azorín. *Obras completas*. 9 vols. 2d ed. Madrid: Aguilar, 1959–63.
Risco, Antonio. *Azorín y la ruptura con la novela tradicional*. Madrid: Alhambra, 1980.

B

Balzac, Honoré de (1799–1850). Flaubert was imaginatively involved with Honoré de Balzac's works from the beginning to the end of his career. In 1849, after spending four days listening to Flaubert read them the first version of his visionary *Tentation de saint Antoine*, his friends Louis Bouilhet and Maxime Du Camp urged him to throw it into the fire and to read Balzac's realistic novels to cure himself of "the cancer of lyricism." Flaubert's last project, "Sous Napoléon III," was planned as a vast Balzacian social fresco. Both authors are masters of static description, but they differ markedly in their treatment of plot and character. Flaubert relies on chance to bring about many key plot shifts in his novels, whereas Balzac loves to deploy melodramatic peripeties (radical, unexpected changes of fortune), surprise appearances, and revelations of identity. Most of Flaubert's characters (with notable exceptions such as Emma Bovary) are weak and indecisive, yielding to impulse. Balzac's characters, in contrast, are willful and determined. Overall, Flaubert planned painstakingly in advance, drafting scenarios, outlines for sections of scenarios, and dialogue fragments for each scene. His proof copies of his typescripts show only minor stylistic retouching of fine points, to avoid word repetition, assure a better rhythm, or achieve a more harmonious sound. Balzac was a rhapsode, an improviser. His proof copies bear heavy, extensive revisions, and during composition, he often yielded to the temptation of hypercreativity, inventing stories for many minor characters, detailing the past history of major ones, and explaining thoughts and motives in enormous detail. When Flaubert's texts are longer than they need to be, it is not because of the ebullience of his inventiveness but because of his fidelity to his sources. Sometimes he is too much the scholar to be an entertaining storyteller. The first five chapters of *Madame Bovary*, for example, could have been condensed into one, but they reported the details of the real-life "Affaire Delamare" on which Emma Bovary's life was modeled, so they stayed (Bardèche 12).

Madame Bovary has been said to draw inspiration from Balzac's *La Muse du département* and from his *Physiologie du mariage* (Sagnes, "Tentations"). *L'Education sentimentale* may ridicule Balzacian clichés about the will and fatality expressed in *Le Lys dans la vallée* and in *Illusions perdues* (Vial). Balzac's *Louis Lambert* may have helped Flaubert describe the ecstatic visions of his Saint Antoine (although Flaubert's own experience of epilepsy was his major source). But Flaubert's main interaction with his precursor was a sustained attempt to purge Balzacian romantic lyricism and narratorial intrusiveness from his style. In his working notes for *L'Education sentimentale*, he warns himself, "Prendre garde au *Lys dans la vallée*" (watch out for Balzac's *The Lily of the Valley*, meaning, be careful to not wallow in the pathos of an older woman's feelings when she has renounced sexual intimacy with a younger man and then has been abandoned by him). For example, as Graham Falconer has shown, when Flaubert revised *Madame Bovary*, he eliminated not a few explicit explanations of motive, leaving places of indeterminacy. Fleeting evocations of a character's inner life, such as "le père Rouault's" after his daughter Emma's wedding, reveal traces of a not-quite-suppressed hypercreativity. But Flaubert ruthlessly damped down poignant language: in the drafts, when Charles Bovary has married Emma, the narrator's comment reads, "He had for himself, the poor lad, all to himself, and for his whole life, this pretty woman he adored." The final version says simply, "But now he had for life this pretty woman he adored." Justin's unrequited passion for Emma is much more fully developed and explained in the earlier versions of *Madame Bovary*. The narrator's hatred for the pharmacist Homais becomes greatly reduced. In general, like Balzac, the Flaubert of the drafts has a much greater social density—the words, acts, and thoughts of many secondary figures—than he does in the final text (Falconer 130–37). (LMP)

References:

Bardèche, Maurice. "Balzac et Flaubert." *L'Année Balzacienne* 1976: 9–29.

Falconer, Graham. "Le Travail de 'débalzacienisation' dans la rédaction de *Madame Bovary." Revue des lettres modernes* 865–72 (1988): 123–56.

Gothot-Mersch, Claudine. "Souvenirs de Balzac." In Claudine Gothot-Mersch, *La Genèse de* Madame Bovary. Paris: Corti, 1966. 50–60.

Raitt, Alan. "Le Balzac de Flaubert." *L'Année Balzacienne* 1991: 335–61.

Sagnes, Guy. "De Balzac à Flaubert: L'Enfance de Deslauriers d'aprés le manuscrit de *L'Education sentimentale*." *Littératures* 1980. 2:17–32.

———. "Tentations balzaciennes dans le manuscrit de *L'Education sentimentale." L'Année Balzacienne* 1981: 53–64.

Steele, H. Meili. *Realism and the Drama of Reference: Strategies of Representation in Balzac, Flaubert, and James*. University Park: The Pennsylvania State University Press, 1988.

Vial, André. *Faits et significations*. Paris: Nizet, 1973. 55–108.

Banville, Théodore de (1823–91). Théodore de Banville was a poet and theorist at the transition between art for art's sake (exemplified by Théophile Gautier) and Parnasse (exemplified by Leconte de Lisle). He and Flaubert both admired the beautiful young Louise Colet. A kindred spirit insofar as he shared Flaubert's cult of formal perfection, he was among the first to praise *L'Education sentimentale* and *La Tentation de saint Antoine* when these works were being attacked in the press. (LMP)

Reference:

Charpentier, John. *Théodore de Banville, l'homme et son œuvre*. 2d ed. Paris: Perrin, 1925.

Barbey d'Aurevilly, Jules Amédée (1808–89). Jules Amédée Barbey d'Aurevilly was a conservative French novelist and critic whose review of *Madame Bovary* (in *Le Pays*, October 6, 1857) exemplified contemporary reactions to the work. He grudgingly praises Flaubert's prose style but criticizes the novel's excessive descriptiveness and lack of spirituality. (DF)

Reference:

Barbey d'Aurevilly, Jules. "M. Gustave Flaubert." Trans. Robert Steele. In Laurence M. Porter, ed., *Critical Essays on Gustave Flaubert*. Boston: Hall, 1986. 50–57.

Barnes, Julian (1946–). Julian Barnes is the author of the witty, delightful *Flaubert's Parrot*, filled with whimsical lore about the author. The narrator imagines himself as a naïve literary historian in search of the stuffed parrot described by Flaubert in "Un cœur simple." There it becomes a fetishistic representation of the Holy Spirit in the mind of the saintly, illiterate servant Félicité. The narrator's quest ranges all over France; he finds many stuffed parrots, but each, for one reason or another, must be disqualified. Finally he discovers a whole batch of stuffed parrots, dusted with insecticide, in a basement. The novel concludes, tongue-in-cheek, "Perhaps it was one of them." (LMP)

References:

Barnes, Julian. *Flaubert's Parrot*. New York: Knopf, 1985.
Moseley, Merritt. *Understanding Julian Barnes*. Columbia: University of South Carolina Press, 1997.

Bart, Benjamin F. (1917–91). Benjamin F. Bart was the author of the definitive biography *Flaubert*, which makes extensive use of unpublished manuscripts. There he offers valuable comments on nearly all the fictional works. He shows that Flaubert, like Baudelaire and Proust, believed in the enduring impact of childhood experiences. Flaubert's mother fixation, feminine tendencies, and unwillingness to undertake lasting commitments to women are tactfully analyzed. However, "love as aspiration would become the central theme of most of his works" (223). Bart underlines the pervasive importance of the experience of pantheistic ecstasy in Flaubert's fictions and lucidly explains his philosophical and religious thought. He also wrote *Flaubert's Landscape Descriptions* (1956) and, with Robert Cook, *The Legendary Sources of Flaubert's* Saint Julien. His articles on "Aesthetic Distance in *Madame Bovary*" and on "Flaubert's Concept of the Novel" remain important sources for understanding Flaubert's aesthetics. Also noteworthy are his psychoanalytically oriented studies of "La Légende de saint Julien l'hospitalier" and of *Salammbô*. (LMP)

References:

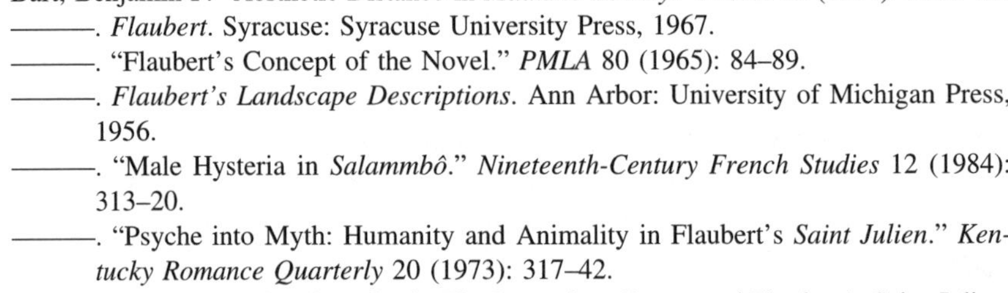

Bart, Benjamin F. "Aesthetic Distance in *Madame Bovary*." *PMLA* 69 (1954): 1113–26.

———. *Flaubert*. Syracuse: Syracuse University Press, 1967.

———. "Flaubert's Concept of the Novel." *PMLA* 80 (1965): 84–89.

———. *Flaubert's Landscape Descriptions*. Ann Arbor: University of Michigan Press, 1956.

———. "Male Hysteria in *Salammbô*." *Nineteenth-Century French Studies* 12 (1984): 313–20.

———. "Psyche into Myth: Humanity and Animality in Flaubert's *Saint Julien*." *Kentucky Romance Quarterly* 20 (1973): 317–42.

Bart, Benjamin F., and Robert Cook. *The Legendary Sources of Flaubert's* Saint Julien. Toronto: University of Toronto Press, 1977.

Porter, Laurence M., ed. *A Man for All Seasons: A Volume of Homage Studies in Honor of Benjamin F. Bart*. Special Issue of *Nineteenth-Century French Studies* 17.1 (Fall 1988): 1–113. Contains T. H. Goetz et al., "The Contributions of Benjamin F. Bart," 5–19.

Barthes, Roland (1915–80). Roland Barthes is the author of three seminal studies of the realist novel that draw heavily on Flaubert. "L'artisanat du style" (1953) claimed that Flaubert exemplified the crisis of literature around 1850. Given the failure of democracy in 1851, fiction seemed irrelevant. Flaubert tried to justify writing by the pains it took to produce it; thus craftsmanship replaces romantic genius as an ideal. "L'Effet du réel" (1968) introduces the concept of descriptive notions whose only apparent function is to announce that "we [objects or settings] are the real," citing the barometer on the piano in "Un cœur simple" and the description of the town of Rouen in *Madame Bovary*. *Le Plaisir du texte* (1973) evokes the euphoric cultural plenitude one experiences in reading Flaubert's richly textured style, contrasting such a *texte de plaisir* with the shocking, surprising *texte de jouissance* (the orgasmic text) and with the banally erotic *texte de désir* (vicarious with fulfillment). (LMP)

References:

Bal, Mieke. *Narratologie*. Paris: Klincksieck, 1977. 87–111.

Barthes, Roland. "L'artisanat du style." In Roland Barthes, *Le Degré zéro de la littérature*. Paris: Seuil, 1953. 89–94. Trans. as *Writing Degree Zero*, by Annette Lavers and Colin Smith. New York: Hill & Wang, 1968. 62–66.

———. "L'Effet du réel." *Communications* 11 (1968): 84–89.

———. *Le Plaisir du texte*. Paris: Seuil, 1973.

Culler, Jonathan. *Flaubert: The Uses of Uncertainty*. 1974. Rev ed. Ithaca: Cornell University Press, 1985.

Porter, Dennis. "*Madame Bovary* and the Question of Pleasure." In Naomi Schor and Henry F. Majewski, eds., *Flaubert and Postmodernism*. Lincoln: University of Nebraska Press, 1984. 116–38.

Baudelaire, Charles (1821–67). Flaubert and Charles Baudelaire were kindred spirits insofar as both believed in art for art's sake as opposed to a didactic, moralizing art, or to art as the imitation of reality. Indeed, it was the journal *Réalisme* that published the harshest attack on *Madame Bovary* for being too well written (Starkie 283, 334–39). When *Madame Bovary* first appeared, Baudelaire wrote a keenly perceptive review, emphasizing Emma's virility but attributing her aberrant behavior to hysteria and pitying her for her limited, unrealistic aspirations. He offered a shrewd analysis of the clubfoot episode. He pointed to affinities between some of Emma's hallucinatory experiences—both visual and auditory—and the vision in *La Tentation de saint Antoine*, of which some selections had been published in 1856. Baudelaire heralded Flaubert's psychological insight. He emphasized that a work of art need not preach morality; if it is crafted well, its style and structure serve as vehicles for a tacit ethical message. Only Baudelaire and Sainte-Beuve published strongly favorable reactions to Flaubert's masterpiece. (LMP)

References:

Baudelaire, Charles. "*Madame Bovary*, par Gustave Flaubert." *L'Artiste*, October 18, 1857. Trans. in Paul de Man, ed., *Madame Bovary*. New York: Norton, 1965. 336–43.

Starkie, Enid. *Flaubert. The Making of the Master*. New York: Atheneum, 1967.

Baudry, Frédéric (1818–85). A philologist who had been a friend of Flaubert's since childhood, Frédéric Baudry attended Flaubert's salon in the 1870s. He later played an important role in the writer's life. As the 1870s ended, Flaubert had been financially ruined by his nephew-in-law Ernest Commanville and urgently needed a job. He and Baudry then became competitors for a position at the Bibliothèque Mazarine. Despite Flaubert's influential friends, Baudry was appointed. Not only was he more qualified, but also he probably benefited from political favoritism: he was the son-in-law of the prominent lawyer Jules Sénard who, ironically, in 1857 had defended Flaubert against the charge of corrupting public morals by publishing his masterpiece, *Madame Bovary*. As a consolation, Baudry proposed another post to Flaubert, but the latter took this offer as an insult. (CG)

Reference:

Lottman, Herbert. *Gustave Flaubert*. New York: Fromm, 1990 (1979).

Berlioz, Hector (1803–69). The great French romantic composer Hector Berlioz reviewed Flaubert's *Salammbô* when it appeared in 1862 and was interested in making it into an opera. They had several conversations in 1863, when Berlioz asked Flaubert's advice on the Carthaginian costumes for the opera *Les Troyens*, and Flaubert treasured his memories of their meetings. He also greatly admired *La Damnation de Faust* (1877), performed again at last after the thirty years of unjust neglect that followed its premiere in 1846.

The composer was the best music critic of his day, and his memoirs (1865) vividly bring his age to life. Flaubert in turn delighted in the angry criticism of society that filled Berlioz's published correspondence, even in the bowdlerized 1879 edition (see Barzun 2:269). He identified with Berlioz as the exemplar of the embattled artist at odds with society. "Voila un homme! et un vrai artiste! Quelle haine de la médiocrité! Quelles belles colères contre l'infâme bourgeois! . . . Je ne m'étonne plus de la sympathie que nous avions l'un pour l'autre. Que ne l'ai-je mieux connu! Je l'aurais adoré!" (There's a man for you! And a real artist! How he hated mediocrity! What splendid diatribes against the vile bourgeoisie! . . . I'm no longer surprised [after reading Berlioz's recently published correspondence] at the sympathy we felt for each other. Why couldn't I have known him better! I would have worshipped him.) (Letter to his niece Caroline Commanville, April 16, 1879, *Corr*. 8:254–55). (LMP)

References:

Barzun, Jacques. *Berlioz and the Romantic Century*. 2 vols. 3rd ed. New York: Columbia University Press, 1969.

Flaubert, Gustave. *Correspondence*. 9 vols. Paris: Conard, 1910–23.

Bernardin de Saint-Pierre, Jacques-Henri (1737–1814). In 1869, a new edition of Jacques-Henri Bernardin de Saint-Pierre's *Paul et Virginie* (1789) was published, making this romantic pastoral as popular as *La Nouvelle Héloïse*. The influence of Bernardin de Saint-Pierre's exotic novel on Flaubert can easily be traced in certain names, situations, narrative techniques, and essential motifs found in "Un cœur simple" (1875). Flaubert, however, abandoned the lyricism of the pastoral: he aimed to reproduce the life and language of his protagonists in a realistic manner. Choosing brief dialogues over theatrical discourses, Flaubert transformed the exotic pastoral into a nineteenth-century short story, or, as he called it, "un conte bonhomme." (CT)

Reference:

Simon, Jean Jacques. *Bernardin de Saint-Pierre ou le triomphe de Flore*. Paris: Nizet, 1967.

bêtise. Flaubert's correspondence is studded with references to *bêtise* (stupidity)—of Parisians, the bourgeoisie, the public, democracy, all of humanity. He wrote to Mlle Leroyer de Chantepie, "Il y a un fond de bêtise dans l'humanité qui est aussi éternel que l'humanité elle-même" (There is a depth of stupidity in humanity that is as eternal as humanity itself) (January 16, 1866, Bruneau, ed., *Corr.* 3:479). It is overwhelming: he says that he feels crushed by the stupidity around him, and he often uses images of depths or oceans to describe it. He includes himself in this judgment, often chiding himself for having done something stupid ("une bêtise"). *Bêtise* oppressed him even as a child: at nine, he pronounced New Year's Day stupid (letter to Ernest Chevalier, January 1, 1831, Bruneau, ed., *Corr.* 1:4). The posthumously published *Dictionnaire des idées reçués*, used extensively for the composition of *Bouvard et Pécuchet*, is a compendium of the stupid things people say.

Benjamin Bart sees Flaubert as waging war on stupidity through his works. His characters' language is filled with clichés and platitudes. But other critics contend that Flaubert cannot escape stupidity himself. They have linked his preoccupation with stupidity to a skepticism about language, language assimilated to the cliché, because of his awareness that language conditions thought. According to Jean-Paul Sartre, "Flaubert ne croit pas *qu'on parle: on est parlé.* . . . Le language pour Flaubert, n'est autre que la bêtise" (Flaubert does not believe that *we speak: we are spoken.* . . . Language, for Flaubert, is nothing but stupidity) (1:623).

Commonplaces such as those Flaubert made his characters say in his novels and that he listed in his *Dictionnaire* are meaningless because they are the fixed, mechanical expression of opinions disconnected from reality. Gaillard sees *bêtise* as more profound than that, however: as the unison of voices speaking for France, expressing the general will, universalizing and homogenizing the idea of France. (CR)

References:

Bart, Benjamin F. *Flaubert.* Syracuse: Syracuse University Press, 1967.

Gaillard, Françoise. "A Little Story about the *bras de fer*; or, How History Is Made." In Naomi Schor and Henry F. Majewski, eds., *Flaubert and Postmodernism.* Lincoln: University of Nebraska Press, 1984: 84–99.

Sartre, Jean-Paul. *L'Idiot de la famille.* 3 vols. Paris: Gallimard: 1971–72. *The Family Idiot.* Trans. Carol Cosman. 5 vols. Chicago: University of Chicago Press, 1981–93.

the Bible (influence on Flaubert). Although Flaubert's family was neither religious nor anticlerical, he read the Bible at an early age. From his *Correspondance* and works of fiction, it is evident that he was deeply influenced not only by the Bible but by other Christian and pagan sources. His own religion, or set of beliefs, was close to the aesthetic Christianity of the romantics: he held a panpsychic view of Creation and God. All religions attracted him. He vehemently condemned fanaticism (not only in Christianity but also in Islam) and the claim of each religion to hold the ultimate truth: "Chaque religion et chaque philosophie a prétendu avoir Dieu à elle, toiser l'infini et connaître la recette du bonheur. Quel orgueil et quel néant!" (Every philosophy and every religion has claimed to have exclusive possession of God, to be able to sound the infinite and to know the recipe for happiness. What vaingloriousness and what a void!) (letter to Mlle Leroyer de Chantepie, October 23, 1863, Bruneau, ed., *Correspondance* 3:353). For Flaubert, religions cannot define God in human terms even though they try: "Mais la manière dont parlent de Dieu toutes les religions me révolte, tant elles le traitent avec certitude, légèreté et familiarité" (But the way that all the religions speak about God inspires my indignation, because they treat him with such self-assurance, frivolousness, and pretentiousness.) (Letter to Edma Roger des Genettes, December 18, 1859, Bruneau, ed., *Correspondance* 3:67). He expressed his "rage antireligieuse" (letter to Edma Roger des Genettes, 1860, Bruneau, ed., *Correspondance* 3:131) and justified it by saying that when he studied the Bible, he found that God was represented as an oriental monarch or Louis XIV, and that religion was unable even to contain the idea of God (letter to Edma Roger des Genettes, Spring 1864, Bruneau, ed., *Correspondance* 3:401).

Like other nineteenth-century writers, Flaubert accepted the God of the New Testament more readily than the God of the Old Testament. In a letter written from Jerusalem (to Louis Bouilhet, August 20, 1850, Bruneau, ed., *Correspondance* 1:665–69), Flaubert expressed his disillusionment with the financial profit that promoters had made of the Holy Land: "On a fait tout ce qu'on a pu pour rendre les saints lieux ridicules" (They've done everything possible to make the holy places ludicrous) (666). He found solace from the bitterness of disappointment by reading the Sermon on the Mount from the Gospel of Matthew. He hoped to reach a mystical level of spirituality by reading the Bible while he was in Jerusalem but found that he could not cross the void that separated the true God from human destructiveness.

Biblical intertextuality or overtones are more evident in Flaubert's overtly religious works: *La Tentation de saint Antoine, Salammbô*, "Hérodias," and "La Légende de saint Julien l'hospitalier." Flaubert also researched historical archives, traveled, and was influenced and inspired by religious paintings, sculptures, churches, and cathedrals before completing his novels and short stories. In all versions of *La Tentation de saint Antoine*, Antoine's temptation by the Devil is similar to Christ's in Matthew 4:1–11. As in some of the tales Flaubert wrote in his youth, Satan takes Antoine into the air to survey the world; in the Bible, Satan tempts a weakened Christ by offering him the kingdoms of this world in exchange for Christ's worshiping him. Antoine drifts in and out of hallucinations and contemplates suicide, but recovers when he sees a vision of Christ's face in the sun; Christ rebukes Satan, and angels minister to Christ's needs.

Before writing *Salammbô*, Flaubert read and annotated fifty-three volumes about Carthage (Bart 398). The novel's biblical inspiration is the Old Testament. There the sun god Moloch, to whom the Carthaginians make sacrifices, appears frequently to incite men to the abominations of human sacrifice and immorality

(Leviticus 20:2–5; Deutoronomy 12:31; I Kings 11:7; II Kings 23:10). Flaubert's description of human sacrifices echoes those in the Bible.

In "Hérodias," Flaubert recounts the prophesied beheading of John the Baptist by Herod. This story is found in the gospels of Matthew 14:1–12 and Mark 6: 17–29. Flaubert's description is more detailed, and he adds a dimension of Roman and Jewish antagonism that the biblical account lacks.

In "La Légende de saint Julien l'hospitalier," the source being, as its title states, a legend and not a biblical story, the biblical references are more subtle. The most obvious allusion is to a chapter from the story of Elisha, an Old Testament prophet. The miracle recounted in II Kings 4:18–37 (more specifically verse 34) is similar to the miracle reported at the end of the tale: a leper asks Saint Julien to keep him warm and to lie on top of him. Spiritual ecstasy ensues, and the leper-turned-Christ takes Saint Julien in his arms and transports him to heaven. Elisha resurrects a boy by lying on him and by putting his mouth, his eyes, and his hands on the child's. The boy instantly rises and walks around his house. The Old Testament miracle of healing is a physical one, whereas the one miracle of Saint Julien is spiritual and metaphysical and redeems the sins of the parricidal and formerly cruel saint.

In "Un cœur simple," Félicité becomes devoted to the God of the New Testament. Flaubert brings a new light to Christianity in this story: during her lifetime, she had "found all the humble things of her daily life recurring in His story and sanctified by His presence," and she identifies her parrot with the Holy Spirit as she dies (Bart 693). By attributing such refreshing naïveté to one of his characters, Flaubert reminds us that our own interpretation of God, however flawed, might suffice us to transcend the foibles of our life. In all the tales of *Trois Contes*, the characters are confronted with God, whether to fulfill a prophecy, to rise from sadism to canonization, or to live and die a simple, loving life. (MMC)

References:

Backès, Jean-Louis. "Le Divin dans *Salammbô.*" *Revue des lettres modernes* 1165–72 (1994): 115–34.

Bart, Benjamin. *Flaubert*. Syracuse: Syracuse University Press, 1967.

Debray-Genette, Raymonde. "Profane, Sacred: Disorder of Utterance in *Trois Contes.*" In Naomi Schor and Henry F. Majewski, eds., *Flaubert and Postmodernism*. eds., Lincoln: University of Nebraska Press, 1984. 13–29.

Flaubert, Gustave. *Correspondance*. Ed. Jean Bruneau. Paris: Gallimard, 1973 (vol. 1), 1991 (vol. 3).

Genette, Gérard. "Demotivation in Hérodias." In Naomi Schor and Henry F. Majewski, eds., *Flaubert and Postmodernism*. Lincoln: University of Nebraska Press, 1984. 192–201.

Retat, Laudyce. "Flaubert, Renan, et l'interrogation des religions." *Revue des lettres modernes* 865–72 (1988): 5–34.

Toulet, Suzanne. *Le Sentiment religieux de Flaubert d'après* La Correspondance. Montréal: Cosmos, 1970.

"Bibliomanie" (1836). Like "Quidquid volueris," though with far fewer of that story's ironic shifts in register, the stylistic exercise "Bibliomanie" is an intriguing short story from Flaubert's teenage years. Through the old Spanish bookseller's possessive and somewhat criminal love for the book as an object, rather than for the knowledge contained therein, the story provides an early example of the fetishism displayed by so many of Flaubert's characters in his mature works. The depiction of the main character's madness shows the influence of the *petits romantiques* such as Petrus Borel. (MCO)

References:

Bruneau, Jean. *Les Débuts littéraires de Gustave Flaubert, 1831–1845.* Paris: Colin, 1962.

Flaubert, Gustave. *Bibliomania. A Tale.* Trans. Theodore Wesley Koch. Evanston, IL: Northwestern University Press, 1929.

———. "Bibliomanie." *Œuvres complètes.* 28 vols. Paris: Conard, 1910–1952. 20: 132–42.

———. *Œuvres complètes.* Ed. Maurice Bordèche. 16 vols. Paris: Club de L'Honnête Homme, 1971–76.

Binet (*MB*). In *Madame Bovary*, Binet is the local tax collector whose hobby is turning objects such as napkin rings and handrail knobs on a lathe. He is unable to sell them; they accumulate in his attic. He is an officer in the local National Guard, known for his punctuality and skill in arithmetic. The pleasure he takes in repetitive, seemingly useless activity makes him a precursor of the two copy clerks Bouvard and Pécuchet. Flaubert mentions the whirring of his lathe, a possible symbol of Fate, in scenes where Emma confronts a psychological crisis. (EFG)

Boileau-Despréaux, Nicolas (1636–1711). Nicolas Boileau-Despréaux was a passionate, mischievous critic and satirist who, tongue-in-cheek, called himself "the legislator of Parnassus" (the mountain where Apollo and the Muses lived and thus, by extension, the domain of the humanities and arts). His *Art poétique* (1674) is the leading French statement of classical aesthetics, according to which inspiration is tempered by reason.

Flaubert, who at first disdained the seventeenth-century poet and theoretician, reversed his opinion in 1846 and 1853 in letters to Louise Colet. Coming to consider in 1846 the unity of a work as central, he acknowledges the authority of Boileau for this principle. At this same time, he derives from the classicist the value of brevity in expression. Flaubert also opposes to romanticism a theory of the primacy of work over natural talent. Remarking that a literary work demands patience and sustained energy, Flaubert echoes Boileau's claim that art requires time and care; it is not the product of an artistic whim. In 1853, Flaubert's general view of classicism shifts significantly after a more careful study of Boileau. The poetician's belief that artistic perfection comes from restraints elevates him in Flaubert's estimation. Flaubert learns from Boileau that what binds a literary work together is the strength of its initial concept, from which structural harmony will flow. This conceptual foundation, as Flaubert gleans it from Boileau, demands hours of reflection to assure clarity of expression. Flaubert describes Boileau as a narrow, shallow stream of utmost clarity in which the depth of reflection is veiled by facility. In 1853, Flaubert also comes to value Boileau's lessons concerning expression and style over those concerning structure. Boileau teaches an exigent classicism that opposes the intemperance of romanticism. (EA)

Reference:

Butler, Ronnie. "Flaubert et Boileau." *Revue d'histoire littéraire de la France* 86 (1986): 856–64.

the book. In many senses, books were Flaubert's world. The first work he published was a short story called "Bibliomanie"; as its title shows, it is about a collector of rare books, for whom, however, the contents of his books and manuscripts hold no interest. Flaubert himself was an omnivorous reader; he did immense research for his trip to Egypt and the Near East and in preparation for his novels, especially *Salammbô* and *Bouvard et Pécuchet*. For the latter, he read more than one hundred volumes on medicine alone (Bart 722). The structure of this novel has been compared to that of a library; its title characters read through the disciplines (agriculture to chemistry to astronomy, and so on), dismissing each in turn. Like her creator, Emma Bovary is a great reader; in keepsakes, novels of romance and adventure, and religious works, she finds models for her life, which, however, never measure up to them. The most important books for Flaubert were of course those he himself wrote: his works were his life, which became increasingly devoted to his art: "J'écris fort lentement, parce qu'un livre est pour moi une manière spéciale de vivre" (I write very slowly, because for me a book is a special way of living) (letter to Maurice Schlésinger, December 20, 1859, *Corr.* 4:359). Flaubert's own library has been preserved in the town hall of Canteleu-Croisset. (CR)

See also art; bovarysme; museums.

References:

Bart, Benjamin F. *Flaubert.* Syracuse: Syracuse University Press, 1967.
Peterson, Carla. *The Determined Reader: Gender and Culture in the Novel from Napoleon to Victoria.* New Brunswick, NJ: Rutgers University Press, 1986.

Bordin, Mme veuve (*BP*). Mme Bordin is a widow who lives on her income in Chavignolles. She thinks for a time of marrying Bouvard. Before, during, and after her flirtation with Bouvard, however, she is preoccupied with her project for purchasing some of his land at a bargain price. Flaubert thus emphasizes bourgeois greed as the ultimate social reality. (LMP)

Borges, Jorge Luis (1899–1986). In two essays on Flaubert, the great Argentine short-story writer Jorge Luis Borges claims that Flaubert's creation of "meta-literature" (writing about writing) in works such as *Bouvard et Pécuchet* prepares the way for the symbolist poet Stéphane Mallarmé (1842–98), who said that the world was made to end up as a book. Thus he anticipates by more than a decade Jean-Paul Sartre's depiction of Flaubert and Mallarmé as socially non-committed "knights of nothingness" in Sartre's *L'Idiot de la famille*. (LMP)

References:

Borges, Jorge Luis. "Vindicación de *Bouvard et Pécuchet*" and "Flaubert y su destino ejemplar." In Jorge Luis Borges, *Discusión*. Buenos Aires: Emecé, 1961 [1957]. 137–43, 145–50.

Sartre, Jean-Paul. *L'Idiot de la famille*. 3 vols. Paris: Gallimard, 1971–72.

Bosquet, Amélie (1815–1904). A journalist and novelist from Rouen, Amélie Bosquet was one of the three women with whom Flaubert discussed literary issues. Her writings tended to express social and feminist ideals. She started writing in *La Revue de Rouen* at twenty-four and published novels between 1845 and 1897; the most admired are considered to be *Louise Meunier, une passion en province* (1861), *Une femme bien élevée* (1866), *Le Roman des ouvrières* (1868), and *Les Trois Prétendants* (1874). Her *la Normandie romanesque et merveilleuse* (1845) still is a useful source for local legends of Flaubert's *pays*. Although she misleadingly claimed to have been the governess of Flaubert's niece, she actually first met him in 1858 at an art exhibit in the Bibliothèque Nationale, when he was already renowned (Starkie 34–39). Her friendship with Flaubert started in 1859; she used to ask his advice about her writings. Although she refused to become his mistress, Flaubert's letters to her continued to be affectionate and flattering. Their relationship ended after December 1869, when she published an ambivalent review of *L'Education sentimentale* in *Le Droit des femmes*. Perhaps she was becoming envious of George Sand's increasingly close literary relationship with Flaubert; or perhaps she saw herself caricatured in the disagreeable character of La Vatnaz. This act ended their friendship. Her "Mémoire" on Flaubert can be found in the Bibliothèque Nationale in Paris. (CBK/LCP)

Reference:

Starkie, Enid. *Flaubert, the Master*. New York: Atheneum, 1971. 34–39.

Bouilhet, Louis Hyacinthe (1821–69). One of Flaubert's classmates, Louis Bouilhet became his closest friend, though not until 1846. In 1842, Bouilhet studied medicine under Flaubert's father while writing poetry in his spare time. In 1846, he quit his studies to dedicate himself to writing, while giving lessons for a living. From then on, Bouilhet and Flaubert showed each other their work and also collaborated on a couple of plays. During the writing of *Madame*

Bovary, "Monsignor," as Flaubert fondly nicknamed Bouilhet, paid weekly visits to Flaubert to discuss their work. He collaborated with Flaubert on the unpublished "La Queue de la poire de la boule de monseigneur," a scatological farce, and provided illustrations. Bouilhet was a known literary figure before Flaubert. When Bouilhet moved to Paris in 1853 following the success of his poem "Melaenis" after its reading in Louise Colet's salon, he and Flaubert started a weekly correspondence. Bouilhet's play *Madame de Montarcy* was a success in 1856. In 1857, he left his fashionable Parisian life when he was appointed librarian, first in Mantes, then in Rouen in 1867. Both before and after Bouilhet's death in 1869, Flaubert took pains to have the latter's work published and staged. Flaubert considered Bouilhet a great poet, but Bouilhet was aware that his name would not reach posterity. Bouilhet's role in Flaubert's work has been underestimated; it goes beyond providing medical information for his novels, such as the symptoms Emma Bovary suffers after swallowing arsenic. He helped Flaubert revise everything that the latter would publish, but was too ill to hear the end of *L'Education sentimentale*. However, Flaubert used elements from his play *Hélène Peyron* (1858) in *L'Education sentimentale*. Bouilhet and Maxime Du Camp firmly rejected the first version of *La Tentation de saint Antoine* in 1849. A thoroughly revised version of that novel appeared only in 1874. Bouilhet also influenced significant scenes of *Salammbô*. Bouilhet and Flaubert's physical resemblance reflects their intellectual affinity; they shared the need for precise documentation and impassibility in their writings. After Bouilhet's death, Flaubert wrote, "I lost my midwife, the man who saw more clearly in my mind than I did myself" (*see* Bart). (CBK/LMP)

References:

Bart, Benjamin F. "Louis Bouilhet, Flaubert's accoucheur." *Symposium* 17 (1963): 183–201.

Bouilhet, Louis. *Œuvres*. Geneva: Slatkine, 1974.

Flaubert, Gustave. *La Queue de la poire de la boule de monseigneur: Pochade rouennaise inédite*. Paris: Nizet, 1958.

Green, Anne. "Flaubert, Bouilhet and the Illegitimate Daughter: A Source for *L'Education sentimentale*." *French Studies* 40 (1986): 304–10.

Bournisien (*MB*). The priest in *Madame Bovary*, Bournisien is sincere and dedicated, but devoid of spirituality. His insensitivity to Emma Bovary's emotional distress helps drive her into adultery. The atheistic pharmacist Homais and he have several comic arguments that punctuate the novel, underscoring the inefficacy of both Catholicism and Enlightenment positivism—the myth of scientific progress as a means to human betterment—in meeting humans' deepest needs. He gives Emma the last rites, but then he and Homais fall asleep together during the wake. (LMP)

Reference:

Jasinski, René. "Le couple Bournisien-Homais." In René Jasinski, *A travers le XIXe siècle*. Paris: Minard, 1975. 249–68.

Bouvard and **Pécuchet** (*BP*). Dryly presented with impersonal, omniscient narration, the two inseparable friends Bouvard and Pécuchet dominate Flaubert's last, unfinished novel throughout. These two copy clerks meet in a park and strike up a conversation. François-Denys-Bartholomée Bouvard works for a business firm; Juste-Romain-Cyrille Pécuchet works for the Naval Ministry. They quickly become deeply attached to each other. Their homosocial bond is a commonplace in Flaubert (Frédéric Moreau and Deslauriers in *L'Education sentimentale* come to mind; see also Kempf). Bouvard often plays the "masculine" role and Pécuchet the "feminine," but the latter himself is excited and sexually initiated by their maid Mélie, from whom he catches syphilis. Bouvard soon inherits enough money for them to quit their humdrum jobs, purchase property in the country, and devote themselves to a quest for knowledge. They do so by consulting manuals devoted to a wide range of activities (agriculture, gymnastics, pedagogy, and so forth) and then by applying their often-contradictory or self-contradictory sources literally, resulting in ludicrous, repeated failures. But they do occasionally succeed. For instance, when they practice phrenology, they read their own personalities, as well as those of their adopted children Victor and Victorine and of others, with reasonable accuracy. Despite their failure to find an authoritative, reliable guide, they obstinately continue to trust in the manuals that they consult. They are *alazons* (overly self-confident persons) continually deflated by experience, but without ever—until near the end—learning a healthy skepticism. Their ineptitude provides a telling commentary on human stupidity, on the presumption that we can master nature, but in Flaubert's laborious research and prodigious note taking, he himself, at times, seems infected by their folly. As Saint Antoine said of the Catoblépas, "Sa stupidité m'attire" (Its stupidity attracts me).

Whereas their creator is excessively bookish, his characters are not. They never learn to organize or synthesize; they heap up curiosities like magpies. Rather than try to impose on externality a system that does not work, as Eugenio Donato claimed, they are "intoxicated" and "astonished" by their contact with the country. Flaubert describes their reactions to the new situation with a vocabulary of ecstasy, not of intellectual control. Polymorphously perverse, sensuously reborn, they love living in the country because they can run around naked there. In their experimentation, too, they lump together what "should have" stayed separate. Their attempts at arboriculture fail, for instance, because they ignore temporal constraints, fail sufficiently to respect the different needs of various special trees, and thus end up simultaneously trimming some trees both at the top and at the root, killing them. When Pécuchet grows melons, he plants different varieties too close together, producing "abominable hybrids." In general, plants have the upper hand over their protagonists because the plants refuse to conform to their gardeners' wishes. Indeed, the characters are in constant opposition to their surroundings. They struggle against plants, birds, and the weather in their attempt to put into practice their theoretical readings. Everything seems in collusion against them. Their efforts to relate knowledge and activity fail.

Bit by bit, the two friends learn to become skeptics. When they study in chapter 4 to write a history of the duc d'Angoulême, for example, they find that he has straight hair in one portrait and curly in another (see Gaillard). Any representation through which an object is knowable, in other words, depends on the arbitrary. Our apprehension of origins, the couple quickly learns, always is filtered through interpretations, which depend on other interpretations in turn. Bouvard's questionable paternity follows this pattern: his paternity is later established by his former uncle/present father's testament.

This questionable heritage reflects Flaubert's questioning of the authority and paternity of his own text and of the very nature of language. Much like his characters, Flaubert is a reader faced with a proliferation of texts. As a writer, however, he communicates to his reader how preponderant a mishmash of scientific and other discourses is in society and, more important, how unoriginal this mishmash is. Flaubert refutes the possibility of origin in science and art and disputes the possibility of total knowledge. Without an origin, how can we assign any responsibility for discourse? Much of Flaubert's irony plays with the fact that when we read Flaubert's text, we are put in a position somewhat similar to that of Bouvard and Pécuchet. Their final decision to abandon the quest for knowledge and to return to copying as before reflects their renunciation of all intellectual control. One can universalize only by limiting the field of examples one considers ("you have to forget before you can begin to think"), and by resolving to copy everything that comes their way, Flaubert's characters do not impose limits. This decision compels them to live in chaos. Perhaps Flaubert suggests that only irony can give one any hope of power over the excess of texts facing a reader. (ENM)

References:

Donato, Eugenio. "The Museum's Furnace: Notes toward a Contextual Reading of *Bouvard et Pécuchet*." In Laurence M. Porter, ed., *Critical Essays on Gustave Flaubert*. Boston: Hall, 1986. 207–22.

Flaubert, Gustave. *Bouvard and Pécuchet*. Trans. T. W. Earp and G. W. Stonier. New York: New Directions, 1954.

Gaillard, Françoise. "Une innarrable histoire." *Flaubert et le comble de l'art*. Paris: Société d'édition d'enseignement supérieur, 1987. 9–22.

Kempf, Roger. "Flaubert: Le double pupitre." In Roger Kempf, *Mœurs: Éthnologie et fiction*. Paris: Seuil, 1976. 69–95.

Mouchard, Claude. "Terre, technologie, roman: A propos du deuxième chapitre de *Bouvard et Pécuchet*." *Littérature* 15 (1974): 65–74.

Porter, Laurence M. "The Rhetoric of Deconstruction: Donato and Flaubert." *Nineteenth-Century French Studies* 20.1–2 (1991–92): 128–36.

Trilling, Lionel. "Introduction." In Gustave Flaubert, *Bouvard et Pécuchet*. Trans. T. W. Earp and G. W. Stonier. New York: New Directions, 1954. v–xxxvii.

Bouvard et Pécuchet (1881). "It's my last will and testament," said Flaubert, "the distillation of all my experiences and my judgment of humankind and its works" (cited by Sabatier). He died while writing the last chapter. His niece Caroline de Commanville made a fair copy of that chapter and oversaw the publication of the work. Cento's critical edition shows her additions.

The story is simple. Two copy clerks meet in a park by chance. Reproducing the classical contrast of the odd couple, Flaubert makes Bouvard stout and Pécuchet lean. The clerks' initial conversation recapitulates the book in advance. As they continue to meet and share their intellectual curiosities, their imagination becomes stimulated. The monotony of their office work becomes painful and humiliating. When Bouvard acquires an unexpected inheritance, they retire to a farm in the country.

Chapter 2 tells of these city dwellers' first encounters with nature. They "felt themselves possessed by an almost religious reverence for the wealth of the soil" (Flaubert 42) and intoxicated by the fresh air. The featherheaded Bouvard encounters a series of disasters: the spontaneous combustion of all his harvested wheat, piled in too great a mass; the explosion of his preserves. A storm ruins their orchard. To learn what caused the explosion, in chapter 3 they turn to physics and chemistry, but they are at length forced to conclude, "Science is constructed according to the data given by a corner of the whole field. Perhaps it doesn't agree with the remainder, of which nothing is known, which is much bigger and can't be discovered" (94). Then they explore geology, which leads them to abandon the hope of finding an underlying order in the world. "Everything passes, crumbles, is transformed. Creation takes place in an up-and-down and haphazard manner" (112).

In chapter 4, they become archaeologists and turn their house into a museum heaped with heteroclite objects that Flaubert enumerates. This study of the past leads them to investigate history: they study the duc d'Angoulême as a test case (an episode that probably suggested to Jean-Paul Sartre his protagonist's meaningless research on the marquis de Rollebon in *La Nausée*), but soon realize that their sources are shaped by individual subjectivity, and that they do not even know what is going on in their own house. So they come to literature, in chapter 5, as a way of learning about human psychology.

Chapter 6 describes their encounters with politics, giving Flaubert an opportunity to satirize socialism. In chapter 7, both men fall in love—Bouvard with their neighbor Mme Bordin, who wants mainly to buy some of their land cheap, and Pécuchet with their servant Mélie, who gives him syphilis. In a homosocial move typical of Flaubert (compare the ending of *L'Education sentimentale*, where Frédéric Moreau and Deslauriers, formerly rivals in love, are reconciled), Flaubert's heroes learn that they have been foolish. They regret the interruption in their friendship caused by the distraction of heterosexual lust, and they embrace tenderly.

In chapter 8, they pursue what one might call the health sciences—gymnastics and hypnotism (then called magnetism)—and finally revert to philosophy, but uncertainty overwhelms them. That they share their skepticism with their neighbors makes them suspect and unwelcome. "Bouvard and Pécuchet enunciated their abominable paradoxes on other occasions. . . . In fact, they undermined all foundations. . . . The evidence of their superiority gave umbrage. . . . Then a pitiable faculty developed in their spirit, that of perceiving stupidity and no longer tolerating it" (258). Too often, critics overlook this and similar passages and treat the heroes as buffoons with no insight.

In chapter 9 (to underline the precariousness of their skeptical insight, which Flaubert shares), Bouvard and Pécuchet experience a religious conversion. They sell their farm to Mme Bordin, who covets it, in exchange for a life annuity. At length they become disillusioned with religion, owing to the intellectual difficulties of accepting miracles and the doctrine of permissive evil (God allows evil to exist as part of a mysterious grand plan—a notion already sketched in the Old Testament Book of Job). But they feel affection for Victor and Victorine, the orphaned children of a convict, who are being sent, respectively, to a reformatory and a convent. They vouch for them and take them in. The sequence of the events in their education recapitulates the experience of Bouvard and Pécuchet, and in the same order. The clerks' wards, however, prove incorrigible, and faulty techniques of education aggravate their defects of character. By implication, Flaubert satirizes Rousseau's novel of education, *Emile*.

Bouvard and Pécuchet lose custody of their wards, who are indifferent to them anyway. The whole town comes to condemn them. They have no more interest in life until they suddenly have an inspiration: "Let's copy as before." (This phrase was actually added by Flaubert's niece after his death, which occurred as he was drafting the final chapter.) As the novel ends, they set to work, more or less at random. But in Flaubert's mind, the passages they were to copy would create a volume 2, consisting of outrageous, contradictory, and ridiculous statements from popular culture and from authorities. Already in the 1840s, he had planned this *Dictionnaire des idées reçues* and had collected materials for it before even envisaging the composition of the novel, which became a gigantic preamble. (LMP)

See also anatomy; Bouvard and Pécuchet; copies, copying; pastoral; socialism.

References:

Bart, Benjamin. *Flaubert*. Syracuse: Syracuse University Press, 1967. 587–620.

Bersani, Leo. "Flaubert's Encyclopedism." *Novel* 21 (1988): 140–46.

Cento Alberto. *Commentaire de* Bouvard et Pécuchet. Naples: Liguori, 1973.

———, ed. *Gustave Flaubert*, Bouvard et Pécuchet. Paris: Nizet, 1964.

Demorest, D. L. *A travers les plans, manuscripts, et dossiers de* Bouvard et Pécuchet. Paris: Conard, 1931.

Durry, Marie Jeanne, and Jean Bruneau. "Lectures de Flaubert et de Bouvard et Pécuchet." *Rivista di letterature moderne e comparate* 15 (1962): 5–45.

Gaillard, Françoise. "Une innarrable histoire." In Pierre Cogny, ed., *Flaubert et le comble de l'art*. Paris: Société d'édition d'enseignement supérieur, 1981. 75–87.

Gothot-Mersch, Claudine. "Le roman interminable: Un aspect de la structure de *Bouvard et Pécuchet*." In Pierre Cogny, ed. *Flaubert et le comble de l'art*. Paris: Société d'édition d'enseignement supérieur, 1981. 9–22.

Kempf, Roger. *Bouvard, Flaubert et Pécuchet*. Paris: Seuil, 1990.

Moussaron, Jean-Pierre. "Une étrange greffe." In Pierre Cogny, ed., *Flaubert et le comble de l'art*. Paris: Société d'édition d'enseignement supérieur, 1981. 89–109.

Sabatier, Auguste. "L'Œuvre posthume de Gustave Flaubert." *Journal de Genève* April 3, 1881.

Schulz-Buschhaus, Ulrich. "Das historische Ort von Flauberts Spätwerk—Interpretationsvorschläge zu *Bouvard et Pécuchet*." *Zeitschrift für französiche Sprache und Literatur* 87 (1977): 193–211.

Terdiman, Richard. "Counter-humorists: Strategies of Ideological Critique in Marx and Flaubert." *Diacritics* 9, 3 (1979): 18–32.

Trilling, Lionel. "Introduction." In Gustave Flaubert, *Bouvard and Pécuchet*. New York: New Directions, 1954. v–xxxvii.

Bovary, Berthe (*MB*). In *Madame Bovary*, Berthe Bovary is the unfortunate daughter of Charles and Emma Bovary. Emma's relationship with her daughter is ambivalent. While Emma was anticipating the birth of the child, she dreamt of having a son, whom she would name Georges (from the Greek *georgos*, farmer), in unconscious, ironic opposition to her romantic dreams of success and freedom for a male child. After the child is born, Emma passes in review all the romantic names she can find, but finally chooses the name Berthe, a name she had heard by chance at the ball at the Vaubyessard château. From the text, it is impossible to determine whether Berthe was one of the aristocratic guests or one of the servants. If we assume the latter, the choice is once again unwittingly ironic. Neglected by her mother, Berthe becomes an impoverished orphan after Emma's suicide and Charles's death: she goes to live with her grandmother Bovary, who dies soon after. Berthe is then sent to work in a cotton mill. Her future could well serve as the basis for a bleakly naturalistic novel by Emile Zola. (EFG)

Bovary, Charles (*MB*). Charles Bovary is Emma's hapless husband in *Madame Bovary*. His limitations underscore the confining world in which she finds herself. She dreams of passionate love; Charles is quiet, plodding, and uncommunicative. She dreams of being married to a successful physician; Charles is only a paramedic (*officier de santé*) who botches the operation on the clubfoot Hippolyte. In school, Charles, condemned to be average, works hard just to stay in the middle of his class. He is mocked by his classmates, ridiculed by the teacher, and made to copy twenty times the expression *ridiculus sum*, an undeserved punishment that nevertheless sums up his life.

Yet Charles does have good qualities, a point often overlooked. He is popular with his patients because he does not take on airs. He enjoys some medical success because he is prudent in his treatments, and he fails only when he accedes to Emma's wish that he attempt a revolutionary operation on the stable boy Hippolyte, an operation that is clearly beyond his capabilities (as well as being illegal for someone who is not a registered physician). Flaubert's depiction of Charles seems cruel, but that may be because we see him mainly through the eyes of others. As Flaubert revised his novel, he progressively eliminated Charles's good qualities. Charles's foolish faithfulness to Emma's memory contributes to his ruin and his death. (EFG)

References:

Falconer, Graham. "Flaubert assassin de Charles." In Michael Issacharoff, ed., *Languages de Flaubert.* Paris: Les Lettres Modernes, 1976. 115–41.

Lesser, Simon O. "The Role of Unconscious Understanding in Flaubert and Dostoevsky." *Daedalus* 92 (1963): 363–82.

Levin, Harry. "Flaubert." In Harry Levin, *The Gates of Horn: A Study of Five French Realists.* New York: Oxford University Press, 1963. 214–304.

Porter, Laurence M. "Emma Bovary's Narcissism Revisited." In Graham Falconer and Mary Donaldson-Evans, eds., *Kaleidoscope: Essays on Nineteenth-Century French Literature in Honor of Thomas H. Goetz.* Toronto: Centre d'Etudes Romantiques Joseph Sablé, 1996. 85–97.

Sinclair, Alison. *The Deceived Husband: A Kleinian Approach to the Literature of Infidelity.* New York: Oxford University Press, 1993.

Bovary, Emma, née Rouault (*MB*). The main character of *Madame Bovary,* Emma Rouault is a farm girl who dreams of a life in high society. Her father sends her to a convent school in Rouen when she turns thirteen, where the program aims at preparing middle- and upper-class women to take their places as wives and mothers (part 1, chapter 6). Critics have often mentioned Emma's convent training, and especially her extracurricular reading, in trying to explain her subsequent vagaries. She is not without intellectual ability—she answers the vicar's most difficult questions of catechism, but she is particularly sensitive to physical sensations: "Elle s'assoupit doucement à la langueur mystique qui s'exhale des parfums de l'autel, de la fraîcheur des bénitiers et du rayonnement des cierges" (she sank softly into the mystical languor of the incense on the altar, the coolness of the holy-water fonts, and the light of the candles), and like Félicité in "Un cœur simple," she is much taken by sentimental images of "la brebis malade" (the ailing sheep) and the like. A washerwoman, a member of an aristocratic family ruined during the Revolution, lends the girls romantic novels, which Emma also reads. Her daydreams will take on the concrete detail of the illustrations in these books, which will become the model onto which she will try to fit the data of lived experience.

When Charles visits her farm home, we see Emma mainly through his eyes; but we do not see Charles from Emma's point of view until after they are married. In like fashion, we also see her through the eyes of the other two men in her life, Léon and Rodolphe, in their initial meetings. However, given her temperament and reading, it is possible to construct a plausible view of Charles, Léon, and Rodolphe as Emma sees them. For example, we can construct an initially idealized Charles who will give way to an exaggeratedly denigrated

Charles as the marriage wears on. This latter view will change briefly as Charles attempts the operation on Hippolyte, and Emma dreams of being married to a successful surgeon (an impossible dream because Charles cannot legally perform surgery). Jules de Gaultier termed this tendency of Emma "bovarysme," "le pouvoir départi à l'homme de se concevoir autre qu'il n'est" (the ability that people have to imagine themselves different from what they are), an ability that can lead to good, but that in Flaubert's works is always accompanied by powerlessness and failure. Flaubert, in what may be an apocryphal remark, is often quoted as having said, "Madame Bovary, c'est moi, d'après moi" (Madame Bovary is I, or based on me, critics often omit the second clause). He shared with Emma Bovary the romantic dreams of exotic places and times and her dissatisfaction with contemporary society, but his dreams resulted in great literature. Emma did not have the ability to break free of the societal constraints of her day and thus move her life in a positive direction. She did not become a George Sand, a Rachel, or an Eugénie Niboyet—that was not the type of story that Flaubert wished to write. Discussions of the novel quite rightly focus on Emma's situation: Does her failure result from societal pressures or her own limitations? Does Flaubert intend that we sympathize with Emma or blame her? Is Emma's case of no significance, or does she somehow represent the average person in a modern, consumer-oriented society? He once said that at any moment, twenty Madame Bovarys were languishing and suffering in little villages throughout France. (EFG)

References:

Bersani, Leo. "Emma Bovary and the Sense of Sex." In Leo Bersani, *A Future for Astyanax: Character and Desire in Literature*. Boston: Little, Brown, 1976. 89–105.

Bloom, Harold, ed. *Emma Bovary*. New York: Chelsea House, 1994.

Kaplan, Louise. *Female Perversions: The Temptations of Emma Bovary*. New York: Doubleday, 1991.

Paris, Bernard J. "The Search for Glory in Madame Bovary: A Horneyan Analysis." *American Journal of Psychoanalysis* 57.1 (1997): 5–24.

Peterson, Carla. *The Determined Reader: Gender and Culture in the Novel from Napoleon to Victoria*. New Brunswick, NJ: Rutgers University Press, 1986. 132–79.

Porter, Laurence M. "Emma Bovary's Narcissism Revisited." In Graham Falconer and Mary Donaldson-Evans, eds., *Kaleidoscope: Essays on Nineteenth-Century French Literature in Honor of Thomas H. Goetz*. Toronto: Centre d'Etudes Romantiques Joseph Sablé, 1996. 85–97.

Rothfield, Lawrence. "From Semiotic to Discursive Intertextuality: The Case of *Madame Bovary*." *Novel* 19 (1985): 57–81.

Bovary, Madame (*MB*; Charles Bovary's first wife). Critics have often wondered why Flaubert created a first wife for Charles Bovary, a decision that, some feel, unnecessarily lengthens the novel. Charles's passive nature is amply demonstrated by his subordination to his mother, when she chooses the widow

Dubuc to be his wife, and then to his first wife. Flaubert emphasizes the contrast between her and Emma Rouault, which helps to explain Charles's blind devotion to Emma. The abrupt, arbitrary death of the first wife (as a narrative device) leaves the way open for Charles to marry Emma, which he does without ever looking back. (EFG)

Bovary, Madame (*MB*; Charles Bovary's mother). Madame Bovary, trapped in an unhappy marriage to a promiscuous drunk, has taken on the nontraditional role of managing the family's financial affairs. (Perhaps her example unconsciously induced Charles later to let his wife Emma do the same, with disastrous results.) She dotes on Charles, spoils him, and insists that he obtain some schooling, first with the local priest, then at school in Rouen. She wants him to have a career. After he is established as an *officier de santé*, she finds an older wife supposedly with a substantial dowry for him, but that wife soon dies. Charles's mother tries to continue to play a role in his life after his second marriage, but cannot supplant Emma in Charles's affection. She strongly disapproves of Emma's laziness, prodigality, and irreverence. When Charles defends Emma, a break between mother and son occurs. After Emma's death, Charles and his mother part definitively because he will not take her good advice. After Charles's death, she cares for her granddaughter Berthe, but dies soon after. (EFG)

Bovary, Monsieur (*MB*; Charles Bovary's father). A surgeon's assistant in the army—ironically, an ancillary role not unlike the one his son will play—forced to resign because of a scandal over recruiting violations, Monsieur Bovary charms a wealthy woman with his good looks and bravado and secures her dowry. At first, she is devoted to him, but her servility, Flaubert observes, only drives her husband further away. He fails at farming and business and then lives on his meager army pension, drinking and whoring. At last, his wife, out of desperation, takes over the complete management of their household and their financial affairs and shuts herself up in a furious silence that will last until her death. He is indifferent to his son: he does not send him to school, lets him go barefoot, and spends time with him only to try unsuccessfully to teach him to drink and blaspheme. Charles's mother plans her son's future, choosing for him a profession, a place to practice it, and an older, unattractive first wife who is supposed to have money. When Charles's parents go to visit their son and Emma, the elder Madame Bovary fears that her husband might try to seduce his daughter-in-law, because "he was a man who respected nothing." Emma enjoys his self-assured manner and his flirtations. His neglect of his son leads to Charles's mother having a disproportionate role in his life and prepares for Charles to be dominated by Emma, as well as establishing the model, unusual for the time, of a woman managing the family finances. Thus Emma can drive herself and her husband into bankruptcy without Charles noticing. Flaubert's implied depiction of the strong influence that paternal neglect can play in deciding a child's destiny exemplifies the subtle subtexts of his novel. (EFG/LMP)

Bovarysme. The term "bovarysme" was coined by Jules de Gaultier in his 1902 book *Le Bovarysme*. He defines it as a basic human faculty, the power to conceive of oneself as other than what one is. In Flaubert's characters, this capacity is deformed and becomes a flaw: not only Emma Bovary but also the characters in *L'Education sentimentale* waste their efforts in futile attempts to imitate idealized models. Gaultier's precursor here is Stendhal, who defines a kind of love (*amour/vanité*) where "les idées de roman vous prenant à la gorge, on croit etre amoureux et mélancolique, car la vanité aspire à se croire une grande passion" (Ideas from novels get you by the throat, you think you are lovesick and melancholy, because vanity aspires to a grand passion) (*De l'amour*, book 1, ch. 1). René Girard applies the concept, under the name "mimetic desire," to *Le Rouge et le noir, Don Quixote*, and Proust as well as to Flaubert, and finds that novelistic truth is the revelation of this romantic "lie." Gaultier sees variants of bovarysme in other works of Flaubert: in *La Tentation de saint Antoine* it is the attempt to surpass human limitations; in *Bouvard et Pécuchet*, it is the disproportion between human knowledge and the individual's illusory attempt to appropriate it.

In Gaultier's book, Flaubert is only a point of departure; and bovarysme, rightly conceived and used, has positive consequences: it enables one to imagine the world in different ways. Therefore, it is essential to the evolution of human thought. We might think, then, that bovarysme could provide a basis for artistic creation. The characters in Flaubert's fiction, however, are unable to take this step. (CR)

References:

Gaultier, Jules de. *Le Bovarysme*. Paris: Mercure de France, 1902.
———. *Bovarysm*. Trans. Gerald M. Spring. New York: Philosophical Library, 1970.
Girard, René. *Mensonge romantique et vérité romanesque*. Paris: Grasset, 1961.
Stendhal (pseud. of Henri Beyle). *De l'amour*. Paris: Le Divan, 1927.

Brainne, Léonie. Léonie Brainne was one of the mature Flaubert's many female friends. They met in 1871, just after the Franco-Prussian War. A widow since 1864, she was the most cherished of Flaubert's "three angels" (the other two were her sister Mme Lapierre and an actress, Mme Pasquier). Living in Rouen by the time their correspondence took place, Mme Brainne once offered to help Flaubert resolve his financial difficulties, but the writer gratefully declined. Despite a few intimate-sounding passages in their letters to each other, Flaubert's biographers could never prove that the couple was physically involved. (LF)

Breughel the younger, Pieter (ca. 1564–1637/38). Flaubert always insisted that the idea for *La Tentation de saint Antoine* came to him from Pieter Breughel's painting of the subject, which he first saw in the Balbi Palace on a trip to Genoa, Italy, in 1845. From 1846 until his death, he had on his wall a copy of that painting in the form of an engraving by Breughel's disciple Jacques Callot (1592–1635). The monsters that assail Antoine are inspired by the grotesque composite forms of Flemish painting and by the even more alarming fusions of plant, animal, and human forms that Breughel may have introduced to painting. (LMP)

References:

Lombard, Alfred. *Flaubert et saint Antoine*. Paris: Attinger, 1934.
Milner, Max. *Le Diable dans la littérature française de Cazotte à Baudelaire, 1772–1861*. 2 vols. Paris: Corti, 1960. 2:213–35.

Brombert, Victor. Victor Brombert has long been an active Flaubert critic; his noteworthy studies include *The Novels of Flaubert*, which underlines Flaubert's morbid eroticism and pessimistic nihilism. *Flaubert par lui-même* richly characterizes Flaubert's imagination. Brombert's expressive criticism seeks reflections of Flaubert's dreams and preoccupations in his texts. "Flaubert and the Status of the Subject," impenitently conservative, disputes that Flaubert could be considered a progenitor of modernism. (LMP)

References:

Brombert, Victor. "Flaubert and the Status of the Subject." In Naomi Schor and Henry F. Majewski, eds., *Flaubert and Postmodernism*. Lincoln: University of Nebraska Press, 1984. 100–115.
———. *Flaubert par lui-même*. Paris: Seuil, 1971.
———. *The Novels of Flaubert: A Study of Themes and Techniques*. Princeton: Princeton University Press, 1966.

Bron, Rosanette (*ES*). The parallelism between Frédéric Moreau and Jacques Arnoux finds an equivalent in the links between Mme Arnoux and Roseannette Bron, usually referred to as "la Maréchale" in reference to the disguise she wears at the fancy-dress ball early in *L'Education sentimentale*. As Arnoux's mistress, she offers a more sensual and more available version of womanhood than does Mme Arnoux, whom she constantly recalls to Frédéric's susceptible imagination, either by the similarity of objects they possess (owing to Arnoux's undiscriminating generosity) or by the contrast between her superficiality and Mme Arnoux's depth, her easy warmth and the apparent coldness of Mme Arnoux. As a very young girl, Rosanette was sold by her mother to a man willing to pay for her. She drifts from lover to lover in the course of the novel, constantly returning, however, to Arnoux. If Frédéric remains attracted to her for so long, the reason lies in her teasing rejection of him. It is one of Flaubert's most bitter ironies that she accepts Frédéric on the evening after Mme Arnoux fails to meet him, and that the episode takes place in the apartment he had prepared for Mme Arnoux. The political symbolism of their affair has often been underlined: Fédéric accepts second-best just as France, failing to achieve a true republic, makes do with a watered-down and short-lived version. Their liaison quickly descends into banality and boredom as Frédéric becomes aware of Rosanette's poor taste, her ignorance, and her behavioral tics. She bears his son, but Frédéric feels nothing but repugnance for the child, whose death seals the end of their affair. At the end of the novel, we learn that she has married one of the richest of her lovers, has become enormously fat, and has adopted a little boy. The embodiment of physical, and, above all, sexual appetite, Rosanette nevertheless retains her individuality, part of Flaubert's endless fascination with the variety of female nature. (RL)

References:

Williams, David. "Sacred and Profane in *L'Education sentimentale.*" *Modern Language Review* 73 (1978): 787–98.

Woestelandt, Evelyne. "Le Corps vénal: Rosanette dans *L'Education sentimentale.*" *Nineteenth-Century French Studies* 16 (1987–88): 120–31.

Bruneau, Jean (1921–). Jean Bruneau is the leading "hard scholar" (one dealing with original sources, manuscripts, and documents) of Flaubert. With Jean-A. Ducourneau, he compiled the *Album Flaubert*, the best collection of documents, sketches, and photographs concerning the author. His study of Flaubert's juvenilia, *Les Débuts littéraires de Gustave Flaubert, 1831–1845* has still not been surpassed. Above all, he has compiled a monumental labor of love, the finest edition of Flaubert's *Correspondance*. (LMP)

References:

Bruneau, Jean. *Les Débuts littéraires de Gustave Flaubert, 1831–1845*. Paris: Colin, 1962.

Bruneau, Jean, and Jean-A. Ducourneau, eds. *Album Flaubert*. Paris: Gallimard, 1972.

Flaubert, Gustave. *Correspondence*. Ed. Jean Bruneau. 5 vols. to date. Paris: Gallimard, 1973– .

Butor, Michel (1926–). One of the experimental New Novelists, Michel Butor has devoted several studies to Flaubert over the years. His 1970 article in *Critique* (partially reprinted in *L'Esprit Créateur*) is a playful identification of the cyclical recurrence of parallel episodes in *La Tentation de saint Antoine*, in which he sees a picturesque parade of temptations, with no real progression. Thus he overlooks the novel's psychodyamic dimension in its depiction of the saint. Butor further argues that unlike the characters in Balzac or Stendhal, where the primary virtue is energy, in Flaubert the fictional characters are enveloped in determinism. They cannot redirect their lives. Instead, they are exposed to temptation. Flaubert is at odds with "the dominant ideology of the chain of decisive individual actions." He always presents processions and parades ironically.

Butor developed his *Improvisations sur Flaubert* from lectures in Mayence, in a course on Flaubert and the problems of literary creation. In *Madame Bovary*, Butor claims, Flaubert passes from "horizontal" to "vertical" writing. Beneath the smooth, icy surface where pronouns and adverbs are made as important as nouns and verbs, and where pronouns are often depersonalized ("on," "quelqu'un"), Flaubert tries to make us occasionally sense the presence of a mask underneath the face. Compare his description of Charles Bovary's ridiculous hat, which has "depths of expression, like an imbecile's face." In this series of lectures, each dealing with a different work, one finds a radical Flaubert in the mode of Butor himself. Flaubert, who often expressed his hatred of the bourgeois, was in Butor's view referring not to a social class but to a language that is a continuing lie, full of clichés that corrupt the population. Flaubert's writing. Butor claimed, was a "war machine" manipulating yet subverting a degraded received language. All Flaubert's characters and settings also fulfill this subversive program. Carthage is Paris, where Hannon incarnates "the bankerly and administrative mind." Bouvard and Pécuchet, like Socrates and Christ, are disturbers of public order, martyred by modern society. Emma, too, is a sacrificial victim who wishes to destroy society. This is a deeply personal reading, debatable but highly suggestive. (EFG/LMP)

References:

Butor, Michel. "Demeures et dieux à Carthage." *Corps-Ecrit* 9 (1984): 127–47.

———. "La Forme de la Tentation." *L'Esprit Créateur* 10.1 (1970): 3–12.

———. *Improvisations sur Flaubert*. Paris: Editions de la différence, 1984.

———. "La Spirale des sept péchés." *Critique* 26 (1970): 387–412. Rpr. in Michel Butor, *Répertoire IV*. Paris: Minuit, 1974. 209–35.

Mason, Barbara. "Language and Ideology in Michel Butor's *Improvisations sur Flaubert*." *Nottingham French Studies* 28.1 (1989): 53–64.

Passias, Katherine. "Deep and Surface Structure of the Narrative Pronoun *vous* in Butor's *La Modification* and Its Relationship to Free Indirect Style." *Language and Style* 9 (1976): 197–212.

Byron, Lord (George Gordon Byron, sixth Baron Byron, 1788–1824). For Flaubert, as for many French romantics, Byron was the Poet, the soul of his epoch. He gave it voice and marked its place in history. As a boy, Flaubert developed a romantic worldview by devouring both Byron's works and contemporary legends about the author, along with the works and legends of other popular romantics. Byron's Don Juan in particular haunted the young Flaubert's imagination. But romanticism was not the only product of Flaubert's youth, nor the only vision that Byron had to offer him: *L'Education sentimentale* and *Bouvard et Pécuchet* also began to take shape during his early period.

Byron's *Don Juan* anticipates and helps prepare Flaubert's satiric realism. There are numerous parallels between the two authors' styles, imagery, and themes. To varying degrees, both works reflect an emerging realism that arises from the impact of reality on romantic expectations and frustrated sense of entitlement. For example, Flaubert draws on the motif of unsatisfied erotic longing and then transforms it into sordid adulteries in *Madame Bovary*. Byron, however, like Heinrich Heine or Alfred de Musset, exemplifies the practice of "romantic irony" in which a personified author defensively, explicitly mocks his own unrealistic aspirations. Flaubert abandons this practice in his mature works. (DF)

Reference:

Schuber, Stephen Paul. "From Romanticism to Realism: The Intrusion of Reality in Byron's *Don Juan* and Flaubert's *Madame Bovary*." Ph.D. diss., University of Oregon, 1976.

C

Cahier intime de jeunesse: Souvenirs, notes, et pensées intimes. *Souvenirs, notes, et pensées intimes* was first mentioned by Jean Bruneau and was subsequently discussed by Jean-Paul Sartre and by Hazel Barnes. Written between sometime in 1838 and January 1841, the forty-four pages of thoughts and maxims, and personal reflections on human nature, art, and the writer's vocation vividly suggest Flaubert's preoccupations during early adulthood. His literary tastes revealed here—a preference for Montaigne over Voltaire, and a disdain for Sade's lack of self-irony—will later change. This work is vitally important for the study of the young Flaubert's artistic development. (MCO)

References:

Barnes, Hazel. *Sartre and Flaubert.* Chicago: University of Chicago Press, 1981.

Bruneau, Jean. *Les Débuts littéraires de Gustave Flaubert, 1831–1845.* Paris: Colin, 1962.

Flaubert, Gustave. *Cahier intime de jeunesse: Souvenirs, notes, et pensées intimes.* Ed. J. P. Germain. Paris: Nizet, 1987.

———. *Souvenirs, notes, et pensées intimes.* Ed. Lucie Chevalley Sabatier. Paris: Buchet-Chastel, 1965.

———. *Souvenirs, notes, et pensées intimes.* In Gustave Flaubert, *Œuvres complètes,* ed. Maurice Bardéche. 16 vols. Paris: Club de l'Honnête Homme, 1971–76. 11: 595–603.

Sartre, Jean-Paul. *L'Idiot de la famille.* 3 vols. Paris: Gallimard, 1971–72. Trans. Carol Cosman, *The Family Idiot.* 5 vols. Chicago: University of Chicago Press, 1983–95.

Le Candidat (1874). *Le Candidat* is a dramatic comedy, the only play of Flaubert's career written entirely by him and the only one produced during his lifetime, from March 11–14, 1874, at the Théâtre du Vaudeville. The critics and the public were unenthusiastic, and although the producers planned a much longer run, the play closed after only four nights. The reviews complained of clownlike characters and stiff dialogue. Flaubert had no political views of his own, aside from resolutely opposing the power and authority wielded by the *haute bourgeoisie*. However, he was fascinated, amused, and dismayed by the variety of opinion (generally loosely held and quickly changed) that marked the politics of the Second Empire and the young Third Republic. *Le Candidat* is best read in conjunction with the chapters of *L'Education sentimentale* and *Bouvard et Pécuchet* devoted to politics. *Le Candidat* has seen other productions, among them a 1980 adaptation in Milan and a 1914 adaptation by Karl Sternberg in Germany. (MCO)

References:

Canu, Jean. *Flaubert, auteur dramatique*. Paris: Ecrits de France, 1946.

Cento, Alberto. "Flaubert e il 'cocu triomphant': un scénario inédito del *Candidat*." *Rivista di letterature moderne e comparate* 20 (1967): 118–22.

Flaubert, Gustave. *Le Candidat*. Ed. Yvan Leclerc. Paris: Le Castor Astral, 1988.

———. *The Candidate. A Humorous Political Drama in Four Acts*. 1904. Repr. New York: Fertig, 1978.

Masson, Bernard. "Théâtre." In *Gustave Flaubert, Œuvres complètes*, ed. B. Masson. 2 vols. Paris: Seuil, 1964. 2:315–16.

Raitt, Alan. *Flaubert et le théâtre*. Bern: Lang, 1998.

Carnets de travail. Pierre-Marc de Biasi has prepared a monumental labor of love to assist Flaubert scholars: a critical, genetic edition of nearly a thousand pages of Flaubert's notes and scenarios now held in the Bibliothèque Historique de la Ville de Paris. They run from 1845 until 1879 and include every major work except *Madame Bovary* and *Trois Contes*. Included are reading notes, records of Flaubert's direct observations, information he gleaned from research interviews, quotations, plans, and lists of future projects (see 39–55 for a clear overview of the eighteen of twenty notebooks that survive). Biasi's copious annotations and his lucid descriptions of how Flaubert's projects took shape in their early stages are invaluable for Flaubert scholars. In an appendix, Biasi lists all the books in Flaubert's library and provides a name index that allows one today to estimate the influence of contemporary authors and events on Flaubert. Biasi's lively, readable style makes his findings accessible to the cultured general reader who knows French. (LMP)

Reference:

Flaubert, Gustave. *Carnets de travail*. Ed. Pierre-Marc de Biasi. Paris: Balland, 1988.

Carthage (*Sal*). Carthage betrays its origins as a Phoenician city by its very name, which means "new city." (The emperor Napoleon's name, a synonym for Naples, has the same root meaning of "new city.") Mâtho, who represents the younger Napoleon Bonaparte (Addison 99, 103, 105), is tempted by the riches of Carthage, while Hamilcar, whose colonial ambition is to found another "new city" in Sicily, views Carthage as a cornucopia or source of supplies and reinforcements (Mullen Hohl 42–43).

The specificity of the city of antiquity lies precisely in the close ties between its political and religious institutions. At once an oligarchy and a democracy, Carthage was hated by other nations of Africa, especially those in the Punic territory, from whom it exacted exorbitant taxes. Moreover, Carthage's obsession with material gain dulled its political acumen; in fact, the city depicted by Flaubert may symbolize the power of gold (Michel 115). Green (61–68) views Carthage as reflecting the political and social conditions of nineteenth-century France, and as a state occupying a place at the end of history, at the end of civilization, much as Flaubert viewed contemporary France. Carthage's domestication of violence demonstrates that social order and what we call history are not a rational continuum, but rather contain the seeds of war that is likely to erupt at any given time in the periodic return of repressed violence. Above all, the city is a sacred place, a temple and the privileged framework for sacrifice, as demonstrated by the closing chapter of *Salammbô* (Michel 117–18).

The primary importance of Carthage in the novel, as opposed to that of Salammbô, has been a topic of debate since publication. Flaubert himself said that the pedestal (the depiction of the city) was too large for the statue (the heroine). However, Flaubert resolved the problem masterfully by adding one more element to the equation "Salammbô equals Tanit." Throughout the novel, he implicitly or explicitly linked the fall of Carthage to Salammbô's "fall" (her sexual intercourse with Mâtho). Rome's will to destroy Carthage, expressed by Cato the Elder's "Delenda est Carthago," known to every student of Latin, is first alluded to in relation to fruitful harvests, a context that implicates Salammbô because she represents the corn goddess Korê/Persephone (Mullen Hohl 89–91). Hamilcar's prediction of the fall of Carthage narratively engenders the representation of his daughter's "fall," and her visit to Mâtho's tent precipitates Giscon's wrath as he curses her and equates her "ignominious" act with the ruin of Carthage. As Salammbô is represented as Tanit, so Tanit is repeatedly represented as Carthage. Both city and goddess are depicted as having the same form, be it that of a slave ship or a horn of plenty.

Finally, what has been considered an atrocious neologism, even in modern French, since it has not become part of the language, marks the shared identity of Salammbô and the city on her doomed wedding day, when she is described as merging with Tanit and becoming the genius of the city, its soul incarnate (*'corporifiée'*). Such a transformation of spirit into matter effectively erases the distinctions on which the dualistic Western aesthetics, rhetoric, and philosophy inherited from Plato depend (Backès 132–33). If Salammbô is Carthage incarnate, then the spasm of titanic joy that anagrammatically enfolds Tanit (tanit/titan) also applies to Hamilcar's daughter, recalling the Festival of Joy celebrating the resurrection of Attis/Adonis. However, Carthage's boundless hope is ironically, immediately undermined by Salammbô's death in response to Narr'Havas's toast to the genius of Carthage, a death that prefigures the destruction of Carthage by the Romans. (AMH)

References:

Addison, Claire. *Where Flaubert Lies: Chronology, Mythology, and History*. Cambridge: Cambridge, University Press. 1996.

Backès, Jean-Louis. "Le Divin dans *Salammbô*." *Revue des lettres modernes* 1165–72 (1994): 115–34.

Green, Anne. *Flaubert and the Historical Novel*: Salammbô *Reassessed*. Cambridge: Cambridge University Press, 1982.

Michel, Alain. "*Salammbô* et la cité antique." In Marie-Claire Bancquart, ed., *Flaubert, la femme, la ville*. Paris: Presses Universitaires de France, 1983. 111–18.

Mullen Hohl, Anne. *Exoticism in* Salammbô: *The Languages of Myth, Religion, and War*. Birmingham, AL: Summa, 1995.

Sainte-Beuve, Charles-Augustin. "*Salammbô*." In Charles-Augustin Sainte-Beuve, *Nouveaux lundis*. Paris: Lévy, 1865. 4: 31–95.

Carvalho (pseud. of Léon Carvaille, 1825–97). Carvalho, one of the best-known producers in France, was the director of the Théâtre du Vaudeville. He initially seemed enthusiastic about *Le Sexe faible*, a play Flaubert had found among Louis Bouilhet's papers. (The title, an antiphrasis, refers to weak men dominated by women.) Flaubert wanted to have it produced in memory of his late friend. He read it to Carvalho in the spring of 1873. The latter promised to produce it the next season if substantial revisions were made, and he offered to consult Flaubert on the casting. Flaubert reworked Bouilhet's play feverishly, but Carvalho became increasingly hesitant to commit himself to a production. At length, Flaubert turned to other theaters, but only the second-rate Cluny Theater accepted it and that theater proposed actors who were so inept that Flaubert withdrew the play in 1875.

The experience of rewriting Bouilhet's play, however, revived Flaubert's interest in the theater; actually, Carvalho was primarily interested in producing a play by Flaubert and encouraged him to develop his outline for *Le Candidat* while postponing the beginning of rehearsals on *Le Sexe faible. Le Candidat*, which Ivan Turgenev, Charles d'Osmoy, and Carvalho had all helped to retouch, agreeing on the necessary changes, promptly went into rehearsal in December 1873. Soon after, however, Carvalho left to manage another theater, and Flaubert had to work with a new person. The opening night came on March 11, 1874. The play was a flop and closed after only four performances. At this point, Flaubert abandoned the theater for good (Bart 621–26; Lottman 263–69). (LMP)

References:

Bart, Benjamin F. *Flaubert*. Syracuse: Syracuse University Press, 1967.

Lottman, Herbert R. *Flaubert: A Biography*. New York: Fromm, 1990.

Cather, Willa Sibert (1873--1947). A voracious reader of French literature, Willa Cather identified Flaubert as one of the three "giants of letters" (the others being Honoré de Balzac and Guy de Maupassant) (Cather, *The World* 1.574). Deprecating much fiction of her contemporary United States as escapist, Cather turned to *Madame Bovary* as a model for her critique of the romantic ideology of love. *My Mortal Enemy* (1926) departs from Flaubert in representing deluded romantic passion as marital rather than adulterous: Myra Henshawe is disinherited because of her romantic elopement and confides to the narrator that her marriage has "been the ruin of us both. We've destroyed each other. . . . People can be lovers and enemies at the same time. . . . A man and woman draw apart from that long embrace, and see what they have done to each other" (77, 88). Heterosexual romance itself appears mystified or even fatal in Cather's fictions. The adulterous subplot of *O Pioneers!* (1913) culminates in a double murder when the jealous husband discovers his wife with a lover, and the affair is represented as inauthentic and clichéd. Female autonomy and creativity appear antithetical to romantic desire, and Cather's strong women typically renounce desire in favor of art (as in *The Song of the Lark*, 1915) or of matriarchal power in the farmland of Cather's native Nebraska (as in *My Antonia*, 1918). Cather's lesbianism complicates and enriches her investigation of the social construction of gender, the commodification of women, and the nineteenth-century ideology of separate spheres that relegated women to childbearing and ornamental domesticity. (ST)

References:

Cather, Willa. "Escapism." In Willa Cather, *On Writing: Critical Studies of Writing as an Art*. New York: Knopf, 1949. 18–29.

———. *My Mortal Enemy*. New York: Vintage, 1954.

———. *The World and the Parish: Willa Cather's Articles and Reviews, 1893–1902*. Ed. William M. Curtin. Lincoln: University of Nebraska Press, 1970.

Gilbert, Sandra M., and Susan Gubar. *No Man's Land: The Place of the Woman Writer in the Twentieth Century*. Vol. 2, *Sexchanges*. New Haven: Yale University Press, 1989.

Haller, Evelyn. " 'Behind the Singer Tower': Willa Cather and Flaubert." *Modern Fiction Studies* 36 (1990): 39–53.

Nelson, Robert J. *Willa Cather and France: In Search of the Lost Language*. Urbana: University of Illinois Press, 1988.

Rosowski, Susan J. "The Novel of Awakening." *Genre* 12 (1979): 313–32.

Stouck, David. "Willa Cather and the Impressionist Novel." In John J. Murphy, ed., *Critical Essays on Willa Cather*. Boston: Hall, 1984: 48–66.

Catoblépas (*TSA*). The Catoblépas is one of the series of monsters meant perhaps to demonstrate that attempts to join fantasy with substance (or, Jean Seznec believes, fantasy with reason and logic) result in monstrous combinations of no significant use, and in frustration. Flaubert called the Catoblépas a "swine lying down." Its name is said to mean "that which looks downward." Antoine is fascinated by its incredible stupidity and drawn to it, because its example offers the possibility of release from the continual mental tension of resisting doubt and despair. (AHP)

Reference:

Seznec, Jean. "Saint Antoine et les monstres." *PMLA* 58 (1943): 195–222.

Cervantes Saavedra, Miguel de (1547–1616). Miguel de Cervantes is generally acknowledged as the greatest author in the Spanish language, a vocation he pursued after years as a soldier and a prisoner of war. He is renowned as the creator of *Don Quixote*, the idealistic fool who tries to re-create the age of chivalry long after it has past, and whose plump, matter-of-fact squire, Sancho Panza, makes a perfect, involuntarily ironic foil to him. Flaubert discovered Cervantes when he was only nine: as a result, he decided to become a novelist rather than a playwright. He later claimed that he had known *Don Quixote* by heart before he was able to read (letter to Louise Colet, June 12, 1852, *Corr.* 6:442), and the Spanish author inspired several of his early works (see Bruneau). Flaubert's letter of September 25, 1852, to Colet declares: "What makes great geniuses stand out is creativity and the ability to generalize. With one type character, they can sum up many scattered traits, and make humankind aware of new kinds of personalities. Don't we believe in the existence of Don Quixote as much as we believe in Caesar's?" (*Corr.* 3:31).

Harry Levin aptly called Emma Bovary a female Don Quixote. Having been seduced by books that they took literally (Don Quixote, by the novel of chivalry *Amadis de Gaula*), both characters imagine themselves as fictional heroes; they have an unrealistic view of their abilities and their possibilities. Both shun the intellectuality and detachment that might inhibit them from plunging avidly into the world. The illusions of their senses are realities for them (Cascardi 234). Cervantes and Flaubert each regard their misguided protagonists with both mockery and warmth; at times, the protagonists' expansive impulses indirectly satirize the mean-spiritedness and self-interested caution of most of the remainder of society—without, however, offering a workable model of behavior that might effectively transcend that society. Like "Voltaire's Candide, nourished on Leibniz's philosophy of optimism, and Stendhal's Julien Sorel, brought up on the writings of Rousseau and Napoleon, Emma fits the paradigm of the fictional character whose reading of the preceding generation's literature has left him or her unable to cope with present-day reality." But despite her flamboyant gestures of independence, Emma, unlike her deluded male counterparts, is mainly condemned passively to await a knight who may come to rescue her (Berg and Martin 35). (LMP)

References:

Berg, William J., and Laurey K. Martin. *Gustave Flaubert*. New York: Twayne, 1997.
Bruneau, Jean. *Les Débuts littéraires de Gustave Flaubert, 1831–1845*. Paris: Colin, 1962.

Cascardi, Anthony J. *The Bounds of Reason: Cervantes, Dostoevsky, Flaubert.* New York: Columbia University Press, 1986. 159–237, 241–43, 263–70.

Girard, René. *Deceit, Desire, and the Novel: Self and Other in Literary Structure.* Trans. Yvonne Freccero. Baltimore: Johns Hopkins Press, 1965. Trans. of *Mensonge romantique et vérité romanesque.* Paris: Grasset, 1961.

Levin, Harry. *The Gates of Horn: A Study of Five French Realist Novelists.* New York: Oxford University Press, 1963. 46–47, 246–52.

Parlej, Piotr. *The Romantic Theory of the Novel: Genre and Reflection in Cervantes, Melville, Flaubert, Joyce, and Kafka.* Baton Rouge: Louisiana State University Press, 1997.

Chabrol, Claude (1930–). Born into a family of pharmacists, Claude Chabrol initially intended to follow the example of his father and grandfather. However, he met François Truffaut at age seventeen and veered off into a different direction, writing for *Arts* and *Cahiers du cinéma,* then collaborating with Eric Rohmer on a book about Alfred Hitchcock in 1957. Thanks to an inheritance from his first wife, he was able to make the transition from critic to filmmaker: his first feature film, *Le Beau Serge,* was released in 1958. Associated with the French New Wave cinema, Chabrol is today one of France's most prolific filmmakers, having more than fifty feature films to his credit. He is known for his vicious portraits of the bourgeoisie and for the Hitchcockian camera techniques used in many of his films.

Chabrol first read *Madame Bovary* at age thirteen. Obsessed with Flaubert's masterpiece, he had long considered adapting it to the screen, but he decided to do so only when Isabelle Huppert agreed to play Emma. The two had worked together previously (Huppert had acted in Chabrol's *Violette* [1978] and *Story of Women* [1988]), and the filmmaker was persuaded that in Huppert he had found the perfect incarnation of Emma Bovary. He exercised equal caution in selecting the actors for the other principal roles, insisting that they have a deep respect for Flaubert's novel. In addition to Huppert, the cast consists of Jean-François Balmer as Charles, Christophe Malavory as Rodolphe, Jean Yanne as Homais, and Lucas Belvaux as Léon.

Filmed on location in Normandy, Chabrol's *Madame Bovary* (1991) is respected for its attention to detail, its authentic re-creation of life in mid-nineteenth-century provincial France, and its fidelity to Flaubert's novel. Chabrol preserved as much of the novel's language as possible in dialogue and voiceover. Moreover, he succeeded in rendering the novel's tone of impersonality, accessing Emma's subjectivity through close-ups and adopting a more distant perspective when Flaubert's text suggests an objective viewpoint. Cuts were, however, inevitable, and Chabrol, viewing *Madame Bovary* as Emma's story, elected to suppress the novel's first chapter. When, during an interview with Chabrol, the literary critic Pierre-Marc de Biasi commented on Flaubert's well-known anger at the idea that illustrations might accompany his text, Chabrol expressed his conviction that Flaubert would have approved of a cinematic adaptation, indeed, that his modus operandi (*gueuloir* or oral composition, for example) was very cinematographic.

Chabrol once remarked that stupidity is infinitely more fascinating than intelligence because it has no limits. This cruelly ironic view of human nature, expressed in many of his films (*Les Cousins* [1959], *Les Bonnes Femmes* [1960], and others) was well suited to Flaubert's novel. *Madame Bovary* was Chabrol's forty-fourth feature film. A more recent film, *La Cérémonie* (1995), also features Isabelle Huppert. (MDE)

References:

Boddaert, François, ed. *Autour d'Emma.* Madame Bovary, *un film de Claude Chabrol.* (interviews). Paris: Hatier, 1991.

Wood, Robin, and Michael Walker. *Claude Chabrol.* New York: Praeger, 1970.

Charpentier, Georges (1846–19?). Georges Charpentier was a publisher and the son of the founder of the Charpentier press, which was the first to publish *La Tentation de saint Antoine*. He was one of "Les Cinq," the loyal friends who shared a realist or naturalist aesthetic and the experience of failure in the theater. They included Edmond de Goncourt, Alphonse Daudet, and Emile Zola as well as Flaubert and Charpentier, and they met regularly at Flaubert's Sunday salon in Paris during the late 1870s. Charpentier and his wife Marguerite joined Ivan Turgenev in trying to obtain a government appointment for Flaubert from Léon Gambetta in 1879, when Flaubert was ill and in desperate need. He was present at Flaubert's funeral. (LMP)

References:

Charpentier, Georges. *Trente Années d'amitié, 1872–1902: Lettres de l'éditeur Georges Charpentier à Emile Zola.* Ed. Colette Becker. Paris: Presses Universitaires de France, 1980.

Robide, Michel. *Le Salon Charpentier et les impressionnistes.* Paris: Bibliothèque des arts, 1958.

Le Château des cœurs. The fairy play in ten tableaux *Le Château des cœurs* was written during 1862–63 in collaboration with Louis Bouilhet and Charles d'Osmoy, though it was not first published until 1880, principally through the efforts of Guy de Maupassant. The authors tried without success to have the work performed. The theater as a vehicle for the fantastic had interested Flaubert since 1847, when he composed *Pierrot au sérail.* Just prior to work on *Le Château*, Flaubert had been elaborating a fairy play of his own (see *Le Rêve et la vie). Le Château* offers some sparkling moments of social satire (e.g., tableaux six and five, "Au royaume du Pot-au-feu," the department-store fantasy of "Au pays de la Toilette"), but it is generally a compromised work, having too many authors among whom only one, Bouilhet, was a playwright. The manuscripts recently rediscovered and kept in Rouen, show Flaubert's contributions to be concerned primarily with satire and the sequences on Paris life, where the characters and milieux are the first working through of material developed the following year in *L'Education sentimentale*. The play is of interest mainly for that reason. (MCO)

References:

Canu, Jean. *Flaubert, auteur dramatique*. Paris: Ecrits de France, 1946.

Douchin, J.-L. "Un tableau inédit du *Château des cœurs.*" *Les Amis de Flaubert* 38 (1971): 5–17.

Flaubert, Gustave. *The Castle of Hearts*, publ. with *The Candidate*. New York: Fertig, 1978 (New York: Dunne, 1904).

———. *Le Château des cœurs*. In Gustave Flaubert, *Théâtre*. In *Les Œuvres de Gustave Flaubert*, ed. Maurice Nadeau. 18 vols. Lausanne: Editions Rencentre. 13: 23–198.

Olds, Marshall C. "*Le Château des cœurs* et la féerie de Flaubert." *Bulletin des Amis de Flaubert et de Maupassant*, forthcoming.

———. *La Féerie de Flaubert: Pensée théâtre et narrative*. Forthcoming.

Chateaubriand, François René de (1768–1848). A writer and political figure, François René de Chateaubriand saw his military career interrupted by the French Revolution. He traveled to the United States in 1791, returned to France when he heard that the king had been arrested, and fought against the armies of the French Republic. After being wounded at the battle of Thionville, Chateaubriand immigrated to England (1793), where he remained till 1800. On his return to France he wrote the novels *Atala* (1801) and *René*, with American Indians as sympathetic characters. His French protagonists struggled against the temptations of fornication and incest while communing with an exotic nature.

Chateaubriand powerfully influenced the adolescent Flaubert, who plagiarized Chateaubriand in his first, unpublished historical tale, "Mort du Duc de Guise" (1835, Bibliothèque Nationale, Nouvelles Acquisitions Françaises 14.138). Flaubert drew heavily on Chateaubriand's *Analyse raisonnée de l'histoire de France* for all the names of the secondary characters, the sequence of scenes, the point of view, and some of the most eloquent sentences (Bruneau 81–82).

In 1811, Chateaubriand's *Itineraire de Paris à Jérusalem* was the first truly romantic French travel journal, recreating the personal musings of the traveler—intimate, digressive, and sentimental. Flaubert's own travel notes, *Voyage aux Pyrénées et en Corse* (1840), conform to this impressionistic model as it was developed by several later writers (Bruneau 288–305). But it was above all Flaubert's novella "Novembre," composed in 1841–42, that bears the mark of Chateaubriand in his pioneering psychological novel *René*. "Flaubert's model, in this last youthful work, is above all Chateaubriand," particularly in his descriptions of nature and of the hero's communing with nature (Bruneau 331). Later in Flaubert's career, many of the romantic cliches satirized in *Madame Bovary* derive from Chateaubriand; and even toward the end of his life, Flaubert loved to recite long passages from *Atala* and *René*. (APZ/LMP)

References:

Barbéris, Pierre. *Chateaubriand: Une réaction au monde moderne.* Paris: Larousse, 1976.

Bart, Benjamin F. "Flaubert Plagiarist of Chateaubriand." *Modern Language Notes* 55 (1950): 336–39.

Bruneau, Jean. *Les Débuts littéraires de Gustave Flaubert, 1831–1845.* Paris: Colin, 1962.

Chateaubriand, François René de. *Analyse raisonnée de l'histoire de France.* In François René de Chateaubriand, *Œuvres complètes.* 12 vols. Paris: Garnier, 1860. Vol. 10.

———. *Itineraire de Paris à Jérusalem.* Ed. Emile Malakis. 2 vols. Paris: Les Belles Lettres, 1946.

Chevalier, Ernest (1820–1887). Sharing Flaubert's love for literature, Ernest Chevalier was his closest childhood friend. Along with Flaubert's sister Caroline, the two boys put on plays (first, of French classic authors such as Molière, then plays of Flaubert's creation). Chevalier moved to Paris to study law, in which he excelled and had a brilliant career. He held prominent positions successively in Corsica, Grenoble, Lyon, Metz, Lille, and Angers. In 1850, his marriage to Louise Leclerc-Thoüin turned him into even more of a bourgeois, much to Flaubert's discontent. After the publication of *Salammbô*, Chevalier sent Flaubert a letter in which he and his middle-class friends praised the novel.

Flaubert lamented Chevalier's loss of passion for literature as Chevalier became increasingly involved in his career and less interested in his previous romantic vision. He retired to Chalonnes-sur-Loire, where he became an elected government official in 1870. The love episodes between Deslauriers and his "grisette" in *L'Education sentimentale* were inspired by Chevalier's lifestyle during his years as a law student in Paris. Chevalier and Flaubert's correspondence was profuse in the 1830s and early 1840s; as the men grew apart, their letters became less frequent. (MMC)

Reference:

Mignot, Albert. *Ernest Chevalier, ancien procureur général, député de Maine-et-Loire. Son intimité avec Gustave Flaubert, lettres inédites de l'auteur de "Madame Bovary," l'affaire X . . . , un scandale judiciaire, révélations, etc. Notes biographiques rédigées et mises en ordie par Albert Mignot, son neveu.* Paris: Dentu, 1888.

Chimera (*TSA*). *See* Sphinx and Chimera.

Chopin, Kate (1851–1904). Kate Chopin, who began to write professionally to support her family when she was widowed at thirty-four, read French fiction throughout her career and regarded George Sand, Guy de Maupassant, and Flaubert as major literary precursors. *The Awakening* (1899), widely condemned for its frank treatment of adultery and then neglected for over half a century after being banned in Chopin's native St. Louis, is now regarded as a masterpiece of the female bildungsroman. The novel, which mixes naturalism with symbolism, alludes extensively and at multiple levels to *Madame Bovary*, notably in its repeated invocations of Flaubert's bird imagery. However, Chopin's "Creole *Bovary*" (as Willa Cather termed it, 697) depicts Edna's discovery of the self and the senses with evident sympathy and identification, in contrast to Flaubert's more detached, more ironic narrator. The problematic nature of Edna's awakening is registered by the text's splitting her desire between Robert (who is represented as a romantic but not sexual object) and Arobin (represented as sexual but not romantic). The novel rejects both the self-denying domesticity of the perpetually pregnant "mother-woman" (26) Mme Ratignolle and the ascetic, "queer" (103) musical artistry of Mlle Reisz, and its second half dramatizes Edna's double flight from conventional domesticity and from the bovarysme of her idealized erotic attachments largely as a withdrawal into the self. Chopin's master trope of the sea revises *Madame Bovary*'s negatively charged, nihilistic images of liquidity (such as the grotesque image of the black liquid that issues from the dead Emma's mouth): the sea in *The Awakening* is an eroticized Whitmanian metaphoric space associated with Aphrodite, both passional and (in Edna's ambiguous final swim) fatal. (ST)

References:

Cather, Willa. *The World and the Parish: Willa Cather's Articles and Reviews, 1893–1902*. Ed. William M. Curtin. Lincoln: University of Nebraska Press, 1970.

Chopin, Kate. *The Awakening*. Boston: Bedford Books, 1993.

Gilbert, Sandra M., and Susan Gubar. *No Man's Land: The Place of the Woman Writer in the Twentieth Century*. Vol. 2, *Sexchanges*. New Haven: Yale University Press, 1989.

Heath, Stephen. "Chopin's Parrot." *Textual Practice* 8 (1994): 11–32.

Petry, Alice Hall, ed. *Critical Essays on Kate Chopin* New York: Hall, 1996.

Pitavy-Souques, Danièle. "De G. Flaubert à K. Chopin, du paraître à l'etre: Notes sur Emma Bovary, Thérèse Lafirme, Edna Pontellier dans *The Awakening*." *Etudes Anglaises* 46 (1993): 477–86.

Rosowski, Susan J. "The Novel of Awakening." *Genre* 12 (1979): 313–32.

Thornton, Lawrence. "*The Awakening*: A Political Romance." *American Literature* 52 (1980): 50–66. Rpr. in Alice Hall Petry, ed., *Critical Essays on Kate Chopin*. New York: Hall, 1996. 85–96.

Cisy (*ES*, 1869). Blessed with an inherited aristocratic rank and a fortune, Cisy initially appears well groomed and refined—he dresses like a dandy—but he is exceptionally stupid. He compensates with bluster and insult for his ineptitude with repartee. He and Frédéric presumably lose their virginity together during a trip to a bordello (Paulson 91), thus symbolically undoing Frédéric's earlier, unsuccessful attempt with Deslauriers. Rosanette Bron later humiliates Frédéric by leaving him in the Café Anglais, in order to go home with Cisy. The irritation that results from this incident leads Frédéric to respond aggressively when Cisy insults Madame Arnoux during a dinner at the Dambreuses. The context of the two young men's exchange was sufficiently ambiguous that one might have supposed it was Rosanette Bron who was insulted; in any event, Frédéric shows himself to be courageous in one of his rare admirable moments. Cisy collapses in terror when he is faced with Frédéric's pistol, lightly cutting himself on the hand and so providing a pretext for ending the duel before a shot has been fired. When reported at a subsequent dinner, Frédéric's romantic role on this occasion leads all three women present—Marie Arnoux, Louise Roque, and Mme Dambreuse—to admire him, thus laying the groundwork for his affair with Mme Dambreuse. By the end of the narrative, Cisy has withdrawn to his bastion of reactionary privilege, married, and sired eight children. (LMP)

Reference:

Paulson, William. *Sentimental Education: The Complexity of Disenchantment.* New York: Twayne, 1992.

class consciousness. *See* socialism.

classicism. Flaubert's interest in classical aesthetics, both ancient and early modern, helped him shape a counterstance to romanticism. Reading Plutarch inspired Flaubert to personify romanticism and classicism by contrasting the fevered Heliogabalus with the tempered Nero. Although as a boy, Flaubert read many classical authors such as Homer, Shakespeare, and Montaigne, it was a live performance rather than a book that inspired his deep appreciation for classical art; in 1840, he saw for the first time on stage the celebrated tragedienne of Greek drama, Rachel, whose acting embodied for him the classical principles of simplicity and purity. Flaubert sought to reproduce in his own prose the calm and beauty he found in classical antiquity. Visiting Athens with Maxime Du Camp, he uncovered a classicism that was vigorous and natural, and whose qualities he wanted to convey in writing. While he was writing *Madame Bovary*, he even learned ancient Greek. Influenced by Nicolas Boileau and Jean de La Fontaine in his maturity, he came to see seventeenth-century classicism as the search for the perfect form, and he felt that each new work required its own poetics. Even in his youth, when he read Corneille, Racine, and Molière, Flaubert had remarked their exemplary limpidity and their terse sentence structure, which stemmed from the seventeenth-century preoccupation with a style that perfectly merged form and content. (EA)

References:

Barnwell, H. T., ed. *The Classical Tradition in French Literature*. London: Grant and Cutler, 1977.
Moreau, Pierre. *Le Classicisme des romantiques*. Paris: Plon, 1932.

cliché. The term *cliché* originally referred only to a printer's plate from which multiple copies of a text or image are made. By the 1860s, it had acquired its figurative sense of a hackneyed idea or expression. Flaubert did not use the term, however. Rather, he used *lieu commun* (commonplace) or *idée réçue* (received idea, platitude); and he collected examples of these throughout his career with a view to publishing his *Dictionnaire des idées reçues*.

Flaubert fills the dialogue of his characters with clichés—not just the speech of satirical figures such as Homais or Bouvard and Pécuchet, but the main characters as well. A famous example is the conversation between Madame Bovary and Léon about romantic landscapes, including Emma's comment, "Je ne trouve rien d'admirable comme les soleils couchants, reprit-elle, mais au bord de la mer, surtout" ("I think nothing is as wonderful as sunsets," she said, "but especially by the seashore") (part 2, chapter 2, 1:601 in Masson, ed.). Because Flaubert has specified where Emma has been in her life, the reader knows that she has never seen the sea and can only be repeating what she has read somewhere. Flaubert was delighted to find the banalities of this fictional conversation almost word for word in a contemporary magazine, commenting, "Et note que ces mêmes gens qui disent 'poésie des lacs,' etc., détestent fort toute cette poésie, toute espèce de nature, toute espèce de lac, si n'est leur pot de chambre qu'ils prennent pour un océan" (Note that the same people who say "the poetry of lakes," etc., really hate all such poetry, all nature, any kind of lake, unless it's their chamber pot, which they take for an ocean) (letter to Louise Colet, June 20, 1853, *Corr.* 2:358).

Flaubert often uses italics to signal the presence of a cliché, especially in *Madame Bovary* (Duchet). He also uses quotation marks, indirect quotation, and the *style indirect libre* (see "free indirect style"). He incorporates not only the clichés of romantic literature, not just the language of the bourgeoisie he so hated, but in general the discourse of society. Through his irony, he distances himself from its *bêtise*. But irony is an invisible trope, and critics disagree about how to interpret passages of Flaubert's novels. We find clichéd language not only in the direct or indirect speech of his characters, but also in the rhetoric of his narrative passages, in worn-out smiles and metaphors, hyperbole, and surprising juxtapositions (Amossy and Rosen). Furthermore, what discourse is not social? How is Flaubert himself to escape the debasement of language?

The cliché has been compared to a kind of prostitution of language, open to everyone (Amossy and Rosen 6). Felman finds this structure in *Novembre*, where the prostitute's body is a kind of common place where all discourses meet. In this novella, the narrator, an aspiring writer, finds in earlier texts his own ideas and expressions and despairs, "Je m'étais cru leur égal et je n'étais plus que leur copiste!" (I thought I was their equal, but I was no longer anything more than their copyist!) (1:254 in Masson, ed.) In such passages, Flaubert shows himself aware that writing is repetition, and that the vocation of a writer is that of Bouvard and Pécuchet: a copyist (Felman 33).

According to Walter Benjamin, with the development of the mechanical means of reproduction in the nineteenth century, the work of art lost its link with the hand of its maker and, consequently, its authority (221). Likewise, the linguistic cliché, endlessly repeated, has no author and no authority. It is becoming almost a commonplace of Flaubert criticism to see him as a postmodern writer, because he realizes that language is always repetition, that the signifier is arbitrary and never original. No language, not even his, can escape the cliché, for language itself is the commonplace (Felman). Flaubert feared falling into banality; he admitted to Louise Colet that when he let himself go in his writing, there were good parts, but the unity of the whole was lacking. His description of the result contains no fewer than four synonyms for the cliché:"les répétitions abondent, les redites, les lieux communs, les locutions banales" (repetitions abound, restatements, commonplaces, banal expressions) (August 26, 1853, *Corr.* 2.416). (CR)

References:

Amossy, Ruth, and Elisheva Rosen. *Les Discours du cliché*. Paris: Société d'édition d'enseignement supérieur, 1982.

Benjamin, Walter. "The Work of Art in the Age of Mechanical Reproduction." In Walter Benjamin, *Illuminations*. Trans. Harry Zohn. Ed. Hannah Arendt. New York: Schocken, 1969. 217–52.

Duchet, Claude. "Signifiance et in-signifiance: Le discours italique dans *Madame Bovary*." In Claudine Gothot-Mersch, ed., *La Production du sens chez Flaubert*. Paris: Union Générale d'Editions, 1975. 358–78.

Felman, Shoshana. "Modernity of the Commonplace." In Laurence M. Porter, ed., *Critical Essays on Gustave Flaubert*. Boston: Hall, 1986. 29–48.

Flaubert, Gustave. *Œuvres complètes*. 2 vols. Ed. Bernard Masson. Paris: Seuil, 1964.

Gaillard, Françoise. "L'En-signement du réel." In Claudine Gothot-Mersch, ed., *La Production du sens chez Flaubert*. Paris: Union Générale d'Editions, 1975. 197–220.

"Un cœur simple" (1875). The first tale of *Trois Contes*, "Un cœur simple," was written in 1875, requiring approximately six months of work. Flaubert chose Pont-L'Evêque as its setting, perhaps to honor the memory of his recently deceased mother, who had grown up there. In addition to similarities between the tale and the circumstances of his own life, there are numerous textual sources. The children's names allude to Jacques-Henri Bernardin de Saint-Pierre's *Paul et Virginie*, which constitutes, along with its companion tale *La Chaumière indienne*, an important intertext (Cronk 154). Both Honoré de Balzac's *Eugénie Grandet* (1833) and Alphonse de Lamartine's *Geneviève: Histoire d'une servante* (1850) feature pious, self-sacrificing female servants (Cronk 157). Haig argues that Flaubert is parroting his own previous writings in "Un cœur simple," as in the example of Catherine Leroux, the servant in *Madame Bovary* with her fifty years of servitude, who also ends up deaf and mute (108). Flaubert's challenge here is to conceive a narrative around another such figure of muteness.

In chapter 1, Flaubert expresses with an extraordinary economy of means the routine that structures fifty years of Félicité's adult life as a servant in Madame

Aubain's household. The chapter contains some forty verbs in the imperfect tense and a mere five in the *passé simple*, emphasizing the perpetually unfinished and therefore seemingly insignificant nature of Félicité's activities.

Chapter 2 enumerates a succession of flawed relationships and subsequent losses experienced by Félicité over the course of her life. The circumstances of her youth borrow from the register of melodrama. After her brutal amorous disillusionment with Théodore, Félicité arrives in Pont-L'Evêque without familial attachments (a fact Flaubert accentuates by not disclosing her family name), seeking a new beginning. A pattern of subjugation is established when Madame Aubain, a widow with two children, agrees to hire Félicité with the proclamation "Soit, je vous accepte!" (Flaubert 594). Félicité's identity is thenceforth largely a construct of the words of others. Her remarkable capacity for self-extrusion first appears in her attachment to Madame Aubain's children, Paul and Virginie. In the single episode in which Félicité displays mastery over external events, she imperils herself to protect her mistress's family from the attack of a bull. Nonetheless, her subalternate status ensures that the children's identification with the servant who nurtures and cherishes them is at best incomplete. Félicité encounters a sister with whom she had lost contact and develops a doting relationship with her nephew Victor. She cooks and mends for him and offers gifts to his family. Madame Aubain haughtily dismisses the relationship with the statement "Évidemment, ils l'exploitaient" (Flaubert 600). Free indirect discourse here implies that this judgment concurs with that of society at large (Killick 312).

In the third chapter, Félicité takes an almost voluptuous pleasure in the rituals of Virginie's daily catechism and first communion. The priest's words translate in Félicité's mind into a series of tableaux, forming the basis of a distorted, idolatrous theology. The deaths of Victor and Virginie and the uneventful passage of time in the deteriorating house leave an emptiness in Félicité's life that is finally alleviated through her acquisition of a live parrot.

Chapter 4 outlines the development of the singular bond between Félicité and Loulou. The parrot's repertoire of three locutions reflects in miniature Félicité's own limited speech repertoire. The increasingly deaf servant and the exotic bird share a playful, ambiguous mutual affection. The narrator describes the parrot as almost a son and a lover. Loulou dies, and Félicité, in a process fraught with difficulties and delays, undertakes to have him stuffed. She comes to confuse him with the Holy Spirit. With the death of Madame Aubain, Félicité disengages from the social sphere, where she had always been cast in a marginalized, subordinate role. Nearly blind and suffering from pneumonia, Félicité prepares to follow her mistress into death and sacrifices her venerated stuffed parrot as a votive offering in the Corpus Christi procession.

Chapter 5 finds Félicité, deaf and blind in her reliquary-like room, suffering the final agony of death while the Corpus Christi procession takes place outside. Her personal mysticism, a blend of the spiritual and the corporal, is seen when she savors the smell of the incense wafting into her room from the censer, closes her eyes, and smiles. The narration of her death combines medical fact and poetic image, contrasting with Madame Aubain's previous stiffly bourgeois avoidance of direct reference to death. As her heart ceases beating and she exhales for the last time, she thinks that she sees a gigantic parrot hovering in the skies above her. After a lifelong series of failed relationships, only her final bond with Loulou affords the fusion with the Other that she had always been denied. The final scene alternates contrapuntally between the horizontal plane, represented by the procession outside, and the vertical plane, seen in the vision of the ascending parrot.

Flaubert wrote the last chapters of "Un cœur simple" in the company of a stuffed parrot borrowed from the Muséum d'histoire naturelle de Rouen. The introduction of a talking bird, paired with a protagonist of limited verbal ability, signals language and its limitations as the tale's focus. The inarticulate protagonist is disadvantaged in her dealings with society by her linguistic passivity. Direct discourse marks the pivotal moments in Félicité's life, although she is typically the receiver rather than the utterer of these directives and statements (Killick 308). This imbalance underlines her lack of control over events. The three phrases in the parrot's repertoire—"Charmant garçon!" "Serviteur, Monsieur!" and "Je vous salue, Marie!"—summarize the affective and spiritual aspects that form the totality of Félicité's limited universe. With its subservient, repetitive discourse, the parrot figures Félicité herself, reflecting a thought process "constrained within the inherited moulds of female, social, and religious dependency" (Killick 309). Loulou's impoverished lexicon and mindless repetition additionally point to the idiocy of banal language. In their repetition, the parrot's utterances constitute a ritualized linguistic routine that gives Félicité a sense of connection to the Other. It is not the meaning of the words, but the reassuringly repetitive gesture of speech that matters for Félicité, although Loulou's words at times create in her imagination a spiritual transcendence.

Félicité's inefficacy in the realm of symbolic thought is shown through her subordination to those more adept at the manipulation of language. It also appears in her reliance on alternative nonverbal modes of communication and self-representation: the corporal language that conveys her emotions and her collection of objects that are remnants of past attachments. When she does speak, her discourse is truncated, grounded in the literal, derivative, repetitive, and lexically limited. Her modest linguistic acumen, inferior to that of virtually all the other human characters in the tale, contributes to her portrayal as a figure of innate goodness. Félicité, unlike Madame Aubain, does not use language as an instrument of domination and control. Of the text's competing modes of discourse, exemplified by the priest (religious), Madame Aubain and Bourais (bourgeois), and Félicité (naïve), only Félicité's lacks manipulative intent. The paradigm of subservience that characterizes her relations with the Aubain family becomes the basis of all her human relationships. Her tolerance of exploitive behavior is far from an ideal means to achieve integration into the social order, but as Killick points out, Félicité becomes an increasingly sympathetic figure as the unreliability, opportunism, and egocentricity of the other characters are gradually exposed. Israel-Pelletier goes so far as to characterize her ignorance as "a form of *wisdom,* which allows her to circumvent and work both inside and outside the system that tries to alienate and confuse her" (26; emphasis added). It is ultimately the limitations inherent in her linguistic ability that enable this simple woman's imagination to recuperate from the losses dealt by a hostile world over her lifetime. (JM)

References:

Cronk, Nicholas. "Reading *Un cœur simple*: The Pleasure of the Intertext." *Nineteenth-Century French Studies* 24. 1–2 (1995–96): 154–61.

Flaubert, Gustave. "Un cœur simple." In Albert Thibaudet and René Dumesnil, eds., *Œuvres.* 2 vols. Paris: Gallimard, 1951–52. 2: 591–622.

Haig, Stirling. "Parrot and Parody: Flaubert." In Emanuel J. Mickel, Jr., ed., *The Shaping of Text: Style, Imagery, and Structure in French Literature.* Lewisburg, PA: Bucknell University Press, 1993. 105–12.

Israel-Pelletier, Aimée. *Flaubert's Straight and Suspect Saints: The Unity of* Trois Contes. Amsterdam: Benjamins, 1991.

Killick, Rachel. " 'The Power and the Glory'? Discourses of Authority and Tricks of Speech in *Trois Contes." Modern Language Review* 88.2 (1993): 307–20.

Stipa, Ingrid. "Desire, Repetition, and the Imaginary in Flaubert's *Un cœur simple." Studies in Short Fiction* 31.4 (1994): 617–26.

Colet, Louise (1810–76). Best known as Flaubert's mistress and correspondent, Louise Colet was also a writer who won several prizes for her poetry. She was eleven years older than he and was married. Atypically for women of her time, she frequented literary salons and invited many writers and members of the intelligentsia to her own salon; she supported herself by her writing; she had several lovers and a child fathered by one of them; and her husband tolerated her affairs as long as she was discreet. When she and Flaubert met, she had already won recognition for her writing, whereas he was unknown. Their relationship lasted seven years, from 1847 to 1854, although Flaubert declared it over between 1849 and 1851.

What began as a physical relationship developed into an epistolary one: they were physically apart more than they were together. Their letters consisted mostly of their thoughts and questions concerning literature and writing. When Colet sent Flaubert a copy of a poem she wished to send for publication, he rewrote most of it, considering his version to be superior. Flaubert called her his Muse because he was able to discuss his works with her as he was writing them. Colet played an important role in the creation of *Madame Bovary* because she encouraged Flaubert to put his ideas on paper and consult her. Her intelligence and writing ability gave him the confidence to ask her opinion, consider her suggestions, and incorporate them into his creative process.

Colet continued to write and publish after meeting Flaubert. Two of her works contain characters based on him: *Une histoire de soldat* (1856) and *Lui, roman contemporain* (1859). Critics have recently begun to rehabilitate her and to question the received opinion that she was a hysterical, untalented social climber. (SM)

References:

Bellet, Roger, ed. *Femmes de lettres au XIXe siècle, autour de Louise Colet*. Lyon: Presses Universitaires de Lyon, 1982.

Duytschaever, Marie-Claude. "Louise Colet, un poète entravé." In Carrol F. Coates, ed., *Repression and Expression: Literary and Social Coding in Nineteenth-Century France*. New York: Lang, 1996. 197–202.

Fisher, Martine. "L'Art des sacrifices: La correspondance de Flaubert avec Louise Colet de 1851 à 1854." In *Les Femmes de lettres: Ecriture féminine ou spécificité générique?* Montreal: University of Montreal Press, 1994. 75–85.

Jackson, John F. *Louise Colet et ses amis littéraires*. New Haven: Yale University Press, 1937.

Steegmuller, Francis. *Flaubert et Madame Bovary: A Double Portrait*. Rev. ed. New York: Farrar, Straus and Giroux, 1968.

collective bovarysme. The term "collective bovarysme," coined at a conference in 1917 by Haitian writer Jean Price-Mars (1876–1969), describes the tendency of his country's intelligentsia to envision their society as other than it is (*La Vocation de l'élite*, 1919). At the basis of his thesis is the concept that the intellectual elite tend to ignore the existence of Haitian voodoo, one of the symbols of the country's popular culture, as beneath their intellectual dignity. Modern criticism often refers to collective bovarysme, derived from Jules de Gaultier's bovarysme theory (*Le Bovarysme, essai sur le pouvoir d'imaginer*, 1902), as Haitian bovarysme. (LCP)

References:

Gautier, Jules de. *Bovarysm*. Trans. Gerald M. Spring. New York: Philosophical Library, 1970.

Price-Mars, Jean. *La Vocation de l'élite*. Port-au-Prince: E. Chenet, 1919.

le Collège Royal. An expensive, prestigious Rouen boarding school in which Flaubert was enrolled at age ten (1832), le Collège Royal was designed to develop leading citizens and enrolled 500–700 pupils at the time. Flaubert appreciated his history teacher, Pierre-Adolphe Chéruel (1809–91), a disciple of Jules Michelet, and his French teacher Gourgand-Dugazon, both of whom encouraged him to write stories. Chéruel was to become an outstanding, productive scholar of French history. However, despite his interest in history, natural history, and philosophy, Flaubert was unhappy at the Collège Royal. The school was run like a military academy, and he could not adjust to the drum rolls, 5:00 A.M. risings, and marching lines. In *Mémoires d'un fou* (1838), he describes how his classmates teased and victimized him for being different. Flaubert's loathing for them evolved to include all those ruled by conformity and intolerance. In response, he and his friends Ernest Chevalier and Alfred Le Poittevin created and enacted "Le Garçon," an imaginary buffoon whose insipid remarks and hypocrisy personified for them the bourgeoisie they so detested.

In 1838, Flaubert became a day student while residing at the Hôtel-Dieu. In December 1839, he was expelled from the school for participating in a student protest against the educational system and for refusing to perform supplementary work assigned as punishment. He spent the next seven months working at home in preparation for the *baccalauréat* exam, which he passed in August 1840. (JWA)

References:

Chaline, Jean-Pierre. "Le Milieu culturel rouennais au temps de Flaubert." In *Flaubert et Maupassant: Écrivains normands*. Colloquium, University of Rouen, May 8–10, 1980. Paris: Presses Universitaires de France, 1981. 17–25.

Dumesnil, René. *Flaubert: Son hérédité, son milieu, sa méthode*. Geneva: Slatkine, 1977.

Fournier, Albert. "De Rouen à Croisset." *Europe* 485–87 (1969): 252–68.

Collier, Gertrude. *See* Tennant, Gertrude (née Collier).

Collier, Harriet (1824–1909). Harriet Colliers's father, a retired British Navy captain, had moved to France because it was cheaper to live there than in England. He summered at Trouville, the Normandy beach resort where the Flauberts went also. The two families met in 1843. Harriet, who was crippled by a spinal disease, would be carried outdoors each day to sit for hours in a park next to the Flauberts' house, enjoying the sea air. She and Flaubert were attached to each other, and he started writing a romantic short story about her. But her father, who knew no French and who was prejudiced against the French people, did not want his daughter to marry a Frenchman who, worse yet, was an aspiring writer and therefore seemed to have no financial prospects. Flaubert's strong mother fixation, and his secret reluctance to give up sexual orgies with prostitutes, were further obstacles to marriage. Dr. Achille Flaubert, however, Flaubert's father, became Harriet's physician, and the Colliers moved for a time to Rouen, while Flaubert returned to Paris to continue studying law. The Colliers subsequently moved to the Champs-Elysées. Flaubert visited her often there, and read much French romantic literature aloud to her. Harriet became more ill, the Colliers moved out to a suburb, Flaubert failed his law exams, and he and the Colliers drifted apart. Then, from January 1844 through April 1845, Flaubert was seriously ill with epilepsy. After he recovered, he visited the Colliers again several times. But he became terrified when he realized she wanted to marry him, and withdrew for five years. In 1851, Flaubert visited her again in London, where she had returned to live. Her health had greatly improved. They exchanged affectionate letters, and she sent her portrait, but she married in 1854 without informing him. The naïve, impulsive, forward Louise Roque in the 1869 *Education sentimentale* was in part modeled on her. (LF)

References:

Bart, Benjamin F. *Flaubert.* Syracuse: Syracuse University Press, 1967.
Flaubert, Gustave. [Untitled short story.] Rouen, Bibliothèque Municipale, MS 92268, folios 198–99.
Spencer, P. "New Light on Flaubert's Youth." *French Studies* 7 (1954): 97–108.
Starkie, Enid. *Flaubert, the Making of the Master.* New York: Atheneum, 1967.

colors. Colors in Flaubert's writing have received most attention in *Madame Bovary*. There he uses them in two strikingly opposite ways. Yellow symbolizes degrading reality, mud, or adultery. The curtains of a room where Emma and Rodolphe have sex are yellow. The coach L'Hirondelle (the swallow), that takes Emma to her rendezvous with Léon every week, is yellow; the curtains of the coach in which she first has sex with him are yellow. Blue, as Haig richly demonstrated, corresponds to the illusion of the ideal, as perceived by the protagonists. Charles first sees Emma in a blue dress; she herself dreams of blue silk; at other moments a blue haze suggests the possibility of happiness. Flaubert uses the potentially pejorative term "bleuâtre" (bluish) to tinge this dream with authorial sarcasm. The use of green appears ambiguous in *Madame Bovary*. It may imply a false hope of transcendence, as in the notations that Rodolphe wears a green velvet frock coat, and that Charles wants to cover Emma's coffin with a green velvet cloth (Hélein-Koss). But green is also associated with the satanic: the landscapes are filled with lush greenery each time Emma is about to succumb to a sexual seduction. And Lheureux, the demonic merchant who successfully tempts Emma to over-extend her credit, initially appears in a greenish twilight. The blind beggar, symbol of the weaknesses and sufferings of the flesh, has a green eye (Duncan).

So far as their reported perceptions are concerned, characters other than Emma and Charles usually appear to inhabit a world of black and white. It is the impersonal narrator who ordinarily notes the touches of red, green, or gold in their surroundings. There are, however, two main exceptions to this principle. First, an abundance of variegated ("bariolées") colors in Flaubert's novelistic descriptions usually connotes kitsch (from the German word for "junk," and designating the results of a bad taste that blends incongruous objects, resulting in monstrosities such as the cap with mixed materials and shapes that Charles Bovary's mother buys for him when she sends him off to school). Homais's pharmacy stands out in Yonville, for example, because of the gleaming red and green liquids in flasks in his display window. The portraits by the inept painter Pellerin in *L'Education sentimentale* are hideous daubs whose garish colors suggest decay and putrescence. Second, gold (the traditional background color for medieval paintings of saints, the Blessed Virgin, or the Trinity, connoting that the figures represented are in paradise) serves Flaubert to suggest an overreaching bourgeois grandiosity. We see it in Homais's name on his shop sign, and on the nut a taxidermist places in the parrot Loulou's beak in "Un cœur simple." That those sensitive enough to perceive colors—including the oafish

Charles—are always deceived in their perceptions intensifies the bitterness of Flaubert's starkly disillusioning world. (LMP)

References:

Demorest, Don-L. *L'expression figurée et symbolique dans l'œuvre de Gustave Flaubert.* Paris: Les Presses Modernes, 1931.

Duncan, Phillip A. "Symbolic Green and Satanic Presence in Flaubert's *Madame Bovary.*" *Nineteenth-Century French Studies* 13. 2–3 (1985): 99–104.

Haig, Stirling. "The *Madame Bovary* Blues." *Romantic Review* 61 (1970): 27–34.

Hélein-Koss, Suzanne. "Le tracé ironique du velours vert dans *Madame Bovary.*" *Nineteenth-Century French Studies* 21.1–2 (Fall–Winter 1992–93): 66–72.

Tipper, Paula Andrew. *The Dream-Machine: Avian Imagery in* Madame Bovary. Durham: University of Durham, 1994.

Comices agricoles (*MB*). *Comices agricoles* is one of the capital scenes of *Madame Bovary* (part 2, chapter 8). An outstanding, often-cited example of Flaubert's technique of the tableau, this description of an agricultural fair operates on multiple levels. It illustrates important aspects of the main characters (Emma, Homais, Rodolphe) and at the same time provides a subtle critique of political ambitions, economic exploitation, religious mystification, obtuse civic pride, and the perversion of language in modern society. On one level, Rodolphe and Emma—their sense of superiority symbolized by their spatial elevation and isolation, as later during the scene of physical seduction—are ensconced on the second floor of the town hall; through the open window, they watch the award ceremony. At this point, Rodolphe begins his verbal seduction of Emma; she is impressed by his insouciant attitude, his costume, and his false romantic melancholy. On another level, on the ground and on the stage, we see an ironic depiction of country life: the review of the National Guard, the empty speeches by minor government officials, the agricultural prizes. Throughout the scene, Flaubert emphasizes the inadequacy and the misuse of language. The introductory speech by the prefect's aide (the prefect himself having decided at the last moment not to appear) is filled with clichés and incoherent metaphors (e.g., the chariot of state sailing on a stormy sea). While the awardees are being announced, Rodolphe pursues his campaign of seduction, using all the worn-out clichés of the romantic era. Flaubert intersperses the two sequences of remarks to make the remarks on the stage, culminating in the expression "Race porcine, prix *ex aequo*" ("Pigs, shared prize") seem an indirect, ironic commentary on Rodolphe's patter.

On yet another level, we see the self-importance of Homais as he explains to Madame Lefrançois the relationship between agronomy and chemistry. Not only is Homais's newspaper article reporting on the fair exaggerated (the failed fireworks display is compared to a scene from the *Thousand and One Nights*), but also it attacks the clergy; Homais regularly uses his position as a newspaperman to further his own agenda. (EFG)

See also tableau.

Reference:

Goldin, Jeanne, ed. and commentator. *Les Comices agricoles de* Madame Bovary *de Flaubert*. 2 vols. Geneva: Droz, 1984.

Commanville, Caroline (née Hamard, 1846–1931). Caroline Commanville was Flaubert's niece. Her mother died when she was two months old. She was raised by her grandmother and by her uncle Flaubert himself. He lovingly tutored her in history and geography and directed her reading to ensure a broad education. She recalls in her reminiscences that between 1852 and 1856, while Flaubert was painstakingly composing *Madame Bovary*, "la Bovary" became in her mind synonymous with working, which for Flaubert meant writing (49). Her *Souvenirs sur Gustave Flaubert*, originally published in 1887 as the preface to the first edition of Flaubert's general correspondence, provides ample information about, in her words, the fanatic who made art his God (22). But she edulcorates and sometimes censors the sexual adventures of her uncle, ambivalently obsessed with love. She does not name Louise Pradier or Elisa Schlésinger, although she mentions Maurice Schlésinger and Louise Colet (36). She impassively reports on her unhappy marriage to Ernest Commanville in 1864, which, as she wrote, changed the course of their lives (66), and on the financial disaster from which Flaubert self-sacrificially saved her and her husband (73–74) after the latter incurred overwhelming debts after the Franco-Prussian War of 1870–71.

Flaubert felt indebted to his niece, who helped his mother care for him, especially when he was bedridden in 1860. Some critics have claimed that her devotion was insincere, and that she shared her unscrupulous husband's avarice. But Flaubert's frequent letters to Caroline show unwavering loyalty to the "daughter" he nurtured until his death in 1880 (see Steegmuller 273, 279–84). After his death, she became the guardian of his papers and his memory. To her credit, she kept most of Flaubert's manuscripts intact. Three years after her husband Ernest Commanville died in 1890, she moved to Antibes. There she named her new house the Villa Tanit (after the moon goddess in *Salammbô*). In 1900, she proposed to and married Dr. Franklin Grout, a childhood friend and son of a student of her father. He died in 1921. Generations of Flaubert scholars made pilgrimages to her retirement home, and in later years she herself became an active Flaubert scholar. On her death in 1931, Flaubert's manuscripts were auctioned off and dispersed, many to parts unknown. (AP/LMP)

References:

Cather, Willa. "Chance Meeting." *Atlantic Monthly* (February 1933): 154ff.

Commanville, Caroline. *Souvenirs sur Gustave Flaubert*. Paris: Ferroud, 1895.

Lottman, Herbert. *Flaubert*. New York: Fromm, 1990. 63–65, 181–89, 193–96, 202–4, 225–30, 243–51, 272–74, 305–7, 309–311, 321–25, 341–45, and passim.

Steegmuller, Francis, ed. *The Letters of Gustave Flaubert*. 2 vols. Cambridge, MA: Harvard University Press, 1980–82.

Commanville, Ernest (1834–90). Ernest Commanville was a wood importer and owner of a sawmill business at Dieppe. Concealing his illegitimacy, on April 6, 1864, he married Caroline Hamard, the niece for whom Flaubert had taken responsibility because she was an orphan. From 1867 until Flaubert's death, Commanville took charge of Flaubert's financial affairs. Among his responsibilities were paying Flaubert's debts, managing his capital, and paying Flaubert the interest on his investments. From this time on, Flaubert never knew where he stood financially; he had difficulty obtaining money from his nephew. When Commanville had financial troubles in 1875, Flaubert sacrificed more than half his fortune to prevent Commanville's bankruptcy. Flaubert's financial ruin is usually attributed either to Commanville's incompetence in business or to his dishonesty, and it is commonly believed that the author's death was hastened by the financial worries that Commanville's bad management caused. (LCP)

Reference:

Bart, Benjamin F. *Flaubert.* Syracuse: Syracuse University Press, 1967.

la Commune. The year 1871 saw the sudden arrival and equally rapid departure of the Commune, a revolutionary government in Paris that endured only from March to May. The exact character of the Commune is difficult to typify: it was founded less as a political program than in opposition to the republican but conservative government of France as a whole. That government had angered the Parisians in two regards, first by signing a peace treaty with Bismarck when Paris had stood ready to fight, second by locating the capital in Versailles rather than Paris. This second action, in addition to affronting the inhabitants of Paris, the traditional capital of France, reinforced suspicions about the monarchist sentiments common in the government.

Though its opponents defined the Commune as socialist (as did the Russian revolutionaries in 1917 who harked back to it as a model), the government of the Commune was in fact dominated by Republicans; the Socialist International received only four seats. Sixteen of the ninety initially elected to the Central Committee refused their seats, opposing the split with Versailles. Once fully constituted, the eighty-one member government pursued a generally progressive agenda, but did not disturb the Bank of France and allowed only unoccupied workshops to be taken over by workers.

On May 21, 1871, government forces, finally arrayed and fully primed with rhetoric about the socialist Commune, attacked, starting what has become known as *la semaine sanglante* (the bloody week). Though the Communards fought fiercely, they did not present a unified front. Barricades varied in strength, and many of the Communards would fight only in their own districts. As the Versaillais (partisans of the government of Versailles) progressed, the Communards set fire to the city. By May 27, Paris was smoldering rubble, but firmly in the hands of the French government. More people, including many women and children, perished at the hands of the invading troops than had been executed during the Reign of Terror of 1793.

The Commune seems to have driven Flaubert from politics for good. Hardly convinced that one man was the equal of another, he saw his worst suspicions about the nature of democracy confirmed in the Commune, which he viewed as both lawless and socialistic. (GB)

See also socialism.

Reference:

Bart, Benjamin F. *Flaubert*. Syracuse: Syracuse University Press, 1967. 554–61.

concordances. A concordance of a literary work is an exhaustive glossary of "keywords in context" (listing all words together with the phrases in which they occur). A concordance helps one find the source of quotations, but it is a useful tool in diverse fields of research. The glossary allows linguists (but also sociocritics and psychocritics) to study a writer's privileged vocabulary (idiolect) or, more widely, the language of a certain period. Aided by a concordance, stylistic studies can help account for the idiosyncrasies of a writer's style, whereas thematic studies can focus on themes and motifs by commenting on the occurrences of all relevant words and on the ways they relate to their context. A more ambitious examination of the entire work of an author can be tackled by comparing the concordances of all that author's writings.

The concordances to Flaubert's texts are remarkable, although they merely display the words in a line (not in a complete sentence), do not distinguish among certain grammatical functions (for instance, *je marche* and *il marche*), and do not take variants into account. They clearly group all occurrences of identical words, distinguish homographs (such as the noun *boucher* and the verb *boucher*), and give precise references (part, chapter, page, and paragraph numbers) to readily available editions. (ELC)

References:

Carlut, Charles, Pierre H. Dubé, and J. Raymond Dugan. *A Concordance to Flaubert's* Bouvard et Pécuchet. 2 vols. New York: Garland, 1980.

———. *A Concordance to Flaubert's* La Tentation de saint Antoine. New York: Garland, 1979.

———. *A Concordance to Flaubert's* L'Education sentimentale. 2 vols. New York: Garland, 1978.

———. *A Concordance to Flaubert's* Madame Bovary. 2 vols. New York: Garland, 1978.

———. *A Concordance to Flaubert's* Salammbô. 2 vols. New York: Garland, 1979.

———. *A Concordance to Flaubert's* Trois Contes. New York: Garland, 1979.

Conrad, Joseph (Teodor Jósef Konrad Korzeniowski, 1857–1924). Flaubert was "the author [Joseph Conrad] admired and revered most" (Hervouet 6). During the decade that Ford Madox Ford worked as Conrad's close friend and collaborator (1898–1908), the two men memorized pages of *Madame Bovary* and other works and imitated Flaubert and Guy de Maupassant as part of their literary apprenticeship. Frederick Karl believes that Flaubert's work was "perhaps the single most compelling literary influence on Conrad's development as a writer. . . . Flaubert is everywhere in Conrad, virtually a divine presence, a guru" (70, 270). In an April 6, 1892 letter in French to Marguerite Poradowska, Conrad praises Flaubert: "In him, we see a man who had enough imagination for two realists. There are few authors who could be as much a creator as he. One never questions for a moment either his characters or his incidents: one would rather doubt one's own existence" (1:111).

The same letter shows that, despite later disclaimers, Conrad was rereading *Madame Bovary* while writing his first book, *Almayer's Folly: A Story of an Eastern River* (1895). Both Almayer and Emma suffer from romantic illusions, covet wealth, and enter a loveless marriage to realize their fantasies. They refuse to accept their own mediocrity and the limitations of their circumstances, which circumstances finally become so badly entangled that death seems the only exit. Almayer also bears some resemblances to Frédéric Moreau, the weak hero of *L'Education sentimentale*. Conrad's tightly unified plot and the narrative impassivity that contrasts with the intrusive narrators in Victorian fiction are inspired by Flaubert. Conrad also used Flaubert's tableau method.

In "An Outcast of the Islands," the motif of romantic delusion recurs, and the farewell scene between Emma and Léon when he leaves Yonville in *Madame Bovary* is echoed in the scene where Willems and Aïssa first hold hands. "The Nigger of the *Narcissus*: A Tale of the Sea" (1896–97) contains closing pages that seem inspired by the description of Emma Bovary's wedding, and she has some resemblances to Donkin. The group of sailors evokes the barbarian mercenaries in *Salammbô*. While Conrad was composing this tale, he read *Salammbô* each day as if it were "my morning coffee." Thornton finds that the first twenty pages of "Karain" were inspired by *Madame Bovary* and by *Salammbô*, although he criticizes Conrad sharply for poor imitations of Flaubert's style and impersonal point of view and for missing Flaubert's complex irony (150–51). Again, in "The Idiots," Thornton finds reminiscences of the Bovary and Rouault (Emma's) families and of their country wedding. Watson complains that "An Outpost of Progress" (1896) represents awkward attempts to move between intimate character analysis and interior monologue, as Flaubert had done in *Bouvard et Pécuchet* (38).

Decisive for the development of Conrad's artistic independence and maturity were, first, the inspiration of Maupassant's "elaborate narrative frames and dramatized narrators" (Watson 39) and, second, the development of the Marlow figure—derived from Conrad's own years as a seaman—in "Youth," *The Heart of Darkness, Lord Jim*, and *Chance*. Marlow's evocations of the ineffable are in contrast with the cool irony of Flaubert's impersonal narrators. Conrad always retained, however, Flaubert's ideal of the cult of art. (LMP)

See also Ford, Ford Madox; tableau.

References:

Conrad, Joseph. *The Collected Letters of Joseph Conrad.* Ed. Frederick R. Karl and Laurence Davies. 5 vols. Cambridge: Cambridge University Press, 1983–[96].

Hervouet, Yves. "Aspects of Flaubertian Influence on Conrad's Fiction." *Revue de littérature comparée* 57.1 (1983): 5–24.

Karl, Frederick R. *Joseph Conrad: The Three Lives.* New York: Farrar, 1979.

Smitten, Jeffrey R. "Flaubert and the Structure of 'The Secret Agent': A Study in Spatial Form." In Wolodymyr T. Zyla and Wendell M. Aycock, eds., *Joseph Conrad: Theory and World Fiction.* Lubbock: Texas Tech University, 1974. 151–66.

Thornton, Lawrence. "Conrad, Flaubert, and Marlow: Possession and Exorcism." *Comparative Literature* 34.2 (1982): 146–56.

Watson, Wallace. " 'The Shade of Old Flaubert' and Maupassant's 'Art Impeccable (Presque)': French Influences on the Development of Conrad's Marlow." *Journal of Narrative Technique* 7 (1977): 37–56.

Watt, Ian. *Conrad in the Nineteenth Century.* Berkeley: University of California Press, 1979. 50–55.

Yelton, Donald C. *Mimesis and Metaphor: An Inquiry into the Genesis and Scope of Conrad's Symbolic Imagery.* The Hague: Mouton, 1967. Chs. 1–4.

copies, copying. A "copy" in its etymological sense suggests abundance (Latin *copia*, as in "copious" or "cornucopia"). In Flaubert's day, before typewriters and computers, and before photographic reproduction had become commonplace, the term usually meant the exact reproduction of a handwritten document by a clerk who would write out the same text again in a handwriting different than that of the original author. That Bouvard and Pécuchet are both "copistes" by profession mirrors this activity thematically. Their job is to transcribe manuscript texts (a French term for written homework, *copies*, still suggests the lack of originality that predominates in imposed assignments). The clerk, then, functions like a human typewriter, a machine. In Herman Melville's "Bartleby the Scrivener," the human machine becomes an uncanny presence by refusing to function. But in any event, the normal copy clerk had no will of his own and copied on demand.

From this bare stem spring numerous side branches. Forgeries are copies (often of paintings) that masquerade as familiar originals; plagiarism is copying that masquerades as a newly created product. Negative connotations cling to these two terms because both of these transgressions involve a pattern or "intent to deceive." Indeed, "plagiarism" derives from the Latin term for kidnapper or seducer (*plagiarius*) and has come to refer to the adoption of thoughts or words of another as one's own without acknowledgment. The protection of literary copyright, which punishes unauthorized reproduction of an author's work, began only at the end of the nineteenth century.

Flaubert's various works bear witness to his manifold techniques for copying. Copy as multiplication forms the core of his mode of irony, which consists of multiplying, fragmenting, and juxtaposing the many often-prescriptive texts he copies. In a text such as *Salammbô*, he makes a collage of unacknowledged borrowings whose unity derives from their historical subject: the rebellion of the barbarian mercenaries cheated of their pay by the city-state Carthage and overwhelmed at last by the vindictive gods they had unwittingly opposed. In *Madame Bovary*, Emma's various daydreams copy episodes from contemporary popular novels, and some of Homais's "scientific" endeavors are copied from a pharmaceutical text. Many details in Emma's death scene come directly from Flaubert's notes on the effects of arsenic, as reported in medical books. His unifying style conceals the rough edges of the disparate sources pasted together.

In contrast, citational irony foregrounds the borrowed source (often by using quotation marks or by naming the source), but defamiliarizes it by embedding it conspicuously within an alien whole. In "Un cœur simple," *Madame Bovary*, or *L'Education sentimentale*, the episodic use of clichés in italics makes us aware for the first time of how a verbal reflex by a member of the despised bourgeoisie betrays how that class functions automatically in society. Powerful because it remains unexamined yet generally accepted, the use of a cliché is always already given by the cultural code. It parallels the economic role of the bourgeoisie, who are consumers (who use objects already "given"), not producers. Flaubert's own masterful style, in which clichés are exposed like flies in amber, heightens the contrast between creativity and mere copying.

Finally, in his last creation, *Bouvard et Pécuchet*, Flaubert creates a kind of metacopying. Initially freed from their imposed task by an unexpected inheritance, the copy clerks play the role of involuntary *eirons* (those who expose and then deflate pretensions). They copy the behaviors prescribed by the written authorities in various branches of theoretical and applied science, in education, and in other fields. At times, their failure to understand and follow directions leads to their discomfiture. Flaubert's writing seems to exemplify the archaic meanings of the words *cop(p)ieur* and *cop(p)ieux*, both of which meant *moqueur* or *railleur* (mocker). He satirizes Bouvard and Pécuchet's absolute belief in what they read; their ensuing failures confirm the stupidity of their belief. In other words, while instructional manuals seek to codify information and instruct the reader, Flaubert uses many how-to books to produce *Bouvard et Pécuchet*, a great "how-not-to" book. His many ironic manipulations of the copied texts subvert whatever authority they might have possessed. Flaubert successfully undermines the supposedly stable, inherent coherence of the printed text through fragmentation and the dislocation of these fragments.

In addition, the Erasmian notion of *copia* promotes many figures of abundance that reappear in highly ironized form in his last work. Such images include the cornucopia (ironized through the characters' failed attempts at gardening), gold (money is spent rapidly here), sexual fertility (which Flaubert transforms into sexual ignorance and venereal disease), and eating (ironized most comically through Flaubert's depiction of Bouvard). Flaubert ironizes the values of military strength (plural *copiae*, "forces") as well, especially when Bouvard and Pécuchet attempt to reenact sections of Amoros's gymnastics manual.

When the clerks finally renounce the quest for knowledge and resolve to copy as before, it is now they who choose to do so—and their documents will come to them at random. Thus they transcend their former profession and the human condition of radical unoriginality that that profession implies by knowingly embracing it, with all its ineluctable limitations. (ENM)

Reference:

Meyer, E. Nicole. "Facts into Fiction in Flaubert's *Bouvard et Pécuchet*." *Nottingham French Studies* 33 (1994): 37–46.

Correspondance. Flaubert's *Correspondance* is unanimously considered one of the most beautiful correspondences of French literature. Although many of the thousands of letters that Flaubert wrote between 1830 and 1880 have been destroyed (including, for instance, most of those to Maxime Du Camp and to Louis Bouilhet), a considerable number have been preserved that constitute an exceptional document for readers and researchers.

The letters are first of all a document on nineteenth-century French society, more precisely on bourgeois and artistic life in Paris and in the provinces, for Flaubert lived most of the time in Croisset, near Rouen. Flaubert often shares his opinions on current issues or topics, for instance, religion and politics. He describes his intellectual life, his early interest in the arts, and later, when his reputation grows, his acquaintance with many artists and writers of the period. Moreover, the letters give a continuous account of his considerable readings: literary readings, of course, encompassing not only classical and contemporary French literature (Rabelais, Montaigne, Balzac, Hugo, and others), but also foreign literature, particularly English and German (Shakespeare, Goethe) and literature from classical antiquity. Flaubert was passionate about contemporary and ancient history and was very knowledgeable in philosophy (for instance, Hegel, Kant, and Spinoza) as well as in the sciences (particularly in medicine). Therefore, the letters contain numerous analyses and comments that illustrate the writer's point of view and reflect the image of a French intellectual at that time.

Obviously, Flaubert never wrote his letters with the intention of being published. Therefore, he wrote with sincerity, exposing fragments of his own life, giving advice, confiding in certain correspondents, and making judgments about his contemporaries. His *Correspondance* is a precious tool for understanding his complex personality. It reveals his vision of life and of the relation between life and art: since the human condition is miserable, life can be legitimated only through an eternal pursuit of art. Whereas the years 1830–51 correspond, above all, to a period of "formation" of the writer, in the following years the letters focus primarily on a long reflection on creation in general and on Flaubertian aesthetics in particular, which explains why the *Correspondance* is considered the best "preface" to Flaubert's work. From the time of his correspondence with Louise Colet (1851–56), which matches the long elaboration of *Madame Bovary*, he expresses his conception of art and genres (especially prose), as well as his problems with composing in diverse literary forms (such as narration, description, and dialogue). He also writes about his anxiety concerning creation and his desperate search for Beauty, which he links to a primordial principle of objectivity. In turn, Flaubert relates this principle to a goal of impersonal and quasi-scientific distance—that is, literature must be *exposante*. The letters bear witness to Flaubert's painful ambition to reach perfection in style, certainly the most important aspect of his writing.

After his separation from Louise Colet, Flaubert never again engages in such an intense dialogue. He continues to convey his critical and aesthetic ideas and ideals in letters to "literary correspondents" (such as Ernest Feydeau, the Goncourt brothers, Charles Baudelaire, and, later, Emile Zola) and to a few acquaintances (Edma Roger des Genettes, Marie-Sophie Leroyer de Chantepie); however, the *Correspondance* often turns into a list of precise details that Flaubert needs for his work, calling on specific individuals to supply him with the necessary information (especially Jules Duplan and then Edmond Laporte and Guy de Maupassant). These letters are in general less explanatory and developed than those to Louise Colet, but they remain useful for a concrete understanding of how Flaubertian creation functions in relation to precise issues (for instance, during the writing of *L'Education sentimentale* and *Bouvard et Pécuchet*).

Moreover, from 1869 (with the death of Louis Bouilhet) and then through the 1870s, after a series of disasters that greatly affect the writer (the Franco-Prussian War as well as the deaths of his mother and intimate friends, and finally the Commanvilles' bankruptcy in 1875), the *Correspondance* reveals an immense loss of energy and increasing pessimism. The reader is left with the impression that Flaubert, whose opinions do not vary with time, cannot help but repeat himself in increasingly succinct formulae, except in some letters to Ivan Turgenev and also in his correspondence with George Sand. Sand, with whom Flaubert differs greatly both in personality and art, engages him in persuasive discussions concerning their shared moral, political, and artistic convictions.

Soon after Flaubert's death, his heirs, particularly Caroline Commanville, realized that they could profit from selling his correspondence. Selected letters appeared in four volumes published by Charpentier from 1887 to 1893. Afterwards, the publisher Conard attempted to release an integral edition of the *Correspondance* in 9 volumes from 1926 to 1933; it contains 1,992 letters. However, this edition lacks numerous letters, and many others are censored (notably because of Flaubert's tone, sometimes considered "indecent," if not "obscene"); furthermore, the text is at times inaccurate, owing to reading mistakes, and some letters are incorrectly dated. These problems urged Conard to publish four additional volumes in 1954 ("*Supplément*"), which offer 1,296 new letters. Gallimard then responded to the increasing interest in correspondences in France by publishing a new integral edition of Flaubert's *Correspondance*, undertaken by Jean Bruneau. This edition had not yet been completed; the last volume is still forthcoming. Thanks to immense and patient research around the world, one can still discover, at the end of the twentieth century, some of Flaubert's letters that remained unpublished; Bruneau also manages to fill lacunae and to correct errors or wrong dates found in many previously published letters (9 previously unpublished letters appear in the first volume, 12 in the second, 74 in the third, 76 in the fourth, and the four volumes reveal 328 newly completed letters). He also identifies letters whose owners have refused to release them. Moreover, as it contains numerous helpful notes, this edition represents an invaluable, definitive tool for the knowledge and study of Flaubert. (ELC)

References:

Beaumont, Barbara, ed. and trans. *Flaubert and Turgenev, a Friendship in Letters: The Complete Correspondence*. London: Athlone, 1985.

Debray-Genette, Raymonde, and Jacques Neefs. *L'Œuvre de l'œuvre: Etudes sur la correspondance de Flaubert*. Saint-Denis: Presses Universitaires de Vincennes, 1993.

Dufief, Pierre-Jean, ed. *Gustave Flaubert—Les Goncourt, correspondance*. Paris: Flammarion, 1998.

Flaubert, Gustave. *Correspondance*. Ed. Jean Bruneau. Paris: Gallimard, 1973 (vol. 1: 1830–51), 1980 (vol. 2; 1851–58), 1988 (vol. 3; 1859–68), 1998 (vol. 4; 1869–75), forthcoming (vol. 5; 1876–80).

———. *Lettres inédites de Gustave Flaubert à son éditeur Michel Lévy*. Ed. Jacques Suffel. Paris: Calmann-Lévy, 1965.

Jacobs, Alphonse, ed. *Correspondance/Gustave Flaubert, George Sand*. Paris: Flammarion, 1981.

Leclerc, Yvan, ed. *Correspondance/Gustave Flaubert—Guy de Maupassant*. Paris: Flammarion, 1993.

Steegmuller, Francis, and Barbara Bray, eds. and trans. *Flaubert—Sand: The Correspondence*. London: Harvill, 1993.

Zviguilski, Alexandre, ed. *Correspondance Flaubert—Tourgéniev*. Paris: Flammarion, 1989.

coup d'état of December 2, 1851. As president under the Second French Republic (1848–51), Louis-Napoleon (later Napoleon III) had the support of the clergy, who were pleased by the Loi Falloux. This law gave the Catholic Church considerable influence over public education between 1850 and 1905, when it was repealed in the aftermath of the anti-Catholic reaction occasioned by the Dreyfus Case. Monarchists (who could not agree on a single candidate to be their heir to the throne) and businessmen, fearful of a return of the instability associated with the 1848 revolution, also were glad to see a strong, authoritarian, conservative leader in power. But according to the laws of the Second Republic, presidents were limited to one four-year term, and the Legislative Assembly's 446–278 vote to amend the constitution had not yet achieved the required supermajority. Therefore, Louis-Napoleon planned a coup to perpetuate his rule beyond its legal limits. His plans were devious, sound, and thorough.

He first selected a new prefect of police in Paris and a new head of the army. He chose the date of the coup, December 2, for its symbolic value as the anniversary of Napoleon I's coronation and his victory at Austerlitz, but also for its practical value; with the Assembly in session, it would be easier to round up its members before they could mount opposition. That same Assembly had furnished justification for the coup. Conservatives had done well in the 1849 legislative elections, but spooked by a surprisingly strong showing by socialists and radical republicans, the Assembly had restricted suffrage, taking the franchise away from some three million Frenchmen in a 433–241 vote. The law was sustained by five votes (353–348) when Louis-Napoleon pressed for abrogation; he was able to come to power thanks to his promise that all Frenchmen would have the right to vote for or against his program.

Late on December 1 and early on December 2, the army and Paris police occupied key locations in Paris while fliers announcing the coup and the return of universal suffrage were plastered all over the city. In the early morning, enemies of Louis-Napoleon were arrested, as were 220 conservative deputies meeting in the tenth arrondissement later in the day. On December 3 and 4, arrests continued and violence broke out, resulting in the death of one deputy on the third and of some sixty citizens on the fourth. Violence also broke out in the provinces, but this disorder only provided the new regime with a further excuse to crack down. Once Louis-Napoleon had established control, he called for a vote on December 20–21. He was elected president for a ten-year term and was charged with creating a new constitution by an overwhelming vote of 7,145,000 to 592,000.

Flaubert was actually in Paris on December 2, 1851. He enjoyed the spectacle of the coup, but, indifferent to government except insofar as it affected the artist, he remained aloof from the politics of the event. (GB)

critical reception. Flaubert has long been considered the dominant novelist of nineteenth-century France—the great age of the novel. At first glance, his preeminence is surprising, because he is less purely entertaining than his great contemporaries. He lacks Balzac's melodramatic intensity and range of character types; Stendhal's wit, verve, and political sophistication; and Zola's violence, raw sex, and visionary fervor. The historical background of Flaubert's "exotic" novels, *Salammbô* and *La Tentation de saint Antoine*, seems remote and labored. The protagonists of his "realistic" novels, *Madame Bovary, L'Education sentimentale*, and *Bouvard et Pécuchet*, are obscure middle-class figures; their conversations are uninteresting; their ideas, clichés; their lives produce only a transient ripple of scandal in society; and at best, they are only dimly aware of the historical processes unfolding around them. So what accounts for Flaubert's durable prestige? His realism and his psychological acuity.

A few kindred spirits, great authors in their own right, appreciated Flaubert from the beginning—Baudelaire, Banville, Sand, Zola, and Proust. Aside from their spontaneous admiration, Flaubert criticism has evolved through three overlapping stages: first, normative criticism, which called Flaubert a realist; next, thematic criticism, which considered him an idealist; and finally, structuralist and poststructuralist criticisms, which consider him an indeterminist, a writer who resists conclusions.

Normative criticism predominated from the appearance of *Madame Bovary* in 1856–57 until the centenary of Flaubert's birth in 1921. The normative critic chooses an aesthetic or moral standard, or both, and then judges literary works according to how closely they conform to that standard. Usually—because the critic's function must be justified—he or she says that the works fall short. Early in the eighteenth century, l'abbé Batteux summed up the underlying presupposition of normative criticism: the proper mission of literature was "l'imitation de la belle nature" (Batteux 20, 22). Literally, this expression means "the imitation of [what is] beautiful [in] nature," but Batteux was not actually recommending a literature of landscape descriptions. By "nature" he meant mainly "human nature," and by "beautiful," what is morally admirable and inspiring in human nature. In other words, literature should propose a good example to its readers. The major corollary to this view was that the reader needed guidance; an author should therefore intervene explicitly to praise virtue and condemn vice, as George Eliot, Victor Hugo, or Charles Dickens did, tugging the reader by the sleeve and telling him or her what to feel.

Since most critics of Flaubert's time adhered to such views, they were too moralistic fully to appreciate realistic literature as we can today. Reacting to *Madame Bovary*, they granted that Flaubert observed people keenly and described them memorably, but they condemned him for selecting only what was base and trivial in human nature and neglecting what could have uplifted readers. Worse yet, they complained, Flaubert did not denounce his characters' baseness. He reported it calmly, impersonally, without telling readers how they should act. His dispassion seemed to condone the immorality he depicted. He also failed to defend the good: when his narrator observes that in adultery Emma Bovary "rediscovered all the platitudes of marriage," marriage and adultery seem equally bad. Critics found Flaubert's detached attitude cynical and depressing.

Thus Edmond Duranty, himself the moving spirit of a journal called *Réalisme*, nevertheless assailed *Madame Bovary* as a novel where "there is no emotion, no feeling, no life" (Porter, ed. 49). Sainte-Beuve, the leading critic of the century, saw only "meanness, misery, pretentiousness, stupidity" in Flaubert's characters. "Why not provide the good in one figure at least, in one charming or venerable face? . . . That provides relief and consolation, and the view of humanity is only more complete" (in Becker, ed. 103). In a more preemptory manner, Barbey d'Aurevilly exclaimed: "Human nature is loath to have a subject in hand without feeling some passion for or against. But Flaubert escapes from this custom which seems a law of the human spirit" (Porter, ed. 50).

During the remainder of Flaubert's career, critics gradually came round to a grudging, backhanded appreciation of *Madame Bovary*, contrasting it with his later novels and claiming that he had outlived his genius. They universally damned *Salammbô* in 1862, finding it contrived, frenetic, and artificial, a cold-blooded orgy of sadism and horror with flat, unbelievable characters. Critics welcomed Flaubert's return to the contemporary world in *L'Education sentimentale* (1869), but once again found that his skill in observation, his keen treatment of detail, and his carefully wrought style were offset by his concentration on the trivial and degrading, while he preserved an inappropriate detachment. They did appreciate his impersonality, however, insofar as it represented a departure from the confessional effusions of the romantics. *La Tentation de saint Antoine*, finally published in 1874, was the last full-length work to appear during Flaubert's lifetime. In it, critics believed, he seemed to have slid back into the incoherent, excessively bookish exoticism of *Salammbô*, depicting a limp-wristed saint passively watching a parade of visions. Henry James condemned the work for consisting entirely of "a strangely artificial and cold-blooded picturesque—abounding in the grotesque and the repulsive. . . . When the author has a really beautiful point to treat—as the assembly of the Greek deities fading and paling away in the light of Christianity [a morally edifying spectacle of The Triumph of the Good]—he becomes singularly commonplace and ineffective" (in Porter, ed. 145). Most readers of the time—like Paul Valéry, Michel Butor, and Jonathan Culler after them—failed to realize that the generative principle of the work was psychic projection (frequently signaled by Flaubert), a defense mechanism that attributes one's own shameful feelings to beings outside oneself. The devils and monsters that beset Antoine in his hallucinations and dreams are extensions of his own personality, embodiments of his memories. Like the fantastic tales of Nodier and Nerval before him, Flaubert's visionary work, on which he labored intermittently for twenty-five years, anticipates depth psychology by exploring the operations of the unconscious and the fantasies to which they give rise.

In 1881, the year after Flaubert died, Maxime Du Camp's *Souvenirs littéraires* revealed that his friend had composed a first version of the *Tentation* early in his career and had suppressed it after harsh criticism from Du Camp and Louis Bouilhet. The posthumous publication of the unfinished *Bouvard et Pécuchet* in the same year showed that Flaubert had reverted to his drably realistic mode as he portrayed two retired copy clerks who try to master all practical applications of human knowledge. These two publishing events in 1881 seemed to reveal a complete trajectory of Flaubert's literary endeavors and thus created a durable image of an author torn between two opposite extremes, yielding first to one and then to the other, binging and then fasting like an anorexic:

Romantic Excess	**Realistic Restraint**
1. *La Tentation* (1849)	2. *Madame Bovary* (1857)
3. *Salammbô* (1862)	4. *L'Education sentimentale* (1869)
5. *La Tentation* (1874)	6. *Bouvard et Pécuchet* (1881)

According to this view, Flaubert first overindulged his imagination, becoming grotesque and incoherent. While he was composing his romantic historical novels (column 1), he tried ineffectually to rein in his fancies through the discipline of exhaustive documentation. The result was that he wrote in a manner that was simultaneously bookish and uncontrolled. He reacted with an excess of self-restraint, choosing for his next subject a trivial contemporary topic, at the cost of becoming dry. Only from the late 1970s on has literary criticism begun consistently to challenge this scheme, emphasizing the psychological realism of the *Tentation* and the relevance of the history in *Salammbô* to Flaubert's own time. Ever since Baudelaire, critics have tellingly analyzed the elements of personal fantasizing (e.g., Flaubert's androgyny) in *Madame Bovary*, but more remains to be done to bring out the intimate obsessions reflected in *L'Education sentimentale* and in *Bouvard et Pécuchet.*

The normative criticism that dominated the Victorian age and the French "Belle Epoque" (1880–1914) reappeared in new guises after World War I. Revulsion at the horrors of the war, added to a groundswell of reaction against late-nineteenth-century positivism and scientism ("vice and virtue are products like sulphuric acid and sugar"), produced strong religious revivals in France and England. As a result, critics such as J. Middleton Murry emerged, condemning Flaubert for not having been Christian. More complex and influential was the position of Marxist criticism. From its viewpoint, the French Revolution had been led by and worked primarily for the benefit of the middle class. This class replaced the feudal system of the formerly dominant aristocracy with capitalism. Middle-class capitalists developed more efficient means of production and accumulated wealth at the expense of a growing urban proletariat. The latter was exploited without mercy. Around the middle of the nineteenth century, writers, also middle-class, recognized themselves as members of a social group that had become morally bankrupt. Seeing no positive values to uphold, they reacted with disillusionment, despair, and nihilism, becoming, in Jean-Paul Sartre's words, "knights of nothingness" (Sartre 3: 193–202).

The most influential representatives of this neo-Marxist school of criticism were Roland Barthes and Jean-Paul Sartre. In *Writing Degree Zero*, Barthes argues that *Madame Bovary* exemplifies a crisis of the loss of values in the novel around 1850: Flaubert tries to revalidate the novel in capitalist terms, on the basis of how much work has gone into producing it. The third volume of Sartre's monumental study of Flaubert, *L'Idiot de la famille*, criticizes Flaubert for sharing the middle class's "bad faith," the convenient self-deception that masks an initial deliberate choice to claim special privileges for oneself at the expense of logic and justice. Sartre argues that Flaubert tried to escape from his own class into a pseudonobility during the last nine years of the Second Empire (1861–70). He accepted the cross of the Legion of Honor in 1866 (having ridiculed his character Homais nine years earlier for having prostituted himself to gain that same cross) and became a regular guest of Princess Mathilde, to whom he referred as "*our* princess." After the disaster of the Franco-Prussian War in 1870, Sartre continues, Flaubert was forced to realize the sham of the bourgeois values by which he lived, but had no recourse but to reaffirm them without conviction. Although he had thought about a satiric novel on the Second Empire, he refrained from writing it because his loss of the special status of honored guest of the imperial family depressed him (3:160–206).

Normative criticism such as Sartre's or Duranty's tries to locate the ultimate meaning of a literary work outside the work, in a parallel but more extensive frame of reference—moral values, the historical process. It is "extrinsic." In contrast, thematic criticism in its broadest sense is "intrinsic": it seeks the work's meaning within itself or within the corpus of the author's works. The assumption is that an author does not explain everything, and that the task of criticism is to bring out what the author has implied or hidden. Normative criticism serves social values; it tries to make them more vivid. Thematic criticism serves the artist, working to disclose his or her richness, complexity, and enduring interest. Normative criticism usually states its presuppositions; thematic criticism takes them for granted. Normative criticism claims to represent values that the work of art is always vehemently suspected of having flouted; thematic criticism sees the work of art either as existing in harmony with its tradition or as inaugurating a new and equally valid one. With the exceptions just noted—Barthes and Sartre—thematic approaches dominated Flaubert criticism from about 1920 to 1970.

Georges Poulet encapsulated the attitudes of thematic criticism by insisting on the organic unity of the work of art. "The main purpose of [*Madame Bovary*] is to create relation and order" ("The Circle" 407). "What man attains in the Flaubertian experience is . . . the intuition of life in its cosmic expansion." Poulet's phenomenological criticism assumes that only our subjective representations of the world—of time and space, self and other, thought and object—are knowable, while that world in and of itself is not. Poulet argues that "Flaubert arrived at an integral phenomenalism. The mind being what it represents, and the object existing only in its representation in the mind, what remains is simply a unique being that can be called indifferently mind or nature" ("Flaubert" 17, 16). Poulet tries to demonstrate how Flaubert enters this state of awareness and then reemerges from it to reconstitute a novel. He considers as part of a single, uniform whole everything that Flaubert wrote, at every period of his life. He takes no account of development or chronological order, assuming that Flaubert's thought was always already fully formed; and he does not adequately consider Flaubert's literary masterpieces. Forty percent of his citations in "Flaubert" refer to the correspondence, and 45 percent more to the youthful works. Nevertheless, Poulet's method works well with nineteenth-century French authors in general, and with Flaubert in particular, because most of them share the organic worldview of romanticism, according to which every part reflects the whole as the DNA in a single cell reflects the organism from which it comes.

As Poulet dominated the thematic criticism of nineteenth-century French literature in general, Victor Brombert dominated the thematic criticism of the nineteenth-century French novel. He discusses "the metaphorical unity [the inevitable word] of *L'Education sentimentale*" in terms of prostitution—literal and figurative, male and female, individual and social. "Society itself, as represented by various groups, corporations or institutions, is the great whore who always embraces the winner" (*Novels*, 127). Anne Green places a similar motif in a broader context by treating the historical novel *Salammbô* as a reflection of the corruption Flaubert deplored in his own day. She explains that Flaubert selected a historical period with features similar to his own. Vitality (the liberal revolution of 1848/the mercenary barbarian armies) confronts decadence (the authoritarian reaction leading to the Second Empire/the decadent city-state of Carthage) only to be defeated; yet triumphant decadence is itself doomed. Carthage was soon to be overwhelmed by Rome, and the similar fate that Flaubert anticipated for the Second Empire was realized eight years later by the Prussian invasion.

Flaubert's fantastic and visionary literature—*La Tentation de saint Antoine*, and "Hérodias" and "La Légende de saint Julien l'hospitalier" from the *Trois Contes*—has lent itself particularly well to a psychologically oriented thematic criticism. Theodor Reik's classic essay applied traditional psychoanalytical methods to studying the repressed contents of Flaubert's unconscious. Unknown to the author, Reik claims, these contents manifest themselves in symbolic disguises in the literary work, linking unresolved, incestuous infantile fantasies and masochistic asceticism. More recent psychoanalytic approaches usually are influenced by ego psychology, which acknowledges the reality of repression but stresses the autotherapeutic, self-healing function of literary creation. According to this view, writing is regression in the service of the ego: it provides a means of getting in touch with primordial fantasies in order to bring them to consciousness. In this vein, Benjamin F. Bart studied the evolution of Flaubert's lifelong struggle to come to terms with his sexuality. He focuses on the core fantasy of a youthful dream and traces its progressive refinement down to the Saint Julian legend written in Flaubert's mid-fifties. Laurence M. Porter analyzed *La Tentation de saint Antoine* in detail, examining how the devil figure projects Anthony's inner religious doubt and stressing how carefully Flaubert revised the work over the years to imply that the sources of Anthony's visions could be situated in his own lived experience. Such studies make it clear that Flaubert was an innovative, sophisticated psychologist who recognized the crucial formative impact of childhood experience.

Jean Rousset, in the most frequently reprinted essay in Flaubert criticism, insists on Flaubert's desire to compose *Madame Bovary* as "a book about nothing, a book without reference outside itself," an enterprise that makes Flaubert "the first in date of the non-figurative novelists" such as Joyce and Woolf (59). Rousset's essay, pointing to Flaubert's nihilism, had been anticipated by Paul Bourget in 1884. But Rousset's great influence in 1962 announced a major shift in thematic criticism. Earlier thematic critics such as Harry Levin had depicted Flaubert as a saint of art, a martyr to style, sequestering himself in an eremitic retreat in order to dedicate himself to his novels. Once Flaubert's letters had become widely known in the 1930s, critics could find abundant evidence of his ideals. More than once, he called himself a "Platonist." To him, that meant that any subject, properly treated, would allow one to approach the ideal. He reported ecstatic visions of perfection. As Charles Du Bos explained in his pioneering essay on Flaubert, "Art had to make demands upon him as strict as those of the strictest religion, as stern even as the most ardent form of mysticism. Only then will art be a complete religion for him, intimate, mystical in an almost Platonic sense, since the exhilaration he derives from the masterpieces fulfills his desire for the absolute" ("On the 'Inner Environment' " 363). This view of Flaubert was echoed in major articles by critics such as Frank Laurence Lucas, Paul Valéry, and Benjamin F. Bart. As recently as 1984, Jacques Derrida found it necessary to oppose the notion of Flaubert's "Platonic idealism."

Once thematic critics such as Rousset had joined the Marxists in proclaiming that Flaubert's novels of disillusionment pointed to no meanings outside themselves, it was only a short step to the structuralist who studies the works as self-contained linguistic systems. The structuralists were ultimately inspired by the International Phonetic Alphabet, a system perfected in the 1920s to describe and categorize the sounds of all known human languages. This great achievement led the Russian Formalists of the 1920s and 1930s to try to extend it to a universal grammar for literary works, one analogous to the grammar and syntax of sentences. The structuralists, further inspired by anthropological classifications of human behavior in the 1950s and 1960s (Marcel Mauss, Claude Lévi-Strauss), tried to continue the work of the Formalists. Titles such as Tzvétan Todorov's *Grammaire du* Décaméron (by Boccaccio) reflect their efforts. Raymonde Debray-Genette states the structuralists' presuppositions unequivocally in her article on Flaubert's "Un cœur simple." She explains that a literary work is organized like a sentence. It is organized "horizontally" (across its successive narrative segments) by a kind of syntax (a set of rules for putting things together) analogous to the syntax of a sentence; it is also organized "vertically" (across multiple levels of meaning) by rhetorical devices such as "the great figures of speech that nourish classical discourse" (asyndeton, repetition, metonymy, metabole, synecdoche, and metaphor) (165). She concludes that such devices "are figures of nothing if not of themselves. They refer to one another, they circulate meaning, they do not halt it" (184). She thus refuses to "interpret" the literary work, that is, to try to connect it to some ultimate meaning inside ("organic unity") or outside (social or moral values) itself. To such postthematic critics, meaning is a system of transactions, of exchanges, of shifting axes rather than fixed points.

The intertextual approach, whose leading exponent is Michael Riffaterre, stands halfway between the old and the new. Inspired in part, as is structuralism, by classical rhetoric, it studies how a complete work can be generated by the elaboration of one of its parts, by saying the same thing (the core concept, or "hypogram") over and over in different ways. But it also studies the relationships between parts of one text and parts of another, like old-fashioned source criticism. It differs from source criticism, from "influence" studies, in at least three ways. It does not limit itself to the impact of one great author on another. It recognizes the existence of "paratexts," of popularized and vulgarized second-hand sources, as frequent, influential vehicles for ideas. Rather than seeing an earlier text as the "cause" of a later text, it sees both texts as parts of an overall system of socially shared meanings. Regarding *Madame Bovary*, for example, Riffaterre finds the development of commonplaces in the "sociolect," the fund of "common knowledge" that we unreflectively share. Flaubert built his novel on the cliché that adultery inevitably leads to degradation. When Riffaterre uses the words "interpret" and "interpretation," he means translating the idiosyncratic sign system of the author into the communal system of social discourse. He does not try to judge that discourse as uplifting or disappointing, wise or foolish, propitious or disadvantageous for the creation of a work of art.

Shoshana Felman's important essay on Flaubert's early works *Mémoires d'un fou* and *Novembre* introduced a semiotic-deconstructionist viewpoint to Flaubert criticism. Semiotics aspires to explain every instance of behavior (and not language alone) as part of a system of signs—the length of one's hair or lawn grass, the make and year of one's car, the conventions of professional wrestling, and so forth. Analogous to psychoanalytic criticism, which explores how concepts are individually and emotionally "loaded," semiotics goes beyond dictionary definitions to explore how behaviors are socially and culturally "loaded." But whereas semiotics tends to work with systems of binary oppositions (e.g., "good and evil"), deconstruction challenges these oppositions as delusions based on their users' vested interests or self-deception. (Compare Nietzsche's challenging title *Beyond Good and Evil* or William Blake's *The Marriage of Heaven and Hell.*) Felman analyzes the connotations of the concept of "madness" to demonstrate Flaubert's rapid maturation as a writer. In *Mémoires d'un fou* he tries to exploit madness as would a romantic, to prove himself different from others, to assert his independence, originality, and creativity. Sanity would refer to the Other, madness, to the unique self. But already in *Novembre*, completed when Flaubert was only twenty-one, "the narrator discovers that the difference once so diligently searched for in 'madness' is in fact found not in the subject, but in the language: insofar as it is the place of the other" (Felman 40). In other words, "sanity" and "madness" both belong to the shared system of conventions that is language. Therefore, one cannot use "madness" to make oneself different.

Eugenio Donato's essay on *Salammbô* deconstructs the traditional dichotomy of "realist" and "romantic." "The opposition between a Flaubert centered upon a contemporary reality and a Flaubert in quest of an exotic bygone Orient is untenable" (87) (Anne Green reached the same conclusion in her excellent conventional study). Because Flaubert writes from the perspective of the death of society and the end of time, he sees the foreignness of ancient Carthage, Alexandria, or Jerusalem as a mere literary illusion with no real referent. Much of the best recent Flaubert criticism argues that his fiction depicts nothingness and functions to abolish difference. It stresses his texts' fragmentation, internal contradictions, and resistance to interpretation—in short, their drift toward entropy. Jonathan Culler's landmark book summed up this view. In contrast, the traditionalist opposition to deconstruction, whose most eloquent recent spokesperson has been Victor Brombert, emphasizes the ultimate coherence, unity, and decodability of Flaubert's texts.

During the last decade, Flaubert criticism has reverted to an attempt to recuperate meaning by recontextualizing his works. Three of the most noteworthy efforts here occur in an impressive revival of the tradition of "hard scholarship" (based on consulting original documents). First, Pierre-Marc de Biasi lavished careful attention on the thousand pages of notes and sketches left among Flaubert's papers, arranging them and clarifying their import (in *Carnets de travail.*) In addition, the new, definitive edition of Flaubert's correspondence by Jean Bruneau is about to be completed and a series of major articles by Eric Le Calvez uses the newly fashionable techniques of "genetic criticism" (studying successive versions of a text to see how it came into being) to examine the creative process that shaped *L'Education sentimentale* and other works. He is a major contributor to this volume. In a similar vein, Claire Addison's *Where Flaubert Lies* explains the hidden meanings of dates in his works—that is, their relationship to history. In various ways, Julian Barnes, Philippe Dufour, Christopher Prendergast, and H. Meili Steele have called into question the notion of Flaubert's "realism," thus applying neodeconstructive insights to undermine the relationship between word and world. The excellent volume edited by Naomi Schor and Henry F. Majewski sums up such antirepresentational insights. David Baguley reveals how thoroughly Flaubert anticipated the naturalist movement in literature.

The late Charles Bernheimer tried to update psychoanalytic criticism so that it could subsume deconstruction. Dorothy Kelly, Lilian Furst, Carla Peterson, Rosemary Lloyd, Mary Orr, Naomi Schor, and Tony Tanner, among many others, have reexamined Flaubert from a feminocentric perspective. Dominick LaCapra and Alison Sinclair have reexamined adultery from a sociological viewpoint. Pierre Bourdieu has applied his mastery of sociological theory to the writer's role in nineteenth-century France. Mark Conroy, Lilian Furst, Patricia Merivale, and Laurence M. Porter, among others, have found new ways of situating Flaubert within world literature. Ross Chambers has lucidly explained the presuppositions of the predominant and more socially conscious critical outlook of today: "Seeking the strange in the familiar, the familiar in the strange, reading makes a text [such as] *Madame Bovary* relevant by producing meanings that inevitably bring into view and make available for examination the social context in which the reading itself is pursued. For meaning . . . is not inherent 'in' or transmitted 'by' a text so much as it is produced [by a reader] in conjunction with a text" ("Relevance" 152). (LMP)

This entry was adapted from the Preface to Laurence M. Porter, ed., *Critical Essays on Gustave Flaubert* (Boston: Hall, 1986).

References:

Addison, Claire. *Where Flaubert Lies: Chronology, Mythology, and History*. Cambridge: Cambridge University Press, 1996.

Baguley, David. *Naturalist Fiction: The Entropic Vision*. Cambridge: Cambridge University Press, 1990.

Barbey d'Aurevilly, Jules. "M. Gustave Flaubert." In Jules Barbey d'Aurevilly, *Les Œuvres et les hommes*. Geneva: Slatkine, 1968 [1865] 4:61–76. Trans. in Laurence M. Porter, ed. *Critical Essays on Gustave Flaubert*. Boston: Hall, 1986. 50–57.

Barnes, Hazel E. *Sartre and Flaubert*. Chicago: University of Chicago Press, 1981.

Barnes, Julian. *Flaubert's Parrot*. London: Cape, 1984.

Bart, Benjamin F. *Flaubert*. Syracuse: Syracuse University Press, 1967.

———. "Flaubert's Concept of the Novel." *PMLA* 80.1 (1965): 84–89.

Barthes, Roland. "L'Artisanat du style." In Roland Barthes, *Le Degré zéro de l'écriture*. Paris: Seuil, 1953. 89–94. In Annette Lavers and Colin Smith, trans., *Writing Degree Zero*. London: Cape, 1967, 68–72.

Batteux, Charles. *Les Beaux Arts réduits à un même principe*. Geneva: Slatkine, 1969. [1746]. 20–22, 159–378.

Baudelaire, Charles. "*Madame Bovary*, par Gustave Flaubert" [1857]. In *Gustave Flaubert*, Madame Bovary: *Its Backgrounds and Sources: Essays in Criticism*, ed. Paul de Man. New York: Norton, 1965. 336–43.

Bernheimer, Charles. *Flaubert and Kafka: Studies in Psychopoetic Structure*. New Haven: Yale University Press, 1982.

Bourdieu, Pierre. *Les Règles de l'art: Genèse et structure du champ littéraire*. Paris: Seuil, 1992. Trans. as *The Field of Cultural Production: Essays on Art and Literature*, Randal Johnson, ed. New York: Columbia University Press, 1993.

Bourget, Paul. "Gustave Flaubert." In Paul Bourget, *Essais de psychologie contemporaine*. Paris: Plon, 1899 [1884]. 97–147, esp. 111–20.

Brombert, Victor. "Flaubert and the Status of the Subject." In Naomi Schor and Henry F. Majewski, eds., *Flaubert and Postmodernism*. Lincoln: University of Nebraska Press, 1984. 100–115.

———. *The Novels of Flaubert: A Study of Themes and Techniques*. Princeton: Princeton University Press, 1966.

Butor, Michel. *Improvisations sur Flaubert*. Paris: La Différence, 1984.

Chambers, Ross. "Relevance, Meaning, and Reading." In Laurence M. Porter and Eugene F. Gray, eds., *Approaches to Teaching Flaubert's* Madame Bovary. New York: Modern Language Association, 1995. 144–52.

———. "Simplicité du coeur et duplicité textuelle: Etude d''Un cœur simple.' " *MLN* 96.4 (1981): 771–91.

Conroy, Mark. *Modernism and Authority: Strategies of Legitimation in Flaubert and Conrad*. Baltimore: Johns Hopkins University Press, 1985.

Culler, Jonathan. *Flaubert: The Uses of Uncertainty*. London: Elek, 1974.

Debray-Genette, Raymonde. "Narrative Figures of Speech in 'A Simple Heart.' " In Laurence M. Porter, ed., *Critical Essays on Gustave Flaubert*. Boston: Hall, 1986. 165–86.

Derrida, Jacques. "An Idea of Flaubert's 'Plato Letter.' " *MLN* 99.4 (1984): 748–68.

Donato, Eugenio. "Flaubert and the Question of History." *MLN* 91 (1976): 850–70. Rpr. in Laurence M. Porter, ed., *Critical Essays on Gustave Flaubert.* Boston: Hall, 1986. 87–103.

Du Bos, Charles. "On the 'Inner Environment' in the Work of Flaubert." In Gustave Flaubert, *Madame Bovary: Backgrounds and Sources: Essays in Criticism*, ed. Paul de Man. New York: Norton, 1965. 360–71.

Du Camp, Maxime. *Souvenirs littéraires.* 2 vols. Paris: Hachette, 1906 [1882–83]. 1: chs. 7, 9–14; 2:chs. 21, 25, 28–30.

Dufour, Philippe. *Flaubert et le pignouf: Essai sur la représentation romanesque du langage.* Saint-Denis: Presses Universitaires de Vincennes, 1993.

Duranty, Edmond. [Review of *Madame Bovary.*] *Réalisme* 5 (March 15, 1857): 79–80. In Laurence M. Porter, ed., *Critical Essays on Gustave Flaubert.* Boston: Hall, 1986. 49.

Felman, Shoshana. *La Folie et la chose littéraire.* Paris: Seuil, 1978. 191–213. Trans. as "Modernity of the Commonplace" in Laurence M. Porter, ed., *Critical Essays on Gustave Flaubert.* Boston: Hall, 1986. 29–48.

Flaubert, Gustave. *Carnets de travail.* Ed. Pierre-Marc de Biasi. Paris: Balland, 1988.

———. *Correspondance.* Ed. Jean Bruneau. 4 vols. to date. Paris: Gallimard, 1973– .

Furst, Lilian R. "Emma Bovary: The Angel Gone Astray." In Laurence M. Porter and Eugene F. Gray, eds., *Approaches to Teaching Flaubert's* Madame Bovary. New York: Modern Language Association, 1995. 21–27.

———. *Fictions of Romantic Irony in European Narrative, 1760–1857.* London: Macmillan, 1984.

Green, Anne. *Flaubert and the Historical Novel*: Salammbô *Reassessed.* Cambridge: Cambridge University Press, 1982.

James, Henry. "Flaubert's *Tentation de Saint Antoine.*" In Henry James, *Literary Reviews and Essays.* New Haven: College and University Press, 1957 [1874]. 145–50.

———. "The Minor French Novelists." *Galaxy* 21 (1876): 224–29.

LaCapra, Dominick. Madame Bovary *on Trial.* Ithaca, NY: Cornell University Press, 1982.

Le Calvez, Eric. *Flaubert topographe:* L'Education sentimentale: *Essai de poétique génétique.* Amsterdam: Rodopi, 1997.

Levin, Harry. *The Gates of Horn: A Study of Five French Realists.* New York: Oxford University Press, 1963. 214–304.

Lloyd, Rosemary. *Madame Bovary.* London: Unwin Hyman, 1990.

Lucas, Frank Laurence. "The Martyr of Letters: Gustave Flaubert." In Frank Laurence Lucas, *Studies French and English.* London: Cassell, 1950 [1934]. 227–47.

Merivale, Patricia. "Learning the Hard Way: Gothic Pedagogy in the Modern Romantic Quest." *Comparative Literature* 36.2 (1984): 146–61.

Murry, J. Middleton. "Flaubert." *The Dial* 71 (1921): 625–36. Rpr. in J. Middleton Murry, *Countries of the Mind: Essays in Literary Criticism.* 2nd ed. London: Oxford University Press, 1931. 158–73.

Peterson, Carla. "The Heroine as Reader in the Nineteenth-Century Novel: Emma Bovary and Maggie Tulliver." *Comparative Literature Studies* 17 (1980): 168–83.

Porter, Laurence M., ed. *Critical Essays on Gustave Flaubert.* Boston: Hall, 1986.

———. "The Devil as Double in Nineteenth-Century Literature: Goethe, Dostoevsky, and Flaubert." *Comparative Literature Studies* 15 (1978): 316–35.

———. *The Literary Dream in French Romanticism: A Psychoanalytic Interpretation.* Detroit: Wayne State University Press, 1979. 47–67. Rpr. in Laurence M. Porter, ed., *Critical Essays on Gustave Flaubert.* Boston: Hall, 1986. 150–64.

Porter, Laurence M., and Eugene F. Gray, eds. *Approaches to Teaching Flaubert's* Madame Bovary. New York. Modern Language Association, 1995.

Poulet, Georges. "The Circle and the Center: Reality and *Madame Bovary.*" [1955]. In Gustave Flaubert, *Madame Bovary: Backgrounds and Sources: Essays in Criticism,* ed. Paul de Man. New York: Norton, 1965. 392–407.

———. "Flaubert." In Georges Poulet, *Studies in Human Time.* Baltimore: Johns Hopkins University Press, 1956. 248–61.

Prendergast, Christopher. *The Order of Mimesis: Balzac, Stendhal, Nerval, Flaubert.* Cambridge: Cambridge University Press, 1986.

Privat, Jean-Marie. *Bovary, Charivari: Essai d'ethno-critique.* Paris: CNRS, 1994.

Proust, Marcel. "A propos du style de Flaubert" [1920]. In Marcel Proust, *Chroniques.* Paris: Gallimard, 1927. 193–211.

Reik, Theodor. *Flaubert und seine* Versuchung des heiligen Antonius. Minden: Bruns, 1912. Selection in Laurence M. Porter, ed., *Critical Essays on Gustave Flaubert.* Boston: Hall, 1986. 145–50.

Riffaterre, Michael. "Flaubert's Presuppositions." *Diacritics* 2 (1981): 2–11.

Rousset, Jean. "*Madame Bovary*: Flaubert's Anti-Novel." In Laurence M. Porter, ed., *Critical Essays on Gustave Flaubert.* Boston: Hall, 1986. 58–75.

Sainte-Beuve, Charles-Augustin. "*Madame Bovary* par M. Gustave Flaubert." In Charles-Augustin Sainte-Beuve, *Causeries de Lundi.* 16 vols. Paris: Garnier, 1850–60. 13:346–63. Rpr. in George Becker, ed., *Documents of Modern Literary Realism.* Princeton: Princeton University Press, 1963. 99–104.

Sartre, Jean-Paul. *L'Idiot de la famille: Gustave Flaubert de 1821–1857.* 3 vols. Paris: Gallimard, 1971–72.

Schor, Naomi. "Salammbô enchaînée; ou, Femme et ville dans Salammbô." In Marie-Claire Bancquart, ed., *Flaubert, la femme, la ville,* Paris: Presses Universitaires de France, 1983. 89–104.

Schor, Naomi, and Henry F. Majewski, eds. *Flaubert and Postmodernism.* Lincoln: University of Nebraska Press, 1984.

Sinclair, Alison. *The Deceived Husband: A Kleinian Approach to the Literature of Infidelity.* New York: Oxford University Press, 1993.

Steele, H. Meili. *Realism and the Drama of Reference: Strategies of Representation in Balzac, Flaubert, and James.* University Park: Pennsylvania State University Press, 1988.

Tanner, Tony. *Adultery in the Novel: Contract and Transgression.* Baltimore: Johns Hopkins University Press, 1979.

Valéry, Paul. "La Tentation de (saint) Flaubert." In Paul Valéry, *Œuvres.* 2 vols. Paris: Gallimard, 1957–60. 1:613–19.

Croisset. Croisset was a village four kilometers from Rouen during Flaubert's time. His father bought a summerhouse here in 1844, in time for the young Gustave to recover from a series of nervous or epileptic attacks. Located on the right bank of the Seine, the eighteenth-century house boasted a garden, a row of lime trees, and a small pavilion used alternatively as a library, study, and garden shed.

Following the deaths of his father and sister in 1846, Gustave wrote intensively at Croisset, spending summers there with his mother and his young niece Caroline, named after her mother. Flaubert delighted in the youngster's presence, and by the time she was six, he began giving her lessons in history and geography. Croisset became their principal residence in 1851, although the dwelling's poor insulation prompted Mme Flaubert to spend her winters in Rouen. Beginning in 1854, Flaubert often resided in Paris during the winter months as well.

Maxime Du Camp and Louis Bouilhet frequently visited Croisset. The latter was Flaubert's literary soul mate, the man with whom he always shared his work until Bouilhet's death in 1869. Bereft of his friend, Flaubert was keenly aware of his absence at Croisset and missed him deeply, as he did his niece when she married Ernest Commanville in 1864. Other guests over the years included Emile Zola, Alphonse Daudet, George Sand, the Goncourt brothers, Théophile Gautier, Ivan Turgenev, Guy de Maupassant, Edmond Laporte, and Princess Mathilde.

From his correspondence, we know that Flaubert loved Croisset, the charming garden, and the serenity that allowed him to write without interruption. The country home was his haven, his retreat from Rouen and Paris. The Prussian occupation of Croisset in late 1870 was for him a psychological invasion; thirteen enemy soldiers were lodged on the premises. He wrote to Caroline that Croisset had lost its charm and that he would never set foot there again (December 19, 1870, *Corr.* 6:191–92). After the Prussians' departure, however, he returned to Croisset in April 1871 and was immediately joyous upon seeing his desk, personal items, and garden (letter to Caroline Commanville, April 5, 1871, *Corr.* 6:219). Following his mother's death in 1872, he continued to live in Croisset not only because her will permitted it (she bequeathed the house to her granddaughter, Caroline, but Gustave was allowed to remain during his lifetime), but also because he was at home there despite his increased loneliness.

By 1875, Ernest Commanville and Caroline were in grave financial difficulties. Worried that they would have to sell Croisset and unable to imagine life elsewhere, Flaubert sold his Deauville farm and thereby sacrificed his modest income to save them from ruin. This left him barely enough to live on until his death at Croisset in 1880. Within a few months, Caroline sold the house. It was razed, all the surrounding trees were felled, and a distillery for corn liquor, with its storerooms, was built on the site. It later was converted to a paper mill. The one-room summerhouse near the river was spared. Early in the twentieth century, a group named Friends of Flaubert acquired it and turned it into a museum. Inside, a stuffed parrot that may have served as the model for Loulou in "Un cœur simple" can still be found (Lottman 342–43). (JWA)

References:

Bancquart, Marie-Claire. "Croisset, haut-lieu de la littérature." *Europe* 485–487 (1969): 129–37.

Dumesnil, René. *Gustave Flaubert, l'homme et l'œuvre*. Paris: Nizet, 1967.

Fournier, Albert. "De Rouen à Croisset." *Europe* 485–87 (1969): 252–68.

Lottman, Herbert. *Flaubert: A Biography*. New York: Fromm, 1990. 63–64, 97–98, 198–99, 244–45, 306–7, and passim.

D

Dambreuse, Mme (*ES*). "Pretty Mme Dambreuse, quoted by the fashion magazines," as Flaubert parodically refers to her early in *L'Education sentimentale*, is instantly perceived by Deslauriers, if not by the more naïve Frédéric, as an essential conquest to be made on the path to Parisian success. In this as in so many other situations in the novel, Frédéric's desire for uniqueness flounders with the realization that Martinon has anticipated him. Twenty years younger than her husband, forced to bring up his illegitimate daughter Cécile as a niece, and further humiliated by her absolute financial dependence on him, Mme Dambreuse takes her revenge where she finds it. If Frédéric initially misreads her refined simplicity as instant sympathy, it is because he fails to grasp the complexity of social mores and is blind to the hidden depths of the women he meets. When he finally determines to seduce Mme Dambreuse, from political rather than financial need, he fails to realize that her rapid acceptance of him follows hard on the heels of Martinon's marriage to Cécile, and that where he cynically urges submission to the force of impulse, she is yielding with equal cynicism to a desire for vengeance. When, after Dambreuse's death, she discovers that he has left most of his wealth to Cécile, reducing her to straitened circumstances that nevertheless represent opulence for Frédéric, the latter believes that his sense of honor rather than his desire for financial comfort impels him to offer to marry her. Yet in a curious but very Flaubertian twist, a deeper sense of honor, freed this time from thoughts of material gain, drives Frédéric to break his liaison with her when her vindictive nature leads her to buy at auction items that Arnoux's bankruptcy has forced Mme Arnoux to sell. (RL)

Reference:

Zaragoza, Georges. "Le Coffret de Madame Arnoux ou l'achèvement d'une éducation." *Revue d'Histoire Littéraire de la France* 89 (1989): 674–88.

Dambreuse, M. (*ES*). Subtle as a Greek and hardworking as a man from the Auvergne, according to Flaubert's opening description of him, Dambreuse is a barometer that constantly reflects the slightest change in the political climate. His name both recalls and denies aristocratic origins, epitomizing the hedging of bets that marks his nature. Declaring his sympathy for the workers ("for after all," he proclaims, "we are all of us workers") or buying Pellerin's painting depicting the Republic in the form of a figure driving a locomotive through virgin forest, Dambreuse offers Frédéric a sardonic model of a certain form of commercial success. He tries in vain to persuade the vacillating Frédéric to place a large sum of venture capital with him. Later, he silently tolerates Frédéric's love affair with his wife, but gets his revenge by disinheriting her. (RL)

Reference:

Burton, Richard. "The Death of Politics: The Significance of Dambreuse's Funeral in *L'Education sentimentale." French Studies* 50.2 (1996): 157–69.

Darío, Rubén (1867–1916). In *Azul*, the Nicaraguan poet Rubén Darío expresses admiration for *La Tentation de saint Antoine*, which he may have perused to seek rare words of Greek and Latin derivation. "Reino interior," one of the final poems in the *Prosas profanas*, may represent Darío's own vision of the *Tentation*. There Flaubert's seven vices become the "siete mancebos," and the temptations, Darío's "siete doncellas." (LMP)

References:

Darío, Rubén. *Páginas escogidas*. Ed. Ricardo Gullón. Madrid: Cátedra, 1979. 200.
———. *Obras poéticas completas*. Ed. Ricardo Gullón. Madrid: Aguilar, 1941. 526–29.
Fiore, Dolores Ackel. *Rubén Darío in Search of Inspiration*. New York: Las Américas, 1963.

Daudet, Alphonse (1840–97). Alphonse Daudet was a French writer whose most enduring works are the autobiographical novel *Le Petit Chose* (1868) and the sketches of Provençal life entitled *Lettres de mon moulin* (1866). His first published work, a volume of poetry entitled *Les Amoureuses* (1858), made him renowned in the Parisian salons. His success continued with the heroic comic trilogy of *Tartarin* (*Tartarin de Tarascon*, 1872; *Tartarin sur les Alpes*, 1885; and *Port Tarascon*, 1890). Associated with the movement of naturalist realism, he was throughout Flaubert's life one of his greatest admirers. He frequently attended Flaubert's Sunday receptions and dedicated his novel *Jack* (1876) to him. *Les Contes du Lundi* (1873), about the fall of the Second Empire, and *Sapho* (1884), where he describes the habits of his contemporaries, are works of this period. (LCP)

References:

Roure, Jacques. *Alphonse Daudet*. Paris: Julliard, 1982.
Sachs, Murray. *The Career of Alphonse Daudet, a Critical Study*. Cambridge, MA: Harvard University Press, 1965.

death and the dance of death. As Sartre demonstrates in his *L'Idiot de la famille*, Flaubert was haunted by death all his life. His mother's melancholy (she lost two children), his father's profession (enabling Flaubert to witness autopsies), Eustache-Hyacinthe Langlois's friendship (introducing him to old churches and graveyards), his own thoughts of suicide after the discovery of his epilepsy, and the untimely loss of his beloved sister and of his dear friend Alfred Le Poittevin all contributed to reinforce his inherited attraction for the melancholy atmosphere characteristic of Rouen and Normandy, a region dominated for centuries by wars, pestilence, and misery. Although craving the pagan South, Flaubert "remains a captive in the Celtic Middle Ages" (Daykns 38). His desire for isolation, contrasting with his lust for life and carnal pleasures, was rooted in his belief that life comes from death—life of the mind comes from a negation of the body, even from a refusal to procreate. Flaubert's *Correspondance*, his *Carnets*, and his traveler's notes testify to his interests in anything having to do with death. Certain that one of his recurrent dreams loaded with death imagery is a warning, he analyzes his and others' feelings toward death. As we see in his *Carnets* and in *Bouvard et Pécuchet*, he inquires about death rituals and customs of different regions, countries, and periods. Truly one of the first nineteenth-century "sociologists" of death, Flaubert shares his era's fascination with the morbid and the macabre; his first writings speak mostly of duels, poisons, horrible crimes, suicides, and the like.

His mature works may appear to go beyond this youthful fascination with death, but this impression is misleading. Until the end, Flaubert remains loyal to his first interests, and death remains at the core of his writing. *Madame Bovary* is the story of two suicides (one by poison, another by grief). *L'Education sentimentale* mentions several deaths: the rich banker's and the bastard child's, but also the idealist revolutionary's, as well as the innocent bystanders'. In that novel, death and decay dominate nineteenth-century bourgeois society. In the epic *Salammbô*, death is triumphant. It appears in bloody wars; its coming is foreshadowed in Flaubert's descriptions of each individual. Death is a curse, but a necessary one: the Sun must sink for the Moon to rise. Death plays a cardinal role in each tale of *Trois Contes*. Of the ten deaths mentioned in "Un cœur simple," Félicité's is the one given as an *exemplum*. Having suffered because of the death of her loved ones, she is redeemed for her sufferings, and death becomes her deliverance.

Unlike Félicité, who dies of natural causes, the hero of "La Légende de saint Julien l'hospitalier" enacts a highly symbolic tale of sadistic impulses and Oedipal murder, which ends in a highly suspect "holy" death. Is it Christ or a demonic Ghost who takes him away? Finally, the decapitation of Saint John the Baptist, whom Flaubert calls "Iaokanaan" in "Hérodias," raises crucial questions. Is he intended as a prefiguration of Christ, or as a figure of God himself? Has the holy Trinity lost its Head? Is God dead? The final version of *La Tentation de saint Antoine* may answer the question: Death is no longer an enemy of mankind, but its Savior. Destroying the past and all the ancient gods effects the renewal of history and inspires a hope for the birth of a new civilization. *Bouvard et Pécuchet* expands on the question, but under the guise of buffoonery. Here Flaubert again raises the eternal question of the meaning of life and death. Having vainly sought an answer in books and on a grotesque mannequin, his heroes contemplate suicide. They finally choose a kind of death by returning to a life of endless copying.

Many critics have recognized this lifelong obsession with death in Flaubert's works and style, but only recently have they linked it to the medieval imagery of the *danse macabre* ("dance of death"). Sarah Goodwin was probably the first to propose that the motif of the dance of death pervaded Flaubert's mental life. Yvonne Bargues-Rollins goes further in *Le Pas de Flaubert* (Flaubert's step): for her, the motif of the dance of death informs the entire Flaubertian corpus, in a complex web of imagery, metonymies, and allusions that hark back to the earliest iconographic and literary examples of the medieval motif.

From his youth, Flaubert was exposed to the thirteenth-century dance of death as an artistic and literary motif, thanks to a family friend, Eustache-Hyacinthe Langlois. This talented painter, engraver, and art historian took Flaubert on archeological expeditions in Old Rouen and its vicinity. Langlois showed him the forgotten sculptures he had discovered on the pillars of the cemetery of the Saint Maclou cloister, as well as a thirteenth-century manuscript of a dance of death found in a nearby church. The contents of Flaubert's private library reveal his firsthand knowledge of the medieval motif as it became known during the nineteenth century, and as it was preserved in the sculptures, drawings, and monuments of Rouen. Flaubert was well aware of frescoes and poems in which grimacing corpses invite each member of society to join in a sarabande; of paintings and tales of three youths meeting three skeletons; and of engravings and stories of maids courted by skeletons, or who discover the mask of death in their mirrors. As a result, the connotative richness of Flaubert's language creates a network of literal and symbolic references to the medieval motif, both dehumanizing and universalizing.

These diverse references to the medieval topos of the dance of death are to be found in Flaubert's juvenilia, not only in his own *Danse des morts* (Dance of the dead), but also in "Smarh" and all the other pieces. For example, *Novembre* and *Mémoires d'un fou* evoke the medieval *Miroir de la Mort* (Death's mirror), the first *Tentation de saint Antoine* (1849) can be read as a *Triomphe de la Mort* (Death's triumph), and so on. In *Madame Bovary*, Flaubert attempts to reconstruct a modern *Danse aux Aveugles* (Dance of the blind), a famous thirteenth-century poem in which Love, Fortune, and Death are described as the three great blind powers that make mankind dance to the tune of their wanton but irrevocable decrees. In that dance, the confusion of Death, Satan, and Time culminates in the fundamental image of "Death as the Equalizer."

With *Salammbô*, Flaubert reverts to the aesthetics of the very first dance of death, which in twelfth-century France was known as *Le Pas de la Mort*. The novel is also a superb *exemplum* of the antique motif of "death at the banquet" and of the eternal coupling of Eros and Thanatos—both avatars of the dance of death. In *L'Education sentimentale*, the motif of the dance of death is woven into the romantic "Death at the Masked Ball." Visible and omnipresent, Death is nevertheless ignored by a society that has lost contact with reality, even when it faces death on the Revolution's barricades. *Trois Contes* can be read as an allegory of the oldest form of the dance of death, *Les Trois Morts et les trois vifs* (The three dead and the three living). The motif is woven into each text's imagery; it unifies Flaubert's trilogy.

Beyond the topos of death inhabiting the living lies the Christian question concerning redemption: is there life after death? In the final version of *La Tentation de saint Antoine* (1874), the allusion to *Les Trois Morts et les trois vifs* becomes clear, and the equalizing power of Death is emphasized more than ever before, although the traditional imagery has been somewhat modernized. The text stresses that Death levels humankind in the "democracy of the [frailty of the] body"; the accent is on the binarity of the dance of death, of the *pas de deux* between Death and her victim. The "dance of death" has become the "dance of the dead," and we remember, "Death is an illusion, a veil hiding the continuity of life." The motif of the *danse macabre* has finally become Flaubert's own, as he will demonstrate in *Bouvard et Pécuchet*. Here a degraded but still-recognizable archeological and popular imagery of the medieval dance of death occurs in some minute, recurring stylistic details. Like the dance of death on the pillars of Old Rouen's cemetery, the novel begins by presenting a couple who might be the grotesque caricature of Adam and Eve, the ones whose Fall caused our destiny, our Death. (YBR)

References:

Bargues-Rollins, Yvonne. *Le Pas de Flaubert: Une Danse macabre*. Paris: Champion, 1998.

Dakyns, Janine R. *The Middle Ages in French Literature, 1851–1900*. Oxford: Oxford University Press, 1973.

Goodwin, Sarah. "Emma Bovary's Dance of Death." *Novel* 19.3 (1986): 197–215.

Goodwin, Sarah, and Elisabeth Bronfen eds. *Death and Representation*. Baltimore: Johns Hopkins University Press, 1993.

Langlois, Eustache-Hyacinthe. *Essai historique, philosophique, et pittoresque sur les danses des morts*. 2 vols. Rouen: Lebrument, 1851.

Sartre, Jean-Paul. *L'Idiot de la famille. Gustave Flaubert de 1821–1857*. 3 vols. Paris: Gallimard, 1971–72.

death scene of Emma Bovary (*MB*). To settle Emma's debts, the Bovarys' household items are to be sold at auction. In desperation, Emma tries to raise money from Léon, Guillaumin, Binet, and Rodolphe. When Rodolphe refuses her, she becomes mentally disoriented, suffers hallucinations, and rushes straight to the druggist's shop, where she induces Justin to let her into the room where arsenic and other dangerous substances are kept. She ingests arsenic by the fistful and returns home to die.

Charles's failure to act, his desperate paralysis in the face of a crisis, in spite of Emma's obvious symptoms of serious illness, is hard for the reader to believe. More than ever before, his incompetence and helpless devotion to his unfaithful wife—who at first insists that nothing is the matter—emerge sharply in this scene. But the scene initiates the folktale motif of triplication, used in a negatively inverted form to satirize medicine. The paramedic Charles does not know what to do; the local doctor Canivet does the wrong thing (prescribing an emetic instead of a vomitive); the master surgeon Larivière arrives too late to save Emma.

Flaubert describes at length Emma's suffering and Charles's grief, creating a scene of extreme bathos. Her agonizing, repellent physical symptoms give the lie to the romantic literary ideal of the noble suicide that Emma had imagined for herself, an act by which the superior but unappreciated person fades away, departing from a world that is unworthy of her. Her painful dying typifies the realistic novel, whose heroes—unlike romantic ones—can be tired or ill, can look ugly, and can feel physical pain. Critics have questioned Flaubert's decision, in this scene, to treat with sympathy characters that previously had been presented ironically. Questions arise also concerning the reasons for Emma's suicide. Does she take her own life because of her indebtedness, or because of her rejection by Léon and Rodolphe, or because she realizes that the romantic vision that obsesses her is unattainable in this world?

By describing her, at the outset of the sacrament of extreme unction, as giving the crucifix "the greatest kiss of love that she had ever given," Flaubert suggests that the spiritual aspirations of even ordinary people may derive from some transcendent reality. At the same time, however, he debunks any possible grand significance of the event in two major ways. First, he weaves into it the grotesque, repetitious religious argument between the narrow-minded priest Bournisien and the shallow, atheistic pharmacist Homais. Second, at the last moment, the blind beggar arrives under Emma's window and signs his song (taken from Nicolas Rétif de La Bretonne) that reduces a shepherdess to a sexual object, creating a sort of *mise en abyme* (reproduction in miniature, embedded within the thing it reproduces) of Emma's life. Ironically, Emma exercises her greatest influence over Charles after her death, "corrupting him from beyond the tomb," as he finally understands and embraces her unviable, stereotyped romantic ideas. (EFG/LMP)

Reference:

Mason, G. "La Veillée et l'enterrement d'Emma Bovary." *French Studies* 13 (1959): 125–34.

decadence. Historiographers and writers of historical fictions who adopt an organicist view of the world often imply that the state is a macrocosm of the individual. The romantics, and notably among them Jules Michelet, the greatest historian of nineteenth-century France, held this view. To invoke the idea of historical "decadence," then, is to imply that a nation or society must age, decline, and die as does the human body. An international intellectual movement, decadence influenced historiography, philosophy, literature, and the visual arts throughout Western Europe and England.

In history, the decline and fall of the ancient Roman and Byzantine empires seemed to foreshadow the degeneracy of nineteenth-century French society for those who lamented the failure of the French Revolution permanently to install democracy, or who missed Napoleonic grandeur, or who lamented the rise of a commercialized society dominated by the bourgeoisie, nonproducers who lived off the labor of others. This impression was intensified after France's humiliating, rapid defeat in the Franco-Prussian War of 1870. Flaubert, who liked to identify himself with the ancient Saint Polycarp, who inveighed against the corruption of his age, anticipated the "high decadent" movement of 1884 to 1914 with the hedonism, amorality, and macabre aspects of two later novels: *Salammbô* (1862) and *La Tentation de saint Antoine* (1849, 1856, 1874). In *Salammbô*, the immense, leprous, rotting body of the lustful Carthaginian general Hannon exemplifies the decadent fictional character, while scenes of the mercenaries' banquet and of torture and starvation exemplify the decadent plot episode, and the imminent collapse of Carthage typifies the decadent historical vision.

With his *Trois Contes* (1877), a triptych about saints, Flaubert anticipated late-nineteenth-century writers' move away from degeneracy to a revival of religious sentiment in French literature, although "La Légende de saint Julien l'hospitalier" retains many morbid traits. This return to religion, exemplified by Joris-Karl Huysmans' series of novels *A rebours* (1884; "the Bible of decadence"), *Là-bas* (from Satanism to faith), and *La Cathédrale* (a paean to the glories of Catholicism), was to flower in the Catholic Renaissance (Claudel, Péguy, Bernanos, Mauriac, and others) during the first half of the twentieth century. (LMP)

See also Polycarp, Saint.

References:

Calinescu, Matei. *Five Faces of Modernity: Modernism, Avant-Garde, Decadence, Kitsch, Postmodernism.* Rev. ed. Durham: Duke University Press, 1987.

Carter, A. E. *The Idea of Decadence in French Literature, 1830–1900.* Toronto: University of Toronto Press, 1958.

Porter, Laurence M. "Decadence and the *Fin-de-Siècle* Novel." In Timothy Unwin, ed., *The French Novel from 1800 to the Present.* Cambridge: Cambridge University Press, 1997. 93–110.

———. "Huysmans's *A rebours*: The Psychodynamics of Regression." *American Imago* 44 (1987): 51–65.

———. "Literary Structure and the Concept of Decadence: Huysmans, D'Annunzio, and Wilde." *Centennial Review* 22 (1978): 188–200.

La Découverte de la vaccine: Tragédie en cinq actes et en vers. *Le Découverte de la vaccine*, sometimes referred to as *Jenner, ou la découverte de la vaccine*, was written in collaboration with Louis Bouilhet and, possibly, Maxime Du Camp around 1846. Flaubert and Bouilhet wrote a number of dramatic scenarios during this period. Anything but a tragedy, this scabrous though amusing collection of fragments in alexandrines is a pastiche of the type of dramatic verse written by Voltaire and the abbé Delille. Its subject is the discovery of a cure for gonorrhea, a malady that just about everyone in the play has caught, or will. This text displays Flaubert's ear for imitating literary styles and for mocking those he found pompous. It also provides the prime example of the *garçon*, the fictitious, Rabelaisian *farceur* whom Flaubert and his intimates liked to impersonate in their letters, and who would be reborn as Alfred Jarry's farcical père Ubu. (MCO)

References:

Bruneau, Jean. *Les Débuts littéraires de Gustave Flaubert, 1838–1845*. Paris: Colin, 1962.

Diamond, Marie. *Flaubert, the Problem of Aesthetic Discontinuity*. Port Washington, NY: Kennikat Press, 1975.

Flaubert, Gustave. *Œuvres complètes*. Ed. Bernard Masson. 2 vols. Paris: Seuil, 1964.

———. *Œuvres complètes*. Ed. Maurice Bardèche. 16 vols. Paris: Club de l'Honnête Homme, 1971.

Delamare, l'affaire. The Delamare case was the historical prototype for Emma Bovary. Eugène Delamare, a medical student of Flaubert's father, had entered a rural practice in the village of Ry as an *officier de santé* (trained somewhat less well than a licensed practical nurse). After a first marriage to an older widow, he married Delphine Couturier, a farm girl. She committed adultery with a law clerk (like Léon) and then with a local squire (like Rodolphe) while falling ever deeper into debt. Eventually, some said, her debts drove her to suicide. On September 19, 1851, Flaubert decided to make her his heroine and to name her Emma Bovary; many of his reminiscences of country life then crystallized around her. (LMP)

Reference:

Bart, Benjamin F. *Flaubert*. Syracuse; Syracuse University Press, 1967. 242.

Delessert, Valentine. Flaubert and Maxime Du Camp met Valentine Delessert's husband, Gabriel Delessert, while they were traveling around the eastern Mediterranean. This fashionable woman had long been the mistress of Prosper Mérimée. In 1851, when Du Camp returned from the East, he began an affair with Delessert that lasted until 1860. In his correspondence, Du Camp claims that his description of Valentine to Flaubert served as the prototype for the character of Madame Dambreuse in *L'Education sentimentale*. (CG)

References:

Descharmes, René. *Flaubert: Sa vie, son caractère, et ses idées avant 1857*. Geneva: Slatkine, 1969.
Lottman, Herbert. *Gustave Flaubert*. New York: Fromm, 1990 (1979).

Delmar (*ES* 1869). Delmar is a vulgar singer and actor for whose affections Rosanette Bron and Mademoiselle Vatnaz are rivals. Under the Second Republic (1848–51), he becomes a star in left-wing political propaganda plays where his role is vehemently to insult monarchs and the institution of monarchy. Because his admirers confuse his humanitarian stage roles with his true convictions, and because their enthusiasm convinces him he has a chance to succeed in politics, he essays a candidacy for public office while attending meetings of the socialist Club de l'Intelligence (which functions as a caucus) after July 1848. With this figure, Flaubert reworks his opera singer Edgar Lagardy, part hairdresser, part toreador, and all sham, from *Madame Bovary* (Part 2, chapter 15), adding self-deception to charlatanism. (LMP)

Reference:

Paulson, William. *Sentimental Education: The Complexity of Disenchantment*. New York: Twayne, 1992.

descriptions. Descriptions showing characters (portraits) or places (interiors and landscapes) consistently interested Flaubert, from the standpoint of either a reader or a writer. For instance, he declared in his correspondence that when he was reading a novel, he was far more stimulated by descriptions and analyses than by action and narration. This predilection is reflected in his early novels, in which descriptions already play an important role; their manuscript variants reveal that Flaubert pays particular attention to the problems description specifically raises as a literary form. In this respect, he wrote in his notebooks (*carnets*) that a *real writer* should be able to write on the same topic, regardless of its length, either a narration, a description, an analysis, or a dialogue, which shows that he considered description as one of the main categories of literary techniques. It is therefore not surprising that descriptions (particularly landscape descriptions) abound in his work. This often irritated literary critics throughout his career. For instance, Jules Barbey d'Aurevilly wrote that the reader of *L'Education sentimentale* often hopes in vain to find in the novel a sentence that does not describe anything, even though the frequency of description decreases in Flaubert's late novels (*L'Education sentimentale* and especially *Bouvard et Pécuchet*) compared to his first published works (*Madame Bovary* and *Salammbô*). The cases of *Trois Contes* and *La Tentation de saint Antoine* are distinct because of the very nature of these texts.

Flaubertian description differs from Balzac's with which it has sometimes been mistakenly compared. In Flaubert even more than in Balzac, description tends to dissect what it represents into minute details, which are often enumerated at length; objects (Charles Bovary's cap is so fragmented that it can no longer be visualized), characters (Salammbô seems to be hidden behind the numerous details composing her costume), and space (Rosanette's boudoir is a mere juxtaposition of diverse small objects that construct the courtesan's universe). Description also interrupts action with still tableaux (the well-known "Flaubertian silences"). Flaubertian description is scattered, and although it is true to say that it usually invades all the layers of the narrative, it is always inserted into specific passages and at strategic moments. It mostly takes the form of one or several short paragraphs and conforms to particular principles of integration that greatly preoccupy Flaubert, as can be seen from certain statements made in the correspondence and also from the extraordinarily multiple corrections found in the manuscripts. To Sainte-Beuve, who reproaches Flaubert's numerous descriptions, he retorts that none of them is isolated or gratuitous; on the contrary, they all serve to depict characters, and they have an influence, whether it be immediate or more remote, on the action. This statement is made in the context of *Salammbô*, but it can be generalized to Flaubert's entire work: description indeed partakes of what he calls the "poétique insciente" (internal and intrinsic poetics) of each individual work.

The structuralist and poststructuralist reading of Flaubert's texts has demonstrated that the aims of Flaubertian description are not merely representative, but also (and perhaps primarily) symbolic, for description is actually related to characters (i.e., it has a psychological function) and, more widely, to action, (i.e., it has what narrative analysis calls a pragmatic function). Most often associated strategically with the characters' vision and, symbolically, with their state(s) of mind, description has a metonymical function that operates more implicitly than explicitly (contrary to the explicitness of description in the romantic novel). Description can also prepare forthcoming action through a complex system of allusions that will be echoed later in the narrative (recurrences of objects, themes, and motifs).

Moreover, that description is associated with a specific moment in the narrative, and especially with the characters' point of view, necessarily implies variations of points of view (focalization). Such variations have several aspects, for they may stem from multiple visions of the same "object" by a single character (Emma as viewed by Rodolphe at different moments in their relationship) and from multiple visions of the very same "object" by different characters (Emma as viewed by Charles, Rodolphe, and Léon). Therefore, the nature of what is represented is less important than the fashion in which it is represented, for it changes constantly. This essential process affects the representation of characters (the most famous example of this is certainly the color of Emma Bovary's eyes: they are alternately brown, black, and even blue) as well as the representation of space (in *L'Education sentimentale*, Paris appears at times beautiful, at other times hideous, depending on—and reflecting—changes in Frédéric's feelings or sensations). Such modes of descriptive significance are usually diverse and, even more important, connotative (as opposed to the generally denotative, explanatory descriptions in the Balzacian novel), which explains why the study of Flaubert's descriptions is complex and challenges the concept of Flaubertian "realism." (ELC)

References:

Adam, Jean-Michel, and André Petitjean. *Le Texte descriptif.* Paris: Nathan, 1989.
Hamon, Philippe. *Introduction à l'analyse du descriptif.* Paris: Hachette, 1981.
Le Calvez, Eric. *Flaubert topographe*: L'Education sentimentale: *Essai de poétique génétique*. Amsterdam: Rodopi, 1997.

Deslauriers (*ES*). By using the oblique focus of Frédéric Moreau's friend Deslauriers, Flaubert is able to show less flattering characteristics of his central character without alienating his reader's sympathy. Deslauriers has all the ambition and drive Frédéric lacks, but neither his charm nor his money. As a child, Frédéric was spoiled by his mother, whereas Deslauriers was beaten and bullied by his father and was forced to work long hours copying documents, the first of the long series of acts of copying that will mark his progress through the novel. Following on Frédéric's heels, he will attempt to seduce Mme Arnoux, will sleep with Rosanette Bron, and will marry Louise Roque, as if Frédéric's evident failure in terms of a career somehow made of him a model for other aspects of existence. Condemned since boyhood to rely on Frédéric for money, Deslauriers sees all his dreams of personal and social success evaporate as his friend chooses to use his wealth for different purposes. At each point where he thought he could rely on Frédéric for companionship or aid, he is abandoned in favor of Mme Arnoux. At the end of the novel, we find him attached to a provincial industrial company, his friendship for Frédéric miraculously untarnished by experience. Seeking the cause of his failure to achieve his dreams of power, he concludes not that he never received the assistance his friend had always promised him, but that he has been too logical, in a gesture that for all the underlying authorial irony nevertheless points to the power of friendship as perhaps the only virtue in Flaubert's vision of existence. (RL)

References:

Layton, Lynne. "Flaubert's *L'Education sentimentale*: A Tragedy of Mind." *French Forum* 11 (1986): 335–51.
Paulson, William. Sentimental Education: *The Complexity of Disenchantment*. New York: Twayne, 1992.

the Devil (*TSA*). The Devil is a character in *La Tentation de saint Antoine* who works actively to persuade Saint Antoine to turn away from God. In part 1, he appears to Saint Antoine with horns, in part 2, carrying on his back the seven mortal sins, and in part 3, disguised as Hilarion, one of Antoine's disciples. Hilarion is first incarnated as a small, misshapen, pathetic-looking child. During their time together, Hilarion grows steadily in stature (as did Victor Hugo's "Le Satyre" confronting the Olympian gods in *La Légende des Siècles*), finally abandoning the role and allowing himself to be seen as a gigantic archangel and at last with a cloven hoof that leaves no doubt about his identity. He uses logic and "science" to undermine the saint's faith, as well as carrying him about through space to show him God cannot be found there. (AHP)

References:

Bem, Jeanne. *Désir et savoir dans L'œuvre de Flaubert: Etude de* La Tentation de saint Antoine. Neuchâtel: La Baconnière, 1979.

Porter, Laurence M. "The Devil as Double in Goethe, Dostoevsky, and Flaubert." *Comparative Literature Studies* 15 (1978): 316–35.

Starr, Peter. "Science and Confusion: On Flaubert's Temptation." *MLN* 99 (1984): 1072–93.

Dictionnaire des idées reçues. As Flaubert died before completing *Bouvard et Pécuchet*, the content of what he called its "second volume" remains somewhat nebulous, yet his notes and correspondence designate the *Dictionnaire des idées reçues* as an integral, long-standing part of the work. Indeed, Alberto Cento proposes that the *Dictionnaire* probably inspired the novel. That Flaubert's letters first refer to the *Dictionnaire* (in 1850) much earlier than they first mention *Bouvard et Pécuchet* (in 1872) seems to support this interpretation. Nevertheless, René Descharmes argues convincingly that although *Bouvard et Pécuchet* incorporates many of the *Dictionnaire*'s conversational clichés, the two works should be considered separately. In modern editions of *Bouvard et Pécuchet*, the *Dictionnaire des idées reçues* usually appears as part of Flaubert's projected second volume.

In his *Dictionnaire des idées reçues*, Flaubert undermines the authority of the discourses that constitute his text through their very inclusion. He disturbs the dictionary's alphabetical ordering by using cross-references, similar definitions for different entries, and extensive prescriptions. Indeed, Flaubert's classification of discourses becomes less an organizing system than a manner of depriving discourses of any stability.

The title of the dictionary already combines two incongruous elements. A normal dictionary provides facts—on whose accuracy the value of the dictionary depends—by defining words. But the importance of Flaubert's "received ideas" (generally accepted commonplaces), although they are not necessarily false, depends less on their factual content than on how they are proclaimed and received. They are presented as unquestionably true—that is, as dogmatic truth—but they remain bound to and limited by the ideological systems that permit their diffusion.

Jane Austen offers a clear, ironic example of "received ideas" at the beginning of her novel *Pride and Prejudice* (1813): "It is a truth universally acknowledged, that a single man in possession of a good fortune must be in want of a wife. However little known the feelings or views of such a man may be on his first entering a neighborhood, this truth is so well fixed in the minds of the surrounding families, that he is considered the rightful property of some one or another of their daughters." The French writer Lautréamont (pseudonym of Isidore Ducasse) culled a collection of received ideas from the maxims of seventeenth- and eighteenth-century *moralistes* (authors of reflections on human nature and society), changed a key word here and there, and ironically called them *Poésies* (1870).

Flaubert finds another way to mock received ideas, by ironically presenting them with a vehicle—the dictionary—that itself has an aura of authority. Like the museum, which can impart significance to whatever disparate objects it may contain, the dictionary format suggests careful research and selection and makes an implied claim to be comprehensive. The alphabetical order presents an unequivocal guide to each entry, and within the latter, we expect to find all the meanings of a selected word.

The *Dictionnaire des idées reçues* differs from a typical dictionary in its brevity and in the way it is read. Because its satiric intent is apparent at once, as in other *sottisiers* (collections of foolish remarks) it cannot serve as a true reference work. The alphabetical order of the individual entries no longer serves as a useful guide—instead, one would need a thematic arrangement—and cross-references work to subvert rather than explain ("Blondes: sexier than brunettes. See 'Brunettes.' " "Brunettes: sexier than blondes. See 'Blondes.' "). As a result, no entry has priority over any other. Flaubert maintains neutrality by adopting the voice of majority opinion, but without either endorsing or openly opposing it. A number of manipulative strategies, however, reveal his own views. The content of the dictionary articles reveals the ignorance of those who pronounce judgments without prior reasoning or reflection. Flaubert exposes the opinions, rules, and slogans that dictate his contemporaries' lives. With this intent, the dictionary's contents extend beyond received ideas to include sayings and proverbs, as well as actual citations from publications of Flaubert's day. (ENM)

References:

Cento, Alberto. *Commentaire de* Bouvard et Pécuchet. Paris: Nizet, 1973.

Descharmes, René. "Le Dictionnaire des idées reçues dans l'œuvre de Flaubert." In René Descharmes, *Autour de* Bouvard et Pécuchet: *Études documentaires et critiques*. Paris: Librairie de France, 1921. 204–54.

Ferrère, E. L. "Introduction." In Gustave Flaubert, *Le Dictionnaire des idées reçues*, Paris: Conard, 1913. 11–37.

Flaubert, Gustave. *Dictionnaire des idées reçues*. Ed. Lea Caminiti. Paris: Nizet, 1966.

Herschberg-Pierrot, Anne. "Bibliothèque d'idées reçues au XIXe siècle." *Revue des lettres modernes* 703–6 (1984): 35–59.

———. *Le Dictionnaire des idées reçues de Flaubert*. Lille: Presses Universitaires de Lille, 1988.

Hobden, L. H. "L'Utilisation du Dictionnaire des idées reçues dans l'œuvre de Flaubert." *Amérique française* [Montreal] 1953: January–February, 40–48; March–April, 38–43; May–June, 54–58; July–August, 37–45; November, 32–40.

Jacquet, Marie Thérèse. *Les Mots de l'absence; ou, Du "Dictionnaire des idées reçues" de Flaubert.* Paris: Nizet, 1987.

Maupassant, Guy de. "Etude sur Gustave Flaubert." In Maurice Nadeau, ed., *Pour Gustave Flaubert.* Paris: Editions Complexe, 1986. 37–111.

Diderot, Denis (1713–84). With Voltaire, Denis Diderot was the main leader of the philosophical Enlightenment movement of the latter half of the eighteenth century. He was one of the main editors of the monumental *Encyclopédie, ou Dictionnaire raisonné des sciences, des arts, et des métiers* (1751–72), dedicated to disseminating knowledge and dispelling superstition. An extraordinarily versatile thinker, Diderot distinguished himself in many domains, notably in literature, philosophy, and the applied sciences.

Around the 1850s, while Flaubert was reflecting on literary creation, he looked back at the eighteenth-century philosophers' doctrines and in particular Diderot's concept of the "modèle intérieur." This notion developed the idea that one writes better when one feels detached from the subject that he is describing. Diderot believed that in order to see clearly the object of his inspiration, the artist should withdraw all of his emotions. He expressed this idea memorably in the essay "Paradoxe sur le comédien" and dramatized it in *Le Neveu de Rameau.* Flaubert sought to apply this concept of cold observation in *Madame Bovary* as a reaction to the romantic cult of inspiration. (CT)

Reference:

Bart, Benjamin F. *Flaubert.* Syracuse: Syracuse University Press, 1967. 330.

diseases. Flaubert's unwise sexual adventuring during his trip to the Middle East in 1849–50 led to his contracting venereal diseases—first syphilis and then, perhaps, chancroids (nonsyphilitic lesions of the genital region). Although he took mercury treatments off and on for years afterward, he probably never recovered from syphilis. He became bald, and his peaceful death, whose cause was diagnosed as a ventricular hemorrhage of the brain, may have been caused by tertiary syphilis (Bart 220–21, 742–43). (LMP)

See also epilepsy.

References:

Bart, Benjamin F. *Flaubert.* Syracuse: Syracuse University Press, 1967.

Pommier, Jean. "Les Maladies de Gustave Flaubert." In Jean Pommier, *Dialogues avec le passé: Etudes et portraits littéraires.* Paris: Nizet, 1967. 281–99.

***Don Quixote,* influence of.** *See* Cervantes Saavedra, Miguel de.

Du Camp, Maxime (1822–94). Raised somewhat independently (his parents died in his youth), Maxime Du Camp was schooled in Paris. By his own admission, he showed little academic promise: often distracted from schoolwork by his literary interests, he began writing in his mid-teens. After receiving his baccalaureate degree in 1841, he fended off family pressure to take up a profession and began a leisurely life revolving around literature, hunting, and womanizing, much of which he paid for by borrowing against the inheritance he was soon to receive. When he met Gustave Flaubert in 1843 (the latter was studying law in Paris at the time), Du Camp was a young literary dilettante living off a comfortable fortune. The two became friends, often dining together in Paris, and Du Camp's affection for, and admiration of, the slightly older and more austere Flaubert was deep. When Flaubert was stricken with epilepsy in 1844, Du Camp made the trek out to Rouen to see his friend and proved himself a solid moral support. This support was to continue during the difficult times to come, and it was to Du Camp that Flaubert wrote the most candidly after the death of his sister Caroline in 1846. The friendship between these two men seems to have been codependent. (Some readers see hints of a homoerotic relationship between the two, but the evidence is slim and inconclusive.) Flaubert gave Du Camp contact with a serious literary mind and a prestigious social connection that the younger man was always eager to display to others, even after they had become less close.

In the early years, Du Camp provided Flaubert with affection and enthusiasm. The two undertook a hiking tour together for three months in 1847, traveling from Anjou to Brittany and then through Normandy. The trip was a substitute for the voyage to the Middle East that they had had to abandon, temporarily, owing to concerns for Flaubert's health. There was a sense of adventure about the trip—for example, they visited Chateaubriand's as-yet-unoccupied tomb on the island of Le Grand Bé (near Saint Malo) and spent hours reading *René* on the shore—and the two collaborated on a literary account of the journey (*Par les champs et par les grèves*, 1886 [written in 1847–48]). This bracing encounter with nature also served another purpose: Du Camp was working to disrupt the stormy relationship Flaubert had with the writer Louise Colet. The Normandy trip was such a success, and Flaubert held up so well, that the two friends resumed planning their trip to the Orient. They left in 1849 and in the next year and a half traversed Egypt, Palestine, Syria, Libya, Asia Minor, and Greece, returning via Italy. Flaubert took notes (the *Voyage en Orient* appeared serially from 1849 to 1851), and Du Camp took pictures—he was one of the first to transport the bulky equipment then necessary for photography into remote regions of the Middle East.

After 1851, the relationship between Flaubert and Du Camp began to cool. Du Camp took up the editorship of the *Revue de Paris*, and it was here that *Madame Bovary* appeared, in serial form, in 1856. Squabbles ensued, for Du Camp insisted on removing risqué passages, cuts that Flaubert steadfastly refused; Du Camp made the changes anyway. Nevertheless, the government censors cracked down, and both Flaubert and the *Revue de Paris* became the objects of a lawsuit, which they eventually won.

After this time, Du Camp and Flaubert kept up an infrequent correspondence and maintained a mostly congenial but lukewarm relationship. Du Camp's literary endeavors were varied: he published some fiction and continued working in literary journalism; from 1869–1875 he published volumes of his interesting (if verbose) *Paris, ses organes, ses fonctions, et sa vie dans la seconde moitié du XIXe siècle*. He continued to read Flaubert. In fact, Du Camp had read much of Flaubert's work in draft stage, beginning with *Novembre* and extending to *Salammbô*, and Flaubert often saw his criticisms as both helpful and hard to bear. Du Camp was elected to the Académie Française in 1880 and in later years wrote his *Souvenirs littéraires*, a rather superficial and unreliable account of his literary life, much of it focusing on Flaubert. (SDC)

References:

Bart, Benjamin F. "Is Maxime Du Camp a Reliable Witness?" *Modern Language Review* 48 (1953): 17–25.

Brombert, Victor H. *Flaubert par lui-même*. Paris: Seuil, 1971.

Bruneau, Jean, ed. *Gustave Flaubert. Correspondance.* 5 vols. Paris: Gallimard, 1968–98.

Commanville, Caroline. *Souvenirs sur Flaubert*. Paris: Ferroud, 1895.

Du Camp, Maxime. *Souvenirs littéraires* 2 vols. Paris: Hachette, 1882–83. I, ch. 7:9–14; II, ch. 21:25, 28–30.

Dumas père, Alexandre (1802–70). Once described as the most popular novelist in France, Alexandre Dumas achieved literary notoriety with *Henri III et sa cour* (1829), a historical drama. Dumas is more famous than ever today for his novels *Les Trois Mousquetaires* (1844) and *Le Comte de Monte-Christo* (1844). His sensational play *Antony* (1831), which epitomized all the extravagant attitudes of romanticism, inaugurated the modern drama in prose. Imitating Antony, Flaubert and his young friends slept with daggers under their pillows.

Dumas père brought Maurice Schlésinger to Trouville in 1836, and was thus indirectly instrumental in triggering Flaubert's lifelong fixation on Mme Elisa Schlésinger, and therefore in providing the initial inspiration for Flaubert's *L'Education sentimentale* (Bart 27). (APZ/LMP)

References:

Bart, Benjamin F. *Flaubert*. Syracuse: Syracuse University Press, 1967.

Brix, Michel. "Alexandre Dumas et l'histoire littéraire." *Œuvres et critiques* 21.1 (1996): 15–21.

Duplan, Jules (?–1870). Jules Duplan was Flaubert's closest friend after Louis Bouilhet and certainly one of his greatest admirers. He scanned all the newspapers he could find, looking for mentions of Flaubert, and sent him the clippings. He also helped Flaubert locate and transcribe materials, especially for the

Sottisier (compendium of stupid remarks). Privately, the two men exchanged very open and even pornographic letters; in them Flaubert addressed his friend as "vieux pédéraste" (old queer). Enid Starkie speculates that they may have shared a homosexual relationship. (LCP)

References:

Bart, Benjamin F. *Flaubert*. Syracuse: Syracuse University Press, 1967.

Starkie, Enid. *Flaubert, The Master*. New York: Atheneum, 1971.

Dupuis, Léon (*MB*). Emma Bovary's second lover, the law clerk Léon Dupuis, is a weak-willed dreamer, exchanging with Emma, at the beginning of part 2 all the romantic clichés of the day. With pungent sarcasm, Flaubert implies his utter mediocrity. He and Emma fall in love, but neither dares take the initiative. After leaving Yonville to study law, Léon encounters Charles and Emma by chance at the opera in Rouen, and Emma's second affair ensues, with Léon playing the passive role. Flaubert observes that he becomes her mistress more than she is his. As Emma descends rapidly toward financial disaster, Léon does nothing to dissuade her. After her death, he renounces his earlier romantic tendencies and marries Miss Léocadie Lebœuf, whose family name continues the bovine motif of complacent stupidity in the novel. (EFG)

References:

Culler, Jonathan. *Flaubert: The Uses of Uncertainty*. Rev. ed. Ithaca: Cornell University Press, 1985.

Gans, Eric. Madame Bovary: *The End of Romance*. Boston: Twayne, 1989.

Knight, Diana. *Flaubert's Characters: The Language of Illusion*. Cambridge: Cambridge University Press, 1985.

Tanner, Tony. *Adultery in the Novel: Contract and Transgression*. Baltimore: Johns Hopkins University Press, 1979.

Dussardier (*ES*). The only sympathetic male character in *L'Education sentimentale*, the worker and revolutionary Dussardier reappears throughout the novel, both to reflect the progress of the political movement in France and to cast an ironic light on Frédéric's own lack of progress. Imbued with a sense of fairness, shaped by seeing the massacres in the rue Transnonain in his boyhood, Dussardier is also the character who brings cynical comments on women to an abrupt stop when he confides that he yearns to love just one, forever. His brutal assassination by Sénécal in the novel's closing pages shows the domination of evil at the dawn of the Second Empire. (RL)

References:

Denommé, Robert T. "From Innocence to Experience: A Retrospective View of Dussardier in *L'Education sentimentale*." *Nineteenth-Century French Studies* 18.3–4 (1990): 424–36.

Grandpré, Chantal de. "Sénécal et Dussardier: La République en effigie." *French Review* 64.4 (1991): 621–31.

E

L'Education sentimentale (1845). According to many critics, 1845 marks the appearance of the first Flaubertian text. This does not, of course, mean that Flaubert had written nothing before that date (most notably, *Mémoires d'un fou* in 1838 and *Novembre* in 1842); rather, it suggests that the first version of *L'Education sentimentale* is a turning point, the work in which Flaubert hits on the aesthetic technique underpinning the masterpieces of the later years. A quirky, somewhat uneven novel, the first *Education sentimentale* is nevertheless compelling in its own right and fascinating for anyone interested in the evolution of Flaubert's aesthetics. As Jacques Neefs has pointed out, it is a "performative" text: at the same time that the novel describes the process of becoming an artist, writing it accomplishes this same development for the author (Neefs 86).

Similar in this respect to the 1869 version of *L'Education sentimentale*, the 1845 novel tells the story of two childhood friends, Henry Gosselin and Jules (whose family name is never given), who have just finished school and are launching their adult lives. Inseparable in their youth, during which they had shared dreams of a glorious literary future, the two are now pulled apart by the exigencies of their social condition. At the novel's opening, the wealthier, more passive Henry has arrived in Paris to continue his studies, while Jules stagnates in the provinces, where his father plans to find him a position as a clerk or civil servant. (The double narrative of Paris and the provinces recalls Balzac's *Illusions perdues*, which had appeared in 1843.) In his letters, Jules complains bitterly of his lot and envies Henry the good fortune that has taken him to the capital, where all is possible. Yet Henry is no better off. Languishing in his lodgings, stultified by the study of law, he finds little appeal in Paris. His interest finally catches, somewhat apathetically, on the wife of M. Renaud, the bumbling director of the student boarding house. Though nearly twice his age, Mme Emilie flirts with him, and since Henry never quite musters the courage to act, she is forced to seduce him.

The romance is torrid, even more because it is clandestine and forbidden. The lovers relive all the commonplaces of adulterous passion, slipping each other endless series of love letters, squeezing the other's hand under the table at dinner, living from tryst to tryst. Meanwhile, Jules's fate rises and falls like the tide. Condemned by his father to an ignominious position in a customs office, Jules chafes at the bit of financial necessity. Then a chance meeting puts him in touch with a theater troupe, leading to a vague commitment to produce an adolescent play Jules has composed and introducing Jules to Mlle Lucinde, an actress in the troupe. But Jules will be undone: after he loans money to the woman he covets, the entire troupe leaves town, dashing hopes both amorous and literary. The experience sobers Jules and hardens him: he begins to turn away from the world, withdrawing into books.

Henry's undoing occurs in a different way. Perplexed by the vagaries of love, the young adulterer and his mistress struggle to keep the fires burning. Exhausting one trick after another, they are eventually reduced to the kind of grand gesture one reads about in books: they escape to the New World. But living such a trip is less enchanting than was reading about it. Henry is sick during the entire crossing; they find little work and even less happiness. Bit by bit, flagging passion gives way to misery and homesickness. When they return to France and separate, Henry is secretly glad, but he keeps up his correspondence with his first mistress mechanically, numbed by the sameness of all the letters.

Such is, in essence, the "sentimental education" Henry and Jules undergo. Both finish this process as changed men, though changed in different ways. Jules undertakes a long internal quest, hoping to find in books the passion that has eluded him in life. Learning Hebrew and Greek and studying history, aesthetics, and philosophy, he gradually frees himself of received ideas and of the illusions of his early education. A key scene in which he encounters a mangy hound assumes mystical proportions in Jules's imagination, and his rejection of the animal coincides with his crossing a threshold in his life. Infatuated with the literary mastery of such figures as Homer and Shakespeare, Jules learns to turn an analytical eye on the world. As he peels off the veneer of social decorum, he uncovers everywhere, without condemning them, the same hypocrisies, the same pettiness, and the same commonplaces. Yet Jules sympathizes with all the flawed people he studies, and he channels these experiences into his art, to which he dedicates himself patiently and painstakingly. Renouncing romantic inspiration, Jules's art is the product of study, concision, and selflessness.

Henry, on the other hand, has undergone a somewhat different metamorphosis. Rebounding from his debacle with Mme Emilie, Henry incarnates the life Jules has renounced. He becomes a ladies' man and a dilettante, learning just enough about standard topics to be conversant with everyone worthy of conversation. His pat phrases and popular opinions, produced with a slight personal panache, make him admired. Henry has chosen the life of society and of surfaces, Jules that of the mind and the depths. Because of old sympathies, the two men still see each other, though they make for an odd pair, and friendship has been replaced by forbearance.

The 1845 version of *L'Education sentimentale* represents a major turning point in Flaubert's writing. It displays an extraordinarily rich (and sometimes chaotic) combination of elements dear to the later Flaubert. As the summary here suggests, the novel has a rather complicated plot, which required considerable narrative versatility (much more so than *Mémoires d'un fou* or *Novembre*). The technique of "parallel composition" (that is, of maintaining two major narrative strands) was new to Flaubert. He would later put it to good use in the 1869 version of the novel, as well as, to lesser degrees, in *Madame Bovary* and *Bouvard et Pécuchet*. Breaking with the narrative technique of the earlier novels, Flaubert here largely abandons first-person narration, beginning to cultivate the "impersonal" style allowed by the third person. Yet he explores an array of other techniques, including long, slightly Balzacian descriptions, epistolary style (principally in the letters between Jules and Henry), and scenes that artfully balance dialogue and narration, and in one scene he even glides into the form of a theatrical script replete with stage directions. The variety of voices creates interesting possibilities. In particular, distancing the third-person narrator from the main characters allows for irony, and in many respects, this tone prefigures the later Flaubert. Sometimes the irony goes too far, turning to caricature (as in the farcical scene between M. Gosselin and M. Renaud), and occasionally, at the other extreme, the narrator seems too credulous (as in the long lyrical passages regarding Jules's discovery of art). Furthermore, the narrator makes frequent and apparently arbitrary first-person interventions, unsettling the narrative distance. Nevertheless, irony is the principal mode, and this feature represents a radical transformation of Flaubert's work. *Mémoires d'un fou* and *Novembre*, which dealt with love stories similar to Henry's, were written in an exalted, romantic style; the great accomplishment of the first *Education sentimentale* is to recycle the love story while ironizing it, as when the narrator shows Henry unable to distinguish between passion and monotony.

In one of Flaubert's favorite chapters (as he wrote to Louise Colet on January 16, 1852, *Corr.* 2: 343), he traces the deterioration of Henry's love for Emilie: the degradation of ideals and the loss of illusions will become major Flaubertian subjects. A glorious passage adumbrating the later works declares:

> L'amour est pour tous le même voyage, fait sur la même route, au galop, en carrosse, à pied, ou en boitant; c'est toujours le même sentier, à travers les mêmes vallons délicieux, au bord des mêmes précipices, sur les mêmes sommets qui touchent au ciel, avec les mêmes éblouissements, la même fatigue, les mêmes regrets. . . . Eternel pélerinage, long pour les uns, plus court pour d'autres, avec un peu moins de pluie ou plus de soleil; les imbéciles le font comme les héros, les tortus comme les bossus, les louches comme les aveugles, les myrmidons comme les géants.
>
> [Love is the same journey for all, traveled on the same road, at a gallop, in a carriage, by foot, or by limping along; it is always the same path, across the same delightful valleys, along the edge of the same cliffs, on the same summits reaching up to the sky, with the same breathtaking moments, the same lassitude, the same regrets. . . . It is the eternal pilgrimage, long for some, shorter for others, with a little more rain or sun; imbeciles travel it just like heroes, the crooked like the hunchbacks, the cross-eyed like the blind, Myrmidons just like giants.] (*ES*, 1845, in Flaubert, (*Œuvres complètes*, 1: 346)

The carefully wrought rhythm of this passage exemplifies the artistic precision Jules embraces later in the novel, just as the acuity of the observation anticipates Jules's vow to analyze underlying truths. Indeed, Jules is an alter ego for Flaubert: the artistic principles the character outlines will shape Flaubert's greatest works. (They are, moreover, consistent with the principles he explains in his letters to Louise Colet.) More important, though, is the repetition in this passage of the very notion of repetition: "le *même* voyage," "la *même* route," "le *même* sentier," and so on.

In the 1845 novel, Flaubert already evinces a fascination with commonplaces, those clichés that his characters inevitably experience as special and entirely personal. This deflation of the fundamentally romantic notion of originality will be at the very heart of the 1869 version of the novel, as well as of *Madame Bovary, Bouvard et Pécuchet*, and *Le Dictionnaire des idées reçues*. (In fact, as Jean Bruneau has pointed out, Henry's father, portrayed as an absolute encyclopedia of commonplace ideas, prefigures Homais in *Madame Bovary* [Bruneau 415].) The commonplace relates to the entire problem of repetition and of copies in Flaubert. Repetition results in degradation, in wear. For example, Henry and Emilie exchange the same whispered endearments until these have lost all their value; Henry finally stops reading her letters because he knows beforehand what they will say, filled as they are with "the same meaningless drivel" ("le même rabâchage insignifiant"; *ES*, 1845, in Flaubert, *Œuvres complètes*, 1:347). Henry's social success will depend on his ability to mimic the ideas of those around him, becoming a republican among the republicans and a monarchist among the monarchists: "Voilà comme il était, merveilleusement propre à accepter toutes sortes d'idées et à agir de toutes sortes de façons; il passait sans difficulté d'une opinion à l'autre, d'une raison à une autre, de la brune à la blonde" (This is how he was, marvelously adept at absorbing all kinds of ideas and at acting in all sorts of ways; he shuttled effortlessly from one opinion to another, from one way of thinking to another, from brunettes to blondes.) (1: 363–64). This practice of parroting popular ideas, Flaubert intimates, progressively hollows one's substance.

Henry, of course, does not see the deterioration inherent in repetition, but Jules does. In the most famous and most perplexing scene in the novel, Jules happens on a hideous, mangy dog one night while walking in the woods. The scene has been read allegorically by many critics (it would represent, variously, Death, the absurd, Jules's past, or Flaubert's nervous illness), but one need not even assign meaning to the scene to recognize its role in the thematics of repetition. The dog is an explicit reiteration—either copy or repetition—of a dog image from earlier in the novel, the young spaniel ("Fox") Jules gives Lucinde. But here the image returns in degraded form, covered in mud, limping, with patches of bare skin showing. Jules's privileged point of view does nothing to preserve him from the dynamics of repetition (appropriately, Jules cannot rid himself of the dog, which follows him all the way home); however, his aesthetic principles may allow him, unlike Henry and others, to recognize the deterioration and wear that accompany repetition. Flaubert retains this insight, for the problem of repetition (linked to a dynamic of substitution) will be a key to the 1869 version of the novel.

While the 1845 version of *L'Education sentimentale* clearly marks a departure in Flaubert's work, it is not clear what, if anything, prompted this aesthetic development. It may simply represent a crystallization or maturation toward which Flaubert had always been headed. A popular though unsubstantiated theory suggests that his nervous illness played an important role, for his first epileptoid attack occurred in January 1844, interrupting his composition of the novel. According to this line of thinking, the attack and convalescence from it turned Flaubert from a more public life in Paris toward the more introspective existence he was to enjoy at Croisset. In short, it would have transformed him from Henry into Jules, which might explain the shifting balance of these two protagonists' relative importance as the novel progresses. (SDC)

References:

Bem, Jeanne. "L'Artiste et son double, dans 'la première *Education sentimentale.*' " *Revue des sciences humaines* 181 (1981): 11–19.

Bruneau, Jean. *Les Débuts littéraires de Gustave Flaubert, 1831–1845.* Paris: Colin, 1962.

Flaubert, Gustave. *Œuvres complètes.* Ed. Bernard Masson. 2 vols. Paris: Seuil, 1964. Vol. 1.

Kudo, Yoko. "La Première *Education sentimentale* de Flaubert," *Etudes de Langue et de Littérature Françaises* 25–26 (1975): 34–49.

Neefs, Jacques. "Ecrits de formation: *L'Education sentimentale* de 1845 et *Le Portrait.*" *Revue des Lettres Modernes* 953–58 (1990): 85–99.

Sartre, Jean-Paul. *L'Idiot de la famille.* 3 vols. Paris: Gallimard, 1971–72.

L'Education sentimentale (1869). Completely different from the 1845 version, the 1869 version of *L'Education sentimentale* shares little more than a title and a strong homosexual bond between the two male protagonists with its precursor. In the closing pages of the 1869 version of *L'Education sentimentale*, Flaubert allows the novel's two protagonists to sum up their failed lives without apparent authorial intervention: dreams of love and dreams of power, we are told, have led to nothing. Frédéric Moreau and Deslauriers were unable either to forge a direct path through life's richness or to take account of life's complexity. Irony is the dominant mode in this ambitious novel of a nation's failed ambitions: irony permeates every aspect of the text and overflows to offer an implicit but unbounded attack on the limitations and failures of literature itself. From the opening scene with its depiction of the ambitious but directionless young hero leaving Paris, pulled along by the river as he will allow life itself to pull him along—his dreams shaped by romanticism, a movement already in decay—to the closing reminiscences that transform an abortive visit to a brothel into the high point of two careers predicated on failure, *L'Education sentimentale* builds its multileveled presentation of midcentury France around a hollow core. Frédéric Moreau, with apparently everything he needs for success—charm, a reasonable fortune, a few good contacts—and with boundless plans for success, like his lifelong friend Deslauriers, whose only hope of success lies in his overriding determination to succeed, embarks on adult life with the hopes and weaknesses of his post-Napoleonic generation. Divided among the fantasies of making a name in painting, writing, the law, or politics, incapable of transforming reverie into reality, Frédéric, an observer incapable of seeing beyond surface glitter, drifts through a Paris shaken by the possibilities of social and governmental reformation. His story is repeated with numerous variations by the rich cast of characters Flaubert establishes around him and is underlined by the story of one of the very few characters who appears to succeed, his classmate, the coldly unsympathetic Martinon. Most pertinently, perhaps, Frédéric's eventual failure is foreshadowed in the slow decline of the man he meets on that initial boat trip and on whom he models so much of his behavior, the art dealer Jacques Arnoux.

However firmly anchored in the years around the 1848 Revolution Frédéric's story may be, Flaubert's multilayered doubling techniques prevent us from seeing his failure as unique to him, or that of his generation as unique to it. Deslauriers's shadowing of Frédéric, his attempts to wrest success from areas in which Frédéric has already failed, in both his career and his love life, together with the extent to which Arnoux, like a distorting mirror, offers the gradually deteriorating image of possible future Frédérics, constantly suggests that no one in this novel is unique, no one anything but a template for his or her peers. The dreams of art, of journalism, of law, and of politics that Frédéric at various stages contemplates are embodied in Pellerin, Hussonet, Deslauriers, and Dambreuse and find further shadowing and disturbing doublings in Arnoux's dabbling in art and journalism and Dambreuse's self-serving manipulation of law and politics. The multiplicity of city life, in other words, reflects merely an endless repetition of the same, for all the individual characters' belief in their own uniqueness. Within this framework, Frédéric's inability to see the women in his life as individuals, rather than variations on the theme of his own desire, is no more than a permutation on the theme of his own lack of distinguishing features. Cisy embodies this inescapable lack of distinction, with his frequently repeated and invariably inane determination to "avoir du cachet" [to have distinction], resulting merely in his stamping his likeness eight times on his sons.

The preparation, unfolding, and ultimate failure of the 1848 revolution provide an ironic background to the interweaving lives in *L'Education sentimentale*. Frédéric's seduction of Mme Arnoux seems about to reach fruition on the night the revolution at last breaks out, after a slow, tortuous buildup that finds a parallel in the young man's flabby wooing. That he spends the night with Rosanette instead of Mme Arnoux in the love nest specially prepared for the latter has often been read as a wry, bitter commentary on how a country on the brink of transforming itself into a republic made do instead with an empire run by a second-rate Napoleon. Far more fierce than this symbolic suggestion, however, is the dichotomy established by another set of doubles, Dussardier and Sénécal.

The first represents the idealist whose vision can never be realized because he lacks the political sense to maneuver his way through his pragmatic, power-seeking opponents; the second exemplifies the self-serving revolutionary whose doctrines are predicated on his own sense of grievance and entitlement. That Sénécal should shoot the unarmed, nonviolent Dussardier before disappearing from sight is both a searing indictment of the motives of many self-styled revolutionaries and Flaubert's most violent rejection of any hope of improving the lot of the common person, at least through politics. Sénécal's intransigent attack on privilege reveals itself as empty sham once he himself is in a position of privilege, however small, while Dussardier, however likeable Flaubert makes him, has no defenses, physical or strategic, against the forces of conservatism. In a sense, this inevitable divorce of principle and practicality in politics is the sardonic insight at the heart of the novel, more vital and more corrosive as social critique than is the weakness of the central figure or the decay of personal ambition.

The collapse of the revolution, the failure of the characters to achieve their initial high ambitions, the mind's idleness, and the heart's inertia all realize their full dimensions in relationship to the novel's depiction of love and desire. Frédéric's romantic encounter with Mme Arnoux on the steamer has all the hallmarks of the great defining moment: her beauty, what he perceives as her exoticism, her status as a married woman, and her role as mother all enable him to place her at a safe remove from himself, a target of dream rather than of love or lust. His inability to contemplate a woman's individuality marks Frédéric's relationships with all the women in the novel: Rosanette Bron passed from man to man among Frédéric's acquaintances; Mme Dambreuse, who functions primarily as an ironic comment on the Balzacian hero's use of women to gain power, fame, and fortune; and Louise Roque, the most individualistic of them all and the one whom Frédéric fails to read accurately—all these women form interwoven motifs in his dreams of erotic or romantic love. His failure to choose among schemes of enrichment and success finds its counterpoint here in his failure to differentiate among the individual women and in the hackneyed molds into which he tries to force them. Deslauriers, following Frédéric here as elsewhere, also fails to establish lasting relationships with any of these women. The problem, Flaubert implies, lies neither with a lack of willpower nor with an excess of willpower, as Deslauriers himself will argue, but with something more profound, something endemic in contemporary relationships between men and women.

In similar ways, Paris, which in so many nineteenth-century novels is presented as the theater of success, is in this novel both the site and the correlative of failure. The famous landmarks are seen only when they are being left behind, the revolutionary uprisings take place on city squares and crossroads whose original purpose is reduced to the utilitarian one of bringing the classes together, streets serve not so much to connect space as to enable random encounters, and racetracks perform above all the metonymic function of emphasizing contests for wealth and influence. As Pierre Bourdieu has pointed out, the distribution of the characters' dwellings across Paris creates a structural, hierarchical space that reflects the ascending and descending social trajectories, transforming Paris from geographical locus to metaphysical construct. With *L'Education sentimentale*, Flaubert has created a work anchored in a particular time and place, a work infused with both personal and political failure, but nevertheless, through its irony and its complexity, unfailingly contemporary and compelling. (RL)

References:

Bourdieu, Pierre. "The Invention of the Artist's Life." *Yale French Studies* 73 (1987): 75–103.

———. "Is the Structure of *Sentimental Education* an Instance of Social Self-analysis?" In Pierre Bourdieu, *The Field of Cultural Production: Essays on Art and Literature*. New York: Columbia University Press, 1999 (1993). 145–60.

Layton, Lynne. "Flaubert's *L'Education sentimentale*: A Tragedy of Mind." *French Forum* 11 (1986): 335–51.

Le Calvez, Eric. *Flaubert topographe*: L'Education sentimentale: *Essai de poétique génétique*. Amsterdam: Rodopi, 1997.

Paulson, William. *Sentimental Education: The Complexity of Disenchantment*. New York: Twayne, 1992.

Williams, David Anthony. "Gustave Flaubert: *Sentimental Education* (1869)." In David Anthony Williams, ed., *The Monster in the Mirror*. Oxford: Oxford University Press, 1978. 75–101.

Egypt. Flaubert spent eight months in all in Egypt during 1850. He and his best friend Maxime Du Camp had arrived in Alexandria in January 1850 after a voyage from Marseilles. They first spent six weeks in Cairo. Flaubert had an official government assignment to gather agricultural statistics, but soon abandoned it. During a five-month charter-boat excursion on the upper Nile, as far as the Second Cataract, he and Du Camp successfully set the broken leg of a member of their crew, as Charles Bovary was to do in *Madame Bovary*. Flaubert practiced the art of landscape description by taking notes as he traveled. He found himself acutely sensitive to changing nuances of color and light and to the shapes of clouds. Because Saint Anthony's hermitage had been on the upper Nile near Thebes, and Flaubert had just completed the unsuccessful first version of *La Tentation de saint Antoine*, he was particularly curious about Egypt. He interviewed Coptic bishops to learn about the desert recluses, and he visited the holes in the cliffs where they had lived. The Sphinx was an electrifying, terrifying sight. The travelers saw the ancient palaces at Thebes and Karnak and took a side trip overland to the Red Sea. Flaubert brought back the written memories "of sights and sounds and smells [that] would give texture to many of his later works—*Salammbô*, [*La Tentation de saint Antoine*, 1856, 1874], and 'Hérodias' directly, and the others indirectly" (Bart 198). (LMP)

References:

Bart, Benjamin F. *Flaubert*. Syracuse; Syracuse University Press, 1967. 189–98.

Said, Edward. *Orientalism*. New York: Pantheon, 1978.

electronic resources. Chief among electronic resources for the study of Flaubert is ARTFL, an indispensable electronic database for textual research in French literature. It is free and accessible via Netscape. Located at the University of Chicago site, this constantly expanding corpus allows one to search hundreds of French fictional texts, including several by Flaubert, for a given word or phrase. The format is keyword-in-context, and the editions used are specified. The ClicNet site provides links to nine Flaubert texts.

Regarding the nineteenth century in particular, and Flaubert himself, many WWW site names and addresses are provided by Unwin. Those he finds best are listed in the References. For CD-ROMs, he recommends the *Bibliorom 98* catalog available through the CPEDERF, and other outlets, and in particular, the two individual items listed in the References. (LMP)

References:

ARTFL (*American and French Research on the Treasury of the French Language*). University of Chicago.

ClicNet. Littérature francophone virtuelle du XIXe siècle. http://www.swarthmore.edu/Humanities/clicnet/litterrature/sujets/XIX.html/

Flaubert, Gustave. *Madame Bovary*. Collection "L'Autre Plume." Paris: Ubi Soft, 1997. Text, background, sound, and graphics on CD-ROM.

———. *L'Œuvre romanesque, texte intégral*. Collection "Catalogue des Lettres." Paris: Egide, 1997. CD-ROM, designed for advanced search functions.

Gustave Flaubert (1821–1880). www://scopus.ch/users/torrent_j/Flaubert.html/.

Internet Movie Database. http://us.imdb.com/.

Le Pavillon Flaubert. www.napoleon.fr/scripts/napoleon-bin/gide-detail.idc:?num=106.

Unwin, Timothy. "A Report on Flaubert and the New Technologies." In Tony Williams and Mary Orr, eds., *New Approaches in Flaubert Studies*. Lewiston, NY: Mellen, 1999. 235–43.

Eliot, T[homas] S[tearns] (1888–1965). T. S. Eliot was an American-born English poet, critic, and playwright. Remy de Gourmont led both Eliot and Ezra Pound to Flaubert. Eliot admired Flaubert's "sophisticated quasi-omniscience" (Greene 242) and the irony that despite Flaubert's title, *The Sentimental Education*, the hero of the novel learns nothing. In a "Lettre d'Angleterre," Eliot called Flaubert "un maître à la fois d'art et de pensée." "Eeldrop and Appleplex," the first part of an unfinished work (1917), was a rewriting of *Bouvard et Pécuchet* in a new setting. The eponymous narrator in Eliot's early poem "The Love Song of J. Alfred Prufrock" is a literary descendant of Frédéric Moreau. They share an awareness of the spiritual decay of society but lack the necessary will and passion to counteract it, preferring introspection to action. (AA/LMP)

References:

Eliot, T. S. "Eeldrop and Appleplex." *Little Review* 4 (1917): May, 7–11; September, 16–19.

———. "Lettre d'Angleterre." *Nouvelle revue française* November 1, 1923: 620.

Greene, Edward J. H. *T. S. Eliot et la France*. Paris: Boivin, 1951.
Strickland, G. R. "Flaubert, Pound, and Eliot." *Cambridge Quarterly* 2 (1967): 242–63.

Enlightenment. The philosophic thinking of the Enlightenment occupies a special place in Flaubert's doctrines. The desire for truth and the search for knowledge, impulses at the core of Denis Diderot's *Encyclopédie*, constitute major subjects in *Bouvard et Pécuchet*, Flaubert's last work, in which he portrays two men in pursuit of intellectual self-advancement. Other themes essential to the Enlightenment philosophers, such as the constant castigation of intolerance, injustice, and received ideas, appear in Flaubert's work. The conversations of the two clerks in *Bouvard et Pécuchet*, made up of clichés and commonplaces about women or politics, demonstrate how stereotyped thinking enslaves humanity, making it impossible for it to attain good judgment. Flaubert was also fascinated with the different genres and styles that flourished during the eighteenth century. The *roman philosophique* exemplified by *Candide* was of particular interest to him and was a source of inspiration for his last work, for it provided a way to interweave serious subjects into the frame of an amusing tale. Flaubert also found the style of the dialogue, as it occurs in Diderot's *Jacques le Fataliste*, an efficient tool for commenting on weighty subjects. Like Jacques and his master, the two clerks are always in conversation with each other, commenting on topics related to the ideals of progress, liberty, and scientific thought. But Flaubert must recognize that if modern times with their quasi-democratic institutions had made better education possible, they had also decreased people's capacity for direct experience and for the use of common sense. Knowledge for everyone as advocated by Kant and other eighteenth-century thinkers became conceivable in the 1850s, but not everybody could benefit from it, as the two protagonists of *Bouvard et Pécuchet* illustrate. They fail in their quest of self-education and finally decide to return to copying. Education, concludes Flaubert, thus diverging from the Enlightenment, is not always the key to self-understanding. (CT)

References:

Gevrey, Françoise. "L'Image de Voltaire dans la correspondance de Flaubert." In Jean-Louis Cabanes, *Voix de l'écrivain*. Toulouse: Presses Universitaires de Toulouse, 1996. 139–49.
Sumberg, Theodore A. "Flaubert against the Enlightenment." *College Language Association Journal* 26.2 (1982): 241–50.

epilepsy. In January 1844, Flaubert suddenly lost consciousness while he was driving the family cabriolet at night. As he describes it, he felt as if he were being carried off by a torrent of flames. His attacks recurred almost daily at first and for the next six months, at least, were brought on by any sort of nervous tension. Even when he did not lose consciousness and remained lucid during the attacks, he felt discomfort and saw streams of light, like fireworks, passing before his eyes. Often an aura of rainbow-colored light would warn him of an onset. His father, a prominent doctor, placed him on a regimen of absolute calm without any stimulants such as Flaubert's beloved pipe. Primitive treatments including bleeding and colonic purging were used, and at one point his father aggravated the problem by accidentally pouring boiling water over his son's arm, causing burns on his right hand that took months to heal. Further study of law, which bored Flaubert at best, became impossible. Jean-Paul Sartre claimed (*passim*) that Flaubert's problem was hysteria, and even his brother diagnosed his condition as "epiletiform," but the most probable diagnosis in the light of contemporary medical knowledge is temporal-lobe epilepsy. Since this condition stigmatized people at the time, Flaubert's family tried to hush it up (Bart 90–98). Both Emma Bovary's visions just before her suicide and some of Saint Anthony's may have been inspired by the author's lived experience. (LMP)

References:

Bart, Benjamin F. *Flaubert*. Syracuse: Syracuse University Press, 1967.
Pommier, Jean. *Dialogues avec le passé: Etudes et portraits littéraires*. Paris: Nizet, 1967. 281–99.
Sartre, Jean–Paul. *L'Idiot de la famille*. 3 vols. Paris: Gallimard, 1971–72.

Eugénie, l'impératrice (1826–1920). Empress of the French (1853–70), a Spanish noblewoman of great beauty and a leader of fashion, Eugénie de Montijo married the emperor Napoleon III in 1853 and took an active part in government. Eugénie had sympathized with Flaubert when his most famous work, *Madame Bovary*, was under official attack for being offensive to religion and morality (1857), but he first met the emperor and the empress only on January 21, 1863, after the success of his novel *Salammbô* with the court. This success changed Flaubert's life and gave him access to the imperial court and to the highest society for seven or eight years, until the Franco-Prussian War. After Napoleon III's deposition in 1870 during the Franco-Prussian War, the empress fled to England. (CB)

Reference:

Bart, Benjamin F. *Flaubert*. Syracuse: Syracuse University Press, 1967. 451–53, 554–57.

exoticism. The eighteenth-century exotic novel, informed by the Enlightenment concept of relativism, typically presented the alterity of the exotic other as attenuated or nullified. In Montesquieu's *Lettres Persanes*, for example, the exotic, unfamiliar culture is shown to have a more highly evolved set of values than first supposed. In the nineteenth-century exotic novel, of which *Salammbô* is an example, the oriental is typically represented with a heightened theatricality in order to postulate an otherness, an exteriority without interiority. This difference can be maintained (and punished) or assimilated into sameness in the end. Salammbô is represented as the ultimate other; a figure of alterity in space, time, and gender. As the last line of the novel specifies, she must be annihilated for having touched the veil of Tanit, a violation of the paternalistic order that designates her as an object of exchange among men.

The problem of the exotic other is also raised in the oppositional relationship between the barbarian army and the Carthaginians in *Salammbô*. A civilization defines its own contours by its conception of the barbaric. Hamilcar and his cohorts, who set the standard against which similarity and difference are measured, represent a bourgeois materialism not unlike that of Flaubert's contemporary France. The mercenary army possesses all the attributes associated with the archetype of the barbarian: brutality, cowardice, treachery, lubricity, lawlessness, rapacity, and inconstancy. Since the alterity of the barbarians cannot be incorporated into the mercantile society of Carthage, they must be annihilated. The gratuitous torture of the barbarian soldier Mâtho by the implacable Carthaginian mob, however, abolishes any doubt that the latter is as capable of atrocities as is the mercenary army. Flaubert's masterful coup in *Salammbô* is to reveal, by a process of axiological reversal, that the "civilized" cultural self initially represented by the prosperous citizens of Carthage is just as hollow as the depersonalized, empty image of the exotic other it projects. In *Salammbô*, otherness is absorbed by sameness in the end, but not because, as in the usual scenario, the exotic or barbaric characters adopt a vision compatible with the dominant Carthaginian perspective. It is rather because the Carthaginian model, with its parallels to the bourgeois, commodity-driven European society in which Flaubert lived and wrote, is presented as being as alien to its own presumed values as it is to the barbarian model. The Carthaginians triumph over the barbarians at the cost of becoming barbaric themselves. The lesson of *Salammbô* seems to be, as Gaillard points out, that the barbarian is not the other; the barbarian is in us (53).

Flaubert's implied author is alienated from both the Carthaginian and barbarian camps. He looks at the barbarians through the disdainful eyes of the nobility, yet the nobility makes him feel complicity with the barbarian. By partially embracing a barbarian identity, Flaubert reverses the terms of the paradigm that the barbarian must always be cast as other. He autoreferentially portrays the Gaulish contingent of the mercenary army as comically inept and among the most bellicose. Although the barbarian is feared and loathed as a threat to the social order, his mythos includes the possibility of regeneration. Flaubert the writer is intrigued by the barbarian as a source of palingenesis, not only for a decadent civilization, but also for a literary tradition he perceives as decadent.

The choice of distant, exotic settings and motifs in Flaubert's orientalist writings expanded the field of the representable. It afforded him the opportunity to describe a luxuriant proliferation of ornamental detail that would have appeared self-indulgent in a European context. Salomé's sartorial excesses in "Hérodias," for example, suggest a feminine conspiracy to undermine masculine power. In *Salammbô*, the exotic setting allowed Flaubert to transpose, consciously or unconsciously, a satiric vision of his own contemporary society in ways that a direct approach might not have permitted. The cruelty that Flaubert depicts in his orientalist writings might not have achieved public and critical acceptance had it been set instead in contemporary France. Finally, for Europeans who dreamed of a colorful, poetic lost paradise, the Orient exerted a strong attraction during the materialistic, increasingly industrialized nineteenth century. (CBK/JM)

See also orientalism.

References:

Gaillard, Françoise. "La Révolte contre la Révolution (*Salammbô*, un autre point de vue sur l'histoire.)" In Alfonso de Toro, ed., *Procédés narratifs et fondements épistémologiques* Tübingen: Narr, 1987. 43–54.

Porter, Dennis. "The Perverse Traveller: Flaubert's *Voyage en Orient*." *L'Esprit Créateur* 29 (1989): 24–36.

Queffelec, Lise. "La construction de l'espace exotique dans le roman d'aventures au XIXe siècle." In Alain Buisine, Norbert Dodille, and Claude Duchet, eds., *L'Exotisme*. Cahiers CRLH-CIRAOI 5. Paris: Didier Erudition, 1988. 353–64.

Said, Edward. *Orientalism*. New York: Random House, 1979 (1978).

Terdiman, Richard. "Ideological Voyages: On a Flaubertian Disorientation." In Richard Terdiman, *Discourse/Counter-Discourse: The Theory and Practice of Symbolic Resistance in Nineteenth-Century France*. Ithaca, NY: Cornell University Press, 1985.

F

The Family Idiot (by Jean-Paul Sartre). *See* critical reception; Sartre, Jean-Paul.

Faulkner, William (1897–1962). William Faulkner claimed to reread *Madame Bovary* once a year (Kinney 222) and revered Flaubert as a craftsman "whose approach towards his language was almost the lapidary's" (Kinney 225). Adapting Flaubert's *style indirect libre* in his use of interior monologue in such works as *The Sound and the Fury* (1929) and *As I Lay Dying* (1930), Faulkner follows Flaubert as a novelist of consciousness who seeks to represent the impressions of a perceiving mind. His most elaborate intertextual engagement with Flaubert occurs in *Sanctuary* (1931) and *Flags in the Dust* (published posthumously in 1973 after appearing in heavily edited form as *Sartoris* in 1929). Both novels recall *Madame Bovary* at thematic, structural, imagistic, and verbal levels in their visions of post–World War I alienation in a decaying Southern town beset by social, psychological, and sexual enervation and corruption. The original text of *Sanctuary* explicitly recalls Flaubert in Horace Benbow's reflection that Popeye "smells like that black stuff that ran out of Bovary's mouth and down upon her bridal veil when they raised her head" (25). *Sanctuary*'s tropes of liquidity and liquefaction associated with sex and death, of eating and vomiting, and of eyes and blindness trace an extensive intertextual conversation with *Madame Bovary*.

Faulkner's work was admired in France by writers such as Jean-Paul Sartre and André Malraux decades before his reputation was established in the United States, and he continues to influence French novelists, including Louis-René des Fôrets, Claude Simon, and Pierre Guyotat, and Francophone Caribbean novelists such as Patrick Chamoiseau or Edouard Glissant. As André Bleikasten observes, Faulkner's major novels "belong as much to the history of the European novel as to that of American fiction" (Bleikasten 1995: 77). (ST)

References:

Bleikasten, André. " 'Cet affreux goût d'encre': Emma Bovary's Ghost in *Sanctuary*." In Michel Gresset and Noel Polk, eds., *Intertextuality in Faulkner*. Jackson: University Press of Mississippi, 1985. 36–56.

———. "Faulkner from a European Perspective." In Philip M. Weinstein, ed., *The Cambridge Companion to William Faulkner*. Cambridge: Cambridge University Press, 1995. 75–95.

Cohen, Philip. "*Madame Bovary* and *Flags in the Dust*: Flaubert's Influence on Faulkner." *Comparative Literature Studies* 22 (1985): 344–61.

Faulkner, William. *Sanctuary: The Original Text*. Ed. Noel Polk. New York: Random House, 1981.

Kinney, Arthur F. "Faulkner and Flaubert." *Journal of Modern Literature* 6 (1977): 222–47.

Niess, Robert. "Flaubert et Faulkner: Deux allégories de la chasse." In Charles Carlut, ed., *Essais sur Flaubert en l'honneur du professeur Don Demorest*. Paris: Nizet, 1979. 363–80.

Félicité (*TC*). Félicité's first name seems to contrast ironically with her life story and her social status as a servant in "Un cœur simple," the first tale of *Trois Contes* (1877). The incipit—"Pendant un demi-siècle, les bourgeoises de Pont-L'Evêque envièrent à Madame Aubain sa servante Félicité" (for half a century, the good ladies of Pont-L'Evêque envied Madame Aubain her servant Félicité [Flaubert 2: 591])—encapsulates fifty years of her adult life, a period marked by repetition rather than linear progress. When her fiancé abruptly abandons her to marry a rich older woman, Félicité is hired as a cook for a young widow with two small children. Her character is introduced with an enumeration of the household tasks she performs for Madame Aubain (who, consistent with her social class, spends her days sitting in an armchair doing needlework). The repetitiveness and monotony of her chores are captured by a succession of verbs in the imperfect tense. Whereas Madame Aubain receives five thousand francs in revenues from her family farms, her loyal servant earns one hundred francs per year for her labor. Félicité's value as a human being is assessed purely according to the principle of economic exchange (Stipa 617). Her character is the embodiment of diligence, frugality, and selfless accommodation of others.

An example of Félicité's innate goodness is seen in the episode in which she risks her safety to save Madame Aubain and her children, Paul and Virginie, from a charging bull. By the second half of the nineteenth century, the virtuous, devoted servant had become a literary topos, exploited by Balzac, Baudelaire, and Flaubert himself in the character of Catherine Leroux in *Madame Bovary* (Cronk 157). Félicité is a figure not only of selflessness, but also of timelessness. As a young woman, she looks older than her age, but after fifty, she seems to exist statically, impervious to the progression of time.

Piety and charity are also among Félicité's defining characteristics. Accompanying Virginie to catechism, Félicité is entranced and moved as she visualizes the priest's descriptions of biblical events. She is touched by liturgical references to the Lamb and the Holy Spirit because they remind her of the lambs and doves that are a familiar presence in her everyday life. Although she cannot readily conceptualize the Holy Spirit, it seems to pervade her universe. She makes no attempt to comprehend dogma, but revels in the imagery and the ritualized gestures of the Catholic faith. In addition to her self-sacrifice for Madame Aubain's and her own sister's children, Félicité, Christlike, moves freely among the sick and dying, giving care and comfort to cholera victims and to a horribly disfigured old indigent man.

Félicité's close relationship to nature reinforces the impression of her simplicity. She was a chaste but not naive maiden during her courtship with Théodore—she had learned the ways of the world from her observation of animals. She intuitively knew how to subdue the enraged bull that menaced Madame Aubain and her children. Her instinctual rapport with the natural realm also appears in her attachment to her pet parrot and fetish object, Loulou. Its connection to her nephew Victor, who perished in the New World, and Loulou's resemblance in her mind to the Holy Spirit converge to make this exotic bird the last focus of Félicité's affection. Loulou plays a prominent role in her truncated spiritual development.

Félicité's life is defined by a succession of attachments: to her fiancé, to her mistress's children, to her nephew, to the old man she takes care of, and finally, to her parrot. When she observes Virginie's first communion or imagines Victor's hardships at sea, her identification with the beloved Other is so complete that she seems to experience the world as if through their senses rather than her own. Each love attachment ends in the loss of the beloved. As Stipa points out, Félicité's relationships to Madame Aubain's daughter Virginie and to her own nephew Victor stand in relief due to the parallels that link them. Both names begin with the letters *vi*. Both characters are associated with the sea, Virginie because of her illness and Victor because of his vocation. Both take Félicité's affection and generosity for granted. Due to delays, Félicité narrowly misses both the opportunity to see Victor off as he departs for the New World and the opportunity to see Virginie before she expires at the convent. Both Virginie's and Victor's deaths can be attributed to dubious medical care. Loulou, a living reminder of Victor due to the bird's exotic origins, becomes a substitute for him and, by extension, for Virginie. The cycle of love and loss ends with Loulou, whose absences always prove temporary. Félicité enjoys a union with Loulou never attained in her relationships with humans. She attributes to the parrot the characteristics of the Holy Spirit and conceives the image of the Holy Spirit in the form of the parrot. This conflation is validated in Félicité's mind by an Epinal color print of Christ's baptism in which the colors evoke the image of Loulou (Stipa 624).

As her contact with the human world becomes more limited, the physical space in which Félicité lives becomes correspondingly more circumscribed. Confined to the enclosed space of her bedroom, Félicité loses her senses of hearing and sight. The echoes of the sacralized parrot's voice keep her from total sensory isolation in her shrinelike room. The sorrow caused by the loss of this succession of loved ones and the isolation that characterizes the end of Félicité's life do not prevent her from attaining a measure of inner happiness and peace. Echoing Rousseau, the more she is distanced from human society, the happier she seems to become (Cronk 155). In a reconciliation of the realistic and the visionary, the "heart" of the tale's title is reinscribed nonfiguratively in the last sentence as she lies dying in a state of grace with the vision of a giant parrot floating overhead in the sky (Haig 110). Drawing her final breath, she finds, in the redemptive image of the son/lover figure who has come to reunite her with the heavenly father, the union between self and other that had been inaccessible all her life. In the perspective of this newfound sense of plenitude and unity, the ironic charge that the name *Félicité* appeared to carry is dissipated. (JM)

References:

Chambers, Ross. *Story and Situation: Narrative Seduction and the Power of Fiction*. Minneapolis: University of Minnesota Press, 1984. 123–50.

Cronk, Nicholas. "Reading *Un cœur simple*: The Pleasure of the Intertext." *Nineteenth-Century French Studies* 24. 1–2 (1995–1996): 154–161.

Erickson, Karen L. "Prophetic Utterance and Irony in *Trois Contes*." In Barbara T. Cooper and Mary Donaldson-Evans, eds., *Modernity and Revolution in Late Nineteenth-Century France*. Newark: University of Delaware Press, 1992. 65–73.

Felman, Shoshana. "Illusion réaliste et répétition romanesque." In Jean Paris, ed., *La Critique générative*. Paris: Seghers-Laffont, 1973.

Flaubert, Gustave. *Œuvres*. 2 vols. Ed. Albert Thibaudet and René Dumesnil. Paris: Gallimard, 1951–52.

Haig, Stirling. "Parrot and Parody: Flaubert." In Emanuel J. Mickel, Jr., ed., *The Shaping of Text: Style, Imagery, and Structure in French Literature*. Lewisburg, PA: Bucknell University Press, 1993. 105–12.

Schulz-Buschhaus, Ulrich. "Die Sprachlosigkeit der Félicité: Zur Interpretation von Flauberts Un cœur simple." *Zeitschrift für französische Sprache und Literatur* 93 (1983): 113–30.

Stipa, Ingrid. "Desire, Repetition, and the Imaginary in Flaubert's *Un cœur simple.*" *Studies in Short Fiction* 31.4 (1994): 617–26.

feminist and gender studies. One of Flaubert's first readers identified oddities of gender in *Madame Bovary*. It was Charles Baudelaire who noted that Emma's desires masculinized her, and he labeled her a "bizarre androgyne." Indeed, in the context of nineteenth-century French expectations about women's conduct, Emma's overt sexuality and far-reaching desire did stand out as alien and unacceptable, as the trial of *Madame Bovary* on charges of offending public morals showed.

Twentieth-century studies of gender in Flaubert take up Baudelaire's theme to examine other oddities of gender identity in Flaubert's works. Emma's behavior is at once obviously feminine in the definitions of her time, but also occasionally masculine, as in her donning of a monocle like a man or being the aggressor and taking the male role in her relation with Léon. Bouvard and Pécuchet have been seen as a male "couple," one masculine, one feminine.

Several important studies of gender in Flaubert take it beyond a thematic analysis to a more general theoretical concern. Naomi Schor describes Emma as a woman who desires to break the chain of passive femininity but who fails to accede to the phallic writing stage. Roger Huss centers similarly on the impossibility of Emma's incorporation of the masculine, the impossibility of gender plenitude, and the problem of difference itself.

The thematic and structural ambiguity of gender has also led more recently to an investigation of hysteria, the psychological malady of gender ambiguity, both of Flaubert and in his works. Flaubert described himself as a hysteric who succumbed periodically to nervous fits. What does it mean that Flaubert assigned himself a predominantly "feminine" disease? Emma Bovary can be seen as an example of a hysterical woman. What does it mean that Flaubert made her the main character of his novel? These are questions now being posed in critical circles.

Cultural analyses of Emma reveal that she is represented as being inserted into the cultural structures of her time, making them visible to us. For example, that Charles is the first character who appears in a novel entitled *Madame Bovary* shows how woman at that time needed to have man place her in a proper context in society. Indeed, Flaubert's focus on the codification of language and identity puts both man and woman in the place of mechanically performing preformed gender identities.

Flaubert's own pronouncements on gender and woman contain flagrant contradictions. On the one hand, Flaubert's attitude toward female identity is perfectly attuned with the bourgeois views of his time, that women were to be objects of enjoyment for male pleasure. In particular, his letters to his male friends describe degrading sexual experiences that reflect the objectification of women and the collusion among men to strengthen their collective power over women.

On the other hand, we see in certain poignant letters Flaubert's understanding of the horrible effects of gender codification on women when he deplores the choices open to his beloved niece. Flaubert saw how education constructs a woman and affects her entire life: "On apprend aux femmes à mentir d'une façon infâme. L'apprentissage dure toute leur vie. . . . J'ai peur du corset moral. Les premières impressions ne s'effacent pas, tu le sais. Nous portons en nous notre passé; pendant toute notre vie nous nous sentons de la nourrice" (We teach women to lie in a degrading manner. This apprenticeship lasts throughout their life. . . . I'm afraid of moral corsets. First impressions don't fade, you know. We bear our past within us; during our whole lifetime we feel the influence of our wetnurse), (Letter to his mother November 14, 1850, *Corr.* 2:257–58).

Thus Flaubert's sustained attention to our coded, clichéd identities leads him to understand that gender identity is not "anatomical." There is no pure grounding of gender identities in our bodies, in the real; instead, social coding and context assign clichéd identities to us, which we in turn perform or reject. However, Flaubert's texts show how understanding that we are enclosed in this prison house of gender is not enough to free us from it. (DJK)

See also androgyny; queer studies.

References:

Bart, Benjamin F. "Male Hysteria in *Salammbô*." *Nineteenth-Century French Studies* 12 (1984): 313–21.

Beizer, Janet. *Ventriloquized Bodies: Narratives of Hysteria in Nineteenth-Century France*. Ithaca: Cornell University Press, 1994.

Huss, Roger. "Flaubert and Realism: Paternity, Authority, and Sexual Difference." In Margaret Cohen and Christopher Prendergast, eds., *Spectacles of Realism: Body, Gender, Genre*. Minneapolis: University of Minnesota Press, 1995. 179–95.

Kelly, Dorothy. *Fictional Genders: Role and Representation in Nineteenth-Century French Narrative*. Lincoln: University of Nebraska Press, 1989.

Schor, Naomi. *Breaking the Chain: Women, Theory, and French Realist Fiction*. New York: Columbia University Press, 1985.

Williams, Tony. "Gender Stereotypes in *Madame Bovary*." *Forum for Modern Language Studies* 28. 2 (1992):130–39.

Wolf, Susan L. "The Same or (M)Other: A Feminist Reading of *Madame Bovary*." In Laurence M. Porter and Eugene F. Gray, eds., *Approaches to Teaching Flaubert's Madame Bovary*. New York: Modern Language Association, 1995. 34–41.

fetishism. Of the three primary categorizations of the fetish—the religious/anthropological, the economic, and the sexual—only the first two were current during Flaubert's lifetime. Yet it is the sexual definition of the fetish, first forged by the French neurologist Alfred Binet in 1888 and much amplified in Sigmund Freud's essay "Fetishism" of 1927, that is most associated with Flaubert's work within the critical corpus. "What reader," queries Charles Bernheimer, "has not noticed the way Frédéric focuses on Mme Arnoux's shoes, the hem of her dress, the fur trim of her black velvet coat?" (160). Sartre's analysis of the extremely important influence of Flaubert's mother underscores the psychological genesis of fetishism in the Freudian sense as the preservation of a myth of sexual likeness with a phallic mother (Barnes 77).

But fetishism as a sexual substitution serving to palliate castration anxiety is in many ways less important in texts such as *Madame Bovary* and *L'Education sentimentale* than the role of the economic fetish, first explicitly theorized in Karl Marx's essay in his *Capital*, "The Fetishism of Commodities and the Secret Thereof" (1867). Marx theorized the transposition of materialism from the religious to the economic domains as a relation between persons expressed as a relation between things. Bernheimer notes that while the sexual fetish is reassuring, the commodity fetish enforces a sense of disintegration. (162). Flaubert attributes an especially fatalistic psychic and social importance to female characters' trafficking in bourgeois fetish commodities such as Algerian scarves.

This motif suggests a critique of mercantile culture's fostering of a peculiar, orientalist susceptibility in the female consumer, parallel to the plying of "natives" with fetish objects during the process of conquest.

Religious materialism, however, plays by far the most important role in Flaubert's poetics of the fetish. In a letter to Mlle Leroyer de Chantepie, he theorized a fundamental cultural parity between "primitive" fetishes and Christian materialist worship: "Je respecte le nègre baisant son fétiche autant que le catholique aux pieds du Sacré-Coeur" (I respect the Negro kissing his fetish as much as [I respect] the Catholic kneeling before the Sacred Heart). Not only his correspondence and travel writings, but also texts such as "Un cœur simple" reflect his desire to repatriate to French culture the "primitive" fetish, the fetish as a hypocritical signifier of barbarous alterity. While Flaubert viewed the acceptance of religious dogma as a form of consensual enslavement, he greatly admired the fetishistic invention of religious mythology as a powerful example of the psychology of object relations: "Chaque dogme en particulier m'est répulsif, mais je considère le sentiment qui les a inventés comme le plus naturel et le plus poétique de l'humanité" (Each dogma in particular is repulsive to me, but I consider the feeling behind their invention to be the most natural and poetic of humanity) (Letter to Mme Leroyer de Chantepie, March 30, 1857). This insight leads him to expand the role of the fetish into many unfamiliar domains such as, in *Bouvard et Pécuchet*, the linguistic fetishism of what Bernheimer calls "codes of social discourse' " (162) (DJ)

References:

Barnes, Hazel E. *Sartre and Flaubert.* Chicago: University of Chicago Press, 1981.

Bernheimer, Charles. "Fetishism and Allegory in *Bouvard et Pécuchet.*" In Naomi Schor and Henry F. Majewski, eds., *Flaubert and Postmodernism.* Lincoln: University of Nebraska Press, 1984. 160–176.

Flaubert, Gustave. Letter to Mlle Leroyer de Chantepie, March 30, 1857. In Gustave Flaubert, *Correspondance, 1850–1859.* Paris: Club de l'Honnête Homme, 1974. 13:67.

Marx, Karl. "The Fetishism of Commodities and the Secret Thereof." In Karl Marx, *Capital: A Critique of Political Economy.* Trans. Samuel Moore and Edward Aveling. New York: International Publishers, 1967. Part 1, Chapter 1, Section 4: 76–87.

Porter, Laurence M. "Projection as Ego Defense in Flaubert's *Tentation de saint Antoine.*" In Laurence M. Porter, ed., *Critical Essays on Gustave Flaubert.* Boston Hall, 1986. 150–164.

Tanner, Tony. "Fetishism: Castles of Cake, Pellets from the Seraglio, and the Damascened Rifle." In Tony Tanner, *Adultery in the Novel: Contract and Transgression.* Baltimore: Johns Hopkins University Press, 1979. 284–91.

Feydeau, Ernest (1821–73). Ernest Feydeau became a friend of Flaubert shortly after *Madame Bovary*'s publication. Originally an archeologist who studied ancient funeral rites, he published the realist novel *Fanny* (1858), which also is a story of adultery, and cashed in on the notoriety of Flaubert's work. *Fanny* was considered scandalous, but was widely read. Feydeau's novel, in which the artistic and philosophical idealism of Flaubert's works is abandoned in favor of a more trivial realism, was the norm for most of the later productions of the naturalist and realist schools. Charles-Augustín Sainte-Beuve, the leading critic of nineteenth-century France, considered *Fanny* the best work of the realist school and praised it more highly than he did *Madame Bovary* itself (*Le Moniteur*, June 14, 1858). The later fictions of Feydeau offered only a prurient pornographic interest, but had a "succès de scandale."

Following in the wake of the painter and writer Eugène Fromentin, Feydeau later exploited interest in the newly pacified French colony of Algeria by writing two travel journals, *Alger* (1862) and *Souna* (1876). He also wrote essays and plays. He and Flaubert became estranged after five years. His son, Georges Feydeau, became a master of imbroglio comedy. (LCP/LMP)

Reference:

Martino, Pierre. *Le Roman réaliste sous le Second Empire*. Paris: Hachette, 1913. 180–204.

"La Fiancée et le tombeau: Conte fantastique." The short story "La Fiancée et le tombeau" from around 1835 was heavily indebted to stories like *Le Lycanthrope* by Pétrus Borel. It is a macabre tale in medieval dress of ideal love spoiled by the local duke's *droit de cuissage* (the right to deflower every virgin in his domain). It also depicts a moral reversal of fortune (compare "La Grande Dame et le joueur de vielle") whereby the vengeful lover will become cruel in death. The story includes the motif of necrophilia, which Flaubert pursues in *Une Nuit de Don Juan*, in the fairy-play projects of 1862–63, and (though subdued) in the Fontainebleau episode of *L'Education sentimentale*. (MCO)

Reference:

Flaubert, Gustave. "La Fiancée et le tombeau: Conte fantastique." In Maurice Bardèche, ed., *Œuvres complètes*. 16 vols. Paris: Club de l'Honnête Homme, 1971–76.

film adaptations of Flaubert's works. Flaubert's fiction has been a source of continual fascination for filmmakers. *La Tentation de saint Antoine* was the first of his works to be filmed, in 1898, by industry pioneer Georges Meliès. *Salammbô* also saw its first adaptation in the silent-film era. The 1924 French/Austrian production directed by Pierre Marodon and starring Jeanne de Balzac as Salammbô, Rolla Norman as Mâtho, and Victor Vina as Hamilcar was highly regarded. Sergio Grieco directed his version of the novel in an Italian/French production of 1959, but the results were disappointing.

There have been two film adaptations of *L'Education sentimentale*, the first in 1962 by the New Wave precursor Alexandre Astruc and the second a made-for-television movie directed by Marcel Cravenne in 1971 and rereleased in

1985. Astruc's adaptation, which features Jean-Claude Brialy as Frédéric Moreau and Marie-José Nat as Madame Arnoux, is entitled *Education sentimentale*, and the omission of the definite article defines this film, which is more "re-creation" than "adaptation." In contrast, Cravenne's television adaptation, which consist of five fifty-five minute episodes and stars Jean-Pierre Léaud as Frédéric and Françoise Fabian as Madame Arnoux, is more faithful to Flaubert's novel, although it too received mixed reviews. An Italian production of "Un cœur simple" ("Un cuore semplice") was released in 1977. Directed by Giorgio Ferrara and starring Adriana Asti as Félicité, this film has been judged too "academic," despite Asti's credible performance. Jean-Claude Carrière's 1989 adaptation of *Bouvard et Pécuchet* (directed by Jean-Daniel Verhaeghe) has also come under criticism, among other things, for its "finished" feel, which is considered antithetical to the spirit of Flaubert's quintessentially unfinished novel.

Madame Bovary has tempted by far the largest number of film directors, nine in all. The first adaptation of this novel was the 1932 Hollywood production entitled *Unholy Love*, directed by Albert Ray and starring Lila Lee as the daughter of a gardener who secretly marries her father's physician, is subsequently unfaithful to him, and ends up committing suicide. Ray sets the story in Rye, New York, and renames all of the characters. Jean Renoir's well-known adaptation was released in 1934. This version of *Madame Bovary* features Valentine Tessier, Pierre Renoir, and Max Dearly. It has not been considered among Renoir's most successful films. Some of its weaknesses can be blamed on Renoir's distributors, who forced him to cut his three-and-a-half-hour version to two hours. The year 1935 saw the release of a German *Madame Bovary*, directed by Gerhardt Lamprecht, with the famous actress of silent-screen fame Pola Negri as Emma. Although in her 1970 memoirs Negri claims that this film adaptation of the Flaubert classic is "considered by cinema buffs the best ever filmed," recent critics are inclined to regard it as merely competent. In 1949, a new adaptation of *Madame Bovary*, directed by Vincente Minnelli, was released in English. Starring Jennifer Jones, Van Heflin, and Louis Jourdan, Minnelli's film frames Emma's story with that of the novel's trial, casting James Mason in the role of Flaubert. In this adaptation, a lucid Charles decides not to perform the clubfoot operation.

Twenty years elapsed before the novel was again adapted to the screen. *Die nackte Bovary*, a German/Italian production (the Italian title is *I Peccati di Madame Bovary*, and the film title was translated into English as *Play the Game or Leave the Bed*), directed by Hans Schott-Schöbinger and featuring Edwige Fenech as Emma, was released in 1969. The most notable innovation of this adaptation was the director's decision to give Emma's story a happy ending. On the verge of committing suicide by leaping from a bridge, the heroine changes her mind and returns to her husband when she hears the sound of a child crying. In 1972, a more faithful but unspectacular television version of the novel was filmed. This *Madame Bovary*, directed by Georges Neveux and starring Nicole Courcel, was released on videotape in 1986 by Films for the Humanities. A

United Kingdom miniseries directed by Rodney Bennett and starring Francesca Annis appeared in 1975. Sixteen years later, in 1991, Claude Chabrol's *Madame Bovary* was released. Considered the most masterful of the adaptations, as well as one of the most faithful, this adaptation nevertheless has had its critics, many of whom have questioned the casting of Isabelle Huppert in the title role. (Chabrol himself, it is said, would have considered no one else for it.) The year 1994 saw the appearance of *Spasi i sohrani* (*Sauve et protège*), a Soviet production directed by Aleksandr Sokhurov and starring Cécile Zervoudaki as Emma. One of the most notable (and most criticized) features of this film was the director's decision to have Emma speak French, while the other characters express themselves in Russian. Of the cinematic adaptations of Flaubert's famous novel, the best known and most widely respected are those directed by Renoir, Minnelli, and Chabrol.

Adapting Flaubert's works to the screen is no easy task, despite the fact that in his penchant for "showing" rather than "telling" and in many of his novelistic techniques, Flaubert is considered precinematic. Not the least of the problems is rendering the polyvalence of Flaubert's tightly constructed works, where plot is ultimately of minor importance and language is paramount. Even *Madame Bovary*, which on its simplest level can be read as the unhappy tale of an adulterous woman, defies cinematic adaptation, owing in part to its shifting point of view and its subtle irony. Forced to condense and elide scenes and characters and to translate words into images, directors have repeatedly incurred the accusation of betraying the author—a common accusation against those who dare to tamper with such sacred texts of world literature as *Madame Bovary*. (MDE)

See also adaptations.

References:

Tibbetts, John, and James M. Welsh, eds. *The Encyclopedia of Novels into Film*. New York: Facts on File, 1998.

Tulard, Jean. *Guide des films*. Nouv. ed. 2 vols. Paris: Laffont, 1997.

Flaubert, Achille (brother of Gustave Flaubert, 1813–82). The firstborn child of Achille-Cléophas and Caroline Flaubert, Achille Flaubert was Gustave's elder by eight years. (Between 1813 and 1821, three other siblings were born, but they died in infancy.) The difference in their ages contributed to their living rather separate lives, for by the time Gustave was a young child, Achille was away at school; when Achille had finished his studies, Gustave was in school himself. In 1839, Achille married, which further removed him from Gustave's life.

The two brothers were of very different temperament. While Gustave was concocting adolescent theatrical productions with his sister Caroline, his older brother was winning awards in his studies, already showing the focus and determination of his father. Fulfilling family expectations, he followed in his father's footsteps and studied medicine, eventually working under his father's supervision at the Hôtel-Dieu (general hospital) of Rouen. Achille was with his brother on the day in January 1844 when Gustave had his first seizure (commonly thought to have been a form of epilepsy), collapsing suddenly in the carriage in which the two of them were traveling. Following traditional medical practices, Achille administered emergency treatment consisting of three bleedings in rapid succession. Gustave survived the treatment and remained under his father's and brother's care for months after their return to Rouen.

In January 1846, when Achille-Cléophas was suffering from an abscess in his thigh, it was his son he called on to operate. The situation had turned dire, and Achille amputated the leg, but to no avail: his father died on January 15. Just a few months later, partially as a result of his brother's lobbying, Achille was named to replace his father as the new chief surgeon of the Hôtel-Dieu, where he spent his career.

The brothers were not particularly close, and Gustave may well have felt some pangs of jealousy, for Achille alone had earned paternal approbation. Gustave found his brother's lifestyle rather too bourgeois, and they visited each other little. Achille sometimes served as a source of medical information—for example, concerning clubfeet (in *Madame Bovary*)—for Gustave's fictions. Flaubert also had occasion to consult Achille's medical library. Achille provided some financial support for his brother, and in 1879, when Gustave was in dire straits, Achille agreed to give him a pension of three thousands francs a year. Seriously ill during the last years of his life, Achille Flaubert died in January 1882. (SDC)

References:

Commanville, Caroline. *Souvenirs sur Flaubert.* Paris: Ferroud, 1895.

Flaubert, Gustave. *Correspondance.* Ed. Jean Bruneau. 4 vols. to date. Paris: Gallimard, 1973– .

Galérant, Germain. *Médecine de campagne: De la Révolution à la Belle Epoque.* Paris: Plon, 1988.

Lottman, Herbert R. *Flaubert: A Biography.* New York: Fromm, 1990.

Flaubert, Achille-Cléophas (father of Gustave Flaubert, 1784–1846). Born in Maizières-la-Grande-Paroisse (region of Champagne) in 1784, the son of a veterinarian, Achille-Cléophas Flaubert completed his secondary education at the Collège de Sens and then studied medicine in Paris. Though he was of modest background, he excelled in his studies, promising a brilliant career. While preparing his doctorate in 1806, he began work at the Hôtel-Dieu, the main hospital of Rouen, where he met Caroline Fleuriot, the ward of the chief surgeon, Jean-Baptiste Laumonier. She was nine years his junior and, unlike Achille-Cléophas, came from a family with some claim to distinction. In 1812, they married, Caroline bringing some property to the marriage as her dowry. After completing his medical degree, Dr. Flaubert moved into a permanent position at the Hôtel-Dieu and became chief surgeon when Laumonier retired in 1815. There he spent the remainder of his career. Living first in central Rouen, the couple moved to the official residence of the chief surgeon on the premises of the Hôtel-Dieu in 1818. They had six children, three of whom died in infancy. Those who survived were Achille (1813), Gustave (1821), and Caroline (1824).

Gustave's relationship with his father seems to have been distant. Achille-Cléophas was a man of science, blessed with great curiosity and energy. Clearly his career commanded more of his attention than did his family, and he dedicated much of his time to medical experimentation, often undertaking operations solely for their interest to science. It has been suggested that Dr. Larivière, the great surgeon who examines Emma toward the end of *Madame Bovary*, is modeled after Achille-Cléophas Flaubert, which hints at the respect Gustave had for his father: in Larivière one finds the portrait of a great man of science, but one who is devoid neither of emotion nor of compassion. On the other hand, at least one critic has pointed out that the pompous speeches of the *comices agricoles* scenes in *Madame Bovary* read much like a particular speech prepared by Achille-Cléophas. In any case, the elder Flaubert was a gifted surgeon, revered by the people of Rouen. He was not always an advocate of modern medical advances: he remained an ardent practitioner of bloodletting at a time when the popularity of this procedure was waning, and he scoffed at newfangled experiments with anesthesia.

Living at the Hôtel-Dieu provided Gustave with much direct exposure to human misery on a grand scale, but it also taught him a kind of precocious emotional distancing. He and his sister Caroline were surrounded by scenes of suffering and witnessed the sometimes-brutal methods employed by the medicine of the time. They used to spy into the operating room, becoming somewhat inured to the sight of blood. Gustave's powers of observation and his attention to detail also seem consistent with skills exemplified by his father. However, he worried about not meeting his father's high standards. His older brother Achille had gone into medicine, and there was family pressure for Gustave to do the same: literature did not strike Achille-Cléophas as a real profession. The compromise struck between science and letters was to be law, the study of which Gustave undertook in Paris. He had little heart for these studies, and he generally channeled his complaints to the family by way of Caroline; his father sometimes reproached him for not being more direct.

The onset of Gustave's nervous disorder (often referred to as epilepsy) in 1844 provided a good excuse for abandoning his stalled law studies and moving back to Rouen, at least temporarily, where his father was able to treat him and where Gustave could devote himself to his true interests. Then, late in 1845, Achille-Cléophas Flaubert developed an infection in his thigh. As the condition worsened, his son Achille, in a desperate attempt to save him, amputated the leg, but to no avail: on January 15, 1846, Achille-Cléophas Flaubert died. The death came as a severe blow to the family and the community. Fortunately for the Flaubert household, Achille-Cléophas had amassed a certain amount of wealth (mostly through the purchase of property), which was to provide for most of their needs, at least in the medium term. (SDC)

References:

Brombert, Victor H. *Flaubert par lui-même*. Paris: Seuil, 1971.
Commanville, Caroline. *Souvenirs sur Flaubert*. Paris: Ferroud, 1895.
Flaubert, Gustave. *Correspondance*. Ed. Jean Bruneau. 4 vols. to date. Paris: Gallimard, 1973– .
Galérant, Germain. *Médecine de campagne: De la Révolution à la Belle Epoque*. Paris: Plon, 1988.
Lottman, Herbert R. *Flaubert: A Biography*. New York: Fromm, 1990.

Flaubert, Caroline (née Fleuriot, mother of Gustave Flaubert, 1793–1872). Anne-Justine-Caroline Fleuriot, Gustave Flaubert's mother, was born in 1793 in the town of Pont-L'Evêque, in Lower Normandy. Family legend attributed a hue of nobility to the Fleuriot name, although the link was dubious at best. Flaubert's grandmother died in childbirth eight days after Caroline came into the world, and this was the beginning of a somewhat dislocated childhood. Her father, Jean-Baptiste, died when she was nine, after which young Caroline was entrusted to relatives. By 1806, she found herself living with her godmother, who was married to Jean-Baptiste Laumonier, the chief surgeon of the Hôtel-Dieu (main hospital) of Rouen. There she met Achille-Cléophas Flaubert, who was undertaking his medical internship and completing his degree. The two married in 1812 and had six children. After Achille (1813) came three children who died in infancy (a girl and two boys), then Gustave in 1821, and Caroline in 1824. The couple lived in central Rouen for a few years and moved into the official residence of the chief surgeon of the Hôtel-Dieu in 1818, some years after Achille-Cléophas's promotion to his post.

The Flaubert household was solidly bourgeois. Although Mme Flaubert governed the domestic sphere, she performed few domestic chores. The family had servants and governesses, and many parental duties were handled by Julie, the faithful servant who joined the Flaubert household when Gustave was only three and who was to care for him until his death. Mme Flaubert was of a fragile constitution, being afflicted with migraines and other indispositions, which further removed her from family interactions. (Ironically, she proved to be the longest lived of all the family, dying at seventy-eight.) She enjoyed country air, and the family made frequent excursions to their country homes, first in Déville and then, after 1844, in Croisset, which was to become their principal residence. Despite her physical frailty, she was strong-willed, as demonstrated by her decision at age fifty-two, after Caroline's death, to raise her granddaughter herself.

Gustave Flaubert had always been attached to his mother, but the death of his father and sister brought the two even closer. Gustave's reclusive lifestyle served both his own work habits and his mother's protective nature. She fretted whenever he left, and Gustave often felt a duty to stay close to home to watch over her. When he and Maxime Du Camp were about to leave for the "Orient" (the Middle East) in 1849, Gustave nearly abandoned the trip, so loath was he to leave his mother. During his travels, she was his most faithful correspondent.

Mme Flaubert could be affectionate (Maxime Du Camp was impressed by her demonstrations of maternal love after the onset of Gustave's epilepsy), but she was also somewhat controlling. Gustave was terrified that his mother would learn of his relationship with Louise Colet, and he flatly denied Colet's requests to visit him at Croisset. One time when she came anyway, he did not let her in. Mme Flaubert was not easily duped, however, and she let her son know that she disapproved of his clandestine relationship with Colet. In the financial realm, she astutely supervised Gustave's budget, and although she allowed him certain excesses, she did what she could to keep her son from exhausting their resources.

Mme Flaubert's health waxed and waned periodically. Early in April 1872, she began to decline rapidly, and she died on April 6. Gustave was devastated for some time, unsure how to continue without this companion of so many years. (SDC)

References:

Brombert, Victor H. *Flaubert par lui-même*. Paris: Seuil, 1971.
Commanville, Caroline. *Souvenirs sur Flaubert*. Paris: Ferroud, 1895.
Flaubert, Gustave. *Correspondance*. Ed. Jean Bruneau. 4 vols. to date. Paris: Gallimard, 1973– .
Lottman, Herbert R. *Flaubert: A Biography*. New York: Fromm, 1990.

Flaubert, Caroline (sister of Gustave Flaubert). *See* Hamard, Caroline.

focalization (focus; establishing point of view in fiction). The French term *focalisation*, coined by Gérard Genette in his writings on narratology (or narrative analysis), replaces the older concept of *point of view*, which was both vague and confusing because it created an ambiguity between *mode* (the *perception*—even more than the vision—that governs the narrative perspective) and *voice* (i.e., that of the narrator). Genette establishes a distinction between *zero focalization* (no perception regulates the perspective, and representation rests on the narrator's knowledge, as is the case with omniscient narrators), *internal focalization* (representation is filtered by the perception of at least one character, and the narrator's knowledge is limited to that of the character in question), and *external focalization* (representation is filtered by a perception that remains indeterminate, and the narrator knows less than the characters; this last type seldom appears in nineteenth-century narratives).

The concept of focalization is essential for analyzing Flaubert's modes of representation and description; he employs this literary technique subtly and with great variety. Some passages are in external focalization. They are usually short, for instance, when a new and anonymous character appears, such as Frédéric in the first page of *L'Education sentimentale*. External focalization, however, can also occur in longer scenes, such as the coach scene in *Madame Bovary*, where the focus of vision is placed *outside* the coach. Many other passages are written in zero focalization (for instance, the description of Yonville at the beginning of the second part of *Madame Bovary*). However, Flaubert mainly uses internal focalization. It is defined as *variable*: the focus of perception is not always related to a single character, although most of the time it is centered on the protagonist. This technique greatly affects representation, as is shown by Flaubert's descriptions, in which what is represented changes constantly according to the state of mind and perception of the contemplating character. For example, Paris in *L'Education sentimentale* appears ugly or beautiful depending on Frédéric's moods. (ELC)

References:

Genette, Gérard. *Figures III*. Paris: Seuil, 1972. Trans. in part by Jane E. Lewin, as *Narrative Discourse, an Essay in Method*. Ithaca: Cornell University Press, 1980.

———. *Narrative Discourse Revisited*. Trans. Jane E. Lewin. Ithaca: Cornell University Press, 1988.

Fontainebleau, Forest of (*ES*). To prepare the magnificent landscape description and novelistic tableau in *L'Education sentimentale*. Flaubert twice visited the beautiful forest surrounding the palace of Fontainebleau outside Paris. In the novel, Frédéric Moreau, the antihero, takes his new mistress, the kept woman Rosanette Bron, there. Despite the idyllic surroundings, the scene, characteristically for Flaubert, is built around ironic contrasts. Frédéric is deeply moved by the place: Rosanette is insensitive and indifferent. In the palace, she unwittingly displays her ignorance and lack of culture. But the lovers feel closer to each other as they ride through the forest, although this emotional intimacy leads Rosanette to confide the sordid story of her loss of virginity when her mother sold her to an older man. The lovers willfully turn their attention away from the revolution of 1848, which is reaching a climax back in Paris. Indeed, for them to visit a former French royal residence represents in itself a symbolic retreat from present political realities. Their idyll, however, is interrupted when Frédéric reads in a newspaper that his friend Deslauriers had been wounded. He hastily returns to Paris, but for nothing. This motif of a homosocial bond taking precedence over a heterosexual, erotic one anticipates the anticlimactic conclusion of the novel. (LMP)

References:

Le Calvez, Eric. "Notes de repérage et descriptions dans *L'Education sentimentale* (II). Genèse de la forêt de Fontainebleau." *Neuphilologische Mitteilungen* 95.3 (1994): 363–83.

———. "Visite guideé (genèse du château de Fontainebleau dans *L'Education sentimentale*)." *Genesis* 5 (1994): 99–116.

Paulson, William. Sentimental Education: *The Complexity of Disenchantment*. New York: Twayne, 1992. 76–77, 120–24.

food. "On mange beaucoup dans les romans de Flaubert" (People eat a great deal in Flaubert's novels) is the famous opening sentence of Jean-Pierre Richard's phenomenological essay. (Phenomenology, a philosophical approach inaugurated by the German philosopher Edmund Husserl [1859–1938] in 1905, studies inner, subjective impressions of the external, objective world.) The banquet scenes in "Les Funérailles du docteur Mathurin," *Madame Bovary* (the wedding feast), and *Salammbô* immediately come to mind. (Saint Antoine's temptation by Gluttony is a purely internal event.) So do the lavish restaurant meals Flaubert had weekly with his friends in the late 1870s. The three fictional treatments of food just mentioned serve various purposes. Dr. Mathurin's last dinner re-creates the classic *cena* (banquet) scene exemplified by Socrates' gatherings with his friends, Christ's Last Supper, or François Rabelais's descriptions of feasts, during all of which the guests are nourished with wisdom as well as food. Emma Bovary's wedding feast serves the purposes of social satire: the rustics try in vain to act dignified, and the celebration degenerates into resentments. The barbarian mercenaries' orgy simultaneously provides an exotic spectacle and introduces the main political conflict that will move the plot: these soldiers have not received their pay. But all these scenes, for which Honoré de Balzac's orgy in *La Peau de chagrin* (1831) serves as a model, represent an extreme form of literary realism: not only does the implied author lovingly describe the material world as if it were a coveted treasure hoard, but also, through the mediation of his fictional characters, he literally ingests it. This marriage of description and ingestion will reach a climax in Joris-Karl Huysmans's "Bible of decadence," *A rebours* (1884). In its extreme, paroxysmal form, description and digestion become one when the object of description is literally liquefied (Emma Bovary after her death, the horde of monsters that swirl around Saint Antoine, the leprous Hannon in *Salammbô*, the fertilizer indiscriminately heaped up by Bouvard in *Bouvard et Pécuchet*). The excess of the verbal creation of form slides into formlessness. (LMP)

Reference:

Richard, Jean-Pierre. "La Création de la forme chez Flaubert." In Jean-Pierre Richard, *Littérature et sensation*. Paris: Seuil, 1954. 117–219. Abridged translation in Raymond Giraud, ed., *Flaubert: A Collection of Critical Essays*. Englewood Cliffs, NJ: Prentice-Hall, 1964. 36–56.

Ford, Ford Madox (1873–1939). Ford Madox Ford said "it is perhaps only Flaubert who ever paid sufficient attention . . . to the French language to reach its thorough understanding" (*Reader* 181). Ford particularly admired Flaubert as a historian; he called *L'Education sentimentale* the greatest novel of all time, in part for its prescient description of a France drifting toward the Franco-

Prussian War (1870). His novel *The Fifth Queen* (1906), concerning the Tudor period under Cromwell, suggests Flaubert's *L'Education sentimentale* and, more remotely, *Salammbô*.

The eponymous Jewish hero of *Mr. Fleight* (1913) is compared by allusion to Flaubert's Saint Julien, but is "a modern saint" whose life has little romance and much pathos. He is an idealist who achieves an ironic, hollow triumph by marrying a gorgeous woman who hates him and by being elected to the House of Commons (Meixner).

Frédéric Moreau's detached stance as a central observer of major historical events inspired the treatment of the viewpoint of Christopher Tietjens during World War I, particularly in the battle scenes of *No More Parades* (1925). The friendship that develops between him and Macmaster during the initial train ride in *Some Do Not . . . (serve, but only stand and wait*; 1924) recalls the bond between Moreau and Deslauriers in *L'Education sentimentale*. (LMP)

References:

Ferguson, Suzanne. "The Face in the Mirror: Authorial Presence in the Multiple Vision of Third-Person Impressionist Narrative." *Criticism* 21 (1979): 230–50.

Ford, Ford Madox. *The Ford Madox Ford Reader*. Ed. Sondra J. Stang. Manchester, UK: Carcanet, 1986. Contains Ford's review of "Un cœur simple" from the *Outlook*, June 5, 1915.

Huntley, H. Robert. "Flaubert and Ford: The Fallacy of 'Le Mot Juste.' " *English Language Notes* 4 (1967): 283–87.

Meixner, John A. *Ford Madox Ford's Novels: A Critical Study*. Minneapolis: University of Minnesota Press, 1962.

Wiley, Paul L. *Novelist of Three Worlds: Ford Madox Ford*. Syracuse: Syracuse University Press, 1962.

Foucaud, Eulalie (1805–?). Eulalie Foucaud was a Creole woman who initiated Flaubert sexually in 1840, coming to his hotel room at night after he had smiled at her. Flaubert, who had just passed his *baccalauréat*, met the thirty-five-year-old woman in Marseilles at the beginning of a family trip to Corsica, on his first trip abroad. They exchanged letters for six months. Some aspects of his novel *Novembre*, published two years after his affair, could be seen as autobiographical and based on this relationship. Thereafter, Flaubert always associated Marseilles with the image of Eulalie Foucaud. He went on a sentimental pilgrimage to the rue de la Darse, where she had lived, when he and his family passed through Marseilles again in 1845, but she had departed without a trace. When Flaubert visited the rue de la Darse again in 1858, on his way to North Africa, Eulalie's room had been changed into a barber shop. (LCP/LMP)

Reference:

Bart, Benjamin F. *Flaubert*. Syracuse: Syracuse University Press, 1967.

France, Anatole (pseud. of Jacques-Anatole-François Thibault, 1844–1924). Anatole France was a fluent, witty literary critic and productive novelist whose last six major works are satires in the spirit of Flaubert, albeit without the older author's dense erudition and somber pessimism. The first of these form a tetralogy, *Histoire contemporaine*, satirizing French politics: *L'Orme du mail* (1897), *Le Mannequin d'osier* (1897), *L'Anneau d'améthyste* (1899), and *Monsieur Bergeret à Paris* (1901). France generalizes his disenchantment with the myth of continual human progress in the fantasy *L'Ile des pingouins* (1908) and gently ridicules Christian dogma in *La Révolte des anges* (1914). His novel *Thaïs* (1890), about a courtesan who achieves sainthood, is written in the spirit if not the manner of Flaubert's exotic *Salammbô* and more so in that of Flaubert's stories of the struggle for salvation in *La Tentation de saint Antoine* and in the *Trois Contes*.

France became acquainted with Flaubert in the late 1870s in Paris and found him rather stupid (Bart 631), as a scholar without social skills can be. France also judged that Flaubert's Saint Antoine was far more learned in ancient heresies than he could plausibly have been in his time. But at length, bemused and resigned, France was won over by Flaubert's enthusiasm; he summed up thus: "He had a prodigious capacity for enthusiasm and sympathy. That is why he was always furious. He used to battle on the slightest pretext, always having some offence to avenge. He was very like Don Quixote, whom he admired so much. . . . They were two good brave hearts. Both carried on a dream of life, with heroic pride, which it was easier to make fun of than to equal. I had scarcely been five minutes with Flaubert, than the little drawing-room, hung with oriental rugs, was dripping with the blood of twenty thousand slaughtered bourgeois!" (France, *La Vie littéraire* 2:19). (LMP)

References:

Bart, Benjamin F. *Flaubert*. Syracuse; Syracuse University Press, 1967.

France, Anatole. *Thaïs*. Paris: Calmann-Lévy, [1906].

———. *Thaïs*. Trans. Basia Gulati. Chicago: University of Chicago Press, 1976.

———. *La Vie Littéraire*. 4 vols. Paris: Calmann-Lévy, 1889–92.

Malinowski, Wieslaw. "Hérodias de Flaubert et Thaïs de France: Quelques affinities artistiques et intellectuelles." *Studia romanica posnaniensia* 7 (1981): 29–38.

Seznec, Jean. "Flaubert, historien des hérésies dans *La Tentation de saint Antoine*." *Romanic Review* 36 (1945): 200–221, 314–28.

Starkie, Enid. *Flaubert, the Master*. New York: Atheneum, 1971.

Franco-Prussian War (1870–71). In 1870, Spain, in search of a king, had come upon Leopold of Hohenzollern-Sigmaringen, a member of Prussia's ruling family. Concerned that Prussia was attempting to extend its power, France demanded that he immediately step down from the Spanish throne. He did so, but the French Assembly further demanded that King William of Prussia promise that there would be no similar actions on the part of the Prussians. King William refused, and on July 19, 1870, France declared war. France was in fact ill prepared for war, and it appears that the French declaration of war was the result of skillful political maneuvering on the part of the Prussian general Bismarck more than anything else. With France cast in the role of aggressor and with numerous political intrigues in play (e.g., Prussia's warning to Austria that supporting France would have serious consequences), France found no allies; the majority of European nations declared neutrality on the question of French and Prussian hostilities.

The superior army of Prussia had little trouble with the French. The situation was bleak, and Napoleon III went to join his troops in defending France. On September 2, 1870, he was captured at Sedan. A hastily formed provisional government immediately sought peace, but the Prussians pressed on, surrounding Paris and capturing Achille Bazaine's troops at Metz before moving into the heart of France.

The radical left-wing politician Léon Gambetta organized a prowar Government of National Defense within Paris, taking the role of Minister of the Interior. After a daring balloon escape from the besieged city, Gambetta traveled across the country seeking to form an army to counterattack, but had little success. Despite his impassioned objections, with Paris finally captured, an armistice was signed on January 28, 1871.

The French were allowed to elect the government that would negotiate the terms of their surrender. These were the loss of Alsace and part of Lorraine. An occupation army was to remain in Paris until a five-billion-franc indemnity had been paid.

From the first, Flaubert was troubled by the prospect of war and saw his country falling into a trap. The invasion of his home at Croisset by fleeing relatives only further irritated him. Often despondent during this period, Flaubert did at one point find enough hope for France's chances to accept a post as a lieutenant in the National Guard at Croisset. When the Prussians arrived, however, all the units in the area surrendered. Flaubert's house was taken over by Prussian troops, and he joined his mother in Rouen after making provisions for the protection of his most precious papers, including a manuscript of *La Tentataion de saint Antoine*. As the war drew to a close, Flaubert's disgust with his countrymen turned to patriotic fervor, and he became fiercely opposed to the surrender of Paris. His dismay at Paris's fate would only grow with the announcement of the Commune. (GB)

References:

Bart, Benjamin F. *Flaubert*. Syracuse: Syracuse University Press, 1967.
Wright, Gordon. *France in Modern Times, from the Enlightenment to the Present*. 2nd ed. Chicago: Rand McNally, 1974.

free indirect style (FIS, *style indirect libre*, represented discourse, *erlebte Rede*). Free indirect style is a form of indirect discourse in which the reported speech is "freed" from the introductory verb of affirmation or questioning (*verbum dicendi*) and its accompanying conjunction (*que* or *si*). The following example shows both standard and free indirect discourse side by side: "M. Bovary, peu soucieux des lettres, disait que ce n'était pas la peine! Auraient-ils jamais de quoi l'entretenir dans les écoles du gouvernement?" (Mr. Bovary, who didn't care much for the humanities, said that it wasn't worth the trouble. Would they ever have the means to send him to a government school?) The second sentence continues Bovary's comments and must not be confused with the narrator's voice, even though there is no overt sign of indirect discourse. FIS is thus related to the important question of point of view. The naïve reader readily attributes to the author statements or opinions that in fact belong to one of the characters. Such a confusion seems to have occurred during the government's trial of Flaubert and the publisher of the *Revue de Paris* when the prosecutor criticized the following sentence in *Madame Bovary*: "Il [le duc de Laverdière] avait vécu à la Cour et couché dans le lit des reines!" (He had lived at Court and slept in the bed of queens!). This sentence obviously reproduces Emma's impressions and perhaps summarizes gossip that she had heard at the dinner table. The clues to this interpretation are contained in the context and in the use of the exclamation point. Other clues to FIS are the presence of familiar or popular language, since Flaubert's narrative voice in fictional works (as opposed to his letters) avoids them. Flaubert also occasionally uses italics to distance himself from the speech of a character: "M. Lheureux se mit, en termes assez nets, à féliciter Emma sur la succession, puis à causer de choses indifférentes, des espaliers, de la récolte et de sa santé à lui, qui allait toujours *couci-couci, entre le zist et le zest*" (M. Lheureux began, in frank terms, to congratulate Emma on her inheritance, then talked about indifferent things, espaliers, the harvest, his health, which was still "so-so" as usual).

FIS can represent a character's thoughts or unformulated feelings as well as speech. Several examples appear in the scene at the opera, for example, "Mais une folie la saisit: il la regardait, c'est sûr!" (But she was mad: he was watching her, for sure!). This example shows Flaubert's versatility; the first verb "saisit," in the *passé défini*, is part of the narration. The second verb "regardait," in the imperfect, is an example of FIS. The third verb "est" is in the present tense and does not conform to the tense transposition characteristic of FIS. L. C. Harmer has dubbed this *style direct libre* (which also can be found in dialogues where the speakers are not identified). Here it seems intended to indicate the vividness of Emma's hallucination.

Although examples of FIS can be found long before 1850 (e.g., in the medieval *Cantilène de sainte Eulalie* or in the eighteenth-century novels of Pierre Carlet de Chamblain de Marivaux), they are rare. Flaubert sensed in the device a useful tool for writing narrative prose. FIS adds variety to passages containing dialogue (Flaubert disliked long strings of direct quotations, as well as the cacophony introduced by the subordinating conjunction *que*) and allows the writer much flexibility in suggesting the speech and thoughts of characters. The danger of the device lies in the possible ambiguity concerning whether a feeling or opinion belongs to a character or to the narrator. Flaubert was careful in his practice; Zola much less so. After Flaubert, FIS became a standard tool of French prose writers. Elsewhere in Europe, unknown to him, he had been anticipated by Jane Austen and by Johann Wolfgang von Goethe, who both experimented with FIS frequently. (EFG)

See also focalization.

References:

Bally, Charles. "Le Style indirect libre en français moderne." *Germanisch-Romanische Monatsschrift* 4 (1912): 549–56, 597–606.

Ginsburg, Michal Peled. *Flaubert Writing: A Study in Narrative Strategies.* Stanford: Stanford University Press, 1986.

Harmer, Lewis Charles. *Uncertainties in French Grammar.* Cambridge: Cambridge University Press, 1979.

Ramazani, Vaheed. *The Free Indirect Mode.* Charlottesville: University Press of Virginia, 1988.

Strauch, Gérard. "De quelques interprétations récentes du style indirect libre." *Recherches anglaises et américaines* 7 (1974): 40–73.

Ullmann, Stephen. "Reported Speech and Internal Monologue in Flaubert." In Stephen Ullmann, *Style in the French Novel.* New York: Barnes & Noble, 1964. 94–120.

"Les Funérailles du docteur Mathurin" (1839). While Flaubert was still in school, he wrote "Les Funérailles du docteur Mathurin," an effervescent tale of a wise old doctor who knows that he must soon die. He decides to spend his last hours enjoying skeptical philosophical discussions and drinking good wine with his friends. Flaubert was first in his class in philosophy, and this story seems inspired by the *cena* (banquet) scene in Plato's *Symposium* and by Socrates' death scene in Plato's *Phaedo.* The motif of exiting on one's own terms anticipates Flaubert's expulsion from school a few months later, when he refused to copy a thousand lines of poetry in punishment for disrupting the class, and organized most of his classmates to sign a petition in protest. He wrote no more short stories until the *Trois Contes* appeared in the 1870s. (LMP)

Reference:

Flaubert, Gustave. "Les Funérailles du Docteur Mathurin." In Maurice Nadeau, ed., *Gustave Flaubert, Œuvres.* 18 vols. Lausanne: Editions Rencontre, 1: 357–78.

funeral (1880). Flaubert died peacefully, probably from a brain hemorrhage caused by his tertiary syphilis, shortly after noon on Saturday, May 8, 1880. Guy de Maupassant kept vigil over the body for three days and readied it for burial. José-Marie de Hérédia, Edmond de Goncourt, Emile Zola, and Alphonse Daudet also attended the burial, which is described at length in Goncourt's *Journal.* Flaubert's niece Caroline promptly sold Flaubert's beloved home, Croisset. The house was razed, and a distillery was built on the site.

Flaubert's nephew-in-law Ernest Commanville, for whom Flaubert had sacrificed his fortune to prevent bankruptcy, behaved ignobly, playing and cheating at cards during the wake and speculating how much money he could make from the sale of his uncle's works and his unpublished love letters (Bart 742–44). (LMP)

References:

Bart, Benjamin F. *Flaubert*. Syracuse: Syracuse University Press, 1967.

Goncourt, Edmond and Jules de. *Journal: Mémoires de la vie littéraire*. 22 vols. Monaco: Imprimerie nationale, 1956–58. [9 vols. Paris: Charpentier, 1891–98]. See Index in vol. 22.

G

Gabrielle. *See* Augier, Emile.

Gallant, Mavis (1922–). Several of Mavis Gallant's short stories have themes and plot lines similar to *Madame Bovary* (1857) and *L'Education sentimentale* (1869). Her most obvious homage to Flaubert is in *Green Water, Green Sky* (1959), in which a woman assumes that her marriage will change her life for the better. There is also a scene involving a clubfoot, reminiscent of *Madame Bovary*, although Gallant changes its significance and purpose in the story. Winfried Siemerling calls her use of this scene "a wink to an interpretive community," mostly lost on the readers of her English-language novels (138). (SM)

Reference:

Siemerling, Winfried. "Perception, Memory, Irony: Mavis Gallant Greets Proust and Flaubert." *Essays on Canadian Writing* 42 (1990): 131–53.

le Garçon. An imaginary character of Flaubert's childhood, le Garçon represented the young Gustave's dislike of bourgeois tastes and habits. Although the character never appears in Flaubert's novels, many of le Garçon's attributes—predictable movements, thoughts, gestures, and responses—are manifest in those of Flaubert's other characters (e.g., Homais) that satirize bourgeois dullness and complacency. The Garçon character evolved as did some of Flaubert's major characters (e.g., Emma Bovary, Bouvard, and Pécuchet). Beginning as the target of harsh satire, le Garçon eventually became endearing, thus simultaneously representing the bourgeois stupidity that Flaubert detested and its opposite, a carnivalesque release from convention.

The most notorious literary descendant of le Garçon, made coarse, repellent, and tyrannical, is the Ubu of Alfred Jarry (1873–1907). Like Flaubert, Jarry had invented this gross character during his schooldays, dramatizing him in puppet shows. In adulthood, Jarry wrote a cycle of Ubu plays: *Ubu roi* (1896), *Ubu cocu* (1897), *Ubu enchaîné* (1900), and *Ubu sur la Butte* (1901). Jarry seemed to become contaminated by his creation, which he increasingly resembled up until his premature death. (LK/LMP)

References:

Arnaud, Noël. *Alfred Jarry, d'Ubu roi au Docteur Faustroll.* Paris: La Table Ronde, 1974.

Shattuck, Roger. *The Banquet Years.* New York: Random House, 1955. 187–254.

Gautier, Théophile (1811–72). Writer and journalist Théophile Gautier was notorious for helping to lead the cabal that defended Victor Hugo's revolutionary *Hernani* when it was first performed in the theater (1830). It was in the 1830s that Gautier wrote *Albertus* (1832) and *Les Jeunes-France* (1833), inscribing himself in a vivacious current of fantasy writers. He became prominent in 1831 with his first fantasy tale, *La Cafetière*, published the same year as Charles Nodier's essay *Du fantastique en littérature.* Though Gautier's works dramatize fragmentation, discontinuity, and evil, the latter is always destabilized and distanced by a benevolent presence. In all his fantasy works, inanimate objects come to life, and *Spirite* (1865), which inspired the conclusion of Victor Hugo's idealistic *L'Homme qui rit* (1869), crystallizes his ideal of an afterlife.

Gautier's school of art for art's sake strongly influenced the young Flaubert, who proclaims his adherence in the first line of *Mémoires d'un fou* (1838). The doctrine of a self-sufficing art resonated strongly with Flaubert, whose strong vocation for writing made him sense that he could not be useful to society as either a doctor or a lawyer. *Novembre* echoes the rebellious sensuousness of Gautier's *Mademoiselle de Maupin*, an unabashed bisexual (Bart 72). In the first, unpublished version of *L'Education sentimentale* (1845), Flaubert experimented with Gautier's device of writing some fictional passages in unattributed dialogue (*style direct libre*; Bart 108). Gautier's death devastated him. (APZ/LMP)

References:

Bart, Benjamin F. *Flaubert.* Syracuse: Syracuse University Press, 1967.

Castex, Pierre. *Le Conte Fantastique en France de Nodier à Maupassant.* Paris: Corti, 1951.

Chambers, Ross. Spirite *de Théophile Gautier: Une lecture.* Paris: Lettres Modernes, 1974.

Henry, Freeman G. "Gautier, Baudelaire: Homo ludens versus homo duplex." *Nineteenth-Century French Studies* 25:1–2 (1996–97): 60–77.

Lefebvre, Anne-Marie. "Théophile Gautier et les spirites et illuminés de son temps." *Bulletin de la société Théophile Gautier* 15 (1993): 291–322.

Ubersfeld, Anne. *Théophile Gautier.* Paris: Stock, 1992.

Whyte, Peter. *Théophile Gautier, conteur fantastique et merveilleux.* Durham: University of Durham, 1996.

gender. *See* feminist and gender studies.

genetic criticism. Genetic criticism (also called "textual genetics"), an approach that emphasized the elaboration of a literary work through its successive drafts and revisions, was born in France during the 1970s. From an epistemological standpoint, this period represented a context that was important historically and ideologically. The critical impetus was provided when the economic recovery of the postwar era coincided with the sudden release of a flood of manuscripts by Heinrich Heine (1797–1856). The German Jewish poet—liberal, admirer of Napoleon, satirist of Prussia, and expatriate (he had lived in Paris since 1831)—was the greatest German writer between Goethe and Thomas Mann, and a thorn in the Nazis' side. Even they had to allow some of his greatest lyrics to remain, attributed to anonymous authors, in anthologies of German literature. As soon as the Germans occupied Paris, Hitler ordered Heine's grave in the Montmartre cemetery to be destroyed. For the French, preserving and cherishing Heine's literary legacy was a sweet revenge.

First, all of Heinrich Heine's suddenly available but fragile manuscripts had to be treated. This situation led to the elaboration of a politics of preservation and utilization of manuscripts, especially since many writers, particularly from the nineteenth century, had decided to save their rough drafts (Victor Hugo is probably the best example of this, for he had specified in his will to donate all of his personal papers to the Bibliothèque nationale), and also since libraries were becoming more and more willing to purchase genetic dossiers. Therefore, the Centre National de la Recherche Scientifique (CNRS) agreed to create a specific research laboratory, which later became the Institut des Textes et Manuscrits Modernes (ITEM). Those premises then necessitated the elaboration of a precise methodology. Even if it is true that genetic criticism grounded itself on traditional philology, it did so by radically distinguishing itself from this traditional discipline. Contrary to a widespread, superficial view of genetic criticism, its principal aim was no longer to obtain "critical editions" or to produce a mere "criticism of sources" in order to elaborate "definitive" texts that alone were considered pertinent. Instead, although it inherited its analytical methods from structuralism, genetic criticism nonetheless resolutely professed opposition to certain structuralist principles such as the closure of the work in the form of a sacrosanct text while it continued structuralism's reflections on textuality. Genetic criticism was therefore established as a part of an epistemological context that corresponds perfectly to modern issues and to questions that are inherent in this modernity: to share, understand, and define the secrets of creation.

Since manuscripts conceal under innumerable deletions the trace of their genesis, of a dynamism that is precisely that of their creation, these documents have to be explored within a methodological framework that can be defined as retracing and explaining the genesis of a creation. In practice, genetic criticism is extremely complex, notably because of the number of drafts that need to be classified, deciphered, and transcribed, and also because of constant interactions between the diachronic and synchronic dimensions that appear merged in the drafts for anyone who contemplates them a posteriori. This also requires making available and legible documents that are no longer viewed as texts but rather as *avant-textes* (an important concept coined by geneticians during the 1970s), which imperative explains the growing importance of genetic editions. However, although genetic criticism is linked with editing the manuscripts or the unpublished works of a writer (which is obvious for Flaubert, because many genetic editions of his manuscripts have been published during the past twenty years), its contribution to literary studies is more precisely based on theoretical ambitions, which complicate the interpretive approach and process.

Despite many technical difficulties involving, in particular, the constant interaction of theory and practice, it is evident that the study of literary drafts helps bypass the mere consideration and interpretation of a finished, published text. Drafts show, above all, how the text is formed and transformed along with multiple corrections and rewritings. The interpretive phase is therefore complex in itself, for *avant-textes* differ from texts and have to be interpreted independently. Deletions, transformations, and additions are not mere "variants" that separate a rough and draft product from a finished and polished product. Between these two points, another dimension appears, a dimension that is completely heterogeneous, in which transformations and dynamism, as well as the dynamism of these transformations, are oriented and merged—often arbitrarily—with the formation of the work. Genetic criticism has therefore defined its methods and ambitions; they are, above all, theoretical. However, it does not—and should not—offer an autonomous theoretical model. Indeed, genetic criticism is not *in itself* a theory. It should not be confused with hermeneutics, because it does not help the critic to interpret the text. What is most relevant is not *why*, but *how* the text is produced as it is, an important principle that must always be remembered in dealing with manuscripts. With this principle in mind, one of the most productive attitudes for genetic criticism has been to postulate that *avant-textes* are *texts*, even if these texts of a new type are still being formed and do not match the same criteria of textuality as the "definitive" texts. The reflection must be focused on textuality, on the writing processes rather than on the text itself. Therefore, making *avant-textes* talk, to understand how they function synchronically and diachronically, consists of applying analytical grids that must remain flexible and depend on a critical choice, a choice that the genetician makes freely and that does not stem from the object of the study per se. That is to say that the genetician needs to apply an immense theoretical background and to question the drafts in relation to the issues raised by textual production, as viewed by narratology, semiotics, linguistics, stylistics, psychoanalysis, and so on. Genetic criticism therefore requires a deep knowledge of literary theory and an enormous amount of patience and passion for research.

A genetic perspective should therefore be defined as using a tool that leads to a theory of text production when it is connected to textual issues. In addition, since the genetic investigation is first a methodology, it is not limited to literary manuscripts. It can be applied to musical, architectural, and even scientific manuscripts and to other types of rough materials (such as former versions of paintings or statues), that is, to any domain where human thought and creativity are at stake. More widely and ambitiously, it is possible to conceive of this approach as a medium for the construction of a general theory of aesthetic creation. However, one must admit that genetic criticism is complex, time-consuming, and at times frustrating and that it therefore unfortunately remains the field of only a group of privileged specialists.

Because Flaubert carefully saved all of his manuscripts, genetic critics consider him an excellent author to investigate. Moreover, the very nature of his work matches the genetic approach particularly well. Flaubert was always extremely interested in the issues raised by creation, poetics, and aesthetics (as is shown throughout his correspondence), and his obsession in reaching the Beauty of Art and the stylistic perfection of the work forced him to correct numerous pages of drafts that illustrate and retrace the history of their painful genesis; indeed, it is not rare that ten pages of rough drafts (sometimes even more) were necessary for him to obtain one definitive page. The Bibliothèque Nationale's acquisition of most of Flaubert's manuscripts in the 1970s incited Raymonde Debray-Genette in 1977 to found a research team (now a part of the ITEM) whose ambition is to focus on the issues related to Flaubertian creation, based on the edition and interpretation of his manuscripts. Thanks to this program, the research team on Flaubert became the source of an inestimable renewal in Flaubertian as well as theoretical studies, producing numerous genetic publications, research seminars, and even, at present, university courses. Moreover, the expansion of genetic studies has widened during the past decade and has overflowed the limits of France: many scholars throughout the world collaborate in the program. (ELC)

References:

Debray-Genette, Raymonde. *Métamorphoses du récit: Autour de Flaubert.* Paris: Seuil, 1988.

Grésillon, Almuth. *Eléments de critique génétique: Lire les manuscrits modernes.* Paris: Presses Universitaires de France, 1994.

Le Calvez, Eric. *Flaubert topographe*: L'Education sentimentale: *Essai de poétique génétique.* Amsterdam: Rodopi, 1997.

genetic editions. The growing importance of genetic criticism incites specialists to publish genetic editions revealing the manuscript corpus of the genesis of a work. Many excerpts from Flaubert's manuscripts (*avant-textes*) have already appeared in articles or books. However, in order to provide readers with the tools that are essential to understanding the writer's work as a whole, the genetic dossiers must be published in their entirety. Editing Flaubert's drafts is extremely complex because of the very nature of his manuscripts. The principal problem stems from the quantity of drafts: to every definitive page correspond at least ten manuscript pages. First, they have to be classified following the chronological order of their elaboration (a complicated task, for Flaubert does not write one page after another, but rather works on several pages at once—for instance, to develop a scene or an episode). Then they have to be deciphered, which is also problematic because of numerous deletions. Finally, they must be precisely transcribed. Whereas the transcriptions of Flaubert's *avant-textes* in the past have often followed *linear* or *semidiplomatic* codes, it is now obvious that genetic transcriptions must be *diplomatic*, that is, they must remain faithful to the original layout of the draft page (additions and deletions appear as they are, in the space between the lines as well as in the margins). They are therefore difficult to edit, even if this has been simplified by the flexibility of word processors. These diverse problems explain why the editions of Flaubert's manuscripts remain unfortunately scarce and expensive, although this situation will improve with the increasing use of the CD-ROM. (ELC)

References:

Diplomatic transcriptions:

Flaubert, Gustave. *Les Comices agricoles de* Madame Bovary *de Flaubert.* Ed. Jeanne Goldin. 2 vols. Geneva: Droz, 1984.

———. *Plans et scénarios de* Madame Bovary. Ed. Yvan Leclerc. Paris: Centre Nationale de la Recherche Scientifique-Zulma, 1995.

Semidiplomatic transcriptions:

Flaubert, Gustave. *Corpus Flaubertianum.* Vol. 1, *Un cœur simple.* Ed. Giovanni Bonaccorso. Paris: Belles Lettres, 1983.

———. *Corpus Flaubertianum.* Vol. 2, *Hérodias.* Ed. Giovanni Bonaccorso. Vol. 1. Paris: Nizet, 1991. Vol. 2. Paris: Sicania: 1995.

———. *Corpus Flaubertianum.* Vol. 3, *La Légende de saint Julien l'hospitalier.* Ed. Giovanni Bonaccorso. Paris: Didier Erudition, 1998.

Genettes, Edma Roger des (1818–91). Flaubert first met Edma Roger des Genettes in Louise Colet's salon. To please Flaubert, she had arranged an evening in honor of Louis Bouilhet at which she read aloud from Bouilhet's *Melaenis.* She at length had a passionate affair with Bouilhet. Flaubert became her intellectual mentor. They enjoyed a chaste, unruffled, and intimate friendship that lasted from 1852 until Flaubert's death in 1880. He read "La Légende de saint Julien l'hospitalier" out loud to her, and she greatly admired it. Most of their relationship was epistolary, but Flaubert's many letters to her are noteworthy for their thoughtful, detailed comments on his work in progress. (LMP)

Reference:

Bart, Benjamin F. *Flaubert.* Syracuse: Syracuse University Press, 1967.

Giscon (*Sal*). In *Salammbô*, Giscon, like Hamilcar, represents the historical general of antiquity, in contrast to Hannon (Thibaudet 145). The inherent Carthaginian division between Elders and suffetes (Ginsburg 116) is manifest in the case of Giscon. The Elders hate him because of his popularity, fearing a master who might have royal pretensions, just as Hamilcar is represented in Moloch's temple. Giscon's courage, his rhetoric, and his astute stratagems all recall Hamilcar. In many ways, he functions as Hamilcar's double. Thus it is Giscon who arrives at the banquet in the Barca gardens, replacing the absent Hamilcar, with an escort of Sacred Legionnaires to defend their exclusive right to drink from their sacred goblets, a priestly honor coveted by the mercenaries. Here, as their former commander and therefore Hamilcar's equivalent, Giscon persuasively argues that their courage indeed merits access to the drinking cups. At the same time, in a gesture of unity often used by Hamilcar, he depicts the Sacred Legion as one of the army's heterogeneous elements whose property must be respected in the same way that Carthage has honored the diverse ethnicities, customs, and religions of the mercenaries (Ginsburg 121). Because Giscon is Hamilcar's replacement, his departure engenders in the soldiers a feeling of abandonment by Hamilcar.

Unlike Hamilcar, Giscon wishes to pay the mercenaries, that is, to attempt to fulfill Hamilcar's promises; accordingly, he arrives with sacks of silver and interpreters to facilitate the payment. A consummate politician, he exploits the opposition between the Carthaginian suffetes in a rhetorical ploy to gain the mercenaries' confidence by declaring the Carthaginians' good faith in sending him, Hannon's eternal adversary, as their negotiator. Giscon demonstrates his good faith by promising to delve into his personal coffers to fulfill the promises made to them. He is represented as distant and dignified even as the mercenaries become increasingly unruly. He is also depicted, however, as the observant, firm disciplinarian or proverbial master who punishes the fraudulent demands of a laborer by decapitation on discovering the lack of signs of military service represented by a saying in agricultural terms, "to have carob beans," or calluses, under the helmet strap. This scene identifies Giscon with the Adonis myth (Mullen Hohl 137). In the characteristically dissolving properties of apparent opposites (Ginsburg 119), Giscon becomes increasingly like Hannon through his links with Tanit/Salammbô, first implicit in his depiction at the banquet as wearing a mantle that merged with Tanit's night aspect.

When the mercenaries murder his interpreters and take him prisoner, they find three images of Tanit and a metonymic meteorite fallen from the moon in his tent. This explains the meaning of his refusal to dishonor Carthage (Tanit), despite her ingratitude and betrayal (Flaubert, *Œuvres*, I: 765). While Giscon brands the paid mercenaries with green, the color of Tanit, the Queen of Greenery, their payment is inscribed in lead by Tanit's characteristic sign, a hole. Like Salammbô, Giscon's death sentence is represented in the text by means of Tanit's signs, here explicitly in terms of the blanks or gaps between the figures in the accounts of the rich, traced in violet (both Adonis's and Tanit's color) on a lambskin, a sign of the scapegoat that Giscon becomes (Mullen Hohl 52–53).

Giscon also represents the father figure when he eavesdrops on Mâtho and Salammbô during their tryst. His judgment of Salammbô seems a reductive reading of the event (Culler 219–20) and a representation of the broken socio-political contract, the law of the father who mediates the relationship of the daughter and the city (Schor 100). Giscon's condemnation of Salammbô has also been interpreted as the functional narrative equivalent of Hamilcar's reaction to Salammbô's visit, since they both reveal what was concealed in the description of the tryst (Rousset 86). Giscon, a longtime prisoner of the mercenaries at this stage, now strangely resembles the monstrous Hannon. His entrance through the bottom of the tent transforms him from eavesdropper to voyeur as he devours Salammbô with his eyes. His lengthy beard and triple curse on Hamilcar's daughter produce an intratextual allusion to the curse of the stag who judges and curses Julien three times. Giscon's discourse functions like a sequel to another father's discourse, that of Schahabarim, the high priest, who directs Salammbô to Mâtho's tent. Giscon's censure reveals the proximity of the Carthaginian encampment and impels her subsequent visit to Hamilcar's tent, where she will act out Giscon's prohibition, displaying the "zaïmph" (the sacred veil of the goddess Taint) to the acclaim of the five Carthaginian armies. Thus it has been proposed that her visits to the tents are programmed by the Father's discourse (Mullen Hohl 85), and that her unusual energy (Schor 101) is motivated as much by a desire for a future encounter in another tent as by the preceding one (Mullen Hohl 85–86).

Like the two other suffetes, Giscon is represented in terms of decapitation, but Giscon loses his whole head, while Hannon loses only part of his (Mullen Hohl 160). Giscon's death or decapitation establishes him squarely within the Tanit/Astarte, Tammouz/Adonis myths, since decapitation/castration is both the ritual offering exacted by Tanit and the sign of Adonis. Because Giscon is a devotee of Tanit, the parabolic trajectory described by his severed head contains multiple versions of Tanit's characteristic triangular shape as it returns to the Punic encampment, while providing the Punic version of the nineteenth-century French fascination with the life of the head after decapitation (Mullen Hohl 155 n. 33). The fact that the fallacious accounts of the rich refer to the reduced price of corn at the height of the war points to the Tammouz/Adonis myth. Although the mercenaries misread the figures inscribed in violet letters, they interpret them as a sign of abundance, which is exactly what corn signifies in the Adonis myth (Mullen Hohl 53). (AMH)

References:

Culler, Jonathan. *Flaubert: The Uses of Uncertainty*. 1974. Rev ed. Ithaca: Cornell University Press, 1985.

Flaubert, Gustave. "La Légende de saint Julien l'Hospitalier." *Œuvres*. 2 vols. Ed. Albert Thibaudet and René Dumesnil. Paris: Gallimard, 1951–52. Vol. 2.

———. *Salammbô*. In Gustave Flaubert, *Œuvres*. 2 vols. Ed. Albert Thibaudet and René Dumesnil. Paris: Gallimard, 1951–52. Vol. 1.

Ginsburg, Michal Peled. *Flaubert Writing*. Stanford: Stanford University Press, 1986.
Mullen Hohl, Anne. *Exoticism in* Salammbô: *The Languages of Myth, Religion, and War*. Birmingham, AL: Summa, 1995.
Rousset, Jean. "Positions, distances, perspectives dans *Salammbô*." In Gérard Genette and Tzvetan Todorov, eds., *Travail de Flaubert*. Paris: Seuil, 1983. 79–92.
Schor, Naomi. "Salammbô enchaînée." In *Flaubert, la femme, la ville*. Journée d'études organisée par l'Institut de Français de l'Université de Paris X. November 26, 1980. Paris: Presses Universitaires de France, 1983. 89–104.
Thibaudet, Albert. *Gustave Flaubert*. Rev. ed. Paris: Gallimard, 1963; Saint-Armand (Cher): S.E.P.C., 1992 (1922).

gods, procession of the (*TSA*, all versions). The procession of the pagan gods, who pass into oblivion, occupies the fifth of seven sections in the definitive published version of Flaubert's *Tentation de saint Antoine*. As these gods pass, they all lament that no one worships them any longer. This episode follows the spectacle of the heretics and the non-Christian miracle workers of antiquity in section four. Antoine's former disciple Hilarion, the devil in disguise, serves as master of ceremonies. Although Flaubert abridged these sections by sixty percent between 1856 and 1874, they still represent sixty percent of the final version. They offer him ample opportunities to display his erudition concerning the religions of antiquity—a temptation to which he had already yielded in *Salammbô*—and display his strong encyclopedic bent, which will become the object of self-parody in his next, final, unfinished novel, *Bouvard et Pécuchet* (1881). Even here, the solemnity of this Twilight of the Gods is undercut by Flaubert's mischievous evocation, just before Jehovah, the final figure, of Crépitus, the Roman god of flatulence. When the parade has ended, Hilarion reveals himself as Satan, in the form of an archangel. He offers to take Antoine on a journey through outer space and does so in the next section, to demonstrate that the Christian God, too, can be found nowhere and that Satan is the only transcendent spiritual reality. (LMP)

References:

Flaubert, Gustave. *La Tentation de saint Antoine*. Ed. Edouard Maynial. Paris: Garnier, 1968.
Seznec, Jean. *Les Sources de l'épisode des Dieux dans* La Tentation de saint Antoine. Paris: Vrin, 1940.

Goethe, Johann Wolfgang von (1749–1832). In his youth, Flaubert was an enthusiastic reader of French translations of Goethe's reflections *Dichtung und Wahrheit* (Poetry and Truth), of *Die Leiden des jungen Werthers* (The Sorrows of Young Werther), and even more so, of the bildungsroman *Wilhelm Meisters Lehrjahre*, which probably inspired the title and the dreamy romantic hero Jules of the first *Education sentimentale* (Bart 111). Goethe's systematic use of *style indirect libre* (*erlebte rede*, represented discourse) in *Wilhelm Meister* provided a model for Flaubert's extensive experiments with that device (which reports a character's words or thoughts without explicit attribution, thus allowing the text to hover between an impersonal authorial viewpoint and an explicitly subjective-mimetic one) in *Madame Bovary*. The Devil as fictional character and the dramatic dialogued form of *La Tentation de saint Antoine* are found in Goethe's *Faust*. Saint Antoine's visions, as well as the opium visions in Flaubert's sketch "La Spirale," may well have been suggested in part by the Witches' Sabbath scene in *Faust*, part 1, and by the Classical Walpurgisnacht in *Faust*, part 2. (LMP)

References:

Bart, Benjamin F. *Flaubert*. Syracuse: Syracuse University Press, 1967.

Demorest, Don-Louis. *L'Expression figurée et symbolique dans l'œuvre de Gustave Flaubert*. Geneva: Slatkine, 1967 (1931).

Goethe, Johann Wolfgang von. *Faust*. Trans. Barker Fairley. Toronto: University of Toronto Press, 1970.

———. *The Sorrows of Young Werther; Elective Affinities: Novella*. Trans. Victor Lang and Judith Ryan. New York: Suhrkamp, 1988.

———. *Wilhelm Meister's Apprenticeship*. Ed. and trans. Eric A. Blackall and Victor Lange. New York: Suhrkamp, 1989.

Lombard, Alfred. *Flaubert et saint Antoine*. Paris: Attinger, 1934.

Merivale, Patricia. "Learning the Hard Way: Gothic Pedagogy in the Modern Romantic Quest." *Comparative Literature* 36 (1984): 146–61.

Porter, Laurence M. "The Devil as Double in Nineteenth-Century Literature: Goethe, Dostoevsky, and Flaubert." *Comparative Literature Studies* 15 (1978): 316–35.

Goncourt, Edmond and Jules de (1822–96; 1830–70). Edmond de Goncourt and Jules de Goncourt were novelists, essayists, historians, and refined esthetes who wrote as one until Jules's death. Like Flaubert, they frequented Princess Mathilde's salon and the Restaurant Magny dinners for writers. Their *Journal* (1851–96) is a mine of bitchy gossip about Paris throughout the second half of the nineteenth-century. Edmond left money in his will to found le Prix Goncourt (1903–), which became France's most famous literary award, as it still is today.

Flaubert first met the Goncourt brothers in 1859 when he visited them to seek some historical information for *Salammbô*. He already admired their writing, and a lifelong friendship began. They shared Flaubert's misogynistic belief that (male) artistic creation and marriage were incompatible. They used Flaubert as a distant model for their disillusioned eponymous hero in their novel *Charles Demailly* (1860). At times, they were ruffled by Flaubert's coarseness, practical jokes, bumptiousness, and bourgeois conservatism, but they frequently visited his Sunday-afternoon salon in Paris. Edmond felt that *La Tentation de saint Antoine* was overburdened with descriptive detail.

Edmond grieved deeply at Flaubert's death. He was indignant at the unscrupulous, grasping, disrespectful behavior of Flaubert's niece and her husband

Ernest Commanville at Flaubert's funeral. His journal preserves our most detailed account of that event. (LMP)

References:

Bascelli, Anthony L. "Flaubert as Seen through the Eyes of the Brothers Goncourt." *Nineteenth-Century French Studies* 5 (1977): 277–95.

Billy, Andre. *The Goncourt Brothers*. Trans. Margaret Shaw. New York: Horizon, 1960.

Goncourt, Edmond and Jules de. *Journal: Mémoires de la vie littéraire*. Ed. Robert Ricatte. 3 vols. Paris: Laffont, 1989.

Gosselin, Henry (*ES*, 1845). Initially the main character of the 1845 version of *L'Education sentimentale*, Henry Gosselin surrenders much of his importance later in the novel. His story tells of lost illusions: having come to Paris to study, he instead falls in love with Mme Renaud and eventually flees with her to America. The New World unfortunately resembles the old one in many respects, and it fails to rekindle their dying passion. They return to France and separate, after which Henry turns into an accomplished man of high society. He takes the middle path in everything and walks this path elegantly, his future is full of a promise that the narrator depicts ironically. His story and that of Jules, his childhood friend, are intertwined. While Henry's story occupies much of the first part of the novel, Jules's development into an author dominates the concluding chapters. Henry is the first of Flaubert's antiheroes. He is a passive, languid character, neither likeable nor particularly odious. In many respects, he prefigures Frédéric Moreau in the 1869 version of the novel. The character seems heavily drawn from two biographical sources: Flaubert himself, who, like Henry, went to Paris to study law, and Maxime Du Camp, for whom the lure of social success was hard to resist. (SDC)

References:

Bruneau, Jean. *Les Débuts littéraires de Gustave Flaubert, 1831–1845*. Paris: Colin, 1962.

Flaubert, Gustave. *L'Education sentimentale* (1845). In Gustave Flaubert, *Œuvres complètes*, ed. Bernard Masson. 2 vols. Paris: Seuil, 1964. Vol. 1.

Gosselin, Monsieur (*ES*, 1845). A secondary character in the 1845 version of *L'Education sentimentale*, Monsieur Gosselin is the father of Henry Gosselin, one of the protagonists. His only direct appearance occurs in the middle of the novel when he confronts Monsieur Renaud over the departure of his son with Renaud's wife. His role in the plot is negligible; what is remarkable is Flaubert's description of the character, in which he depicts Monsieur Gosselin as a compilation of commonplaces and clichés, as in this character description: "Pour lui toute jeune fille était *pure*, tout jeune homme était un *farceur*, tout mari un *cocu*, tout pauvre un *voleur*, tout gendarme un *brutal*, et toute campagne *délicieuse*" (For him, all young girls were *pure*, all young men *jokesters*, all husbands *cuckolds*, all beggars *thieves*, all policemen *brutes*, and all countrysides *delightful* (*ES*, 1845, 1:346). Foreshadowing such characters as Jacques Arnoux (*L'Education sentimentale* of 1869) and Homais (*Madame Bovary*), Monsieur Gosselin's existence is intertwined with the germination of the *Dictionnaire des idées reçues*. (SDC)

References:

Bruneau, Jean. *Les Débuts littéraires de Gustave Flaubert, 1831–1845*. Paris: Colin, 1962.

Flaubert, Gustave. *L'Education sentimentale* (1845). In Gustave Flaubert, *Œuvres complètes*, ed. Bernard Masson, 2 vols. Paris: Seuil, 1964. Vol. 1.

"La Grande Dame et le joueur de vielle, ou, La mère et le cercueil." A theater scenario, *Deux Amours et deux cercueils (La mère et le cercueil)*, dating from 1835 or 1836 allows us to suppose the same period for "La Grande Dame et le joueur de vielle, ou, La mère et le cercueil," an outline for a short story. Indebted to *petits romantiques* such as Petrus Borel for the elements of incest and gruesome death as well as to the Tristram saga for the unrecognized minstrel lover, the story traces a double reversal of fortune, both economic and moral, the kind to which Flaubert would remain attached, especially in *L'Education sentimentale*. While mainly a stylistic exercise, these few pages show an early, developing use of irony, though not as a purely rhetorical device. (MCO)

Reference:

Flaubert, Gustave. *Œuvres complètes*, ed. Maurice Bardèche. 16 vols. Paris: Club de l'Honnête Homme, 1971–76.

Greece. On their trip through Italy and the Middle East, Flaubert and Maxime Du Camp spent seven weeks in Greece, from December 1850 through January 1851. The intense light and the dramatic terrain inspired Flaubert to create new landscape descriptions for the beginning and the ending of *La Tentation de saint Antoine*. The Acropolis in particular corresponded to Flaubert's dream of the perfect harmony and flawless craftsmanship of self-sufficing art. (LMP)

Reference:

Bart, Benjamin. *Flaubert*. Syracuse: Syracuse University Press, 1967. 205–13.

le gueuloir (oral composition). Flaubert, like most other French prose writers, tried to avoid "vers caractérisés," embedded syllabic groups corresponding to traditional lines of verse such as the octosyllable (eight-syllable line) and the alexandrine (twelve-syllable line). He also avoided tinny, jingling repetitions that would create obvious internal rhymes ("You're a poet and don't know it"), alliteration (dense repetition of the same consonant), and assonance (dense repetition of the same vowel sound). He detested the cacophony of repeated *quis* and *ques*. But he considered the more subtle rhymes and rhythms of prose to be of supreme importance; therefore he often tested his drafts by reading them to himself or to his friends out loud, at times raising his voice to an enthusiastic shout. In his letters, he refers to this process of revision as filtering his prose through *le gueuloir*, an invented word derived from *'la gueule'* (slang for mouth, as in "ta gueule!" [shut up!]) and *gueuler* (to speak or sing loud). At times, he also uses *gueuler* to mean "protest against" the corruption, mediocrity, and inanity of his times. (LMP)

H

Hamard, Caroline (née Flaubert, 1824–46). Caroline Flaubert, Gustave's sister, was born on July 15, 1824. Three years his junior, she was far closer to Gustave in age and intimacy than was their brother Achille (born in 1813). The two remained close until Caroline's premature death in 1846.

In their early youth and adolescence, Caroline and Gustave spent long periods together. For Gustave, who clowned a good deal, Caroline made an appreciative audience and apprentice. She enjoyed her brother's incarnations of le Garçon (regularly conjured up by Flaubert and his friends), a two-faced character who both mimicked and scoffed at bourgeois banalities. Le Garçon was particularly cherished by the two for his raucous laugh.

From their correspondence, it is clear that the relationship between Gustave and Caroline was both tender and spirited. Caroline was an educated, perspicacious young woman; Gustave had directed her readings, and she was accomplished at piano and drawing. (Maxime Du Camp once referred to her as one of the most exquisite women he had ever met.) While Gustave did not relate to her as an equal, he clearly respected her and relished her company. His letters to her are filled with affectionate nicknames ("mon bon rat," "mon vieux raton," "mon bon Carolo," and others). Gustave's separation from the family during his studies in Paris (1841–44) pained Caroline as much as it did her brother, and they eased the absence by making fun—sometimes rather sardonically—of the events and people surrounding them. Caroline was Gustave's main channel of communication with his family, and she occasionally mediated his requests for money. For Gustave, who missed the close-knit family life he had led in Normandy, Caroline's reports of family events were invaluable, helping him tolerate months of "dreary" Parisian life.

In 1845, Caroline married Emile Hamard, who had gone to lycée with Gustave and was no stranger to the family, although Gustave thought him a bit of a dolt. Gustave traveled with the newlyweds to Italy and back during the spring of 1845, and on their return, Caroline and Emile settled in Paris. While the summer of 1845 was happy for Gustave, reunited with his family in Croisset, this happiness was not to last. In January 1846, his father, Achille-Cléophas, died from complications of an infection. In the same month, his beloved Caroline gave birth to her first child and soon fell ill with puerperal fever. Her weakness was perhaps not entirely surprising, for Caroline had always been frail, and she and Gustave had regularly exchanged notes about their health. By March, she was declining rapidly. After a few days of delirium, she expired peacefully on March 10. Gustave relates the aftermath in a heart-wrenching letter to Maxime Du Camp (March 25, 1846, *Corr.* 1: 197–98): he describes the vigil he kept over the body the day before burial, the final kiss he laid upon her brow, and the vulgar events of the burial itself, when the coffin would not fit in the grave without considerable shoving and trampling by the gravediggers.

Before her funeral, Gustave had Caroline's hands and face cast in plaster; he had a bust sculpted to serve as a personal relic. But he kept Caroline's memory quietly, and throughout the rest of his life one finds few references to this woman whom he had cherished as much as or more than any other. In his sister's absence, Gustave lavished affection on her infant daughter, named Caroline after her mother; the relationship with his niece was to be long and close. (SDC)

References:

Brombert, Victor H. *Flaubert par lui-même*. Paris: Seuil, 1971.
Commanville, Caroline. *Souvenirs sur Flaubert*. Paris: Ferroud, 1895.
Du Camp, Maxime. *Souvenirs littéraires*. 2 vols. Paris: Hachette, 1882–83.
Flaubert, Gustave. *Correspondance*. Ed. Jean Bruneau. 4 vols. to date. Paris: Gallimard, 1973– .

Hamard, Emile (Flaubert's brother-in-law, 1821–77). Emile Hamard was a schoolmate of Flaubert at the Collège Royal in Rouen since 1840. "He is so stupid that you feel sorry for him," Flaubert confided to his diary (Starkie 8). He helped Flaubert move into an apartment when the writer went to Paris to study law. He had courted Flaubert's beloved sister Caroline for some time and married her in March 1845, after he completed his law studies. Flaubert and his parents accompanied the newlyweds on their honeymoon to Italy. Caroline gave birth to a girl, Désirée-Caroline, on January 21, 1846, six days after her father's death. But she had contracted puerperal fever, and she died in March. The Flaubert family, who disliked Hamard and considered him unstable and incompetent, retained custody of the child. Hamard, devastated by his wife's premature death, took to drink. The Flaubert family had to obtain a restraining order to keep him away from his daughter. He had always seemed eccentric, and soon he went patently insane, but he lived until March 3, 1877. (LMP)

Reference:

Starkie, Enid. *Flaubert, the Making of the Master*. New York: Atheneum, 1967.

Hamilcar (*Sal*). Hamilcar has been viewed as the figure of the ancient general such as he was depicted by historians of antiquity, in a historical style (Thibaudet 143). He has also been seen as the hero locked in an age-old struggle for hegemony with his rival, Mâtho, their conflict taking on a superhuman grandeur (Gaillard 50–51). Both Hamilcar and Mâtho have been found to be embodiments of Napoleon (Addison 102–4, 121–23). His political rise to power has been interpreted as heralding a totalitarian regime (Neefs 233, 238). However, ambivalence pervades Hamilcar's relationships with Salammbô and the mercenaries. This very ambiguity heightens the memory of the absent suffete, both as father and master, so that like a god or legendary hero, his presence is continually felt and desired.

At the mercenaries' banquet at Hamilcar's palace, his gardens, the Barca fish, and Salammbô have all been seen as metonymic substitutions for Hamilcar (Ginsburg 125–26). Moreover, Salammbô's description of the genius of the Barca residence, the black serpent, demonstrates its function at least as a metonym, if not a metaphor, for Hamilcar (Mullen Hohl, *Exoticism*, 74–75), who is later continually referred to as the genius of Carthage, an identity he shares with Tanit/Salammbô. The mercenaries' feelings of abandonment by Hamilcar and their resentment at his unfulfilled, extravagant promises motivate their escalating demands for compensation, but they experience the least surprise on his return, since in their opinion he is a man who cannot die.

His actual arrival, after a third of the novel, bears all the trappings of a miraculous event, as though it had been engendered by the holocausts offered for his safe return by the repentant peace party. His defiant stance on Moloch's altar as he takes a vow of silence with regard to his daughter and Mâtho has been similarly interpreted as miraculous (Bart 415). Ironically, it is at this meeting that he predicts the fall of Carthage, which Giscon will later equate with the "fall" of Salammbô. Here the conflict between Hamilcar and the Council of Elders is marked by his condemnation of the Elders' failure to reject or to divide and rule the mercenaries in his absence, which immediately generates ambivalently a declaration of his identity as the mercenaries' master, united with them by the hatred of the Elders. Hamilcar's alternate stratagems to woo back the mercenaries and threaten them with annihilation recur throughout the novel, notably in his repetition of Giscon's rhetorical ploy, inscribed on a sheepskin (Mullen Hohl, *Exoticism*, 52–53). Just as Hamilcar displays his anger at the Elders for withholding supplies during the Punic War, his anger at their neglect during the truceless war engenders signs of the political division among the Carthaginians (Ginsburg 116), coupled with a desire for union with the mercenaries and the destruction of Carthage.

Larger than life, Hamilcar surpasses the other characters of the novel by his astuteness, his cleverness, his colonial ambitions (Mullen Hohl, *Exoticism*, 42–43), his extreme cruelty, and his delight in the spectacle of his awful vengeance, as well as by his unbounded pride. It has been observed that much as his daughter conducts her love affair, he conducts the war by avoiding contact. Thus his military masterpiece consists of a strategy of continual evasion, which ends in his enticing the mercenaries into the gorge where they will die of starvation or exterminate each other at Hamilcar's command (Rousset 85). Significantly, the only military engagement between Hamilcar and the mercenaries is at the Macar River, in which the cruel pleasure of close bodily contact is represented as a voluptuous embrace. Thus battle becomes a carnal engagement in the novel. Thereafter, the Punic suffete resumes his tactic of distance by disappearing (Rousset 85). Hamilcar's appearances and disappearances have also been found to represent him in terms of the paradigm of the death and resurrection of Eschmoun/Tammouz/Adonis, and the battle scenes to function as fertility rites (Mullen Hohl, *Exoticism*, 82–83, 108–13).

Hamilcar's hope for a son is betrayed by the birth of his daughter, Salammbô. Accordingly, his gift to her at birth is the curse of the father, since daughters were considered a calamity in religions of the sun. Thus he initiates her life under the sign of betrayal. Hannibal, however, is his pride and joy. It has been noted that there is no substitute sacrificial victim for Salammbô, as opposed to Hannibal (Schor, "Débat," 106). In the case of his son, Hamilcar is willing to brave the wrath of Moloch by substituting for the requisite Hannibal a slave child whom he sends to be sacrificed to Moloch in Salammbô's shoes, thus foreshadowing her fate. The duplication between the timing of Emma Bovary's death and the sacrificial substitution (Addison 99) is explained by the intertextual relationship between *Salammbô* and *Madame Bovary* (Mullen Hohl, "Flaubert's *Salammbô*," 21). With regard to his son, Hamilcar's behavior is described as that of a mother who has found her lost firstborn, a comparison heavily freighted with irony, because it is the loss of several male children that provokes Hamilcar's curse on Salammbô. His display of affectionate emotion toward Hannibal is interpreted as a sign of Hamilcar's androgyny by Suhner-Schluep, but is also seen in conjunction with his behavior, described as that of a female professional mourner, as a manifestation of hysteria (Mullen Hohl, *Exoticism*, 130–31). His legacy to his son is an inexpiable hatred of Rome, and his view of his son's destiny is that of perpetuation of the Barca colonial ambitions rather than personal accomplishment (Gaillard 49).

The description of Hamilcar's riches has frequently provoked critical commentary. It has been viewed as demeaning the great statesman Hamilcar by representing him as violent and greedy (Sainte-Beuve, 65–66). It has also been thought out of character for Hamilcar, the general of antiquity, to be depicted as an avid Carthaginian (Thibaudet 143). His display of gems has been considered almost surrealistic, a Parnassian element (Brombert 106–8). Details that render him comic (Culler 115) have also been shown to depict him as a sun god, as it happens, Eschmoûn/Tammouz/Adonis (Mullen Hohl, *Exoticism*, 89–90, 151–52 n. 12). The blinding display of jewels and other symbols of luxury functions as a narrative veil, deflecting attention from the most important aspects of Hamilcar's riches, his pharmacy, which identifies him with the god of healing, Asclepius/Eschmoûn (Mullen Hohl, *Exoticism*, 69), and his supply of corn, which renders the suffete a type of Frugifer/Tammouz, or corn god, to Salammbô's Persephone/Koré (Mullen Hohl, *Exoticism*, 90–92). Moreover, he bears the identifying sign of Eschmoûn/Tammouz/Adonis, inscribed in the shape of a snakelike scar between his eyebrows. This sign is revealed in Moloch's temple when he removes his mystic tiara, whose eight tiers represent the coiled configuration of the snake, eight being the number of solar increase. It is by means of the Adonis myth that Hamilcar is linked with both Salammbô's proposed husband and her lover Mâtho, giving a representation of incest and constituting an intertextual allusion to Madame Arnoux's farewell to Frédédic in *L'Education sentimentale* (Mullen Hohl, *Exoticism*, 82–93). (AMH)

References:

Addison, Claire. *Where Flaubert Lies: Chronology, Mythology, and History*. Cambridge: Cambridge University Press, 1996.

Bart, Benjamin. *Flaubert*. Syracuse, NY: Syracuse University Press, 1967.

Brombert, Victor. *The Novels of Flaubert: A Study of Themes and Techniques*. Princeton: Princeton University Press, 1966.

Culler, Jonathan. *Flaubert: The Uses of Uncertainty*. 1974. Rev. ed. Ithaca: Cornell University Press, 1985.

Flaubert, Gustave. *L'Education sentimentale*. In Gustave Flaubert, *Œuvres* vol. 2. Bibliothèque de la Pléiade. Dijon: Gallimard, 1952.

Gaillard, Françoise. "La Révolte contre la révolution (*Salammbô,* un autre point de vue sur l'histoire)." In Alfonso de Toro, ed., *Procédés narratifs et fondements épistémologiques*. Tübingen: Narr, 1987. 43–54.

Ginsburg, Michal Peled. *Flaubert Writing*. Stanford: Stanford University Press, 1986.

Mullen Hohl, Anne. *Exoticism in* Salammbô: *The Languages of Myth, Religion, and War*. Birmingham, AL: Summa, 1995.

Neefs, Jacques. "Le Parcours du Zaïmph." In Claudine Gothot-Mersch, ed., *La Production du sens chez Flaubert*. Paris: Union Générale d'Editions, 1975. 227–41.

Rousset, Jean. "Positions, distances, perspectives dans *Salammbô*." *Poétique* 6 (1971): 145–54.

Sainte-Beuve, Charles-Augustin. "*Salammbô*." In Charles-Augustin Sainte-Beuve, *Nouveaux Lundis*. Paris: Lévy, 1865. 4:31–95.

Schor, Naomi. "Salammbô Bound." In Naomi Schor, *Breaking the Chain: Women, Theory, and French Realist Fiction*. New York: Columbia University Press, 1985: 111–26.

Suhner-Schluep, Heidi. *L'Imagination du feu; ou, La Dialectique du soleil et de la lune dans* Salammbô *de G. Flaubert*. Zurich: Juris, 1970.

Thibaudet, Albert. *Gustave Flaubert*. Rev. ed. Paris: Gallimard, 1963; Saint-Armand (Cher); S.E.P.C., 1992 (1922).

Hannibal (*Sal*). Hannibal's childhood has been viewed as obviously miraculous, prefiguring that of Saint Julien l'Hospitalier, with whom he shares a prodigious talent for hunting (Bart 404–5). The combat between Hannibal and the eagle foreshadows Julien's struggle to finish killing a pigeon (Mullen Hohl 33–34). The description of this event is proffered by the slave Iddibal, who has raised him, as an example of his strength and fearlessness, thus identifying him with

Salammbô's representation of her father at the mercenaries' banquet (Mullen Hohl 75). The depiction of Hannibal locked in conflict with an eagle represents a carnal embrace as their blood mingles, producing a variant of the battle scenes as fertility rites (Mullen Hohl 109–14). In the Punic sacred system, the holiest of feasts, the resurrection of the year is symbolized by the flight of the eagle, believed to be a means of connecting with the sun's strength. It so happens that the resurrection of the year for the Hebrews and the Canaanites occurs twice a year at the vernal and the autumn equinoxes; thus the year is a doubled phenomenon of two six-month periods, exploited by Flaubert as a veiling technique in the novel to escape censure (Addison 89). Melkarth is the Punic equivalent of Hercules (*New Larousse* 83), and Hannibal is identified in the French sociolect with Hercules, owing to Livy's writings (Mullen Hohl 33). Thus at a time when Hannibal is supposed to be utterly ignorant both of Carthaginian traditions and its system of the sacred, as well as the identity of his father, Hamilcar, he is represented as a sun god, like his father, in union with the eagle, the sign of communion of the Carthaginian people with their god. The relationship between Hamilcar and Hannibal has been considered one of the most perplexing elements of the novel (Addison 98–99). If Hamilcar forbids Iddibal to inform Hannibal of his true identity, this would seem to be a safety precaution against the "molk" or sacrifice of children to Moloch, especially since he enjoins Iddibal shortly after his return to love his son and eventually, at Iddibal's urging, agrees to have Iddibal talk to Hannibal about his father.

Salammbô's theogony describes Melkarth as the father of her family and therefore Hannibal's ancestor too. But Melkarth is also depicted as god of the Sidonians in Salammbô's theogony, although in fact it was Eschumoûn/Adonis/Asclepius, who became a god of healing, that was worshiped at Sidon, where Ashtart/Astarte was also venerated (*New Larousse* 81). Thus once again a technique of narrative veiling (Mullen Hohl 133–34) is at work, concealing that the whole Barca family is absorbed into the Adonis myth. So it is that the serpentine-haired Lamia, the African version of Medusa, who is also Salammbô/Tanit/Astarte and whose name is contained anagrammatically by Hamilcar's holds no fear for Hannibal, just as Hamilcar is designated as disdaining Tanit, together with the Punic pantheon. Father and son are also represented as inspiring godlike feelings in each other. Thus the thought of Hannibal fills Hamilcar with peace, as if he had been touched by a god, who is evidently an extension of himself, while the terrible tenderness of his father fills Hannibal with dread, as if he were in contact with a god, and reduces him for once to silence. (AMH)

References:

Addison, Claire. *Where Flaubert Lies: Chronology, Mythology, and History*. Cambridge: Cambridge University Press, 1996.

Bart, Benjamin. *Flaubert*. Syracuse: Syracuse University Press, 1967.

Flaubert, Gustave. "La Légende de saint Julien l'Hospitalier." In Gustave Flaubert, *Trois Contes, Œuvres*, vol. 2. Dijon: Gallimard, 1952.

———. *Salammbô*. In Gustave Flaubert, *Œuvres*, vol. 1. Dijon: Gallimard, 1951.
Mullen Hohl, Anne. *Exoticism in* Salammbô: *The Languages of Myth, Religion, and War*. Birmingham, AL: Summa, 1995.
New Larousse Encyclopedia of Mythology. 1959. Hong Kong: Toppan for Hamlyn, 1968.

Hannon (*Sal*). The grotesque figure of Hannon is a foil for the two other Carthaginian commanders, Giscon and Hamilcar. The latter two exemplify conventional heroic portraits of the generals of antiquity, whereas Hannon reflects the banal picturesqueness of a character in a modern historical novel. He also represents the inner political divisions of the city-state Carthage, which deliberately promoted hatred between its two suffetes (commanders-in-chief) so that neither of them would grow too powerful. This strategy succeeds particularly well in influencing Hannon: so much does he detest Hamilcar that he offers to deliver him to the barbarian rebel leader Mâtho to avoid his own imminent crucifixion by the mercenaries. In exchange, he offers that Mâtho and he will enter Carthage together as kings. This offer is highly ironic in the context of the accusations of regal ambitions, anathema to the Carthaginians, that Hannon hurled at Hamilcar during the meeting of the Elders in Moloch's temple.

Hannon is a parody of excess. Every aspect of his appearance reflects his obsession with material details: his overflowing body, whose excess compensates for the missing parts of his mutilated face; the sartorial ornamentation; and his refusal to engage in battle until every detail of costume and armor is complete, down to the minute features of the regalia worn by the elephants and their drivers. A true Carthaginian, Hannon represents the master-slave paradigm. When he is dealing with the mercenaries, he repeatedly refers to himself as the proverbial master. When he is visiting them at Sicca, he arrives with all the trappings of luxury, sprinkling his discourse with proverbs and moral fables illustrating the needs of the master. His refusal to pay the mercenaries is an attempt to reduce them to slaves, just as he sold the Libyan captives from the battle of Hecatompylus as slaves, for his personal profit, while reporting them as dead to the Republic of Carthage. To add insult to injury, he speaks to the mercenaries in Punic, the language of the master, which the mercenaries do not understand and, in the event, cannot hear. Because Hannon, as suffete, is also judge, here he dramatizes the Rabelaisian dictum that what lawyers sell is words.

Hannon explicitly represents the sadistic imagination as he delights in contemplating the terrible punishment he intends for his prisoners of war. The mercenaries' counterattack interrupts his plans to cut off their hands; he has the prisoners beheaded instead, washing his hands in their blood as a cure for his leprosy. Decapitation, a variant of castration, is repeatedly linked with him. He wishes to decapitate the mercenaries rather than pay them; in turn, they ask for his head as proof of Carthage's friendship.

The mythological underpinnings of the text explain the unexpected symbolic similarities between Salammbô and Hannon, which are mediated by the moon goddess Tanit. Both characters are lavishly adorned, covering themselves with the pearls formed by Tanit. The moon goddess also produces monsters and putrefaction. Hannon's elephantiasis and leprosy, the latter of which supposedly sent by the moon, render him progressively more monstrous as the novel runs its course. As Salammbô is motivated by recovering Tanit's veil from the barbarians, Hannon too is associated with a veil, which he wears to cover the gaping hole formed by the erosion of his nose and lips. By stealing back the veil, Salammbô as servant of the moon goddess symbolically castrates Mâtho; Tanit's castrating aspect likewise afflicts Hannon's face.

Hannon's diseased body also incorporates the paradigm of multiplicity and mutilation characteristic of the Adonis myth. Flaubert frequently describes him as a statue or an idol and represents him as Tammouz/Adonis on his litter covered with fleece, the functional equivalent of Tammouz's legendary hoard of women's hair. Thus Tammouz's catafalque was adorned during the mourning rites for Adonis. As Hannon's illness progresses, the part (hair) is represented by the whole (women thrown into his litter to be raped). Hannon also is likened to Eschmoûn/Adonis's serpent, both by the color and texture of his skin and by his use of vipers as a remedy for his illness, in a manner reminiscent of Salammbô entwining herself with the sacred serpent. The first martial encounter with the mercenaries under Hannon's command is not at all a military engagement: symbolically it represents a fertility rite, in which Hannon is depicted alternately as the dying and the resurrected god Tammouz. (AMH)

References:

Ginsburg, Michal Peled. *Flaubert Writing*. Stanford: Stanford University Press, 1986.

Green, Anne. *Flaubert and the Historical Novel*: Salammbô *Reassessed*. Cambridge: Cambridge University Press, 1982.

Mullen Hohl, Anne. *Exoticism in* Salammbô: *The Languages of Myth, Religion, and War*. Birmingham, AL: Summa, 1995.

Thibaudet, Albert. *Gustave Flaubert*. Rev. ed. Paris: Gallimard, 1963, Saint-Armand (Cher): S.E.P.C., 1992 (1922).

Hegel, Georg Wilhelm Friedrich (1770–1831). The thought of the German philosopher Georg Wilhelm Friedrich Hegel, combined with that of Martin Heidegger, had a decisive influence on continental philosophies such as phenomenology, existentialism, and deconstruction. Hegel speculated that being and thought composed a single principle, the Idea, which developed in three stages: thesis, antithesis, and synthesis (the Hegelian dialectic). Flaubert encountered Hegelian thought at secondary school through the teaching of his philosophy teacher, Charles Auguste Mallet (1807–75), who had absorbed Victor Cousin's eclectic idealism in Paris. Hegel's aesthetic ideas helped shape Flaubert's depiction of Jules in the first *Education sentimentale* (1845). Hegel rejects the traditional distinction between form and content and claims that art is truer than either nature or history because it relates more closely than they to the realm of ideas. Later, Hegel's views of religion and morality as essences that may be fully present and fully valuable in a simpleminded, limited life appear to have shaped the depiction of Flaubert's heroine Félicité in "Un cœur simple" (Bart 48, 117, 647). (LMP)

References:

Bart, Benjamin F. *Flaubert*. Syracuse: Syracuse University Press, 1967.

Cigada, Sergio. *Il pensiero estetico di Flaubert*. Milan: Istituto di filologia moderna. Contributi Serie Francese 3 (1964): 186–453.

Mallet, Charles Auguste. *Etudes philosophiques*. 2 vols. Paris: Mme Maire-Nyon, 1836–38.

———. *Mélanges philosophiques*. 6 vols. Paris: n.p., 1842–63.

Hennique, Léon (1851–1935). Léon Hennique was a minor writer belonging to the naturalist group along with J. K. Huysmans and Henri Céard. He contributed a short story to *Les Soirées de Médan* (1880), a collaboration by six authors including Huysmans and Zola. They all used the occasion to satirize the folly of the Franco-Prussian War and to oppose the militaristic, revanchist spirit of their times. This text provoked scandal and, owing to its aggressive preface, was seen as a founding manifesto of naturalism. Hennique also wrote novels and had plays produced in André Antoine's pioneering, naturalistic Théâtre Libre (1887–94).

In the 1870s, Hennique regularly attended Flaubert's salon in Paris, where prominent and promising writers met every Sunday afternoon. Among them were Ivan Turgenev, Alphonse Daudet, Emile Zola, Hippolyte Taine, Edmond de Goncourt, and Guy de Maupassant. Although Flaubert was not fond of the naturalist movement, he tried to encourage these new writers. Hennique received several letters from Flaubert and was among the few writers to attend his funeral in Croisset. (CG/LMP)

References:

Hennique-Valentin, Nicolette. *Mon Père: Léon Hennique*. Paris Editions du Dauphin, 1959.

Huysmans, Joris-Karl. "Léon Hennique." *Marges* 9 (1930): 91–93.

Morgan, Owen R. "Léon Hennique and the Disintegration of Naturalism." *Nottingham French Studies* 1 (1962): 24–33.

———. "The Plays of Léon Hennique." *Nottingham French Studies* 5 (1966): 89–99; 6 (1967): 19–29.

Rheault, Raymond. "Emile Zola: Lettres inédites à Léon Hennique (1884–1902)." *Cahiers naturalistes* 57 (1983): 179–210.

Herbert, Juliet (1829–1909). Juliet Herbert was the second English governess of Caroline, Gustave Flaubert's niece. She started to work at the Flaubert home in Normandy in 1853. She taught English and Shakespeare to Flaubert, and exchanged summer visits with him through 1866. She probably left in 1864, when Caroline got married. It is known today that Flaubert had a long intimate relationship with Herbert, but very little evidence of their relationship remains. Their love affair probably started in 1855 and continued for years, as on several occasions Flaubert visited her secretly in London and Paris as late as 1877. It is notable that in his correspondence, Flaubert never mentioned the terms of this relationship. He burned hundreds of letters, probably including hers, one night in May 1879. After her return to England, Juliet became a writer. (CG)

References:

Lottman, Herbert. *Gustave Flaubert*. New York: Fromm, 1990. 199–223, 367–68.
Oliver, Hermia, *Flaubert and an English Governess: The Quest for Juliet Herbert*. Oxford: Clarendon Press, 1980.

Hérode (*TC*). Son of Herod the Great, Herod Antipas was tetrarch of Galilee and Peraea from 4 B.C. to 39 A.D. The appointment was nominal since the Jewish kingdom was under the direct rule of Vitellius, the Roman governor of Syria. Flaubert's "Hérodias" takes place in 28 A.D. during the reign of Emperor Tiberius. In the first chapter, Hérode dominates the sweeping landscape he surveys from the terrace of his palace. From that point forward, his domination becomes increasingly more tenuous. More fully than those who had reworked the biblical anecdote before him, Flaubert develops a web of internal conflicts that diminishes the importance of the Salomé/Iaokanann opposition and foregrounds Hérode's political difficulties. Parallel binary oppositions include the relationships of alterity between Hérode and Hérodias, between Hérode and Iaokanann, between Hérode and the Arab troops camped outside the citadel, between the Essene Phanuel and the Samaritan Mannaeï, between the Pharisees and the Sadducees, and between the Latins and the Jews. Hérode struggles in isolation at the center of all the political and amorous conflicts of the tale.

The political, racial, and religious cleavages that Hérode must mediate are conveyed in visual "scenes" that are almost theatrical in their conception. The successive unveiling of his military stockrooms by Vitellius shows the tetrarch as a compromised and threatened leader. Political and religious tensions are highlighted again in the banquet scene. The sacrilegious serving of forbidden foods dramatizes the intractable cultural incompatibilities among the sects. The Pharisees shatter dishes, enraged at having been served a "viande immonde" (an unclean meat, Flaubert 197). The florid descriptive excess of the architectural setting, of the overflowing serving tables, and of the ceremonial clothing visually doubles the proliferation of peoples, beliefs, and conflicts present at the banquet. Through their carefully staged behavior and attire, Hérode and his spouse court the allegiance of the diverse, unruly crowd.

In Roman tradition, a female dancer performs after a feast. Unveiled little by little, Salomé appears to Hérode as the resurrection of Hérodias in her youth. The focus reverts to the central conflict between Hérodias and Iaokanann, played out through Salomé and Hérode. Crazed by the vertiginous spectacle of the dithyrambic dance, Hérode regretfully grants the request that Hérodias has prompted Salomé to make—the head of Iaokanann. The scene ends with the ineffectual ruler Hérode defeated and alone in the banquet room, gazing uncomprehendingly at the prophet's disembodied head. Flaubert's somewhat sympathetic portrayal of Hérode emphasizes the difficulty of the tetrarch's position vis-à-vis John the Baptist and his other potential political rivals. His capitulation to the feminine machinations of Hérodias ensures his downfall. (JM)

References:

Brombert, Victor. *The Novels of Flaubert: A Study of Themes and Techniques*. Princeton: Princeton University Press, 1966.

Flaubert, Gustave. *Trois Contes*. ed. Edouard Maynial. Paris: Garnier, 1956.

Issacharoff, Michael. "*Trois Contes* et le problème de la non-linéarité." *Littérature* 15 (1974): 27–40.

Knapp, Bettina L. "Herodias/Salome: Mother/Daughter Identification." *Nineteenth-Century French Studies* 25.1–2 (1996–97): 179–202.

"Hérodias" (*TC*). The third of the *Trois Contes*, "Hérodias," is set in biblical antiquity. Although Hérodias and Salomé had been represented in John the Baptist hagiographies for centuries, it was not until the mid-to-late nineteenth century that these terrifyingly destructive, amoral women captured the collective imagination of artists and writers in Europe to become the primary subject of a large number of works of art and literature. Flaubert's vivid, erudite retelling of the tale testifies to his dual penchants for methodical historical research and for detailed descriptions of topography, setting, decor, and costume. Through the voice of Iaokanann (Flaubert's name for John), he illustrates the incantatory power of language in biblical times. His pictorial writing style, in which the fabula is advanced by a series of visual tableaux, explores the power that icons exert on the "primitive" imagination.

The events of the drama, which are few, occur within one day. The narrative is divided into three chapters, the first set in the early morning hours, the second at midday, and the third stretching from evening to dawn. Chapter 1 consists of four main scenes, showing Antipas alone, Antipas and Mannaeï, Antipas and Hérodias, and Antipas and Phanuel. The two major scenes in the second chapter elaborate the political power of the Romans and the spiritual power of Iaokanann. The third chapter tells of the banquet and its epilogue. In a series of tableaux spanning all three chapters, Flaubert establishes the backdrop of accumulated tensions among individuals and factions that conspire to bring about the inevitable decapitation.

Since Iaokanann possesses the qualities Hérode Antipas lacks as a leader, the latter harbors ambivalent feelings toward the future saint. Nonetheless, at the outset he has no desire to betray the precursor of Christ. Only because he offended Hérodias is Iaokanann subjected to the ultimate punishment. In its oppositional structure, which includes internal and external obstacles, in its unity of time, space, and setting, and in its dénouement, the tale resembles a classical tragedy. With Phanuel's prediction at the end of the second chapter of "la mort d'un homme considérable, cette nuit même, dans Machaerous" (Flaubert 194), the notion of fate enters the narrative. The device of the oracle also derives from classical drama. Flaubert aspired to be a playwright before turning to prose; his narrative style often reflects his affinity for the theater.

Flaubert's transformation of the biblical anecdote diverges from other reinterpretations that emphasize the titillating episode of the dance to the point that they become little more than warnings of the horror of unfettered feminine sensuality and cruelty. Flaubert's tale is expanded to include conflicts between races and religions as well as the conflict between the sexes. The tale opens by delineating a number of conflicts between characters and groups of characters, the primary one being the animosity between Hérodias and Iaokanann. The latter's fanatical asceticism (which casts Hérodias as the incarnation of evil) is the counterpart to her obsessive desire to see him eliminated before he further undermines her power. Secondary tensions woven into this narrative set in a universe of alterity include those between the Romans and the Jews; between Arabs and Jews; and between the Jewish sects of the Pharisees and the Sadducees. Amorous intrigue also figures in the constellation of conflicts. Hérodias is decried by Iaokanann for permitting herself to divorce and remarry. Hérode Antipas himself offended the Arabs by marrying Hérodias instead of the Arab princess to whom he was betrothed.

The third chapter, where Phanuel's prophecy is fulfilled, is composed of the banquet Hérode gives to placate his various constituencies and by its aftermath. The lively discussions and ritual gorging that precede the dance that Hérodias stages in order to induce Antipas to execute Iaokanann suggest a "mounting frenzy of the mind and body" (Brombert 247). Salomé is the daughter of Hérodias and of Hérode Philippe who is the half brother of Hérode Antipas, making her both the niece and the stepdaughter of Antipas. Salomé was raised in Rome, and Antipas has never met her before the fateful evening. Hérodias correctly calculates that her younger double, Salomé, will be able to extract whatever she desires from Antipas after performing a dance before him. In a hazy, vertigo-inducing ambiance of unsteady light, scintillating jewels, shimmering fabrics, and a swirling together of colors, vapors, and sounds, Salomé executes an acrobatic dance that induces the tetrarch to grant her any wish. The wish, expressed by Salomé but scripted by Hérodias, is that Iaokanann's head should be presented to her on a platter. Gustave Moreau painted a memorable representation of this scene.

The radical separation of Iaokanann's head from his body gives concrete form to the spirit/body duality that he spoke of in his sermons and imprecations. According to the asceticism he practiced, the head, where qualities reside, must overrule the body, which is governed by animal impulses. The female sex, in Iaokanann's worldview, is closely tied to the body and, by extension, to the animal aspects of humanity. While the prophet's strength derives in part from his renunciation of the female and the feminine, Hérode's weakness is his susceptibility to the same. In the spectacle of Salomé's dance, this split is figured in the ostentatious display of her ornamented, mobile body, followed by the executioner's display of John's lifeless head on a charger.

Victor Brombert writes of "Hérodias" that "from contradiction arises neither a purifying conflict nor a definitive debate, but dizziness and surrender" (252). It becomes clear that in spite of Antipas's affinity for Iaokanann—he admits "Malgré moi, je l'aime" (Flaubert 190)—the prophet is destined to be sacrificed. Flaubert's innovation is to dissociate the presumed cause from its effect: it seems that the precursor is not sacrificed simply due to the machinations of Hérodias, which become almost incidental, but rather to the inexorable spirit of Molochism, which in the eyes of the eternal pessimist Flaubert animates the march of humanity. In the end, the causal relationships among events in the classically conceived fabula are ironically revealed as a mirage. (JM)

References:

Bart, Benjamin F. *Flaubert*. Syracuse: Syracuse University Press, 1967. 698–704.

Brombert, Victor. *The Novels of Flaubert: A Study of Themes and Techniques*. Princeton: Princeton University Press, 1966.

Dottin-Orsini, Mireille. *Cette femme qu'ils disent fatale*. Paris: Grasset, 1993.

Flaubert, Gustave. *Trois Contes*, ed. Edward Maynial. Paris: Garnier, 1956.

Issacharoff, Michael. "*Trois Contes* et le probléme de la non-linéarité." *Littérature* 15 (1974): 27–40.

Knapp, Bettina L. "Herodias/Salome: Mother/Daughter Identification." *Nineteenth-Century French Studies* 25.1–2 (1996–97): 179–202.

Hérodias (*TC*). The title character of the third tale of Flaubert's *Trois Contes*, Hérodias is the wife of Hérode Antipas, the mother of Salomé, and the avowed enemy of John the Baptist (also known as Iaokanann). Hérodias embodies "the Great Mother archetype in her avatar as castrator" (Knapp 179). The biblical bit player Hérodias occupies a place in history alongside the legendary destructive female figures of Eve, Judith, Dalilah, Jezebel, and Medea.

As Hérode Antipas's wife, Hérodias acts as both an ally and an adversary. She is described as having always dreamed of a great empire. When John the Baptist denounces her marriage as contrary to Jewish law, she fears that her power in the public sphere, and possibly even in her marriage, will diminish. To end the humiliation of John the Baptist's public imprecations against her, she manipulates her husband into destroying her vociferous accuser. Hérode has already incarcerated the prophet, perhaps because of the political threat he poses, but Hérodias will settle for no less than his definitive silencing.

As the mother of Salomé, an adolescent daughter by an earlier marriage, Hérodias is shown as a ruthless figure who exploits her daughter's sensuality to her own ends. Like Hamilcar in Flaubert's novel *Salammbô*, Hérodias calculatedly endeavors to deploy the spectacle of her daughter's luscious virginity to aid her quest for power. Hérodias is characterized as a single-minded, relentless adversary to John the Baptist. In contrast to Flaubert's poetically undeveloped and childlike Salomé, his Hérodias is a coherent, complete dramatic figure (Dottin-Orsini 148). Unknown to Hérode, all of her initiatives are motivated by a desire for vengeance against the icon of patriarchal Christianity, John the Baptist. Ironically, the beheading of John the Baptist fails to achieve its objective. (JM)

References:

Dottin-Orsini, Mireille. *Cette femme qu'ils disent fatale*. Paris: Grasset, 1993.

Hubert, Judd D. "Representations of Decapitation: Mallarmé's Hérodiade and Flaubert's Hérodias." *French Forum* 7.3 (1982): 245–51.

Knapp, Bettina L. "Herodias/Salome: Mother/Daughter Identification." *Nineteenth-Century French Studies* 25. 1–2 (1996–97): 179–202.

Hilarion (*TSA*). Like the historical Saint Hilarion of Cyprus (also said to be of Gaza, ca. 291–ca. 371), the fictional character was one of Saint Anthony's disciples. Legend has it that using Anthony as his model, the ascetic Saint Hilarion struggled against the temptations of demons while living as an anchorite in the Thebaid. He had considerable influence on eremitical life in the desert. Through him, many monasteries were established in Palestine and elsewhere.

In Flaubert's *Tentation*, Satan assumes the guise of Hilarion, representing logic and science. He uses reason to challenge Antoine's faith and existence itself. The satanic Hilarion chastises Antoine for real and imagined sins, and as the hermit's appetites respond to the stimulus of thinking about sins, Hilarion grows in size until he assumes the shape of a luminous but devilish archangel. (AHP)

References:

Attwater, Donald. *The Penguin Dictionary of Saints*. Harmondsworth: Penguin, 1965.

Louis Réau. *Iconographie de l'art chrétien*. Tome 3, *Iconographie des saints*. Paris: Presses Universitaires de France, 1958. 1:101–15.

history, Flaubert's treatment of. Both history and notions of how to present history play important roles in Flaubert's fiction. At times, the unfolding of actual historical events coincides with the lives of his characters. For example, Flaubert made extensive chronologies and did considerable research regarding the historical events that provide the setting for *Salammbô* and *L'Education sentimentale*. For *Salammbô*, he drew upon the ancient historians Polybius and Livy, among others. As the events that provide a backdrop for *L'Education sentimentale* were almost contemporary, he served as his own historian, visiting numerous sites and consulting many people in search of information regarding the events depicted, particularly the revolution of 1848. In other cases, for example, *Madame Bovary*, the historical context within which the characters act lends authenticity to the work, although historical events themselves do not generally intrude into the narrative. *Bouvard et Pécuchet* discusses both the methods of historiography and the revolution of 1848 (chapter 4).

In the presentation of history, Flaubert's realist style corresponds to concurrent trends in historiography. To pursue an objective or scientific history, historians of his time were turning away from the grand narrative of times past in favor of the documentation of the facts as known (a tendency also displayed by the recent Annales school of French historiography). Flaubert similarly rejected the grand narrative by effacing the omniscient narrator while limiting value judgments to those made through the eyes of individual characters when the story was being told. The relationship between Flaubert and the professional historian becomes particularly clear in *L'Education sentimentale*, in which major historical events are sometimes scanted because Frédéric Moreau, otherwise occupied, is not available to witness and interpret. (His visit to the Forest of Fontainebleau with Rosanette Bron is a striking example.) In the traditional historical novel, the narrator would present these events, but Flaubert refrains from commenting on whatever happens outside the direct experience of his characters, much as a professional historian would refrain from commenting on the past without direct evidence. (GB)

References:

Addison, Claire. *Where Flaubert Lies; Chronology, Mythology, and History*. Cambridge: Cambridge University Press, 1996.

Campion, Pierre. "Roman et histoire dans *L'Education sentimentale.*" *Poétique* 22.85 (1991): 35–52.

Falconer, Graham. "Le Statut de l'histoire dans *L'Education sentimentale*." In G. T. Harris and P. M. Wetherill, eds. *Littérature et révolutions en France*. Amsterdam: Rodopi, 1990. 106–20.

Green, Anne. "Time and History in *Madame Bovary.*" *French Studies* 49.3 (1995): 283–91.

Lowe, Lisa. "Nationalism and Exoticism: Nineteenth-Century Others in Flaubert's *Salammbô* and *L'Education sentimentale*." In Jonathan Arac and Harriet Ritvo, eds., *Macropolitics of Nineteenth-Century Literature: Nationalism, Exoticism, Imperialism*. Philadelphia: University of Pennsylvania Press, 1991. 213–42.

Niang, P. M. "L'Insertion de l'histoire dans *L'Education sentimentale* de Gustave Flaubert." In G. T. Harris and P. M. Wetherill, eds., *Littérature et révolutions en France*. Amsterdam: Rodopi, 1990. 77–105.

Wetherill, P. M. "Roman et histoire: Un Problème de situation." *Neuphilologische Mitteilungen* 93.1 (1992): 61–73.

Homais (*MB*). In *Madame Bovary*, Homais, the pharmacist of Yonville, is a mentor to Charles and at the same time paves the way for his and Emma's destruction. He does not appear in the earliest scenarios, but winds up being a prime motive force in the plot. His literary origins clearly lie in the many satiric representations of the bourgeois of the first half of the century, in the genre known as *physiologie*, in the character of Henry Monnier's Joseph Prudhomme, and in caricatures such as Honoré Daumier's and Charles Philipon's Robert Macaire or Charles Joseph Traviès's (1804–59) Mayeux. Critics beginning with Emile Zola have generally written about Homais as a reincarnation of Joseph Prudhomme, a somewhat harmless, bumbling buffoon known for his fractured sayings and for his fine penmanship (cf. Bourais in "Un cœur simple," also known for his penmanship), neglecting the possible affiliation with Robert Macaire and Mayeux, both of whom have a decidedly dark side. Although it is certainly true that Homais can be pompous and ridiculous, strewing incongruous sayings right and left, uttering pretentious statements, and taking on an air of importance at the *comices agricoles*, he too can be sinister.

The reader can infer much about Homais just from the description of his pharmacy. On its sign, the name Homais is written in large gold letters along the width of the façade. The narrator's description of Homais in the inn before the Bovarys arrive shows that the pharmacist possesses much knowledge, but in undigested form—he is a walking almanac. He has in his library "the best authors," Voltaire, Rousseau, Delille, Walter Scott, and *L'Echo des Feuilletons* (a magazine similar to the Reader's Digest Condensed Books series) and subscribes to the Rouen newspaper. He gives Charles a short course on the medical situation in the area. Homais's head is "plus remplie de recettes que sa pharmacie ne l'était de bocaux" (more filled with recipes than his pharmacy was with bottles). He knows how to make all sorts of jams, preserves, and liqueurs and how to preserve cheese and treat diseased grapevines. Yet he is singularly obtuse, for he believes that Justin is in love with the Bovarys' maid. His knowledge profits no one but himself and can even have disastrous consequences. After reading about a new technique for operating on clubfeet, Homais begins a publicity campaign to convince the community that Yonville needs such an operation in order to be up-to-date, wisely beginning his arguments with Emma. He also encourages Charles to take Emma to the theater for a performance of *Lucia di Lammermoor*, which leads to the chance meeting with Léon and to Emma's subsequent affair. His dark side becomes clear in his campaign against the blind beggar, whom he causes to be locked up as a public nuisance because he is unable to cure the beggar's affliction. Homais does not hesitate to use his position as a journalist to conduct this nefarious campaign. Later he plays a role in the prefect's political campaign. That Homais finally succeeds in receiving the medal of the Legion of Honor (France's most prestigious award for civilians) passes Flaubert's unequivocal judgment on the debased values of modern society. (EFG)

References:

Bersani, Leo. "Flaubert and the Threats of Imagination." In Leo Bersani, *Balzac to Beckett: Center and Circumference in French Fiction*. New York: Oxford University Press, 1970. 140–91.

Jasinski, René. "Le Couple Bournisien-Homais." In René Jasinski, *A travers le XIXe siècle*. Paris: Minard, 1975. 249–68.

Russel, André, ed. *Le Charivari: Un journal révolutionnaire.* Paris: La Courtille, 1971.
Traviès de Villers, Charles Joseph. *Album Traviès: 20 lithographies.* Paris: Pannier, 1843.

Homer. When Flaubert was supposed to be studying law in Paris, he had a daily predawn ritual of reading Homer while sitting at his window and smoking. He liked to declaim Homer's verses aloud. He read the *Iliad* in preparation for his trip to Greece, and the *Odyssey* while he was traveling on the Nile (Bart 64, 196; Lottman 77, 90). The most obvious resonances of Homer's *Iliad* appear in *Salammbô*, in such characteristically epic scenes (known in criticism as elements of "thematic composition") as the council or the gathering of the armies. (LMP)

References:

Bart, Benjamin F. *Flaubert.* Syracuse: Syracuse University Press, 1967.
Lottman, Herbert R. *Flaubert: A Biography.* New York: Fromm, 1990.

homosexuality. The question of homosexuality has always been thorny in Flaubert scholarship, partly because of the perceived delicate or even immoral nature of homosexual acts, partly because they were acts ascribed to one of the canonic immortals, and partly because they have seemed aberrations in an otherwise exemplary (at least in terms of the bourgeoisie of the time) heterosexual life. Why complicate Flaubert's sex life with such foibles? Let us admit for the moment that even from the point of view of social constructivism, we are dealing, largely, with a modern vision of homosexuality. Most famous, of course, is Flaubert's own account of his homosexual activity in a bathhouse in Cairo during his trip to the Orient. Later in the trip, while he was in Beirut, he seems to have continued or repeated such activity; evidence shows that he contracted syphilis from a fourteen-year-old Maronite boy in Beirut in 1850. While we have only Flaubert's statement that he engaged in homosexual activity, as critical (in all senses of the word) a reader as Jean-Paul Sartre indicates flatly that he does not believe Flaubert, that this is an invention, an imaginary case of temporary homosexuality that fits the stereotypical trip to the East, in which the tourist, far from the eyes of home and hearth and well into the Sotadic (licentious, scurrilous) zone where everyone is bisexual, engages in illicit activity for its own sake. Thus for Sartre, Flaubert invents the activity to make himself a better tourist. However, most other critics who discuss this matter accept Flaubert's statements, though not always at face value.

It can be hypothesized that Flaubert was not homosexual nor even bisexual, but simply engaged in experimentation when he had the opportunity. Yet there seem to be echoes of homosexuality throughout Flaubert's life. Julian Barnes, ventriloquizing Louise Colet's voice, says that Flaubert's life was marked by "sodality confirmed by sodomy." Enid Starkie indicates that Flaubert's friendship with Alfred Le Poittevin, though not necessarily sexual, was certainly a romantic friendship. Perhaps his most personal novel, *L'Education sentimentale*, is marked by a homoerotic friendship between Frédéric and Deslauriers that is, after all, the only lasting relationship in the whole novel. Indeed, as Mary Orr points out, there is an "other" sentimental education, the signs and indications of at least potential bisexuality and (latent) homosexuality in the work. Sartre was clearly wrong: we must believe Flaubert and must consider that even if the homosexual and homoerotic experiences were few and far between over the course of his life, they marked him as much as the vision of Elisa Schlésinger that helped him maintain an androgynous spirit. They fed into the structures of his writing and the construction of his narratives, from the voice of the feminine in *Madame Bovary* to the latent homosexual couple of his last novel, *Bouvard et Pécuchet*, living life as an old married couple in the country, surrounded by their acquisitions and with their adopted children in tow. (LRS)

References:

Barnes, Julian. *Flaubert's Parrot*. New York: Knopf, 1985.
Douchin, Jacques-Louis. *La Vie érotique de Flaubert*. Paris: Pauvert, 1984.
Dumesnil, René. *Le Grand Amour de Flaubert*. Geneva: Editions du Milieu du Monde, 1945.
Orr, Mary. *Flaubert: Writing the Masculine*. Oxford: Oxford University Press, 2000.
Sartre, Jean-Paul. *L'Idiot de la famille*. 3 vols. Paris: Gallimard, 1971–72. Rev ed. 1988.
Starkie, Enid. *Flaubert: The Making of the Master*. London: Weidenfeld and Nicolson, 1967.
Troyat, Henri. *Flaubert*. Trans. Joan Pinkham. New York: Viking, 1992.

l'Hôtel-Dieu (municipal hospital, Rouen). The Hôtel-Dieu was the hospital where Flaubert was born (December 12, 1821) and where his father was chief surgeon. Built under Louis XV, the 600-bed, two-story structure was old and gloomy. Dr. Achille-Cléophas Flaubert housed his family in one wing. Gustave's room overlooked the entrance courtyard planted with two rows of elms and an acacia outside his window. He and his younger sister Caroline often climbed a trellis to peer into the garden where their father dissected cadavers. This environment affected Gustave and haunted him forever. He once wrote to Louise Colet that he could not gaze on an infant without seeing an aged person, or on a naked woman without seeing her skeleton (August 8, 1848, *Corr.* 1:221).

The Flaubert's maidservant Julie and Father Mignot, an elderly neighbor, told Gustave stories and sparked his love for fiction. By age ten he had written plays and performed them in the hospital's billiard room with Caroline and their friends Ernest Chevalier and Alfred and Laure Le Poittevin. Both Ernest and Alfred shared Gustave's passion for literature.

Later in life, Gustave occasionally returned to the Hôtel-Dieu to take steam baths or dine with his brother, Achille, who inherited his father's post after the elder Flaubert's death in 1846. Gustave spent at least one night at the Hôtel-Dieu in December 1870 when Croisset was inhabited by Prussian soldiers. In

June 1874, he took Julie back to the hospital, where Achille operated on her eyes. (JWA)

References:

Descharmes, René. *Flaubert; Sa vie, son caractère, et ses idées avant 1857*. Paris: Ferroud, 1909.

Dumesnil, René. *Flaubert: Son hérédité, son milieu, sa méthode*. Geneva: Slatkine, 1977.

Hugo, Victor (1802–85). Having tried to reconcile classicism and romanticism, Victor Hugo became the leader of the romantic movement with the preface to *Cromwell* (1827). He defended the principle of art for art's sake in the "Préface des *Orientales*" (1829). It was *Hernani* (1830), a play inspired by Shakespearean themes and German romanticism, that provoked the literary battle between classics and moderns. Among Hugo's most famous novels are *Notre-Dame de Paris* (1831), symbol of the Gothic revival for the romantics of the period, and *Les Misérables* (1862), an epic of human spiritual redemption in the face of social injustice. Hugo devoted himself to politics after the death of his daughter Léopoldine (1843), advocating a humanitarian and liberal democracy. In exile throughout the Second Empire (1851–70), he published *Les Châtiments* (1853), a diatribe directed at Napoleon after the December 1851 coup. *Les Contemplations* (1856), a collection of poems inspired by his daughter's death, meditated on a theory of punitive reincarnation and universal redemption at the end of time.

Flaubert first met Hugo at the sculptor James Pradier's Paris studio in 1842. Hugo was one of the few to recognize at once that *Madame Bovary* was a masterpiece. He later supported Flaubert strongly for election to the Académie Française and still later for a government post that could alleviate Flaubert's financial woes. (APZ/LMP)

References:

Jullien, Dominique. "Biography of an Immortal." *Comparative Literature* 47 (1995): 136–59.

Porter, Laurence M. *Victor Hugo*. New York: Twayne, 1999.

Ward, Patricia. "Victor Hugo; ou, Le Calcul des profondeurs." *French Review* 71 (1997): 290–91.

Hussonet (*ES*, 1869). Hussonet forms part of the *Art Industriel* circle that has gathered around Jacques Arnoux's art journal and art dealership in *L'Education sentimentale*. He enjoys frequenting artists, and compensates for his own lack of creative talent through eccentricity—notably, by affecting an archaic spoken French. He also systematically, mechanically adopts contrarian views in conversation, to try to make himself seem interesting. Frédéric Moreau sees through him, and is merely bored and irritated by Hussonet. The latter seeks easy, lucrative literary triumphs as a hack journalist and playwright, and after that, as a conservative political pen for hire. Enjoying an unmerited but ironically apposite success, under the Second Empire he ends up as Chief Censor. If we recall Flaubert's trial on the charge of having offended public and religious morals with *Madame Bovary*, we can imagine the distaste and contempt with which he viewed his unsympathetic character Hussonet. (LMP)

Reference:

Paulson, William. *Sentimental Education: The Complexity of Disenchantment.* New York: Twayne, 1992.

I

iconography. At present there are at least four major sources of images concerning Flaubert and his creations: printed materials, films, CD-ROMs, and Web resources. The last three of these four also often accompany images with text and with sound. Since students', teachers' and readers' cognitive/learning styles vary widely, and since persons whose special abilities involve color, sound, or the perception of spatial relationships are often disadvantaged and discouraged in the conventional text-centered classroom or in the experience of personal reading, it seems desirable to reinforce their learning experience by using more than one channel of communication. Moreover, because, starting in primary school, many students now regularly prepare assignments involving use of and downloading from the Web, and because the visual experience of television watching fills several hours a day for many people, to make the classroom experience more congruent with students' everyday lives appears a practical strategy. Professor Timothy Unwin at the University of Liverpool maintains a World Wide Web site there, *Dix-Neuf,* that lists nineteenth-century French and Francophone resources in discography and "webliography." The *Internet Movie Database* includes television adaptations, information concerning actors and directors, plot summaries, and directions on how to purchase or consult films. The Ubi Soft CD-ROM of *Madame Bovary* includes sound and graphics. Among conventional printed materials, the *Album Flaubert* edited by Jean Bruneau and Jean-A. Ducourneau has an excellent collection of documents, sketches, and photographs, although some images are small. René Dumesnil's compilation provides images of Flaubert, his family, friends, homes, and haunts. Peter Wetherill's volume on *L'Education sentimentale* offers many contemporary portraits and images that may roughly correspond to what Flaubert saw or imagined while composing this novel. (LMP)

See also electronic resources; film adaptations of Flaubert's works.

References:

Bruneau Jean, and Jean-A. Ducourneau, eds. *Album Flaubert.* Paris: Gallimard, 1972.
Dix-neuf. http://www.liv.ac.uk/french/dix-neuf.
Dumesnil, René. *Flaubert et* L'Education sentimentale. Paris: Les Belles Lettres, 1943.
Flaubert, Gustave. *Madame Bovary* (CD-ROM). Paris: Ubi Soft, 1997.
Internet Movie Database. http://us.imdb.com/.
Wetherill, Peter M., ed. and comp. L'Education sentimentale: *Images et documents.* Paris: Garnier, 1985.

image and **metaphor.** In his well-known battle against his effusive romantic tendencies, Flaubert worked hard to limit the metaphors in his texts: "Rassure-toi, d'ailleurs: je me prive de métaphores, je jeûne de comparaisons et dégueule fort peu de psychologie" (Anyhow, you may rest assured: I've stopped consuming metaphors, I'm severely limiting my intake of similes, and I'm barfing up very little psychology) (Letter to Louis Bouilhet, May 24, 1835, *Corr.* 4: 72). Yet Flaubert claims to have loved metaphors: "Les grandes tournures, les larges et pleines périodes se déroulant comme des fleuves, la multiplicité des métaphores, les grands éclats du style, tout ce que j'aime enfin, n'y sera pas" (Grandiloquence; wide, full periodic sentences that flow like rivers; crowds of metaphors, starbursts of style—in a word, everything I love—won't be found here) (Letter to Louise Colet, May 21–22, 1853, *Corr.* 2: 202).

Don-Louis Demorest's study demonstrates that Flaubert indeed had a natural tendency to write metaphors, as shown by the many images in his early letters and youthful writings. Drafts of his well-honed works show that he consistently eliminated metaphors. Not surprisingly, the more ironic, realist texts such as *L'Education sentimentale* and *Bouvard et Pécuchet* do indeed contain fewer metaphors and images than the exotic, romantic texts such as *Salammbô* and "Hérodias."

Flaubert's effort to eliminate the narrator's voice from his stories helps produce this limitation of metaphor, since a metaphor sometimes serves to reflect an impersonal narrator's point of view. For instance, when Rodolphe finds that Emma's language is rife with empty clichés, the narrator intervenes to contradict that opinion with a comparison: "Il ne distinguait pas, cet homme si plein de pratique, la dissemblance des sentiments sous la parité des expressions . . . [O]n en devait rabattre, pensait-il, les discours exagérés cachant les affections médiocres; comme si la plénitude de l'âme ne débordait pas quelquefois par les métaphores les plus vides, puisque personne, jamais, ne peut donner l'exact mesure de ses besoins, ni de ses conceptions ni de ses douleurs, et que la parole humaine est comme un chaudron fêlé où nous battons des mélodies à faire danser les ours, quand on voudrait attendrir les étoiles" (Despite all his experience with women, the equivalence of expressions prevented him from discerning the differences in feelings. She ought to tone it down, he thought: her exaggerated language conceals the ordinariness of her attachment to me—as if a soul bursting with love could not sometimes brim over with the emptiest metaphors: no one ever can express the precise dimensions of her needs, her conceptions, or her sufferings. Human speech is like a cracked cauldron on which we beat out tunes fit only to set bears dancing, although we yearn to make the stars weep in sympathy) (259).

The metaphors that Flaubert does use (some 10,000 according to Demorest) are well adapted to the worlds of the works, as they should be according to the rules of rhetoric. In "Un cœur simple," the images correspond to Félicité's simple world and draw mainly on what she might experience or know. When she flees from the bull in the field, the comparison of its hoofbeats with hammers is one that she might make. In *Madame Bovary*, a sardonic image of Charles corresponds perfectly to the idea, to Charles, and to Emma's own possibilities of imagining this metaphor: "La conversation de Charles était plate comme un trottoir de rue" (Charles's conversation was as flat as a sidewalk) (101).

In *Salammbô*, by contrast, the images are rich and majestic and correspond to the ancient world's possibilities. Flaubert introduces us to Salammbô through the viewpoint of the soldiers who see her, and this permits him to add a comparison that might come from them: "Des soldats l'avaient aperçue la nuit, sur le haut de son palais, à genoux devant les étoiles, entre les tourbillons des cassolettes allumées. C'était la lune qui l'avait rendue si pâle, et quelque chose des dieux l'enveloppait comme une vapeur subtile" (Some soldiers had seen her on the roof of her palace, kneeling beneath the stars, among the swirling flames of braziers. It was the moon that had made her look so pale, and an aura from the gods enveloped her like a fine mist) (*Salammbô* 14). These images can be remarkably expressive: "Au bas de Malqua, des filets de pêcheurs s'étendaient d'une maison à l'autre, comme de gigantesques chauves-souris déployant leurs ailes" (At the foot of Malqua, fisherman's nets were stretched between the houses, like enormous bats spreading their wings) (*Salammbô* 47). It is perhaps this restricted use of images that makes those that survive so striking and memorable in an otherwise impersonal transcription of events. (DJK)

References:

Demorest, Don-Louis. *L'Expression figurée et symbolique dans l'œuvre de Gustave Flaubert*. Geneva: Slatkine, 1967 (1931).

Flaubert, Gustave. *Madame Bovary*. Ed. Bernard Ajac. Paris: Flammarion, 1986.

———. *Salammbô*. Paris: Les Belles Lettres, 1944.

Proust, Marcel. "A propos du style de Flaubert." In Marcel Proust, *Chroniques*. Paris: Gallimard, 1927.

indeterminacy. Critics often juxtapose Flaubert with Balzac to show how Balzac's texts summarize, lecture, and conclude, whereas Flaubert's texts leave us somewhat at a loss; they seem to make us unsure of our conclusions. Flaubertian indeterminacy has many contributing factors, which have attracted much attention in recent years.

First, Flaubert's novels do not show us many heroes. The reader cannot find a character with whom to identify, because all the characters have major flaws that we would not like to admit in ourselves. Emma Bovary dreams of a better life, but in pursuing her dreams, she trivializes and debases them. We would not wish to be so foolish, yet we do value the desire to better one's life. What should we think of Emma? Frédéric Moreau, although he is the main character of *L'Education sentimentale*, squanders his life through indecision; indeed, indecision, or perhaps indeterminacy, becomes the subject of the novel itself. But what other main character in the novel is more meritorious? Félicité, in "Un cœur simple," is an honest, hardworking, faithful servant, but she is so simple-minded that we cannot elect her as our heroine. At the end of their stories, Flaubert's characters leave us in a state of indecision, an effect of the indeterminate value of his characters.

Many other elements of Flaubert's style enhance this indeterminacy. Free indirect discourse, because it presents at least two different narrative voices, leaves us hovering between the narrator and the characters. What, for instance, does the exclamation point mean in this sentence: "Ils arrivèrent, en effet, ces fameux Comices!" (And indeed, the day of that splendid fair arrived!) (Flaubert 197)? Is it the emotion of the "on," the townspeople who anxiously await the day? Or is it the expression of anticipation by Rodolphe, the subject of the preceding section, who plans to meet with Emma then? Or is it the irony expressed by the narrator that such a commonplace ceremony should create such expectancy? Irony itself, of course, participates in indeterminacy, because often one is not quite certain whether the text is ironic.

Furthermore, the multiple narrative points of view in many of Flaubert's texts destabilize any particular perception of events. Even Charles presents his dreams to us. This indeterminacy of viewpoint can lead to wonderfully comic effects, as when the carriage in which Emma and Léon make love is seen "continuellement" (318) by the very indeterminate "on" of Rouen. Finally, descriptions, seemingly unmotivated by anything but the presentation of disconnected details, leave us with no orienting consciousness, no definite meaning.

At the end of Flaubert's works, then, one is left with questions—questions about values, dreams, meaning—that Flaubert refuses to answer. Such indeterminacy forces one to turn the spotlight inward, to question oneself and to question human life itself. Do I have dreams like Emma's? Do I believe that life has meaning as it does in novels? Do I behave like Félicité? Should I or should I not? Flaubert himself warns against definitive answers in this well-known pronouncement: "Oui, la bêtise consiste à vouloir conclure. Nous sommes un fil et nous voulons savoir la trame" (Yes, stupidity consists in wanting to reach conclusions. We are a single thread and we want to comprehend the entire warp and woof) (Letter to Louis Bouilhet, September 4, 1850, *Corr.* 2: 239). (DJK)

References:

Culler, Jonathan. *Flaubert: The Uses of Uncertainty*. 1974. Rev. ed. Ithaca: Cornell University Press, 1985.

Flaubert, Gustave. *Madame Bovary*. Ed. Bernard Ajac. Paris: Garnier, 1986.

Prince, Gerald. "A Narratological Approach to *Madame Bovary*." In Laurence M. Porter and Eugene F. Gray, eds., *Approaches to Teaching Flaubert's* Madame Bovary. New York: Modern Language Association, 1995. 84–89.

inédits (unpublished works). Flaubert's unpublished works fall into two principal categories, depending on the nature of a particular work and on the reason why he did not publish it; on the one hand, texts that remained unpublished during Flaubert's lifetime; on the other, texts still unpublished today. In the first category are texts that Flaubert did not wish to appear, mainly for aesthetic reasons; this applies to nearly all of the works written before *Madame Bovary*, a novel that marks Flaubert's first major publication. There are also all of the writer's "personal papers," that is, the manuscripts, whether they are drafts, correspondence, isolated notes, or notebooks (*Carnets de lecture* and *Carnets de voyages*), which Flaubert obviously never meant to publish.

The second category is comprised of texts that have appeared since his death. Actually, the publication of Flaubert's *inédits* began early. *Bouvard et Pécuchet* is a good example of this: its writing was interrupted by the author's unexpected death (in the middle of the final chapter of what is called the "first volume," the second volume being "conjectural"), and the unfinished novel was published a year later, in 1881. Since then, the requirements of literary research have incited specialists to edit Flaubert's early works (juvenilia), correspondence, and, later, manuscripts, rapidly decreasing the number of Flaubert's unpublished texts. Flaubert is the most studied French author of the nineteenth century, about whom an immense amount of documentation has been discovered, so that almost all of his works, either finished or unfinished, are now available in print. They have appeared mainly in Flaubert's *Œuvres complètes*, but even today, it is still possible to discover previously unpublished letters that further enrich the volumes of the *Correspondence* (and many owners of known letters have refused to release them).

Many manuscripts are progressively being published in critical editions (for instance, those of the *Carnets* and of the *Voyage en Orient*) or in articles, particularly when they correspond to minor works (such as *De la littérature romantique en France* and *Louis XIII*) or even to reading notes (such as "Esdras et Néhémias, Tobie, Judith, Esther, Job, les Psaumes"). However, the most important works that remain unpublished are the manuscripts of Flaubert's major texts, that is, the *avant-textes* themselves (scenarios and sketches, drafts, and autograph manuscripts). Although they should appear in the form of genetic editions, this type of edition remains unfortunately rare for reasons of length, complexity, and cost (some excerpts of the drafts are also published in diverse genetic publications). Therefore, the majority of the drafts for *Madame Bovary* (apart from the plans and scenarios of the novel, which have appeared in an excellent edition) and all of the drafts for *Salammbô, L'Education sentimentale, La Tentation de saint Antoine*, and *Bouvard et Pécuchet* are still unpublished, although in principle these may be ordered from the microfilms department of the Bibliothèque Nationale. (ELC)

References:

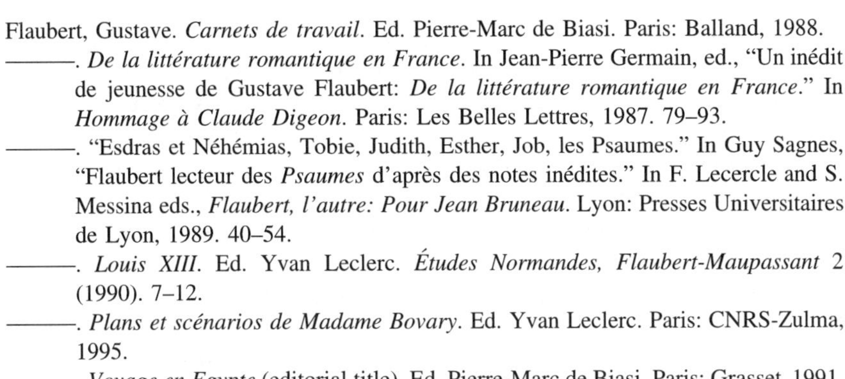

Flaubert, Gustave. *Carnets de travail*. Ed. Pierre-Marc de Biasi. Paris: Balland, 1988.

———. *De la littérature romantique en France*. In Jean-Pierre Germain, ed., "Un inédit de jeunesse de Gustave Flaubert: *De la littérature romantique en France*." In *Hommage à Claude Digeon*. Paris: Les Belles Lettres, 1987. 79–93.

———. "Esdras et Néhémias, Tobie, Judith, Esther, Job, les Psaumes." In Guy Sagnes, "Flaubert lecteur des *Psaumes* d'après des notes inédites." In F. Lecercle and S. Messina eds., *Flaubert, l'autre: Pour Jean Bruneau*. Lyon: Presses Universitaires de Lyon, 1989. 40–54.

———. *Louis XIII*. Ed. Yvan Leclerc. *Études Normandes, Flaubert-Maupassant* 2 (1990). 7–12.

———. *Plans et scénarios de Madame Bovary*. Ed. Yvan Leclerc. Paris: CNRS-Zulma, 1995.

———. *Voyage en Egypte* (editorial title). Ed. Pierre-Marc de Biasi. Paris: Grasset, 1991.

irony. Without in any way exhausting the subject or covering all its possible subdivisions, one may use an interactive model to distinguish four main varieties of irony, which pit the world against the self, the self against the self, or the self against the other. Cosmic irony in literature presents a world blind or hostile to human hopes and desires, and it is nearly always present in Flaubert's works. When Charles Bovary, meeting his dead wife's lover Rodolphe, says, "Fate was to blame," the unprincipled Rodolphe scorns Charles because it was he, Rodolphe, who "had directed that fatality" after finding a target of opportunity in Emma. But on a deeper level, any Flaubertian character who hopes for more than money or power is bound to be disappointed. When the loving, devoted, unappreciated servant Félicité in "Un cœur simple" loses everyone she had cherished, and even her stuffed parrot, cosmic irony again seems at work, but Flaubert equivocally reverses it with a final apotheosis. A further implication of cosmic irony is that the world never can be understood—as implied by Matthew Arnold's description of it as a place where "ignorant armies clash by night" ("Dover Beach"). To Flaubert, history seems an "entirely unintelligible disorder" (Ramazani, "Historical Cliché," 122).

A generalized, explicitly verbal form of cosmic irony is incommunicability (the chronic inability of language to make us understood). When Rodolphe misreads Emma Bovary's expressions of passionate devotion to him as clichés, the narrator intervenes with a generalization: "Human speech is like a cracked cauldron on which we beat out tunes fit only to set bears to dancing, when we would have wished to make the stars weep in sympathy." Vaheed Ramazani offers an interesting discussion of this issue as it affects the writer. Because language must be a shared repertory for communication to occur, this language, which the author had hoped to use to express and affirm a unique vision, is always the least common denominator. That books in the nineteenth century are mass manufactured and distributed for commercial gain further deprives the literary work of art of any claim to transcendence ("Historical Cliché" 121, 132–33).

Tragic irony again pits the world against the self, but this time the reader feels that if only the protagonist had known more, a tragedy could have been avoided. Racine's Theseus, in *Phèdre*, curses his son Hippolytus and brings about his death because he does not realize that Hippolytus has been falsely accused. Such irony is uncommon in Flaubert because most of his characters lack the will and intelligence to change their world, no matter how much they know, and the villains, focused on their material self-interest, ordinarily know everything they need to know.

Romantic irony, characteristic of the nineteenth-century writers Lord Byron, Heinrich Heine, and Alfred de Musset, pits the self against the self when the author intervenes in his or her own work to mock its quality, originality, and insight. Again, such irony is uncommon in Flaubert, who aspired to be "like God in His universe, everywhere influential and nowhere visible." As might be expected, one can find more traces of such irony in Flaubert's early works, when he still strongly feels the influence of romanticism. In the first chapter of *Mémoires d'un fou*, for example, after saying that he will pour out to us all of his thoughts and feelings, the narrator adds, "It weighs on me, however, that I'm going to crush the tips of a bunch of quill pens, that I'm going to waste a bottle of ink, that I'm going to bore the reader and bore myself" (*Early Writings* 162; translation modified).

Finally, figural or verbal irony pits the self—the implied author or a representative—against the other. For example, when the fatuous pharmacist Homais's wife asks anxiously about his blood pressure after Emma's death in *Madame Bovary*, Doctor Larivière answers, "Ce n'est pas le sang [sens] ce qui le gene" (It's not an excess of blood/common sense that is his problem). The irony is compounded because Mme Homais does not understand the pun. Most often, instances of verbal irony, like romantic irony and unlike cosmic or tragic irony, are segmental (localized) rather than pervasive (generalized). There are exceptions, however. Intertextual citation and allusion to a particular ludicrous motif can pervade a work (see the discussion of the tissue of ironic references to the "beatus ille" topos—"fortunate is the person who can live in the peace of the country"—in *Bouvard et Pécuchet* in the entry on pastoral). Because irony is one of the few figures of speech that can be dramatized, that is, embodied in fictional characters, the entire work *Bouvard et Pécuchet* represents an evolution of the title characters from *alazons* (braggarts and pretentious know-it-alls who are always mistaken) to *eirons* (those who deflate the pretensions of others). (LMP)

References:

Felman, Shoshana. "Flaubert's Signature: *The Legend of Saint Julian the Hospitable.*" In Naomi Schor and Henry F. Majewski, eds., *Flaubert and Postmodernism.* Lincoln: University of Nebraska Press, 1984. 46–75.

Flaubert, Gustave. "Diary of a Madman." In Gustave Flaubert, *Early Writings*, trans. and ed. Robert Griffin. Lincoln: University of Nebraska Press, 1991. 161–203.

Haig, Stirling. *Flaubert and the Gift of Speech: Dialogue and Discourse in Four Modern Novels.* Cambridge: Cambridge University Press, 1986.

Ramazani, Vaheed. *The Free Indirect Mode: Flaubert and the Poetics of Irony.* Charlottesville: University Press of Virginia, 1988.

———. "Historical Cliché: Irony and the Sublime in *L'Education sentimentale.*" *PMLA* 108.1 (1993): 121–35.

———. "Lacan/Flaubert: Towards a Psychopoetics of Irony." *Romanic Review* 80 (1989): 548–59.

Italy. Italy was the destination of Flaubert's trip with his family in 1845 and again in 1851, as the final leg of his trip to the Orient with Maxime Du Camp. The first visit lasted three weeks: Flaubert and his parents accompanied his sister Caroline and her husband Emile Hamard on their honeymoon. Influenced by romantic authors' idealization of Italy, Flaubert admired the vistas, streets, narrow houses, and barefoot women and children. Genoa's architectural beauty also impressed him, and he found Como very "Italian" with its pleasure boats and "Shakespearean" landscape around the lakes (Flaubert 1:44–45). Flaubert visited many museums and marveled at Antonio Canova's *Love and Psyche* in Como and Pieter Breughel's *Temptation of Saint Anthony* at the Balbi Palace in Genoa.

During his second visit (February–June 1851), Flaubert sought Italy's ancient past. Disappointed with Rome's Renaissance trappings, he wrote to Louis Bouilhet: "I was looking for Nero's Rome but found only that of Sixtus V" (April 9, 1851, *Corr.* 2:304–5). The presence of Christian churches and art also clouded Flaubert's mental image of ancient Rome. Naples, the promenade lined with oaks at La Chiaia, and Venice pleased him. His *Notes de voyage* from this trip include learned descriptions of the art he encountered. In Rome, he was impressed by the Vatican, the Sistine Chapel, and Michelangelo's *Last Judgment.* (JWA)

References:

Bruneau, Jean. "Les Deux Voyages de Gustave Flaubert en Italie." In *Connaissance de L'Etranger: Mélanges offerts à la mémoire de Jean-Marie Carré.* Paris: Didier, 1964. 164–80.

Claudon, Francis. "A propos des voyages de Flaubert: Le *Voyage en Italie et en Suisse* (1845)." In *Flaubert et Maupassant: Ecrivains normands.* Paris: Presses Universitaires de France, 1981. 91–109.

Flaubert, Gustave. *Notes de voyages.* In Gustave Flaubert, *Œuvres complètes.* 28 vols. Paris: Conard, 1910–54. Vols. 3–4.

Gut, Philippe. "L'Italie vue par Flaubert." *Les Amis de Flaubert* 47 (1975): 4–12.

J

James, Henry (1843–1916). Henry James was introduced by Ivan Turgenev to Flaubert's literary circle (which he characterized to William Dean Howells as "the little *coterie* of the young realists in fiction") during his residence in Paris in the winter of 1875–76 (James, *Letters* 116). While James counted among his precursors numerous British and continental novelists, Flaubert occupied a unique place in James's literary consciousness. His four essays on Flaubert written between 1874 and 1902 reflect an ambivalent, shifting valuation of Flaubert's achievement and narrative procedures, but the 1902 essay, the longest and most important of these, lauds *Madame Bovary* as the most literary of novels and its author as the "novelists' novelist," (346), from whom "there is endlessly much to be learned" (316). James singles out for particular praise "the dignity of Madame Bovary herself as a vessel of experience" (325), though he finds her character portrayal "comparatively meager" (336) and insufficiently self-conscious. (In effect, he faults Emma Bovary for not being a Jamesian center of consciousness.) James reinterprets Flaubert's *style indirect libre* for his limited third-person point of view, using the conditional mood much as Flaubert uses the imperfect tense to modulate subtly between perspectives. Especially in such late works as *The Sacred Fount* (1901), *The Beast in the Jungle* (1903), and *The Golden Bowl* (1904), James follows Flaubert in attenuating plot in favor of representing complex dramas of consciousness.

A telling instance of James's redefinition of novelistic event as interior and psychological occurs in Isabel Archer's unwitting allusion in *The Portrait of a Lady* (1881) to Emma's dream of fleeing to Italy with Rodolphe: she confides to Henrietta Stackpole, "A swift carriage, of a dark night, rattling with four horses over roads that one can't see—that's my idea of happiness" (James, *Portrait* 187). The allusion underscores Isabel's internalization of Emma's romanticism, as the male object of Emma's desire is replaced by Isabel's idealized relation to her own imagination. Though Isabel suffers for her peculiarly Emersonian version of bovarysme, consciousness remains for James—as for Flaubert—a limitless domain. (ST)

References:

Balsamo, Gian. "Henry James and Emma Bovary." *Canadian Review of Comparative Literature* 18 (1991): 547–56.

Cook, David A. "James and Flaubert: The Evolution of Perception." *Comparative Literature* 25 (1973): 289–307.

Ferguson, Suzanne. "The Face in the Mirror: Authorial Presence in the Multiple Vision of Third-Person Impressionist Narrative." *Criticism* 21 (1979): 230–50.

Gervais, David. *Flaubert and Henry James: A Study in Contrasts*. London: Macmillan, 1978.

Grover, Philip. *Henry James and the French Novel: A Study in Inspiration*. London: Elek, 1973.

James, Henry. *Letters, Fictions, Lives. Henry James and William Dean Howells*, ed. Michael Anesco. New York: Oxford University Press, 1997.

———. *Literary Criticism: French Writers, Other European Writers*. New York: Library of America, 1984. Contains a revised version of Gustave Flaubert, *Madame Bovary*, "Introduction." New York: Appleton, 1902.

———. *The Portrait of a Lady*, ed. Nicola Bradbury. Oxford: Oxford University Press, 1995.

Purdy, Strother B. "Henry James, Gustave Flaubert, and the Ideal Style." *Language and Style* 3 (1970): 163–84.

Weinstein, Philip M. "A Round of Visits: James among Some European Peers." In Daniel Mark Fogel, ed., *A Companion to Henry James Studies*. Westport, CT: Greenwood Press, 1993. 235–64.

Jarry, Alfred. *See* le Garçon.

Jelinek, Elfriede (1946–). Elfriede Jelinek is a prolific Austrian writer whose scandalous novel *Lust* ("Desire," 1989) has evoked parallels with *Madame Bovary*. The action of both novels unfolds in a small, provincial town, and in both, an unhappy wife's attempt to free herself through adultery leads only to her being sexually exploited. Jelinek's fictive husband Hermann, however, unlike the gentle, devoted Charles Bovary, is a brutal oppressor who considers both his wife and the factory workers he employs to be "human trash" (Lehnert 37). He beats his wife Gerti and forces her to lick his penis clean each time he rapes her, and to dry it with her hair. Her lover half-rapes her and then betrays her by abandoning her to her husband. Like Medea, Gerti exacts a self-destructive revenge by killing her son; but in Jelinek's grim world, this son is little more than one more material possession—Emma's bankrupting her husband Charles is therefore closer to Gerti's revenge than it would at first appear. Jelinek, unlike Flaubert, does not analyze the wife's feelings in detail, but does imply that the husband's godlike patriarchal dominance belongs to a system of hegemony to which the woman has in part consented, exchanging her body for financial support. "In Jelinek's vision of a marriage there is nothing outside such sexual politics, and that is why everything seems so hopeless" (Lehnert 41). Moreover, Jelinek suggests that in the heterodiegetic dimension of her novel, the author's patriarchal power sustains itself by once again exploiting—and literally consuming—its female victim inside the text. (LMP)

References:

Jelinek, Elfriede. *Lust.* Reinbek bei Hamburg: Rowohlt, 1989.

Lehnert, Gertrude. "Elfriede Jelinek's *Lust* and *Madame Bovary*." In Jorun B. Johns and Katherine Arens, eds., *Elfriede Jelinek: Framed by Language.* Riverside, CA: Ariadne Press, 1994. 35–47.

Schestag, Uda. *Sprachspiel als Lebensform: Strukturuntersuchungen zur erzählenden Prosa Elfriede Jelineks.* Bielefeld: Aisthesis, 1997.

Schlich, Jutta. *Phänomenologie der Wahrnehmung von Literatur: Am Beispeil von Elfriede Jelineks* Lust *(1989).* Tübingen: Nìemeyer, 1989.

Jenner, ou la découverte de la vaccine. *See La Découverte de la vaccine.*

Jerusalem. Flaubert had hoped to find faith in the Holy City; as he entered it, he had a vision of Christ. But he was soon dismayed by the local commercialism and exploitation of tourists. Rival Christian sects fought so fiercely over the Holy Sepulcher that the local pasha had to keep the keys to it. Flaubert became profoundly disappointed with God, with the Christians, and with the other local inhabitants (Bart 200–203). (LMP)

Reference:

Bart, Benjamin F. *Flaubert.* Syracuse: Syracuse University Press, 1967.

Joyce, James (1882–1941). James Joyce claimed to have read all of Flaubert, who was a critical precursor for English modernism in general and Joyce in particular. Ezra Pound declared "English prose catches up with Flaubert" in Joyce's *Dubliners* (1914: Pound, "Past History" 351). Pound also described *Ulysses* (1922) as "the first [book] which, inheriting from Flaubert, continues the development of Flaubertian art from the point where he left it in his last unfinished book," *Bouvard et Pécuchet* (Pound, *Polite Essays* 82–83). The collage, catalog, and encyclopedic strategies of *Bouvard et Pécuchet* are reworked in *Ulysses* and especially *Finnegans Wake* (1939), in which the anarchic proliferation of seemingly random or meaningless linguistic units both parodies the pseudo-scientific procedures of naturalism and challenges the referential assumptions of realism. *Ulysses* and *Finnegans Wake* also contain numerous formal and thematic allusions to *La Tentation de saint Antoine*. Joyce's œuvre bears the clear imprint of Flaubert's protomodernist attenuation of plot in favor of exploring the minute play of consciousness. Joyce's use of interior monologue creates a dominant third-person subjectivity (such as Stephen's in *A Portrait of* *the Artist as a Young Man*, 1916) rather than the intermittent third-person subjectivity presented through the use of *style indirect libre* in precursors such as Jane Austen, Johann Wolfgang von Goethe, or Flaubert. As with *style indirect libre*, however, interior monologue remains indeterminate because the author introduces an intermittent ironic distance between character and narrator. (ST)

References:

Bernheimer, Charles. "Grammacentricity and Modernism." *Mosaic* 11 (1977): 103–16.

Cross, Richard K. *Flaubert and Joyce: The Rite of Fiction*. Princeton: Princeton University Press, 1971.

Hayman, David. "A De-Simplified Heart: Flaubert through a Joycean Optic." In Reingard M. Nischik and Barbara Korte, eds., *Modes of Narrative: Approaches to American, Canadian, and British Fiction*. Würzburg: Königshausen & Neumann, 1990. 45–56.

———. "*A Portrait of the Artist as a Young Man* and *L'Education sentimentale*: The Structural Affinities." *Orbis Litterarum* 19 (1964): 161–75.

Kenner, Hugh. *Flaubert, Joyce, and Beckett: The Stoic Comedians*. Boston: Beacon Press, 1962.

Pound, Ezra. "Past History." *The English Journal* 22 (1933): 351.

———. *Polite Essays*. Norfolk, CT: New Directions, 1940.

———. *Pound/Joyce; The Letters of Ezra Pound to James Joyce, with Pound's Essays on Joyce*, ed. Forrest Read. New York: New Directions, 1967.

Revue des Lettres Modernes 953–58 (1990). Special issue on Flaubert and Joyce.

Spiegel, Alan. "Flaubert to Joyce: Evolution of a Cinematographic Form." *Novel: A Forum on Fiction* 6 (1973): 229–43.

Viswanathan, Jacqueline. "Spectacles de l'esprit: Flaubert, Hardy, Joyce." *Poétique* 19 (1988): 373–91.

Jules (*ES*, 1845). In the 1845 version of *L'Education sentimentale*, Jules (whose family name is never given) is one of the two protagonists. Originally conceived of by Flaubert as a simple foil for Henry Gosselin, Jules ends up with a privileged role. Denied the opportunities afforded Henry, Jules remains in the provinces, where, after being rebuffed in love, he turns away from the world. After his mystical encounter with a hideous dog, he abandons his past and throws himself into the passion of books and art. The introversion of Jules leads to rigorous study and, eventually, to an overarching principle of aesthetics based on analysis, concision, and objectivity mixed with compassion. His mature self may have been modeled in part on Daniel d'Arthez, the idealized writer figure in Honoré de Balzac's *Illusions perdues*.

While the intense early friendship between Jules and Henry calls to mind that between Flaubert and Alfred Le Poittevin, or even Maxime Du Camp, Jules clearly evolves into a kind of alter ego for Flaubert himself, for the principles attributed to the character are the very ones being tested in the composition of the novel. Structurally the role of Jules will become like that of Deslauriers in the 1869 version of the novel, although Deslauriers has none of Jules's artistry or integrity. The twinning of Jules and Henry also foreshadows another famous Flaubertian pair, Bouvard and Pécuchet. (SDC)

References:

Bruneau, Jean. *Les Débuts littéraires de Gustave Flaubert, 1831–1845*. Paris: Colin, 1962.

Diamond, Marie J. *Flaubert: The Problem of Æsthetic Discontinuity*. Port Washington, NY: Kennikat Press, 1975.

Ginsburg, Michal Peled. *Flaubert Writing: A Study in Narrative Strategies*. Stanford: Stanford University Press, 1986. 16–45.

Justin (*MB*). Justin is the young pharmacist's apprentice in *Madame Bovary* who secretly admires and loves Emma. He seeks every pretext he can think of to be near her or her clothing, helping her maid and polishing the muddy boots she wore to her assignations with Rodolphe—a Cherubino with a fetishist bent. His employer, Homais, scolds him for reading a manual on *Conjugal Love*. By a cruel twist of fate, he is the one who leads Emma to the place where the arsenic that she consumes is stored. After her death, the gravedigger Lestiboudois catches him weeping at night on her grave and jumps to the conclusion that it is Justin who has been stealing his potatoes, which he sacrilegiously grows among the tombs. In microcosm, this last incident sums up two major themes of the novel: the sacred (the tombs of the dead) is profaned by commercialism (cultivating tubers among them), and the deepest, purest devotion (Justin's for Emma, like Charles's for Emma or hers for Rodolphe) will always be unrecognized and unappreciated by its recipient. (EFG/LMP)

Reference:

Gothot-Mersch, Claudine. *La Genèse de* Madame Bovary. Paris: Corti, 1966.

K

Kafka, Franz (1883–1924). Franz Kafka is one of the greatest authors in the German language. Goethe and Flaubert's cult of art, which Kafka shared, made him rate them above all other authors. He particularly savored Flaubert's journals.

Kafka's novels *Amerika, The Castle*, and *The Trial* and his powerful, dismaying stories such as "The Hunger Artist," "Metamorphosis," and "The Penal Colony" emphasize the absurdity of the human condition, the futility of our striving, and the failure of communication. Jorge Luis Borges situates him at the end of a satiric continuum that runs from Jonathan Swift through Flaubert, claiming that his foolish, involuntary *eirons* (fictional characters whose remarks deflate the vainglorious pretensions of others) unwittingly speak deep truths and shatter the conventional frame of the novel. Here one could invoke as harbingers not only Flaubert's Bouvard and Pécuchet, whose naïve questions call all academic, sociological, and scientific disciplines into question, but also Charles Bovary at the end of his novel. He excuses Emma's infidelities by saying, "Fate was to blame," and Flaubert's omniscient narrator observes, "That was the most profound remark he ever made in his life." Rodolphe, "who had directed that fatality," scorns Charles for his spinelessness, but the author means that regardless of our strength of will or character, we have little control over our lives. Charles Bernheimer's study *Flaubert and Kafka* offers an excellent analysis of Flaubert's fetishism, but does not attempt a systematic comparison of the two authors. Walter Sokel's groundbreaking book emphasizes the tragic irony of the situations in which Kafka's protagonists find themselves; they inevitably lack the knowledge that would allow them to act effectively or to understand their accursed destinies. Most of Flaubert's characters are equally blind, but they create their own problems and their own derisory successes, whereas Kafka's universe is implacably hostile.

Regarding their differences, James Rolleston sharply contrasts Flaubert's supremely realist, detailed descriptive style and Kafka's seamless style, in which realism is impossible. Although Flaubert's mimesis seems an end in itself, dates and a historical context can be intuited, whereas Kafka's nightmare worlds seem to float in a void. In the social microcosm, Kafka depicts oppressive families and numerous paternal surrogates, whereas Flaubert portrays disintegrating families that fail to perpetuate themselves. (LMP)

See also fetishism.

References:

Bem, Jeanne. "Flaubert lecteur de Kafka; ou, L'Ecriture de l'existence." *Revue d'histoire littéraire de la France* 81. 4–5 (1981): 677–87.

Bernheimer, Charles. *Flaubert and Kafka: Studies in Psychopoetic Structure*. New Haven: Yale University Press, 1982.

Corngold, Stanley. "The Curtain Half Drawn: Prereading in Flaubert and Kafka." In Clayton Koelb and Susan Noakes, eds., *The Comparative Perspective on Literature: Approaches to Theory and Practice*. Ithaca: Cornell University Press, 1988. 263–83.

Parlej, Piotr. *The Romantic Theory of the Novel: Genre and Reflection in Cervantes, Melville, Flaubert, Joyce, and Kafka*. Baton Rouge: Louisiana State University Press, 1997.

Rolleston, James. "Kafka's Time Machines," In Ruth V. Gross, ed., *Critical Essays on Franz Kafka*. Boston: Hall, 1990. 85–88.

Sokel, Walter H. *Franz Kafka: Tragik und Ironie: Zur Struktur einer Kunst*. Munich: Langen, 1964.

Weinstein, Leo. "Altered States of Consciousness in Flaubert's *Madame Bovary* and Kafka's 'A Country Doctor.' " In Raymond J. Cormier, ed., *Voices of Conscience: Essays on Medieval and Modern French Literature in Memory of James D. Powell and Rosemary Hodgins*. Philadelphia: Temple University Press, 1977. 215–29.

Karr, Alphonse. (1808–90). The journalist Alphonse Karr became the director of *Le Figaro* in 1839. He created a newspaper, *Les Guêpes* (1839–49), that satirized politics, letters, and the arts; he also wrote mediocre novels. In *Les Guêpes* of June 1840, he insinuated that Louise Colet's child was fathered by her lover Victor Cousin. Colet, incensed, went to Karr's house and attempted to stab him with a kitchen knife. After wresting the knife from her, Karr hung it on the wall of his study under the inscription "Donné par Madame Colet, née Revoil, dans le dos." (MMC)

Reference:

Scales, Derek P. *Alphonse Karr, sa vie et son oeuvre*. Geneva: Droz, 1959.

"The Kugelmass Episode." *See* Allen, Woody.

L

Lagier, Suzanne (Honorine-Suzanne-Marie-Louise, 1833–93). One of Flaubert's many actress friends, Suzanne Lagier made her debut in Charles Dupeuty's one-act vaudeville, *La Veuve de quinze ans*, in 1846 and later played Marguerite de Bourgogne in Alexandre Dumas's famous *La Tour de Nesle* (first written in 1832), a production that greatly intensified the medievalist vogue of French romanticism. After 1865, Lagier gained renown among the aristocrats, artists, and writers who gathered to hear her licentious songs at the *caf'-conc'* (a coffeehouse, with live entertainment) on the Boulevard de Strasbourg in Paris. The Goncourts' *Journal* portrays her as a witty, bold, lascivious woman known for her ribald tongue. Among her lovers were Alexandre Dumas fils, Sainte-Beuve, Maupassant, and Flaubert, whom she later visited in his beloved home at Croisset, near Rouen, during the last decade of his life. Concerning her affairs, she allegedly said, "J'en ai eu cent, cent-cinquante, est-ce que je sais? Un homme, pour m'aimer, aurait eu trop de choses à me reprocher" (I've had a hundred lovers, a hundred fifty, what do I know? A man who loved me [as a husband or committed partner] would have had too many things for which to reproach me). Rosanette Bron's story of the loss of her virginity, in *L'Education sentimentale* of 1869 (her mother sold her to an older man), comes from Suzanne Lagier's life (Bart 516). (APZ)

References:

Bart, Benjamin F. *Flaubert.* Syracuse: Syracuse University Press, 1967.

Morembert, T. de. "Suzanne Lagier." *Dictionnaire de biographie français* 19:254–55. Paris: Letouzet et Ané, 1995.

Lamartine, Alphonse de (1790–1869). A lyric poet and liberal politician, Alphonse de Lamartine was for three months the head of the Second Republic in 1848. His *Méditations poétiques et religieuses* (1820) inaugurated the second generation of French romanticism. Flaubert at least twice used the romantic cliché of two young lovers' ride on a lake, inspired by Lamartine's poem "Le Lac"—seriously in *Mémoires d'un fou* and satirically in *Madame Bovary*. Jules, the writer hero of the first *Education sentimentale* (1845), comes to reject as insipid "the lake with its tedious boat and its perpetual moonlight" (Starkie 112). Some details from idyllic descriptions of nature in Lamartine reappear in the episode of the Forest of Fontainebleau in the second *Education sentimentale* (1869). Although Lamartine objected to the brutal realism of Emma Bovary's death scene, he at first courageously volunteered to write a letter to help defend Flaubert against the imperial government's accusation of having offended public morals. Once he reread the novel more carefully, however, and realized that it was making fun of him, he withdrew his support (Starkie 153–54). Nevertheless, his initial admiring letter proved useful at the trial. (LMP)

Reference:

Starkie, Enid. *Flaubert: The Making of the Master*. New York: Atheneum, 1967.

Langlois, Eustache-Hyacinthe (1777–1837). Eustache-Hyacinthe Langlois was a painter, engraver, and art teacher at the Ecole municipale de Rouen. In 1831, he took Flaubert and his classmates to visit the church of Caudebec-en-Caux, which contains a statue of Saint Julian and a stained-glass window depicting the legend of Saint Eustache; the two saints' stories are similar. Langlois's 1832 *Essai historique et descriptif sur la peinture sur verre ancienne et moderne* included an interpretation of the story of Saint Julian as shown in the Rouen cathedral's stained-glass windows; Langlois's version influenced Flaubert's interpretation of "La Légende de saint Julien l'Hospitalier." Flaubert declared to his publisher Charpentier that to illustrate the deluxe edition of his story, he would accept only a line drawing from Langlois's book, depicting the Saint Julian window. (MMC)

Reference:

Bart, Benjamin F., and Robert F. Cook. *The Legendary Sources of Flaubert's* Saint Julien. Toronto: University of Toronto Press, 1977.

Lapierre, Marie-Valérie. Marie-Valérie Lapierre was the wife of Flaubert's friend Charles Lapierre, the owner and editor of *Le Nouvelliste de Rouen*. Flaubert fondly called her, her sister, Madame Charles Brainne, and their actress friend Madame Alix-Marie-Angèle-Sein Pasca "my three angels." ("Pasca" was a stage name for "Pasquier".) These charming women provided a welcome distraction from the financial hardships Flaubert endured in the 1870s to rescue his niece and her husband from bankruptcy. Nevertheless, after an evening spent with the Lapierres, Flaubert admitted to Caroline that "my angels are pretty silly. . . . I think they love the man in me, but as for the mind I'm aware that I often shock them or seem mad" (quoted in Steegmuller 2: 194n).

Flaubert had chosen Saint Polycarp as his patron, ostensibly from sympathy with the saint's supposed lament "Oh God, oh God, in what an age thou hast made me live!" Madame Lapierre organized an annual Saint Polycarp celebration for Flaubert at her Rouen home; Charles Lapierre gives an account of the last one, just before Flaubert's death in 1880 (38–44). (APZ)

References:

Lapierre, Charles. *Esquisse sur Flaubert intime*. Evreux: Hérissey, 1898.

Steegmuller, Francis, ed. *The Letters of Gustave Flaubert*. 2 vols. Cambridge, MA: Harvard University Press, 1980–82.

Laporte, Edmond (1832–1906). Edmond Laporte was a devoted friend of Flaubert. The two men met in the mid-1860s. Laporte was then running a small lace factory near Croisset. In 1868, he became Flaubert's assistant. He helped to copy materials and gather information and even accompanied the writer on an investigative tour through Normandy. Beginning in 1875, Laporte agreed to sign several promissory notes for Flaubert's niece. Laporte found himself caught in a dangerous chain of events; being in financial straits, he decided in 1879 to stop being a guarantor. Angry about Laporte's retraction, the Commanvilles induced Flaubert to end his friendship abruptly. Later, Caroline censored all references to the quarrel in the *Correspondence*. (CG)

Reference:

Bart, Benjamin F. *Flaubert*. Syracuse: Syracuse University Press, 1967.

Larivière Dr. (*MB*). Charles Bovary's former teacher in paramedical school, Dr. Larivière assumes epic proportions when he is called to minister to Emma after she takes arsenic. Despite being depicted as approaching godhood, Larivière is powerless to save Emma, saying only, "That's fine, that's fine," in response to Dr. Canivet's remarks. He strongly reprimands both the pharmacist Homais and Canivet for their incompetent choice of treatment for Emma and mocks Homais with a pun that passes unnoticed. His gaze, "plus tranchant que ses bistouris, vous descendait droit dans l'âme at et désarticulait tout mensonge" (sharper than his scalpels, would penetrate you to the depths of your soul and dismember every lie). He is the only character in the book with this godlike, penetrating vision. Some biographers believe that his portrait is derived from Flaubert's own father, head surgeon at the Rouen hospital. (EFG)

Reference:

Bart, Benjamin F. *Flaubert*. Syracuse: Syracuse University Press, 1967.

Le Poittevin, Alfred (1816–48). Alfred Le Poittevin was Flaubert's closest childhood friend from 1837 on. His mother had been a girlhood friend of Flaubert's mother; Flaubert's father was Le Poittevin's godfather; and Le Poittevin's father was Flaubert's godfather. The two boys and their two sisters were constant companions.

Le Poittevin was sensitive, withdrawn, gloomy, and morbid. He wanted above all else to become a writer. He greatly contributed to forming Flaubert's literary and philosophical tastes. Both boys published precociously in a biweekly Rouen little magazine, *Le Colibri* (The hummingbird), which Le Poittevin edited. Later, Le Poittevin and Maxime Du Camp became fierce rivals for Flaubert's friendship. When Le Poittevin married in 1846 and left Rouen for Paris, Flaubert felt jealous and envious, but he was already beginning to nurture a new friendship with Louis Bouilhet, to whom he would remain devoted for the rest of his life. All his old feelings returned, however, when he watched over Le Poittevin on his deathbed (his premature demise may have been caused by alcoholism), and afterward, Flaubert felt his friend's influence more intensely than ever (Starkie 35–41, 107–8, 156–59). (LMP)

References:

Bardèche, Maurice. *L'Œuvre de Flaubert*. Paris: Les Sept Couleurs, 1974; Paris: La Table Ronde, 1988.

Starkie, Enid. *Flaubert, the Making of the Master*. New York: Atheneum, 1967.

Le Poittevin, Laure (1821–?). Laure Le Poittevin was the sister of Alfred Poittevin and a beloved childhood friend of Flaubert. The Le Poittevins, Caroline, and Gustave Flaubert were constant companions. Laure married Gustave de Maupassant, but separated to raise her two sons, Guy and Hervé, alone. She and Flaubert remained in touch, and her son Guy, the future writer, became Flaubert's surrogate son and protégé. Rumors that Guy was Flaubert's biological son have never been convincingly supported. (LMP)

Reference:

Bart, Benjamin F. *Flaubert*. Syracuse: Syracuse University Press, 1967.

"Une Leçon d'histoire naturelle, genre commis" (1837). "Une Leçon d'histoire naturelle, genre commis" is a Voltairean mockery of the hubristic efforts of contemporary zoologists, represented by the famous efforts of Baron Georges Cuvier (1769–1832) and Henri Blainville (1777–1850) who contradicted Cuvier, his mentor, to classify all living things. Flaubert pretends to extend their efforts to the genus "Clerk," a being he describes as subhuman. Its thoroughly predictable habits and its major activity, making fair copies of handwritten texts, anticipate *Bouvard et Pécuchet* forty-four years later and express the adolescent Flaubert's disdain for the prospect of "settling down." Herman Melville's "Bartleby the Scrivener" carries such satire one step further, depicting a clerk in whom routine becomes paralyzing psychosis. (LMP)

Reference:

Flaubert, Gustave. "A Lecture on Natural History—Genus:*Clerk*." In Gustave Flaubert, *Early Writings*, trans. and ed. Robert Griffin. Lincoln: University of Nebraska Press, 1991. 45–49.

Leconte de Lisle, Charles-Marie (1818–94). Charles-Marie Leconte de Lisle was the leader of the Parnassian school of poetry, characterized by its insistence on formal perfection, its cult of classical antiquity, its impassivity, and its exotic subjects. In 1900, polls showed that the public rated him second only to Victor Hugo among nineteenth-century French poets. He was a friend of Flaubert, who considered him a kindred spirit. In *L'Idiot de la Famille*, Jean-Paul Sartre groups him with Flaubert as a "knight of nothingness" (3:193–202), someone who champions detachment and disengagement. (LMP)

Reference:

Sartre, Jean-Paul. *L'Idiot de la famille*. 3 vols. Paris: Gallimard, 1971–72.

"La Légende de saint Julien l'hospitalier" (1876). The center of the triptych formed by *Trois Contes*, "La Légende de saint Julien l'hospitalier" was written over six months in 1875–76. Flaubert sought respite from the grueling composition of *Bouvard et Pécuchet*; he also hoped to recover some financial stability after rescuing his niece from insolvency. Inspired by the stained-glass window in the cathedral of Rouen that traced Saint Julian's life, the project dated from 1856 (Bart and Cook 29–39). The tale combines a reworking of the Oedipus myth with its biblical antecedents by introducing an oracle, a parricide, and the flight and wanderings of the protagonist. Mostly in free indirect discourse, the narrative relates Julien's journey toward self-definition and self-determination.

The tale is symmetrically structured: transgression is followed by expiation. The young Julian commits progressively more sadistic carnage, deriving voluptuous gratification from taking life. At last, after he had mortally wounded a stag in an orgiastic massacre, the creature, who embodies the displaced voice of Julien's father, curses him three times and prophesies that the cruel youth will murder his own parents. After this encounter, Julien represses his compulsion to hunt, becomes despondent, and then, despite the stag's admonition, seeks once again to slaughter animals—this time without success. In his absence, his wife has welcomed his parents and has put them in her and Julien's bed. Thinking that she has committed adultery, Julien kills them both in the dark. In retrospect, this profoundly inhospitable act and unwitting violation of filial piety makes his previous savage killings of game seem displaced aggressions against his parents.

In the second part, Julien reacts to his crime with suicidal depression, but then has an epiphany. Having recognized his father's image in his own reflection, he seems to overcome his narcissism. He begins an ascetic life of charitable service as a hyperbolically hospitable ferryman, moving from his wife's castle to a squalid mud hut—a place of decay and decomposition. One day, he helps a dying leper, who demands food, shelter, and, finally, the warmth of Julien's embrace in bed. When Julien complies, the leper transforms himself into Jesus Christ and carries Julien off to heaven. This ascension recalls the imagined apotheosis of the stuffed parrot, another figure of transformation, at the conclusion of "Un cœur simple." Aimée Israel-Pelletier draws a speculative parallel between Julien and Jesus Christ, calling them both rebellious sons who defied the concept of God the Father as One (79).

The initial sentences of "Un cœur simple" and "Hérodias" refer, respectively, to Mme Aubain and to the citadel of Machaerous, each representing those existing structures of class and political power that the protagonist will challenge. The incipit of "La Légende de saint Julien l'hospitalier" similarly evokes figures of parental authority—Julien's mother, his father, and their castle. Julien's pious mother is visited by a prophetic figure who predicts that her son will become a saint. His more worldly father receives a prophetic message that his son will be an emperor. The infant Julien's life, either way, is presented as an already-written text from the outset. A conventional reading proposes a hagiography inscribed in the tradition of medieval saints' lives. Israel-Pelletier's alternative reading surpasses the binary opposition of sinner and saint to focus on Julien as the unformed self attempting to create its own meaning by opposing previously imposed parental texts. Julien does finally fulfill the hagiographic and worldly texts of his parents, but not before achieving his own rewriting of the self, dictated by his own desires. He seeks communion with nature and the primordial energies absent from the rigid, bloodless civilization to which his parents belong.

In earlier works such as *Salammbô* (1862), Flaubert depicts the savage or barbarian as an ambivalent force, carrying both the threat of unspeakable horror and death and the promise of regeneration and rebirth. His savage impulses make Julien similarly ambivalent: for all his saintly self-sacrifice, he remains remorseless, with no love for humanity. He does, however, triumph over the corrupt material world of his father through his perfect spiritual union with Christ. Despite its hagiographic foundations, Flaubert's tale has been emptied of the moral content typical of the narratives of medieval saints' lives.

The stained-glass window Flaubert gives as a reference point contains a sequence of medallions representing many scenes not present in Flaubert's narrative, such as Julian transporting the Devil in his boat, or Julian and his wife ascending to the heavens. Conversely, the hunting scenes, the leper, the apotheosis, and many other episodes related in Flaubert's legend do not appear in the iconography of the window. The retrospective, ecphrastic nature of the narrative becomes explicit when it begins, "Et voilà l'histoire de Saint Julien l'hospitalier, telle à peu près qu'on la trouve, sur un vitrail d'église, dans mon pays" (And here is the story of Saint Julian the Hospitalor, more or less as it can be found on a stained-glass window where I came from). Typographically detached, this sentence can be seen as the key controlling the whole tale as it strips narrative of its purported objective status and challenges the discourse of religious authority enshrined within it (Killick 315). The variance between Flaubert's version of the legend and the historical document on which it was based, combined with his desire to reproduce the stained-glass window along with the text, shows his intent to violate the traditional historiographical legend.

The hunting motif can be understood as a metaphorical treatment of writing. Both Flaubert and Julien in a sense destroy the world—with pens or with arrows, respectively (Israel-Pelletier 81). Julien's effortless killing in his youth would correspond to Flaubert's early, lyrical writing, which came more easily to him than did his writing on contemporary subjects because it was based on the referent of the self rather than on the unifying principles of style that inform his mature works. Such a reading equates Julien, fearful and guilt-stricken after slaying his parents, with Flaubert, equally fearful and guilty for having slain the classical literary models of the past. Julien's later difficulties in striking his targets would reflect Flaubert's growing sense of language's troubled relationship to the world and his resulting sense of impotence as a writer. For Israel-Pelletier, Julien's ultimate fusion with Christ figures Flaubert's solution to the problem of writing in a language not dominated by his father, and thus subject to difference and violence. Flaubert cannot assert himself as an original writer, cannot break away from tradition, without enacting a symbolic murder of his literary forebears and thus becoming guilty of an Oedipal transgression. Flaubert evades this aporia by embracing Christ as the surrogate mother whose disintegrating leprous body paradoxically effects the dissolution of difference, while using her as a model for writing against the father in a language that both reflects and transforms the world. (JM)

References:

Bart, Benjamin F. *Flaubert.* Syracuse: Syracuse University Press, 1967. 670–86.

Bart, Benjamin F., and Robert Francis Cook. *The Legendary Sources of Flaubert's* Saint Julien. Toronto: University of Toronto Press, 1977.

Israel-Pelletier, Aimée. *Flaubert's Straight and Suspect Saints: The Unity of* Trois Contes. Amsterdam: Benjamins, 1991.

Killick, Rachel. " 'The Power and the Glory'? Discourses of Authority and Tricks of Speech in *Trois Contes" Modern Language Review* 88.2 (1993): 307–20.

Weber-Caflisch, Antoinette. "La Place de la culpabilité dans *L'Education sentimentale* et 'La Légende de saint Julien l'hospitalier.' " *Travaux de littérature* 8 (1995): 287–317.

Léon Dupuis (*MB*). *See* Dupuis, Léon.

Leroux, Catherine (*MB*). Catherine Leroux is the servant in *Madame Bovary* who receives a silver medal at the agricultural fair for her "54 years of service." Her portrait is typically Flaubertian, with the external point of view, the characteristic physical details of the person, and the cynical comments of the spectators who witness her single-minded religious faith. One is reminded of Félicité, the servant in "Un coeur simple." The reader cannot help but feel sympathy for this elderly woman whose only recompense for a "half-century of servitude" is a medal. (EFG)

Reference:

Goldin, Jeanne, ed. *Les Comices agricoles de* Madame Bovary *de Flaubert.* 2 vols. Geneva: Droz, 1984.

Leroyer de Chantepie, Marie-Sophie (1800–1885). A resident of Angers, the spinster Marie-Sophie Leroyer de Chantepie first wrote Flaubert on December 18, 1856, having finished the last installment of *Madame Bovary* published in *La Revue de Paris.* Voicing her heartfelt identification with Flaubert's "poor Madame Bovary," Mlle Leroyer de Chantepie offered a striking testimonial to the novel's realism. "Monsieur . . . I saw, from the first, that you had composed a masterpiece of truth and naturalness. Yes indeed! These are truly the customs of that province where I was born and where I spent my life! That is sufficient to explain to you how I understood the sadness, the boredom, the unhappiness of that poor Madame Bovary. From the outset I recognized her and loved her as a friend. I identified myself so much with her life that it seemed to me that it was I, that it was she! No, that story isn't fiction, it is truth, that woman has existed, you must have been a witness of her life, of her death, of her suffering." Leroyer de Chantepie then asked Flaubert where he had acquired "this perfect knowledge of human nature," which she described as "the scalpel applied to the human heart, to the soul" (Starkie 267–68; translation modified). This enthusiastic praise inspired an intimate, affectionate epistolary relationship that lasted for twelve years. The two correspondents never met, but their lengthy exchanges reflect a meeting of the minds based on a nineteenth-century woman's social and spiritual discontents as they intersect with Flaubert's aesthetic and religious views. As Flaubert wrote her on November 4, 1857 (*Corr.* 4:231), "The more experience I acquire in my art, the more tormenting that art becomes. . . . You cling to the religious ideas that cause you so much suffering, and I to the chimera of style, which consumes me body and soul. But perhaps we are worth something only because of our sufferings, for these are all aspirations." (APZ)

References:

Starkie, Enid. *Flaubert, the Making of the Master.* New York: Atheneum, 1967.

Steegmuller, Francis, ed. *The Letters of Gustave Flaubert.* 2 vols. Cambridge, MA: Harvard University Press, 1980–82.

Lestiboudois (*MB*). Lestiboudois is the sexton who insensitively plants potatoes in the church graveyard, even though the priest protests, "You're feeding yourself with the dead." Always alert for a profit, he rents out chairs from his church during the agricultural fair. When he surprises Justin weeping on Emma's grave at night, and the young man flees, Lestiboudois assumes that it is Justin who has been stealing his potatoes. Flaubert uses these comically concrete episodes to make a point about conventional spirituality: even those appointed as guardians of the official state religion heedlessly profane it. (LMP)

Lévy, Michel (1821–75). By 1856, the Paris publisher Michel Lévy was rapidly becoming established in the literary world: he had already published Baudelaire, Dumas fils, Gautier, Hugo, Mérimée, Sand, and Stendhal. Perhaps more important to Flaubert, his dear friend Louis Bouilhet had just signed two contracts with Lévy. Maxime Du Camp had serialized *Madame Bovary* in *La Revue de Paris* in 1856–57. Lévy quickly recognized its importance and purchased the rights to it on Christmas Eve, 1856, for only 800 francs (about three weeks' wages for a clerk). The first run was 6,750 copies (Lottman 139–40). Lévy issued a new edition in 1861.

In 1862, he purchased *Salammbô* after intense negotiations: he wanted to see the text in advance of acceptance, he wanted it illustrated, and he also asked for right of first refusal on Flaubert's next novel on a modern subject. Flaubert detested the idea of illustrations and wanted 20,000–30,000 francs. As the author's expectations rose together with his fame, he began to betray an unattractive anti-Semitic side in his private references to Lévy. Author and publisher finally settled on 10,000 francs, a sizable sum in those days. The novel quickly went into a third printing.

George Sand, whose complete works were being published by Lévy, went to the publisher on Flaubert's behalf to negotiate the contractual price for *L'Education sentimentale*. Three thousand copies were printed, but they had not sold out after four years, perhaps because of their high price. The publisher then issued a less expensive edition. Flaubert finally broke with Lévy over a misunderstanding about who would pay the printing costs for a posthumous volume of poetry by Flaubert's beloved friend Louis Bouilhet. Without consulting Lévy, Flaubert had insisted on a lavish format to make the slim volume appear full-length. Flaubert then held back *La Tentation de saint Antoine* until 1873, when his contract with Lévy expired. Sand tried in vain to engineer a reconciliation. Flaubert was so angry when Lévy was awarded the medal of the Legion of Honor that he stopped wearing his own decoration until the publisher died in 1875, and even then he remarked that Lévy had not deserved his peaceful death. Georges Charpentier then purchased the rights to Flaubert's works and reissued them, with hundreds of minor stylistic retouches by the author. (LMP)

References:

Flaubert, Gustave. *Lettres inédites de Gustave Flaubert à son éditeur Michel Lévy*, ed. Jacques Suffel. Paris: Calmann-Lévy, 1965.

Lottman, Herbert. *Flaubert: A Biography*. New York: Fromm, 1990.

Lewis, (Harry) Sinclair (1885–1951). Sinclair Lewis's criticism of American small-town narrow-mindedness and bourgeois philistinism through the protagonist in *Main Street* evokes the bourgeois critique in Flaubert's *Madame Bovary*. Carol Kennicott's reactions to disappointing experiences convey Lewis's vision of middle-class values. Like Emma in Yonville—although her character is not as much affected by love—Carol has read literature only to find grotesque approximations of her dreams in the provincial reality of Gopher Prairie. Flaubertian hostility toward small-town mentality further shows through Lewis's depicting the village impersonally, much as Flaubert's portrayal of rural Normandy lets the reader infer the author's satirical intentions from it. Lewis himself, however, in his interview with Austin, denied that Flaubert had influenced him. (IC)

References:

Austin, Allen. "An Interview with Sinclair." *University of Kansas City Review* 24 (Spring 1958): [199]–210.

David, Simone. "Carol Kennicott de *Main Street* et sa lignée européenne." *Revue de littérature comparée* 19 (1939): 407–16.

Schorer, Mark. *Sinclair Lewis: An American Life*. New York: McGraw–Hill, 1961.

Lheureux (*MB*). Lheureux is a minor but a masterful portrait of the wheedling, seductive, ruthless salesman. He repeatedly tempts Emma Bovary to buy expensive things she does not need, lends her money when she does not have enough, and finally takes advantage of her unpaid debts to have all her and Charles's household effects confiscated. He ruins others as well and obviously represents the modern age of commerce and credit for which Flaubert felt great disdain.

An original, speculative study by Mary Orr emphasizes his ambiguous sexuality, his Protean character, his love for deception, and his sadism. "The fetishist *par excellence*" (Orr 53), he preserves tokens from his victims. Control of money provides him with a power that compensates for his deficient masculinity. The text hints that he may even overwhelm Homais, who embodies the triumph of energetic mediocrity, in the end. (EFG/LMP)

Reference:

Orr, Mary. "Reversible Roles: Gender Trouble in *Madame Bovary*." In Tony Williams and Mary Orr, eds., *New Approaches in Flaubert Studies*. Lewiston, NY: Mellen, 1999. 49–64.

life (1821–80). Gustave Flaubert was born in Rouen on December 12, 1821. His father was head of surgery at the local hospital. Flaubert's older brother Achille followed his father's example; his younger sister Caroline was a beloved childhood companion, but she married young and died in childbirth. He was schooled at home by his mother until he went to the Collège Royal in Rouen. At times he appeared lost in thought to an extent that suggested the presence of the temporal-lobe epilepsy that would later give him frequent seizures. But despite Jean-Paul Sartre's claim that he was dyslexic, Flaubert wrote and acted out plays with his friends, starting before he was ten. Since he displayed no signs of a medical vocation, he was sent to Paris to study law, the default career choice for well-to-do young men who could decide on nothing else. The onset of overt epilepsy in 1844 freed him from this unwelcome obligation, and from then on he was able to write at home, to travel, or to visit Paris as he pleased. His father's premature death in 1846 left Flaubert with a comfortable inheritance, and he stayed in the family house at Croisset, on the bank of the Seine just outside Rouen, for the rest of his life. He was devoted to his mother, who died only eight years before he did. Together, they raised his ungrateful niece Caroline, who would eventually find her identity in becoming the main custodian of his memory and of his manuscripts and a bit of a Flaubert scholar.

Biographers have made much of Flaubert's childhood infatuation with Elisa Schlésinger and of his stormy liaison with the writer Louise Colet, but most of his life was his work. He proceeded slowly, after elaborate documentation and many preliminary sketches. In 1849, he completed the manuscript of his first major work, *La Tentation de saint Antoine*, but his friends discouraged him from trying to publish it, and he was to hold it back until 1874, except for some portions published in 1856. It blends extensive research on early church history with memories of epileptic visions. A parade of demonic figures and false gods tries to distract Saint Antoine from prayer. Flaubert's twenty-month journey through the Middle East and down the Nile in 1849–51 revived his interest in *La Tentation* by leaving him with vivid mental images of the places and peoples among which the action of his novel had been set.

On his return, he set to work on *Madame Bovary*, his masterpiece. This novel treated what Flaubert knew best: it satirized small-town, middle-class mediocrity in Normandy, jarringly contrasted with the impractical, selfish dreams of a pretty farmer's daughter. Initially it was published in installments in *La Revue de Paris*, edited by Maxime Du Camp. The imperial prosecutor Ernest Pinard promptly indicted the author and the publisher for offenses against public morals and religion, but a masterful defense by the defense attorney Jules Sénard got them off with a judicial reprimand. At the time of publication, only a few kindred spirits fully appreciated *Madame Bovary*; later, critics gave Flaubert backhanded praise by comparing his later works unfavorably to it. However, Flaubert found an admirer in Princess Mathilde, a cousin of the reigning emperor, Napoléon III. He enjoyed invitations to her salon and started one of his own in Paris that met from one to seven on Sunday afternoons. It attracted several great writers who were loyal to Flaubert, but he never gained enough support in intellectual milieux to win a much-deserved election to the Académie Française.

Flaubert was embittered by the Prussian occupation of France and of his own house in 1870 and was devastated by the loss of his mother in 1872 and the financial disasters of his nephew-in-law Ernest Commanville, to whom he sacrificed most of his modest resources from 1875 on. His writings take a decidedly somber turn during the final decade of his life, but at the same time, his friendship with the great writer George Sand inspired him with a renewed idealism expressed in his *Trois Contes* (1877), three stories about saints. Among them, the Saint Julian legend and "Un cœur simple" won unrestricted praise and, thanks to Flaubert's friend Ivan Turgenev, were promptly translated into Russian.

The remainder of Flaubert's life can be largely summed up by listing his ensuing works: *Salammbô* (1862), *L'Education sentimentale* (1869), *La Tentation de saint Antoine* (1874), and the posthumous *Bouvard et Pécuchet* (1881). Although they were not written for publication, Flaubert's letters at their best form another masterpiece. He was one of the greatest and most prolific correspondents of his century, in contrast, say, to the vapid, routine, or ceremonial letters of Victor Hugo. He died on May 8, 1880, probably from a brain hemorrhage, likely resulting from the third stage of the syphilis contracted thirty years earlier in the Middle East. His niece immediately took charge of his manuscripts and preserved most of them intact, although on her death they were scattered among several museums. Flaubert's enduring importance can be gauged by such signs as that in the definitive *Critical Bibliography of French Literature*, volume 5, *The Nineteenth Century* only Baudelaire and Balzac receive more space, and Stendhal about the same; or that in the United Kingdom, more *dix-neuvièmistes* today identify themselves as Flaubert scholars than as specialists of any other author. (LMP)

References:

Bart, Benjamin F. *Flaubert*. Syracuse: Syracuse University Press, 1967.

Gray, Eugene F., and Laurence M. Porter. "Gustave Flaubert." In David Baguley, ed., *A Critical Bibliography of French Literature*. Vol. 5: *The Nineteenth Century*. Syracuse: Syracuse University Press, 1994. 801–66.

Lottman, Herbert. *Flaubert: A Biography*. New York: Fromm, 1990.

Sartre, Jean-Paul. *L'Idiot de la famille*. 3 vols. Paris: Gallimard, 1971–72. Rev. 1988.

Starkie, Enid. *Flaubert: The Making of the Master*. New York: Atheneum, 1967.

———. *Flaubert, the Master*. New York: Atheneum, 1971.

Steegmuller, Francis. *Flaubert and Madame Bovary: A Double Portrait*. Rev. ed. New York: Farrar, Straus & Giroux, 1968 (1939).

Louis-Philippe (1773–1850). King of the French (1830–48), Louis-Philippe, duke of Orléans, was the son of Louis-Philippe d'Orléans and Louise-Marie de Bourbon-Penthièvre. He joined the army of the French Revolution, but deserted (1793) and remained in exile until the Bourbon Restoration (1814). He was chosen as king of France after the revolution of 1830 (Monarchy of July). Flaubert grew to maturity under Louis-Philippe (nicknamed the "bourgeois monarch"). Louis-Philippe became increasingly unpopular with both the right and the left. The king's removal of the liberal marquis de Lafayette from the government had aroused the indignation of even the apolitical Flaubert. He despised Louis-Philippe, whom he considered a traitor. Campaigns against the government led to Louis-Philippe's abdication in February 1848 in favor of his grandson. Flaubert vividly described scenes from the 1848 revolution in *L'Education sentimentale* (1869). The Second Republic was declared; Louis-Philippe then fled to England, where he died. (CB/GB)

Reference:

Wright, Gordon. *France in Modern Times, from the Enlightenment to the Present.* New York: Norton, 1988 (1968).

Lucia di Lammermoor. The opera *Lucia di Lammermoor* by Gaetano Donizetti is based on a novel by Sir Walter Scott. Emma Bovary goes with Charles to see it in Rouen because Homais has suggested the outing as a distraction for the depressed Emma. There she meets Léon again; her affair with him follows. (LMP)

See also opera scene.

Ludovica. *See* Pradier, Louise.

lust and death (*TSA*, all versions). The Devil ostensibly abandons Saint Antoine at the beginning of the seventh and final section of the definitive 1874 version of *La Tentation de saint Antoine*. But the saint is promptly tormented by sexual fantasies about his childhood acquaintance Ammonaria—the only woman other than his mother whom he has ever known. Despair at his continuing moral weakness leads him to contemplate suicide by leaping off the cliff beside the Nile where he lives. At this sinful thought, an aged, emaciated women appears. She first resembles Antoine's mother come to life. She tempts him with the prideful thought that he could undo God's creation by killing himself, and with the prospect of relief from the sufferings of his arduous life. But then a marvelously beautiful woman appears to tempt him by telling him where he can find a skillful prostitute. The two apparitions vie for Antoine, offering him permanent repose or ecstasy by turns. Soon their robes part, revealing a sensuous body and a skeleton. They continue to tempt him, and then merge into a single undulating figure: a death's head atop a naked woman's torso with a wormlike tail. When this vision disappears, Antoine realizes "Encore une fois c'était le Diable, et sous son double aspect: l'esprit de fornication et l'esprit de destruction" (Once again, it was the Devil in his twofold guise: the spirit of fornication and the spirit of destruction [257]). He rejects both happiness and death as illusions, and proclaims his faith in the immortality of the soul. The devil will not return. (LMP)

Reference:

Flaubert, Gustave. *La Tentation de saint Antoine*, Ed. Edouard Maynial. Paris: Garnier, 1968.

M

Madame Bovary (serialized, 1856; as book, 1857). *Madame Bovary* is Flaubert's best-known novel and one of the seminal novels of the nineteenth century. The origins of the novel have been the subject of some debate, but one must conclude that Flaubert's sources were multiple. Maxime Du Camp reports in his *Souvenirs littéraires* that during their trip to Egypt, Flaubert was already thinking about his future novel and one day cried out, "Eureka! Je l'appelerai Emma Bovary." Du Camp's recollection is mistaken on this point. On the other hand, his contention that the novel is based on the real-life story of an *officier de santé* (a public health officer, roughly equivalent to a registered nurse) and his wife who lived in the village of Ry, near Rouen, is accurate in its broad outlines. Eugène Delamare married, as his second wife, a young woman named Delphine Couturier. They had a daughter; she had a number of affairs, went into debt, and died in 1848 at age twenty-six; he died a year later. Rumors spread that they both died of poison, but there is no documentary evidence of it. How did Flaubert learn about the Delamare story? Louis Bouilhet, who had been a medical student of Flaubert's father, was apparently the first one to suggest the subject. But Delamare also studied with the older Flaubert, and the story may well have been a subject of discussion at the Flaubert dinner table. In addition, it appears that Flaubert's mother knew Delamare's mother. The Delamare story provides only the skimpiest outline for the action of the novel; there are many other sources for the story, and it would be a mistake to equate Yonville and Ry, Emma and Delphine, and Charles and Delamare, as some have done. One of the most curious sources is a document titled "Mémoires de Madame Ludovica," an account of the amorous and financial extravagances of Louise Pradier, the wife of the sculptor James Pradier, whom Flaubert knew. Other possible sources are the memoirs of Madame Lafarge, convicted of poisoning her husband in 1840, Honoré de Balzac's *Muse du département* and *Physiologie du mariage*,

Flaubert's relationship with Louise Colet, conversations with friends and acquaintances, and, for the clubfoot chapter, a treatise by Dr. Vincent Duval.

Flaubert spent about five years writing *Madame Bovary*, setting to work on September 19, 1851, and sending the finished manuscript to Maxime Du Camp, of *La Revue de Paris*, on May 31, 1856. Serial publication began in the October issue. The editors, shocked by the realism of the novel and fearing a lawsuit and suppression of the journal, made several serious cuts (for example, Léon's and Emma's cab ride, during which he seduces her). Flaubert, for whom artistic concerns were far more important than political ones, was furious. The novel finally appeared in book form in April 1857. Unfortunately, none of the editions that appeared in Flaubert's lifetime reproduced his manuscript exactly, although the edition published by Charpentier in 1873 (called "définitive") came closest. The next major event in the history of Flaubert's book was the lawsuit brought by the government against Flaubert and *La Revue de Paris* for "outrage à la morale publique et religieuse et aux bonnes mœurs" (offenses to public morals, religious morals, and common decency). After the acquittal, Flaubert was famous, but the whole affair disgusted him. Reviews of the book were almost universally harsh. Reviewers saw in it a new literary form that they deplored: realism. They were repelled by the stark reality of everyday, banal events described with no evidence of emotion, with no uplifting sentiments. Sainte-Beuve, while praising Flaubert's stylistic abilities, found the author cruel and lamented the lack of admirable characters and of consoling thoughts. He thought that the novel contained the characteristics of a new literary form: science, observation, force, and harshness. His last statement (Sainte-Beuve 363) sums up his judgment: "Anatomistes et physiologistes, je vous retrouve partout" (Anatomists and physiologists, I find you everywhere). Baudelaire, on the other hand, did not classify Flaubert as a realist, praising rather his powers of imagination and poetry. For Baudelaire, Emma, far from being the unworthy character seen by most critics, was virile and sublime. Readers may wonder how such a banal story can have inspired so much critical interest for over 140 years. The answer lies in Flaubert's choice of a setting and of characters that could easily be transposed into the twentieth century, and in the artistic application of an ironic and ambiguous style that challenges readers to reach their own conclusions. (EFG)

References:

Auerbach, Erich. *Mimesis: The Representation of Reality in Western Literature*. Trans. Willard R. Trask. Princeton: Princeton University Press, 1953.

Bopp, Léon. *Commentaire sur* Madame Bovary. Neuchatel: La Baconnière, 1951.

Brombert, Victor. *The Novels of Flaubert*. Princeton: Princeton University Press, 1966.

Culler, Jonathan. *Flaubert: The Uses of Uncertainty*. Rev. ed. Ithaca: Cornell University Press, 1985.

Du Camp, Maxime. *Souvenirs littéraires*. 2 vols. Paris: Hachette, 1906.

Gothot-Mersch, Claudine. *La Genèse de* Madame Bovary. Paris: Corti, 1966.
Lloyd, Rosemary. *Madame Bovary*. London: Unwin Hyman, 1990.
Porter, Laurence M., and Eugene F. Gray, eds. *Approaches to Teaching Flaubert's* Madame Bovary. New York: Modern Language Association, 1995.
Sainte-Beuve, Charles-Augustin. "*Madame Bovary* par Gustave Flaubert." In Charles-Augustin Sainte-Beuve, *Causeries du lundi*. Paris: Garnier, 1858. 13: 346–63.
Tanner, Tony. *Adultery in the Novel: Contract and Transgression*. Baltimore: Johns Hopkins University Press, 1979.

Madame Bovary. *See* Bovary, Emma; Bovary, Madame (Charles Bovary's first wife); Bovary, Madame (Charles Bovary's mother).

Madame Bovary, la mort de. *See* death scene of Emma Bovary.

Mann, Heinrich (1871–1950). Heinrich Mann was the brother of the novelist Thomas Mann and, in his own right, a prominent German writer and critic of the early twentieth century. He left Germany for Nice as soon as Hitler took power, and worked for the French Resistance. In 1940, he fled to the United States, where he died in Los Angeles in 1950. He greatly admired Flaubert's antipathy toward the bourgeoisie, use of the grotesque, and impersonal narration combined with intense imaginativeness and sensitivity. His left-wing views contrasted sharply with his brother's conservatism.

Mann's major essay on Flaubert appears in *Geist und Tat*, a volume that also treats Choderlos de Laclos, Stendhal, Hugo, and Zola. In this statement, Mann mystifies Flaubert's cult of art until it attains a visionary, Proustian intensity. Later, Mann also devoted a book to Flaubert's warm friendship with the idealist novelist George Sand. Flaubert greatly influenced Heinrich Mann's "Pippo Spano." Moreover, *Die kleine Stadt* contains many parallels with *Madame Bovary*. (LMP)

References:

Banuls, André. "L'éducation sentimentale." In André Banuls, *Heinrich Mann: Le Poète et la politique*. Paris: Klincksieck, 1966. 161–84.
Mann, Heinrich. *Eine Freundschaft: Gustave Flaubert und George Sand*. Ed. Renate Werner. Munich: Hanser, 1976 (1971).
———. *Geist und Tat: Franzosen, 1780–1930*. Berlin: Keipenheuer, 1931.
———. "Zola." In Heinrich Mann, *Macht und Mensch*. Munich: Wolff, 1919. 25–131. Extract in David Baguley, ed., *Critical Essays on Emile Zola*. Boston: Hall, 1986. 75–80.
Roberts, David. "The Critique of the Artist: Heinrich Mann's Flaubert Essay." *Australian Journal of French Studies* 9 (1974): 23–39.
Weisstein, Ulrich. "Heinrich Mann und Gustave Flaubert." *Euphorion* 57 (1963): 132–55.

Mann, Thomas (1875–1955). One of the greatest twentieth-century German novelists, Thomas Mann won the Nobel Prize in 1929 and later immigrated to the United States. "Before I began to write [the tetralogy *Joseph and His Brothers*], I reread [Flaubert's exotic historical novel] *Salammbô* in order to see how not to do it [to write a historical novel] today. None of this archaeological brocade! None of this scholarly-artsy stuff and none of this deliberately anti-bourgeois cult of crass exoticism!" (Mann, *Werke*, 11:626). However, as Clayton Koelb and Reena Spicehandler explain, there are two fundamental resemblances between important plot elements in *Salammbô* and the *Joseph* novels. The robe veil belonging to Rachel and Joseph seems modeled on the zaïmph, the mystical, untouchable veil of the moon goddess Tanit, the tutelary spirit of Carthage. Rachel and Joseph themselves are identified with the moon goddess Ishtar. Nevertheless, the two goddesses function quite differently: Flaubert's Tanit afflicts Salammbô and Mâtho with an unquenchable sexual passion for each other, which leads to their sadistic destruction. The scene of Flaubert's novel shows Mâtho tortured to death while Salammbô must watch. Then she herself drops dead. The last line dryly observes, "Thus perished the daughter of Hamilcar, for having touched the veil of Tanit" (which she had recovered to save her town). Mann's Ishtar, in contrast, leads her protégés to spiritual fulfillment (LMP)

References:

Furst, Lilian R. "Reading 'Nasty' Great Books." In Virgil Nemoianu and Robert Royal, eds., *The Hospitable Canon: Essays on Literary Play, Scholarly Choice, and Popular Pressures*. Philadelphia: Benjamins, 1991. 39–51.

Koelb, Clayton, and Reena Spicehandler. "The Influence of Flaubert's *Salammbô* on Mann's *Joseph und seine Bruder*." *Comparative Literature Studies* 13 (1976): 315–22.

Mann, Thomas. *Gesammelte Werke*. 12 vols. Munich: Fischer, 1960.

manuscripts. Flaubert belongs to a tradition of writers, especially from the nineteenth century, who decided to save all of their manuscripts. In general, Flaubert's manuscripts have been remarkably preserved, although the ink has a natural tendency to fade with the passing of time, which explains why libraries are often reluctant to give the dossiers to the public (in addition, some manuscripts—for example, many of Flaubert's letters—belong to private collections and therefore are not accessible). Nevertheless, most of the manuscripts have been reproduced on microfilms and are readily available to researchers. The case of Flaubert is therefore privileged for genetic critics and also for editors who need to compare passages from the published texts with their corresponding manuscripts.

Flaubert's manuscripts are heterogeneous, a situation that stems from his writing method. In general, when Flaubert worked on a project, he first wrote *scénarios d'ensemble* (general sketches), in which he drafted the text in broad lines; he then developed *scénarios partiels* (partial sketches), in which the text evolved in a more detailed way, usually one chapter after another. After this second phase, he began to work on the *brouillons* (rough drafts) themselves while writing, in parallel, *scénarios ponctuels* (localized sketches), in which shorter textual fragments germinated along with many details (generally arranged one scene after another). When he finished working on the drafts of a single passage, Flaubert copied the text fragment by fragment on a final manuscript (called the autograph manuscript) that he corrected again and finally gave to a copyist for recopying and then to the publisher. This method, related to Flaubert's well-known obsession with Beauty and stylistic perfection, explains why each work covers thousands of manuscript pages. Besides these drafts, the genetic dossiers also contain *carnets* (notebooks), in which Flaubert took notes regarding information pertinent to the work in progress and locations he visited to check topographic details to be inserted into the narrative. There are also *travel notebooks* (for instance, the *Voyage en Orient*), as well as numerous reading notes. Thanks to the increasing importance of genetic criticism, Flaubert's manuscripts are more and more studied and published, whether it be partially (in genetic publications) or in their entirety (in the form of genetic editions), a trend that progressively reduces the number of Flaubert's *inédits* (unpublished works).

As for the most famous of Flaubert's texts, many manuscripts are preserved in the Bibliothèque Nationale de France in Paris (noted hereinafter "BNF"). These include the dossiers of *L'Education sentimentale* (thirteen volumes), *Salammbô* (seven volumes), *La Tentation de saint Antoine* (eight volumes), and the *Trois Contes* (2 volumes); some of the manuscripts of *La Tentation* are also preserved in Rouen, New York's Pierpont Morgan Library, and Geneva's Fonds Bodmer). The Bibliothèque Municipale de Rouen (noted hereinafter "Rouen") holds a rich collection: the manuscripts of *Madame Bovary* (nine volumes; some notes for *Madame Bovary* are also kept in the Fonds Bodmer in Geneva) and the enormous dossiers for *Bouvard et Pécuchet* and the *Dictionnaire des idées reçues* (fifteen volumes). Flaubert's reading notebooks (*Carnets de lecture*, eighteen volumes) are preserved in the Bibliothèque Historique de la Ville de Paris, as are his travel notebooks (*Carnets de voyage*, thirteen volumes). Among the dossiers concerning Flaubert's reading notes are found the manuscripts on "Bernard Palissy" (Rouen), "Empereurs romains Commode-Julien" (BNF), "Histoire de la République de Gênes" (BNF), "Mythologie" (BNF), "Nalus, épisode du Maba-Bharata" (BNF), "Notes sur Port-Royal de Sainte-Beuve" (Geneva, Fonds Bodmer), and "Philostrate, Vie d'Apollonius de Tyane" (BNF).

Flaubert also wrote, in his youth, many texts (juvenilia) that he never wanted to publish. The rough drafts of *Mémoires d'un fou, Novembre*, and the first version of *L'Education sentimentale* have all disappeared (only the autograph manuscript of the first *Education sentimentale* has been discovered). However, many early manuscripts are accessible (some correspond to texts that Flaubert wrote entirely and others to unfinished projects): *Agonies* (BNF), *Chant de la courtisane* (Geneva, Fonds Bodmer), *Chronique normande du Xe siècle* (BNF),

Composition d'histoire (Rouen), *La Danse des morts* (BNF), *De la littérature romantique en France* (BNF), *Décomposition de la société romaine par les mœurs et les idées de la Grèce* (Geneva, Fonds Bodmer), *Dumesnil, candidat pour la mairie* (BNF), *Etude sur Rabelais* (BNF), *La Femme du monde* (BNF), "La Fiancée et la tombe" (BNF), "les Funérailles du docteur Mathurin" (BNF), "La Grande Dame et le joueur de vielle" (BNF), *Histoire moderne* (BNF), *Influence des Arabes* (Manchester, John Rylands University Library), *Ivre et mort* (BNF), "Une Leçon d'histoire naturelle, genre commis" (BNF), *Louis XIII* (BNF), *La Lutte du Sacerdoce et de l'Empire* (Austin, Humanities Research Center), *La Main de fer* (BNF), *Mademoiselle Rachel* (BNF), *Narrations et discours* (BNF), *Opuscules historiques* (BNF), "Un Parfum à sentir" (BNF), "Passion et vertu" (BNF), "La Peste à Florence" (BNF), "Quidquid Volueris" (BNF), "Rage et impuissance" (BNF), *Rédactions d'histoire naturelle* (Rouen), *Rêve d'enfer* (BNF), *Rome et les Césars* (BNF), "Un Secret de Philippe le Prudent, roi d'Espagne" (BNF), "Les Sept fils du derviche" (BNF), "Smarh" (BNF), and *Souvenirs, notes, et pensées intimes* (BNF).

Flaubert also wrote for the theater. He published only a few plays and kept his early works unpublished, many of which remained in the form of projects. In addition, some plays or projects were written or planned with the collaboration of Louis Bouilhet (noted hereinafter "with LB"). The dossiers of Flaubert's published theater correspond to the manuscripts of *Le Candidat* (BNF, Rouen, and Harvard University, Houghton Library), *Le Sexe faible* (BNF and Rouen) and *Le Château des cœurs* (with LB and Charles d'Osmoy, BNF and Rouen). The manuscripts of unpublished plays or projects include *La Découverte de la vaccine* (with LB, BNF), *Deux Amours et deux cercueils* (project, BNF), *Les Deux pirates* (project, with LB, BNF), *Madame d'Ecouy* (project, BNF), *Marie Dufau* (project with LB, BNF), *Le Marquis de Pombal* (project with LB, BNF), *Parisina* (project with LB, BNF), *La Partie de barres* (project, with LB, BNF), *Pierrot au sérail* (project with LB, BNF), *Le Pivot* (project with LB, BNF), *La Queue de la poire de la boule de Monseigneur* (Austin, Humanities Research Center), *Le Rêve et la vie* (project, Harvard University, Houghton Library) and finally *La Tache de sang* (project with LB, BNF). (ELC)

Reference:

Guidis, Odile de. "Répertoire des manuscrits de Flaubert." In Y. Leclerc, ed., *Plans et scénarios de* Madame Bovary. Paris: CNRS-Zulma, 1995.

Martin du Gard, Roger (1881–1958). Roger Martin du Gard, a French novelist, won the Nobel Prize in 1937. His best-known novels are *Jean Barois* (1913) and the ten-volume chronicle of a middle-class family, *Les Thibault* (1922–40). In *Jean Barois*, Martin du Gard experiments with consistently using theatrical-style dialogue to refract through the protagonist's life the ideological struggles between right-wing Catholicism and scientism at the turn of the twentieth century. Such dialogue had often been used before—for example, by Flaubert in *La Tentation de saint Antoine*, by the Comtesse Sophie de Ségur in her best-selling children's books, and by Victor Hugo in his memorable debate between Danton, Marat, and Robespierre in the historical novel *Quatrevignt-treize* (1874). It had not often been used, however, to represent a mature, central perceiving consciousness in an objective setting. *Les Thibault* shows the intellectual Catholicism of one generation being displaced by the atheistic humanism of the next—without either position successfully resolving ethical dilemmas. Martin du Gard sought to be quite independent of his literary precursors, but he, like Flaubert, sought totally to conceal the author's personality in his fictions, making his representation of events transparent. Flaubert himself (who decried such slips in his own writer's diaries), Martin du Gard believed, was sometimes too heavy-handed with his narrative transitions (Letter to Marcel de Coppet, May 8, 1906, 1:189).

Yet Martin du Gard greatly admired Flaubert's craft: "I'm feeling intense emotion as I finish reading *Madame Bovary*. I am delighted to have reread this prodigious book for the nth time. At the beginning, I had reservations. The story opens clumsily, but by the middle, perfection is achieved, and from then right to the end it's a splendid dramatic crescendo in a perfectly balanced work of art. You don't die as much as other people do when you leave works like that behind" (Letter to his wife, October 13, 1918, 1: 981). He always considered Flaubert a kindred spirit because of their shared hatred for the middle class (Letter to Agnes Thompson, December 7, 1899, 1:17–18). Martin admired Flaubert's correspondence so much that he took it with him on his honeymoon (Sicard, 1996, 278–79). His first, unpublished project for a novel was a saint's life, apparently suggested by Flaubert's *Tentation de saint Antoine* and by the *Trois Contes*. Flaubert's incisive descriptions of the monotonous Norman towns and countryside inspired Martin du Gard: the hero of his first published novel, *Devenir!*, echoes the illusions and disappointments of both Emma Bovary and Frédéric Moreau (*ES*). In this depiction, Martin du Gard was strongly influenced by Jules de Gaultier's *Le Bovarysme*, which defined "the inherent capacity of human beings to imagine themselves otherwise than as they are" (13). Flaubert's *Bouvard et Pécuchet* provided an additional source for Martin du Gard's bourgeois critique (Sicard, 1976). So strong were Martin du Gard's affinities with Flaubert that in 1932 the publisher Gaston Gallimard asked him to write the screenplay for a film version of *Madame Bovary*, to be directed by Jacques Feyder. A disagreement between the publisher and director prevented the project from being accomplished, but Martin du Gard's preliminary plans have survived (Sicard, 1996, 284–85). (LMP)

References:

Gaultier, Jules de. *Le Bovarysme*. Paris: Mercure de France, 1902.

Martin du Gard, Roger. *Journal, textes autobiographiques, 1892–1919*. Vol. 1. Ed. Claude Sicard. Paris: Gallimard, 1992.

Sicard, Claude. *Roger Martin du Gard, Les Années d'apprentissage littéraire (1881–1910)*. Paris: Champion, 1976.

———. "Roger Martin du Gard et Gustave Flaubert." In Jean-Louis-Cabanes, ed., *Voix de l'écrivain: mélanges offerts à Guy Sagnes*. Toulouse: Presses Universitaires du Mirail, 1996. 277–87.

Martinon (*ES*, 1869). Martinon, an arch-conformist, appears plodding and undistinguished, but he actually has a keen eye for the main chance, and has no scruples against engaging in any safe scheme that may further his advancement. He becomes the stylish Mme Dambreuse's lover, and then uses his entrée into her circle to court her rich, unattractive, illegitimate stepdaughter. Frédéric, unaware of this previous liaison, assumes his role as Mme Dambreuse's lover. Ironically, he does not conceal this relationship as Martinon had done: consequently, M. Dambreuse, while dying, surreptitiously changes his will to disinherit his wife. Thus, his illegitimate daughter—who passes as a niece—and Martinon are enriched at Mme Dambreuse and Frédéric's expense. (LMP)

Reference:

Paulson, William. *Sentimental Education: The Complexity of Disenchantment*. New York: Twayne, 1992.

Mathilde, la princesse (1820–1904). The daughter of Lucien Bonaparte, cousin of Emperor Napoleon III, and niece of the tsar of Russia, Mathilde Demidof married a multimillionaire Russian, separated from him with a large alimony, and settled in Paris in 1841. Princesse Mathilde was a patroness of the arts and letters and one of the most famous hostesses of the Second Empire. Her friendship with the novelist Gustave Flaubert began after the success of his novel *Salammbô* (1862). Princesse Mathilde frequently invited him to her salon, and a long, mutually admiring correspondence began. She was a patron to Flaubert and gave him entry to the imperial court; she obtained for him the cross of Chevalier de la Légion d'honneur in 1866. It is said that Flaubert composed *L'Education sentimentale* (1869) for her. In 1870, Princesse Mathilde took refuge in Belgium from the Franco-Prussian War. When the war and the Commune were over, she returned to France. She and Flaubert then resumed their friendship, which lasted until his death in 1880. (CB)

Reference:

Bart, Benjamin F. *Flaubert*. Syracuse: Syracuse University Press, 1967.

Mâtho (*Sal*). The Libyan mercenary's name Mâtho has been found to be a synonym for Gustave. According to the Egyptian solar calendar, the celebration of the Staff of the Sun occurs on December 12, Flaubert's birthday, which coincides with the beginning of the Inexpiable War (Addison 96–97). Mâtho has been identified with Richard Wagner's Tristan and has been viewed as a simple soldier before he drank the potion of love that bewitched him (Thibaudet 140–41). He has been seen as embodying animality, specifically that of the bull, who attracts Salammbô/Pasiphaë and is tamed by her (Green 104). Mâtho has also been defined in terms of his conflict with Hamilcar, which has been interpreted as the eternal struggle of rivals for hegemony, Mâtho being impelled by his desire for Salammbô, and the suffete by his will to power. Their ferocious, uncompromising confrontation is considered to have a superhuman grandeur, almost to be a sacred act that, because of their identical courage, becomes a fratricidal tragedy (Gaillard 50–51). Mâtho's equivalency with Hamilcar underlies his identification with the suffete as the embodiment of Napoleon, whose name is derived from the Greek Apollon, signifying the relationship between the sign Leo and the sun. Mâtho's wearing a Herculean lion's skin for bed and battle establishes a link between the sun god and Napoleon Bonaparte, the Desert Lion, while Hamilcar is considered the older aspect, Napoleon I, in quest of a global empire (Addison 94, 103, 105). Hamilcar's former slave Spendius's substitution of his Carthaginian master for Mâtho further demonstrates their equivalency. While Spendius has been associated with Fouché, whose relationship with Napoleon never progressed beyond that of servant and master, the personal friendship that develops between Mâtho and Spendius has been deemed exemplary of the spirit of fraternity and solidarity demonstrated by the mercenaries/barbarians (Addison 11–13).

Mâtho's first encounter with Salammbô at the banquet is mediated both by the father figure Hamilcar and by the desire of Mâtho's other rival, Narr'Havas, the young Numidian chieftain who becomes her betrothed. These latter two characters are contrasted throughout the novel: for example, Mâtho's masculinity is opposed to Narr'Havas's femininity (Ginsburg 126–27). However, Mâtho has also been found to identify himself with Salammbô in a manner that in Flaubertian terms may be considered her femininity; he feels that she has become his soul and has a sense of being penetrated by her. Moreover, he "becomes" Salammbô when he mimics her gestures and voice as he repeats verbatim her recital of the sacred origins of her family, a telling mimetic discrepancy, since the text declares that the barbarians do not understand the old Canaanite language of Salammbô's theogony (Mullen Hohl 73–74). Thus he reveals the same sexual ambiguity as Saint Antoine, who has been depicted in relation to his encounter with the Queen of Sheba as imagining that he was Salammbô (Danger 189). Moreover, Mâtho evinces the wish to sell himself and become her slave, which in the context of the Barca household signifies castration (Mullen Hohl 39–40, 73–74). Such an interpretation is consistent with Mâtho's hysterical behavior (Bart 313–21; Mullen Hohl 59, 131). It also casts light on the representation in terms of penetration of Mâtho and Spendius's invasion of Tanit's temple to steal the zaïmph and Salammbô's journey to retrieve it from Mâtho's tent (Neefs 228–29), especially since Tanit's temple has been found to represent her body, just as Mâtho's body is represented as a temple of healing (Mullen Hohl 34–36, 69–70).

The representation of Mâtho's body as a temple of healing identifies him with Asclepius/Eschmoûn, just as Hamilcar's pharmacy functions as a sign of his equivalence with Asclepius. Both Mâtho and Hamilcar are depicted as Eschmoûn through their shifting identity as master or lord of the barbarians. By making good Hamilcar's debt to the mercenaries (an idea of Spendius), Mâtho replaces him and acquires the title "schalischim," or head of the barbarians, a title that, from the Carthaginian perspective, is further transmuted into king, thus reinforcing the link with Hamilcar. The latter's initial refusal to command the Punic forces at the request of Eschmoûn's pontiff immediately generates the Adonis/Eschmoûn/Tammouz hypogram representing Mâtho as Tammouz, robber of the zaïmph in the month of Tammouz, and comparing him in terms of Adonis with Hamilcar, whose response is to reveal himself under the aspect of Eschmoûn on Moloch's altar (Mullen Hohl 76–77, 83). Within the novel's complex system of time (Addison 88–129), the presence of the Adonis/Tammouz hypogram dictates the figuration of the month of Tammouz for this event. Multiple signs of Mâtho's and Hamilcar's interchangeability as representatives of Eschmoûn are repeatedly embedded in *Salammbô* (Mullen Hohl 68–93). Tammouz and the lion, a sacred solar animal, were both beloved of Tanit/Astarte/Ishtar; thus Salammbô's necklace, as she welcomes Hamilcar attired as the goddess, figures two upright lions, found to be Mâtho and Hamilcar (Mullen Hohl 77–78). Since Hamilcar and Mâtho have been associated with Napoleon, the Desert Lion, the lions who devour the last barbarians in the gorge are linked with Hamilcar/Napoleon (Addison 123), while Mâtho is represented as the lion scapegoat. It is because Mâtho is depicted both as a lion and Tammouz that he is finally caught in a net, for the benefit of Hamilcar, that other Tammouz who thus becomes Lord of the Net (Mullen Hohl 122–23).

Mâtho has been shown to be a Christ figure, both in the scene where Spendius tempts him to plunder Carthage after the banquet and in his torture or Passion, in which the double "hostie" as (archaic) sacrificial victim and the Christian Host must be retained (Green, 110–11). While Mâtho is represented as the ultimate scapegoat during his "Passion," and Salammbô's reaction to his broken body is presented in terms of his suffering for her, it is the many lions crucified by the Carthaginians that function textually as scapegoats. In particular, the first one perceived by the mercenaries on their way to Sicca is represented in terms of Christ's Crucifixion, implying that Christ was a sun god (Mullen Hohl 124–25). In this context, Mâtho's declaration to Salammbô in his tent by carrying wood on his shoulders for others and his description of the marvelous land where they will live have been seen as Christological discourse, the former representing Christ carrying his cross and the latter his teaching that his kingdom is not of this world (Mullen Hohl 124–25). If Mâtho's epigraph is Salammbô's name, which when broken down gives "salaam," the Muslim salutation meaning "peace," for which Christ is said to have died, Salammbô is the temple that is rent on his death (Mullen Hohl 101). Moreover, Schahabarim's slicing of Mâtho's heart from his cadaver and its subsequent offering to the sun give an unusually literal version of the figurative dictum "Sursum corda" (Raise up your hearts) used in Roman Catholic masses at times of celebration. The bleeding heart also produces a novel form of consubstantiation, in which the body and blood are present under one species. Thus this sacrifice has been considered a Red Mass, celebrating both death and resurrection (Mullen Hohl 99–100, 133). (AMH)

References:

Addison, Claire. *Where Flaubert Lies: Chronology, Mythology, and History*. Cambridge: Cambridge University Press, 1996.

Bart, Benjamin. "Male Hysteria in *Salammbô.*" *Nineteenth-Century French Studies* 12.3 (Spring 1984). 313–21.

Danger, Pierre. "Sainteté et castration dans *La Tentation de Saint Antoine*." In Charles Carlut, ed., *Essais sur Flaubert en l'honneur du professeur Don Demorest*. Paris: Nizet, 1979. 185–202.

Flaubert, Gustave. *Salammbô*. In Gustave Flaubert, *Œuvres*, vol. 1. Bibliothèque de la Pléïade. Dijon: Gallimard, 1951.

Gaillard, Françoise. "La Révolte contre la révolution (*Salammbô*: un autre point de vue sur l'histoire.)" In Alfonso de Toro, ed., *Procédés narratifs et fondements épistémologiques*. Tübingen: Narr, 1987. 43–54.

Ginsburg, Michal Peled. *Flaubert Writing*. Stanford: Stanford University Press, 1986.

Green, Anne. *Flaubert and the Historical Novel*: Salammbô *Reassessed*. Cambridge: Cambridge University Press, 1982.

Mullen Hohl, Anne. *Exoticism in* Salammbô: *The Languages of Myth, Religion, and War*. Birmingham, AL: Summa, 1995.

Neefs, Jacques. "Le Parcours du Zaïmph." In Claudine Gothot-Mersch, ed., *La Production du sens chez Flaubert*. Paris: Union Générale d'Editions, 1975. 227–41.

Thibaudet, Albert. *Gustave Flaubert*. Rev. ed. Paris: Gallimard, 1963; Saint-Armand (Cher): S.E.P.C., 1992 (1922).

Maugham, Somerset (1874–1965). The British novelist and playwright Somerset Maugham was born in Paris, spent the first eight years of his life there, and at first hardly spoke English. A modest independent income allowed him to devote himself to writing, and by 1908 the success of his plays ensured him financial security for life. He adopted a conservative compositional style, in the sober tradition of realism.

In World War I, Maugham served first in the medical corps as a wound dresser and later as a British spy. A homosexual who was for a time married and had one child, he worked out his tormented sexual identity directly in the heavily autobiographical *Of Human Bondage* (1915). He also explored his identity theme indirectly, through gender reversal. He found himself drawn repeatedly to rework *Madame Bovary* in a series of novels: *Mrs. Craddock* (1902), *The Painted Veil* (1925), and *The Razor's Edge* (1944). For the man unfaithful to his wife in thought and deed because he is attracted to other men, Maugham substitutes the woman unfaithful by being attracted to men other than her husband.

It appears that Maugham first learned about *Madame Bovary* by reading a well-known, early adaptation by "Miss [Mary Elizabeth] Braddon" (1837–1915), who was known in nineteenth-century England as "the Queen of the circulating libraries." Her novel *The Doctor's Wife* (1864), like Flaubert's novel and like *Mrs. Craddock*, tells of a sensitive, romantic, book-loving heroine, Isabel Sleaford, who is frustrated by her marriage to a boorish husband, George Gilbert. Like Emma Bovary, intoxicated with clichéd romantic ideas, Isabel has been seduced by "secondhand Platonism, borrowed from the misty pages of Shelley" (280). Her provincial society, depicted satirically, aggravates her discontent. Attracted to a romantic lover, she plans but then declines to elope with him. There are no suicides in Miss Braddon's or Maugham's versions: the unsuspecting husbands die early, and their wives remain unmarried. Miss Braddon heavily censors the idea that Isabel might rejoice in her widowhood. She "had no such loathesome thoughts" (357). Maugham instead keeps the widow and her potential lover separated, but adds a Bovaryesque passion, "an insane fire in the blood, irresistible" (315).

An even more obvious imitation of Miss Braddon and Flaubert occurs in Maugham's *The Painted Veil*. From the beginning, Kitty Fane is absorbed in an adulterous affair. She bears her lover's child and is again seduced in her final meeting with her lover. Unlike Emma, she feels painfully guilty. Unlike Charles, her husband Walter Fane is perspicacious and hostile. Kitty returns to fidelity when her husband threatens her with divorce and her cowardly lover, Charlie Townsend, then refuses to divorce his own wife.

In *The Razor's Edge*, Isabel Bradley meets her love, Laurence Darrell, before marriage. Like Byron, Darrell travels restlessly, questions God and the established political order, and expresses democratic sympathies. Isabel marries another man, Gray Maturin, for financial security and stability for her future children. In a parallel to Emma's financial problems, the stock-market crash of 1929 drives Isabel first into genteel poverty in South Carolina and next to the less fashionable and then very provincial town of Dallas, Texas. Like Maugham, she "neither satisfies nor overcomes desire" (Heywood 68). (LMP)

References:

Braddon, Mary Elizabeth. *The Doctor's Wife*. New York: Oxford University Press, 1998 (1864).

Heywood, C. "Somerset Maugham's Debt to *Madame Bovary* and Miss Braddon's *The Doctor's Wife*." *Etudes Anglaises* 19 (1966): 64–69.

Maugham, W. Somerset. *Mrs. Craddock*. London: Heinemann, 1955 (1902).

———. *The Painted Veil*. London: Heinemann, 1951 (1925).

———. *The Razor's Edge*. London: Heinemann, 1953 (1944).

Maupassant, Guy de (1850–93). "Flaubert's most ardent admirer" (Wallace 13), the naturalist writer Guy de Maupassant was "adopted" and "trained," as it were, by Flaubert, who became his literary mentor. "He is *my* disciple," Flaubert said, "and I love him as a son" (cited by Stivale 214 n. 25). Flaubert preached the virtues of hard work in solitude and the cult of art as a religion. He also encouraged Maupassant to publish his breakthrough story "Boule de Suif" (1880) about a good-hearted prostitute and the ungrateful people she rescues, which led to financial success substantial enough to allow Maupassant to quit his job and devote himself to creative writing. Flaubert introduced Maupassant to Ivan Turgenev, who would prove an effective literary agent, and to the naturalist coterie.

Maupassant's novel *Une Vie* (1883) presents many similarities to *Madame Bovary*. Maupassant's *Pierre et Jean* (1888) adopts Flaubert's favorite satiric motif of the triumph of insensitive mediocrity. In both writers, this topic is treated from the viewpoint of the dry, detached social critic, rather than—as it would have been treated in romantic literature—from the viewpoint of the victim. Maupassant is best known for his short stories. "Décoré" depicts a Homais-like "M. Sacrement," obsessed with social distinction and striving to win the award of the Legion of Honor (Wallace 33). "La Petite Roque" takes its eponymous victim's last name from Louise Roque in *L'Education sentimentale*. The last scene of that novel, reminiscences about a visit to a whorehouse, also inspired "A La Feuille de Rose: Maison Turque" (Stivale 78, 141). Adultery frequently occurs in Maupassant's fictions, as in Flaubert's, and these writers share a pessimistic attitude and contempt for society.

Flaubert's example clearly influenced Maupassant's style and his ideas on literature. During his lifetime, it was rumored that he was Flaubert's illegitimate son, an idea rejected by most modern critics. However, the families of Maupassant's and Flaubert's mothers had deep Norman roots, and Flaubert's best friend as a young man was Alfred Le Poittevin (1816–48), the brother of Maupassant's mother. (EFG)

References:

Bismut, Roger. "Un cas privilégié de filiation littéraire: *Une Vie* de Guy de Maupassant." In Charles Carlut, ed., *Essais sur Flaubert en l'honneur du professeur Don Demorest*. Paris: Nizet, 1979. 97–119.

Fournier, Louis. "Trois Lecteurs de *Bouvard et Pécuchet*: Maupassant, Thibaudet, Sabatier." *French Studies* 49.1 (1995): 29–48.

Killick, Rachel. "Maupassant, Flaubert, et *Trois Contes*." In Christopher Lloyd and Robert Lethbridge, eds., *Maupassant conteur et romancier*. Durham, England: University of Durham, 1994. 41–56.

Maupassant, Guy de. Preface to *Pierre et Jean*. In Guy de Maupassant, *Romans*, ed. Louis Forestier. Paris: Gallimard, 1987.

Smirnoff, Renée de. "Réminiscences flaubertiennes dans *Pierre et Jean*." In Jean-Louis Cabanes, ed., *Voix de l'écrivain*. Toulouse: Presses Universitaires du Mirail, 1996. 151–61.

Stivale, Charles J. *The Art of Rupture: Narrative Desire and Duplicity in the Tales of Guy de Maupassant*. Ann Arbor: University of Michigan Press, 1994.

Suwala, Halina. "Zola et Maupassant, lecteurs de Flaubert." *Cahiers naturalistes* 65 (1991): 57–77.

Wallace, A. H. *Guy de Maupassant*. New York: Twayne, 1973.

Maupassant, Laure de. *See* Le Poittevin, Laure.

Maurice, Barthélemy (1801–?). After Flaubert's death, Alphonse Daudet and Edmond de Goncourt claimed that he had plagiarized Maurice's short story "Les Deux Greffiers" (1841) to write *Bouvard et Pécuchet.* Both works tell of two copy clerks who retire to the country and eventually return to copying there, as a hobby. But this claim identifies only superficial resemblances, and even so, it has shaky foundations. Maurice's characters start copying again merely to ward off boredom: the message seems to be that one should enjoy life fully while one can. Flaubert's clerks, in contrast, return to copying to record and expose all the absurdities of human thought in the "Sottisier" (compilation of foolish remarks) that Flaubert had been collecting since the middle 1840s. (His initial inspiration probably was Voltaire, a militant social satirist whom he had read and annotated heavily at that time, without, however, accepting all of Voltaire's remarks uncritically.) He planned to gather these cliches and stupidities in a second volume to which *Bouvard et Pécuchet* was intended only as a preamble. Although one can find some verbal echoes of Maurice's tale in *Bouvard et Pécuchet,* one can also find many echoes of an earlier story about clerks by Flaubert, "Leçon d'histoire naturelle, genre commis" (1837), in Maurice, as Zagona points out. Then again, it seems that Maurice had published an earlier version of his tale (1833) in a more obscure publication. Alongside the hypothesis of Flaubert's plagiarism, then, one must lay two equally plausible hypotheses: either Maurice plagiarized Flaubert, or both authors drew on a widespread sociolect of commonly held opinions about copy clerks. This sociolect can be observed in the caricaturist Henry Monnier's prose sketches with accompanying drawings. (LMP)

See also Monnier, Henry.

References:

Cento, Alberto, ed. *Bouvard et Pécuchet.* Paris: Nizet, 1964. xix–xx.

Descharmes, René, and René Dumesnil. "Les Ancêtres de *Bouvard et Pécuchet.*" In René Descharmes and René Dumesnil, *Autour de Flaubert.* 2 vols. Paris: Mercure de France, 1912. 2: 6–38 (includes the text of "Les Deux Greffiers").

Flaubert, Gustave. "Leçon d'histoire naturelle, genre commis." *Le Colibri,* 1837. Rpr. in *Gustave Flaubert, œuvres complètes,* ed. Maurice Bardèche. 16 vols. Paris: L'Honnête Homme, 1967–71. 11: 305–9.

Maurice, Barthélemy. "Les Deux Greffiers." *Gazette des Tribunaux,* April 14, 1841. Rpr. in Gustave Flaubert, *Bouvard et Pécuchet,* ed. Claudine Gothot-Mersch. Paris: Gallimard, 1979. 558–65.

Zagona, Helen G. *Flaubert's* Roman philosophique *and the Voltairian Heritage.* Lanham, MD: University Press of America, 1985. 111–18.

Maury, Louis-Ferdinand-Alfred (1817–92). Alfred Maury was a pioneering researcher in comparative religion and a friend of Flaubert's. His writings helped prepare Flaubert's depiction of ancient Carthage in *Salammbô.* His *Essai sur les*

Légendes pieuses du Moyen-Age (1843) probably steered Flaubert toward a modern version of *"La Légende de Saint Julien le Pauvre, d'aprés un manuscrit de la Bibliothèque* d'Alençon" (Starkie 246). (LMP)

References:

Lecointre-Dupont, G.-F.-G. "La Légende de Saint-Julien le Pauvre, d'apres un manuscrit de la Bibliothèque d'Alençon." *Mémoires de la Société des Antiquaires de l'ouest.* 1838. Poitiers: Saurin, 1839.

Maury, Louis-Ferdinand-Alfred. *Essai sur les Légendes pieuses du Moyen-Age.* Paris: Lagrange, 1843.

Starkie, Enid. *Flaubert, the Master.* New York: Atheneum, 1971.

medievalism. The Middle Ages provided both fond and bitter preoccupations for French historians and writers of fiction from the enlightenment through the nineteenth century. "Medievalism," as this interest has come to be called, underwent change after change as writers from François-René de Chateaubriand to Joris-Karl Huysmans saw in their chivalric past either an "époque féerique" (a magical era) or a "temps maudit" (a blighted age), according to prevailing tastes and politics. For the Enlighteners, this earlier period was charming myth; for the romantics, exuberance and exotic terror; for writers of the Second Empire, a revered or reviled contrast to an increasingly materialistic bourgeoisie; and for the symbolists, a field of free play for the subjective imagination.

For Flaubert, the Middle Ages provided material for the masterpiece of prose fiction that is his "Légende de saint Julien l'Hospitalier" (1877), a "saint's life" that presents itself both as fiction (it is the second of Flaubert's *Trois Contes*) and as a legend in the full hagiographical tradition of which the Julian story is a part. Following the lead both of medieval and of more modern accounts, and inspired by a stained-glass window in the cathedral in Rouen (especially as it had been described by his friend Eustache-Hyacinthe Langlois in the latter's *Essai historique et descriptif sur la peinture sur verre ancienne et moderne* [1832], Flaubert creates a tale spectacular for its medieval detail, true to the legend's original topic of error and redemption in the face of overwhelming fate, and whose envisioned world is governed by that "immanence of meaning" characteristic of the medieval period—the sense that nothing takes place outside the divine will, and that "chance," as R. Howard Bloch points out, "has no place" (19).

But if the design Flaubert weaves into his tale richly recalls a medieval and folkloric past, providing perhaps the final form to a legend whose lengthy process of transformation had begun in the mid-twelfth century, the texture he achieves is entirely modern. The Julien of Flaubert is a personality of intricate complexity whose passion for violence (he is convulsed with "savage and tumultuous pleasure" as he strangles a pigeon) almost subverts the religious frame his story so carefully establishes. This legendary tale—an "uncanny superimposition of the myths of Oedipus and of Christ" (Felman 46); a depiction of a figure both saintly and perversely narcissistic (Israel-Pelletier 62)—comes to life in a language capable of rendering the depths of the human psyche, and in narrative tones that provide exquisite form to a medieval image that remains nonetheless intact.

Critics have long debated Flaubert's precise use of earlier texts in shaping his own, some insisting on the attention he paid to original medieval accounts such as Jacobus da Voragine's in his thirteenth-century *Legenda aurea*, others (especially Bart and Cook) pointing to the greater importance for him of such nineteenth-century romantic retellings as G.-F.-G. Lecointre-Dupont's "Légende de Saint-Julien le Pauvre, d'après un manuscrit de la Bibliothèque d'Alençon" (1838). Janine Dakyns underlines the critical role Flaubert's medievalism would play in setting the scene for the freedom that characterized the symbolists' use of the medieval period in the 1880s and 1890s. All agree on the power of the text that emerges from the deft, self-conscious mingling of medieval legend with art. For all his meticulous efforts at documentation, his enthusiasm for a bygone age, and his desire to flee the political and moral climate of his own times, Flaubert also realized that "history is only the reflection of the present upon the past," and the world "un clavecin" for the artist (*Corr. Supp.* 2:19 and 1:95). Understanding that his use of the Middle Ages was not a means for re-creating the past but a vehicle for a very present vision of beauty and artistic truth, Flaubert made his "Saint Julien" the apogee of nineteenth-century medievalism, and of medievalism one more infallible tool in the arsenal of his distinctive craft. (DH)

References:

Bart, Benjamin F., and Robert Francis Cook. *The Legendary Sources of Flaubert's* Saint Julien. Toronto: University of Toronto Press, 1977.

Bloch, R. Howard. *Medieval French Literature and Law*. Berkeley: University of California Press, 1977.

Dakyns, Janine. *The Middle Ages in French Literature, 1851–1900*. Oxford: Oxford University Press, 1973.

Felman, Shoshana. "Flaubert's Signature: *The Legend of Saint Julian the Hospitable*," In Naomi Schor and Henry F. Majewski, eds., *Flaubert and Postmodernism*. Lincoln: University of Nebraska Press, 1984. 46–75.

Israel-Pelletier, Aimée. *Flaubert's Straight and Suspect Saints: The Unity of* Trois Contes. Amsterdam: Benjamins, 1991.

Jameson, Fredric. "Flaubert's Libidinal Historicism: *Trois Contes.*" In Naomi Schor and Henry F. Majewski, eds. *Flaubert and Postmodernism*. Lincoln: University of Nebraska Press, 1984. 76–83.

Schwob, Marcel. "Préface." In Gustave Flaubert, *La Légende de Saint Julien l'Hospitalier*. Paris: Ferroud, 1895. Rpr. in Marcel Schwob, *Spicilège*. Paris: Mercure de France, 1896.

Mélie (*BP*). Mélie is the servant to Bouvard and Pécuchet who gives Pécuchet his first sexual experience, and syphilis. She illustrates the phallocratic myth that woman is the source of all men's ills, a belief illustrated in the stories of Pandora, Eve, and Emile Zola's *Nana*, among others. (LMP)

Mémoires d'un fou (1838). *Mémoires d'un fou* is a fictive diary dedicated to Alfred Le Poittevin and divided into twenty-three short chapters. Characteristically for the frenetic strain of European romanticism, which exaggerates the posturing of the self-justifying Rousseauistic confession, the writer first aggressively addresses the complacent reader, defying him or her to claim superiority. The writer asserts the prerogative of pouring disconnected dreams, reflections, and memories onto the page and depreciates his efforts. He then, typically for certain French romantics suffering from the *mal du siècle*, says that he is still young and has few experiences to report from the world of action, but many from the world of thought. The protagonist presents his writing from two conflicting points of view: both as the expression of his "madness" and as an exploration that may help him regain contact with reality (chapters 1–9; see Unwin 115). Fundamentally inadaptable to society, he was mocked by his schoolmates and his teachers while he was lost in a dream of glory. A vivid nightmare of his mother's drowning (chapter 4) has more than once been used in psychological studies of Flaubert. Increasingly as he matures, he becomes critical of society and feels smothered by ennui (in the strong, etymological sense of finding everything hateful).

Chapter 10 begins a new section that reports autobiographical memories of his chaste childhood love for "Maria" (Elisa Schlésinger). From a distance, he watches her swim every morning and feels excited by how her wet clothing clings to her body. The Oedipal motif of the rival husband looks back to the historical author's infatuation and forward to Frédéric's fixation on Mme Arnoux in *L'Education sentimentale* of 1869. The crucial difference is that the fictive hero did not love her at the time of their acquaintance and loves her only in and by virtue of the willful revival of memory (chapters 10–14). Chapter 13 describes a boat ride with her on a lake—a reminiscence of Alphonse de Lamartine's poem "Le Lac" that will recur with Emma and Léon in *Madame Bovary*.

Chapter 15, concerning two English sisters, seems detached from the rest. Because the manuscript of *Mémoires d'un fou* has been lost, one cannot tell whether this episode reflects Flaubert's friendship with Harriet and Gertrude Collier in 1842; with a Caroline Anne Heuland in 1838; with another, unknown person; or with a mere fiction (see Andrieu). This chapter is jarringly interrupted with impatient, disparaging remarks by personified hearers, which recall the manner of Charles Nodier in his *Histoire du roi de Bohème et de ses sept châteaux* (1830).

Chapter 16 tells of the narrator's disillusioning experience of sexual love, which seems a profanation of his earlier ideals. The relatively long concluding section reports his disenchantment with everything, even with art; his yearning for an impossible union with the infinite (a lifelong theme); and his enduring nostalgia for "Maria." Like many a languishing romantic author, he anticipates his own death (chapters 17–23). The entire work is filled with grandiose philosophical aphorisms, often in the first person. Unremarkable so far as its literary qualities are concerned, this apprentice romantic's sampler remains of interest because it preserves a record of the naïve, enthusiastic voice that appears in Flaubert's mature work mainly as the target of ridicule. (LMP)

References:

Andrieu, Lucien. "Un amour inconnu de Flaubert: Caroline Anne Heuland, l'Anglaise probable de *Mémoires d'un fou." Les Amis de Flaubert* 23 (1963): 27–29.

Bruneau, Jean. *Les Débuts littéraires de Gustave Flaubert, 1831–1845*. Paris: Colin, 1962.

Diamond, Marie J. *Flaubert: The Problem of Aesthetic Discontinuity*. Port Washington, NY: Kennikat, 1975.

Duchet, Claude. "L'Ecriture de jeunesse dans le texte flaubertien." *Nineteenth-Century French Studies* 12 (1984): 297–312.

Felman, Shoshana. *La Folie et la chose littéraire*. Paris: Seuil, 1978. 170–90.

———. *Writing and Madness*, (trans. of *La Folie et la chose littéraire*). Ithaca: Cornell University Press, 1985. 78–100.

Flaubert, Gustave. "Diary of a Madman." In Gustave Flaubert, *Early Writings*, ed. and trans. Robert Griffin. Lincoln: University of Nebraska Press, 1991. 161–203.

Schor, Naomi. "Fetishism and Its Ironies." *Nineteenth-Century French Studies* 17 (1988–89): 89–97.

Unwin, Timothy. *Art et infini: L'Œuvre de jeunesse de Gustave Flaubert*. Amsterdam: Rodopi, 1991. 113–31.

Mérimée, Prosper (1803–70). Prosper Mérimée was a government-employed archaeologist and the author of several well-known short stories and novellas, notably "Carmen" (the source of Georges Bizet's opera in 1875) and "La Vénus d'Ille." Mérimée and Flaubert each had affairs with Louise Colet, who attacked them and many others in her *roman à clef, Lui*. Maxime Du Camp claimed that Mérimée's longtime mistress Valentine Delessert (who was also Du Camp's mistress) was the prototype for Madame Dambreuse, Frédéric's last major liaison in *L'Education sentimentale*. The female characters who have made a bad marriage in Mérimée's *La Double Méprise* (1831) and Balzac's *La Muse du département* (1843) probably served as prototypes for the more complex character of Emma Bovary. (DF)

References:

Pommier, Jean. "*La Muse du département* et le thème de la femme mal mariée chez Balzac, Mérimée et Flaubert." *L'Année Balzacienne* (1961): 191–221.

metaphor. *See* image and metaphor.

Michelet, Jules (Paris 1798–Hyères 1874). Jules Michelet was the greatest historian of nineteenth-century France and a central figure, before 1848, in fomenting the discontent that delegitimized the July Monarchy. He wrote *Le Peuple* (1846), a Rousseauistic approach to the natural qualities of people. Fascinated by history, which he viewed as a struggle of human freedom against social and material fatality, he wrote his *Histoire de France* (1833–73). He also published *Histoire de la révolution française* (1847–53) to understand absolute monarchy better. In 1851, his polemics against the clergy and the government led to the suspension of his lectures at the Collège de France.

In secondary school, Flaubert had become enthusiastic about the study of history thanks to Adolphe Chéruel (1809–1891), a former pupil of Michelet. Flaubert devoured Michelet's *Histoire de la république romaine*, which was to become a major background source for *Salammbô* (Bart 137, 415). Like Michelet's writings, three of Flaubert's major novels—*Salammbô, L'Education sentimentale*, and *La Tentation de saint Antoine*—have detailed, carefully researched historical settings. Flaubert wrote to Michelet in 1867 that "you are certainly the French author whom I have most often read, and reread" (*Correspondance*, ed. Bruneau, 3: 701). (APZ/LMP)

References:

Bart, Benjamin F. *Flaubert.* Syracuse: Syracuse University Press, 1967.

Barthes, Roland, *Michelet.* Trans. Richard Howard. Berkeley: University of California Press, 1992.

Dumesnil, René. *La Vocation de Gustave Flaubert.* Paris: Gallimard, 1961.

Febvre, Lucien. *Michelet et la Renaissance.* Paris: Flammarion, 1992.

Flaubert, Gustave. *Correspondance.* Ed. Jean Bruneau. 4 vols. to date. Paris: Gallimard, 1973– .

Gossman, Lionel. *Between History and Literature.* Cambridge, MA: Harvard University Press, 1990.

Kaplan, Edward. *Michelet's Poetic Vision: A Romantic Philosophy of Nature, Man, and Woman.* Amherst: University of Massachusetts Press, 1977.

Le Goff, Jacques. "The Several Middle Ages of Jules Michelet." In Jacques Le Goff, *Time, Work and Culture in the Middle Ages*, trans. Arthur Goldhammer. Chicago: University of Chicago Press, 1980. 3–28.

Mitzman, Arthur. *Michelet, Historian: Rebirth and Romanticism in Nineteenth-Century France.* New Haven: Yale University Press, 1990.

Orr, Linda. *Jules Michelet: Nature, History, and Language.* Ithaca: Cornell University Press, 1976.

Minnelli, Vincente (1903–86). An American filmmaker with thirty-five films to his credit and a directorial career that spanned thirty-three years, Vincente Minnelli was born Lester Anthony Minnelli in Chicago in 1903, the last of five children and the only one to survive infancy. His father, Vincent Charles Minnelli, was a musical conductor and co-impresario of the Minnelli Brothers' Tent Theater; his mother, Mina, was the leading lady of the itinerant troupe. Working first as a display artist at a Chicago department store, then moving to theater as a costume designer, and from there to Broadway, Minnelli took a Latinized version of his father's name before he accepted a position as art director at Radio City Music Hall in 1932. After ten years in theater in New York City, he signed a contract with MGM in 1940 and directed his first film, *Cabin in the Sky*, in 1943. During production of his next film, *Meet Me in St. Louis* (1944), he came to know Judy Garland, and the two married in 1945. His films are marked by an unusual use of color and by their dream sequences.

Minnelli had made his reputation by directing musical comedies. In 1949, an invitation to film *Madame Bovary* gave him the opportunity to show that he was also capable of directing serious films. One of the least faithful of the adaptations, Minnelli's *Madame Bovary* (screenplay by Robert Ardrey) reflects the ebullience of the postwar era, an era ill suited to understand the overriding ennui depicted in Flaubert's novel. With a cast that includes Jennifer Jones as Emma, Van Heflin as Charles, Louis Jourdan as Rodolphe, and Christopher Kent as Léon, the Minnelli production frames Emma's story with a courtroom scene in which a dashing James Mason as Flaubert defends his heroine, a "kitchen drudge who dreamed of love and beauty." A highly inaccurate description of the convent-educated Emma Rouault, this idiosyncratic interpretation is followed by another, since the courtroom frame established Flaubert himself as the narrator, and it is his voice that is heard in the film's several voiceovers. Yet another departure from the novel lies in the character portrayals. Minnelli's rather-too-handsome Charles, painfully aware of his limitations ("I'm a blunderer"), decides against performing the clubfoot operation; Rodolphe, no longer the unrepentant playboy, truly loves Emma, and a deeply smitten Léon sacrifices his legal career to her. In short, the coquettish, self-absorbed Emma has only herself to blame for her fate; even Yonville, as Minnelli re-creates it, is too charming to be the site of such intolerable despair. It has been said that fear of censorship led Minnelli to adopt the courtroom frame, in hopes that his censors would not want to be associated with those who accused Flaubert of immorality. The strategy was successful. To what extent Minnelli's negative portrayal of an adulterous woman was determined by fear of censorship is open to debate; some say that Emma's character owes more to the problems that Minnelli was having with his wife Judy Garland, from whom he separated in 1950.

Notwithstanding the considerable liberties it took with the novel, Minnelli's *Madame Bovary* was a cinematic triumph, its ball sequence at La Vaubyessard considered one of the best set pieces in film history. Modestly successful at the box office, but critically acclaimed, it retains its reputation as one of Minnelli's most skillful melodramas, equal in quality to his best-known musicals (*An American in Paris* [1951], *Brigadoon* [1954], *Gigi* [1958]) and comedies (*Father of the Bride* [1950] and *Goodbye Charlie* [1964]). (MDE)

References:

Harvey, Stephen. *Directed by Vincente Minnelli.* New York: Museum of Modern Art, 1989.

Wagner, Geoffrey. *The Novel and the Cinema*. Rutherford, NJ: Fairleigh Dickinson University Press, 1975.

mirror symbolism. In several famous passages, Emma Bovary looks at herself in the mirror. She strikes resigned poses when she has decided to remain virtuous although Léon loves her. But after giving herself to Rodolphe, she looks at her reflection and exclaims, "J'ai un amant! un amant!" (I have a lover! a lover!) (Flaubert, part 2, chapter 9: 1, 629). Hazel Barnes finds her inauthentic in this scene, unlike during her seduction, when she was surrounded by nature and gave herself over to her sensations (353). Finally, Emma asks for her mirror on her deathbed, and great tears fall from her eyes: at this moment the "aveugle" (blind) Emma sees herself for what she is. Throughout the novel, in a figurative sense, Emma finds reflections of herself in the books she reads, as in the keepsakes she discovers in the convent, filled with images of beautiful women Emma would like to emulate (*see* bovarysme).

In *L'Education sentimentale*, the protagonist Frédéric also looks in the mirror. He finds himself handsome when he is planning to conquer Paris and be a great painter. Like Emma, he looks at himself again at a dramatic moment, before a duel, wondering whether he is afraid. These passages and the many allusions to mirrors in the setting underscore Frédéric's uncertain sense of identity.

Sartre bases his interpretation of Flaubert as passive and feminine partly on a passage from *Novembre* in which the hero would like to be a woman looking at her reflection in the water (Sartre, *L'Idiot,* 2:683, 694). Sartre also sees gender confusion in Flaubert's projection of himself into a female heroine: the masculine Emma is, for him, a mirror reflection of the feminine Flaubert. (CR)

References:

Barnes, Hazel. *Sartre and Flaubert*. Chicago: University of Chicago Press, 1981.

Flaubert, Gustave. *Madame Bovary*. In Gustave Flaubert, *Œuvres complètes*, ed. Bernard Masson. 2 vols. Paris: Seuil, 1964.

Sartre, Jean-Paul. *L'Idiot de la famille*. 3 vols. Paris: Gallimard, 1971–72. Trans. as *The Family Idiot*. Trans. Carol Cosman. 5 vols. Chicago: University of Chicago Press, 1981–93.

Thornton, Lawrence. "The Fairest of Them All: Modes of Vision in *Madame Bovary.*" *PMLA* 93.5 (1978): 982–91.

Moloch (*Sal*). Moloch, the sun god, has been seen as a Minotaur figure (Green 104–6) and as Saturn, both being supernatural figures who devoured young human beings. The former was killed by Theseus, and the latter was castrated by Jupiter. In keeping with the archaic tradition of descriptive periphrastic naming, Moloch is given several hyphenated titles that reflect a prominent trait, for example, "Moloch-à-tête-de-taureau" (bull-headed Moloch), "Moloch Dévorateur" (Moloch who devours), and "Moloch-Homicide" (Moloch the killer). Moloch's method of possession, be it in love, war, or sacrifice, is by fire, which is his sign.

Like Tanit, the moon goddess, Moloch is a polymorphic deity whose mode of existence is linked to a specific statue and place (for example, Moloch's Colossus), which is the privileged equivalent of many other forms of the divinity (Backès 132). So it is that Eschmoûn/Adonis/Tammouz, who has been found to play such a dominant but covert role in the novel, is a pervasive presence in descriptions of Moloch's statue and temple. Eschmoûn is a title that means "the name" or "no name" (Weston 38 n. 6). Thus he is the Other whom one must not name, according to Punic doctrine, since the Carthaginians believed that by concealing their gods' names and chaining their statues, they could prevent their access to others. In accordance with the technique of narrative veiling and obfuscation prevalent in the novel, signs of Eschmoûn, the planetary aspect of the supreme Baal or sun god, are dispersed in descriptions of Moloch's statue and temple. Access to Moloch's statue is through an egg-shaped room whose walls are studded with seven different-colored square doors signifying the planets, with the conjunction of egg and planetary signs representing Tanit/Eschmoûn, just as these deities are represented in terms of the serpent's relation to Tanit's earth aspect in the Punic system of beliefs, in the prelude to Salammbô's dance, and again at her never-to-be wedding, when the sun under its astral sign incorporates Moloch. Moreover, the curtains in Moloch's temple, which are raised to unite the Colossus with the sun at sunrise in a portrayal of birth/animation, are dyed in Eschmoûn's characteristic hyacinth shade. Most important, during the "mol'k" (the holocaust of the Carthaginian children), Eschmoûn's paradigm of death and rebirth occurs in a traditional burst of song.

The descriptions of Moloch's hybrid statue are also characterized by dispersal; they represent the godhead in terms of diverse parts of varied mythological monsters without giving a complete idea of the whole deity, in keeping with the novel's miragelike technique. Certain elements are emphasized by repetition. First is the human chest consisting of gaping apertures; they constitute the seven planetary compartments shielded by gratings, as is the entrance to Tanit's temple. Second are the inordinately long arms that extend the statue's hands to the ground, producing the familiar feature of an orangutan and an intratextual connection with *"Quidquid Volueris,"* whose very title mimes "monstrous" names, such as "Quodvultdeus" given to children who had escaped the "mol'k" by means of the substitution called "molchomor" (Charles-Picard and Charles-Picard 151). Another recurring element underscoring the heterogeneity of the statue is Moloch's lengthy wings, described in his temple in the manner of Tanit's attached/detachable veil spread out on the temple wall, but which, at the "mol'k," are separated from the temple and seen with their points immersed in the flame of the sacrificial pyre between the Colossus's feet.

Moloch and Tanit share life-giving powers as well as powers of destruction. Bart notes that Salammbô was intended to represent a daring contradiction, a hysterical statue (*Flaubert* 407), which is precisely what is realized in the case of Moloch's statue, since his chest is unmistakably represented as an upwardly displaced womb according to the ancient theory of hysteria. This detail points to an equivalence with Salammbô and Tanit, reflected in the similarities between Tanit and Moloch's statues (Mullen Hohl 131–33). In relation to Moloch's representation, one critic has been moved to speak of "womb envy" (Addison 124–25). Like the sacrilege portrayed by the theft of the veil, the statue of Moloch itself symbolizes desecration and looting, inasmuch as the Bull of Phalaris was pillaged by the Carthaginians during the sack of Agrigentum and returned to Sicily only at the close of the Third Punic War (Addison 103).

The representation of the "mol'k" functions as the equivalent of Salammbô's visit to the encampments and martial engagements; both are rites intended to fertilize the ground, that is, Tanit under her terrestrial aspect (Mullen Hohl 113–15). The result engendered by the "mol'k" is the voice of Moloch, that is, thunder, which is traditionally associated with rainmaking, and which engenders Tanit's rain-child.

The prayers at the "mol'k" representing the self-replicating god transcode the Nicene Creed by which Roman Catholics profess their faith. Moreover, the excessive number of victims or scapegoats has an intratextual connection with the ending of an unpublished version of *La Tentation de Saint Antoine* in which Christ is addressed as "Moloch à toison d'agneau," that is, Moloch in lamb's clothing, for whom a deluge of human blood was spilled (Mullen Hohl 118–20). The "mol'k" takes place during Passover. Thus it commemorates the Flight into Egypt that saved Christ; the children who died in his stead are celebrated in Roman Catholic liturgy as the Holy Innocents who received the crown of martyrdom. They represent a type of scapegoat, like the Carthaginian children burned in the holocaust to Moloch. In the description of the sacrifice, there is a further transcoding of the Lamb of God celebrated as a sacrificial offering, or scapegoat, in the Roman Catholic Mass. Christ's Crucifixion, commemorated in the Mass, points to an intratextual connection with the sacrament of extreme unction, or last rites, as when Emma Bovary is dying (Mullen Hohl 117–22). The date of her death corresponds with that of Hamilcar's substitution of a slave for Hannibal before the "mol'k" (Addison 124–25). A transposition of Roman Catholic worship also appears in the representation of Christ's birth, since "The Word was made Flesh" is inverted by the Carthaginian holocaust of children, in which their flesh is reduced to ashes so that the voice of Moloch (thunder) may be heard. Thunder will in turn will render Tanit fertile, thus constituting the Punic version, "The Flesh was made Word" (Mullen Hohl 130–33). (AMH)

References:

Bart, Benjamin F. *Flaubert*. Syracuse: Syracuse University Press, 1967.

Addison, Claire. *Where Flaubert Lies: Chronology, Mythology, and History*. Cambridge: Cambridge University Press, 1996.

Backès, Jean-Louis. "Le Divin dans *Salammbô*." *Revue des lettres modernes* 1165–72 (1994): 115–34.

Charles-Picard, Gilbert, and Colette Charles-Picard. *Daily Life in Carthage at the Time of Hannibal*. Trans. A. E. Foster. New York: Macmillan, 1961.

Green, Anne. *Flaubert and the Historical Novel*: Salammbô *Reassessed*. Cambridge: Cambridge University Press, 1982.
Mullen Hohl, Anne. *Exoticism in* Salammbô: *The Languages of Myth, Religion, and War*. Birmingham, AL: Summa, 1995.
Weston, Jessie. *From Ritual to Romance*. Garden City, NY: Doubleday, 1957 (1920).

Monnier, Henry (1799–1877). Henry Monnier was a celebrated caricaturist and popular writer whose creation, "M. Prudhomme," clearly foreshadowed Flaubert's "le Garçon" and the pharmacist Homais in *Madame Bovary*, as well as Honoré de Balzac's Bixiou in Balzac's *Scènes de la vie privée*. In turn, these figures became ancestors of Jules Romains' Dr. Knock and Albert Jarry's Ubu. Both Monnier and Flaubert saw their grotesque characters as a revenge on complacent bourgeois. Moreover, Flaubert's youthful work, "Une leçon d'histoire naturelle: genre commis," undoubtedly owes much of its inspiration de Monnier's *Scènes de la vie bureaucratique*, which forms part of the 1835 edition of Monnier's *Scènes populaires* published in Belgium and reissued from 1836–39 in Paris. Monnier's and Flaubert's copy clerks have similar clothing, habits, and turns of phrase.

Monnier wrote satiric dialogue sketches from everyday life, illustrated with drawings. He frequently expanded these sketches as they passed through as many as a dozen editions during his lifetime. M. Prudhomme first appeared in "Le Dîner bourgeois" episode of Monnier's *Scènes populaires* (1830). Prudhomme reappears in Félix Auguste Duvert's play *La Famille improvisée* (1831), in the sketch "M. Prudhomme, membre de l'institut." Monnier, as an actor, played the romantic lead and all four character parts for this production. He also played the lead role in the successful farce *Grandeur et décadence de M. Joseph Prudhomme* at the Théâtre de l'Odéon in November 1852, and in a shortened version at the Théâtre des Variétés during June 1856. On December 30, 1857, Monnier cheekily wrote Flaubert to present him with a fait accompli: Monnier announced that he had dramatized *Madame Bovary*, and intended to play the part of Homais. The pharmacist's deistic professions of faith closely resemble Prudhomme's.

One cannot be certain whether Monnier and Flaubert ever met, but Flaubert frequently alludes to Prudhomme in his letters, especially after 1870. Flaubert even signed "Joseph Prudhomme" to a humorous letter in florid style written to the Baroness Lepic (September 24, 1872, *Corr.* 6: 417–19). Many entries in Flaubert's *Dictionnaire des idées reçues*, the projected second volume to *Bouvard et Pécuchet*, for which Flaubert had been gathering material all his life, are verbal parallels to Monnier's parodic assertions. (LMP)

References:

Flaubert, Gustave. "Une leçon d'histoire naturelle: genre commis." In Gustave Flaubert, *Œuvres de jeunesse inédits*, in Flaubert, *Œuvres complètes*. 28 vols. Paris: Conard, 1910–54. 1:198–293.

Melcher, Edith. *The Life and Times of Henry Monnier 1799–1877.* Cambridge: Harvard University Press, 1950. 179–85.
Monnier, Henry. *Mémoires de M. Joseph Prudhomme.* Paris: Librairie Nouvelle, 1857.
———. *Scènes populaires.* 4 vols. Paris: Dumont, 1836–39.
———. *Scènes populaires, dessinées à la plume.* Paris: Levavasseur, 1830.
———, and Gustave Vaez (pseud.). *Grandeur et décadence de M. Joseph Prudhomme.* Paris: Lévy, 1854.

monsters, episode of (*TSA*, all versions). The episode of the monsters occurs in the seventh and final section of the definitive version of Flaubert's *Tentation de saint Antoine* (1874), between the scene with the Sphinx and Chimera (representing Matter and Thought, respectively) and the saint's pantheistic ecstasy, which precedes the concluding epiphany of Christ's face in the sun. The very diversity of these monstrous forms suggests an underlying unity that is the secret of life, while their grotesqueness affords Flaubert an opportunity for implied anti-bourgeois satire. As Antoine contemplates them, he is no longer afraid and enters into a delirious pantheistic frenzy: "O bonheur! bonheur! j'ai vu naître la vie, j'ai vu le mouvement commencer. Le sang de mes veines bat si fort qu'il va les rompre. J'ai envie de voler, de nager, d'aboyer, de beugler, de hurler. Je voudrais avoir des ailes, une carapace, une écorce, souffler de la fumée, porter une trompe, tordre mon corps, me diviser partout, être en tout, . . . pénétrer chaque atome, descendre jusqu'au fond de la matière,—être la matière!" (O rapture, rapture! I've seen the origins of life, I've seen movement begin. My blood is pounding so hard that it's going to burst my veins. I feel like flying, swimming, barking, bellowing, howling. I would like to have wings, a shell, a coat of bark, to breathe out smoke, to have a trunk, to writhe like a serpent, to parcel myself out everywhere, to be in everything, . . . penetrate each atom, descend to the depths of matter—to be matter!) (275–76). Whereas the devil invites an estrangement from Creation, this ecstasy reconciles Antoine with Creation: dawn rises, Christ's face shines from the sun, and Antoine once again can pray. (LMP)

References:

Flaubert, Gustave. *La Tentation de saint Antoine*, ed. Edouard Maynial. Paris: Garnier, 1968.
Seznec, Jean. "Saint Antoine et les monstres. Essai sur les sources et la signification du fantastique chez Flaubert." *PMLA* 58 (March 1943): 195–222.

morbidity. Flaubert had a lifelong preoccupation with the early mystic Saint Anthony, who is said in his vita to have lived for some time in the tombs of the dead as a form of asceticism. In Flaubert's *La Tentation de saint Antoine*, the mystic's frustrated chagrin at having been in the wrong place at the wrong time and therefore having missed out on undergoing a martyr's execution has a comic effect. The documents from the trial of *Madame Bovary* debate whether her death makes a moral example of her or not, but the violently vivid details of her blood-chilling suicide in the novel are surely the most explosively blasphemous aspect of the text. Throughout Flaubert's œuvre, morbidity poses the question whether the social being can and will accept the conditions of social existence set by her or his peers and era.

It was while Flaubert was watching over his sister's corpse and reading Montaigne, according to Eugenio Donato, that he realized with a kind of morbid exhilaration that form and content are noncongruent. Reading at wakes was undeniably important for Flaubert; near the corpse of his beloved friend Alfred Le Poittevin, he read Georg Friedrich Creuzer's *Religions de l'antiquité*, a foundational text for his lifelong project *La Tentation de saint Antoine*. This reading beside corpses and about corpses presages Flaubert's literary tendency either to exhibit his characters as dead bodies or to have them view dead bodies within the framework of his novels. Madame Bovary, like Caroline Flaubert, wears her wedding dress to the grave, a tiny trickle of black bile belying the illusion of virginal expectation. Saint Antoine is portrayed by Flaubert as experiencing a visceral identification with the husband of a young dead woman. Félicité in "Un cœur simple" feels a quiet surprise when her loving gaze fails to resurrect little Virginie.

Certainly for Flaubert, death represents representation itself, by unveiling the fallacy of the ideal of the true imitation. But this metatextual role of death should not obscure its uses for uncensored social commentary. The realist mode in the visual arts of the 1840s and 1850s, for example, Gustave Courbet's *L'Enterrement à Ornans*, is drawn to the subject of the corpse, in which only materiality remains. To censor that materiality would be to censor the unredeemable. When the conditions of social existence have been refused, through suicide or ascetic mysticism or the delusions of invalid old age, morbidity then raises the issue whether society can and will accept the representation of that refusal.(DJ)

References:

Creuzer, Georg Friedrich. *Religions de l'antiquité*. 4 vols. bound in 10 parts. Paris: Treuttel et Würtz, 1825–51.

Donato, Eugenio. "The Crypt of Flaubert." In Naomi Schor and Henry F. Majewski, eds., *Flaubert and Postmodernism*. Lincoln: University of Nebraska Press, 1984. 30–45.

White, Nicholas. "Dying for Flaubert: Two Naturalist Versions of the Death of the Subject." *New Zealand Journal of French Studies* 18 (1997): 20–29.

Moreau, Frédéric (*ES*). When we first meet the main character of *L'Education sentimentale*, newly graduated from high school and preparing to study law, the eighteen-year-old Frédéric Moreau is already convinced that the happiness to which he has a right is slow in coming. At the end of the novel, all ambition abandoned, he lives "en petit bourgeois" in the provinces. That unfocused, directionless search for happiness through an array of possible careers and chance relationships forms the sardonic center of Flaubert's *L'Education sentimentale*. The novel's blend of external focalization and internal monologue allows Flaubert both direct comment (the list of Frédéric's literary enthusiasms, for instance, is followed by "and others that were more mediocre filled him with almost equal enthusiasm") and direct access to the mediocrity of his protagonist's own mind, as, for example, in the following revealing meditation: "The thought of the Dambreuses came to him; he would use them; then he remembered Deslauriers."

Unequivocally described as "the man who had all the weaknesses," Frédéric not only represents Flaubert's vision of contemporary France, but is reflected and refracted through the novel's other characters. His vaguely formulated ambition to succeed in the law, for example, is exemplified in the colorless figure of Martinon; his dreams of painting a great work of art find an ironic commentary in the character Pellerin; his hopes of making his name as a writer are mockingly refracted in the journalist Hussonet.

Frédéric's dreams of love are equally vague, becoming increasingly etiolated by his inability to focus on a specific goal or even a specific woman and by his substitution of money for intrinsic values when he attempts to draw attention to himself. Boasting of his inheritance to Mme Arnoux or buying for Rosanette Bron the objects he hopes will win her over typifies his failure to discover in himself or in the external world anything of real value.

That failure is carried over into the political arena. Watching one of the bloodier incidents in the 1848 revolution, Frédéric is unable to perceive it as real, reducing it to spectacle and amusement in his inability to comprehend the reality of what he is seeing. Likewise, when he attempts to run for public office, his inability to understand is sardonically if comically reflected in the long speech in Spanish that one of the visitors makes, holding the crowd's attention where Frédéric's own bromides had signally failed. Observing always from the outside, tagging along rather than participating, let alone leading, Frédéric reveals the impossibility of remaining neutral in a postindustrial world, but he also indicates how much the mass of modern humanity fails to make the kind of personal or social decisions that might lead to change or create some kind of meaning for existence. (RL)

References:

Bourdieu, Pierre. "The Invention of the Artist's Life." *Yale French Studies* 73 (1987): 75–103.

Brix, Michel. "Portrait d'un jeune homme 'entortillé par sa maman': Le Personnage de Frédéric Moreau dans *L'Education sentimentale*." *Lettres romanes* 44.3 (1990): 297–313.

Festa-Peyre, Diana. "Aging by Default: Frédéric Moreau and His Times in Flaubert's *Sentimental Education*" *Symposium* 47.3 (1993) 201–18.

Raitt, A. W. "The Art of Decharacterization in *L'Education sentimentale*." In Laurence M. Porter, ed. *Critical Essays on Gustave Flaubert*. Boston: Hall, 1986: 130–39.

Morel (*ES*, 1845). A secondary character in the 1845 version of *L'Education sentimentale*, Morel is a friend of the Gosselin family, and Henry Gosselin visits him in Paris. Rubbing elbows with high society, Morel is a boor devoid of illusions and aesthetic sensitivity. A social chameleon, he hires out his skills as a writer, later working as a lawyer, businessman, entrepreneur, and more. Henry despises Morel, but ends up strangely resembling him, with this difference: while Morel is, by the end of the novel, condemned to a rustic life on the family farm, Henry's future seems full of promise (although Flaubert depicts this promise ironically). Morel has no clear corollary in the 1869 version of the novel, nor in Flaubert's life. (SDC)

museums. Flaubert had a keen interest in art. He visited the Louvre as well as museums and galleries on his travels in Italy, Greece, Egypt, and the Near East, and he describes many of them in *Par les champs et par les grèves*, and in his correspondence. In July 1876, he borrowed several objects from the museum in Rouen, including a parrot to use as a model for Loulou in "Un cœur simple." In *Flaubert's Parrot*, Julian Barnes describes visits to that museum and to the one at Croisset, each of which exhibits what it claims is the original for Loulou.

Donato likens *Bouvard et Pécuchet*'s project to that of a natural history museum, an attempt to classify knowledge and impose order on nature as do geology and archeology (endeavors he dismisses as failures). Responding to Donato, Porter points out that Bouvard and Pécuchet are anything but systematizers and that their failures lead them to a skeptical stance toward human knowledge. How appropriate that at Croisset, in the summer pavilion that is all that remains of Flaubert's estate, the exhibits are "carelessly laid out, catch your heart at random" (Barnes 20). (CR)

References:

Barnes, Julian. *Flaubert's Parrot*. New York: Knopf, 1985.

Donato, Eugenio. "The Museum's Furnace: Notes toward a Contextual Reading of *Bouvard and Pécuchet*." In Josué V. Harari, ed., *Textual Strategies*. Ithaca: Cornell University Press 1979. 213–38.

Porter, Laurence M. "The Rhetoric of Deconstruction: Donato and Flaubert." *Nineteenth-Century French Studies* 20 (1991–92): 128–36.

Musset, Alfred de (1810–57). Alfred de Musset was an immensely gifted poet, playwright, and novelist who ruined his health and died young because of drink. Like Flaubert, he frequented Louise Colet's salon. When Flaubert returned from his long trip through the Middle East in 1851 and resumed his affair with Colet without much enthusiasm, she started a second liaison with Musset, perhaps to make Flaubert jealous, but he remained amused and indifferent. She excoriated both of them in her book *Lui* (1859). Some of the Colet-Musset correspondence and a few surviving letters from her to Flaubert are reproduced in volume 2 of

Bruneau's edition of Flaubert's correspondence. The evidence of the letters appears partially to rehabilitate Colet and Maxime Du Camp, whom scholars have tended to vilify when describing their relations with Flaubert. (LMP)

References:

Flaubert, Gustave. *Correspondance*. Ed. Jean Bruneau. 4 vols. to date. Paris: Gallimard, 1973– .

Gérard-Gailly, Emile. *Autour de Gustave Flaubert: Les Véhémences de Louise Colet, d'après des documents inédits*. Paris: Mercure de France, 1934.

N

Nabokov, Vladimir (1899–1977). A true cosmopolitan, Vladimir Nabokov lived in Russia until 1919, studied French and Russian literature at Trinity College, Cambridge, England, and then lived in Berlin and in Paris before moving to the United States. There he worked as a literary critic, novelist, poet, and translator while teaching literature at Cornell, Harvard, Stanford, and Wellesley College. *Lolita* (1955) proved so profitable as a novel and film that Nabokov was able to retire from teaching and devote himself to writing. He ended his career in Montreux, Switzerland (1961–77). The hapless European professor transplanted to the United States often plays a major role in his works (*Lolita, Pnin, Pale Fire*). Nabokov tends to use simple plot lines with a strong central focus, but displays an enormously rich vocabulary with much multilinguistic punning. He enjoys using two or three adjectives to modify a word.

Nabokov strongly admired Flaubert and identified with his novelistic art, which, in his mind, Joyce barely surpassed. *Madame Bovary* inspired a lecture by Nabokov condensing much of what has since been written about Flaubert's style and composition: that they produce the effect of poetry in prose. Thus Nabokov explores how various vignettes such as the layering motif (e.g., Charles's cap, Emma's wedding cake, and eventually the embedded coffins wherein he buries her) or the equine motif whose thread is interwoven with Emma's love life disseminate poetic cues throughout the novel. He examines how such recurring details, in turn, symbolize the protagonist's inner struggle while objectifying the poet's vision of Emma's life. They participate in Flaubertian pictorial art just as his use of ironic counterpoint does, by providing trivial but seemingly factual details and by underlining the shallowness of provincial bourgeois life, as in the love duet during the agriculture fair or in the cathedral scene between the beadle, Léon, and Emma. Thus creating a wealth of echoes, of associations of themes and ideas, while fostering narrative movements from one image to the next, Flaubert succeeds beautifully and artistically,

Nabokov claims, in painting the drab reality of Emma's life and surroundings. (IC/LMP)

Reference:

Nabokov, Vladimir. "Gustave Flaubert: *Madame Bovary*." In Vladimir Nabokov, *Lectures on Literature*, ed. Fredson Bowers. New York: Harcourt Brace Jovanovich, 1980: 125–77.

Napoleon III (Charles-Louis-Napoleon Bonaparte, 1808–73). The son of Louis Bonaparte, king of Holland, Charles-Louis-Napoleon Bonaparte twice tried to overthrow Louis-Philippe and have himself proclaimed emperor (1836, 1840). Sentenced to life imprisonment, he escaped and took refuge in London. After the revolution of 1848, he returned to France and skillfully appealed to both liberals and conservatives. Although he swore to uphold the constitution of the Second Republic when he was elected as its president (December 10, 1848), within three years he engineered a coup that installed him as emperor. He reigned from 1851 to 1870, when he unwisely responded to Prussian provocations, declared war, and was soundly defeated and captured at Sedan. Not long after, he died in exile in England.

Flaubert remained aloof from politics throughout the Second Empire, but both Empress Eugénie and her young relative, Princess Mathilde, admired *Madame Bovary* and defended it when the novel, its publisher, and its author were put on trial for immorality. Princess Mathilde became a good friend to Flaubert, and after he published *Salammbô* (a work she privately considered inferior to the first novel), she frequently invited him to her parties and balls, where he met the emperor and empress from time to time. He reveled in his access to high society and campaigned for the Legion of Honor, a decoration he received in 1866. Like Jean-Paul Sartre after him, Louis Bouilhet complained that Flaubert had renounced the cult of art and sold out to materialism, but Flaubert enjoyed his busy, impressive social life too much to abandon it, although he seriously overspent his income during this time (Bart 450–54). (GB/LMP)

See also Coup d'état of December 2, 1851.

Reference:

Bart, Benjamin F. *Flaubert*. Syracuse: Syracuse University Press 1967.

narrator. As is often noted, Flaubert's realist style qua style erases itself, almost as if reality were telling its own story without a human narrator. Flaubert himself comments on this invisibility of the creator in this well-known phrase: "L'artiste doit être dans son œuvre comme Dieu dans la création, invisible et tout-puissant; qu'on le sente partout, mais qu'on ne le voie pas" (The artist should be invisible and all-powerful in his work, as God is in creation: let him be felt everywhere, but seen nowhere) (Letter to Mlle Leroyer de Chantepie, March 18, 1857 *Corr.* 4:164). This impersonal narrative voice is sometimes omniscient, sometimes exterior to people and to their thoughts, sometimes interior to one character's and then another's point of view; these shifts leave the reader shuttling among different perspectives without any unifying vision.

These shifting points of view are possible in part because the Flaubertian narrator is not a character who can give us an individual, unified point of view to help us with our interpretation (there are some minor and ephemeral exceptions such as the "Nous" that begins *Madame Bovary*). Nor does the third-person narrator pronounce obvious, subjective judgments of characters and events that an author such as Stendhal makes in *Le Rouge et le Noir*.

Even though the impersonal narrative voice in Flaubert is less prone to make judgments and offer opinions than it is in Stendhal or Balzac, the narrator's voice and opinions do come through clearly at times. For instance, the ironic, superior point of view of the narrative voice criticizes the petty banality of Rodolphe's understanding of language: "Il ne distinguait pas, cet homme si plein de pratique, la dissemblance des sentiments sous la parité des expressions" (Although he was so experienced with women, [Rodolphe] could not distinguish differences among feelings beneath the similarity of the words used to express them) (Flaubert, part 2, chapter 12:1, 466). Flaubert worked to eliminate as much of this personal voice as possible, but some clear judgments remain.

The decenteredness resulting from the multiplicity of narrative perspectives crops up again in realist descriptions. With no clear narrator, there is no clear spot from which to view the real. As Jonathan Culler has shown, random bits of observation put together, as in the following passage, create an odd indirection and disunity: "Les toits de chaume, comme des bonnets de fourrure rabattus sur des yeux, descendent jusqu'au tiers à peu près des fenêtres basses, dont les gros verres bombés sont garnis d'un nœud dans le milieu, à la façon des culs de bouteilles. Sur le mur de plâtre que traversent en diagonale des lambourdes noires, s'accroche parfois quelque maigre poirier, et les rez-de-chaussée ont à leur porte une petite barrière tournante pour les défendre des poussins qui viennent picorer, sur le seuil, des miettes de pain bis trempé de cidre" (The thatched roofs, like fur bonnets pulled down over the eyes, cover nearly a third of the low windows, whose thick, bowed panes are embellished with a lump in the middle, like bottle glass. On the plaster wall criss-crossed with blackened beams, a scrawny pear tree is attached here and there, and the ground-floor entrances have a little turnstyle in the doorways, to keep out the chicks who come to the doorstep to peck at crumbs of bread soaked in cider) (Flaubert, part 2, chapter 1: 1, 355) We go from specific to general and back again with little reason for the whole and with no unification from a central narrative consciousness. Such techniques of decentering leave the reader floundering in search of a definite conclusion, a clear perspective on the work, when none is available. (DJK)

References:

Culler, Jonathan. *Flaubert: The Uses of Uncertainty* 1974. Rev. ed. Ithaca: Cornell University Press, 1985.

Flaubert, Gustave. *Madame Bovary*. In Gustave Flaubert, *Œuvres*, ed. Albert Thibaudet and René Dumesnil. 2 vols. Paris: Gallimard, 1951–82. Vol 1.

Ginsburg, Michal Peled. *Flaubert Writing: A Study in Narrative Strategies*. Stanford Stanford University Press, 1986.

Narr'Havas (*Sal*). Narr'Havas, chief of the Numidians, owes his presence at the mercenaries' banquet to his father's propensity for forging alliances. As the novel runs its course, he becomes so successful at making and undoing alliances that he effectively becomes his father and acquires the title of king of the Numidians. He has been seen as crafty and fickle (Thibaudet 143); in a work rife with betrayal, he epitomizes treachery. Neither Carthaginian nor barbarian, the Numidian prince is the quintessential outsider who changes sides constantly, his alliances dictated by the prevailing winds of power (Neefs 235–36). As is true of Salammbô, also represented as a traitor, he circulates in both camps. In fact, both characters pursue similar objectives, she to retrieve the zaïmph, whose absence from Carthage provokes a popular denunciation of Tanit as a defector, and he to ally himself with the army whose power derives from its possession.

In a series of shifting triangular configurations, Narr'Havas is first Mâtho's rival as they both demonstrate their interest in Salammbô at the mercenaries' banquet, during which Narr'Havas wounds Mâtho. Then he is identified with Hamilcar in relation to Salammbô, as is Mâtho. From both Mâtho's and Salammbô's point of view, Narr'Havas is also depicted as feminine. Salammbô is enthralled by Narr'Havas's femininity and considers him a sister god sent for her protection, in contrast to Mâtho's violence, which she desires. In other words, he is like a woman, as Mâtho and Hamilcar were found to be. These characteristics, in conjunction with a series of temporal coincidences in *Salammbô*, have led to Narr'Havas's interpretation as a composite figure, a conflation of Henri de Navarre, Murat, and Alexander I, all three sharing his propensity for charm, marriage alliances, and betrayal (Addison 105–9).

The mercenaries' banquet and the final wedding banquet are marriages of blood (Rousset 91). In the former, Narr'Havas prefigures Schahabarim's mutilation of Mâtho's corpse when he wounds Mâtho. The wound is in Mâtho's arm, an area that will later identify him with Eschmoûn as he commences his descent to his Passion. At the putative marriage feast, the triangular configuration is repeated. Narr'Havas, the presumed victorious rival and never-to-be, yet already-cuckolded, husband, is witness to what has been called the true marriage of Salammbô and Mâtho (Rousset 91).

A third feast is accompanied by what may well be called another marriage of blood. It is the sacrificial meal that seals the alliance between Narr'Havas and Mâtho. Here the victims are a white bull and a black ewe, which symbolize day and night—that is, time. Narr'Havas, in a notable gesture, calls on the gods to bear witness as he curses Carthage. This is the first and only reference in the novel to his connection with the sacred. The blood of the victims is collected in a ditch, reminiscent of Attis's sacramental meal and baptism of blood at the vernal equinox (Frazer 408), and Narr'Havas and Mâtho plunge their arms into the blood bath. Subsequently, each of them leaves the blood imprint of his hand on the other's chest and tent, with the use of the word *stigmata* in the text functioning here as a sign of Mâtho's identification with Christ. The feast takes place exactly two months after the mercenaries' banquet, that is, at the summer solstice, which occurs just after the appearance of the Asclepius/Eschmoûn constellation. By means of a complex, disguised doubling of time, the dates of the feast in the tent correspond to both the summer solstice and the winter solstice, on which is superimposed the vernal equinox (Addison 95). After the betrayal of their alliance by Narr'Havas, Mâtho burns his own tent, on which the red imprint of Narr'Havas's hand is still visible.

Both Narr'Havas and Mâtho are skilled in hunting elephants, animals sacred to the sun god, so it is no small irony that Narr'Havas catches Mâtho/Adonis/Tammouz, Lord of the Net (Weston 128), in a net and brings him triumphantly into Carthage, his body tied in the shape of a cross on an elephant's back. The description of the unbounded joy expressed by the population of Carthage corresponds to the Festival of Joy celebrating the resurrection of Attis/Adonis (Frazer 407). Hence, just as Henri de Navarre said in his famous statement, "Paris is worth a Mass," as he converted to Catholicism, so Narr'Havas clearly thought that Carthage was worth a Red Mass. The text, however, closes on an appropriately ironic note by illustrating the proverb "Pride goeth before a fall," since Narr'Havas is represented as intoxicated by the pride of possessing Salammbô, Carthage incarnate, just before she falls down dead. (AMH)

References:

Addison, Claire. *Where Flaubert Lies: Chronology, Mythology, and History*. Cambridge: Cambridge University Press, 1996.

Frazer, Sir James. *The Golden Bough*. Abridged ed. New York: Macmillan, 1951.

Mullen Hohl, Anne. *Exoticism in* Salammbô: *The Languages of Myth, Religion, and War*. Birmingham, AL: Summa, 1995.

Neefs, Jacques. "Le Parcours du Zaïmph." In Claudine Gothot-Mersch, ed., *La Production du sens chez Flaubert*. Paris: Union Générale d'Editions, 1975. 227–41.

Rousset, Jean. "Positions, distances, perspectives dans *Salammbô*." *Poétique* 6 (1971): 145–54.

Thibaudet, Albert. *Gustave Flaubert*. Rev. ed. Paris: Gallimard, 1963; Saint-Armand (Cher): S.E.P.C., 1992 (1922).

Weston, Jessie. *From Ritual to Romance*. Garden City, NY: Doubleday, 1957 (1920).

naturalism. Naturalist novelists considered themselves disciples of Flaubert, but did not imitate him in every respect. Unlike Flaubert's realism, naturalism in Emile Zola's view treated working-class rather than middle-class characters and held heredity to be a decisive causal factor. Guy de Maupassant followed Flaubert most closely (see his novel *Une Vie*, 1883), but his novels and short stories do not have the profundity of *Madame Bovary*. Zola adopted techniques like the tableau, *style indirect libre* ("free indirect style" or represented discourse), and abundant and accurate description, but did not follow Flaubert's dicta on art nor imitate his mania for the well-turned sentence. (EFG)

Reference:

Brunetière, Ferdinand. "Le Naturalisme français: Etude sur Gustave Flaubert." In Ferdinand Brunetière, *Le Roman naturaliste*. Paris: Calmann-Lévy, 1896 [1883]. 149–203.

neurosis. Flaubert's early correspondence conceives of professional employment as a capitulation to the world's absurdity. "Me voilà sur le point de *choisir un état*," he wrote to Ernest Chevalier. "Il me reste encore les grands chemins, les voies toutes faites, les habits à vendre, les places, mille trous qu'on bouche avec des imbéciles. Je serai donc bouche-trou dans la société" (Here I am, about to choose a profession. All that's left for me is the highways, well-beaten paths, clothes to sell, positions, a thousand holes you can plug with an imbecile. So I'll be a plug for holes in society). Flaubert was definitively prevented from becoming a *bouche-trou*, however, by the nervous crisis that occurred in January 1844 as he drove a carriage near Pont-L'Evêque with his brother Achille. It is with a certain irony, then, that in a letter of February 1844 to Ernest Chevalier he qualifies as the "récit de mes douleurs" (the account of my sorrows) the announcement that he will have to withdraw from his legal studies in Paris and devote himself on a quasi-permanent basis to taking in "l'air de la mer, beaucoup d'exercice, and surtout beaucoup de calme" (The sea air, a lot of physical exercise, and above all, much peace and quiet). Scholars are divided on whether this crisis was epilepsy or hysteria. Jean-Paul Sartre believed that Flaubert's nervous attacks were hysterical. Hazel Barnes convincingly argues, however, that Flaubert himself viewed the attacks as the consequence of the reciprocal influence of bodily and psychic processes (208). This reciprocity is illustrated, according to Barnes, by the alarm that greeted Flaubert's mimetic portrayal of epilepsy during adolescent performances that centered around imitations of odd characters such as an epileptic beggar at the beach (205). Flaubert's own family and friends saw the attacks as "epileptiform" rather than epileptic. However, they now fall under a specific epileptic diagnosis (Lottman 55).

Whether the origins of Flaubert's nervous condition were psychic, physical, or a reciprocal combination of the two, his position on the sidelines of professional life was a central facet of his existence. Many of his novelistic characters share this marginalized position. The ambiguous effect of Flaubert's nerves parallels the complex effects of money on Frédéric in *L'Education sentimentale*, of gender on Emma Bovary in *Madame Bovary*, and of mystical hallucinations on Saint Antoine in *La Tentation de saint Antoine*. Saint Antoine reflects morosely at one point that without his visions, he could have been a toll taker rather than a hermit. (DJ)

References:

Barnes, Hazel E. *Sartre and Flaubert*. Chicago: University of Chicago Press, 1981. 182–224.

Flaubert, Gustave. Letters to Ernest Chevalier, July 23, 1839, and February 1, 1844. In Gustave Flaubert, *Correspondance*, ed. Bernard Masson. Paris: Gallimard, 1998. 41–42, 51–52.

Lottman, Herbert R. *Gustave Flaubert*. New York: Fromm, 1990. 54–58.

Sartre, Jean-Paul. *L'Idiot de la famille*. 3 vols. Paris: Gallimard, 1971–72.

nihilism. The debate about the role of nihilism in Flaubert's work is nowhere better exemplified than in his last work, *Bouvard et Pécuchet*. Jean-Paul Sartre read the suggestion in *La Tentation de saint Antoine* that suicide's creation of nothingness is equivalent to the nothingness from which God creates the world. If Being is suffering, Nothingness is Better, writes Sartre of Flaubert's nihilism. Flaubert's nihilism is indeed strikingly evident in the pattern of suicides or contemplations of suicides that traverses his work from "Quidquid Volueris" on. The seduction of nothingness is often seen as an effect of his profound critique of the bourgeoisie, but as Victor Brombert notes, Flaubert's nihilism is often most developed when the end fails to come: it is the tragedy of the very absence of tragedy (90). The tragedy of the absence of tragedy often creates a postmodern effect. *Bouvard et Pécuchet* particularly embodies this form of nihilism: the life of the copy here spells the death of the original. But this quandary raises the question whether Flaubert's nihilism is, in the absence of tragedy, comic. Even more problematic, Flaubert's comic nihilism is not exclusively ironic; as in the case of Félicité's *bêtise*, Bouvard and Pécuchet's earnest errors are saturated with feeling. One might perhaps conclude that Flaubert's faux nihilism does not take one to an end but to the creation of new tropes generated from nothingness. (DJ)

References:

Brombert, Victor. *The Novels of Flaubert: A Study of Themes and Techniques*. Princeton: Princeton University Press, 1966.

Fournier, Louis. "Flaubert Nihiliste: une idée reçue?" *Lettres romanes* 51. 1–2 (1997): 53–73.

McKenna, Andrew. "Mass Media: Flaubert and the Art of Nihilism." *Enclitic* 1. 1 (1977): 71–76.

Sartre, Jean-Paul. *L'Idiot de la famille*. 3 vols. Paris: Gallimard, 1971–72.

Novembre (1842). *Novembre* is perhaps the most polished of Flaubert's juvenilia and is commonly considered the most nearly autobiographical of Flaubert's works (although *Mémoires d'un fou* can be considered a close competitor, retelling the same stories). The fine opening pages express the narrator's delight in autumn; his sense of union with nature recalls young Werther in Goethe's *The Sorrows of Young Werther* (1774). He longs for love, but has been disillusioned by his experiences in a Paris brothel, where he meets the prostitute Marie (the road not taken by the weak hero of *L'Education sentimentale* of 1869, who ran away without entering the bordello, and who remembers the illusions he thus preserved as the happiest experience of his life). Their love-making is described with a keen, daring sensuality inspired by Théophile Gautier's descriptions of the bisexual Mademoiselle de Maupin. At this point, the narrative digresses into fantasy when Marie falls in love with him and says that he is the man for whom she has been searching. But still he can find no lasting satisfaction with her (Bart 76). A relay narrator now takes over, reporting that the hero had considered and then rejected suicide, but had died shortly after anyway.

In *Mémoires d'un fou*, Felman points out, in what is the best essay on the juvenilia, Flaubert still tries awkwardly to use fictive madness like a romantic, to prove that he is different from others. In *Novembre*, he must acknowledge the unpalatable truth that "madness" has always already been situated in the linguistic and social "common place" previously occupied by others. Madness and the narrator's death themselves become clichés that undermine the status of the narrative as an original creation whose originality can validate its author. *Novembre*, Felman adds, may be even more modern than the 1845 version of *L'Education sentimentale* because it denounces the referential illusion that words can reliably correspond to something in externality. Ginsburg develops the thought that *Novembre* exposes the dilemma of the narrator threatened with annihilation both as protagonist and as narrator by the fictive double that he has created. He must die as an "I" to survive as a narcissistic projection. Experience itself has the structure of representation; desire is nonoriginal and nonoriginary (compare René Girard's reflections on "mediated desire" in his *Deceit, Desire, and the Novel*). Extrapolating from the text to Flaubert's life, Henri Guillemin speculates that the work reflects an adolescent identity crisis, unsatisfactorily resolved through a despairing self-sacrifice to Flaubert's father's wishes that his son learn and pursue a useful profession (LMP)

See also neurosis.

References:

Bart, Benjamin. *Flaubert*. Syracuse: Syracuse University Press, 1967. 68–79.

Brombert, Victor. "Usure et rupture chez Flaubert: L'Exemple de 'Novembre'. " In Charles Carlut, ed., *Essais sur Flaubert en l'honneur du professeur Don Demorest*, Paris: Nizet, 1979. 145–54.

Bruneau, Jean. *Les Débuts littéraires de Gustave Flaubert, 1831–1845*. Paris: Colin, 1962.

Felman, Shoshana. "Modernity of the Commonplace." In Laurence M. Porter, ed., *Critical Essays on Gustave Flaubert*. Boston: Hall, 1986. 29–48.

Ginsburg, Michal Peled. *Flaubert Writing: A Study in Narrative Strategies*. Stanford: Stanford University Press, 1986. 16–45.

Girard, René. *Deceit, Desire, and the Novel: Self and Other in Literary Structure*. Trans. Yvonne Freccero. Baltimore: Johns Hopkins University Press, 1965.

Guillemin, Henri. "Introduction." In Gustave Flaubert, *Novembre*. Neuchâtel: Ides et calendes, 1961. 7–42.

Une Nuit de Don Juan. *Une Nuit de Don Juan* is a dramatic scenario with some dialogue, 1850–51, perhaps transcribed in preparation for writing a novel.

This subject was one of three Flaubert mentioned in a letter to Louis Bouilhet (November 14, 1850, *Corr.* 2:253), all treating the same theme of the conflation of "les deux formes de l'amour terrestre [self-centered and generous] et l'amour mystique [the two forms of earthly and mystical love]." Flaubert seems to have pursued this subject intermittently throughout his travels in the Middle East (see the letters of February 10 and April 9, 1851 to Louis Bouilhet, *Corr.* 2:293–99; to Ernest Chevalier, *Corr.* 2:307–11) and then to have abandoned it on his return in favor of *Madame Bovary*, with which it shares many preoccupations, though without the irony of loss. In this relatively optimistic scenario, the love given to the Don by Thérèse "ne périt pas quand la statue du Commandeur l'engouffra" (did not die when the Commander's statue engulfed him). (MCO)

References:

Bruneau, Jean. *Les Débuts littéraires de Gustave Flaubert, 1831–1845*. Paris: Colin, 1962.

Flaubert, Gustave. *Correspondance*. In Flaubert, *Œuvres complètes*, ed. Maurice Bardèche. 16 vols. Paris: Club de l'Honnête Homme, 1971–76.

———. *Œuvres complètes*. Ed. Bernard Masson. 2 vols. Paris: Seuil, 1964.

O

Oedipus complex. According to Jean-Paul Sartre, Hazel Barnes, and William Berg, among others, Flaubert's unresolved mother fixation appears in many biographical data and in Flaubert's literary productions. The massive accumulation of such evidence carries conviction. Flaubert remained emotionally dependent on his mother for most of his life; he wrote her almost daily during his twenty-month trip through the Middle East. Both his great unrequited love Elisa Schlésinger and his longtime mistress Louise Colet were distinctly older than he. He never married and, sexually, was most comfortable with prostitutes.

The maternal older woman is idealized in both versions of *L'Education sentimentale* (1845 and 1869). Sartre stresses the importance for understanding Flaubert's psyche of four works written from the time Flaubert was fourteen until he was sixteen: "La Fiancée et le tombeau"; "La Dame et le joueur d'orgue," containing literal but innocent incest; *Madame d'Ecouy*, depicting accidental incest; and *Deux Amours et deux cercueils*, where the son is a chaste avenger. All these depict the punishment of a mother-surrogate for having been unfaithful—voluntarily or involuntarily—to her fiancé, lover, or son. Moreover, the dream of the death of the mother in *Mémoires d'un fou* shows her symbolic fall (in the river) and punishment (by drowning).

The most flagrant dramatization of the Oedipus complex in Flaubert's mature work occurs in "La Légende de saint Julien l'hospitalier." Returning home from the hunt at night, Julien finds a couple in his bed and kills them, believing them to be his wife and a lover. Instead, they are his parents, who had arrived unexpectedly, and to whom his wife had offered hospitality. Julien's sadistic massacres of animals can be seen as displaced hostility toward his father; they cease after his father's death. He eventually wins sainthood despite killing his parents (Barnes 329). Flaubert moves earlier versions of the legend of Saint Julian closer to a primordial Oedipal tale by suppressing his wife as a companion of the repentant man after the murders and by eliminating Julian's visit to the pope (a symbolic, spiritual father). In real life, the death of Flaubert's father was wish-fulfilling: it removed a disapproving rival, left Flaubert alone with his mother, and, through inheritance, freed him from the need to work other than as a creative writer. His compulsive drudgery in later years could be read as self-justification and as symbolic atonement to his father. (LMP)

References:

Barnes, Hazel. *Sartre and Flaubert.* Chicago: University of Chicago Press, 1981.

Berg, William J., Michel Grimaud, and George Moskos. *Saint/Oedipus: Psychocritical Approaches to Flaubert's Art.* Ithaca: Cornell University Press, 1982.

Sartre, Jean-Paul. *L'Idiot de la famille: Gustave Flaubert de 1821–1857.* 3 vols. Paris: Gallimard, 1971–72. Trans. as *The Family Idiot.* Trans. Carol Cosman. 5 vols. Chicago: University of Chicago Press, 1981–93.

opera scene (*MB*). Found in *Madame Bovary*, part 2, chapter 15, the opera scene is one of the outstanding scenes of the novel and an example of Flaubert's technique of the tableau. At Homais's suggestion, Charles takes Emma to the opera in Rouen to see Gaetano Donizetti's *Lucia di Lammermoor* in order to cheer her up after her severe depression following the break with Rodolphe. Emma easily follows the plot because of her earlier reading of Sir Walter Scott's novel *The Bride of Lammermoor*, but Charles is hopelessly lost. At first, Emma is completely absorbed in the scene, associating events on the stage with events in her own life. Without knowing the opera libretto, it is difficult for the reader to follow the action, for much of it is presented in fragmentary fashion, from Emma's point of view, with occasional notations from the narrator. For example, we read that the painted sets shake as the actors walk across the stage, reminding us that Emma is viewing a fiction (at several removes, since it is a French libretto derived from an Italian libretto based on a novel by a Scottish novelist). The description of the tenor Lagardy borders on caricature—he is a charlatan, a cross between a hairdresser and a toreador. As the action progresses, Emma recognizes the artificiality and exaggeration of art, and the reader begins to believe that Emma has finally been cured. But no, her fantasies fasten on the tenor Lagardy, whose flamboyant career fascinates Emma, just as she had been fascinated at La Vaubyessard by the decrepit Duke of Laverdière, the supposed former lover of Marie Antoinette. She imagines what life would have been like with Lagardy, sharing his fame, being the object of his love. Once again her fantasy takes on the immediacy of reality as she imagines that Lagardy is looking directly at her, and she is tempted to call to him to take her away with him (as she had earlier done with Rodolphe). But Flaubert, in typical fashion, ends her fantasy abruptly as the curtain descends at the end of act 1. The chance meeting with Léon during the intermission propels the plot in a different direction. (EFG)

See also tableau.

Reference:

Daniels, Graham. "Emma Bovary's Opera: Flaubert, Scott, and Donizetti." *French Studies* 32 (1978): 285–303.

orientalism. To most French people, "l'Orient" has meant the Middle East, not the Far East. Literary works such as Voltaire's tragedy *L'Orphelin de la Chine* (1755) were most unusual, and some of the best-known texts that deal with the Far East—Judith Gautier's assisted translations of Chinese poetry, André Malraux's *La Condition humaine*, or Paul Claudel's prose poem cycle *Connaissance de l'Est* ("The East I Know")—did not yet exist in Flaubert's time. Napoleon's expedition to Egypt had excited great interest at the turn of the nineteenth century, and the French colonization of Algeria, which lasted from 1830 to 1871, maintained awareness of that area in France, as Eugène Delacroix's paintings vividly demonstrate. The major influence on French awareness of the Middle East, however, was the revival of the Catholic faith after the French Revolution, which led to pilgrimages and excursions to the Holy Land. François-René de Chateaubriand's *Itinéraire de Paris à Jérusalem* (1811), relating his journey through Constantinople, Jerusalem, Egypt, and Carthage during 1806, provided a prestigious model for later works such as Flaubert's (taken in 1849–51) or Gérard de Nerval's *Voyage en Orient* (taken in 1843, published in 1851). As Flaubert's travel diaries and intimate correspondence make clear, the Middle East quickly became a favorite locale for sexual tourism—a motif still prominent in André Gide's *L'Immoraliste* (1902) (on Flaubert, see Said 188–90).

Edward Said's groundbreaking study, *Orientalism*, explains that this multifaceted term refers, variously, to area studies; to a categorical opposition of "East" to "West"; and to a complex effort at intellectual and discursive domination of the Others and their culture by framing the conditions under which the Other will be exploited and judged. The goal of this cultural project is hegemony, power exercised with the consent of the governed. Said explains that Flaubert and Nerval are exceptions to the exploitation of a dehumanized oriental Other for commercial gain, in their imaginative literature. Each elaborated a personal myth—in *La Tentation de saint Antoine*, "Hérodias," and *Salammbô*, for example. An essential part of the integrity of this myth, Said believes, is that Flaubert does not ever believe that he can "capture" the Orient—not even decoratively or semantically (180–90). In a negative form, Flaubert's modesty regarding the Orient reappears even in *Bouvard et Pécuchet*, a work that, by satirizing the projects and representations of its naïve heroes, debunks the widespread nineteenth-century European myth of an Asia (including, in the romantic model, the Middle East) destined eventually to be regenerated by Europe (Said 114–16). (LMP)

References:

Bruneau, Jean. *Le "Conte oriental" de Flaubert*. Paris: Denoël, 1973.

Carré, Jean-Marie. *Voyageurs et écrivains français en Egypte*. 2 vols. Cairo: Institut Français d'Archéologie orientale, 1932.

El-Nouty, Hassan. *Le Proche-Orient dans la littérature française de Nerval à Barrès*. Paris: Nizet, 1958.
Flaubert, Gustave. *Correspondance*. Ed. Jean Bruneau. Paris: Gallimard, 1973. 1: 518ff.
Lamartine, Alphonse de. *Voyage en Orient*. Paris: Hachette, 1887 (1835).
Said, Edward W. *Orientalism*. New York: Vintage Books, 1979.

P

pantheism. Pantheism is the belief that God and the universe are identical, that God does not exist as a distinct personality, but rather as the expression of physical forces of nature. Flaubert's descriptions of nature frequently give the feeling that he is at least occasionally a pantheist. His friend Alfred Le Poittevin claimed to be one, and Baruch Spinoza had provided a philosophical structure for the belief. Flaubert's readings in Near Eastern religions gave him considerable knowledge of pantheism, as is readily apparent in *La Tentation de saint Antoine*. (AHP)

References:

Bart, Benjamin F. "Psyche into Myth: Humanity and Animality in Flaubert's Saint-Julien." *Kentucky Romance Quarterly* 20 (1973): 317–42.

Seznec, Jean. "Saint Antoine et les monstres: Essai sur les sources et la signification du fantastique chez Flaubert." *PMLA* 58 (1943): 195–222.

Par les champs et par les grèves (1847–48). Flaubert and his friend Maxime Du Camp hiked through the Loire valley and around the Breton peninsula from May through early August 1847. Starting in Brest, Flaubert's mother followed their route in a carriage and met them in the inns where they stopped for the evening. In Brittany, the two young men found a harsh contrast between tawdry modern bourgeois civilization and the idealized ancient Celtic kingdom with its Druid priestesses, described in Chateaubriand's *Les Martyrs* (Bart 160). Observing the Breton cult of the Virgin Mary, Flaubert recognized the diffuse, atavistic sensuality inseparable—in his view—from religious sentiment (Bart 167). He also once again experienced the pantheistic ecstasy of fusion of his self and of the landscape that he had first known in Corsica in 1840 (Bart 173–75).

Flaubert and Du Camp had planned to write a picturesque travel diary in which they would alternate chapters. In their desire to preserve memories of a vanishing past, they joined the current of romantic medievalism exemplified by Charles Nodier, the Baron Justin Taylor, and Alphonse de Cailleux in their *Voyages pittoresques et romantiques dans l'ancienne France*, a multivolume folio series with magnificent engravings that appeared between 1820 and 1845. But to allow themselves the pleasure of digressions and coarse humor, Du Camp and Flaubert decided not to try to publish their diary (Bart 164). Flaubert kept revising and adding to his sections throughout his life; they were posthumously published in 1886. Dumesnil's edition of the *Voyages* suggestively compares the manuscript to the published version. (LMP)

References:

Bart, Benjamin F. *Flaubert*. Syracuse: Syracuse University Press, 1967.

Flaubert, Gustave. "Les Pierres de Carnac et l'archéologie celtique." *L'Artiste*, April 18, 1858. Rpr. Gustave Flaubert, *Par les champs et par les grèves*, vol. 2: 236–43 in Maurice Nadeau, ed., *Œuvres complètes*. 18 vols. Lausanne: Editions Rencoutre, 1964.

———. *Voyages*. Ed. René Dumesnil. 2 vols. Paris: Les Belles Lettres, 1948. Vol. 1.

Starkie, Enid. *Flaubert: The Making of the Master*. New York: Atheneum, 1967. 151–54.

Tooke, Adrianne J. "Prolégomènes à une édition nouvelle de *Par les champs et par les grèves* de Gustave Flaubert et Maxime Du Camp." *Studi francese* 25 (1981): 291–99.

Pardo Bazán, Emilia, Condessa de (1852–1921). Emilia Pardo Bazán was a Galician, raised in a very conservative Catholic and monarchist milieu. She quickly transcended her upbringing, however: she visited Victor Hugo (a symbol of liberal intransigence) in Paris in 1874, shortly after his return from nineteen years in exile for opposing Emperor Napoleon III. She became a committed feminist who also supported the then-scandalous movement of literary naturalism led by Emile Zola in France; and she published *La literatura francesa moderna* in 1910. Chapter 2 of this work analyzes Flaubert's *Tentation de saint Antoine*.

Pardo Bazán seems to have first read Flaubert, Honoré de Balzac, the Goncourts, and Alphonse Daudet while taking a liver cure at Vichy in 1880. French realist and naturalist novelists had begun to be publicized in Spain from 1879 on, and particularly after Zola's shocking *Nana*—the tale of a prostitute who corrupts an entire society—appeared in 1880. Reading Flaubert as well as the great peninsular novelists Benito Pérez Galdós, José María de Pereda, and Juan Valera gave her the idea of becoming a novelist herself. Her *Un viaje de Novios* (1881) introduces Leocadia, a secondary character who, like Emma Bovary, is sensitive but mediocre; disillusioned in love, she dies in order to escape reality.

Pardo Bazán treats Flaubert in *La cuestión palpitante*, chapter 10, first published in serial form in the Madrid newspaper *La Epoca* from November 1882 through April 1884. She calls him the first true realist, free of the melodramatic exaggerations of Balzac. Flaubert's repressed subjectivity, she finds, can be detected in his despairing pessimism. However, she was particularly impressed by the visionary *Tentation de saint Antoine*, which she saw as a sort of *auto sacramental* (a devotional act—a phrase applied to Spanish religious theater of the Golden Age). As she reads Flaubert's visionary work, the soul struggles with doubts, emerges victorious, and reaffirms its faith in Christ.

Like *Madame Bovary*, Pardo Bazán's novel *El cisne de Vilamorta* (The Swan of Deadsville, 1885) sets unrealistic, romantic characters in a realistic setting where they are bound to fail. The title, referring to a weak, unscrupulous male who fancies himself an artist and to a boring, isolated town, is ironic. Like Emma Bovary, a woman sacrifices her child to her passion and poisons herself rather than accept the loss of her illusions. A minor character, a pharmacist, reminds one of Homais. The omniscient narrator preserves an aloof tone while continually deflating his characters with matter-of-fact remarks.

Pardo Bazán's *La Quimera* (The Chimera, 1905), her masterpiece, at first glance seems inspired by Zola's *L'Œuvre*. It depicts a young painter consumed by ambition. But Flaubert's Pellerin in *L'Education sentimentale* also provided a comic prototype. Moreover, the title of Pardo Bazán's novel came from the dialogue between Flaubert's Sphinx and Chimera in part 7 of *La Tentation*. This dialogue also gave Pardo Bazán the idea for the title of *La Esfinge* (The Sphinx), planned for the unfinished first part of the unfinished second volume of *La Quimera*—a struggle between mysticism and science. On examination, the young painter Silvio, the solitary figure striving for perfection and beset with dreams and hallucinations, seems closer to Saint Antoine than to Zola's protagonist. One of them involves the temptation of pantheism that also afflicts Saint Antoine. (Other visions, which Silvio experiences while standing in front of the cathedral of Notre-Dame de Paris, recall Victor Hugo.) *La Quimera* starts with a mood of despair, as does Flaubert's novel, and the one-act marionette play, *Sinfonía*, that opens *La Quimera* experiments with a lyrical prose again derived from *La Tentation de saint Antoine*. Silvio asks his patroness to read *La Tentation de saint Antoine* aloud to him. This intelligent but physically unattractive woman ruins herself financially to support the young painter, who fails and kills himself. The perverse Espina Porcel recalls Flaubert's Queen of Sheba. Finally, in 1911, Pardo Bazán's novel *Dulce Dueño* seems to be inspired by the richly detailed antiquarian descriptions of Flaubert's *Salammbô*.

Thanks to my colleague Dr. Patricia Greene for calling my attention to this literary relationship. (LMP)

References:

Clemessy, Nelly. *Emilia Pardo Bazán romancière (La critique, la théorie, la pratique)*. 2 vols. Paris: Centre de Recherches Hispaniques, 1973. 599–610 and passim.

González-Arias, Francisca. *Portrait of a Woman as Artist: Emilia Pardo Bazán and the Modern Novel in France and Spain*. New York: Garland, 1992. 165–200.

Pattison, Walter T. *Emilia Pardo Bazán*. New York: Twayne, 1971. 47, 85–89.

"Un Parfum à sentir, ou Les Baladins" (1836). "Un Parfum à sentir" is the tale of an indigent female clown with two children who has lost her looks and her ability to perform on the tightrope, and who is scorned, betrayed, and beaten by her husband and mocked by the rest of society until she finally despairs and commits suicide. The narrator exhaustively analyzes her emotional and physical sufferings. This self-conscious narrator's sympathetic, indignant comments also interrupt and frame the story with social criticism. Crudely written and obviously derivative of recent romantic texts such as Balzac's *La Peau de chagrin* (in the gambling scene) and Victor Hugo's *Notre-Dame de Paris*, this text is nevertheless interesting as an early example of the artist-as-clown motif that was to become prominent in the creations of premodernist and modernist figures such as Charles Baudelaire, Pablo Picasso, and Guillaume Apollinaire. (LMP)

Reference:

Flaubert, Gustave. "A Fragrance to Smell." *Early Writings*, In Gustave Flaubert, ed. and trans. Robert Griffin. Lincoln: University of Nebraska Press, 1991. 5–33.

Paris. Flaubert spent many extended sojourns in Paris. In November 1841, he enrolled in the Faculté de Droit to study law and took an occasional hotel room near the residence of friends Elisa and Maurice Schlésinger. Gustave also visited the Colliers, whose daughters he had befriended at Trouville, and he haunted the art studio of James Pradier, a neoclassic sculptor. Fellow law students and friends included Alfred Le Poittevin, his companion since childhood, and Louis de Cormenin. It was not until November 1842 that Flaubert rented his first apartment overlooking the Luxembourg gardens. In 1843 he met Baron Maxime Du Camp, a writer who became Flaubert's close friend.

As a student in Paris, Flaubert was bored and homesick. He quickly tired of its attractions and complained that success in the city required one to be *chic* (Letter to Pradier, September 21, 1846, *Corr.* 1: 329). The awkwardness he felt never dissipated; years later he still asserted that Paris caused his entire being, his personality to disappear (Letter to Mme Roger des Genettes, May 27, 1878, *Corr.* 8: 117). His novel *L'Education sentimentale* (1869) depicts the capital as a source of failure and disappointment, its topography disjointed and its people obsessed with appearances.

Although Flaubert passed the exam covering his first year of study in December 1842, he neglected his studies in favor of writing and fell into a pattern of debauchery. Finally he endured a series of epileptic or nervous attacks that, coupled with his inability to pass subsequent exams, terminated his law studies. In 1846, he met the poet Louise Colet in Paris and began a tumultuous sexual affair that lasted several years. Soon, however, it became mainly intellectual and epistolary. Flaubert broke off relations in early 1855.

Between 1851 and 1856, Flaubert worked on *Madame Bovary* (1857) at his home in Croisset and came to Paris only infrequently, although he did witness the coup d'état in 1851. By 1854, he had begun spending winter months in the capital, where his friend Louis Bouilhet had moved. In 1856, Du Camp agreed to publish installments of *Madame Bovary* in his *Revue de Paris*; shortly thereafter, an assertive young publisher, Michel Lévy, offered to publish the book. Claiming that the novel was a flagrant insult to morals and religion, the government sued Flaubert and the *Revue* in what became known as the trial of *Madame Bovary*. They were acquitted in February 1857.

During the 1860s, Flaubert continued to winter in Paris and published *Salammbô* (1862) and *L'Education sentimentale* (1869). A wide circle of literary acquaintances attended Sunday receptions at his apartment. They included the Goncourt brothers, Bouilhet and Du Camp, Théophile Gautier, the Russian novelist Ivan Turgenev, Charles-Augustin Sainte-Beuve, Emile Zola, Alphonse Daudet, Guy de Maupassant, and Joris-Karl Huysmans. Flaubert was also a welcome guest at Princess Mathilde's. The Prussian invasion in 1870 upset him and revealed to him his love for the city despite its faults ("ce Paris maudit et adoré," (Letter to Princess Mathilde, May 1871, *Corr.* 6: 240).

A play, *Le Candidat* (1873), and the visionary novel *La Tentation de saint Antoine* (1874) were rejected by the Parisian public; however, *Trois Contes* (1877) was well received, and Flaubert was fêted. In the years preceding his death (1880), he spent less time in Paris. (JWA)

References:

Bancquart, Marie-Claire. "L'Espace urbain de *L'Education sentimentale*: Intérieurs, extérieurs." In Marie-Claire Bancquart, ed., *Flaubert, la femme, la ville*. Paris: Presses Universitaires de France, 1983. 143–57.

Fournier, Albert. "De Rouen à Croisset." *Europe* 485–87 (1969): 252–68.

Wetherill, P. M. "Paris dans *L'Education sentimentale*." In *Flaubert, la femme, la ville*. Paris: Presses Universitaires de France, 1982. 123–35.

Pasca, Mme (pseud. for Alix-Marie-Angèle Sein Pasquier). Madame Pasca was one of Flaubert's "Three Angels," the attractive, flirtatious younger women whose friendship comforted him after the Franco-Prussian War of 1870–71. Mme Pasca starred in Alexandre Dumas fils's plays. (LMP)

References:

Laney, Pierre. *Le Théâtre d'Alexandre Dumas fils*. Paris: Presses Universitaires de France, 1928.

Schwarz, H. Stanley. *Alexandre Dumas fils, dramatist*. New York: New York University Press, 1927.

"Passion et vertu: Conte philosophique" (1837). "Passion et vertu" was the prototype for *Madame Bovary*, perhaps inspired by a newspaper account of a trial in *Le Journal de Rouen*, October 4, 1837. Ernest, a cynical and sadistic seducer who anticipates Rodolphe in *Madame Bovary*—to the point of using some of the same expressions—courts Mazza, a virtuous, thirty-year-old married woman who recalls Mme de Rênal in Stendhal's *Le Rouge et le Noir* (1830). Her integrity, sincere resistance, and regrets make her far more sympathetic than

Emma Bovary. When Ernest stops loving her and accepts an assignment in Mexico, she pursues him to the port, but in vain. She poisons her husband and then her two children to become free for Ernest. When he sends her a coldly dismissive letter, she sends a confession to the chief of police and then poisons herself. Flaubert's androgynous identification with her feelings is striking. (LMP)

References:

Bruneau, Jean. *Les Débuts littéraires de Gustave Flaubert, 1831–1845.* Paris: Colin, 1962.

Flaubert, Gustave. "Passion and Virtue." In Gustave Flaubert, *Early Writings*, trans. and ed. Robert Griffin. Lincoln: University of Nebraska Press, 1991. 103–28.

Herval, René. *Les Véritables Origines de* Madame Bovary. Paris: Nizet, 1957.

Starkie, Enid. *Flaubert: The Making of the Master.* New York: Atheneum, 1967. 31–34.

passivity. As a child, Flaubert would sit quietly for long periods, apparently unaware of his surroundings. Jean-Paul Sartre (*L'Idiot* 1:54) interprets this behavior as self-protection against being inadequately loved. The protagonists in Flaubert's youthful works, like Flaubert himself as a child, appear prematurely aged and apparently tired of life. Because Flaubert's older brother Achille had already won all the academic honors and had followed successfully in his father's footsteps by becoming a surgeon, there was no incentive for Flaubert to strive for distinction at school (Barnes 123). His repeated failures at his law exams—and perhaps even his epileptoid seizures—were therefore effective acts of passive aggression.

The young Flaubert never wanted to work for a living; he felt that his father's fortune should be adequate to support him as a writer. His idea of sexual enjoyment also seemed "a consenting, expectant passivity, a swooning self-abandonment" (Barnes 83) while being caressed. The pantheistic ecstasies common in Flaubert's work are a subsexual form of the same style of relating to the world. Instances of impressionistic narration, the long, detailed descriptions that often slow the progress of his mature works and that seem at times to have no meaning other than to signify the predominant, nonhuman part of our world, reflect the same passive stance by the writer, who implicitly presents himself as observer rather than as creator. Flaubert's sardonic pastiches of trite remarks and of unexamined opinions also require passivity on the part of the author. At the supreme moment of such passivity, at the conclusion of Flaubert's last work, *Bouvard et Pécuchet*, the two eponymous characters resolve to spend the rest of their days copying documents: thus others' writing overwhelms personal writing, and further creativity would become impossible. (LMP)

References:

Barnes, Hazel. *Sartre and Flaubert.* Chicago: University of Chicago Press, 1981.

Sartre, Jean-Paul. *L'Idiot de la famille: Gustave Flaubert de 1821–1857.* 3 vols. Paris: Gallimard, 1971–72. Trans. as *The Family Idiot.* Trans. Carol Cosman. 5 vols. Chicago: University of Chicago Press, 1981–93.

pastoral. The pastoral is a form of utopia set in the countryside, "a pictorial form seeking to project within certain arbitrary limits a vision of the good life" (Magowan 7). The bucolic poetry of Vergil and Theocritus, and Longus's narrative *Daphnis and Chloe* are canonical works in this tradition. As a depiction of idyllic repose, pastoral contrasts with the strife of the epic (one society against another) and with comedy and tragedy, wherein society heals itself via integration or expulsion, respectively, of its disturbing elements. Epic, comedy, tragedy, and pastoral were the four great genres of ancient literary theory, but today pastoral has been all but forgotten. In modern times, it appears mainly in ironic modes, as a vision of a lost paradise receding ever further into the past; its heroes must face the tests of aging and of death. Nicolas Poussin's seventeenth-century painting *Et in Arcadia ego* (I [death] too am found in Arcady), depicting a small group of peasants contemplating a gravestone, is the locus classicus of such awareness. Jacopo Sannazaro, Torquato Tasso, Edmund Spenser, Sir Philip Sidney, Andrew Marvell, and Lope de Vega are only a few of the practitioners of the genre since antiquity. More recently, Eugène Fromentin, George Sand, Alain-Fournier, Sarah Orne Jewett, and Isak Dinesen have perpetuated it. Stendhal ironizes it memorably in part 2, chapter 1, of *Le Rouge et le Noir*.

The pastoral genre in Honoré d'Urfé's *L'Astrée* (1607–27) best exemplifies the pastoral genre in French literature. The novel depicts the careless life of idealized, sentimentalized shepherds and their idylls in the countryside. The genre began to disappear in the eighteenth century, although traces can still be found in Jean-Jacques Rousseau's *La Nouvelle Héloïse* (1761) and in Queen Marie Antoinette's toy farm, Le Hameau, which has been preserved to this day in the gardens of Versailles (she became queen in 1774). Nevertheless, the desire to discover a heaven on earth continues to pervade the literature of the nineteenth century, and the influence of the pastoral can be seen ironically presented in Flaubert's work, particularly in *Bouvard et Pécuchet* (1881). The genre of the pastoral can be traced through schematic descriptions of the shepherd's life, but it also appears to have been treated in an ambivalent manner. In descriptive passages, bucolic settings fail to provide the reader with the sense of eternity specific to the genre. In the novel as a whole, it is not romantic love but rather love of discourse and knowledge that constitutes the object of desire. The use of language then becomes a space of innocence and happiness that defy eternity. Flaubert applies the components of the pastoral genre to the narrative structure of *Bouvard et Pécuchet*, suspending time. Literal-minded critics have noted that the two clerks, already retired when they retreat to the country, would have had to live at least till eighty or ninety to complete all the experiments Flaubert describes. Yet they must face the eventual ending of the world through geological cataclysm or entropy. Time is in a sense totally suspended throughout the second volume—a compendium of maxims from writers and from everyday life—where language helps the reader to escape the reality of a growing bourgeois culture in the very act of confronting its banality. (CT/LMP)

References:

Lalonde, Normand. "*Bouvard et Pécuchet*, poème bucolique." *French Studies* 49.2 (1995): 155–63.

Magowan, Robin. *Narcissus and Orpheus: Pastoral in Sand, Fromentin, Jewett, Alain-Fournier, and Dinesen.* New York: Garland, 1988.

Von der Thusen, Joachim. "Flaubert and the Transformation of Idyll." In Harald Hendrix, ed., *The Search for a New Alphabet: Literary Studies in a Changing World.* Amsterdam: Benjamins, 1996. 245–49.

Pécuchet (*BP*). *See* Bouvard and Pécuchet.

Pellerin (*ES*). Pellerin is an artist whose grandiose dreams end in failure. Wishing to become an artist in order to get closer to Mme Arnoux, whose husband is an art dealer, Frédéric arranges to take painting lessons with Pellerin, but nothing comes of it. He paints a hideous portrait of Rosanette Bron and then displays it in his shop window with the notation "Belongs to M. Frédéric Moreau" in hopes of blackmailing him into purchasing it. He later creates a grotesque painted allegory of Progress. Although he lacks several dimensions of Victor Hugo's evil Thénardier in *Les Misérables* (1862), his warped vision and his ambitions as an artist recall this earlier figure. Recently, in accordance with literary critics' natural tendency to grant to artist figures in fiction an importance disproportionate to the textual space that they occupy, criticism has emphasized Pellerin's importance in Flaubert's skeptical vision. (LMP)

References:

Bourdieu, Pierre. "The Invention of the Artist's Life." *Yale French Studies* 73 (1987): 75–103.

Paulson, William. Sentimental Education: *The Complexity of Disenchantment.* New York: Twayne, 1992. 54–56.

Pelouze, Mme. Mme Pelouze was the wealthy restorer of the lovely Château de Chenonceaux, which lies across the Loire River. She had influence in financial circles, and in 1877 Flaubert asked her to help raise capital for his nephew-in-law Ernest Commanville. She delivered 50,000 French francs in liquid cash and asked for more from her friends, but still Commanville could not raise enough capital to resume operations in his sawmill. Finally, in 1878, it had to be sold (Bart 723–25). (LMP)

Reference:

Bart, Benjamin F. *Flaubert.* Syracuse: Syracuse University Press, 1967.

Perec, Georges (1936–82). Georges Perec was influenced by Flaubert's detached descriptive style and his conception of the problems of writing. He constantly consulted his copies of *L'Education sentimentale, Bouvard et Pécuchet,* and the *Correspondance*. He suggested in a 1980 article that his Flaubert borrowings came from wanting to be Flaubert. Perec acknowledged that his breakthrough work, *Les Choses* (1965), contains thirteen sentences copied from *L'Education sentimentale*. Perec's pastiche of a literature textbook was the script for a short film entitled *Gustave Flaubert* (1975). In an appendix to *La Vie, mode d'emploi* (1978) and in his article in *L'Arc* (1980), Perec divulges Flaubert's presence in the work as pastiche and/or direct quotation. (LK)

References:

Bellos, David. *Georges Perec: A Life in Words*. London: Harvill, 1993.
Burgelin, Claude. *Georges Perec*. Paris: Seuil, 1988.
———. "Perec, lecteur de Flaubert." *Revue des lettres modernes* 703–6 (1984): 135–71.
Miguet, Marie. "Sentiments filiaux d'un prétendu parricide: Perec." *Poétique* 13.54 (1983): 135–47.
Perec, Georges. "Emprunts à Flaubert." *L'Arc* 79 (1980): 49–50.
———. *La Vie, mode d'emploi*. Paris: Hachette, 1978.
Petruso, Thomas F. "Madame Bovary in the Consumer Society." *Qui parle* 1.1 (1985): 46–59.

Person, Béatrix (1828–84). Béatrix Person was an actress and Flaubert's mistress. In April 1854, during the composition of *Madame Bovary*, Flaubert broke up with Louise Colet. Around that time, he began a relationship with Béatrix Person. Although it was never very serious, they saw each other sporadically for several years during Flaubert's trips to Paris. Flaubert mentioned a letter from Béatrix in which she revealed that she had compromised herself with him. "Il m'est tombé une lettre éperdue de Paris. La Per[son] perdait la tête. Tout était découvert, sa position compromise, etc." (A frantic letter from Paris just dropped into my lap. That Per[son] woman was going out of her mind with worry. They knew everything [about us], she was seriously compromised, and so forth) (to Louis Bouilhet, August 2, 1854, *Corr.* 2:562). (CG)

"La Peste à Florence" (1836). In the short story "La Peste à Florence," the older of two brothers, François, succeeds at everything, as an old woman had foretold. Finally he becomes a cardìnal. His younger brother Garcia has long been consumed with envy. At the ball celebrating François's appointment, Garcia faints from an excess of repressed rage. Later he kills his brother on a hunt. When he is accused of the murder, he collapses beside his brother's corpse. His father kills him and announces that both his sons have died of the plague. Flaubert's sense that he was forever foredoomed to suffer inferiority to his brother and rejection by his father is an obvious suggestion. (LMP)

References:

Bruneau, Jean. *Les Débuts littéraires de Gustave Flaubert, 1831–1845*. Paris: Colin, 1962.

Griffin, Robert, trans. and ed. *Early Writings*. Lincoln: University of Nebraska Press, 1991.

physical appearance. By all accounts, Flaubert grew into a striking, handsome young adult. He was six feet tall, with large gray eyes. As a young adult, he was tall and slim, with golden brown hair, white skin, and pink cheeks. He grew a beard as a young adult, which was later shorn, to leave, as portraits and photographs attest, only a moustache. By 1851, Flaubert was already starting to go bald, with clumps of hair falling out in what is called *alopécie en clairière*, a symptom of secondary syphilis. He took mercury treatments for the syphilis starting in 1852, but as a result of these treatments, he lost almost all his teeth, with only one tooth left in the 1870s. At his death, his niece Caroline wanted a cast of his hand at death, but this proved to be impossible because his hand was clenched in a tight fist as a result of his final seizure. (LRS).

References:

Barnes, Julian. *Flaubert's Parrot*. New York: Knopf, 1985.
Lottman, Herbert. *Flaubert: A Biography*. New York: Fromm, 1990.
Starkie, Enid. *Flaubert: The Making of the Master*. New York: Atheneum, 1967.

Pierrot au Sérail: Pantomime en six actes, suivie de l'Apothéose de Pierrot dans le Paradis de Mahomet. *Pierrot au Sérail* is one of the many scenarios that Flaubert composed around 1847 with his friend Louis Bouilhet. This droll little farce is of interest on several counts. It is Flaubert's first attempt to project the fantastic into a theatrical space (as opposed to the narrative one of the *conte oriental*), an ambition he would pursue in 1849 and thereafter in the different versions of *La Tentation de saint Antoine* and in 1863 in the fairy play *Le Château des cœurs*. There are two manuscripts of the work, the first on the unmarked paper Flaubert used during the 1840s, and the second on the Rives-Heaume vellum (high-quality paper) that he first used in the manuscript for *Madame Bovary*, beginning in September 1851. *Pierrot* thus offers perhaps the most important example of paper used to date some of Flaubert's manuscripts. His interest in the work manifestly continued. Flaubert's decision to call the play a pantomime arose with the later manuscript, when he evidently decided that the addition of dialogue was not necessary and that the scenic and stage directions could stand alone. (MCO).

References:

Flaubert, Gustave. *Œuvres complètes*. 2 vols. Ed. Bernard Masson. Paris: Seuil, 1964.
———. *Œuvres complètes*. 18 vols. Ed. Maurice Bardèche. Paris: Club de l'Honnête Homme, 1971–76.
Olds, Marshall C. "From Stage to Page: The Impossible Theaters of Flaubert and Mallarmé." In Alice N. Benston and Marshall C. Olds, eds., *Essays in European*

Literature for Walter A. Strauss. Manhattan, KS: Studies in Twentieth Century Literature Monographs, 1990. 85–98.

Pig (*TSA*). A character in the first and second versions of Flaubert's novel *La Tentation de Saint Antoine*, the pig represents pure egotism, the desire for fleshly gratification, and materialism. In traditional iconography, Saint Anthony's constant companion was a pig, not so much because it symbolized the temptations that assailed him, but because its lard was thought to be an effective remedy for erysipelas (also known as St. Anthony's fire, an acute streptococcus infection of the skin). Providing an ironic counterpoint to Anthony's asceticism, Flaubert's pig espouses a materialistic philosophy significantly influenced by Spinoza. Consequently, in a fit of depression, it wants to be reduced to ham. (AHP).

Reference:

Réau, Louis. *Iconographie de l'art chrétien*. Tome 3, *Iconographie des saints*. Paris: Presses Universitaires de France, 1958. 1:105.

Pinard, Ernest. Ernest Pinard was the imperial prosecutor in Flaubert's trial for having corrupted public morals by writing *Madame Bovary*. He particularly deplored the absence of admirable characters (as Sainte-Beuve had also done) or redeeming social values. He attacked the two seduction scenes, Emma's transient, narcissistic infatuation with religion, and her horrifying death. Adultery seemed to have been treated with morbid delectation. To demonstrate a pattern of depravity, he cited passages from the 1856 version of Flaubert's *Tentation de saint Antoine*, published piecemeal in Théophile Gautier's *L'Artiste* from December 1856 through early February 1857. Years later, in 1879, Flaubert had the ironic satisfaction of seeing Pinard unmasked as the author of pornographic verse. (LMP)

Reference:

LaCapra, Dominick. Madame Bovary *on Trial*. Ithaca: Cornell University Press, 1982.

political views. *See* socialism.

Polycarp, Saint, as role. Flaubert's fondness for nicknames mingled the world of fiction with the world of intimate role playing. He often called his niece Caroline "Loulou," the same name Félicité gives her beloved parrot in "Un cœur simple," and the genealogy of this pet name may stretch back to his correspondence with his sister Caroline whom he referred to as "boudou." Through nicknames, Flaubert wove fetishistic details of love relationships between literature and life, creating an extraliterary reality for his texts and a superreal text for his life.

He was delighted when his friends extended his own playful identification with Saint Polycarp (d. ca. 155 A.D.) to the celebration of the saint's name day.

On April 27, 1880, Guy de Maupassant contributed to la [fête de] saint Polycarpe with a dozen farcical birthday letters from personages such as the archbishop of Rouen and a merchant of *objets de sainteté* (holy objects). Why choose Saint Polycarp, a bishop of Smyrna and the subject of the first known biography of a martyr, who is mentioned only once in *La Tentation de saint Antoine* ("le sang de Polycarpe éteignait les flammes de son bûcher" [Polycarp's blood put out the flames of his funeral pyre])?

In 1853, Flaubert had written Louise Colet that "Saint Polycarp had the habit of repeating, while holding his hands over his ears: 'In what an age, my God, did you make me be born!' " (August 21–22, Maurice Nadeau, ed., *OC* 7: 230–39 [238]). One can also appreciate the name's comic phonological and etymological resonances. *Poly* is the Greek prefix indicating multiplicity ("polygon"), and *carpe* is a homonym for the fish, often used to figure muteness, as in the expression "mute as a carp." In this fishy sense, Saint Polycarp as a role recalls Flaubert's childhood attachment to animal identifications, which Jean-Paul Sartre interprets as a symptom of a common childhood resistance to acculturation. (DJ)

Reference:

Barnes, Hazel E. *Sartre and Flaubert.* Chicago: University of Chicago Press, 1981. 17–99.

Sartre, Jean-Paul. *L'Idiot de la famille.* 3 vols. Paris: Gallimard, 1971–72.

Ponge, Francis (1899–1988). Francis Ponge was a French poet. His first well-known work, *Le Parti pris des choses* (1942), announced a fascination with objects that later extended to his own texts and their genesis, as exemplified by *La Fabrique du pré* (1971). His poems describing and defining objects reveal an attention to detail and a labor-intensive writing process reminiscent of Flaubert. As indicated by the title of his final work, *Pratiques d'écriture; ou, L'Inachèvement perpétuel* (1984), he renounces the possibility of a perfectly polished work: his *écriture à processus* (writing as work in progress) thus contrasts with Flaubert's *écriture à programme* (preplanned writing). (AA).

References:

Andrew, Chris. *Poetry and Cosmogony: Science in the Writing of Francis Ponge.* Amsterdam. Rodopi, 1999.

Derrida, Jacques. *Signéponge.* Paris: Seuil, 1988.

———. *Signsponge.* Trans. Richard Rand. New York: Columbia University Press, 1994.

"Portrait de lord Byron" (1835). "Portrait de lord Byron" is a school exercise that reflects a change in the curriculum after the revolution of 1830: modern authors began to replace Latin texts. Flaubert conventionally depicts a passionate rebel who believed in nothing except his own genius, freedom, passion, and will. (LMP)

References:

Bruneau, Jean. *Les Débuts littéraires de Gustave Flaubert, 1831–1845*. Paris: Colin, 1962. 26–27.

Flaubert, Gustave. *Early Writings*. Ed. and trans. Robert Griffin. Lincoln: University of Nebraska Press, 1991. 3–4.

postmodernism. Modernism, a literary movement between the two world wars (1919–39), abandons the optimism and faith in progress common to many romantics, but preserves faith in an artistic vision that can apprehend a decaying world. T. S. Eliot, James Joyce, and Ezra Pound exemplify this tendency. Postmodernism replaces the cult of significant, referential art with ludic, aleatory compositions. Marcel Duchamp, Pablo Picasso, Erik Satie, and Guillaume Apollinaire, among others, introduced this trend in France even before World War I. Collage in the visual arts, serial composition in music, and fragmentation in all the arts illustrate the postmodernist vision, which no longer seeks to convey deep truths about "human nature." In prose fiction, digressions, multiple plot lines, and frequently shifting points of view are traits of a postmodernist style. Georges Perec's jigsaw puzzle of a novel, *La Vie, mode d'emploi* (Life: A user's manual, 1978), along with Julio Cortázar's *Rayuela* (Hopscotch) and Italo Calvino's *Cosmicomics*, characterize the movement.

The ironic detachment of Flaubert's implied authors, in contrast to the passionate involvement of impersonal narrators in Honoré de Balzac, Stendhal, or Emile Zola, makes him an easy target for annexation as a precursor. His denunciation of the inadequacy of language to express our humanity and its failure to signify at all reaches a pre-postmodernist climax in *Bouvard et Pécuchet* and its unfinished sequel, the *Dictionnaire des idées reçues*. These works especially are used to justify a postmodernist "harrowing of hell" that—as virtuous pagans who had never heard of Christ were rescued by him during his three days in the tomb—redeems Flaubert from the mire of novelistic convention in the nineteenth century. Shoshana Felman in particular, and the contributors to the outstanding collection *Flaubert and Postmodernism* in general, have extended the postmodernist perspective to many of the author's earlier works, showing that he still speaks to our condition. (LMP)

References:

Felman, Shoshana. *La folie et la chose littéraire*. Paris: Seuil, 1978. 191–213. Trans. by Debora V. Traas in Laurence M. Porter, ed., *Critical Essays on Gustave Flaubert*. Boston: Hall, 1986. 29–48.

Schor, Naomi, and Henry F. Majewski, eds. *Flaubert and Postmodernism*. Lincoln: University of Nebraska Press, 1984.

Pound, Ezra (1885–1972). While Ezra Pound was composing his *Cantos* and searching how to relate modern consciousness to the literary traditions of ancient epics and more recent prose narratives, his interest was kindled by *Bouvard et*

Pécuchet. With an epic scope as wide as modern humanity, Flaubert told the journey of mediocre men caught up in their disorganized applications of encyclopedic knowledge. Pound saw Flaubert's major influence on Joyce. Like both of them, he subsumed his own research and experience into the monumental task of expressing modern civilization. To him, Bouvard, Pécuchet, Frédéric Moreau, Stephen Dedalus, and Bloom, serving as his own Mauberley, were the day's Odyssean figures. (IC)

References:

Bart, Benjamin F. *Flaubert.* Syracuse: Syracuse University Press, 1967.
Read, Forrest. "Pound, Joyce, and Flaubert: The Odysseans." In Eva Hesse, ed., *New Approaches to Ezra Pound: A Coordinated Investigation of Pound's Poetry and Ideas.* Berkeley: University of California Press, 1969. 125–44.
Strickland, G. B. "Flaubert, Pound and Eliot." *The Cambridge Quarterly* 2 (1967): 242–63.

Pradier, James (Jean-Jacques) (1790–1852). James Pradier was a sculptor whose statues and statuettes in the eighteenth-century neoclassical style were much admired in his day. His works were distributed by the manufacturers at Sévres. He and David d'Angers were the favorite sculptors of Louis-Philippe. Flaubert met Victor Hugo in Pradier's studio in 1843, and Louise Colet (of whom Pradier was making a bust) in 1846. Flaubert had gone there to commission a bust of his sister Caroline. Pradier sculpted one from her death mask. Louise Pradier ("Ludovica") was his extravagant, unfaithful wife. They separated in 1845. Pradier had a daughter, Claire, by the actress Juliette Drouet, who was to become Victor Hugo's mistress for half a century. (MMC)

Reference:

Bart, Benjamin F. *Flaubert.* Syracuse: Syracuse University Press, 1967.

Pradier, Louise (née Louise d'Arcet). Called "Ludovica" by her friends, with etymological and psychological connotations of obsessive play, Louise Pradier was "the gay, extravagant, and unfaithful wife" (Starkie 92) of the eminent sculptor James Pradier, who eventually separated from her in 1845. Frequenting the Pradier household, where his artistic contemporaries gathered, Flaubert secretly longed to become one of her lovers. They had an affair in 1847 after his ardor for Louise Colet had waned. He had described her to Colet as "the very type and model of woman with all her instincts, an orchestra of female sentiments" (Bart 156). The *Mémoires de Madame Ludovica,* found to be an anonymous source for *Madame Bovary* (Leleu), relate her adulteries and her financial ruin. Douglas Siler has more recently identified the author of the *Mémoires* as Louise Françoise Bové, a friend of Louise Pradier, and has dated the work to 1847 or 1848. Episodes of Ludovica's life that exemplify her "poetic need of luxury" (Bart 268) provided a model—and, at times, a script (see Siler 1973)—for Flaubert's psychological portrayal of Emma Bovary. (AP)

References:

Bart, Benjamin F. *Flaubert.* Syracuse: Syracuse University Press, 1967.
Leleu, Gabrielle. "Une Source inconnue de *Madame Bovary*: Le Document Pradier." *Revue d'Histoire Littéraire de la France* 47 (July–September 1947): 227–44.
Siler, Douglas. "Autour de Flaubert et Louise Pradier: Lettres et documents inédits." *Studi francesi* 61–62 (1977): 141–50.
———. "Du nouveau sur la genèse de 'Madame Bovary.' " *Revue d'Histoire Littéraire de la France* 79 (1979):26–49.
———. "Du nouveau sur les 'Mémoires de Madame Ludovica.' " *Revue d'Histoire Littéraire de la France* 78 (1978): 36–46.
———, ed. *Flaubert et Louise Pradier: Le Texte Intégral des* Mémoires de Madame Ludovica. Paris: Minard, 1973.
Starkie, Enid. *Flaubert: The Making of the Master.* New York: Atheneum, 1967.

Proust, Marcel (1871–1922). Marcel Proust was a French novelist, believed by some to be the greatest in his language. His life contains several coincidental resemblances to Flaubert's: both men had a father and a brother who were doctors; both had a childhood in Normandy; both suffered from nervous illness with physical complications; both were emotionally androgynous (Naturel 12–12). Proust's seven-volume masterpiece, *A la recherche du temps perdu* (1913–22), scarcely mentions Flaubert. Instead, the novel emphasizes the importance, for the narrator's childhood, of George Sand's sentimental, idealized tale of rural life, *François le Champi* (Francis the Foundling, 1850). Proust's 1920 essay on Flaubert pointed to the ternary rhythm (the use of threefold parallel phrases or clauses) that had come to characterize Proust's own style. But Proust also attacked what he called Flaubert's superficial, ornamental use of imagery as opposed to Proust's own totalizing metaphors that reflect Proust's organic world view, in which each part reflects the whole. As Muller points out, however, Flaubert unlike other writers appears in Proust's text through the operation of involuntary memory, the very element Proust considers essential to the creative process.

Proust, like Flaubert, adopts an impressionistic style in which the protagonists' sense impressions trigger perception and action. The strong affective bonds of male pairs in Flaubert (Henry and Jules in the 1845 *Education sentimentale*; Frédéric and Deslauriers in the 1869 version of that novel; the eponymous characters in *Bouvard et Pécuchet*) become intensified, in Proust, into patently homosexual and lesbian relationships—but Flaubert offered Proust rich, detailed models for depicting male bonding. Proust, however, replaces Flaubert's painstaking, sometimes labored research in scholarly background sources with a deep literary and artistic context whose contemporary models can be identified (Naturel 353): Proust's ultimate referent always is art.

The awkward way that mentions of Flaubert are inserted into and then edited out of Proust's writings as these texts develop (Naturel 9, *passim*) perfectly illustrates the effects of the anxiety of influence, according to which psychic principle a dominant, revered precursor must be disparaged and misinterpreted in order to free an emerging author to express his or her own originality. Two published pastiches of Flaubert (in *Les Plaisirs et les jours,* 1896: in *Le Figaro*, March 14, 1908—both reproduced in *Contre Sainte-Beuve*) reveal Proust's strong sense of rivalry with Flaubert. Proust contributed to the post-World War I debate surrounding the correctness of Flaubert's French by faulting him for a lack of mastery in the use of metaphor (1920). However, Proust openly admired Flaubert's habitual use of the imperfect past tense to create a new style. By praising Flaubert's "imparfait éternel" as an innovation in the representation of time that makes event blend with memory and with repetition, Proust obliquely acknowledged Flaubert as his precursor. (AA/LMP)

References:

Muller, Marcel. "Proust et Flaubert: Une dimension intertextuelle de *A la recherché du temps perdu*." In John Erickson and Irène Pagès, eds., *Proust et le texte producteur*. Guelph, Ontario: University of Guelph, 1980.

Naturel, Mireille. *Proust et Flaubert: un secret d'écriture*. Amsterdam: Rodopi, 1999.

Proust, Marcel. "A propos du 'style' de Flaubert." *Nouvelle Revue Française*, January 1, 1920." In Marcel Proust, *Contre Sainte-Beuve; précedé de* Pastiches et Mélanges; *et suivi de* Essais et Articles. Ed. Pierre Clarac. Paris: Gallimard, 1971.

———. *Contre Sainte-Beuve; précedé de* Pastiches et Mélanges; *et suivi de* Essais et Articles. Ed. Pierre Clarac. Paris: Gallimard, 1971.

Q

Queen of Sheba (*TSA*). In the Bible and in antiquity, the Queen of Sheba was the ruler of a very prosperous kingdom southwest of what is today Yemen who visited Solomon and was dazzled by his wealth. Legend paints her as an incredibly desirable woman who seduced the Hebrew king. In *La Tentation de saint Antoine*, she acquires the characteristics of such Near Eastern fertility goddesses as Venus or Cybele. According to André Chastel, she is the first incarnation of the Devil, prepared by Antoine's love for his sweetheart, Ammonaria, and by the beautiful girl being whipped before the temple of Serapis, an Egyptian god of the dead, of healing, and of fertility. Flaubert's Queen of Sheba represents lust (*luxuria*). She offers Antoine unimaginable wealth and endless sexual delight. When he crosses himself, she hops away (lameness being a traditional attribute of the Devil, who has assumed her form) with her face in her hands. (AHP)

Reference:

Chastel, André. "La Reine de Saba." *Romanic Review* 40 (1949): 261–67.

queer studies. The question of queer studies is more a speculative one about a developing field than an attestation of Flaubert scholarship. Aside from Mary Orr's excellent articles on Lheureux's sadistic identification with women in *Madame Bovary* and on the homoerotic and homosexual subtext in *L'Education sentimentale*, work on "queer Flaubert" mostly remains to be done. Certainly a study of motifs of androgyny and homosexuality would itself be useful to the readership at large, especially as they figure in the dialectics of Western and oriental. It must be remembered that while Flaubert's own homoerotic experiences are situated within the structures of Western friendship, the few cases of his acknowledged homosexual activity relate to a structure of orientalism. If *Madame Bovary* seems the quintessence of heterosexual ideology, the very fact that Flaubert constantly puts that ideology into question at all levels leads the reader to wonder about the structuring of sexuality in this work. Whether it is the identification of Emma with the woman as victim or the repartition of masculinity into the three figures of Charles, Léon, and Rodolphe, this novel puts sexual structures and definitions into question. The separation of sex and gender and the performativity of certain gender choices envisioned by some queer theorists are pertinent here.

Another fertile area for exploration is *L'Education sentimentale*. Aside from the homoerotic interplay of some of the female characters (La Vatnaz and Rosalie, for example), there is the palpable latent homosexuality both individually in Frédéric Moreau and Deslauriers and dyadically between them; this is a relation repeated and expanded in Flaubert's last work, *Bouvard et Pécuchet*. In this volume, the relation between the two characters, while not homosexual as such, resembles nothing more than a long-term marriage. Flaubert's construction of the male-male couple is somewhat reminiscent of Balzac's couple of Pons and Schmucke in *Le Cousin Pons*, here set in a seriocomic vein, but it goes further in an exploration of the dyad and its dynamics, their function as an economic and signifying unit. Other areas in which queer studies or queer theory can be useful are the constructions of femininity in *Salammbô* and "Hérodias" and the figures of masculinity in "La Légende de St. Julien l'hospitalier" and *Salammbô* as well. Aside from matters relating to the social construction of gender, queer studies has much to say about the vehicles for desire, the figures in which desire is carried, and the interrelation between the means of representation and the structures of desire. Attention could be paid to the roles of desire in *Bouvard et Pécuchet* and the means by which representation is enacted in that novel, as well as in works like *L'Education sentimentale* and *Madame Bovary*. (LRS)

See also androgyny; feminist and gender studies.

References:

Orr, Mary. "Reading the Other: Flaubert's *L'Éducation sentimentale* Revisited." *French Studies* 46.4 (1992): 412–23.

———. "Reversible Roles: Gender Trouble in *Madame Bovary*." In Tony Williams and Mary Orr, eds., *New Approaches in Flaubert Studies*. Lewiston, NY: Mellen, 1999. 49–64.

Queirós, Eça de (1845–1900). The greatest Portuguese realist novelist of his century, Eça de Queirós appears to have been influenced by *Madame Bovary* in his *O primo Bazilio: Episodio domestico* (1878). The plot structure of the two works is similar, Luisa's personality resembles that of Emma Bovary, and many details correspond. Both novels tell of the inevitable "fall" of a young married woman whose convent education has left her unprepared for life and without effective religious beliefs. Both women enjoy reading romantic fiction. Many details of the adulterous affairs correspond, and Queirós uses a scene similar to

Emma's with the lawyer Guillaumin, who tries to buy her when she asks for help in extricating herself from her financial straits.

The two works differ in some key respects: compared to Luisa, Emma is lower-class, provincial, and strong-willed. Luisa's money problems result from blackmail by a vindictive servant. Luisa's episodes of decisive action, borrowed from Emma, seem inconsistent with most of her character depiction, and her death from illness, although prepared by several advance mentions, appears arbitrary. (LMP)

References:

Queirós, Eça de. *Cousin Bazilio*. Manchester, UK: Carcanet, 1992.
Stevens, James R. "Eça and Flaubert." *Luso-Brazilian Review* 3.1 (1966): 47–61.

La Queue de la poire de la boule de Monseigneur. *La Queue de la poire de la boule de Monseigneur* is a theatrical farce from around 1866. One of the riotous amusements enjoyed by Flaubert and his local pals, including especially Louis Bouilhet, in their ceaseless mocking of Rouen and its inhabitants was the invention of a fictitious diocese. In fact, Bouilhet's nickname in the correspondence is *Monseigneur*, and Flaubert's, *le grand vicaire*. The two collaborated in writing this short work, although from the manuscript, Flaubert was responsible for the largest part. The play has as its subject a vexing case of constipation and its final cure. In his letter of July 27, 1867, Flaubert went so far as to suggest to George Sand that the work be staged at her home theater in Nohant. (MCO)

References:

Bruneau, Jean, ed. *Gustave Flaubert. Correspondance*. 5 vols. Paris: Gallimard, 1973–98. 3: 368–69.
Flaubert, Gustave. *Œuvres complètes*. 28 vols. Paris: Conard, 1910–54.
———. *La Queue de la poire de la boule de Monseigneur*. Paris: Nizet, 1958.

"Quidquid volueris" (1837). "Quidquid volueris" is a short story that is certainly among the most interesting and complete of the juvenilia. This playful work offers pastiches of a variety of prose styles ranging from the *petits romantiques* to Chateaubriand, Hugo, and Balzac. Published on the heels of Balzac's *Eugénie Grandet* (1833) and *Le Père Goriot* (1835), "Quidquid volueris" uses the topos of the opportunistic Parisian who has enriched himself in America through inhumane means and has brought back a caricatural romantic "monster" in the person of the half-human, half-ape Djalioh. The story is an important prototype of Flaubert's mature work, not only as a stylistic exercise, but also for the continued interest in the monstrous and in aphasiac characters. Jean-Paul Sartre relies on this story for his analyses of Flaubert's character in *L'Idiot de la famille*. The title is Latin for "comme tu voudras" or "as you like [it]" and alludes to Rabelais's liberated Abbey of Thélème. (MCO)

References:

Flaubert, Gustave. "Quidquid volueris." In Maurice Nadeau, ed., *Œuvres complètes*. 18 vols. Lausanne: Editions Rencontre, 1964. 1:139–74.

———. "Whatever You Want." In Robert Griffin, ed. and trans., *Early Writings*. Lincoln: University of Nebraska Press, 1991. 76–102.

Olds, Marshall C. "Value and Social Mobility in Flaubert." In B. T. Cooper and M. Donaldson-Evans, eds., *Moving Forward. Holding Fast: The Dynamics of Nineteenth-Century French Culture*. Amsterdam: Rodopi, 1997. 81–90.

Perrone-Moisés, Leyla. "*Quidquid volueris*: The Scriptural Education." In Naomi Schor and Henry F. Majewski, eds., *Flaubert and Postmodernism*. Lincoln: University of Nebraska Press, 1984. 139–59.

Sartre, Jean-Paul. *L'Idiot de la famille*. 3 vols. Paris: Gallimard, 1971–72.

R

Rabelais, François (d. 1553). François Rabelais's *Gargantua,* his *Pantagruel,* and his other three books using these comical giants as instruments to satirize society and to propose visions of utopias glorifying Renaissance learning were bedside reading for Flaubert (see his letter to Louis de Cormenin of June 7, 1844, *Corr.* 1:153). He mentions Rabelais repeatedly in his unpublished *Œuvres de jeunesse* (the editorial title for three volumes in the Conard edition, Paris, 1910–54). The Renaissance author taught him that the hearty enjoyment of life's physical pleasures, good companions, and a mocking laugh were the best response to the absurdity of existence. The youthful "Funérailles du docteur Mathurin" presents this philosophy of life with vigor. (LMP)

References:

Flaubert, Gustave. *Œuvres de jeunesse inédites*. 3 vols. In Gustave Flaubert, *Œuvres complètes*, 28 vols. Paris: Conard, 1910–1954. Vols. 20–22.

Martin, Andrew. "Chez Jules: Nutrition and Cognition in the Novels of Jules Verne." *French Studies* 37 (1983): 47–58.

"Rage et impuissance" (1836). In the short story "Rage et impuissance," a doctor named Ohmlin, exhausted, takes an opium pill to sleep. Because he shows no vital signs, he is buried alive. Both the opium dream and his futile struggles to escape the grave are vividly rendered. This early story is noteworthy for its social density: the forebodings of the doctor's old servant, Berthe, and of his dog are presented in some detail. A rationalist himself, he unwisely ignores them. Flaubert's sadism is apparent, and one can also see in this tale a covert revenge on his own father. (LMP)

References:

Bruneau, Jean. *Les Débuts littéraires de Gustave Flaubert, 1831–1845*. Paris: Colin, 1962.

Flaubert, Gustave. *Early Writings*. Ed. and trans. Robert Griffin. Lincoln: University of Nebraska Press, 1991. 34–44.

Unwin, Timothy. *Art et infini: L'Œuvre de jeunesse de Gustave Flaubert*. Amsterdam: Rodopi, 1991. 108–11.

realism. The realist movement began with the painter Gustave Courbet (1819–77); at the time of the revolution of 1848 and the Second French Republic that followed (1848–51), he emphasized the importance of sincerity and authenticity in art, in a socialist context. As a literary tendency current in Western Europe around the middle of the nineteenth century and in the United States during the 1920s and 1930s, its influence has continued up to the present. Literary realism arose as a reaction to the "excesses" of romanticism—improbable or impossible situations and plots; unrealistically noble, idealized heroes and heroines; the pathetic fallacy (the belief that a personified nature sympathizes with and can preserve the memory of our feelings); vapid religiosity; and lyrical effusions. Realism stresses observation, documentation, and reproduction of real life; average, believable characters; a neutral (for the most part) narrator; a great deal of description of physical reality; and reproduction of ordinary speech, including, on occasion, dialect. The protagonists often succumb to the pressures of society and renounce their ideals, or fail for hard-to-define reasons ("l'univers est ironique," in Flaubert's words). The names usually associated with this movement are Champfleury (*Le Réalisme*, a collection of his articles originally inspired by Courbet, appeared in 1857), Flaubert (although he hated the label), and the Goncourt brothers, although some romantic writers such as Balzac, Stendhal, and Mérimée are usually said by literary historians to display and anticipate realist tendencies. (EFG/LMP)

References:

Auerbach, Erich. *Mimesis: The Representation of Reality in Western Literature*. Trans. W. R. Trask. Princeton, NJ: Princeton University Press, 1953.

Furst, Lilian, ed. *Realism*. New York: Longman, 1992.

Lukacs, Gyorgy. *Studies in European Realism*. Trans. Edith Bone. New York: Grosset & Dunlap, 1964 (1960).

Prendergast, Christopher. *The Order of Mimesis: Balzac, Stendhal, Nerval, Flaubert*. Cambridge: Cambridge University Press, 1986.

Wellek, René. "The Concept of Realism in Literary Scholarship." In René Wellek, *Concepts of Criticism*, New Haven: Yale University Press, 1963. 222–55.

religiosity. The subject of Flaubert's approach to religion is as omnipresent in his work and as complicated as the subject of the role of the author. Flaubert in his correspondence equates the role of the author with that of God: "L'auteur, dans son œuvre, doit être comme Dieu dans l'univers" (The author, in his oeuvre, should be like God in the universe) (letter to Mme Leroyer de Chantepie, March 18, 1857, *Corr.* 4: 164). But since Flaubert found himself unable to believe, the power suggested in that formula of the omnipresent author-god is dramatically undercut. "Ce matin, dans le saint sépulchre, il est de fait qu'un chien aurait été plus ému que moi" (The truth is that this morning in the Holy Sepulcher a dog would have been more moved than I) (Flaubert, *Voyage* 5:214) wrote Flaubert at Jerusalem. In "Un cœur simple," Flaubert experimented with a character who, like the dog, is more moved by religion than is Flaubert, but whose dogged belief presents a singular challenge to literate representation. Numerous critics have read that challenge either as a philosophical exploration of the polarities of irony and pathos or as a collapse of that very polarity, as in Jonathan Culler's definition of the sacred in Flaubert as "the sentimental purified by irony, emptied of its content" (Culler 226).

Hazel Barnes, following Jean-Paul Sartre, differentiates between Flaubert's lack of religion, on the one hand, and on the other hand his very marked religiosity, meaning his recuperation of religion for its aesthetic, imaginative, and philosophical "riches" (Barnes 17–70). Laurence Porter adds psychology to this list of riches, noting that Flaubert ultimately identified God as "our soul projected onto objects," a tendency to be overcome by "demythologizing" (61; compare the letter to Mlle Leroyer de Chantepie, February 18, 1857, *Corr.* 9: 203). The temptation of these riches for Flaubert was clearly substantial, as roughly half his mature works engage religions deeply in some sense.

As the self-styled "hermit of Croisset," Flaubert overlaid his vocation as a writer with the solitude of the mystic. But in *La Tentation de saint Antoine*, mystical solitude is crowded with the cacophony of centuries of dissent. Donato proposes that Flaubert privileges the Gnostic heresies precisely because of the "secondary" and "composite" nature of their ideologies, contextualizing religion as a "linguistic museum" (85)—and, one might add, as a cultural battlefield for the freedom to explore apparently inevitable spiritual dramas to the point of personal lucidity. (DJ)

References:

Barnes, Hazel E. *Sartre and Flaubert.* Chicago: University of Chicago Press, 1981. 17–70.

Culler, Jonathan. *Flaubert: The Uses of Uncertainty.* 1974. Rev. ed. Ithaca: Cornell University Press, 1985. 207–28.

Donato, Eugenio. *The Script of Decadence: Essays on the Fictions of Flaubert and the Poetics of Romanticism.* New York: Oxford University Press, 1993. 80–99.

Flaubert, Gustave. *Correspondance.* 9 vols. In Gustave Flaubert, *Œuvres complètes.* 28 vols. Paris: Conard, 1910–54.

———. *Voyage en orient.* In Gustave Flaubert, *Œuvres complètes.* 18 vols. Ed. Maurice Nadeau. Lausanne: Editions Rencontre, 1964. 5:214.

Porter, Laurence M. *The Literary Dream in French Romanticism: A Psychoanalytic Interpretation,* Detroit: Wayne State University Press, 1979. 47–67.

Sartre, Jean-Paul. *L'Idiot de la famille.* 3 vols. Paris: Gallimard, 1971–72. 1:523.

Renan, Joseph Ernest (1823–92). A kindred spirit, torn, as was Flaubert, between religious yearnings and an ineradicable skepticism, Ernest Renan was a

Breton whose doubts had led him to leave the seminary. His revisionist, scandalous *Vie de Jésus* (1863) was a popular success. A believer in the myth of progress and influenced by the Hegelian dialectic, he held that religious belief among early humans had been superseded by the skeptical spirit of scientific examination, but that both religion and science would eventually blend in a synthesis that would realize the ultimate perfectibility of the human spirit.

Renan was a friend of Flaubert's, and his pioneering studies in comparative religion and historiography and his view that character was shaped by history contributed substantially to the conceptual basis of Flaubert's re-creation of ancient Carthage in his historical novel *Salammbô*. Renan's biographical *Saint Paul* helped inspire Flaubert's depiction of early Christianity in the final version of *La Tentation de saint Antoine* (1874). Renan's view that religion embodied a culture also informed Flaubert's depiction of the Roman household gods in Antoine's hallucination of the twilight of the gods in that final version. Renan contributed to the development of Flaubert's religious skepticism. His often-anthologized "Prière sur l'Acropole" (1876), in which he reluctantly abandons his cult of Minerva, goddess of wisdom, echoed the Götterdämmerung of the procession of the gods in *La Tentation* two years earlier. He and Flaubert went to George Sand's funeral together. (LMP)

References:

Chadbourne, Richard. *Ernest Renan as an Essayist*. Ithaca: Cornell University Press, 1957.

Renan, Ernest. *Saint Paul*. Paris: Lévy, 1869.

Rétat, Laudyce. *Religion et imagination religieuse: Leurs formes et leurs rapports dans l'œuvre d'Ernest Renan*. Paris: Klincksieck, 1977.

Renaud, Emilie (*ES*, 1845). A character in the 1845 version of *L'Education sentimentale*, Emilie Renaud is the wife of Monsieur Renaud, the director of the student boarding house in which Henry Gosselin takes lodging. Physically similar to many of Flaubert's female protagonists, she attracts young Henry's gaze by her dark eyes and hair, her large breasts, and her small feet. Although only slightly flirtatious at first, she coyly seduces Henry, and the two live their adulterous love under the nose of her husband for months before escaping to America. In the New World, however, their love wears thin, and they eventually return home, after which they drift apart.

Structurally, Emilie Renaud will become Mme Arnoux in the 1869 version of the novel. However, in her small-mindedness and wantonness, she more closely resembles Rosanette Bron in the 1869 version, or even more closely, Emma Bovary. Biographically, as Jean Bruneau has pointed out, Emilie Renaud recalls two women: Elisa Schlésinger and Eulalie Foucaud (Bruneau 409). (SDC)

Reference:

Bruneau, Jean. *Les Débuts littérres de Gustave Flaubert, 1831–1845*. Paris: Colin, 1962.

Renaud, Monsieur (*ES*, 1845). A character in the 1845 version of *L'Education sentimentale*, Monsieur Renaud (he is given no first name) runs the student boarding house in which Henry Gosselin lives while studying law. Henry seduces Renaud's wife, Emilie, and flees with her to New York. Some years later the aging Renaud meets his former rival in the street and engages him in a jealous brawl, only to be taken away by the police. His bonhomie, his womanizing, and his physical and social deterioration throughout the novel show him to be a precursor to Jacques Arnoux in the 1869 version of the novel. Biographically he is related to Maurice Schlésinger, the publisher whose wife, Elisa Schlésinger, the young Flaubert coveted. (SDC)

Reference:

Bruneau, Jean. *Les Débuts littéraires de Gustave Flaubert, 1831–1845*. Paris: Colin, 1962.

Renoir, Jean (1894–1979). Born the son of the impressionist painter Pierre-Auguste Renoir, Jean Renoir began his film career in the silent-film era. However, his best-known films were produced after the introduction of sound. *La Grande Illusion* (1937) and *La Règle du jeu* (1939), considered to be his masterpieces, illustrate his penchant for social satire. The influence of the impressionists can be seen in such early films as *Nana* (1926), based upon Emile Zola's 1880 novel, and the unfinished *Une Partie de campagne* (1936), adapted from Guy de Maupassant's short story of the same name. Renoir was misunderstood by his contemporaries, and after 1940 he sought relief from the criticism by going to Hollywood, although he returned to France to make films following World War II. But it was his work of the 1930s that had the greatest influence on the industry, making its mark in particular upon the Italian film director Luchino Visconti, who was Renoir's assistant from 1936 to 1940.

When Renoir received a phone call from a producer asking him whether he would make *Madame Bovary*, he accepted on the spot, seeing in the project the opportunity to treat once again a theme that was central in *La Chienne* (1931) and *Boudu sauvé des eaux* (1932), that of the individual in conflict with society. He cast theater actors in the principal roles, Valentine Tessier as Emma and his brother Pierre Renoir as Charles. Secondary roles were played by Fernand Fabre (Rodolphe), Daniel Lecourtois (Léon), and Max Dearly (Homais). Renoir began filming in 1933, shooting first near Rouen, then moving to the studio in September 1933. The film was released in 1934, but not before Renoir's three-and-a-half-hour version had been cut to two hours at the insistence of the distributors. Renoir himself expressed displeasure at the result, which has been criticized for presenting a disconnected series of grand scenes, with insufficient attention to the humdrum nature of daily life that is at the core of Emma's dissatisfaction. As for the casting, only Pierre Renoir's performance has been deemed worthy of praise, and Valentine Tessier, whose performance has been described as "wooden," is considered too mature for the part of Emma. Furthermore, the film has come under attack for its theatricality. Eric Rohmer was among the few who lauded this *Madame Bovary*, pointing to its fidelity to the spirit of the 1850s. The film was a commercial failure. Clearly, Renoir underestimated the complexities of filming Flaubert's classic novel. Fortunately, the filmmaker's reputation rests solidly on his more successful efforts. (MDE)

References:

Durgnat, Raymond. *Jean Renoir*. Berkeley: University of California Press, 1974.

Sesonske, Alexander. *Jean Renoir: The French Films, 1924–1939*. Cambridge, MA: Harvard University Press, 1980.

repetition. Repetition in Flaubert's works fills two functions. As pure form, repetition in "Un cœur simple" and *Madame Bovary* deadens meaning. Repetition in *L'Education sentimentale*, however, adds meaning to certain passages. Several scenes (e.g., the opening and second voyage scenes and the final chapter's crowd scene) repeat a pattern evoking oscillation through rhythmic sounds and fluidity. Recurring plurals in description also conjure waves of repeating forms. These seemingly meaningless repetitions invariably foreshadow the frustration of Frédéric's immediate plan. The motif of oscillation in these passages echoes Frédéric's wavering attention and desire throughout the novel and appears symbolic of his hollow, uncommitted character. (LK)

Reference:

Kelly, Dorothy. "Oscillation and Its Effects: Flaubert's *Education Sentimentale*." *Romanic Review* 80 (1989): 207–17.

Rétif de La Bretonne, Nicolas Edmé (1734–1806). The influence of Nicolas Edmé Rétif de La Bretonne's work on Flaubert is minimal. According to D. Anthony Williams, Flaubert rarely read Rétif's novels, and the latter was never mentioned in the author's correspondence. In *Madame Bovary*, however, a character known as "the blind man" sings a number that was adapted by Flaubert from a song he found in the first volume of Rétif's *L'Année des dames nationales*. The song, which deeply distresses Emma, becomes more than an allusion soon after her death. Upon the protagonist's demise, the lyric appears fully transcribed. It remains doubtful whether Rétif de La Bretonne is the actual writer of the verses or whether he used a popular source instead. (LF)

Reference:

Williams, D. Anthony. "Une Chanson de Rétif et sa réécriture par Flaubert." *Revue d'histoire littéraire de la France* 91 (1991): 239–42.

Rêve d'enfer (1837). *Rêve d'enfer* is a skillful example of the frenetic Gothic. Duke Arthur Alamaroës, a superhuman being superior to Satan, lives in a ruined castle and has no soul. When Satan is challenged and taunted, he tries in vain to subdue the duke with physical force and with the desperate love of a beautiful woman, but the duke feels nothing, and he cannot die. Satan himself is envious and frantic because, as an insubstantial spirit, he can enjoy none of the physical joys of humanness. This dialogue of unfeeling matter and bodiless spirit anticipates the dialogue of the Sphinx and Chimera in the seventh and a last section of *La Tentation de saint Antoine*. (LMP)

References:

Bruneau, Jean. *Les Débuts littéraires de Gustave Flaubert, 1831–1845*. Paris: Colin, 1962.

Flaubert, Gustave. "Dream of Hell." In Gustave Flaubert, *Early Writings*, ed. and trans. Robert Griffin. Lincoln: University of Nebraska Press, 1991. 50–75.

Le Rêve et la vie. *Le Rêve et la vie* is the longest of the unfinished scenarios for *féeries* that Flaubert wrote, probably from 1861 to August or September 1863, before abandoning his project in favor of Louis Bouilhet's. This latter would become *Le Château des cœurs*. The other titles for these scenarios are *Les Trois Epiciers ou la fille du voisin* (in *Carnets de travail*, 19), *Les Trois Épiciers* (unpublished) and *Les Trois Frères* (in Kovács). Rather than rely on the naïve artifice of supernatural beings such as fairies, Flaubert's novel conception was to have the fantastic spring from speculative scientific sources of the day related to magnetism, and from the literal realization of hackneyed metaphors. The scenario's ambulatory form consisted of a series of thematically based tableaux culminating in an apotheosis. Referred to in both *L'Education sentimentale* and *Bouvard et Pécuchet*, the *féerie* was an interesting formal experiment that would bear especially on the final *Tentation de saint Antoine* and *Bouvard et Pécuchet*. Thematic elements also appear in *Bouvard et Pécuchet* and "Un cœur simple." (MCO)

References:

Durry, Marie-Jeanne. *Flaubert et ses projets inédits*. Paris: Nizet, 1950.

Flaubert, Gustave. *Carnets de travail*. Ed. Pierre-Marc de Biasi. Paris: Balland, 1988.

———. *Le Rêve et la vie: A Theatrical Experiment by Gustave Flaubert*. Presented by Katherine Singer Kovács. Harvard Studies in Romance Languages, 38. Lexington, KY: French Forum, 1981.

Olds, Marshall C. "De didascalie en diégèse: Le Fantastique moderne et *Un cœur simple*." In C. F. Coates, ed., *Repression and Expression: Literary and Social Coding in Nineteenth-Century France*. New York: Lang, 1996. 55–63.

La Revue de Paris. Together with Théophile Gautier and Louis de Cormenin, Flaubert's intimate friend Maxime Du Camp revived the already-famous periodical *La Revue de Paris* in 1851. Its initial editorial announcement in October 1851, just before Napoleon III's coup d'état, promised that the journal would be completely independent and would censor no one. Flaubert decided not to abridge and select from the first version of *La Tentation de saint Antoine* for serialization, as Du Camp had suggested, but Du Camp purchased the rights to serial publication of *Madame Bovary* in 1856. However, he and his editors insisted on many cuts affecting the scenes of Emma's wedding, the *comices agricoles*, the clubfoot operation, the extreme unction administered to Emma, and the debate between the priest Bournisien and the Voltairean pharmacist Homais as they keep vigil by her body. By then, Napoleon III had imposed a severe censorship. Du Camp had to retreat from his initial announcement: he rightly feared the conservative government's hostility to bourgeois critique and to wordings that implied disapproval for traditional sexual morality and for religion. The *Revue* had already been warned twice after expressing liberal views; it was to be suspended briefly early in 1857 and was ordered to cease publication in 1858, after a failed assassination attempt on the emperor. Flaubert quarreled with Du Camp over the latter's insistence that Léon's sexual seduction of Emma in the horse-drawn carriage in part 3 be deleted; Flaubert then insisted on adding a disclaimer that he no longer recognized the *Revue de Paris* version as his work. He and the *Revue* were indeed put on trial in January 1857 for having offended religion and morality. The novel, and the publicity from the trial, consolidated Flaubert's reputation. (LMP)

References:

Bart, Benjamin F. *Flaubert*. Syracuse: Syracuse University Press, 1967. 354–61.
Starkie, Enid. *Flaubert: The Making of the Master*. New York: Atheneum, 1967. 225–38.

Reyer (pseud. of Ernest Rey, 1823–1909). Reyer was an opera composer influenced by the Wagnerian tradition. Flaubert's novel *Salammbô* (1862), exotic and replete with crowd scenes, heroic warriors, treacherous politicians, and star-crossed lovers, obviously provided an ideal canvas for a grand stage spectacle. Flaubert's reputation, moreover, had reached a peak after the scandalous success of *Madame Bovary* in 1857. Reyer approached Flaubert as soon as he knew about *Salammbô*. The librettist Reyer planned to engage, Camille Du Commun du Locle (1832–1903), was highly qualified. Du Locle was a talented writer with poetic sensitivity; he later codirected the Opéra Comique and was to work on the libretti for Giuseppe Verdi's *Aïda* and *Otello*. Flaubert was pleased: he even wrote a shrewd scenario for Du Locle, suggesting which eight scenes to keep.

For various reasons, the project was completed only after Flaubert's death. The opera premiered in Brussels (February 10, 1890), and then moved to Rouen (at the Théâtre des Arts, November 23, 1890) and to Paris (May 16, 1892). Rose Caron (1857–1930) sang the lead role. The heroine was transformed from an ingenuous instrument of fate to a courageous warrior preoccupied with the destiny of her people. Following the tradition of Verdi's *Il Trovatore* (1835), the moon and the sun were systematically contrasted, faithful to Flaubert's own opposition of the moon-goddess Tânit, associated with Salammbô the Carthaginian princess, and the sun-god Moloch, associated with Mâtho the barbarian leader. Most of the political intrigue and the military conflicts were sacrificed, as were the scenes of the naked Salammbô's ritual intertwining with the sacred serpent, the sacrifice of children in the ovens of the sun-god Moloch, and the starvation of the mercenary army in the Défilé de la Hâche. Instead of having the captive rebel leader Mâtho be tortured to death, a scene concluding when his heart is ripped out to be offered to the gods, and having Salammbô mysteriously drop dead "for having touched the [forbidden] veil of [the moon-goddess] Tânit" as she watches this sacrifice, Du Locle switched the emphasis of the conclusion from the sacred to the romantic. He imitated *Romeo and Juliet* and similar stories, by having first Salammbô and then Mâtho die by stabbing themselves. The reviewers' reactions were evenly divided between praise for Reyer and Du Locle having achieved a tricky conversion from erudite novel to theatrical event, and blame for having robbed the heroine of her mystery. (LMP)

Reference:

Bailbé, Joseph-Marc. "*Salammbô* de Reyer: Du roman à l'opéra." *Romantisme* 38 (1982): 93–103.

Rodolphe (*MB*). Rodolphe is Emma's first lover in *Madame Bovary*. The early scenarios projected him as Emma's second lover, but Léon's passive nature and inexperience dictated that Léon admire her silently at first. In his notes, Flaubert sees Rodolphe as "le type du brac [read 'braque'] mais plutôt extérieurement" (the typical madcap, but externally). A bon vivant and provincial Don Juan, Rodolphe is struck by Emma's beauty and resolves to seduce her. As a man of experience, but also "de tempérament brutal et d'intelligence perspicace" (brutal and perspicacious), as the narrator tells us, at a glance Rodolphe understands Emma's desperation. As Flaubert describes Rodolphe walking across the fields toward his house after meeting Emma for the first time, he represents Rodolphe's brutality with a subtle stylistic device typical of Flaubert's prose: "Tandis qu'il trottine à ses malades, elle reste à ravauder des chaussettes. Et on s'ennuie! on voudrait habiter la ville, danser la polka tous les soirs! Pauvre petite femme! Ça bâille après l'amour, comme une carpe après l'eau sur une table de cuisine" (While he is out making his rounds, she stays home darning his socks. And she is bored! She would like to live in the city, dance the polka every evening. Poor little woman! She gapes after love, as a carp gapes after water on the kitchen table). The sequence of subject pronouns is telling—first "elle," the standard personal pronoun, then "on," which removes individuality, then "ça," scornful and totally impersonal. The final, visual note that concisely sums up Rodolphe's personality comes as Rodolphe makes his decision to seduce Emma "en écrasant, d'un coup de bâton, une motte de terre devant lui" (shattering with his walking stick a clod of earth in front of him). Rodolphe is all surface, projecting a certain elegance and savoir faire that entrances Emma. His letter breaking off their affair (part 2 chapter 13) is a model of cruel cynicism. (EFG)

Reference:

Reynaud-Pactat, Patricia. "La Lettre de rupture de Rudolphe à Emma Bovary: L'énonciation parle l'économie." *Nineteenth-Century French Studies* 19.1 (1990): 83–94.

Roger des Genettes, Edma. *See* Genettes, Edma Roger des.

Romains, Jules (pseud. for Louis Farigoule, 1885–1972). Jules Romains was elected to the Académie Française in 1946. He wrote poems, plays, essays, and novels, but is best known for his monumental roman-fleuve, *Les Hommes de bonne volonté* (1932–46), and for his brief, lyrical unanimist novel *Mort de quelqu'un* (1911). His farcical play *Knock, ou le triomphe de la médecine* (1923) consolidated his popularity. Like Flaubert's pharmacist Homais in *Madame Bovary*, Doctor Knock creates a flourishing practice in a small country town. Rather than offer free consultations and then sell costly medicines and therapeutic devices, however, Knock succeeds by terrifying the healthy inhabitants into believing they are ill. This crude, boisterous character also derives from the Ubu of Alfred Jarry (1873–1907), who in turn has elements of Flaubert's Garçon, Shakespeare's Falstaff, Rabelais's giants, and the comic-scatological devils of the medieval *mystères*—to mention only a few such traditional buffoons and trickster figures. Flaubert more explicitly associated medical practice with the carnivalesque in his youthful works "Les Funerailles du docteur Mathurin" (1839) and "La Découverte de la vaccine" (ca. 1846). (LMP)

See also Découverte de la vaccine, La; Funerailles du docteur Mathurin; Garçon, le.

References:

Bruneau, Jean. *Les Débuts littéraires de Gustave Flaubert, 1831–1845*. Paris: Colin, 1962.

Romains, Jules. *Doctor Knock: A Comedy in Three Acts*. Trans. Harley Granville-Baker. New York: S. French, 1925.

———. *Knock: ou, le triomphe de la médecine: comédie en trois actes*. Ed. J. B. Alton. London: Longmans, 1973.

romanticism. Romanticism was a literary movement current in Western Europe in the second half of the eighteenth century and the first half of the nineteenth. In France, its earlier major manifesto was Germaine de Staël's *De l'Allemagne* (1813), advocating the marriage of French logic and wit with Germanic sensibility and spirituality. The movement reached its apogee in France in the early 1830s with Victor Hugo's *Hernani*, Stendhal's *Le Rouge et le Noir*, Eugène Delacroix's *La Liberté guidant le peuple*, the election of the poet Alphonse de Lamartine to the Académie française, and Hector Berlioz's *Symphonie fantastique*. In France, romanticism grew out of a reaction to classicism and neoclassicism, seen by Stendhal, for example, as the set of values of his great-grandparents, whereas romanticism represents the values of contemporary society (cf. Baudelaire in his *Salon de 1846*: "Qui dit romantisme dit art moderne" [Whoever says Romanticism is saying Modern Art]). The romantics' interest in the strange and exotic led them to choose the Middle Ages, Africa, North America, and Asia as backdrops and inspired them to travel to exotic settings. Inspired by the historical novels of Sir Walter Scott and by the history plays of Shakespeare, they also explored their national heritage. Romantic writers generally interested themselves in the individual's struggle with society, sympathizing with the individual, foregrounding creativity, emotions, the irrational, the spontaneous, and the transcendental, and often creating larger-than-life heroes and heroines embodying these characteristics. During the romantic period, there developed a basic contempt for the bourgeois, seen as the ultimate philistine, the enemy of everything the romantics stood for. This led (in part) to the rising popularity of the caricatures of Honoré Daumier and Henry Monnier and to the genre known as *physiologie*. (At age fifteen, Flaubert published a *physiologie* titled "Une Leçon d'histoire naturelle, genre commis.") As a writer, Flaubert lived romanticism during the 1840s, only to scoff at it in his mature works. (EFG).

References:

Baudelaire, Charles. "Qu'est-ce que le romantisme?" In Baudelaire, *Salon de 1846*. In Marcel A. Ruff, ed., Baudelaire, *Œuvres complètes*. Paris: Seuil, 1968. 230.

Bowman, Frank Paul. *French Romanticism: Intertextual and Interdisciplinary Readings*. Baltimore: Johns Hopkins University Press, 1990.

Charleton, D. G., ed. *The French Romantics*. 2 vols. Cambridge: Cambridge University Press, 1984.

Douchin, Jacques-Louis. "L'Influence des publications populaires sur l'œuvre de Flaubert." In *Flaubert et Maupassant: Ecrivains normands*. Paris: Presses Universitaires de France, 1981. 27–38.

Peyre, Henri. *Qu'est-ce que le romantisme?* Paris: Presses Universitaires de France, 1971.

Porter, Laurence M. "The Present Directions of French Romantic Studies, 1960–75." *Nineteenth-Century French Studies* 6.1–2 (1978): 1–20.

Wellek, René. "The Concept of Romanticism in Literary History." In René Wellek, *Concepts of Criticism*. New Haven: Yale University Press, 1963, 128–98.

Roque, Louise (*ES*). Louise Roque is the wild, unsocialized girl child who falls in love with Frédéric Moreau, the antihero, before she is in her teens. She is legitimized when Old Roque, a neighbor, marries his maid. At first he cheats Frédéric's mother of much of her fortune, but when he realizes his daughter's feelings for Frédéric—whom he considers an advantageous connection—he changes his behavior and tries to throw himself in the young man's way repeatedly, as if by accident. In Paris, Frédéric forgets about her, but when he returns to Nogent, finds that she has become attractive and realizes that she is actively pursuing him, he is flattered and is tempted to marry her. His mother urges him to do so. As usual, however, Frédéric vacillates. When he again returns to his hometown, Nogent, he finds that Louise has just married his friend and rival Deslauriers. Later still we learn, with no details, that Louise has left Deslauriers to run off with another man. This episode underscores by contrast the force of the homosocial bond between the two male friends, who end up together despite all their mutual betrayals. Louise also completes a quaternity of possible types of women to love: the idealistic married woman (Mme Arnoux), the cynical married woman (Mme Dambreuse), the demimondaine (Rosanette Bron), and the virginal child (Louise Roque). None of these relationships can succeed or bring happiness.

The real-life prototype of "la petite Roque" (the little Roque girl) was Harriet Collier.

Flaubert's protégé Guy de Maupassant used Louise's full name for the eponymous murder victim of one of his fantastic tales. (LMP)

See also Collier, Harriet.

References:

Layton, Lynne. "Flaubert's *L'Education sentimentale*: A Tragedy of Mind." *French Forum* 11 (1986): 335–51.

Sherrington, R. J. "Louise Roque and *L'Education sentimentale*." *French Studies* 25 (1971): 427–36.

Starkie, Enid. *Flaubert: The Making of the Master*. New York: Atheneum, 1967.

Rouault, le père (*MB*). Rouault is Emma's father in *Madame Bovary*. A farmer who appears to be prosperous, he is in reality on the brink of ruin, owing in large measure to his self-indulgence. He is unable to understand his daughter's romantic tendencies, although he unwittingly fostered them by sending her to a convent school for an education unusual for a farm woman. Presumably, once he had been widowed, he did not know what to do with her. It is when Charles is called to the farm to treat Rouault's broken leg that he sees Emma for the first time. Flaubert's treatment of the father's letter to his daughter is done with great sympathy (part 2, chapter 10), as are his memories of his own deceased wife. He is not sorry to see Emma married, however; she is of no use around the farm. (EFG/LMP)

Rouen. Flaubert was born in Rouen (1821) and spent much of his life there. The nineteenth-century industrial town was often veiled in fog and smog; Flaubert portrayed the city's colorless gloom in *Madame Bovary* (1857). Achille-Cléophas Flaubert, Gustave's father, housed his family at the Hôtel-Dieu, (the municipal hospital), where he was chief surgeon. After his father's death, Gustave and his mother left the hospital but remained residents of Rouen until 1851, when they moved to Croisset (Mme Flaubert later wintered in Rouen). Throughout his life, Gustave used the library, attended concerts, art exhibitions, plays, marriages, and funerals, and visited his brother, niece, and acquaintances in Rouen. These acquaintances included Charles Lapierre, editor; Félix Pouchet, scientist; and Louis Bouilhet, a former schoolmate who became one of Flaubert's best friends and with whom he shared his work.

Anticipating the Prussians' arrival in Rouen (December 1870), Flaubert became lieutenant of the National Guard of Croisset and went to Rouen to learn military tactics. He quickly resigned, however, and he was indignant at the city's decision to capitulate (Letter to Caroline Commanville, October 1870, *Corr.* 6: 162). When the Prussians invaded Croisset, Flaubert and his mother took refuge in his niece Caroline's Rouen apartment.

Records reveal that the Rouennais were avid readers who collected art and supported two theaters as well as literary and musical salons. Rouen's prestigious lycée, the Collège Royal, trained Flaubert and his classmates in the classics. Nonetheless, Flaubert developed enmity toward Rouen's bourgeoisie, thereby dissociating himself from them. He inveighed against their pretentiousness, poor taste in the arts and literature, and intolerance for the unorthodox. His disdain peaked in December 1871 when the city council temporarily refused to erect a monument to Louis Bouilhet. Benjamin Bart rightly underscores Flaubert's love/hate relationship with the city. (JWA)

References:

Andrieu, Lucien. "Les maisons de la famille Flaubert dans la région rouennaise." *Les Amis de Flaubert* 30 (1967): 9–14.

Bart, Benjamin. *Flaubert's Landscape Descriptions.* Ann Arbor: University of Michigan Press, 1956.

Chaline, Jean-Pierre. "Le Milieu culturel rouennais au temps de Flaubert." In *Flaubert et Maupassant: Ecrivains normands.* Paris: Presses Universitaires de France, 1981. 17–25.

S

Saba, la reine de. *See* Queen of Sheba.

Sabatier, Apollonie ("La Présidente") (1822–?). Apollonie Sabatier was a demimondaine idolized by Charles Baudelaire. The sculptor Jean-Baptiste Clésinger immortalized her with the intensely sensuous, writhing naked marble statue called *Femme piquée par un serpent* (woman bitten by a poisonous snake). She was celebrated as a kind, warmhearted hostess, as well as for her extraordinary beauty. Flaubert sometimes went to her Sunday soirees when he was in Paris. The life of the kept woman Rosanette Bron in *L'Education sentimentale* was in part modeled after hers. (LMP)

References:

Billy, André. *La Présidente et ses amis*. Paris: Flammarion, 1949.
Moss, Armand. *Baudelaire et Madame Sabatier*. New ed. Paris: Nizet, 1978.
Pia, Pascal, ed. *Théophile Gautier. Lettres à la Présidente et poésies, libertines*. Paris: Cercle du livre précieux, 1960.

Sade, Donatien, marquis de (1740–1814). The Marquis de Sade exercised noteworthy influence on Flaubert's works. Despite there being no direct mention of Sade in Flaubert's correspondence, the Goncourt brothers describe in their journal various gatherings at Parisian cafes in which Flaubert openly expressed his admiration of the marquis. It remains uncertain, however, whether Flaubert's early writings such as *Rêve d'enfer* (1837) and *La Danse des morts* (1838) were inspired by Sade or were composed under the influence of the Bouzingot school. The latter dates from the 1830s and presents as one of its chief characteristics the portrayal of repulsive or lugubrious subjects. In subsequent works, particularly in *Salammbô* (1862), *La Tentation de saint Antoine* (1874), and "La Légende de saint Julien l'hospitalier" (1877), numerous passages abound in painstaking narrations of sadistic behavior, gratuitous cruelty, and various perversions. In addition to Flaubert's fascination with ghastly themes and violence, Sade's influence also becomes discernible in the writer's passion for excess and repetition, as observed, for example, in *Bouvard et Pécuchet* (1881). Furthermore, the use of circularity unites both writers. Like Sade, moreover, Flaubert repeatedly develops his characters and story lines through the motif of confinement. (LF)

Reference:

Tondeur, Claire-Lise. "Flaubert et Sade; ou, La Fascination de l'excès." *Nineteenth-Century French Studies* 10. 1–2 (1981–82): 75–84.

sadism. The Marquis de Sade was a favorite author of Flaubert's from the time he was seventeen. Several of his early tales contain gruesome scenes. In "Rage et impuissance," a man buried alive eats his own forearm. In "Quidquid Volueris," an ape-man rapes and mutilates a woman and then kills himself by smashing his skull into a wall. Traveling in Egypt, Flaubert showed a morbid fascination for the tortures used by tax collectors on their debtors. *Salammbô* evokes homosexual bonds between some barbarian soldiers, ritual prostitution of the priestesses of Tanit, drinking the blood of a freshly killed enemy, and, frequently, tortures. The leprous, lecherous Hannon, whose spongy body is literally disintegrating, rapes the more attractive female captives. The slow death from starvation of an army of 40,000 in the Défilé de la Hache in *Salammbô*, their despairing cannibalism, and the survivors' being crushed to death under the feet of Hamilcar's war elephants exploited horrors that Flaubert had found lacking in Sade. Perhaps as a result, in a review, Francisque Sarcey was later to compare the author of *L'Education sentimentale* to Sade, whom Sarcey admittedly had not read (Starkie 2.137). The young Saint Julien's bloodthirsty massacres of animals provide a final sadistic echo near the end of Flaubert's career. (LMP)

Reference:

Starkie, Enid. *Flaubert, the Master*. New York: Atheneum, 1971.

Sainte-Beuve, Charles-Augustin (1804–69). After an early career as a romantic poet (*Vie, poésies, et pensées de Joseph Delorme*, 1829; *Volupté*, 1834) and confessional novelist, Charles-Augustin Sainte-Beuve became the most prominent literary critic of nineteenth-century France, a member of the Académie Française, and sénateur during the Second Empire. He immediately recognized a masterpiece, and the beginning of a new literary generation of realism in the novel, in *Madame Bovary*. He praised Flaubert's style, descriptions of Normandy, and character portrayals, which he compared to surgical dissections. However, he complained of Flaubert's "cruelty" and of the lack of an idealized figure who could have interjected a note of hope.

Later, Sainte-Beuve devoted three articles to *Salammbô*. He was respectful, but expressed concern over that novel's sadism. Flaubert often attended the celebrated writers' dinners at the Restaurant Magny that Sainte-Beuve had inaugurated in 1862; he enjoyed Saint-Beuve's company and respected his understanding of literature. He regretted that Sainte-Beuve had not lived to read *L'Education sentimentale*. (LMP)

References:

Chadbourne, Richard M. *Charles-Augustin Sainte-Beuve*. Boston: Twayne, 1977.
Starkie, Enid. *Flaubert: The Making of the Master*. New York: Atheneum, 1967. 28.
———. *Flaubert, the Master*. New York: Atheneum, 1971. 347.

Saintsbury, George Edward Bateman (1845–1933). One of the most influential writers and academic critics of the late Victorian period and early twentieth century, George Saintsbury believed in the supremacy of form over content. Educated in London and Oxford, Saintsbury was later appointed chair of rhetoric and English literature at Edinburgh (1895). He had a thorough knowledge of French and English literature. He contributed numerous articles to British journals and newspapers and produced hundreds of essays and reviews, in addition to literary histories, anthologies, and critical editions. He published *A Primer of French Literature* (1880), *A Short History of French Literature* (1882), *A History of Elizabethan Literature* (1887), and articles for the *Encyclopaedia Britannica*. His *Essays on French Novelists* (1891) included what was for a long time the most sensitive criticism in English on Gustave Flaubert's work. He retired to Bath and published *A History of the French Novel* (1917–19). (CB)

References:

Saintsbury, George. *Essays on French Novelists*. New York: Scribners, 1891. 334–80.
———. *A History of the French Novel*. 2 vols. London: Macmillan, 1917–19.

Salammbô (1862). Following their defeat by the Romans in the First Punic War (third century B.C.), the Carthaginians refused to pay the mercenary army that had fought for them. In response, the mercenaries revolted and threatened the very existence of Carthage, setting the stage for the truceless war described by the Greek historian Polybius in his *Histories* and taken up later by Jules Michelet in his *Histoire de la république romaine. Salammbô* is inspired by this mortal struggle. As is well known, the only extant texts written about Carthaginian history and civilization are those written by outsiders (for example, Livy's history of Rome). After more than five years of meticulous research, in 1862 Flaubert produced a wonderfully complex work that evokes the shades of an ancient time, masterfully interweaving an intricate tapestry of myth, religion, and war filled with passion, jealousy, rivalry, treachery, revenge, violence, and death. Because *Salammbô* is one of Flaubert's most problematic works, it may be useful to summarize it briefly.

In a series of sleights of hand reflecting the novel's mirage effects (Bart, *Flaubert*, 418; Donato 38), the Council of Carthage adopts the subterfuge of attempting to pacify the mercenaries without paying them. The Council designates the home of the absent Hamilcar Barca, their former general, as the site of a banquet for the mercenaries. Hamilcar becomes the target of the mercenaries' fury, believing as they do that he has abandoned them and has feigned disagreement with the Council in order to destroy them. Ironically, the havoc they wreak on Hamilcar's property will in turn motivate him to become the supreme commander of the Punic forces and take terrible revenge on the mercenaries, destroying them down to the last one.

Meanwhile, during Hamilcar's prolonged absence, in the characteristically oscillatory movement of the novel, the mercenaries are persuaded to withdraw from Carthage to Sicca to await remuneration. At Sicca, the suffete (commander) Hannon patently attempts to dupe them, proffering them bombastic, empty discourse in lieu of payment, and is ignominiously routed by the mercenaries, who return to lay siege to Carthage. A third attempt is made to assuage the mercenaries by the commander Giscon, who is represented as genuinely wishing to pay the mercenaries their dues, but is betrayed by the treacherous wartime accounting of the Carthaginian Elders and is taken prisoner by the mercenaries, incited by groundless rumors spread by Spendius (Ginsburg 123), together with thirty Carthaginian notables.

Hamilcar's daughter Salammbô represents the mystical and mythical aspects of the novel in her capacity as priestess of the moon goddess Tanit. It is she who arrives at the mercenaries' banquet, accompanied by a train of Tanit's priests, to upbraid the soldiers for their destruction of the Barca property and ostensibly to restore peace and calm. Her presence, however, provokes another type of dissension among the soldiers when, unconsciously drawn toward the Libyan soldier Mâtho, she offers him a long draft of wine and commands him to slake his thirst, thus arousing Mâtho's desire and provoking the jealousy of her intended, the Numidian prince Narr'Havas.

During the mercenaries' siege of Carthage, Mâtho and Hamilcar's former slave Spendius (who has been freed by the mercenaries at the banquet), acting at the latter's suggestion, penetrate the city's walls, violate Tanit's temple, and steal her sacred veil, the zaïmph, which Mâtho insists on bringing to Salammbô's bedroom. Attracted and horrified by the sight of the veil, Salammbô sounds the alarm, and Mâtho and Spendius flee for their lives. Through his possession of the zaïmph, Mâtho becomes the master or lord of the mercenaries and ironically forms an alliance with Narr'Havas.

In the continued absence of Hamilcar, the Carthaginians' favorite suffete, Hannon, is named commander-in-chief, but in a series of reversals, he fails miserably in a battle he believes that he has won and is once again routed by the mercenaries when Spendius sets pigs aflame and drives them among the elephants, provoking a stampede. Upon Hamilcar's eventual return from war, the high priest of Eschmoûn, an aspect of the sun god, offers him the command of the Punic forces, which Hamilcar ultimately accepts on discovering the damage caused by the mercenaries at the banquet (Ginsburg 128). Despite his subsequent victory at the battle of the Macar, Hamilcar suffers severe setbacks. It is when Salammbô, obeying Tanit's high priest, Schahabarim, engages in a ritual dance with the Barca serpent and then visits Mâtho's tent to retrieve the veil that the tide of war begins to turn in Hamilcar's favor. Narr'Havas returns to offer Hamilcar his allegiance and becomes Salammbô's betrothed. Spendius's subsequent destruction of the aqueduct, however, leaves Carthage without water and reminds the Carthaginians of the necessity of placating the sun god Moloch by offering him a holocaust of their children. Their prayers are answered, and Tanit, dominated by Moloch, produces a torrential downpour that replenishes Carthage with water.

In a novel redolent with cruelty, death, and violence, Hamilcar's strategy of forcing the mercenaries, whom he has lured into a gorge without exit, either to die of starvation or be killed by each other, is particularly sadistic. Mâtho becomes the ultimate scapegoat, the representative of the mercenaries in the eyes of the Carthaginians, and his torture and death at their hands commemorates Hamilcar's massacre of the mercenaries and Salammbô's victory in Mâtho's tent when she retrieves the zaïmph. With great irony on her wedding day, the sight of Mâtho's bleeding body triggers her memories of his words and caresses in his tent, arousing ineluctably her fatal desire for him. Her death, attributed mimetically to her touching Tanit's veil, is thus semiotically inseparable from her tryst with Mâtho. This mystic marriage (Rousset 91) can be seen as the ironic meeting of Salammbô's heart with Mâtho's, torn from his corpse by Tanit's former high priest, Schahabarim, who masterminded Salammbô's visit to the tent only to subsequently reproach her for it. The closure of the novel generates a powerfully ironic statement about desire and death and may be viewed as creating a compelling intratextual link with *Madame Bovary*.

Since its publication in 1862, *Salammbô* has been repeatedly described as strange and enigmatic, with its most persistently debated aspect being its status as a historical novel (Brombert 92–93). Criticized for its obscure historical subject matter, which was thought to be of no interest to the contemporary reader by contrast with the history of Carthage's rival, Rome (Sainte-Beuve 84), it was declared archeologically erroneous and hopelessly opaque because of its unusual vocabulary, giving rise to the derisive coinage "carthaginoiserie" in reference to the description of Salammbô's bedroom (Froehner, CHH, 384). It has been simultaneously accused of being both too modern (psychologically) and too distant (historically) (Sainte-Beuve 45; Lukács 146–47), resulting in the insightful commentary that two such critically and aesthetically divergent critics as Sainte-Beuve and Lukács could arrive at such similar conclusions (Donato 36).

Salammbô has also been viewed as an unorthodox historical novel with close parallels between Carthage's doomed civilization and events in French nineteenth-century history (Green 58–73). Ironically, these parallels have also been used to prove that *Salammbô* was not a historical novel at all, but rather illustrated the notion of the end of history, the end of civilization (Donato 43), a view of France held by contemporary nineteenth-century intellectuals. *Salammbô* has even been denounced as sounding the death knell of the historical novel (Lukács 199). In a similar vein, the novel has often been described as an epic filled with excesses, especially of cruelty and bloodshed (Sainte-Beuve 71; Brombert 94–97; Porter 101). In fact, the Marquis de Sade's name in anagrammatic form is inscribed in the representation of one of the most gruesome episodes of willful cruelty (Mullen Hohl). But the novel has also been praised as an epic poem by Théophile Gautier and championed by Charles Baudelaire.

The notion that *Salammbô* reflects contemporary social and political reality has been challenged by the interpretation of the novel as an endeavor to rethink revolution in terms of a dynamic that produces an "other" or different social configuration, one that is not diametrically opposed to the system it replaces (Ginsburg 130). The displacement of the novel in time and space implies the representation of "otherness" (Mullen Hohl 1–2; Ginsburg 108–9). However, the strangeness of the novel is counterbalanced by a sustained system of translation that mitigates the unfamiliar and ensures intelligibility, thereby maintaining communication with the reader (Mullen Hohl 16–18; Ginsburg 109). In fact, it has been postulated that the choice of Carthage by Flaubert was motivated by the need to find "otherness" that could be a form of sameness, in which what seems different is an illusion created by the familiar mirage effect (Donato 51).

The conflict between two strange and unfamiliar armies, the Carthaginians and the mercenaries, increases the area of the unknown and consequently the possibilities of ambiguity. Thus it is scarcely surprising that interpretations of the novel reflect this inherent ambiguity (Ginsburg 109). It has been pointed out that the novel has frequently been interpreted in recent times in terms of binary oppositions (Frier-Wantiez 34–43; Ginsburg 113–14), most frequently motivated by the polar dialectic between the moon and the sun, such as the male/female antithesis (Thibaudet 139–40; Neefs 236; Rousset 92). The structure of the novel has been seen as a diptych (Rousset 79–82), and speech and vision have been viewed as dominant oppositions (Forrest-Thomson 787), while centralization has been contrasted with dispersal of power in the Carthaginians and mercenaries, respectively (Neefs 232–33). The novel lends itself to this type of interpretation, motivated most probably by the explicit opposition of the astral powers, the moon goddess (Tanit) and the sun god (Moloch). The text further encourages such readings because of the acquisition of godlike powers by both Mâtho and Salammbô, who read each other's attributes as divine. However, on closer examination, the oppositions dissolve (Ginsburg 114–19), and Tanit and Moloch are found to share certain characteristics, not least their powers of life and death and their androgyny.

The mythological and religious aspects of *Salammbô* have escaped no one's attention and are fundamental to understanding the text. The mythological element has been traditionally interpreted as motivated by the polar dialectic between the moon and the sun, the male and the female, even by those who have interpreted similar manifestations quite differently in *La Tentation de saint Antoine* (Danger, "Sainteté," 187–89). The sacred has been seen as one of the keys to understanding the novel (Forrest-Thomson 792; Culler 220–26; Neefs 236; Rousset 90–92). The myth of Pasiphaë has been proposed as the organizing structure of the work, linking the cycle of the seasons and the orbits of the moon and the sun to the pattern of the war, thus engendering the notion, favored by Flaubert, of history as eternal repetition. According to this particular mythological structure, Salammbô plays a Pasiphaë, lunar goddess and daughter of the sun, to Mâtho's bull, representing the ancient belief in the union of the moon and the sun in springtime and the subsequent fecundation of the land by the moon. In this framework, a parody of Christian symbolism has been found to link the biblical references to the figure of the sun god (Green 103–13).

It has been argued, however, that another mythical structure of Phoenician origin permeates *Salammbô*: the myth of Adonis represented by the sun god, Eschmoûn (Mullen Hohl 68–101). This underlying mythical structure can be found in the Carthaginian version of the laments and festivals, the mourning and celebration of the death and resurrection of the god Adonis. Adonis is the son of the legendary Phoenician king of Cyprus, Cinyras, who is said to have instituted the practice of sacred prostitution at Paphos when he begot his son Adonis with his daughter Myrrha at a corn festival. According to myth, it was Adonis, wounded or castrated by the tusk of a boar, whose blood fertilized the ground to produce such blood-red flowers as the anemone and the hyacinth (Frazer 390). Adonis is the hellenized version of the Semitic *adoni*, meaning lord or master, and is also Eschmoûn or Tammouz, the living and dying god of corn and vegetation. Ishtar/Astarte—that is, Tanit—was the lover of Tammouz and was responsible for effecting his resurrection or return to earth. The myth of Adonis produces the paradigm of multiplicity and mutilation that permeates the novel. Both Hamilcar and Mâtho represent compelling embodiments of Eschmoûn, and Hamilcar and Hannon represent the living and dying aspects, respectively, of the god (Mullen Hohl 74–93, 97).

In *Salammbô*, reflecting the sacred harlotry instituted by Cinyras and the incest that produced Adonis, incest is represented at the mythical level, figuring Eschmoûn theriomorphically as a snake born of the land, and Tanit as the land, mother of all serpents. Similarly, the inversion of the construct of the mother/son consort has been demonstrated in the father/daughter relationship of Hamilcar and Salammbô, constituting an intratextual connection with Madame Arnoux and Frédéric in *L'Education sentimentale* (Mullen Hohl 82–96). In this light, Salammbô's sudden energy issuing from the breaking of her chain in Mâtho's tent (Schor 101) is motivated by her desire to reach another (Hamilcar's) tent. Thus the sacred harlotry engaged in by Tanit's priestesses can be seen as a fertility rite, explaining why Salammbô's visit to Mâtho's tent is also represented as a sacred rite. Similarly, the "mol'k" or holocaust of the Carthaginian children can be viewed as a fertility rite to appease the sun god and induce rain. In this mythological framework, then, the battle scenes also become fertility rites, soaking the land with the blood of armies (Mullen Hohl 103–20).

It is because Adonis's priests, who were castrated in the image of their godhead, wore red robes, that Schahabarim is depicted at the close of the novel wearing such robes, engaged in a blood sacrifice or Red Mass. Further, the songs and prayers that represent the cult of Adonis are a Punicized version of Roman Catholic liturgy, as are certain sacrifices, such as the death of the scapegoat Mâtho, and the "mol'k" becomes a Carthaginian version of the massacre of the Holy Innocents, which constitutes an intratextual reference to the as yet unpublished text (in 1862) of *La Tentation de saint Antoine*. That both Mâtho and Salammbô are repositories for Christ signs adds another level of sexual ambiguity and obfuscates the transcoding process of Roman Catholic liturgy. Salammbô (Lukács 189; Donato 53), Mâtho (Bart 313, "Male Hysteria") and Hamilcar all exhibit, in varying degrees, qualities of a hysteric. Sexual ambiguity and the concomitant dispersal of signs for Roman Catholic liturgy are aspects of narrative veiling or obfuscation that have long obscured the textual implications of *Salammbô*. (AMH)

References:

Bart, Benjamin. *Flaubert*. Syracuse: Syracuse University Press, 1967.

———. "Male Hysteria in *Salammbô*." *Nineteenth-Century French Studies* 12.3 (1984): 313–21.

Brombert, Victor. *The Novels of Flaubert: A Study of Themes and Techniques*. Princeton: Princeton University Press, 1966.

Culler, Jonathan. *Flaubert: The Uses of Uncertainty*. 1974. Rev. ed. Ithaca: Cornell University Press, 1985.

Danger, Pierre. "Sainteté et castration dans *La Tentation de Saint Antoine*." In Charles Carlut, ed., *Essais sur Flaubert en l'honneur du professeur Don Demorest*. Paris: Nizet, 1979. 185–202.

———. *Sensations et objets dans le roman de Flaubert*. Paris: Colin, 1973.

Donato, Eugenio. *The Script of Decadence*. New York: Oxford University Press, 1993.

Flaubert, Gustave. [replies to Froehner and to Sainte–Beuve]. *Œuvres*. 2 vols. Ed. Albert Thibaudet and René Dumesnil. Paris: Gallimard, 1951–52. 1: 997–1013.

Forrest-Thomson, Veronica. "The Ritual of Reading *Salammbô*." *Modern Language Review* 67.4 (1972): 787–98.

Frazer, Sir James. *The Golden Bough*. Abridged ed. New York: Macmillan, 1951.

Frier-Wantiez, Martine. *Sémiotique du fantastique: Analyse textuelle de* Salammbô. Publications Universitaires Européennes. Berne: Lang, 1979.

Froehner, Guillaume. "Le Roman archéologique en France. Gustave Flaubert. *Salammbô*." *Revue contemporaine* December 31, 1862; February 15, 1863. Rpr. in the Appendix to *Salammbô*. Paris: Club de l'Honnête Homme, 1971.

Ginsburg, Michal Peled. *Flaubert Writing*. Stanford: Stanford University Press, 1986.

Green, Anne. *Flaubert and the Historical Novel*: Salammbô *Reassessed*. Cambridge: Cambridge University Press, 1982.

Lukács, Georg. *The Historical Novel.* Trans. Hannah Mitchell and Stanley Mitchell. London: Merlin Press, 1962.

Mullen Hohl, Anne. *Exoticism in* Salammbô: *The Languages of Myth, Religion, and War.* Birmingham, AL: Summa, 1995.

Neefs, Jacques. "Le Parcours du Zaïmph." In Claudine Gothot-Mersch, ed., *La Production du sens chez Flaubert.* Paris: Union Générale d'Editions, 1975. 227–41.

Porter, Denis. "Aestheticism versus the Novel: The Example of *Salammbô.*" *Novel: A Forum on Fiction* 3.4 (1971): 101–6.

Rousset, Jean. "Positions, distances, perspectives dans *Salammbô.*" In Raymonde Debray-Genette, ed., *Travail de Flaubert.* Paris: Seuil, 1983. 79–92.

Sainte-Beuve, Charles-Augustin. "*Salammbô.*" In Charles-Augustin Sainte-Beuve, *Nouveaux lundis.* Paris: Lévy, 1865. 4: 31–95.

Schor, Naomi. "Salammbô enchaînée." In Marie-Claire Bancquart, ed., *Flaubert, la femme, la ville.* Paris: Presses Universitaires de France, 1983. 89–104.

Suhner-Schluep, Heidi. *L'Imagination du feu; ou La Dialectique du soleil et de la lune dans* Salammbô *de G. Flaubert.* Zurich: Juris, 1970.

Thibaudet, Albert. *Gustave Flaubert.* Rev. ed. Paris: Gallimard, 1963; Saint-Armand (Cher): SEPC, 1992 (1922).

Weston, Jessie. *From Ritual to Romance.* Garden City, NY: Doubleday, 1957 (1920).

Salammbô (*Sal*). During the first hundred years after *Salammbô* appeared, the degree to which its title character was denigrated or ignored by critics is remarkable, since she is one of the few characters who develop and are transformed by time and events. It is as though she had been destined to suffer the same misunderstanding and neglect as the book that bears her name.

Salammbô has been described as strange and titillating, but failing to animate the work or interest the reader (Sainte-Beuve 437; Bardèche 18). It has been suggested that Salammbô functions merely as a romantic pretext that should have been eliminated from the novel, since the love poetry she inspires creates an irreconcilable conflict with the concept of the historical novel (Bardèche 18). While she, like Pasiphaë, has the gift of calming dissension (Green 104), she concomitantly produces another (sexual) type of dissension, which initiates the rivalry between Narr'Havas and Mâtho. That she clearly savors the commotion she produces among the men of the army has not escaped critical notice; being multilingual, she is able to appeal to each group of soldiers in an intimate way (Ginsburg 126). She has been described as the eternal Eve (Thibaudet 139) and a seductive, destructive temptress (Bart 409).

The novel has also been criticized for the disproportionate emphasis given to Salammbô by the title in relation to her restricted role in the text (Thibaudet 136). Underlying this judgment is Flaubert's well-known metaphor alluding to the discrepancy between the size of the statue (Salammbô) and the pedestal (*Salammbô*), a metaphor with textual significance discussed later. Critics have noted the fusion of Salammbô's body with her clothing and the mesmerizing effect of their splendor on Mâtho in his tent (Bart 412; Schor 93), and Naomi Schor compares her to a clothed statue. Indeed, the impossibility of separating

Salammbô's body from her jewels and apparel has been ingeniously demonstrated in a penetrating analysis that goes on to categorize the novel as an "ornamental text," a prefiguration of postmodernism (Schor 92–94) that is confirmed by other examples of postmodernism in the novel (Mullen Hohl 19–21). The gap produced by Salammbô's ruptured chain becomes the focus of Schor's attention.

The foregoing analysis of Salammbô interprets the shackling or binding of her ankles by a gold chain—sign of her rank and virginity—as a fetish implying female castration, which is masked by the chain's rupture in Mâtho's tent (Schor 95–98). Breaking the chain means breaking the social contract that binds Salammbô to her father Hamilcar. By dying as she does on the day of her arranged wedding, she breaks the law of the father by frustrating Hamilcar's political ambitions and further violates the law of the father in other ways: since her hair is in disarray, she is breaching the rules of decorum, and if she dies (as the text indicates) for having touched the goddess's veil, she is in effect dying for having violated the father's taboo (Schor 103).

Salammbô, the daughter of Hamilcar, traces her ancestry to the sun god and is destined to return to the sun, according to Schahabarim, the high priest of the moon goddess. Her worship of the moon and the sun (Bart 408) is confirmed by the enumeration of her many pilgrimages. It is the pure aspects of the lunar cult, however, that absorb her completely at the beginning of the novel. It has been astutely observed that Salammbô's purity stems from her ignorance of the significance of her erotic desires and concomitant hysteria (Bart 421). This ignorance is maintained by the will of her father, who has forbidden her to join the college of priestesses or have any knowledge of the erotic practices of Tanit's cult, since he plans a marriage for her that would further his political ambitions. Her father's interdiction produces Salammbô's obsession with Tanit's sacred veil, the zaïmph, which resides in the depth of the moon goddess's temple. Like Saint Antoine, she is consumed by the ardent desire for sacred knowledge, represented by the form of the veil, which is thus set up as the perfect decoy that Mâtho can use to tempt her. While the delicate nuance and prescience of the representation of incipient love, frustration, and resulting hysteria well in advance of Freud have been greatly appreciated, the dispersal of its elements has been regretted (Bart 408). But this dispersal mechanism, characteristic of the text, functions as a means of obfuscation and textual veiling.

After her visit to Mâtho's tent, Salammbô is increasingly identified with Tanit, the moon goddess, and on the day of her wedding and death, she is described as incarnating the soul of Carthage and therefore as equivalent to Tanit. It is as though her carnal knowledge—or, as Brombert terms it, her practice of sacred prostitution (*Flaubert* 86)—has enabled her to absorb both sides of the cult, therefore representing Tanit completely. Since Tanit is described in precisely the same terms as the Roman Catholic God, a sun god who is everywhere but resides specifically under the sacred veil/tabernacle, it is not surprising to find many dispersed signs of Christ in the representation of Salammbô.

For example, Salammbô is represented as a fish on her wedding day, and previously, at the mercenaries' banquet, the depiction of her jewels in terms of the scales of eels had identified her with the sacred Barca fish, descended from the original eels that hatched the mystic egg from which Tanit emerged (Ginsburg 125). According to Cumont (168), it was a sacrilege punishable by tumors and ulcers to capture the goddess's fish except at certain times of the year for mystic banquets, at which people believed that they were eating the goddess's body as they consumed the sacred fish. Moreover, Salammbô's wedding-day headdress is made of peacock feathers, which are also found in her garden when she receives Narr'Havas, her betrothed. The peacock was a sign of Christ's resurrection in early Christian iconography (Campbell 501–3), and Christ took the brazen serpent of Moses, which protected against the bite of fiery serpents, as a type of his resurrection (Frye 172). Thus Salammbô's death wish for Mâtho, also a Christ figure, is represented as an attempt to rid herself of her obsessive memory of the tryst in his tent and is rendered through the equivalence of curing vipers' bites by crushing additional vipers on the wound (Mullen Hohl 129). Since Salammbô herself is represented in snake code, her dance of initiation with the Barca serpent produces a mating dance of vipers. The depiction of hysterical pregnancy stems also from interaction with the Barca snake.

The myth of Adonis structures the novel, reflecting multiplicity or fertility and mutilation or castration. In this respect, Salammbô's visit to Mâtho's tent, masterminded by the apostate Schahabarim, Tanit's high priest, may be viewed as an act resonant of the sacred harlotry practiced by Phoenician women when, mourning the death of Adonis, they offered themselves to strangers for the price of gold coins, which they then gave to the goddess's temple. It was believed that the women represented the goddess and the strangers Adonis (Vellay, cited in Weston 104). The inscription of myth here explains why the visit to Mâtho's tent is perceived by both participants in terms of a sacred rite in which the offering of gold is displaced to Salammbô's ruptured gold chain. During the period of mourning Adonis, women wore their hair undone, just as Salammbô's is described both in her bedroom when Mâtho visits and at her death. Moreover, she is represented as Medusa of the serpentine tresses who produced a stupefying effect on men, a variant of the famous Flaubertian *bêtise*, which manifests the equivalence between Mâtho's fantasy of beheading (castrating) the symbolic father (Hamilcar) and the daughter's death.

Salammbô is represented as Tanit/Ishtar to Mâtho's Adonis/Eschmoûn, both in his tent and in the prelude to his passion and death, when he is described in the sun god's serpent code, descending from an unnamed temple that has been found to be Eschmoûn's. Here Mâtho's arms are represented as a mutilated version of Salammbô's chain, or pieces of a serpent. Salammbô is also represented as Tanit/Ishtar in relation to Hamilcar: at the mercenaries' banquet, Salammbô laments the absent father/master, his absence being the dying aspect of the god, and during her welcome ceremony on his return to his palace in Megara, he is repeatedly depicted as the resurrected Tammouz/Eschmoûn, giving a representation of father/daughter incest (Mullen Hohl 64–66, 74–89).

More significant in this context of father/daughter incest, Salammbô is depicted as a statue when she has harvested the veil, that is, has made her father master of the veil in Mâtho's stead when she visits Hamilcar's tent immediately after leaving Mâtho's. She is also represented as Proserpine (Green 105) or Korê to Hamilcar's Frugifer/Pluto (Mullen Hohl 90–91). Pygmalion (or Pumiyathon) was reputed to have had a sacred marriage ceremony with an image of Astarte, but perhaps less well known is that Pygmalion was the father-in-law of Cinyras (Frazer 386–87), who instituted sacred harlotry at Paphos and begot Adonis through incest with his daughter Myrrha (Frazer 385–86). This mythological incest motivates the many statuary comparisons in the novel that have contributed to its categorization as a Parnassian epic, a work of "uncanny" immobility (Brombert, *Novels* 108). The Adonis myth's generative network, however, uncovers a specific resurrection of the past that actually accounts for the "uncanny" effect by its incestuous aspects, as well as the representation of Tanit's priestesses as idols/statues and the constant use of segments of their description to represent Salammbô as a sacred harlot.

If the banquets that frame the novel have been interpreted at one level as festivals of mourning and celebration of Adonis, they have also been found to transcode a cycle of Roman Catholic liturgy in which the mercenaries' banquet where the fish/Salammbô/Christ are consumed is a version of the Last Supper, or First Mass, during which Christ gave his Body and Blood in the form of bread and wine to be eaten by his disciples. The would-be wedding banquet thus becomes a Red Mass, with Mâtho presented as the ultimate scapegoat, replete with signs of Christ and the dying aspect of the god Adonis (Mullen Hohl 122–25), while Hamilcar, attired as Tammouz/Adonis, represents the living/resurrected aspect of the god.

Salammbô may also be seen as a virgin mother through her identification with Tanit. This is how she represents herself during her discourse at Hamilcar's welcome ceremony, which has been found to transcode Roman Catholic prayers such as the Gloria and the Magnificat, just as her prayers to Tanit, portions of which are addressed to her in turn by Mâtho in his tent, have been found to constitute a version of the Hail Mary, which celebrates the fruitfulness of the Virgin Mother. (AMH)

References:

Bardèche, Maurice. "Preface to *Salammbô*." In Gustave Flaubert, *Salammbô*. Paris: Club de l'Honnête Homme, 1971.

Bart, Benjamin. *Flaubert*. Syracuse: Syracuse University Press, 1967.

Brombert, Victor. *Flaubert par lui-même*. Paris: Seuil, 1971.

———. *The Novels of Flaubert: A Study of Themes and Techniques*. Princeton: Princeton University Press, 1966.

Campbell, Joseph. *The Masks of God: Creative Mythology*. Harmondsworth, UK: Penguin, 1983 [1968].

Cumont, Franz Valéry Marie. *Les Religions orientales dans le paganisme romain, conférences faites au Collège de France en 1905*. 4th rev. ed. Paris: Geuthier, 1929.

Flaubert, Gustave. Letter to Sainte-Beuve. December 23–24, 1862.

Frazer, Sir James. *The Golden Bough*. Abridged ed. New York: Macmillan, 1951.
Frye, Northrop. *The Great Code: The Bible and Literature*. New York: Harcourt Brace Jovanovich, 1982.
Ginsburg, Michal Peled. *Flaubert Writing*. Stanford: Stanford University Press, 1986.
Green, Anne. *Flaubert and the Historical Novel*: Salammbô *Reassessed*. Cambridge: Cambridge University Press, 1982.
Mullen Hohl, Anne. *Exoticism in* Salammbô: *The Languages of Myth, Religion, and War*. Birmingham, AL: Summa, 1995.
Sainte-Beuve, Charles-Augustin. *"Salammbô."* In Chârles-Augustin Sainte-Beuve, *Nouveaux Lundis*. 13 vols. Paris: Levy, 1864–84. 4:31–95.
Schor, Naomi. "Salammbô enchaînée." In Marie-Claire Bancquart, ed., *Flaubert, la femme, la ville*. Paris. Presses Universitaires de France, 1983. 89–104.
Thibaudet, Albert. *Gustave Flaubert*. Rev. ed. Paris: Gallimard, 1963; Saint-Armand (Cher): S.E.P.C., 1992 (1922).
Vellay, Charles. *Le Culte et les fêtes d'Adônis-Thammouz, dans l'Orient autique*. Paris: Leroux, 1904.
Weston, Jessie. *From Ritual to Romance*. Garden City, NY: Doubleday, 1957 (1920).

Salinger, Jerome David (1919–). J. D. Salinger listed Flaubert as one of his favorite authors in a rare interview with William Maxwell in 1951. "The Flaubert of American fiction, insofar as he is religiously committed to style" (Dev 81), is mainly indebted to the French master for his own cult of *le mot juste*. In the story "Franny" (1955) of *Franny and Zooey* (1961), however, Flaubertian influence extends to the narrative irony structuring the tale. Lane, a pretentious undergraduate major in literature, tries to impress his date, Franny, with "some perfectly harmless test-tubey paper on Flaubert." But Lane's own style is grotesquely non-Flaubertian: redundant, floridly rhetorical, and filled with clichés. Echoing Rodolphe's romantic platitudes to Emma amidst announcements from the agricultural show below them, Lane's clichéd speech fails to convince Franny—more interested in sipping her martini—that his "goddam paper" is publishable. Her disinterested remarks puncture Lane's pride. Later, her letter to him parodies his clumsy style. Through this exchange and through the topic of Lane's paper—Flaubert's neurotic craftsmanship—Salinger, self-mockingly conveying his ambition to equal Flaubert, may be ironically questioning the validity of stylistic perfectionism.

In "Seymour: An Introduction" (1959) in Salinger's *Raise High the Roof Beam, Carpenters* (1963), a character disparages Flaubert for not following his heart. Leslie Fiedler also associates the motif of the initiation of the innocent in *L'Education sentimentale* with Salinger's *The Catcher in the Rye* (1951). (IC/LMP)

References:

Dev, Jai. "Franny and Flaubert." *Journal of American Studies* 25.1 (1991): 81–85.
Fiedler, Leslie. "The Eye of Innocence." In Henry Anatole Grunwald, ed., *Salinger: A Critical and Personal Portrait*. New York: Harper & Row, 1962. 218–45.

Salinger, J. D. "J. D. Salinger." Interview with William Maxwell. *Book of the Month Club News* (Midsummer 1951): 5–6.

Salomé (*TC*). The legend of Salomé, on which Flaubert's "Hérodias" is based, expands a brief episode in Mark 6:14–29 and Matthew 14:1–12 in which the nameless daughter of Hérodias (or its variant Hérodiade) obtains, in a spectacular manner, the head of the prophet John the Baptist (or Iaokanann, as he is known in Hebrew). Herod Antipas consents to the prophet's martyrdom to please the young dancer who stirs his desire. Herod's desire for Salomé is incestuous, since she is the daughter of his wife, Hérodias. His relationship with Hérodias is itself technically incestuous because she had previously been married to Herod's half brother. Iaokanann condemned this first incest and so incurred the mortal wrath of Hérodias, who deploys her daughter's powers of seduction to induce the dissipated Tetrarch Herod to behead the prophet. To her tormentor Iaokanann's vociferous asceticism, Hérodias opposes the antithetical mute sensuality of her daughter's dance. "Language, the instrument of prophecy, finally reveals itself to be inadequate" (Peterson 249). Imprisonment and finally decapitation, exacted from Herod through the instrument of Salomé's dance, reduce the prophet to silence.

Flaubert's portrayal of Salomé derives from convergent influences that included memories of Ruchiouk Hânem, the Egyptian *almée* (dancer–prostitute) whose dancing Flaubert describes in his *Voyage en Orient* (102–6), and the John the Baptist sculpture cycle on the tympanum of the cathedral of Rouen that represents Salomé dancing on her hands as she does in "Hérodias." Flaubert's portrayal of Salomé reflects the combination that inspired many fin-de-siècle writers and painters: the virgin and the devouress (Meltzer 18). One feature particularly emphasized in Flaubert's version of Salomé is her youth. He attributes to her character a childish lisp, suggesting that the dance is less a manifestation of Salomé's sexual voracity than a performance delivered to achieve maternal approval. Ironically, Salomé has no awareness of the conflict between spirit and body that Iaokanann exemplifies. (JM)

References:

Flaubert, Gustave. *Voyage en Orient.* In Maurice Nadeau, ed., Flaubert, *Œuvres complètes.* 18 vols. Lausanne, Editions rencontre, 1964. Vol. 5.

Meltzer, Françoise. *Salomé and the Dance of Writing: Portraits of Mimesis in Literature.* Chicago: University of Chicago Press, 1987.

Peterson, Carla L. "The Trinity in Flaubert's *Trois Contes*: Deconstructing History." *French Forum* 8 (1985): 243–57.

Sand, George (1804–76). Among Flaubert's many correspondents, George Sand was the most influential in encouraging him in both his writing and his private life. Their correspondence was intimate and tender. She called him her "troubadour," and he called her "Chère maître" (Dear [feminine] master [masculine]).

In addressing her this way, he was recognizing her position as the best-known female writer of her time, acknowledging the difference in their ages (she was seventeen years older), and showing his respect for her intellect and writing ability. She wrote a positive review of *Salammbô* (1862), and when he wrote to thank her, their voluminous correspondence began.

Their letters included discussions of life, death, illness, love, politics, and the art of writing. Their relationship filled a gap each had in life and also complemented the missing parts of their personalities. They were opposites in many ways: she loved to be surrounded by friends and family, he spent most of his time alone, living in seclusion with his mother and niece; she wrote quickly and easily, he chose his words carefully; she believed in the basic goodness of humanity, he was cynical and critical; she loved people of all classes, he leaned toward elitism. Even their physical appearances were opposite: she was quite petite, he was very tall.

Sand attempted to help Flaubert when he was depressed and lonely, encouraging him to marry and have a family. She also suggested that he try to write a story with some hope in it. He did so, calling it "Un cœur simple" (1877), which he wrote for her. She died before she could read it, so he was never to know her opinion of it. Her literary influence can also be found in his novel *L'Education sentimentale* (1869), in which his main character, Frédéric Moreau, shares the antihero traits of Sand's *Horace* (1842).

In addition to her literary advice and influence, Sand also encouraged Flaubert to participate in her family gatherings. He visited her several times, including Christmas of 1869. During these visits, they spent hours together, discussing literature and reading aloud from their own current projects. Flaubert even invited Sand to visit him on two occasions.

Their letters depict a trusting, confiding relationship. Flaubert revealed his feelings of sexual ambivalence to her, telling her that he felt at times as if he were both male and female. Sand's reply is that of a true mentor; she confirmed that his feelings were normal and that one day society would discover that there is only one sex. This is but one example of her similarity to Flaubert despite their many differences. After her death, Flaubert wept at her grave and wrote to a friend of the immense tenderness he had found in the midst of her genius. She had provided the combination of those attributes that he needed, and her importance in his life and work should not be underestimated. (SM)

References:

Bayley, John. "An Unexpected Attachment." *Yale Review* 81.4 (1993): 99–105.

Winegarten, Renee. *The Double Life of George Sand, Woman and Writer*. New York: Basic Books, 1978.

Sand, Maurice (1823–89). Maurice Sand's mother, George Sand, included Flaubert in her life as a kind of adopted son, and Flaubert felt some jealousy of Maurice, envying his mother, his family life, and his children. Flaubert spent

Christmas of 1869 with the family, during which he professed an extreme dislike of the marionettes that Maurice created and used in plays for the family's entertainment. Maurice wrote that Flaubert hated the puppets, criticized everything, and refused to join in the frivolity of it all. He also, however, praised Flaubert's writing, of which Maurice, himself an aspiring author, may have felt somewhat envious. (SM)

Reference:

Barry, Joseph. *Infamous Woman: The Life of George Sand.* Garden City, NY: Doubleday, 1977.

Sarraute, Nathalie (1902–99). For the contemporary French novelist Nathalie Sarraute, language was a powerful instrument of social control. In many of her works, she undermines language's authority by fragmenting and manipulating the discourses of her text. Her interest in the clichéd nature of language, the way in which the language we speak always and necessarily belongs to someone else, and her sense of the difficulty of achieving originality or narrative authority owe much to Flaubert. But in contrast to Flaubert's satiric use of the *style indirect libre*, the impersonal pronoun *on*, and the copying of many sources, Sarraute manipulates a variety of pronouns and clichés to make the novel's viewpoint ambiguous and to demonstrate that all discourse is in fact general. Both Flaubert and Sarraute reject the commonplace because of its incapacity to express the individual. They both find stupidity an integral part of language, one that overwhelms its textual setting through superabundant description.

Sarraute's aim of challenging authority and her narrative stratagems for copying and subverting official language resemble the goals and tactics of Flaubert's modernist irony. Much as with Flaubert's readers, Sarraute's are forced to do the work of interpretation, to discover the meanings behind the words. Sarraute's texts do not name—nor even, at times, gender—characters; language and its inability to capture feelings occupies the foreground. Sarraute herself values Flaubert's ability to create or re-create a new psychic substance. Indeed, such a stance may reflect Flaubert's greatest influence on Sarraute's writing. (ENM)

Her essay on "Flaubert le précurseur" (1965) asserted that "at this moment, Flaubert is the master for all of us [writers]. Our judgment of him has become unanimous: he is the precursor of the modern novel." *Madame Bovary*, she explains, is a masterpiece for its depiction of inauthentic feelings, and inauthenticity becomes the very substance of *Bouvard et Pécuchet*. Sarraute analyzes and praises the style of *Salammbô*, calling it always perfectly under control, never ecstatic or rhapsodic. The extreme precision of the descriptions in that work shows Flaubert's affinity with the Parnassian poets. On the other hand, Sarraute finds *L'Education sentimentale* overrated, lacking in psychological penetration, and showing a hero who merely lives out clichés. In her own works, clichés consistently create an ironic subtext. (LMP)

References:

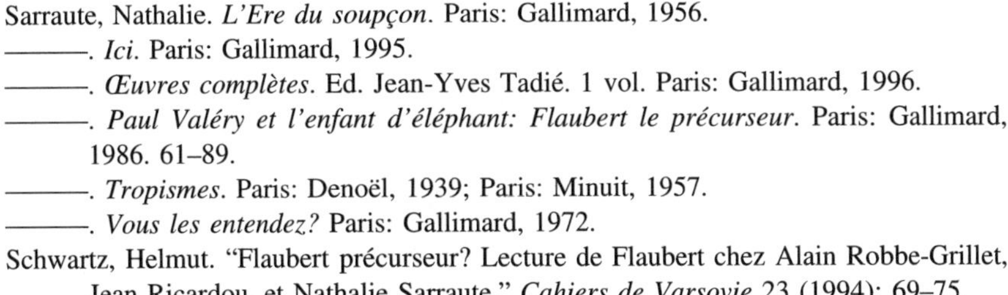

Sarraute, Nathalie. *L'Ere du soupçon*. Paris: Gallimard, 1956.
———. *Ici*. Paris: Gallimard, 1995.
———. *Œuvres complètes*. Ed. Jean-Yves Tadié. 1 vol. Paris: Gallimard, 1996.
———. *Paul Valéry et l'enfant d'éléphant: Flaubert le précurseur*. Paris: Gallimard, 1986. 61–89.
———. *Tropismes*. Paris: Denoël, 1939; Paris: Minuit, 1957.
———. *Vous les entendez?* Paris: Gallimard, 1972.
Schwartz, Helmut. "Flaubert précurseur? Lecture de Flaubert chez Alain Robbe-Grillet, Jean Ricardou, et Nathalie Sarraute." *Cahiers de Varsovie* 23 (1994): 69–75.

Sartre, Jean-Paul (1905–80). Jean-Paul Sartre was France's most influential existentialist philosopher, drawing on Hegel, Marx, Husserl, and Heidegger. He studied phenomenology in Berlin at the outset of the Nazi era. He founded the leading postwar intellectual journal, *Les Temps Modernes*, in 1945. Among his major works are the philosophical treatise *L'Etre et le néant* (1943), a series of excellent plays in the 1940s, and speculative psychobiographies of Baudelaire (1947), Genet (1951), and Flaubert (1971–72). This last work runs 3,000 pages. His autobiography *Les Mots* (1964) is also noteworthy. After the war, he consistently supported human rights, but lost some credibility by blindly and stubbornly supporting Stalinist Communism long after others had recognized its atrocities. His *Critique de la raison dialectique* (1960) tries to reconcile Marxist materialism (i.e., the recognition of how we are shaped by socioeconomic forces and a hierarchical class structure) with his intransigent advocacy of human freedom of action and total moral responsibility. Sartre's analyses of "bad faith"—self-justification based on our suppression of the awareness that our behaviors are based on choice—are particularly rich and subtle in his literary criticism. He denounces as evasions any claims that our lives are determined by chance, luck, or Providence, and that we are ever totally constrained so that we have no choices and therefore no opportunities for self-definition through action.

Sartre frequently returned to Flaubert, who fascinated him, perhaps because social withdrawal and the cult of art tempted Sartre himself. His articles in *Les Temps Modernes* examine Flaubert's youthful writings of the 1830s to find the key to the dualism of the lyrical and the ideal in Flaubert: his hope of escaping his condition as a bourgeois by assuming the aristocratic essence of a writer, and his "misunderstood child's" disgust at those who think too basely to appreciate him. "Smarh," Sartre claims, is the key to understanding Flaubert. Sartre's "Question de méthode" uses his insights into Flaubert to criticize the Marxists, whom Sartre says overlook the formative influence of childhood on the individual and the mediating role of the family in inserting an individual into his or her class. Sartre characterizes Flaubert's father fixation and "the explosive mixture of naïve scientism and godless religion" that composes his psyche, and that he tries to overcome through his cult of artistic form. *Madame Bovary* is hardly "realist," Sartre claims, but is instead a veiled, lyrical, metaphysical confession of a man disguised as Emma Bovary.

Sartre's monumental *L'Idiot de la famille* sees Flaubert as a hysterical neurotic. Sartre speculates that Flaubert was raised conscientiously but without love by his mother, who wanted a girl, and was scorned by his family when he proved dyslexic during his early school years. The nihilism of *Madame Bovary* reflected the bankrupt ideology of the bourgeoisie, with whom Flaubert shared a collective neurosis. He projects his contempt for his own class onto all humanity. Sartre cleverly combines Freud with Marx when he demonstrates how Flaubert learned to defend himself against reality by substituting the imaginary for the real. But he does not explain Flaubert's exhaustive documentation and revision and his satire of his own sympathetic characters. He seems to project unrecognized autobiography and self-hatred onto his portrait of Flaubert. Still, Sartre's psychobiography has been as influential as any study of Flaubert since World War II. (LMP)

References:

Barnes, Hazel. *Sartre and Flaubert*. Chicago: University of Chicago Press, 1981.

Bellemin-Noël, Jean. "Gustave, Poulou, Julien, et nous autres." *Revue des lettres modernes* 1165–72 (1994): 3–20.

Caws, Peter. "Choosing Emotions: The Late Sartre and the Early Flaubert." *Bulletin de la Société américaine de philosophie de langue française* 4.2–3 (1992): 209–17.

Fabre-Luce, Alfred. "Sartre par Flaubert." *Nouvelle Revue des deux mondes*, October–December 1971:44–61.

Ginsburg, Michal Peled. "La Tentation du biographe." *Revue des lettres modernes* 1165–72 (1994): 21–42.

Howells, Christina. "Flaubert's Blind Spot: The Fetishization of Subjectivity: Some Notes on the Constitution of Gustave in Sartre's *L'Idiot de la famille*." In Jean-François Fourny and Charles D. Minahen, eds., *Situating Sartre in Twentieth-Century Thought and Culture*. New York: St. Martin's, 1997. 29–38.

Sartre, Jean-Paul. "La Conscience de classe chez Flaubert." *Temps Modernes* 21 (1966): 1921–51, 2114–53.

———. "Flaubert: Du poète à l'artiste." *Temps Modernes* 22 (1966): 197–253, 423–81, 598–674.

———. *L'Idiot de la famille: Gustave Flaubert de 1821–1857*. 3 vols. Paris: Gallimard, 1971–72. Trans. Carol Cosman, *The Family Idiot*. 5 vols. Chicago: University of Chicago Press, 1981–93.

———. "Question de méthode." In Jean-Paul Sartre, *Critique de la raison dialectique* vol. 1, *Théorie des ensembles poétiques*. Paris: Gallimard, 1960. 15–111.

Suhl, Benjamin. *Jean-Paul Sartre: The Philosopher as a Literary Critic*. New York: Columbia University Press, 1970.

Uitti, Karl D. "Sartre's *L'Idiot de la famille*: A Contribution to the Theory of Narrative Style." *Romanic Review* 68 (1977): 217–34.

Wilcocks, Robert. "The Resurrectionist; or, November in Le Havre." In Ronald Aronson and Adrian van den Hoven, eds., *Sartre Alive*. Detroit: Wayne State University Press, 1991. 240–69.

Schahabarim (*Sal*). The central political and religious importance of Schahabarim, Tanit's high priest in *Salammbô*, cannot be overestimated. Schahabarim, the most erudite man in Carthage, is depicted as transformed in the image of his godhead. Just as the goddess's veil has been found to have an intertextual relationship with Honoré de Balzac's *La Peau de chagrin*, Schahabarim's emasculation, in characteristic Freudian inversion, is inscribed accordingly in his facial skin in Balzacian terms (Mullen Hohl 62–66). Similarly, the *im* ending of his name links him phonetically with the scared veil of Tanit, the zaïmph, while its repeated middle syllables, *haha*, may be seen to compensate for his mutilation, in the way that the paradigm of multiplicity and mutilation have been found to structure the novel at every level (Mullen Hohl 41, 135–36). His name also constitutes, however, an authorial joke at the evasion of censorship (Mullen Hohl 133–34). He has been viewed, together with Giscon and Hannon, as representing aspects of Tallyrand, diplomat and apostate bishop of Autun (Addison 115).

Schahabarim's influence on the course of events in the novel is subtly implied at the Elders' war council in Moloch's temple. The only headwear described at the meeting is Schahabarim's pointed cap and Hamilcar's mystic tiara, which will later be conflated in the pointed tiaras worn by Eschmoûn's priests at the "mol'k" (the sacrifice of children to Moloch). It so happens that the mention of Schahabarim's cap generates a sadomasochistic sequence in which the Elders' delight in Hamilcar's discomfort at their elliptical allusions to Salammbô's purported fall produces the Adonis hypogram, equating both Mâtho and Hamilcar with Eschmoûn/Tammouz (Mullen Hohl 76–77). Since the other distinguishing feature of Schahabarim's representation is his remaining in his seat while everyone rushes forward to attack Hamilcar, his role is one of observer, much like the narrator or the author. As he knows, the Elders' reports that he hears are not accurate in their core accusation of Salammbô's yielding to Mâtho. It has been keenly noted, however, that since Salammbô does eventually become Mâtho's lover, the allegations are retrospectively confirmed, while the love scene in his tent is at the same time an end product of these allegations (Ginsburg 127). Thus Schahabarim, the avid learner who until then has strictly observed Hamilcar's orders concerning his daughter's adherence to the pure aspect of Tanit's cult, will now take a powerful step in transforming the narrative and enact her initiation by setting in motion the train of events that confirms the Elders' allegations, that is, by sending Salammbô to Mâtho's tent to retrieve the veil and allegedly renew his own faith in his godhead.

It is scarcely coincidental that Schahabarim's relationship with Salammbô is a sadomasochistic one (Bart 405). He takes pleasure in her suffering for his goddess, Tanit, which is also his lot. He further identifies with her as sharing a common sex. His ambivalence is manifested by his jealousy of her beauty and purity. Her function in his arid life, however, is that of a flower in the crack of a sepulcher. Put another way, Schahabarim, like Hannon, is represented in terms of death-in-life (Addison 117) and of the living/dying aspect of Adonis (Mullen

Hohl 109–10). Taken in conjunction with his descent into the caves of Persephone (whom Salammbô has been found to represent; Mullen Hohl 27, 89), we have an allusion to the Adonis myth, since Adonis lived with Persephone in the underworld for part of the year (Frazer 380). It is therefore not surprising that on Salammbô's return from Mâtho's tent, Schahabarim's reaction is expressed in terms of the unnameable or the inconceivable, in keeping with the god Eschmoûn, "the name" or no name to whom he will eventually turn, as manifested by the final scene of the novel (Mullen Hohl 104).

The rejection by Moloch's priests of the apostate Schahabarim at the "mol'k" is explicitly attributed to his emasculation. Adonis's Phrygian counterpart, Attis, was beloved of Tanit's equivalent, Cybele, etymologically the goddess of caverns (*New Larousse* 150), one of the holy sites visited by Schahabarim. Attis's priests, the Galli, were given to mutilating themselves voluntarily in the image of their godhead (Frazer 404). Moloch's priests wore purple robes, as did the 'Galli', the color being associated with Attis's fertilizing blood, which was thought to produce flowers of similar shades, such as the hyacinth and the violet (Frazer 405). These are the hues most often used in descriptions of Salammbô/Tanit's attire and that of Eschmoûn/Adonis's priests. At the "mol'k," Eschmoûn is depicted as one of the Canaanite gods who replicate or are split off from the supreme Baal, the sun god. Hence the manner in which Schahabarim could pontificate at a ceremony of the solar divinity, wearing Moloch's mantle, is by transferring his allegiance to Eschmoûn/Adonis, who already has a relationship with Tanit/Astarte. Traditionally, Attis's Archigallus, or high priest, engaged in a blood sacrifice on the Day of Blood, marking Attis's death and burial, followed by his resurrection, celebrated by the Festival of Joy (Frazer 405–8). Thus Schahabarim is represented as an Archigallus as he mutilates Mâtho's corpse and offers his heart to the sun. Since Mâtho/Adonis's heart is textually linked to the sun through the latter's rays at the moment of its daily death (Mullen Hohl 70) as it buries itself in Tanit's marine aspect, Schahabarim's act is not the radical act of apostasy that one has been led to expect. Instead, the mutilation incorporates the union of the two godheads, the sun and the moon, which is perfectly in keeping with the tenor of the closing chapter.

The myth of the daily resurrection of the sun has been found to be an explanation for the journey of Saint John the Baptist's head at the end of "Hérodias" (Debray-Genette, 341), thus creating an intertextual relationship between the two texts. There is also an intertextual connection between the description of Mâtho's heart being offered to the sun and the depiction of Christ's death in the 1849 version of *La Tentation de saint Antoine*, which has revealed the sun god (God the Father) annexing the son. Likewise, the end of the 1874 version of *La Tentation* has been found to be a variant in astral code of the unpublished version (Mullen Hohl 100–101).

The selection of Mâtho's heart as the sacrifice to be offered up to the sun gives a literal rendering of "Sursum corda," the customary address to the faithful at Roman Catholic masses celebrating joyous occasions, such as feast days or the end of war. Mâtho is a Christ figure (Green 110–11; Mullen Hohl 99–101), and the Mass is a sacrifice commemorating both the death and resurrection of Christ. Schahabarim's raising up the heart on a gold spoon mimes the moment of the consecration, when the bread and wine become the body and blood of Christ. His body and blood are present in each substance according to the doctrine of consubstantiation, so the heart, consisting of blood and flesh, provides a literal rendition (Mullen Hohl 99–100). The complex system of narrative obfuscation and ambiguity that cloaks the novel thus serves effectively as a powerful defense against censorship by the prevailing judicial system (Mullen Hohl 133–34). (AMH)

References:

Addison, Claire. *Where Flaubert Lies: Chronology, Mythology, and History.* Cambridge: Cambridge University Press, 1996.

Bart, Benjamin. *Flaubert.* Syracuse: Syracuse University Press, 1967.

Debray-Genette, Raymonde, ed. "Re-Présentation 'd'Hérodias.' " In Claudine Gothot-Mersch, ed., *La Production du sens chez Flaubert.* Paris: Union Générale d'Editions, 1975. 328–44.

Flaubert, Gustave. *Salammbô.* In Gustave Flaubert, *Œuvres,* vol 1. Dijon: Gallimard, 1951.

Frazer, Sir James. *The Golden Bough.* Abridged ed. New York: Macmillan, 1951.

Ginsburg, Michal Peled. *Flaubert Writing.* Stanford: Stanford University Press, 1986.

Green, Anne. *Flaubert and the Historical Novel*: Salammbô *Reassessed.* Cambridge: Cambridge University Press, 1982.

Mullen Hohl, Anne. *Exoticism in* Salammbô: *The Languages of Myth, Religion, and War.* Birmingham, AL: Summa, 1995.

New Larousse Encyclopedia of Mythology. 1959. Hong Kong: Tappan for Hamlyn, 1968.

Schlésinger, Elisa (1810–88). Flaubert first met Elisa Schlésinger in the Norman fishing and resort village of Trouville in 1836, when he rescued her beach robe from the rising tide. At the time, she was nursing a three-month-old child. He fell in love with her at once, and Emile Gérard-Gailly claims that she was his "great," his "only" passion throughout his life (aside, one must add, from his mother; cf. Starkie xv). The scene was transposed in the opening of the 1869 version of *L'Education sentimentale* involving Frédéric Moreau and Madame Arnoux. She also appears to have inspired the character Maria in Flaubert's *Mémoires d'un fou* and Marie in his *Novembre*; one can also suppose that some of Léon's feelings for Emma Bovary as a young mother, apparently virtuous and unapproachable, in the first part of *Madame Bovary* recall the young Flaubert's response to Elisa.

Married secretly to another man, she lived a lie with Maurice Schlésinger, her supposed husband. She may have spent some time in prostitution before they met, but Maurice generously acknowledged her first child, born in 1836, as his own. They were legally married only in 1840 after the first husband died in 1839. Maurice was regularly unfaithful. Elisa was later to spend some time in an asylum during the 1860s, and again in 1875 and 1881 (Bart 639). After Maurice died, Flaubert more openly expressed his affection to her (see his letters of May 22, 1871, September 6, 1871, and October 5, 1872), hoping that he could spend the end of his life near her and that she could visit him and his mother. But she had returned to Germany, where Flaubert could not bear to go after the Franco-Prussian War, and when Elisa visited Trouville in 1871 to look after her property, the illness of Flaubert's mother prevented his going to see her (Starkie 353–54). (LMP)

References:

Flaubert, Gustave. *Œuvres complètes*. Ed. Maurice Nadeau. 18 vols. Lausanne: Editions recentre, 1964. 7:77–78, 126, 317–18.
Gérard-Gailly, Emile. *Le Grand Amour de Flaubert*. Aubier: Editions Montaigne, 1944.
Lottman, Herbert. *Flaubert: A Biography*. New York: Fromm, 1990. 26–28.
Starkie, Enid. *Flaubert: The Making of the Master*. New York: Atheneum, 1967. 24–26 and passim.

Schlésinger, Maurice (1798–1871). Maurice Schlésinger was the model for Jacques Arnoux in *L'Education sentimentale*. His father had published music and edited a prominent music journal in Berlin. After service in the Prussian army at the end of the Napoleonic Wars, Maurice came to France to sell sheet music and musical instruments. A Jew converted to Catholicism, this ingratiating, womanizing, unscrupulous, and vulgar music promoter supported and exploited the young Richard Wagner for two years as an underpaid music critic. He founded the respected *Revue et Gazette musicale de Paris* to advance his commercial interests. His speculative purchase of a hotel in the Norman beach resort of Trouville brought his companion Elisa and Flaubert together again after their first chance meeting on the beach in 1836. He and Flaubert became close friends and spent much time together. Flaubert's correspondence shows that they were still confidants after the *Madame Bovary* trial. Like his literary counterpart Jacques Arnoux, Maurice eventually became nearly destitute through unsound investments. (LMP)

References:

Gérard-Gailly, Emile. *Le Grand Amour de Flaubert*. Aubier: Editions Montaigne, 1944.
Lottman, Herbert. *Flaubert: A Biography*. New York: Fromm, 1990. 26–28.

Scott, Sir Walter (First Baronet, 1771–1832). In "Quidquid volueris" (1837), the adolescent Flaubert draws on the orangutan Sylvanus in Sir Walter Scott's *Count Robert of Paris* (1831) to depict the demonic, tortured ape-man Djalioh. Both characters lack speech, thus remaining on the brink of desire and humanity. In Flaubert's last work, commenting on Scott, Bouvard and Pécuchet first echo the French romantics' enchantment with the English author, but later come to believe that Scott's style is repetitious, artificial, intolerably prudish, and overburdened with dialogue—criticisms characteristic of Flaubert's generation. (DF)

Reference:

Perrone-Moisés, Leyla. "*Quidquid volueris*: The Scriptural Education." In Naomi Schor and Henry F. Majewski, eds., *Flaubert and Postmodernism*. Lincoln: University of Nebraska Press, 1984. 139–59.

"Un Secret de Philippe le Prudent, roi d'Espagne: Conte historique," (1836). "Un Secret de Philippe le Prudent, roi d'Espagne" is an unfinished short story. The few pages that the young Flaubert completed show a remarkable mastery of the fast-moving, descriptive, and dialogic style of an Alexandre Dumas. The fragment we have is not at all a scenario or sketch. The setting in sixteenth-century Spain allowed Flaubert to indulge his love of historical subjects, although the immediate inspiration for the story is thought to be a play by Casimir Delavigne produced in 1835, *Don Juan d'Autriche; ou, La Vocation.* The story offers a subtle *mise-en-abyme* by first focusing on Philip II, who has come fairly recently to the throne following the abdication of his father, Carlos Quinto, and then shifting to Philip's son, Carlos, who is a virtual prisoner in the royal palace. (MCO)

Reference:

Bruneau, Jean. *Les Débuts littéraires de Gustave Flaubert, 1831–1845.* Paris: Colin, 1962.

Flaubert, Gustave. *Œuvres complètes*, 16 vols. Ed. Maurice Bardèche. Paris: Club de l'Honnête Homme, 1971–76.

———. *Œuvres complètes*, 2 vols. Ed. Bernard Masson. Paris: Seuil, 1964.

Sénard, Jules (1800–1885). A prominent Rouen lawyer with liberal views, Jules Sénard had served as president of the Assemblée nationale and as minister of the interior. He was a longtime friend of the Flaubert family, and Flaubert immediately called on him for help when he and *Madame Bovary*'s publisher were indicted for having affronted morality. Masterfully using quotations from the Bible, from the great writers of antiquity, and from a variety of consecrated French authors, Sénard showed that Flaubert's novel was more restrained than their works in its depiction of sexuality and of the rites of the Catholic church. He successfully argued that *Madame Bovary* was a profoundly moral work: Emma Bovary, dying horribly from arsenic poisoning, had suffered an exemplary punishment for her adultery. The court scolded but acquitted the author and publisher. In gratitude, Flaubert dedicated the novel to Sénard. (LMP)

References:

Brière, Max. "Des Amitiés rouennaises de Flaubert, les frères Baudry." *Etudes normandes* 1 (1981): 41–42.

Joubert, Jean. *Jules Sénard: de la défense de Flaubert à la défense de la république*. Paris: Presses du Palais-Royal, 1984.

Sénécal (*ES*). It is through Deslauriers that Frédéric Moreau meets Sénécal, whom Deslauriers presents to us as a mathematics coach, a man of republican convictions, and a future Saint-Just. This connection with the controversial ideologue of the French Revolution, one of the most zealous advocates of the Reign of Terror, who was arrested and guillotined in the Thermidorian Reaction, not only reveals Deslauriers's tendency to inflate the potential of his friends, but also indicates Sénécal's intrinsic brutality. As we see him progressing from coach to overseer in Arnoux's factory, Flaubert depicts him as paradigmatic of the self-centered individual whose support for republican ideals lasts only as long as he himself does not hold any power. Once he is in a position to exert authority over others, he adopts the repressive, brutal practices of those against whom he had previously railed for holding his own abilities in check. Flaubert completes this transformation of Sénécal from individual into symbol when he has him, as a member of the military police, gun down his former friend Dussardier as the latter, unarmed, cries out his support for the Republic. Typical of the novel's biting irony, in the final passage, where the destinies of so many of the characters are succinctly summed up, Sénécal is reported simply as "unaccounted for." (RL)

Reference:

Grandpré, Chantal de. "Sénécal et Dussardier: La République en effigie." *French Review* 64.4 (1991): 621–31.

"Les Sept Fils du derviche" (1837). "Les Sept Fils du derviche" was inspired by Voltaire's *Contes*, Cervantes's *Don Quixote*, and *The Thousand and One Nights*. Each son is obsessed by a fixed idea, but the one who can enjoy riches in thought will be the happiest. (LMP)

References:

Bruneau, Jean. *Le* Conte oriental *de Gustave Flaubert: Documents inédits*. Paris: Les Lettres nouvelles, (1973).

Flaubert, Gustave. "Les Sept Fils du derviche." In Gustave Flaubert, *Œuvres complètes*, ed. Maurice Bardèche. 16 vols. Paris: Club de l'Honnête Homme, 1971–76. 12: 143–70.

les Sept Péchés Mortels (*TSA*). The Seven Deadly Sins, the vices considered the source of all sin, are avarice (*avaritia*), anger (*ira*), pride (*superbia*), lust (*luxuria*), gluttony (*gula*), envy (*invidia*), and sloth (*acedia* or *accidia*). They enter Antoine's life through the direct intervention of the Devil, whom they serve. (AHP)

sex life. Like many young men from his bourgeois milieu, Flaubert considered prostitution as an escape valve. Many of his dalliances were with prostitutes and courtesans, but there were also some long-standing relationships, as well as an erotic fascination with older women that started when he was an adolescent. In 1836, when he was only fourteen and a half, he met Elisa Schlésinger, a twenty-six-year-old woman who fascinated Flaubert from their first encounter. This attraction was the real-life kernel at the heart of Frédéric Moreau's infatuation with Mme Arnoux in *L'Education sentimentale.* Flaubert's first actual sexual experience, however, was not to come until four years later. In Marseilles, in 1840, he lost his virginity to Eulalie Foucaud, a dark-haired, amber-skinned, thirty-five-year-old Creole woman.

According to the Goncourts' journal of November 2, 1863, Flaubert said that he did not engage in sexual relations between the ages of twenty and twenty-four, that is, from 1842 to 1846. In 1846, he met one of the most important women in his life, Louise Colet. On July 29, 1846, he first encountered Colet (née Revoil), who had been born in Aix-en-Provence in 1810. At the time of their meeting, she was still married to Hippolyte Colet, but she was at that time the mistress of the philosopher Victor Cousin, a relation that had begun in 1838. Colet and Flaubert became lovers on August 4, 1846, and engaged in a relationship that lasted until 1848. After a break of several years, they resumed their relationship in July 1851 and continued it until October 1854, after which they never saw one another again. They often met in Mantes, roughly halfway between Paris and Croisset, to consummate their relations. Between the two periods of their involvement came Flaubert's famous trip to the Orient, which was remarkable on several counts. He left Croisset on October 22, 1849, accompanied by Maxime Du Camp. They left Marseilles on November 4. During the trip, Flaubert had an encounter in Esnak with one of the most famous courtesans of the time, Ruchiouk-Hânem, a courtesan who did the erotic dance "de l'abeille" (of the bee) for him, after which they spent the night together. This trip is also notable for Flaubert's homosexual encounters: on one or more occasions in Cairo bathhouses, Flaubert engaged in anal intercourse with young men. He contracted syphilis on March 24, 1850, in Beirut from a fourteen-year-old Maronite boy named Mohammed.

After the break with Colet, Flaubert had two more long-term relationships, though they both seem to have been sporadic in nature. First, chronologically (although the two do overlap), was the relationship with Juliet Herbert, whom Jacques-Louis Douchin characterizes as the great love of Flaubert's life. Born on April 27, 1829 and living until November 17, 1909, Herbert met Flaubert in 1855, but they did not consummate their relationship until the spring of 1857. These relations seem to have continued sporadically until almost the end of his life. Finally, he met Suzanne Lagier, an actress and singer who was born in 1833 and died in 1893. Their first tryst was in 1861 at the latest, with relations continuing through 1867 or 1868 and reprised in 1876, lasting perhaps through 1878. (LRS)

References:

Barnes, Julian. *Flaubert's Parrot*. New York: Knopf, 1985.
Douchin, Jacques-Louis. *La Vie érotique de Flaubert*. Paris: Carrère/J. J. Pauvert, 1984.
Gérard–Gailly, Emile. *Le Grand Amour de Flaubert*. Aubier: Editions Montaigne, 1944.
Starkie, Enid. *Flaubert: The Making of the Master*, London: Weidenfeld and Nicolson, 1967.
Troyat, Henri. *Flaubert*. Trans. Joan Pinkham. New York: Viking, 1992.

Le Sexe faible. *Le Sexe faible* is a dramatic comedy written in 1872–73. Louis Bouilhet, a playwright and Flaubert's closest friend, died in 1869, leaving his most recent manuscript unfinished. As a *travail d'hommage*, Flaubert undertook completing the play, which he did somewhat rapidly, as he was offered production of a play of his own if he would write one (which he did: *Le Candidat*). The weaker sex of the title is, of course, the male one, and the play has some of the light tone and rapid movement of a Feydeau vaudeville. Never one for dramatic dialogue, preferring to relate conversations in his novels through indirect discourse, Flaubert complained during this period that writing dialogue was as irritating as drinking soda water. We can only guess how much of the finished work was actually written by Flaubert, because his and Bouilhet's manuscripts have never come to light. The play has been performed at least once: a 1984 production in Geneva. (MCO)

References:

Canu, Jean. *Flaubert, auteur dramatique*. Paris: Ecrits de France, 1946.
Masson, Bernard. "Théâtre." In Gustave Flaubert, *Œuvres complètes*, ed. B. Masson. 2 vols. Paris: Seuil, 1964. 2:315–16.
Raitt, Alan. *Flaubert et le théâtre*. Bern: Lang, 1998.

Simon Magus (*TSA*, 1849, 1856, 1874). Simon Magus was a renowned magician of Samaria in the first century A.D. Converted by the Apostles Peter and John, he tried to purchase from them the power to bestow the Holy Spirit to whomever he chose—thence the word "simony" (Acts 8:9–24). Having been rebuked, he begged for pardon. However, he later went to Rome and passed himself off as the Messiah; a statue was erected to him there. In the fourth section of the definitive version of Flaubert's *Tentation de saint Antoine* (122–30), the Devil appears in the form of Simon, accompanied by a woman called Ennoia (both the Greek for "thought," and a figuration of Helen of Troy as universal courtesan); he tempts Antoine and tries to baptize him. When Antoine rejects him, the illusion dissipates, only to be replaced by the even more compelling one of Apollonius of Tyana, a first-century Pythagorean philosopher and magician who, in the third century, came to be worshipped as a demigod (Flaubert 293–95, nn. 252–53, 264, 266). (LMP)

Reference:

Flaubert, Gustave. *La Tentation de saint Antoine*. Ed. Edouard Maynial. Paris: Garnier, 1968.

"Smarh" (1839). "Smarh" is a dream sequence in which Satan repeatedly tempts the hermit Smarh. It prefigures Flaubert's *La Tentation de saint Antoine* (versions in 1849, 1856, and 1874), but differs in its boastful prologue, spoken by the Devil, and its conclusion, in which the spirit of the grotesque, Yuk, robs both Satan and Smarh of the fallen female angel they wish to love. An allegorical figuration of Truth, she is smothered in Yuk's monstrous embrace. Much of the middle section consists of a philosophical dialogue concerning theodicy, which foreshadows Antoine's discussions with his disciple Hilarion (the Devil in disguise) in a late section of *La Tentation*. The motif of the inadequacy of language to render our intuitions and our aspirations is prominent (Unwin 49–51); philosophy is also seen as radically incapable to apprehend or to explain Creation or its opposite, the void, to say nothing of the infinite that contains both of them. Yuk, characterized above all by his ironic derision, illustrates the insight already expressed in the Rabelaisian "Funerailles du docteur Mathurin": one way of solving a problem is to laugh at it. (LMP)

References:

Bruneau, Jean. *Les Débuts littéraires de Gustave Flaubert, 1831–1845*. Paris: Colin, 1962.

Flaubert, Gustave. "Smarh." In Gustave Flaubert, *Early Writings*, ed. and trans. Robert Griffin. Lincoln: University of Nebraska Press, 1991. 204–75.

Hilliard, Aouicha. "Le Rythme de 'Smarh': Deux modes contrastés du vœu de désintégration chez Gustave Flaubert." *Romanic Review* 77 (1986): 56–70.

Milner, Max. *Le Diable dans la littérature française de Cazotte à Baudelaire, 1772–1861*. 2 vols. Paris: Corti, 1960. 2: 213–35.

Unwin, Timothy. "Le sujet absolu: 'Smarh.' " In Timothy Unwin, *Art et infini: L'Œuvre de jeunesse de Gustave Flaubert*. Amsterdam: Rodopi, 1991. 49–62.

socialism. In Flaubert's day, socialism was associated primarily with the impractical utopian visions of an ideal community (according to Charles Fourier, Père Enfantin, Claude-Henri de Saint-Simon, and others), although the French revolutionary tradition, protofeminism, the quest to form an enduring republic rather than a monarchy, and the struggles for workers' rights and unionization also contributed to the loose congeries of ideas that constituted left-wing politics in the mid-nineteenth century. An organized French Socialist party was formed only in 1905, thanks to Jean Jaurès.

Flaubert delighted in satirizing the authoritarian, regimenting tendencies of this supposedly liberal movement, although he equally deplored the brutal repression employed by the conservative forces of the day and the bourgeois worship of money and property. His scathing political comments appear most memorably in *L'Education sentimentale* (1869 version), the play *Le Candidat*, and *Bouvard et Pécuchet*. In the first, Old Roque and Sénécal (a tag name evoking the Stoic, ancient Roman virtues of Seneca) each shoot an unarmed, nonthreatening man point-blank and kill him. Flaubert's dry mockery of the conservatives and liberals alike occurs pungently in part 3, chapter 2 of *L'Education*: "Then [in reaction to the alarming establishment of the Second French Republic by the revolution of 1848], [the principle of the sanctity of private] Property rose in people's esteem to the level of Religion, and was confused with God. The attacks on this ideal seemed sacrilegious, almost as savage as cannibalism." On the other hand, the procuress La Vatnaz becomes a rabid propagandist seeking revenge for her lowly social status: "The liberation of the proletariat, according to her, could be achieved only by liberating women. She wanted all jobs to be open to women . . . that wet nurses and midwives be salaried state employees . . . that there be special presses for women, a technical high school for women, a national guard for women, everything for women!" In 1848 or 1869, these commonsense ideas seemed utterly mad to Flaubert and his contemporaries.

Similarly, chapter 6 in *Bouvard et Pécuchet* exposes the absurdities of the opposite extreme views of divine-right monarchy and of the sovereignty of the people. Flaubert rightly observes that left-wing systems proposed by Jean-Jacques Rousseau's *Social Contract* and by Charles Fourier's utopianism are both tyrannical and archconservative at bottom. Like Flaubert, his title characters become disgusted with politics and lose all desire to seek public office. The Prussian invasion of 1870 reignited Flaubert's patriotism (he even volunteered briefly for the National Guard), but he still could find no compatible political party. (LMP)

References:

Bart, Benjamin F. *Flaubert*. Syracuse: Syracuse University Press, 1967.

Carlut, Charles. *La Correspondance de Flaubert: Etude et répertoire critique*. Columbus: Ohio State University Press, 1968. 641–46.

Levin, Harry. *Flaubert*. In Harry Levin, *The Gates of Horn: A Study of Five French Realists*. New York: Oxford University Press, 1963. 214–304.

Sartre, Jean-Paul. *L'Idiot de la famille*. 3 vols. Paris: Gallimard, 1971–72. Vol. 3.

Shroder, Maurice Z. "Gustave Flaubert: The Artist as Raging Saint." In Maurice Z. Shroder, *Icarus: The Image of the Artist in French Romanticism*. Cambridge: Harvard University Press, 1961. 151–80.

Spendius (*Sal*). Spendius combines the traits of Ulysses and Alcibiades (Thibaudet 141) and of a decadent Ulysses, representative of the cunning mind (Brombert 111). As a Greek, he is considered the genius of the mercenaries' army, the man who triggers action, the natural choice to mobilize the heterogeneous army, owing to his craftiness and guile, his shrewdness, and his propensity for intrigue (Thibaudet 141). In this, he mimes his former master,

Hamilcar, whose slave he had become before being liberated by the mercenaries at the banquet. The paradigm of master and slave dominates his behavior (Ginsburg 120). A political opportunist, he is quick to seize the significance of the mercenaries' revolt (Culler 213–14). First he tempts the soldiers to commit a sacrilegious act by demanding to drink from the sacred goblets of the Carthaginian Sacred Legion, an act that is foiled by the persuasive handling of the mercenaries by the Punic commander Giscon, acting in Hamilcar's stead. Later he tempts Mâtho with the immediate conquest of Carthage as they look down on the city (Green 10–11). No longer Hamilcar's slave, he wishes to become Mâtho's and in turn purchases his own slave as soon as he is in a position to do so (Ginsburg 120). Thus he is represented as a social climber in his intertextual relationship with both Stendhal's hero, Julien Sorel, and Balzac's Rastignac (Mullen Hohl 10–11) as he assumes his master's colonial ambitions.

Spendius is also the master translator or mistranslator (Mullen Hohl 11, 13; Ginsburg 122–24). It is he who first informs the reader of the Greek equivalents of Eschmoûn, that is, Esculape/Asclepius, as he holds aloft a cantharus or vase consecrated to Bacchus/Dionysius, linked to the Adonis myth by his love for Adonis's, daughter, Beroë (*New Larousse* 159). Although he is depicted as believing uniquely in the oracle, Asclepius, god of medicine and healing, is the only god to whom Spendius prays, and he will be depicted both in terms of the god's snake sign as he penetrates Tanit's temple and his capacity to heal (Mullen Hohl 62, 69). It is precisely his disregard for the religious beliefs of others that enables him to lead Mâtho to steal the zaïmph (the sacred veil) in Tanit's temple, since he rightly reckons that although it may not benefit the mercenaries, its absence will demoralize the Carthaginians. In this way, he lives out both sides of his genealogy, using the persuasive powers inherited from his father, a Greek rhetorician, and perpetuating his Campanian mother's profession of prostitution, thus in turn enslaving women.

During the war, Spendius alternates between horrific cowardice and bombast, mirroring the suffete Hannon's behavior. Eventually, as one of the mercenaries' ambassadors at the end of the war, he trembles slavelike before Hamilcar, ready to do his every bidding. Outmaneuvered by the master, he ends up on the cross like Hannon, the Carthaginian commander. Unlike Hannon, however, but like Julien Sorel, this is his finest moment, since the certainty of everlasting emancipation confers on him a strange courage, enabling him to scorn life and die with dignity in the stoic manner so admired by Flaubert. (AMH)

References:

Brombert, Victor. *The Novels of Flaubert: A Study of Themes and Techniques*. Princeton: Princeton University Press, 1966.

Culler, Jonathan. *Flaubert: The Uses of Uncertainty*. 1974. Rev. ed. Ithaca, New York: Cornell University Press, 1985.

Flaubert, Gustave. In Gustave Flaubert, *Salammbô. Œuvres*, ed. Maurice Nadeau. 2 vols. Paris: Gallimard, 1951–52. Vol. 1.

Ginsburg, Michal Peled. *Flaubert Writing*. Stanford: Stanford University Press, 1986.
Green, Anne. *Flaubert and the Historical Novel*: Salammbô *Reassessed*. Cambridge: Cambridge University Press, 1982.
Mullen Hohl, Anne. *Exoticism in* Salammbô: *The Languages of Myth, Religion, and War*. Birmingham, AL: Summa, 1995.
New Larousse Encyclopedia of Mythology. 1959. Hong Kong: Toppan for Hamlyn, 1968.
Thibaudet, Albert. *Gustave Flaubert*. Rev. ed. Paris: Gallimard, 1963; Saint-Armand (Cher): S.E.P.C., 1992 (1922).

Sphinx and **Chimera** (*TSA*, part 7). The Sphinx at Thebes had the head and breasts of a woman, the body of a bull or dog, the claws of a lion, the tail of a dragon, and the wings of a bird. As the symbolic representation of an enigma, the Sphinx was thought to guard an ultimate meaning that must remain forever beyond man's reach. Esoteric tradition has it that the Gizeh Sphinx synthesizes all the science of the past, embracing and unifying the essence of both heaven and earth and, as well, the four elements. In Flaubert's mischievous hands, the Sphinx claims to have thought so much that it has nothing left to say. The Chimera, with the head of the lion, the body of a goat, and the tail of a dragon, snorts fire. Said to be a complex symbol of creations of the imagination, it destroys those who submit to it. Kitty Mrosovsky calls attention to two of Flaubert's notes: "The Sphinx and the Chimera outline, contain every order of Nature," and "The Chimera is the appearance [*l'aspect*] and the Sphinx, the substance [*le fond*]." She suggests that the monstrous beings dramatize a contrast between the Chimera's rapid movement and the Sphinx's "absorbed immobility." "Each creature . . . suffers, the Sphinx from the aridity of its stillness, the Chimera from the emptiness of its innovations." It seems possible that the pair indicate that the ultimate answer of mankind's quest for absolute knowledge is unknowable. Because the Idea and Matter cannot embrace, the two monsters that represent these abstractions cannot mate and are thus sterile. (AHP)

References:

Chevalier, Jean, and Alain Gheerbrant. *Dictionnaire des symboles: Mythes, rêves, coutumes, gestes, formes, figures, couleurs, nombres*. Paris: Laffont, 1969.
Mrosovsky, Kitty, ed. "Introduction." In Gustave Flaubert, *The Temptation of Saint Anthony*. Ithaca: Cornell University Press, 1981. 45–48.

Spinoza, Baruch (1632–77). It remains debatable whether the seventeenth-century Dutch philosopher Baruch Spinoza directly influenced the writings and beliefs of Flaubert or whether he simply reinforced Flaubert's belief in pantheism, of which Spinoza is considered one of the greatest proponents in Western thought. Spinoza's influence, along with that of German philosophers and writers, was strongly felt by the French romantics in both direct and mediated forms. Flaubert's first reading of Spinoza late in 1843 postdates his avowed fascination with pantheism in 1840. From 1840 on, the Norman writer firmly believed in a unified universe whose effects were completely determined. He expresses these sentiments in the first *Education Sentimentale* (1845) through Jules, the protagonist, who endorses a pantheistic or crudely Spinozistic view. Influenced by Alfred Le Poittevin, in 1843 Flaubert began his readings of Spinoza with the Latin version of the *Ethics*, from which he derived much of his aesthetics; he discovered the *Theologico-Political Treatise* only in 1870. Before his death, Flaubert read much of Spinoza's oeuvre three times. Spinoza gave Flaubert intellectual support for a position counter to that of the spiritualists. The spiritualists, supported by church and university, held a dualist conception of the world, as opposed to the monist perspective of the pantheists. Like Spinoza, Flaubert believed that "good" and "evil" were only relative terms. Flaubert transferred Spinoza's depiction of the thinker to the artist whose task is to re-create, in calm isolation, the harmony of the universe. Furthermore, the artist, like Spinoza's God, must be impassive and impersonal vis-à-vis his creation. While Bouvard and Pécuchet encounter difficulties attempting to adopt Spinoza's lessons, their efforts point ironically to the complex relationship between the novelist and the philosopher. (EA)

References:

Brown, Andrew. " 'Un assez vague spinozisme': Flaubert and Spinoza." *Modern Language Review* 91 (1996): 848–65.

Bruneau, Jean. *Les Débuts littéraires de Gustave Flaubert, 1831–1845*. Paris: Colin, 1962 (esp. 442–54).

Gyergyai, Albert. "Flaubert et Spinoza." *Les Amis de Flaubert* 39 (1971): 11–22.

"La Spirale." Flaubert planned "La Spirale" in 1852 or 1853 (perhaps in 1860 or 1861) but never wrote it. Most important, it was to deal with epilepsy, almost certainly the disorder from which Flaubert suffered, and the hallucinations that the sickness causes. The imagination is a drug for the mad protagonist. He enters the madhouse with relief, for there he can enjoy a dream more vivid and real than life. Flaubert's notes indicate that the work was also to be a historical piece that included material from the "fabulous Orient" and thus would reflect many of the interests that underlay *La Tentation de saint Antoine*. (AHP)

References:

Bruneau, Jean. *Les Débuts littéraires de Gustave Flaubert, 1831–1845*. Paris: Colin, 1962.

Fischer, E. W. "Une trouvaille." *Table Ronde* 124 (1958): 96–124.

Flaubert, Gustave. *Le Rêve et la vie: A Theatrical Experiment by Flaubert*, ed. Katherine S. Kovács. Lexington, KY: French Forum, 1981. E. W. Fischer's transcription of "La Spirale" is given in the Appendix.

Staël, Germaine de (née Necker, 1766–1817). Flaubert visited Switzerland in 1845. There he saw a portrait of Madame de Staël and studied it carefully. His detailed description of this portrait is given in *Par les champs et par les grèves* (1847). He also wrote down some thoughts concerning her ideas and examples of her romanticism, which he suspected of being less sincere than she claimed it to be. He admired Madame de Staël for her intellect and considered her, like George Sand and Madame de Sévigné, to be both male and female: a masculine brain in a female body. (SM)

Reference:

Flaubert, Gustave, and Maxime Du Camp. *Par les champs et par les grèves*. Ed. Adrianne J. Tooke. Geneva: Droz, 1987.

Stein, Gertrude (1874–1946). Gertrude Stein lived in Paris for much of the time after 1903, except during the two world wars. She studied Flaubert's letters. In "A Transatlantic Interview, 1946," she declared that "everything I have done has been influenced by Flaubert and Cézanne, and this gives me a new feeling about composition" (cited in Hoffman 140). In *The Autobiography of Alice B. Toklas*, she claims to have begun her novel *Three Lives* (1909), her first book, by attempting a translation of Flaubert's *Trois Contes* while sitting beneath Cézanne's portrait of his wife, which she owned. Although in this work she emphasizes character portraiture relatively more than does Flaubert, there are striking similarities between Stein's "The Good Anna" and "The Gentle Lena" and Flaubert's "Un cœur simple" (1877). Inspired by the childlike servant girls who worked for her while she was a medical student at Johns Hopkins University, Stein uses the same type of naïve protagonist as did Flaubert, a similar plot, and even a parrot. Stein's treatment of the plot is more starkly modern, however; Anna's world has less imagination than does Félicité's. More generally, Stein is one of the writers who drew upon Flaubert's pessimistic model of the modern love story. In *L'Education sentimentale* (1869), the main protagonists never really know each other. Stein continues this traditional depiction of incommunicability in her work. She, like Flaubert, is obsessed with perfecting her style and discovering *le mot juste*. (SM/LMP)

References:

Hoffman, Michael J. *Gertrude Stein*. Boston: Twayne, 1976.
Johnston, Georgia. "Reading Anna Backwards: Gertrude Stein Writing Modernism out of the Nineteenth Century." *Studies in the Literary Imagination* 25.2 (1992): 31–37.
Moers, Ellen. *Literary Women*. New York: Oxford University Press, 1985 (1976).
Stein, William Bysshe. "Madame Bovary and Cupid Unmasked." *Sewanee Review* 73 (1965): 197–209.

Sternheim, Carl (1878–1942). Carl Sternheim's admiration for Flaubert led him to suppress personal narration in his novellas. Primarily a dramatist, he adapted Flaubert's play *Le Candidat*, a satire of political campaigns, as *Der Kandidat*, and it was staged in Vienna in 1915. His ex-wife's memories of their twenty years together, from 1907 to 1927, provide a valuable source of anecdotes about Sternheim's interest in Flaubert. (LMP)

References:

Sternheim, Thea. *Erinnerungen*. Ed. Helmtrud Mauser and Traute Hensch. Freiburg: Kore, 1995 (1930).

Williams, Rhys W. "Carl Sternheim's Debt to Flaubert: Aspects of a Literary Relationship." *Arcadia* 15 (1980): 149–63.

style. *See* stylistic studies.

style indirect libre. *See* free indirect style.

stylistic studies. Flaubert has long been considered a master of French prose style. His struggles to find the appropriate expression ("les affres du style" or the torments of style) are legendary, accounting for the long gestation time of his novels (about five years each for *Madame Bovary, Salammbô*, and *L'Education sentimentale*). Emile Zola recounted a conversation between Flaubert and Ivan Turgenev in which the Russian writer asked Flaubert why he felt that Prosper Mérimée was a poor writer. Flaubert read a page from "Colomba," finding fault with every line—syllables whose sounds clashed, clichés, illogical punctuation, trite sentence endings, and so forth. Turgenev was amazed, contending that no writer had ever paid that close attention to style. But Flaubert did, and studies of his style form an essential part of Flaubert criticism, although they are necessarily closed to those with an imperfect knowledge of French.

One of the earliest critics to study Flaubert's style was Ferdinand Brunetière, whose 1880 article in the *Revue des deux mondes* perceptively examined a number of procedures that would continue to interest critics. These included the use of light to highlight objects; the representation of feelings by means of sensations; the "poetic" use of the imperfect tense; the "immobilization" of a character while events of his or her life are recounted; the use of the tableau and the short, striking conclusion to a sentence.

Flaubert's innovations in narrative point of view have attracted a great deal of attention. Discussions of point of view involve the ways in which the actions, feelings, sensations, impressions, thoughts, and speech of fictional characters are communicated to the reader. Earlier authors, for example, Balzac, generally created an omniscient narrator who reported on a character's thoughts, actions, and so on from a global, godlike stance. Flaubert used shifting points of view, sometimes employing an omniscient narrator, sometimes presenting events from the restricted vantage point of a character in the novel, or sometimes from that of an anonymous witness. In Flaubert's writing, there are many examples of the presentation of an event from a restricted point of view, such as the following description of the arrival of the wedding guests in *Madame Bovary*: "De temps à autre, on entendait des coups de fouet derrière la haie; bientôt la barrière s'ouvrait: c'était une carriole qui entrait" (From time to time was heard the crack of a whip behind the hedge; soon the gate would open: it was a carriage entering the yard) (*Œuvres* 1:314). The order of presentation of details parallels the temporal sequence of their perception by a presumed observer, an "iconic" or "impressionistic" technique. Other passages present events as experienced by one of the characters: "Emma, de loin, l' [Léon] entendait venir; elle se penchait en écoutant; et le jeune homme glissait derrière le rideau" (Emma heard Leon approach from afar; she leaned over, listening; and the young man slid by on the other side of the curtain) (*Œuvres* 1:379). The verb "glissait" represents Emma's perception as Léon passes through her field of vision on the other side of the window.

The exposition of *Madame Bovary* furnishes a longer example and contrasts with the beginning of Balzac's novels. The first word of Flaubert's novel is "nous," representing an anonymous witness to Charles Bovary's first day in school. The reader perceives what the witness perceives, and Charles's naïveté and shyness are communicated through the description of external characteristics: dress and actions. Occasionally the narrative voice intervenes, as in the description of Charles's cap, which is termed "une de ces pauvres choses, enfin, dont la laideur muette a des profondeurs d'expression comme le visage d'un imbécile" (one of those pitiful things of which the mute ugliness is as profoundly expressive as the face of an imbecile) (*Œuvres* 1:294), or in the summary of the early years of the Bovary family that occurs somewhat later. The pronoun "nous" disappears shortly thereafter, but the technique of restricted point of view continues, shifting to Charles's and eventually to Emma's viewpoint.

When Charles enters the Bertaux farm for the first time, the reader sees Emma through Charles's eyes: "Une jeune femme, en robe de mérinos bleu garnie de trois volants" (A young woman, in a blue merino dress with three flounces) (*Œuvres* 1:304). Charles's perception of Emma is fragmentary and incomplete because of the weak morning light, the darkened kitchen, or, in a later scene, the light filtered through Emma's parasol. In like fashion, Emma's vision, too, is often blurred—Flaubert regularly places her in situations of insufficient light, even violating the principle of verisimilitude (e.g., the horseback ride of Rodolphe and Emma, which lasts until early evening) to do so. Because of this technique of presenting fragments of reality, a technique that becomes more pronounced in works after *Madame Bovary*, the reader, like Charles or Emma, must construct Flaubert's fictional world. Reading becomes an active, rather than a passive, activity.

The imperfect tense often becomes an element in controlling point of view, partly through its use in *style indirect libre* (free indirect style). Flaubert also uses the imperfect tense to represent the immediacy of an event, or to present a scene, or to render the impressions of a character. In "Un cœur simple," Félicité, Madame Aubain, and the latter's children are chased by a bull as they cross a field: "Il [le taureau] avança vers les deux femmes. . . . Ses sabots, comme des marteaux, battaient l'herbe de la prairie; voilà qu'il galopait maintenant!" (It [the bull] advanced toward the two women. . . . Its hooves were pounding the grass of the field like hammers; now he was galloping!) (*Œuvres* 2:597). Here the imperfect places the reader in front of the scene, as if in front of a film. Shortly thereafter Flaubert wrote: "Sa bave lui rejaillissait à la figure, une seconde de plus il l'éventrait" ([the bull's] drool spurted onto her face, a second more and he would have disemboweled her). In this case, one would expect the second verb to be in the conditional mode; the imperfect indicative suggests that Félicité had a close call.

Flaubert's descriptions have attracted the attention of numerous critics, initially because of their abundance, later because of their form and function (or lack thereof). Flaubert wrote to Charles-Augustin Sainte-Beuve, à propos of *Salammbô*, that all his descriptions serve a purpose, yet some modern critics have questioned the appropriateness of Flaubert's descriptions. Roland Barthes claimed that Flaubert's descriptions had no other purpose than to denote reality, to say, in effect, "We are the real." Jonathan Culler maintained that Flaubert's descriptions serve no purpose at all and that it is impossible to derive any meaning from them (Culler 15). Not all critics are convinced, contending that Flaubert's descriptions not only have a function, but contribute to the overall meaning of his works.

In his descriptions, Flaubert organizes space and utilizes light in striking ways, often following a well-defined pattern as he moves from element to element of an object, a technique that might be termed "vectorial." The description of Charles's cap proceeds from top to bottom, that of the wedding cake from bottom to top. Descriptions are often built up of geometric forms—ovals, circles, polygons, and diamonds in the case of Charles's cap; columns, squares, and spheres in the case of the wedding cake. The description of the procession of carriages along the Champs-Elysées in *L'Education sentimentale* (first mentioned by Brunetière 1880) is an outstanding example of Flaubert's use of light to highlight objects illuminated by the setting sun. Other examples in *Madame Bovary* are the description of the portrait gallery at the château de la Vaubyessard (part 1, chapter 8) and the description of the dining room as Emma enters.

The presence of irony in many of Flaubert's works has been the focus of much study. Because the point of view shifts frequently among the various characters and the omniscient narrator, and because Flaubert believed that the author should not intervene in his work, readers are often perplexed as to how certain passages are to be read and whether Flaubert exhibits sympathy or disdain for his characters. When Charles and Emma are discussing whether she should accept Rodolphe's invitation to go horseback riding for her health, she at first demurs. She cannot go because she has no riding outfit. Charles says that she should buy one. The narrator dryly tells us, "L'amazone la décida" (The riding outfit was decisive). When the outfit was ready, Charles wrote to Rodolphe that "que sa femme était à sa disposition, et qu'ils comptaient sur sa complaisance" (his wife was at his disposal, and that they were counting on his indulgence) (*Œuvres* 1:435). How much of the irony in these sentences is intended? How does the reader react to the self-centeredness of Emma and the blindness of Charles?

Flaubert read voraciously and regularly embedded in his texts popular expressions and citations from his reading. The intent of these embedded expressions is often ironic. The problem for the reader is to identify these citations and then to interpret them correctly. At times Flaubert used italics to maintain an ironic distance from certain expressions in the text that are not part of his active personal vocabulary. Yonville is linked to other towns by a road *de grande vicinalité* (bureaucratic jargon); Emma seeks the true meaning of words like *félicité, passion, ivresse* (romantic clichés); every evening Homais stops by to talk about what was *dans le journal* (a more formally correct expression would be *sur le journal*—and Flaubert's contempt for journalistic writing is well known). Other distancing techniques are used, as in the narrator's summary of Emma's reading in the convent: "Ce n'étaient qu'amours, amants, amantes, dames persécutées s'évanouissant dans des pavillons solitaires, postillons qu'on tue à tous les relais, chevaux qu'on crève à toutes les pages, forêts sombres, troubles du cœur, serments, sanglots, larmes et baisers, nacelles au clair de lune, rossignols dans les bosquets, *messieurs* braves comme des lions, doux comme des agneaux, vertueux comme on ne l'est pas, toujours bien mis, et qui pleurent comme des urnes" (There was nothing but love, lovers, persecuted ladies fainting in solitary pavilions, postilions killed at every relay station, horses ridden to death on every page, dark forests, troubled hearts, sacred promises, sobs, tears and kisses, boats in the moonlight, nightingales in the bushes, gentlemen as brave as lions, as meek as lambs, virtuous like no one you have ever seen, always well dressed, and who cry like pitchers) (*Œuvres* 1:324–325). The restricting expression "Ce n'étaient que," the list of nominal expressions, the obvious clichés and exaggerations, and the sarcastic, dismissive brevity with which each item is mentioned—all converge to connote an ironic point of view.

Quotations embedded in the text and taken from the *Dictionnaire des idées reçues* (Dictionary of clichés, a collection of gaffes and stupid expressions that Flaubert had been collecting at least since 1850, and that was to be the nucleus of *Bouvard et Pécuchet*), are a veiled source of irony, made clear by consulting the *Dictionnaire*. For example, Flaubert calls attention to the fact that Homais wears a *bonnet grec* (a soft felt hat with a tassel): "Homais demanda la permission de garder son bonnet grec, de peur des coryzas" (Homais asked permission to keep his cap on, for fear of catching cold). The entry for *bonnet grec* in the *Dictionnaire* brings to light Homais's pretentiousness: "BONNET GREC. Indispensable à l'homme de cabinet—donne de la majesté au visage" (Indispensable for intellectuals—gives an air of majesty to one's face). In similar fashion, one can find in the *Dictionnaire* the romantic clichés exchanged by Emma and Léon in part 2, chapter 2, and many of the clichés of Homais, for example, in part 2, chapter 6.

Another type of irony occurs in the contrast between exalted or glorified names and the commonplace reality that they denote. The stagecoach *Hirondelle* (the swallow) is described as a yellow box mounted on huge wheels that prevent the travelers from seeing the countryside and that throw dirt up on their shoulders. Rodolphe Boulanger, who so impresses Emma with his elegance, is merely a prosaic Rudy Baker. His property, which he recently purchased, is called La Huchette (little box). Emma's second lover, Léon (lion) turns out to be pusillanimous. Finally, Emma herself is saddled with names of an ironic nature. Her maiden name Rouault suggests a wheel and the circular nature of her life. In order to escape the farm, she marries a Bovary (suggesting *bœuf*, ox). The meanings of names in *Madame Bovary* are not always out of character with their bearer, however. Hippolyte (tamer of horses) is a stable boy; Canivet (from *canif*, penknife) performs the amputation of Hippolyte's leg; Lheureux (fortunate) does very well financially, Binet (perhaps via aphaeresis from *bobiner*, to wind) has a lathe; Charles Bovary is somewhat bovine in nature, and so forth.

Attempts to derive meaning from descriptive details are varied and complex. Such details often acquire symbolic value through repetition with variations. Consider as one example the plaster statue of the priest in the Bovarys' garden in Tostes. The first mention of it (part 1, chapter 4) seems to be one of those unrecuperable details mentioned by Culler: "Tout au fond sous les sapinettes, un curé de plâtre lisait son bréviaire" (Way in the back under the spruces, a plaster priest was reading his breviary). The second mention (part 1, chapter 8) is even shorter as Emma paces to and fro in the garden after the ball at the Vaubyessard château. The third mention (part 1, chapter 9) occurs during the depth of Emma's depression in Tostes: "Dans les sapinettes, près de la haie, le curé en tricorne qui lisait son bréviaire avait perdu le pied droit et même le plâtre s'écaillant à la gelée, avait fait des gales blanches sur sa figure" (Among the spruces, near the hedge, the priest, wearing a three-cornered hat and reading his breviary, had lost his right foot, and the plaster, spalling from the frost, had created white scales on his face). In this case, the reader is naturally tempted to associate the deterioration of the statue with Emma's state of mind and even to see a possible hint of the future amputation of Hippolyte's leg. The last mention of the statue informs the reader that the plaster statue fell onto the pavement during the move to Yonville and broke into a thousand pieces, a possible foreshadowing of Emma's loss of moral restraint or of her own physical destruction, or both.

The repetition of details in different contexts, a technique adopted by Guy de Maupassant in *Une Vie*, can be a vehicle of meaning, as in the descriptions of the plaster statue, or of a statue of Cupid, or in the scene where Emma watches Charles leave on his rounds: "Elle se mettait à la fenêtre pour le voir partir; et elle restait accoudée sur le bord, entre deux pots de géraniums, vêtue de son peignoir, qui était lâche autour d'elle. Charles, dans la rue, bouclait ses éperons sur la borne; et elle continuait à lui parler d'en haut, tout en arrachant avec sa bouche quelque bride de fleur ou de verdure qu'elle soufflait vers lui, et qui voltigeant, se soutenant, faisant dans l'air des demi-cercles comme un oiseau, allait, avant de tomber, s'accrocher aux crins mal peignés de la vieille jument blanche, immobile à la porte" (She would station herself at the window to watch him leave, leaning on the windowsill, between two pots of geraniums, dressed in her peignoir, which hung loosely about her. Charles, down in the street, would buckle on his spurs with his foot on a stone; and she would continue talking to him from up above, while detaching with her mouth a bit of flower or greenery that she would blow down toward him and that would turn, floating in the air, describing semicircles like a bird, and catch on the unkempt mane of his white mare, standing immobile at the door) (*Œuvres* 1:321). The reader will perceive in this passage an ironic reenactment of Emma's readings in the convent.

A more complex pattern of meaning has been elaborated by Alfred Engstrom, who focuses on possible suggestions of the theme of fate, a romantic cliché (*fatalité*) that occurs in the text in Rodolphe's farewell letter to Emma (part 2, chapter 13) and in Charles's pathetic remark to Rodolphe at their last meeting (part 3, chapter 11). Details that would seem to have no purpose in the text, such as images of the spider or images of spinning, suggest the presence of the three Fates, Clotho, Lachesis, and Atropos, who preside over the life of the individual. Clotho spins the thread of life, Lachesis unwinds it, Atropos cuts it. According to Engstrom, a concentration of these symbols appears near the end of Emma's life; Madame Rolet is spinning flax during Emma's last visit to her hovel, and there is a spider spinning on the ceiling; Binet's lathe, whose sound is mentioned during critical periods of Emma's life, is prominently mentioned; and the blind man, whom many critics have identified with death, is present under Emma's window during her last moments.

Because Flaubert kept his notes, outlines, and drafts, many of which have been published, genetic studies have occupied an important place in Flaubert criticism, especially in recent years. These studies show that Flaubert would begin a work by setting onto paper brief notations of characters and scenes, along with pithy summaries of character, gradually expanding these notes in successive versions until he had several pages of narrative. He would then proceed to the next scene or section of narrative. To reach the final version of a text, Flaubert would take out many precise details, sometimes eliminating completely polished paragraphs, such that the final text became more ambiguous than the earlier versions. The reader can follow this process for *Madame Bovary* by consulting the edition with variants compiled by Jean Pommier and Gabrielle Leleu. (EFG).

See also cliché; descriptions; focalization; free indirect style; *le gueuloir*; image and metaphor; indeterminacy; irony; narrator; repetition; tableau.

References:

Barthes, Roland. *Writing Degree Zero*. Trans. Annette Lavers and Colin Smith. New York: Noonday, 1967.

Brunetière, Ferdinand. "Le naturalisme français: Etude sur Gustave Flaubert." *Revue des Deux Mondes*, 1880: 135–95. Rpr. in Ferdinand Brunetière, *Le Roman naturaliste*. Paris: Calmann Lévy, [1883] 1896.

Culler, Jonathan. *Flaubert: The Uses of Uncertainty*. 1974. Rev. ed. Ithaca: Cornell University Press, 1985.
Debray-Genette, Raymonde. *Métamorphoses du récit*. Paris: Seuil, 1988.
Engstrom, Alfred. "Echoes in the Dark Corridor: Flaubert's Vision of Life and Death in *Madame Bovary*." In Alfred Engstrom, *Darkness and Light*. University, MS: Romance Monographs, 1975. 35–58.
Flaubert, Gustave. "Lettre à Sainte-Beuve." In Gustave Flaubert, *Œuvres*. 2 vols. Ed. Albert Thibaudet and René Dumesnil. Paris: Gallimard, 1951–52. 1:997–1005.
———. *Madame Bovary: Nouvelle Version, précédée de scénarios inédits*. Ed. Jean Pommier and Gabrielle Leleu. Paris: Corti, 1949.
———. *Œuvres*. 2 vols. Ed. Albert Thibaudet and René Dumesnil. Paris: Gallimard, 1951–52.
Gothot-Mersch, Claudine. *La Genèse de* Madame Bovary. Geneva: Slatkine, 1980 (1966).
Hamon, Philippe. *Introduction à l'analyse du descriptif*. Paris: Hachette, 1981.
Houston, John Porter. "Flaubert." In John Porter Houston, *The Traditions of French Prose Style: A Rhetorical Study*. Baton Rouge: Louisiana State University Press, 1981. 204–31.
Le Calvez, Eric. *Flaubert topographe*: L'Education sentimentale. *Essai de poétique génétique*. Amsterdam: Rodopi, 1997.
Ramazani, Vaheed. *The Free Indirect Mode: Flaubert and the Poetics of Irony*. Charlottesville: University Press of Virginia, 1988.
Rousset, Jean. *Forme et signification*. Paris: Corti, 1962.
Zola, Emile. *Les Romanciers naturalistes*. Paris: Fasquelle, 1881. 125–30.

suicide. The major index of the difference between the realistic and the idealistic strands in nineteenth-century French literature—if not in all literature—is the motif of suicide. Idealistic characters hold certain values dearer than their life (cf. Rousseau's motto "vitam impendere vero," to sacrifice life for the truth), and whether in exaltation or despair, willingly commit suicide (or allow themselves to die) in order to affirm or realize these values. This attitude exemplifies the temporal sublime, the choice of a short, glorious life over a long, obscure one, as Achilles chose in Homer's *Iliad*. Nearly all the protagonists of Victor Hugo's major works exemplify this strategy, as does the world-weary title character in Villiers de l'Isle-Adam's famous decadent play *Axël*: "Live? The servants can do that for us."

That the character who commits suicide in Flaubert's early tale "Quidquid volueris" is a grotesque ape-man already suggests some dissociation from this idealistic attitude. The horrible suffering, terrified death, and physical decomposition of Emma Bovary, who had imagined suicide as a romantic swooning away before she took poison, definitively debunks the sublime attitude toward suicide. Emma's death marks Flaubert's embrace of realism, which contrasts with the hybrid of romanticism and realism found in the novels and the noble deaths of some protagonists in Balzac and Stendhal. The final illness and death of Balzac's Old Goriot, however, although involuntary, anticipates such uncompromising realism, exposing the cause the hero dies for as a delusion. (LMP)

References:

Chambers, Ross. "On the Suicidal Style in Modern Literature (Goethe, Nerval, Flaubert)." *Cincinnati Romance Review* 6 (1987): 9–41.

Jasin, Soledad Herrero Ducloux. "Sex and Suicide in *Madame Bovary*, *Anna Karenina*, *The Awakening*, and *The House of Mirth*." Ph.D. diss. Texas, 1996. Dissertation Abstracts International DA 9632483.

Mitchell, Giles. "Flaubert's Emma Bovary: Narcissism and Suicide." *American Imago* 44.2 (1987): 107–28.

Switzerland. Flaubert and his parents accompanied his sister Caroline and her husband, Emile Hamard, on their honeymoon to Italy and Switzerland in 1845. Flaubert admired Switzerland's landscape and enjoyed visiting the haunts of his literary predecessors. Although the house of J-J. Rousseau's protectress, Mme de Warens, had disappeared, Flaubert described the setting and meditated on Rousseau in Vevey and Geneva (*Notes de voyages* 1:52 and 55). He also visited and described Mme de Staël's castle.

In July 1874, when Flaubert's nervous disorder required several weeks of relaxation at Kaltbad-Righi, he was bored beyond measure. He now claimed that nature moved him less than art (letter to Ivan Turgenev, July 2, 1874, *Corr.* 7: 158) and that only a geologist or botanist could enjoy himself in Switzerland (letter to Princess Mathilde, July 10, 1874, *Corr.* 7: 166). (JWA)

References:

Claudon, Francis. "A propos des voyages de Flaubert: Le *Voyage en Italie et en Suisse* (1845)." In *Flaubert et Maupassant: Ecrivains normands*. Paris: Presses Universitaires de France, 1981. 91–109.

Flaubert, Gustave. *Correspondance*. 9 vols. Ed. Caroline Franklin-Grout. Paris: Conard, 1926–33.

———. *Notes de Voyages*. In Maurice Nadeau, ed., Gustave Flaubert, *Œuvres complètes*. 18 vols. Lausanne: Editions Recontre, 1964. Vols. 1–2.

T

tableau. A tableau is a set piece. This technique of composition, much used by Flaubert and later by naturalist writers, consists of an apparent slowing down of the forward movement of narrated events and a concomitant accumulation of details. In *Madame Bovary*, there are four tableaux: the wedding scene, the ball at the Vaubyessard château, the *comices agricoles*, and the opera. (EFG)

See also comices agricoles; opera scene.

Taine, Hippolyte (1828–93). A critic, historian, and philosopher, Hippolyte Taine is best known for his deterministic view that "la race, le milieu, et le moment" (heredity, society, and the age in which one lives) allow one to explain both artistic creations and historical events. Flaubert admired him for his sure judgment and for his enthusiasm for literature, although Flaubert himself gave relatively less weight to tradition and more to the individual talent. The two men exchanged information on the role of pathological hallucinations—such as those sometimes experienced in epilepsy, a disorder from which Flaubert suffered—in the artistic imagination. Taine eagerly questioned Flaubert to learn how his imagination functioned.

When *L'Education sentimentale* (1869) appeared, Taine wondered why none of the characters had any distinguished abilities or redeeming features. Later, however, he admired the rendering of the hallucinations in *La Tentation de saint Antoine* (1874) and Flaubert's evocation of ancient Roman and Jewish culture in "Hérodias" (1877). Taine became a regular guest at Flaubert's Sunday-afternoon salon in Paris in the 1870s. Worried about Flaubert's financial straits in 1878–79, he and Ivan Turgenev took the lead in trying to have Flaubert appointed to the sinecure of librarian at the Bibliothèque Mazarine. (LMP)

Reference:

Bart, Benjamin F. *Flaubert*. Syracuse: Syracuse University Press, 1967.

Tanit (*Sal*). Tanit, the moon goddess, her sacred veil, the zaïmph, and Salammbô are a poetic rendering of a threefold reality, similar to the notion of antiquity concerning the three faces of Diana (Thibaudet 138). According to the logic of the Carthaginian system of the sacred, the gods tend to merge with their statues (Backès 126), an interpretation that sheds new light on the blending of Salammbô's clothing with her body when Mâtho identifies her with both Tanit and the veil, and on her merging with Tanit on her wedding day. Metonym of the goddess, the sacred veil derives its power from her divinity. It is both the exemplary object signifying strangeness (Frier-Wantiez 111) and a narrative cursor that generates the erotic mythical and political axes of the novel and is always present at high points of transformation in the text (Neefs 238–39). The zaïmph's method of functioning, however, is negative, entailing deprivation and wear and tear (Neefs 230). That is, it functions like Balzac's "peau de chagrin" (a magical animal skin that represents the owner's life and shrinks every time one of his wishes is granted) and has a direct intratextual relationship with "Hérodias."

The goddess of fertility, Tanit is also a force for death and destruction. Her temple is constructed in the image of her body, and the frescoes on the temple walls are the pictorial version of Schahabarim's cosmogony, representing Tanit as the source of all forms of life and, specifically, of monsters. The veil, multiple and mutilated, is the functional equivalent of the frescoes as the locus of creation. According to Schahabarim's cosmogony, the initial form of life was "Matter." Thus Tanit is "Matter" and as such constitutes an intratextual allusion to Antoine's delirious delivery at the close of *La Tentation de saint Antoine*, in which his desire to penetrate matter corresponds to Mâtho's desire to penetrate Tanit, while Antoine's wish "to be matter" is equivalent to Mâtho's sense of being penetrated by Salammbô.

Salammbô's invocations represent Tanit as the Carthaginian Virgin Mother, among whose titles is Astarte, the moon goddess beloved of Adonis, and therefore the equivalent of Ishtar and her consort, Tammouz. Since Tanit under her land aspect is depicted as mother of snakes and of Eschmoûn, under his serpentine aspect as both her son and consort, the moon goddess is represented as having an incestuous relationship with the sun god. Moreover, as the monstrous mother of all monsters, Tanit must in some way be mother of Moloch (a god of the Ammonites and Phoenicians, represented by a man with the head of a bull, and to whom children were sacrificed by burning), whose hermaphrodism she shares. Most strikingly, Salammbô and both gods are represented in terms of the ancient theory of hysteria, that is, the upward displacement of the womb. The inherent sexual ambiguity in Tanit's representation provides a cover, or narrative veil, that obfuscates her identification in terms of the Roman Catholic doctrine of God's presence being everywhere, but specifically under the tabernacle/sacred veil. Salammbô's prayers transcode utterances from the Roman Catholic Litany to the Virgin and the Hail Mary, which commemorates the Annunciation, celebrating Mary's conception of Jesus. Similarly, Salammbô's greetings to her father transcode the Magnificat, which celebrates the conception of Christ by the Virgin Mother. (AMH)

References:

Backès, Jean-Louis. "Le Divin dans *Salammbô*." *Revue des lettres modernes* 1165–72 (1994): 115–34.

Frier-Wantiez, Martine. *Sémiotique du fantastique: Analyse textuelle de* Salammbô. Berne: Lang, 1979.

Ginsburg, Michal Peled. *Flaubert Writing*. Stanford: Stanford University Press, 1986.

Mullen Hohl, Anne. *Exoticism in* Salammbô: *The Languages of Myth, Religion, and War*. Birmingham, AL: Summa, 1995.

Neefs, Jacques. "Le Parcours du Zaïmph." In *La Production du sens chez Flaubert*. Paris: Union Générale d'Editions, 1975. 227–52.

Thibaudet, Albert. *Gustave Flaubert*. Rev. ed. Paris: Gallimard, 1963; Saint-Armand (Cher): S.E.P.C., 1992 [1922].

temptation (*TSA*). A temptation is an attraction, a lure, an enticement, or an inducement that makes someone want to do something. In traditional Catholic theology, there are three sources and three degrees of temptation. The sources are the world (materialism and corrupt social values that surround and influence us unless we retreat, as Saint Anthony did, into the desert), the flesh (our inescapable physical impulses and needs, which have afflicted us ever since the Fall of Adam and Eve), and the Devil (an active supernatural principle that seeks to undermine Creation and lead God's human creatures into damnation).

The first degree of temptation is the surprise of the senses, when we innocently notice an attractive forbidden object or when the idea of doing something sinful comes into our heads; even the most virtuous persons occasionally experience this form of temptation, and so did Christ (Matthew 4:1–11; Luke 4: 1–13). The traditional formula for representing resistance at this stage is the formula "Get thee behind me, Satan" (*Vade retro, Satanas*). Equivalents frequently occur in Antoine's speech in *La Tentation de saint Antoine*. The second is morbid delectation, when we dwell on a forbidden feeling, object, or act. For example, Antoine has withdrawn into an obscure, ascetic life, but he occasionally envies his brother monks who have remained in the world and who enjoy fame and comfort there. Christ was immune to morbid delectation, but much of the monologue and dialogue in *La Tentation de saint Antoine* is shaped by the saint's alternately yielding to and then resisting it. The more artful temptations of the Devil operate by presenting an innocent allurement (e.g., the visit of Hilarion, a former disciple, to the lonely Antoine), which then gradually becomes perverse (the irreverent, skeptical arguments used by Hilarion—the Devil in disguise—to undermine Antoine's faith in "that phantom you call [a personal] God"). The third is the consent of the will, meaning that we actively try to accomplish sinful acts or allow ourselves to utter sinful words. The "homme moyen sensuel" (the average sensual person) typically alternates, as did Emma

Bovary, between this stage and velleities of virtue. Antoine himself never falls so far.

In Flaubert's novel, the saint is tempted on a number of different levels: first by the seven deadly sins, then by the heresies of Arianism and Gnosticism that were widespread in his day, by philosophy (or "science") and by pantheism, and finally in the quintessential temptation of desiring to become one with God. Only after refusing these temptations is Antoine able to return to prayer. His atonement with God is signaled at the conclusion by the radiant apparition of Christ's face in the sun.

Traditional theology identifies two master forms of temptation, which are in essence the same experience seen from two different perspectives and representing two possible outcomes. *Tentatio subversionis* (subversion) is the Devil's attempt to trick us into committing acts—mortal sins—that will damn us irrevocably unless God grants us a portion of the supererogatory merit accumulated by the saints and through Christ's sacrifice. Literary examples, more common in the dour world of certain Protestantisms, are Matthew "Monk" Lewis's *The Monk*, Charles Williams's *Descent into Hell*, Thomas Mann's *Doctor Faustus*, or Cormac McCarthy's *Blood Meridian. Tentatio probationis* (trial, ordeal) is the temptation that God allows us to undergo ("permissive evil") in order to give us the opportunity to strengthen, refine, and purify our character and to merit the grace of salvation. Besides *La Tentation de saint Antoine*, some literary examples are the Book of Job, Goethe's *Faust*, C. S. Lewis's *The Screwtape Letters*, or Georges Bernanos's *Diary of a Country Priest*. Convincingly to describe the "higher" spiritual state achieved after temptation presents a difficult literary problem that is often solved by obliterating the protagonist's memories of his or her sins and tribulations. After destroying all Job's sons and daughters (Job 1:18–19), for example, God eventually gives him a new set of children (Job 42:13–15)—but wouldn't he miss the first ones? After seducing, impregnating, and abandoning Gretchen and being responsible for the deaths of herself and all her family, Goethe's Faust has his memories erased at the beginning of part 2 so that he can continue to function. Flaubert wisely avoids such issues by cutting *La Tentation* short at the ending and suggesting that Anthony's renewed ability to pray—his spiritual reunion with God—is a full and perfect resolution. (LMP)

References:

Allenspach, Max. *Gustave Flaubert*: La Tentation de saint Antoine, *eine literarästhetische Untersuchung*. Braunfels: Mehl, 1923.

Bem, Jeanne. *Désir et savoir dans l'œuvre de Flaubert: Etude de* La Tentation de saint Antoine. Neuchâtel: La Baconnière, 1979.

Butor, Michel. "La Spirale des sept péchés." In Michel Butor, *Répertoire IV*. Paris: Minuit, 1974. 209–35.

Jung, Carl Gustav. *Psychological Types; or The Psychology of Individuation*. London: Kegan Paul, 1946. 18–33, 70–75.

Porter, Laurence M. "Projection as Ego-Defense: Flaubert's *Tentation de saint Antoine*." In Laurence M. Porter, *The Literary Dream in French Romanticism*. Detroit: Wayne State University Press, 1979. 47–67.

Reik, Theodor. *Flaubert und seine* Versuchung des heiligen Antonius: *Ein Beitrag zur Künstlerpsychologie*. Minden: J. C. C. Bruns, 1912.

Tennant, Gertrude (née Collier, 1819–1918). Gertrude Tennant was the oldest daughter of a captain of the English Royal Navy who moved from England to France in 1823. She spoke excellent French, and knew much of Shakespeare by heart. She was twenty-three when she and Flaubert met in Trouville during the summer of 1842. At the time, Gertrude seemed to be in love with Flaubert, but he did not respond. Five years after their first encounter, she married Charles Tennant, to whom she eventually bore two daughters. In 1857, Flaubert sent her a copy of *Madame Bovary* in which he wrote "Souvenir d'une inaltérable affection." However, there are no records of letters exchanged between them until 1876, when Flaubert and Gertrude met again in Paris while he was writing "Un cœur simple" and longing for the days at Trouville. Gertrude became, to the mature Flaubert, an emblem of his youth. From that moment on, their friendship was nurtured through letters and sporadic visits. They even discussed the possibility of her doing illustrations for "Un cœur simple." Gertrude died in 1918, leaving behind three volumes of papers. The last and most important is "Memoir." She recounts in it the summer of 1842 at Trouville. "Memoir" was written to Flaubert's niece in 1884 and still remains a dependable source of information on Flaubert's character when he was twenty-one years old. (LF)

References:

Bart, Benjamin F. *Flaubert*. Syracuse; Syracuse University Press, 1967.

Spencer, P. "New Light on Flaubert's Youth." *French Studies* 7 (1954): 97–108.

La Tentation de saint Antoine (1874). While thousands of pages have been devoted to the novel *La Tentation de saint Antoine* by lovers and critics of Flaubert, there is little critical unanimity. We still cannot be sure we understand it. The author himself provides few clues to how readers should approach the work, much less to how to analyze and interpret it. Most of Flaubert's comments about the novel in his correspondence turn around his background reading and his difficulty in providing the creation with a framework that would tie it all together. Thanks to Flaubert's notes and the work of such major critics as Jean Seznec, we know a considerable amount about the sources and the genesis, but the novel itself continues to pose a conundrum.

As early as 1849, Flaubert finished a first version of *La Tentation* that he read to Louis Bouilhet and Maxime Du Camp. His two friends were firmly committed to the new emphasis on realism, and they did their best to exorcise from the nascent novelist what they considered his regrettable romanticism. They suggested that he learn to control his exuberance by writing something down-to-earth, such as a recent news item about a doctor's wife who after indulging in a series of foolish love affairs, poisoned herself. Flaubert followed their advice, but the exercise of writing *Madame Bovary* did not diminish his love for the fourth-century saint. We can tell from his manuscripts and letters that he revised *La Tentation* in 1856. But he was still not satisfied, perhaps because the fragments he tried out on the public were not welcomed, and he left the unpublished *Tentation* to turn to another idea, *L'Education sentimentale*, published in 1869. The final reworking of the *Tentation* manuscript was not published until 1874.

La Tentation de saint Antoine falls between genres. In terms of content, one could call it an "anatomy" in Northrop Frye's sense—an encyclopedic compendium of information, in this instance, involving the heresies of the early Christian period. In terms of form, it blends two genres. Extensively written in dialogue form, as though it were a play, it also includes long descriptions and monologues like those of a novel. It enhances the resemblance to a printed play by presenting descriptions (which might be termed "stage" directions) in smaller type than the speech, a technique that encourages the reader both to make and to maintain distinctions recognizing the traditional, theatrical distance between play and audience. Part 1 opens to a vivid setting of Saint Antoine's hut high on a cliff overlooking the Nile and the desert of the Thebaid, the area around Thebes. The saint is making mats near a cross. Finally, he speaks, but only to complain: "Another day! One more day gone!" (32). The "fountain of grace" that used to pour over him has gone dry, leaving him confused, bored, and forlorn. He remembers leaving home and pursuing sanctity. Eventually, he studied the Bible under Blind Didymus, a fourth-century teacher. Antoine then left for Colzim, where he indulged in the extreme penitence that led him to lose his fear of God, despite the biblical warning of Proverbs 9.10: "The fear of the Lord is the beginning of wisdom." Antoine continues to review his past, concentrating on the triumphs. When, for example, a group of anchorites had gathered around him, he was able to establish a practical rule for the group that helped control physical temptations while avoiding the spiritual excesses of the Gnostics and the rationalistic extremes of the philosophers.

There is no doubt that Antoine has lost the peace he once enjoyed and is now bitterly unhappy and filled with self-pity. When the shadows of the arms of his cross assume the shape of horns, we know that the hallucinations have begun. Antoine dreams of meat, grapes, women, money, authority, and the admiration of the masses. His old palm tree takes the shape of a woman leaning over the abyss. A parade of vertiginous images passes before his eyes until he collapses on his mat. The spiritually weak Antoine seems easy prey to sin and Satan.

Part 2 opens with the devil carrying the Seven Deadly Sins as he leans on the hut, while Antoine stretches out and begins to revel in his inactivity. The temptations come one by one: sloth, greed, anger, envy, pride. Although Antoine resists gluttony with a kick, he gives in to the other temptations. Even when he is so filled with self-disgust that he begins to lacerate himself, he finds erotic pleasure in the pain. This sensual surge prepares the arrival of the Queen of

Sheba, who offers him the wealth of nations and the indescribable pleasures of her bed. Only by crossing himself does he send her hopping on her way (her lameness reveals that she is really the Devil in disguise).

Part 3 introduces Hilarion, the most important incarnation of the Devil. At first he appears as a dwarfish but sturdy child who had once been the saint's disciple. He soon adopts the subversive role of logic and science, however, visibly incarnating the temptations and doubts of a rationalistic mind. Naturally, as one would expect of the Devil, he appeals to Antoine's pride, suggesting that he criticize his disciple (and future biographer) Athanasius's intelligence. As Antoine listens, the child grows, speaks more loudly, and points out, for instance, that if the Word of God is confirmed by miracles, there is a problem when we find miraculous works by patently pagan Egyptian sorcerers. Hilarion raises issues that other theologians had attempted to disprove and set aside. Antoine equivocates, unable to silence his former disciple, but soon ready to accept Hilarion's invitation to explore esoteric doctrines of angels, numbers, and metamorphoses. The disciple will serve as the master's guide.

Part 4 reveals Antoine tempted by the belief that only the spirit matters, and it is consequently dominated by the Arian and Gnostic heresies, spokespeople for which surround him. At the outset, Hilarion tempts the stumbling saint to seek knowledge, like one of the sect's visionaries. To believe that one can approach God and achieve salvation through spiritual illumination is heretical, but Antoine does not hesitate. The Gnostics claim that only the spirit matters manifests itself in two contrary ways: by "so many fleshly excesses and [by] spiritual aberrations." Antoine laughs at the Gnostics' absurdity, equivocates, throws himself back in dismay, weeps, fulminates, and then faints with horror, though he subsequently watches a group of martyrs indulge in an orgy with seeming equanimity. He begins to doubt all reality. Simon the Magician arrives to tempt him; he leaves only when Antoine wishes for Holy Water. Apollonius the Pythagorean tempts him to seek illumination, departing only when Antoine cries out to Jesus and throws himself at the foot of the cross.

Hilarion comes back in part 5, but he has grown considerably. Antoine is busy watching a parade "of idols from all nations and from all ages, made out of wood, metal, granite, feathers, sewn skins." At first he now seems safe. Why would he be tempted by mere material objects? But Hilarion is there to point out that the saint's God shares many traits with these pagan gods. He too demanded sacrifices, he too is fragmented. After all, though he is "one single person," he has three parts. Antoine watches various gods mutate, assuming a multitude of forms. Then he sees a man who claims to be a god that has come to save the world. After passing through a number of tests, he became the Buddha, who believes that he knows the essence of all things. Most important, he understands that all things will pass away. Then the gods begin to go into convulsions and die. More gods come. Antoine sadly thinks of the souls lost by hearkening to such gods, while Hilarion suggests that these divinities represent a truth that lies behind God the Father, and Antoine recites a garbled, abbreviated version of the Nicene Creed. Myriads of gods go by, tumbling one after another into a black pit. Suddenly a voice claiming to be the Hebrew Lord of Hosts comes from the darkness, but it too falls silent. All these deities have vanished except Hilarion, now transfigured as an archangel who says that he is really Science/Knowledge, though Antoine recognizes him as the Devil and is repelled. Still, the backsliding saint cannot tear his gaze from him, for he is curious to see him as he really is. He does not resist the invitation of the cloven-footed Devil, who throws him between his horns and carries him off to explore the universe.

In part 6, the Devil takes Antoine into space, inexorably showing him the predominance of illusion in human experience. No longer weighted down by his body, free of suffering, Antoine revels in how his intelligence seems to embrace the order of the universe while he struggles against the Devil's observations that question the omnipotence of God the Father. Antoine wonders about the purpose of the planets, and the Devil tells him that there is none. There is only an unlimited empty expanse. The thought frightens Antoine, and the Devil encourages his sense of helplessness. "You can never know the full expanse of the universe; consequently, you can never grasp its cause or have a just notion of God." The Devil then suggests that Antoine turn from God and worship him, cursing the "ghost" that he calls God, but the saint raises his eyes in an implicit prayer, and the Devil lets him go.

In the concluding part 7, Antoine takes stock. The result of his overweening desire to "unite myself with God!" he realizes, is that his "heart is dryer than a rock [while] it used to spill over with love." At this point, he considers suicide. An old woman appears before him to encourage him to do away with himself: "Do something," she says, "that makes you equal with God. Think about it! He made you; you will destroy his work freely, with your courage." Another woman, this one young and beautiful, arrives to invite him to a life overflowing with the pleasures of lust, wealth, and sloth. Slowly the women change to reveal their identities; the old woman increasingly resembles the skeleton of Death, while the young one's robe splits and reveals the body of lust personified. Antoine considers them as a debate ensues between two forms of the Devil's invitation: the spirit of fornication and that of destruction, both of which lead to death. He continues his search for an explanation of reality. The women give place to a new hallucination, the Sphinx, representing substance, and the Chimera, symbolizing fantasy. They attempt to couple and fail in the attempt. That imagination cannot form a permanent unity with substance is demonstrated in the subsequent pullulating monsters and, next, in several monstrous creations. Seznec has tracked down the sources of these monsters and concludes that they result from Flaubert's erudition rather than from his imagination. Their function seems, however, to show the amazing imaginative constructions produced by fantasy run wild, to illustrate that Antoine's desire for unity results only in teratological creations and frustration. After tracing the bizarre combinations to the sea, to plants, and to insects, Antoine recognizes the power of God in these multiple creations and humbly accepts the lowest position: "I want to . . . descend to the lowest level of matter—to be matter." As the sun comes up, he sees the image of Jesus imprinted in the solar disk, and he crosses himself, once again reunited with God and able to pray.

Contrary to the conclusions of critics who see the ending as a sign of the saint's insanity (Foucault), or of Flaubert's irresistible need to turn from reality to his neuroses and to give preference to nothingness (Sartre), or as another example of the saint's submission to desire and illusion (Butor), it seems clear that the last few paragraphs of *La Tentation de saint Antoine* leave an Antoine who has been freed of the ultimate temptation: he no longer wants to unite with God, a desire that he terms madness and that has brought him to the brink of suicide. He has awakened from the bizarre hallucinations that paraded by, Astomis, Nisnas, Blemmyes, Sciapodes, the Catoblépas, the Griffon—fabulous creatures from around the known world—and he turns to the reality of Creation, where the myriads of forms no longer frighten him. Delirious with joy, he wants to fuse with this Creation. Humbly recognizing his inability to understand an all-powerful, transcendent God, he submits, agreeing to be nothing but "matter." (Compare Job 42:6, "I abhor myself, and repent in dust and ashes.") As Antoine crosses himself in total submission, God is restored to him in the powerful, concluding image of a sun bearing the image of Christ. Only then is he able once again to return to prayer. (AHP)

This entry was adapted from "A Fourth Version of Flaubert's *Tentation de saint Antoine* (1869)," by Laurence M. Porter (*Nineteenth-Century French Studies* 4 [1975]: 53–66).

References:

Bem, Jeanne. *Désir et savoir dans l'œuvre de Flaubert: Etude de* La Tentation de saint Antoine. Neuchâtel: La Baconnière, 1979.

Butor, Michel. "La Spirale des sept péchés." In Michel Butor, *Répertoire IV*. Paris: Minuit, 1974. 209–35.

Carmody, Francis J. "Further Sources of *La Tentation de saint Antoine," Romanic Review* 49 (1958): 278–92.

Flaubert, Gustave. *La Tentation de saint Antoine*. Ed. Edouard Maynial. Paris: Garnier, 1968.

Foucault, Michel. "Fantasia of the Library." In Michel Foucault, *Language, Counter-Memory, Practice: Selected Essays and Interviews*, trans. Donald Bouchard. Ithaca: Cornell University Press, 1977. 87–109.

Frye, Northrup. *The Anatomy of Criticism*. Princeton, NJ: Princeton University Press, 1957.

Ginsburg, Michal Peled. *Flaubert Writing: A Study in Narrative Strategies*. Stanford: Stanford University Press, 1986.

Leal, R. B. "The Unity of Flaubert's *Tentation de saint Antoine." Modern Language Review* 85.2 (1990): 330–40.

Mrosovsky, Kitty, ed. "Introduction." In Gustave Flaubert, *The Temptation of Saint Anthony*. Ithaca: Cornell University Press, 1981. 3–56.

Olds, Marshall C. "Hallucination and Point of View in *La Tentation de saint Antoine." Nineteenth-Century French Studies* 17 (1989): 170–85.

Porter, Laurence M. "A Fourth Version of Flaubert's *Tentation de saint Antoine* (1869)." *Essays in Honor of Jean Seznec. Nineteenth-Century French Studies* 4 (1975): 53–66.

———. *The Literary Dream in French Romanticism: A Psychoanalytic Interpretation.* Detroit: Wayne State University Press, 1979. 47–67.

Sartre, Jean-Paul. *L'Idiot de la famille: Gustave Flaubert de 1821–1857.* 3 vols. Paris: Gallimard, 1971–72. 1:549–56.

Seznec, Jean. "Flaubert historien des hérésies, dans la *Tentation.*" *Romanic Review* 36 (1945): 200–21, 314–28.

———. *Nouvelles etudes sur* La Tentation de saint Antoine. London: Warburg Institute, University of London, 1949.

———. "Saint Antoine et les monstres." *PMLA* 58 (1943): 195–222.

———. *Les Sources de l'épisode des dieux dans* La Tentation de saint Antoine *(Première Version, 1849).* Paris: Vrin, 1940.

***La Tentation de saint Antoine,* versions** (1849, 1856, 1869, 1874). Whereas the two versions of Flaubert's *L'Education sentimentale* represent two radically different novels, *La Tentation de saint Antoine* occupied him throughout twenty-five years of his adult life. A comparison of the different versions therefore offers us a privileged insight into both the evolution and the continuity of Flaubert's imaginative world. In 1848–49, he composed an allegorical, picturesque, and broadly comic panorama of fourth-century Alexandria, a crossroads for religious beliefs, seen through the visions of the hermit-saint. Lively, substantial speeches were given to the saint's pet pig—the embodiment of the baser forms of *cupiditas* (lust and greed; compare the proverb "radix omnium malorum cupiditas," lust, greed, and envy are the root of all evil)—and to each of the Seven Deadly Sins; to Logic and to Science; and to the Three Theological Virtues (Faith, Hope, and Charity). When Flaubert had completed this version, he read it out loud to his best friends Louis Bouilhet and Maxime Du Camp. They had agreed to listen without interrupting him. The reading took four days, and when Flaubert had finished it, his dismayed friends, overwhelmed by the masses of static description and superfluous detail, urged him to burn the manuscript and never think of it again (if Du Camp's account is accurate). His long trip to the Middle East was in part therapy for this stunning disappointment.

Flaubert revised *La Tentation* in 1856. He reduced the text by half, nearly suppressed the pig, and eliminated many exuberantly obscene passages, but did not fundamentally alter the work. During the winter of 1856–57, he published the most striking episodes in the journal *L'Artiste* as a test of the public's reaction. These included the scenes involving Nebuchadnezzar and the Queen of Sheba; the courtesan; Apollonius of Tyana, the thaumaturge; the Sphinx and the Chimera; and the monsters. He also intended to publish the procession of the gods there. He obviously intended to publish the whole of *La Tentation* in 1857 (see Dumesnil and Demorest 171–73). Discouraged for various reasons, he again abandoned the project. He realized that the work was disorganized, and that a more coherent sense of the saint's personality would be needed to unify it.

Flaubert's correspondence shows him taking up *La Tentation* for a third time in June 1869, after he had published *L'Education sentimentale*. He said that the older versions would provide only some fragments. He nearly eliminated certain episodes that seemed digressive: those of the Sphinx and the Chimera, of certain pagan gods, and of the monsters. He also eliminated the strong personalities from history and legend who overshadowed Saint Antoine: Simon the Magician and Apollonius of Tyana. He sharply reduced in importance those allegorical figures such as the pig and the Three Theological Virtues whose presence risked submerging the depiction of the saint's individual personality beneath a conventionally medieval Christian, comic-epic narration of the unending struggle between Good and Evil. As he neared the end of his abridgment, however, Flaubert realized that he had gone too far in sacrificing material: he restored much of what had been provisionally deleted from the procession of the gods, as he was later to restore the major scenes concerning heretics.

During January through March 1870, he wrote of doing additional research in church history; in July and August of that year, he claimed to be rewriting the work completely; in April 1871, he discussed a possible scene (never introduced) in which weeping relatives would visit the graves of Christian martyrs by night, but end their lamentations with a sexual debauch. His work was interrupted in 1869 by the death of his best friend Louis Bouilhet, and in 1870–71 by the Franco-Prussian War, during which the invading troops occupied Flaubert's beloved suburban home, at Croisset. Moreover, angered at his longtime publisher Michel Lévy, he withheld his work from publication until his contract with Lévy expired.

When Flaubert returned to intensive work on *La Tentation* in 1871–72, he had discovered a unifying principle: the origins of Antoine's visions could be found in his memories from throughout his life. These sources were added to the physiological explanations of Antoine's visions provided in the earlier versions—hunger, thirst, dampness, moonlight, the morning erection. Once the coherence of the work had been assured by associating the hallucinations with events in Antoine's past experience, Flaubert could reintroduce the powerful episodes omitted or truncated in 1869. Simon and Apollonius now express, in extreme form, the saint's hubristic desires to be a miracle worker and to possess ultimate truth. The dying gods' despair reflects the saint's own despair at being unable to impose a structure on the universe through his rational and imaginative mental processes. The episode of the monsters, moved significantly to the end, imposes a more nearly personal, and characteristically ambivalent, interpretation on the ending of the work. On the one hand, the saint's final exclamation "to be matter!" betrays a defeat for the orthodox Catholic subjugated by an overwhelming experience of hylozoism. On the other hand, the Deity and matter are not incompatible. In 1874, Satan and his temptations depart before the vision of the monsters, and this vision is no longer separated from the final vision of Christ's face in the sun by an adversative "but." Antoine does not condemn himself after experiencing the vision of the monsters, as he had done after his earlier visions, for it was not a sin. The final version of the ending implicitly grants Antoine a wisdom shared with the pantheist Baruch Spinoza, whom Flaubert had called the most religious of men "because [his philosophical system] allowed only for God" (letter to Mme Roger des Genettes, November 1879, *Corr.* 8:327). He means that the spiritual is not what remains once the material has been taken away, by means of rationality or asceticism: the spiritual is anything in a right relationship to God. (LMP)

References:

Dumesnil, René, and Don-L. Demorest. "Bibliographie de Gustave Flaubert." *Bulletin du bibliophile et du bibliothécaire* 1938: 27–29, 135–38, 315–17, 408–13.

Flaubert, Gustave. *Œuvres complètes*. Paris: Conard, 1910–54. Vol. 17 (1924), Appendix. Reproduces NAF 23664 and 23665 (manuscripts).

France. Bibliothèque Nationale. Nouvelle Acquisitions Françaises 23664–23671 (manuscripts).

Porter, Laurence M. "A Fourth Version of Flaubert's *Tentation de saint Antoine* (1869)." In Benjamin F. Bart, ed., *Patterns of Inquiry: Essays in Honor of Jean Seznec. Nineteenth-Century French Studies* 4.1–2 (1975–76): 53–66.

Seznec, Jean. *Nouvelles Etudes sur* La Tentation de saint Antoine. London: Warburg Institute, 1949.

———. *Les Sources de l'épisode des Dieux dans* La Tentation de Saint Antoine. Paris: Vrin, 1940.

theater. Flaubert had a lifelong fascination with the theater. He was exposed to it early: Rouen had two active theaters. There, in 1840, he saw Rachel (pseud. of Elisa Félix), the greatest actress of her generation. Flaubert's parents also frequently took him to plays in Paris when they were passing through on their way to visit relatives.

Throughout Flaubert's life, he wrote scenarios to help him imagine living people enacting his stories. Flaubert refused, however, two offers to have *Madame Bovary* dramatized, in 1857 and 1858. He mistrusted transpositions from one literary genre to another.

In 1862–63, he and Louis Bouilhet spent eighteen months writing *Le Château de cœurs*, but he realized that the result was mediocre, and indeed, no one willing to produce it could be found. Once he had completed *L'Education sentimentale* in 1869, Flaubert rewrote his late beloved friend Louis Bouilhet's last work *Mademoiselle Aïssé*, a *féerie*, as well as *Le Château de cœurs*. The latter was again rejected by two producers. Flaubert finally persuaded the Odéon theater to produce *Mademoiselle Aïssé* in 1871, but the play failed miserably. During these attempts, Flaubert found a manuscript of a five-act play, *Le Sexe faible*, among Bouilhet's papers. Carvalho, the director of the Théâtre du Vaudeville, at first seemed enthusiastic about producing it, provided that it were heavily rewritten. Flaubert hoped to help Bouilhet's mistress and son financially. Carvalho later had second thoughts, however, and refused to start rehearsals; Flaubert could find no other producer.

Disgusted with the new Third Republic (1870–1940), Flaubert wrote a political satire play, *Le Candidat*. Carvalho approved it, and rehearsals began in

December 1873. Flaubert managed to circumvent the government censors, and the play opened on March 11, 1874. But the characters were flat caricatures, and the play failed after four performances. Flaubert had to abandon his theatrical ambitions forever. In the late 1870s, he and four younger friends who had also failed in the theater formed a literary discussion group they called "Les Cinq": Emile Zola, Alphonse Daudet, Edmond de Goncourt, Georges Charpentier, and Flaubert. (LMP)

References:

Bouilhet, Louis. *Mademoiselle Aïssé*. Paris: Lévy, 1872.
Canu, Jean. *Flaubert auteur dramatique*. Paris: Ecrits de France, 1946.
Descharmes, René, and René Dumesnil. "Flaubert et le théâtre: *Le Candidat* et *Le Sexe faible*." In René Descharmes and René Dumesnil, *Autour de Flaubert*. 2 vols. Paris: Mercure de France, 1912. 1: 200–262.

Thebaid (*TSA*). The Thebaid is the area surrounding Thebes in Upper Egypt, about 400 miles south and east of Cairo. It provides the setting for *La Tentation de saint Antoine*, which (aside from the sites of the saint's hallucinations and memories) occurs entirely around the hermit's cave high on the cliffs overlooking the Nile. (AHP)

Third French Republic (1870–1940). Disgusted by the scramble for power that Flaubert saw under the new, ostensibly democratic regime of the Third Republic, he wrote a satirical political play, *Le Candidat*, which Carvalho, the director of the Théâtre du Vaudeville, prepared for production. It was briefly performed in 1874. At the time, and until 1875, the monarchists were still in the majority in the Chamber of Deputies, but they failed to align themselves behind a single candidate. The power of the discredited church increased for a time. The cathedral of the Sacré Cœur, constructed between 1875 and 1914, was intended as a monument of national expiation for the spiritual guilt of a godless nation supposedly punished by defeat in the Franco-Prussian War of 1870. As late as 1887, a return to dictatorship seemed possible when General Georges Boulanger, the minister of war, attempted a coup d'état. Flaubert's attitude was essentially "a plague on both your houses"—on all political factions. (LMP)

Reference:

Wright, Gordon. *France in Modern Times, from the Enlightenment to the Present*. New York: Norton, 1988 (1968).

Tolstoy, Leo, graf (1828–1910). Leo Tolstoy was a celebrated nineteenth-century Russian novelist, in his time second only to Fyodor Dostoevsky. His epic masterpiece of the Napoleonic Wars, *War and Peace*, appeared in 1865–69. Ivan Turgenev introduced Flaubert to this novel. In a letter to Turgenev on January 2, 1880, Flaubert exclaimed that *War and Peace* had some of Shakespeare's power. "It's first rate. What a painter and what a psychologist! The first two [Volumes] are sublime, but the third goes terribly to pieces. He repeats himself and he philosophizes! In fact the man, the author, the Russian are visible, whereas up until then one had seen only Nature and Humanity" (Beaumont 174). Tolstoy, true to the realist tradition, came to consider Balzac, Stendhal, and Flaubert as the greatest French novelists.

Anna Karenina (1874–77), a novel of adultery and suicide, has many parallels with *Madame Bovary*. A ballroom scene and waltz occur at a crucial moment in each, as does an opera scene. Tolstoy's Oblonsky, like Flaubert's Homais, is the ignorant, self-satisfied dramatic mover who receives an unmerited award at the conclusion. In each novel, the heroine is a woman in her twenties with a young child. She is married to a man whom she finds dull, and who has certain distasteful traits. She finds a passionate lover; the motifs of a horse and of mist are associated with her affair. After a time, the relationship degenerates into sensuality. She fears losing her lover and becomes more demanding, thus driving him away. Feeling that she has nothing left, she impulsively commits suicide. Coincidentally, Tolstoy first arrived in Paris just two weeks after Flaubert and his publisher Maxime Du Camp were acquitted of offending public morals with *Madame Bovary* (February 21, 1857). Turgenev was a mutual friend to Tolstoy and Flaubert. In the 1870s, Tolstoy had the Russian translation of *Madame Bovary* bound together with Shakespeare's *Othello*, suggesting a preoccupation with the motif of adultery and with Flaubert as a guide for treating the motif.

However, Tolstoy does not mention Flaubert in his diaries, and since before 1891 there is no evidence that Tolstoy read the French author with appreciation, the resemblances between their two novels may well be adventitious. Romain Rolland, André Maurois, and Jean Jaurès, among others, reject the possibility of influence, arguing that Flaubert is concerned with form, and Tolstoy with moral problems. Comparing *Anna Karenina* and *Madame Bovary*, Matthew Arnold finds Flaubert lacking in magnanimity and spirituality compared to Tolstoy: bitter and cruel, Flaubert pursues Emma "with malignity." In an interview in 1904, Tolstoy himself finally expressed generous admiration for Flaubert: "One of my most favorite writers is your incomparable Flaubert. There is a truly magnificent artist, strong, precise, harmonious, full-blooded, perfect. His style is filled with the purest beauty. Can one say this of many writers?" (Bourdon) (LMP)

References:

Arnold, Matthew. "Count Leo Tolstoy." In Matthew Arnold, *Essays in Criticism: Second Series*. New York: Macmillan, 1888: 253–99.

Beaumont, Barbara, ed. *Flaubert and Turgenev: A Friendship in Letters*. New York: Norton, 1989.

Bourdon, Georges Henri. "En écoutant Tolstoy." *Le Figaro* March 15, 1904.

Meyer, Priscilla. "*Anna Karenina*: Tolstoy's Polemic with *Madame Bovary*." *Russian Review* 54.2 (1995): 243–59.

Straus, Nina Pelikan. "Emma, Anna, Tess: Skepticism, Betrayal, and Displacement." *Philosophy and Literature* 18.1 (1994): 72–90.

Tanner, Tony. *Adultery and the Novel: Contract and Transgression*. Baltimore: Johns Hopkins University Press, 1979.

Troyat, Henry. *Tolstoy*. Garden City, NY: Doubleday, 1967.

Tostes (*MB*). Tostes is the town in Normandy where Charles Bovary's mother sends him to practice medicine and to marry an unattractive but supposedly wealthy widow. There he meets Emma Rouault on a nearby farm when he goes there to set her father's broken leg. When Charles, a widower, has remarried to Emma, and she tires of the small town, the young couple moves to Yonville, although Charles has just been getting established in his practice. (LMP)

Tourbey, Jeanne de (or **Detourbey**) (1837–1908). Marie-Anne Detourbey, the illegitimate daughter of an illegitimate waitress, changed her name to Jeanne de Tourbey in 1853 when she moved to Paris. There she was introduced to prominent literary figures such as Charles-Augustin Sainte-Beuve, who educated her. She became a patron of the arts and in 1858 started one of the most distinguished literary salons of nineteenth-century France. Flaubert met her in the second half of 1857 and sent her a copy of *Madame Bovary*. It is unlikely that they became lovers, but their friendship remained steady, especially during Flaubert's mid-forties. (MMC)

Reference:

Bart, Benjamin F. *Flaubert*. Syracuse: Syracuse University Press, 1967.

Tournier, Michel (1924–). When the subject is reputation, literary or otherwise, Michel Tournier has never been a humble man. As a youth enamored of philosophy, he proclaimed his intention to become the Hegel of his generation, and only after failing an important university examination in philosophy (the *agrégation*) did he redirect his ambitions toward literature. In time, he won the Prix Goncourt, France's highest literary award, for *Le Roi des aulnes* (*The Ogre*). Given Tournier's self-confidence, his interest in the novel, and his knowledge of literary history, it is not surprising that he would have an intense, albeit ambiguous, relationship with Flaubert.

Tournier's collection of essays *Le Vol du vampire* (1981) contains two essays devoted to Flaubert, "Une mystique étouffée: *Madame Bovary*" and "Nécessité et liberté dans les *Trois Contes* de Flaubert." Both are laudatory, and in the former, he suggests that *Madame Bovary* is perhaps the most celebrated novel in French literature. But scholars have been quick to show that Flaubert is more than an object of admiration for Tournier. He copies elements of Flaubert's style in various texts; he uses Flaubert's penchant for alluding to multiple myths throughout his œuve; and in an interview, Tournier admitted that his *Le Roi des aulnes* (1970) is so heavily inspired by his predecessor that it is practically an anthology of the older novelist's works. Yet if the influence is omnipresent, it is not without a whiff of anxiety, and nowhere is this more evident than in *Gaspard, Melchior, et Balthazar* (1980), Tournier's idiosyncratic version of *Salammbô.*

The two novels have obvious similarities. Both have exotic settings that seem atypical of the works on which the fame of their authors rests. Eating and drinking are obsessive topics in each, as is the constant movement occasionally offset by periods of encirclement or imprisonment. Homoeroticism is a leitmotif in *Salammbô*, while homosexuality is the explicit sexual orientation of a whole society in *Gaspard, Melchior, et Balthazar.* Tournier has, however, weighed these parallels strongly in his favor. While Flaubert's Carthage is fated to fade from history, Tournier's Holy Land will give birth to Christ; Mâtho's consumption of food and wine is a sign of weakness, but Taor's hunger and thirst lead him to a place at the Last Supper. If Mâtho is cannibalized by angry Carthaginians, Taor consumes the body and blood of Christ. Mâtho's voyage is circular, Taor's leads to a place in heaven. The pagan soldiers' love of men is replaced in *Gaspard* by the adoration of the Son of Man.

One could explain Tournier's treatment of Flaubert's work as an example of parody that bespeaks homage. However, there is another possibility. To turn for a moment to one of Flaubert's beloved stained-glass windows in the Rouen cathedral, it is tempting to consider that the younger novelist imagines his distinguished predecessor as an Old Testament prophet in one such window, with a smiling Michel Tournier perched on his shoulders, triumphantly proclaiming the superiority of his own new text. (WC)

References:

Cloonan, William J. *Michel Tournier.* Boston: Twayne, 1985.
Tournier, Michel. *Le Vol du vampire: Notes de lecture.* Paris: Mercure de France, 1981.

travels. In 1840, at age eighteen, Flaubert spent ten weeks traveling with a group of family friends in the Pyrenees and Corsica. In Marseilles, he had an affair with Eulalie Foucaud, who was fifteen years older, and whom he never could find again when he returned (this episode may have contributed to the love affair in Flaubert's *Novembre*). He kept a travel journal, and his careful observations and descriptions in it helped prepare him to be a realist novelist. They distracted him from the self-absorbed, self-pitying stance of his earlier works. His encounter with Roman monuments in the south of France brought history alive for him. He came to realize that the strength of style lay in form; he found himself increasingly drawn to the disciplined art of French classicism. He took another trip to Italy and back through Switzerland with his family in 1845. His notes on Italian paintings reveal his awakening visual sensibility.

In the spring of 1847, he took a three-month hiking trip through the Touraine and in Brittany with his then best friend Maxime Du Camp. Flaubert was fascinated by the aging romantic writer and statesman Chateaubriand and visited his still-unoccupied memorial. On their return, Flaubert and Du Camp wrote alternate chapters of *Par les champs et par les grèves*, which was to be first published only in 1886. There Flaubert developed his art of landscape description—valuable training for the historical and realistic novel (Bart 56–61).

During twenty months from late October 1849 until 1851, Flaubert and Du Camp took a monumental journey down the Rhone to Marseilles, then to Egypt, where they stayed for months in Cairo. They took a long private boat trip up the Nile to the Second Cataract and en route traveled overland to the Red Sea. They continued from Beirut to Jerusalem, Damascus, Baalbek, and Constantinople; they spent weeks in Athens and months in Italy, staying longest in Naples, Rome, and Venice. Robbers with firearms attacked them in Syria; Flaubert had a vision of Christ as they entered Jerusalem. Soon, however, that city's commercialism sharply disappointed him, Flaubert was thrilled by the Greek, Roman, and Etruscan antiquities in the museum of Naples, but Rome disappointed him until he became aware of its Renaissance and baroque art treasures. His mother met him there. After four and a half days in Venice, the discomforts of venereal disease made him cut short their trip.

Du Camp brought a complete set of photographic equipment and achieved "the first comprehensive photographic survey of any region, the first important French book to be illustrated with photographs, the first published work containing photographic coverage of the Middle East" (Lottman 89). Flaubert again kept notebooks with descriptions of what he saw. In the spring of 1858, he took his last long trip through Algeria to Carthage and Tunis in order to add realism to the Carthaginian novel *Salammbô* by viewing the sites where the action of that story occurred. (LMP)

References:

Bart, Benjamin F. *Flaubert*. Syracuse: Syracuse University Press, 1967. 56–61, 184–239.

Bourin, André. "L'Aventure Egyptienne de Flaubert et Du Camp." *Revue des Deux Mondes* (May 1988): 199–203.

Du Camp, Maxime. *Egypte, Nubie, Palestine, et Syrie: Dessins photographiques recueillis pendant les années 1849, 1850, et 1851*. Paris: Gide, 1852.

Lottman, Herbert. *Flaubert: A Biography*. New York: Fromm, 1990. 84–91.

Starkie, Enid. *Flaubert: The Making of the Master*. New York: Atheneum, 1967. 167–82.

trial of *Madame Bovary* (1857). The unflattering depiction of the sacred institutions of marriage, motherhood, and the church in Flaubert's first published novel, and its chaste but enthusiastic descriptions of adulterous sex, promptly drew on him the ire of the governmental censors. Flaubert had some good friends in high places, but after initial skirmishing behind the scenes, they could not prevent the state from bringing him and his publisher Maxime Du Camp, editor-in-chief of the prestigious *Revue de Paris*, to court on a charge of offending against public morals. The family friend Jules Sénard, a prominent attorney, defended Flaubert masterfully and reduced the state prosecutor, Ernest Pinard (the same man who was charged with bringing Charles Baudelaire to trial in the same year for the alleged immorality *Les Fleurs du Mal*) to ridicule. He argued that Emma's horrible death was fitting punishment for her transgressions, and he cited many passages from the Bible, from canonical authors of antiquity and from classic French authors taught in schools to prove that Flaubert's descriptions of sexual love were more chaste than those of his unimpeachable precursors. Flaubert and Du Camp escaped with a reprimand. Years later, Flaubert had the delicious vindication of learning that Pinard had been caught writing and publishing obscene poetry. Several recent editions of *Madame Bovary* reproduce in full the transcript of the trial. (LMP)

See also Du Camp, Maxime; *Madame Bovary*; Pinard, Ernest; Sénard, Jules.

Reference:

LaCapra, Dominick. Madame Bovary *on Trial*. Ithaca: Cornell University Press, 1982.

Trois Contes (1877). After selling his Deauville farm to ameliorate the catastrophic financial situation of Ernest Commanville, the husband of his beloved niece Caroline, Flaubert set aside his novel in progress, *Bouvard et Pécuchet*, to focus on shorter works. "La Légende de saint Julien l'hospitalier" was begun in 1875 and completed in 1876. Flaubert wanted a companion tale in order to have a volume to publish in the fall, because "Un cœur simple" had also been written in 1875. When he had nearly finished this tale of a Norman servant, Flaubert conceived the idea for a third tale, "Hérodias" (1875–76). The collection of the three tales was published in April 1877, amid continuing financial struggles and poor health for Flaubert. Each story is set in a different period and geographical setting. "Un cœur simple" is a contemporary tale of the Norman countryside. The action of "La Légende de saint Julien l'hospitalier" unfolds in a medieval setting. "Hérodias" takes place in the Levant in biblical times. Together, the three classically spare, lapidary narratives form a succinct synthesis of Flaubert's literary universe. Whereas the first two tales span the lives of the principal characters, "Hérodias" relates events within a twenty-four-hour period, and the eponymous character is but one of three main characters. Although the tales differ widely in their temporal and spatial settings, each work deals in some way with the notion of saintliness, and each treats the themes of the power and the limitations of language.

Critics often compare the characters and settings of the tales to those of Flaubert's previous novelistic works: "Un cœur simple" echoes *Madame Bovary*; "Saint Julien" is related to *La Tentation de saint Antoine*, and "Hérodias" to *Salammbô*. Aimée Israel-Pelletier identifies a key difference: the main characters of *Trois Contes* are gloriously redeemed, whereas the characters of the earlier novels are undercut by a reality that exposes their aspirations as illusory. Félicité, Julien, and Iaokanann are all visionaries who disrupt the established order. Each in some way exposes the corruption of the society that oppresses them (Israel-

Pelletier 1). The protagonists' subversive desires are legitimized and valorized. Contrastingly, characters from the earlier novels who challenge the social order are punished or annihilated. The saintly figures of the three tales imaginatively resist the corrupt prevailing order with their fantasies and illusions. Instead of causing their downfall, as happens to Emma Bovary, imagination and illusion become powerful tools whereby the three visionaries transform the self and society (Israel-Pelletier 14).

Israel-Pelletier points out that in Flaubert's writing before *Trois Contes* "the victory of the bourgeoisie, or of the dominant class, over the individual is a common [subject]" (111). In each of the *Trois Contes*, however, an outsider triumphs over the class in power. Whereas the iconic bourgeois figure Homais is revered in Yonville society, his counterpart Bourais is discredited and must flee Pont-L'Evêque. In "Un cœur simple," Félicité undermines patriarchal values on the individual level by excluding men from her life and by creating a kind of personalized pantheism that exists outside the bounds of scriptural authority. In the second and third tales, the protagonist deliberately or accidentally attacks the parental couple that represents the word of law, which forms the basis for a corrupt civilization. Iaokanann's voice triumphs over Hérode, the king and father figure who reveals his impotence as a leader by failing to uphold the law forbidding incest and by failing to comprehend the meaning of events and prophecies. While Félicité and Julien are figures of covert subversion, Iaokanann vociferously expresses a similar message of subversion. The first two tales end with an image of expansion along a vertical axis. The ending of "Hérodias" differs because its final image of expansion is horizontal rather than ascensional.

One can speculate about why the ordering of the tales in the final edition differs from their original order. Israel-Pelletier offers one explanation, which also speaks to the unity of the tripartite work, for the sequence Flaubert elected. In *Trois Contes*, expansion and dilation are represented as enlightenment and dissemination (114). The first two narratives begin on the earth and end in the heavens. The third begins on an elevation (the citadel of Machaerous) and ends at ground level, with the head of Iaokanann, heavy with potential for spiritual dissemination, being carried horizontally to spread his message of hope. The conclusion to "Hérodias" thus seems to conclude the ensemble. In each tale, a new order successfully challenges the status quo. Ironically, Iaokanann's discourse, which upsets the ancient established order, is an early version of the oppressive discourse of religious authority subverted by Félicité in "Un cœur simple."

Although "Un cœur simple" is the only tale of the trilogy without a prophetic figure, the kinds of speech, linguistic problems, and misinterpretations seen in the others are conveyed in it through Loulou, the parrot (Erickson 68). The prophets in the second and third tales are characterized by the extreme volume and expansion of their voices and by an unusually intense gaze. When Loulou returns from the taxidermist's, Félicité is struck by the play of light reflected by his glass eye. Loulou's locutions reverberate like the prophets' voices in the other tales, as in the shrieks of laughter elicited from the bird by the presence of the respected bourgeois, Bourais. Loulou's unmasking of Madame Aubain's financial advisor as a man of dubious scruples reminds the reader of Iaokanann's strident, public denunciations of Hérodias (Erickson 69). The caged parrot repeating fragments of human speech ironically presages Iaokanann repeating prophecies in his prison in "Hérodias." The multiplicity of possible interpretations that the prophecies invite implies a profoundly modern critique of language.

Each tale reflects Flaubert's oscillation between the symbolically charged Orient (the land of the rising sun) and the Occident (the land of the setting sun). For Félicité as for Flaubert, Normandy is the motherland, the locus of childhood memories, and the reality against which all subsequent realities will be measured. Félicité dreams of an exotic New World associated in her mind with Victor. Bourais's atlas is useless to her, but Loulou becomes her imaginative conduit to that far-off land. Julien's parents arrive one evening from the West and are killed by their son the following morning. The symbolism of East and West, of here and elsewhere, of beginnings and endings, is also at play in "Hérodias." The Orient of Hérode Antipas coexists uneasily with the Occident of Vitellius. The decadent old order that Antipas represents resists the threat posed by the rise of Christianity with its message of hope and redemption. The West is seen as rational, utilitarian, bourgeois, and masculine, while the East is viewed as mystical, gratuitous, anarchical, and feminine.

Like Marcel Duchamp's *Boîte en valise, Trois Contes* reflects Flaubert's attempt to recover both his personal past, in "Un cœur simple," and his literary past, in miniaturized reworkings of earlier themes and characters. Flaubert was discouraged with the unfinished project that was to become *Bouvard et Pécuchet*, and wanted to see not only whether he could still write, but also whether writing could still mean something to him. Therefore, he chooses the most sublime of all subjects: sainthood in ancient, medieval, and modern times. Israel-Pelletier sees the writing of *Trois Contes* as an "attempt to recover a lost sense of wonder and optimism about the capacity of language to express being and to transform the self, to reflect the world and to transfigure that world" (124). Just as Iaokanann's prophecies clear the way for Christianity, *Trois Contes* ushers in a new conception of the field of novelistic representation. (JM)

References:

Bart, Benjamin F. *Flaubert*. Syracuse: Syracuse University Press, 1967. 670–706.

Erickson, Karen L. "Prophetic Utterance and Irony in *Trois Contes*." In Barbara T. Cooper and Mary Donaldson-Evans, eds. *Modernity and Revolution in Late Nineteenth-Century France*. Newark: University of Delaware Press, 1992. 65–73.

Israel-Pelletier, Aimée. *Flaubert's Straight and Suspect Saints: The Unity of* Trois Contes. Amsterdam: Benjamins, 1991.

Marotin, François. "Les *Trois Contes*: Un carrefour dans l'œuvre de Flaubert." In François Marotin, ed., *Frontières du Conte*. Paris: Centre National de la Recherche Scientifique, 1982. 111–18.

Trouville. Trouville is a town on the Normandy coast where Flaubert spent summer vacations with his family. Before it was transformed into a resort in the early 1840s, Flaubert loved this village, with its fresh salt air, deserted shoreline, and sunsets. His family resided in a one-story house on the beach. Gustave's famous encounter with Elisa Schlésinger, prompted by his rescue of her scarf from the tide, took place in 1836. The young Gustave fell in love with Elisa, then mother of an infant child and companion to Maurice Schlésinger, a music publisher. Flaubert befriended the couple and spent many hours in their company. Later trips to Trouville reminded him of the passion and distress he had experienced that summer (Letter to Louise Colet, August 21–22, 1853, *Corr.* 3:308). Elisa became the principal source for Mme Arnoux in *L'Education sentimentale* (1869). Flaubert's moonlit arrival on foot from Pont-L'Evêque (a distance of twelve kilometers) after his first year of law studies in 1843 remained a poignant memory as well (Letter to Louise Colet, August 9, 1853, *Corr.* 3: 286).

Between 1835 and 1837, Gustave also befriended the Collier sisters, Harriet and Gertrude, daughters of an Englishman who had lost his fortune and was living on the Continent to escape creditors. Gustave became deeply attached to Harriet, whose spinal condition confined her to bed and to whom he read. Both women later visited the Flauberts in Paris; however, it was Gertrude who remained in contact and visited Flaubert regularly until his death. (JWA)

Reference:

Spencer, Philip. "New Light on Flaubert's Youth." *French Studies* 8 (1954): 97–108.

Turgenev, Ivan Sergeyevich (1818–83). Ivan Sergeyevich Turgenev was the author of *A Sportsman's Notebook, Fathers and Sons*, and other works notable for their depiction of Russian popular culture and everyday life. Flaubert first met the Russian novelist in 1863 at one of the Restaurant Magny dinners for writers inaugurated by Charles-Augustin Sainte-Beuve. They quickly became friends; Flaubert relished the translations of Turgenev's work that the latter sent to him and appreciated Turgenev's warmth and informality. Turgenev enjoyed Flaubert's short stories, and he helped assure the appearance of a Russian translation of *La Tentation de saint Antoine* in 1874. He also began to attend the Sunday-afternoon salons Flaubert hosted in Paris, and he served as an unpaid but effective literary agent for Flaubert's beloved protégé, Guy de Maupassant. In 1879, Turgenev worked hard to secure for Flaubert the sinecure of the post of librarian at the Bibliothèque Mazarine, but the more deserving career librarian Frédéric Baudry was awarded that post instead. (LMP).

References:

Bart, Benjamin F. *Flaubert*. Syracuse: Syracuse University Press, 1967.

Beaumont, Barbara, ed. *Flaubert and Turgenev, a Friendship in Letters. The Complete Correspondence*. New York: Norton, 1985.

U-V-W

Unamuno, Miguel de (1864–1936). The Spanish author Miguel de Unamuno wrote a play, *La Esfinge* (1898), the title of which may have been borrowed from Flaubert's Sphinx in part 7 of *La Tentation de saint Antoine* (1874)—either directly, or through the mediation of Emilia Pardo Bazán. Unamuno, however, particularly admired Flaubert's *Bouvard et Pécuchet* and his correspondence, both of which he saw as prefiguring his own detestation of clichés and the commonplace. The epigraph to *La Novela de Don Sandalio, jugador de ajedrez* (The Novel of Don Sandalio, Chessplayer), and its explanation of the narrator's withdrawal from life, come explicitly from *Bouvard et Pécuchet*: "The truth is that I am prey to the same lamentable tendency as that which, according to Gustave Flaubert, marked the susceptible souls of his Bouvard and his Pécuchet, and that is the tendency to see stupidity everywhere and not be able to tolerate it" (181). In *Amor y pedagogía* (1902), Unamuno mocks the religion of science (Balzac, among others, had anticipated such mockery in his *La Peau de chagrin* of 1831). Bouvard and Pécuchet's disastrous failure in raising the orphans Victor and Victorine is echoed by Unamuno when Don Avito Carrascal vainly asks his good friend Don Fulgencio Entradosmares for clear advice on raising his son, who eventually commits suicide. Both Unamuno and Flaubert satirize the Urwerk on indulgent child rearing, Rousseau's *Emile*. The French writer Maurice Barrès *Les Déracinés* (1897) should also be considered in this antiscientistic lineage. Nancy Gray Díaz offers a more speculative parallel, pointing out that both Flaubert, in *L'Education sentimentale*, and Unamuno, in *Niebla*, repeatedly introduce fog, mist, and smoke into their landscapes to suggest the deluded protagonists' flawed, limited capacity for perception. Eugene F. Gray has made a similar observation: notations of inadequate lighting hint that Charles Bovary cannot really "see" Emma Rouault, the future wife who will ruin him. For Flaubert, however, flawed perception is an inevitable symptom of human mediocrity. For the tragic existentialist Unamuno, flawed perception does not wholly preclude choice; and for the more optimistic Sartre and Camus, a generation later, instances of brilliant lighting connote "gifts" of heightened awareness that invite the protagonists to accept their personal responsibility and to make choices. (LMP)

See also Bouvard et Pécuchet; Pardo Bazán, Emilia; *La Tentation de saint Antoine*.

References:

Clavería, Carlos. "Unamuno y la 'Enfermedad de Flaubert.' " In Carlos Clavería, *Temas de Unamuno*. Madrid: Gredos, 1953. 59–91.

Díaz, Nancy Gray. "Imagery and the Theme of Perception: *L'Education sentimentale* and *Niebla." Comparative Literature Studies* 17 (1980): 429–38.

Gray, Eugene F. "Emma by Twilight: Flawed Perception in *Madame Bovary." Nineteenth-Century French Studies* 6.3–4 (1978): 231–40.

Nozick, Martin. *Miguel de Unamuno*. New York: Twayne, 1971. 141–47.

Unamuno, Miguel de. *The Novel of Don Sandalio, Chessplayer*. In Miguel de Unamuno, *Ficciones: Four Stories and a Play*, trans. Anthony Kerrigan and Martin Nozick. Princeton: Princeton University Press, 1976. 181–226.

unpublished materials. *See inédits*.

Vargas Llosa, Mario (1936–). The Peruvian writer Mario Vargas Llosa judges all other novels against the standard set by Flaubert. The first chapter of *Madame Bovary* seems to have suggested the setting for Vargas Llosa's *La Ciudad y los perros* (The City and the Dogs). *Conversación en la catedral* alludes to the seduction scene between Léon Dupuis and Emma Bovary in the cathedral of Rouen and intertwines two discourses, each happening in a different time and place, recalling how the conversation between Rodolphe and Emma in the town hall is interwoven with the turgid speeches and trite award announcements at the agricultural fair outside, in an ironic counterpoint. *La Guerra del fin del mundo* (The War of the End of the World) recalls *Salammbô* as an epic reconstruction of history through documents. The comic *Pantaleón y las visitadoras* (1973) echoes the satire of bureaucracy in Flaubert's *Bouvard et Pécuchet*, but applied this time to the enterprise of providing sexual services for military troops (compare also the film *McCabe and Mrs. Miller* starring Warren Beatty and Julie Christie). (LMP)

References:

Kovacs, Katherine S. "The Bureaucratization of Knowledge and Sex in Flaubert and Vargas Llosa." *Comparative Literature Studies* 21.1 (1984): 30–51.

Vargas Llosa, Mario. *La Ciudad y los perros*. Barcelona: Seix Barral, 1966 (1962).

———. *Conversación en la catedral*. Rev. ed. Madrid: Alfaguara, 1999.

———. *Conversation in the Cathedral*. Trans. Gregory Rabassa. New York: Harper and Row, 1975.

———. *La Guerra del fin del mundo*. Barcelona: Seix Barral, 1981.

———. *Pantaleón y las visitadoras.* Barcelona: Seix Barral, 1973.

———. *The War of the End of the World.* Trans Helen R. Lane. New York: Farrar, Straus & Giroux, 1984.

la Vatnaz (*ES* 1869). La Vatnaz, a bluestocking who appears to support herself as a procuress—she lines up rich sugar daddies for Rosanette Bron, and mistresses for Jacques Arnoux (with vague suggestions of much similar activity on behalf of others)—is the unsuccessful rival of Rosanette for the actor and singer Delmar. To avenge herself for her defeat, she reveals Rosanette's affair with Delmar to Frédéric Moreau. Selfish and deceitful, she unexpectedly ends up for a time with the most idealistic, loving person in the novel, Dussardier, whom she nurses after he has been wounded during the July Days of the Revolution of 1848. Ironically, in that way she interferes with a homosocial relationship: Frédéric leaves his idyll with Rosanette in Fontainebleau to come care for Dussardier when he reads in the newspapers that his friend has been wounded, only to find that La Vatnaz has anticipated him. She wishes to marry Dussardier, but when he realizes that her apparently selfless concern was motivated by self-interest, he recoils. This motif of the wounded male, who must be symbolically castrated in order to become sufficiently vulnerable to be preyed on by the designing female, echoes Lawrence Sterne's *Tristram Shandy.* (LMP)

References:

Gothot-Mersch, Claudine. "Méandres de la création flaubertienne: La Vatnaz dans les manuscrits de *L'Education sentimentale.*" *Texte* 7 (1988): 81–101.

Orr, Mary. *Flaubert: Writing the Masculine.* Oxford: Oxford University Press, 2000. 107–9.

Paulson, William. *Sentimental Education: The Complexity of Disenchantment.* New York: Twayne, 1992.

Verga, Giovanni (1840–1922). Giovanni Verga was an Italian author whose novel *Il marito di Elena* (1882) depicts a vain, unrealistically romantic woman in the provinces, saddled with a plodding husband and plunging into a disastrous affair. The boring, isolated town is also satirized, like Yonville in *Madame Bovary.* Verga expresses sympathy for the husband, whose goodness is genuine. The novel is told from his point of view, rather than—as in Flaubert's novel—from the perspective of the adulterous wife. (LMP)

References:

Bergin, Thomas Goddard. *Giovanni Verga.* New Haven: Yale University Press, 1931. 66–71.

Di Benedetto, Arnaldo. "Flaubert in Verga." *Arcadia* 18.3 (1983): 258–69.

Ginsburg, Michal Peled. "Free Indirect Discourse: Theme and Narrative Voice in Flaubert, George Eliot, and Verga." Ph.D. diss., Yale University. *Dissertation Abstracts International* 39 (1978): 2236A.

Guzzetta, Lia Fava. "Verga fra Manzoni e Flaubert." *Lettere Italiane* 41.3 (1989): 334–55.
Pomilio, Mario. *Dal naturalismo al verismo*. Naples: Liguori, 1963.
Woolf, David. *An Aspect of Fiction: Its Logical Structure and Interpretation*. Ravenna: Longo, 1980.

Victor and **Victorine** (*BP*). The abandoned children of the convict Touache, Victor and Victorine are adopted and raised by Bouvard and Pécuchet in order to apply and test the theories of child rearing and education they have learned. The ludicrous and sad results form the major episode of chapter 10, the conclusion, underscoring the lesson of the first nine chapters—knowledge cannot be had—with a demonstration that knowledge cannot be transferred either. (LMP)

Voltaire (pseud. of François-Marie Arouet, 1694–1778). Among the many eighteenth-century authors of the Enlightenment, Voltaire was probably the one who most influenced Flaubert. In a letter to Mme Edma Roger des Genettes, he wrote of the old man of Ferney, "C'est pour moi un Saint" (1859–60? *Corr.* 4: 363). He particularly admired Voltaire's *Candide*; in a letter to Louise Colet (August 26, 1853), he said that *Candide* "sums up all Voltaire's works; it is the distillation of sixty written volumes and half a century of effort" (*Corr.* 3:332).

Toward the end of 1845, Flaubert undertook to write summaries of all Voltaire's plays and to take copious notes on the *Dictionnaire philosophique*. The notes reveal his deep interest in Voltaire during the first planning stages of the *Dictionnaire des idées reçues*, which was the projected second volume of *Bouvard et Pécuchet*. The prototype for *Bouvard et Pécuchet*, Flaubert's first published work, "Les Sept Fils du derviche" (1837), was modeled on Voltaire's oriental tales and on *Candide*. The first volume of Flaubert's never-finished final work could be viewed as a nineteenth-century *Candide*, whereas the collection of notes found in the second part is strongly inspired by the *Dictionnaire philosophique*. Voltaire's philosophic preoccupation with the relativity of truth, the limitation of human reason, and intellectual, political, or religious injustice reappears at the core of *Bouvard et Pécuchet*, and both that work and *Candide* adopt the archetypal pattern of withdrawal, enlightenment, and return. The common source for *Bouvard et Pécuchet* and for *Candide* was the dialogues of Lucian of Samosata (second century A.D.), the earliest known writer of comic satiric dialogue, interlarded with farcical narration.

But if Flaubert always saw eye-to-eye with the philosopher's condemnation of dogmatism, he revealed more than once his independent judgment regarding specific topics such as the great achievements of the ancients, whom Voltaire sometimes disparaged. Flaubert, unlike Voltaire, was skeptical about progress. Moreover, volume 2 of *Bouvard et Pécuchet* includes a number of comments directed against Voltaire, showing that if Flaubert admired the enlightened philosopher, he nevertheless refused to accept uncritically everything the latter wrote. Flaubert's admiration for *Candide* was so deep, however—especially for the scene of the visit to the jaded Pococurante, and for the conclusion recommending regular work as the only means to find contentment—that the tale inspired the narrative portion of his last novel. After carefully observing the political and social life of the period, both works reflect on the human condition. Both writers seek to demonstrate how established intellectual systems can lead to the destruction of men's common sense. Finally, as Voltaire does in *Candide*, Flaubert comes to realize that in this unstable world, work might be the key to happiness. The best lesson Flaubert drew from the Voltairean philosophy is that everyone needs to develop his own critical judgment. This is precisely what he did with respect to Voltaire's ideas. (CT/LMP)

References:

Bruneau, Jean. *Le* Conte oriental *de Gustave Flaubert.* Paris: Les Lettres Nouvelles, (1973).

———. *Les Débuts littéraires de Gustave Flaubert, 1831–1845.* Paris: Colin, 1962.

Flaubert, Gustave. *Correspondance*, 9 vols. In Gustave Flaubert, *Œuvres complètes*. 28 vols. Paris: Conard, 1910–54.

———. "Les Sept Fils du derviche." *Le Colibri*, 1837. Rpr. in Gustave Flaubert, *Œuvres complètes*, ed. Maurice Bardèche, 16 vols. Paris: Club de l'Honnête Homme, 1971–76. 11:305–9.

Zagona, Helen G. *Flaubert's* Roman philosophique *and the Voltairian Heritage*. Lanham, MD: University Press of America, 1985.

"Voyage en enfer" (1835). The short text "Voyage en enfer" was designed for number 2 of Flaubert's weekly schoolboy newspaper *Art et progrès* (of which he was the sole writer). It is a symbolic drama, several paragraphs of which reappear in his "Agonies." Satan takes the narrator on a tour of the world, pointing out its cruelties and injustice and revealing that this world is actually Hell (Lottman 21). Because Satan serves as the narrator's guide, the work is considered a precursor of *La Tentation de saint Antoine*. (AHP)

References:

Bruneau, Jean. *Les Débuts littéraires de Gustave Flaubert, 1831–1845*. Paris: Colin, 1962.

Flaubert, Gustave. "A Trip to Hell." In Gustave Flaubert, *Early Writings*, ed. and trans. Robert Griffin. Lincoln: University of Nebraska Press, 1991. 1–2.

———. *Trois Contes de jeunesse*. Ed. T. A. Unwin. Exeter: University of Exeter Press, 1981.

Lottman, Herbert. *Flaubert: A Biography*. New York: Fromm, 1990. 21.

Voyage en Orient. *Voyage en Orient* is the title given to Flaubert's account of his eighteen-month journey to the Middle East in 1849–51 with his friend Maxime Du Camp. Sent on a mission to gather statistics for the Ministry of Commerce and Agriculture, he undertook this trip for health reasons, as well as to escape the banality of bourgeois Europe for a more stimulating civilization.

During this tour through Egypt, Palestine, Syria, Lebanon, Turkey, Greece, and Italy, Flaubert regularly took notes ranging from a few words to lengthy passages recording his impressions and describing places, people, and mores that were exotic to him. He later rewrote his observations but never published them. Consequently, the narrative, a wealth of ethnographic description, remains fragmented. In contrast to his contemporaries, Flaubert valorizes the oriental (meaning the Middle Eastern) over the Western culture of his time; he even wore oriental clothing in his effort to experience the local culture. However, many notes deplore the marks of colonialism and tourism that pervade the region, as well as a feeling of déjà vu, since the Orient was well known and Flaubert had done extensive reading about it. The most famous episode of his travel account is his sexual encounter with an Egyptian dancer-prostitute named Ruchiouk-Hânem. (CBK)

References:

Flaubert, Gustave. *Voyage en Orient*. In Maurice Nadeau, ed., Flaubert. *Œuvres complètes*. 18 vols. Lausanne: Editions Rencontre, 1964. vol. 5.

Said, Edward. *Orientalism*. New York: Vintage Books, 1979

Warren, Robert Penn (1905–89). Robert Penn Warren was the first poet laureate of the United States, named in 1986. His poem "Flaubert in Egypt" was published in his collection *Or Else*. A series of impressionistic vignettes, it was closely inspired by the 1972 translation of Maxime Du Camp's travel journal, written when he accompanied Flaubert on their trip through the Middle East and up the Nile in 1849–51. Only two passages in Warren's poem lack verbal sources in Du Camp. These parallels are reproduced in Floyd C. Watkins's appendix.

Whereas Flaubert as cited by Du Camp remains dispassionate in the face of wretched poverty, disease, homosexuality, and sex slavery, Warren's version shows disapproval. But he also introduces his own poetic sensibility into the account. First, he projects his idiomatic search for selfhood onto Flaubert's just-begun journey. Then, among the many monuments visited by the French novelist, Warren focuses on the mysterious Sphinx as a most powerful transition from the details of the expedition to those of self-discovery through sexual adventures. Flaubert thus joins the pantheon of fascinating yet devious figures Warren so admires. (IC/LMP)

References:

Flaubert, Gustave. *Flaubert in Egypt: A Sensibility on Tour. A Narrative Drawn from Gustave Flaubert's Travel Notes and Letters*. Trans. and ed. Francis Steegmuller. Boston: Little, Brown, 1972.

Warren, Robert Penn. *The Collected Poems of Robert Penn Warren*. Ed. John Burt. Baton Rouge: Louisiana State University Press, 1998. 297–99.

Watkins, Floyd C. "Sex and Art on Tour: Warren's 'Flaubert in Egypt.' " *Papers on Language and Literature* 20.3 (1984): 326–38.

Y-Z

Yeats, William Butler (1865–1939). Irish poet and playwright William Butler Yeats's admiration for Flaubert led him to criticize the National Library of Ireland in 1903 for its refusal to carry his works. He praised Flaubert's unforgettable and richly detailed scenes (*Essays and Introductions*, 1961) and considered *La Tentation de saint Antoine* the last important work of the romantic period (*Uncollected Prose*, vol. 2, 1976). The latter work inspired in part Yeats's unfinished novel *The Speckled Bird*. Yeats may also have drawn on Flaubert for the Sphinx in "The Second Coming" (*Collected Poems*, 1956). (AA)

References:

Yeats, William Butler. *Collected Poems*. New York: Macmillan, 1956.
———. *Essays and Introductions*. New York: Macmillan, 1961.
———. *The Speckled Bird*. 2 vols. Dublin: Cuala, 1973–74.
———. *Uncollected Prose*. Ed. John P. Frayne. 2 vols. New York: Columbia University Press, 1970–.

Yonville (*MB*). Yonville is the town where Charles and Emma Bovary finally settle, and where most of the action of the novel occurs. Its inhabitants typify ludicrous mediocrity interwoven with callous greed and unscrupulous ambition, so dreary that Emma's narcissistic lust at times seems almost refreshing by comparison. Emilia Pardo Bazán's "Vilamorta" and Sinclair Lewis's *Main Street* would exploit the same motif: the satire of smalltown life. (LMP)

Yuk ("Smarh"). Yuk is a Rabelaisian embodiment of the grotesque who reduces even the narrator's guide, Satan, to insignificance. Robert Griffin (Flaubert 208n) sums up several variant but equally plausible interpretations: "Yuk is really the God of Language, which is both grotesque and creative, the true form of immortality in that nothing exists outside it" (Culler, 52); René Dumesnil proposes le Garçon as a model; René Descharmes suggests Edgar Quinet's "Mob" from *Ahasvérus* (1838) as a likely model. Yuk also strongly suggests Mephistopheles from Goethe's *Faust*, part 1. (Indeed, in the last paragraph, the harshly critical frame narrator tells the supposed author that "you saw yourself as a minor Goethe," but because you have no talent after all, you should stop writing [275].) When a beginning student comes to consult Faust for career guidance, Mephistopheles takes Faust's place and preaches the pleasure and profit found in various forms of corruption; he also serves as go-between to help Faust seduce the innocent Marguerite (also referred to as Gretchen). Flaubert's Yuk diverts into thoughts of her sexuality a woman who has come to consult Smarh about religion. In a later scene, although he is presented as Satan's servant, he calls himself "the God of the grotesque" and defines life as "a death shroud spattered with wine, an orgy where everyone gets drunk, sings, and then gets sick" (230), evoking Auerbach's Tavern in *Faust*, part 1. In a role similar to Goethe's "der Geist, der stets verneint" (the spirit of contradiction), Yuk leads Smarh on a tour of the city, mocking everything, and then induces him to wallow in the deadly sins of pride, lust, and greed (237–40). Satan baits a beggar into killing Yuk for his rich purse and becoming a fugitive from justice, only see Yuk to rise again, irrepressibly. From time to time, Yuk unexpectedly intervenes like a malicious Greek chorus to laugh raucously at the human spectacle, and defies Death himself as limited in comparison to Yuk's grotesque eternity. When the Angel of Truth comes to love and to rescue Smarh, Yuk suffocates her in a terrible embrace, and Smarh is doomed to eternal wandering. Yuk more than any other character created by Flaubert anticipates and exemplifies his author's sardonic outlook on Creation, religion, and society. (LMP)

References:

Culler, Jonathan. *Flaubert: The Uses of Uncertainty*, 1974. Rev. ed. Ithaca: Cornell University Press, 1985.

Descharmes, René. *Flaubert*. Paris: Ferroud, 1909. 116–21.

Flaubert, Gustave. *Early Writings*. Ed. and trans. Robert Griffin. Lincoln: University of Nebraska Press, 1991. 204–75.

Zola, Emile (1840–1902). Emile Zola made his first allusion to *Madame Bovary*, which he greatly admired, in 1864. Because of it, he considered Flaubert "the pioneer of our age, the portraitist and philosopher of the modern world" (Dubuc 136). He found in Flaubert a unique combination of impassioned lyricism and cold-eyed observation (Suwala 58). He and Flaubert met in 1869; Zola was at first overwhelmed by Flaubert's nonstop monologues and ranting, but the two became fast friends during the 1870s. They formed part of a group of cronies called "Les Cinq" united by their taste for realist-naturalist literature and social critique and by their failures as playwrights; the others were Georges Charpentier, Alphonse Daudet, and Edmond de Goncourt. In 1877, Flaubert wrote Maupassant thus concerning Zola: "That great man is neither a poet nor a writer, but those limitations don't prevent him from being a great man. Today I admire him much less than before, because I am becoming increasingly enamored of perfection, but perhaps I'm the one to blame" (Dubuc 130). They met regularly at Flaubert's Paris salon and in restaurants. Flaubert actively aided Zola in his unsuccessful quest to receive the medal of the Legion of Honor for distinguished service to his country. During the last years of Flaubert's life, Zola devotedly tried to secure him a government pension, because Flaubert had impoverished himself to pay his nephew-in-law's debts.

Gilbert Chaitin explains how Flaubert's narrative practice, innovative in its subtle and extensive use of free indirect discourse (a mode of reporting thoughts, words, and impressions that hover between the characters' and the narrator's consciousness), prepared the way for Zola's more nearly cinematic writing. Flaubert's practice of free indirect discourse marked a transition from the intrusive romantic narrator to the narrator who listens. The next step was dialogue resulting from "the progressive effacement of narrative voice" (Chaitin 1024) and the increasing importance of "scène" rather than "récit" in the novel, an emphasis characteristic of Zola and a harbinger of the naturalistic novels of the United States in the early twentieth century. (LMP)

References:

Chaitin, Gilbert D. "Listening Power: Flaubert, Zola, and the Politics of *style indirect libre." French Review* 72.6 (1999): 1023–37.

Dubuc, André. "Une amitié littéraire: Gustave Flaubert et Emile Zola." *Cahiers naturalistes* 10 (1964): 129–36.

Imbert, Patrick. "Sémiostyle: La Description chez Balzac, Flaubert, et Zola." *Littérature* 38 (1980): 106–28.

Shillony, Helena. "L'Art dans *L'Education sentimentale* et *L'Œuvre*: (Re)production et originalité." *Australian Journal of French Studies* 19.1 (1982): 41–50.

Suwala, Halina. "Zola et Maupassant, lecteurs de Flaubert." *Cahiers Naturalistes* 37 (1991): 57–77.

SELECTED BIBLIOGRAPHY

This chapter includes the works recommended in an international survey of college and university teachers of Flaubert, with some additions.

BACKGROUND MATERIALS: AUDIOVISUAL

Bruneau, Jean, and Jean-A. Ducourneau. *Album Flaubert* (iconography). Paris: Gallimard, 1972.

Chabrol, Claude, dir. *Madame Bovary*. With Isabelle Huppert, Jean-François Balmer, Christophe Malavoy, Jean Yanne, and Lucas Belvaux. MK2 Productions, 1991.

Clark, Kenneth. "The Fallacies of Hope." In Kenneth Clark, *Civilisation*, part 12 (on romanticism). BBC, 1970. Distr. Time-Life Films, 1000 Eisenhower Drive, Paramus, NJ 07652.

Flaubert, Gustave. *Madame Bovary*. Collection "L'Autre Plume." Paris: Ubi Soft, 1997. Text, background, sound, and graphics on CD-ROM.

———. *L'Œuvre romanesque, texte intégral*. Collection "Catalogue des Lettres." Paris: Egide, 1997. CD-ROM, designed for advanced search functions.

Gustave Flaubert (1821–1880). www://scopus.ch/users/torrent_j/Flaubert.html/.

Internet Movie Database. http://us.imdb.com/.

Minelli, Vincente, dir. *Madame Bovary*. With James Mason, Louis Jourdan, Jennifer Jones, Van Heflin, and Christopher Kent. MGM, 1949.

Le Pavillon Flaubert. www.napoleon.fr/scripts/napoleon-bin/gide-detail.idc?num=106.

Renoir, Jean, dir. *Madame Bovary*. With Pierre Renoir, Robert LeVigan, Max Dearly, and Valentine Tessier. Editions Gallimard, 1934.

Sherrard, Jean, dir. *Madame Bovary*. Adapt. Jean Sherrard and John Siscoe. Based on the Francis Steegmuller trans. National Public Radio Playhouse. Globe Radio Repertory Theatre, Seattle, 1986.

Unwin, Timothy. "A Report on Flaubert and the New Technologies." In Tony Williams and Mary Orr, eds., *New Approaches in Flaubert Studies*. Lewiston, NY: Mellen, 1999. 235–43.

BACKGROUND MATERIALS: PRINT MEDIA

Becker, George Joseph. "Modern Realism as a Literary Movement." In George Joseph Becker, ed., *Documents of Modern Literary Realism*. Princeton: Princeton University Press, 1963. 3–38.

Briggs, Asa, ed. *The Nineteenth Century: The Contradictions of Progress*. New York: McGraw-Hill, 1970.

Genette, Gérard. *Narrative Discourse: An Essay in Method*. Ithaca: Cornell University Press, 1980. Original French version in Gérard Génette, *Figures III*. Paris: Seuil, 1972. 65–282.

———. *Narrative Discourse Revisited*. Ithaca: Cornell University Press, 1988.

Grana, Cesar. *Bohemian versus Bourgeois: French Society and the French Man of Letters in the Nineteenth Century*. New York: Basic Books, 1964.

Hemmings, F.W.J. *The Age of Realism*. Baltimore: Penguin, 1974.

———. *Culture and Society in France, 1789–1848*. Leicester: Leicester University Press, 1987.

———. *Culture and Society in France, 1848–1898: Dissidents and Philistines*. London: Batsford, 1971.

LaCapra, Dominick. Madame Bovary *on Trial*. Ithaca: Cornell University Press, 1982.

Martin, Wallace. *Recent Theories of Narrative*. Ithaca: Cornell University Press, 1986.

Pichois, Claude. *Le romantisme*. Vol. 2, *1843–1869*. Paris: Arthaud, 1979.

Prince, Gerald. *A Dictionary of Narratology*. Lincoln: University of Nebraska Press, 1987.

———. *Narratology: The Form and Functioning of Narrative*. New York: Mouton, 1982.

Raimond, Michel. *Le Roman depuis la révolution*. Paris: Colin, 1981.

Rothfield, Lawrence. "From Semiotic to Discursive Intertextuality: The Case of *Madame Bovary*." *Novel* 19 (1985): 57–81.

Seymour-Smith, Martin. *A Reader's Guide to Fifty European Novels*. London: Heinemann, 1980.

Weber, Eugen. *Peasants into Frenchmen*. Stanford: Stanford University Press, 1976.

Weinberg, Bernard. *French Realism: The Critical Reaction, 1830–1870*. London: Oxford University Press, 1937.

Wright, Gordon. *France in Modern Times: From the Enlightenment to the Present*. 4th ed. New York: Norton, 1987.

Zeldin, Theodore. *France, 1848–1945*. 2 vols. Oxford: Clarendon Press, Oxford University Press, 1973–77. Vol. 2 rev. Oxford: Oxford University Press, 1980.

BIBLIOGRAPHIES

Colwell, David J. *Bibliographie des études sur G. Flaubert*. 4 vols. Egham, Surrey: Runnymede, 1988–90.

Gray, Eugene F., and Laurence M. Porter. "Gustave Flaubert." In David Baguley, ed., *The Nineteenth Century*. Vol. 5 of *A Critical Bibliography of French Literature*. Syracuse: Syracuse University Press, 1994. 801–66.

Klapp, Otto. *Bibliographie der französischen Literaturwissenschaft* (annual). Frankfurt: Klostermann, 1960–.

MLA Annual Bibliography (in print, CD-ROM, and URL formats).

Porter, Laurence M., ed. *Critical Essays on Gustave Flaubert*. Boston: Hall, 1986.
The Year's Work in Modern Language Studies (annual).

BIOGRAPHIES

Barnes, Hazel. *Sartre and Flaubert*. Chicago: University of Chicago Press, 1981.
Bart, Benjamin F. *Flaubert*. Syracuse: Syracuse University Press, 1967.
Brombert, Victor. *Flaubert par lui-même*. Paris: Seuil, 1971.
Du Camp, Maxime. *Souvenirs littéraires*. 2 vols. Paris: Hachette, 1906. Vol. 1, chs. 7, 9–14; vol. 2, chs. 21, 25, 28–30.
Lottman, Herbert R. *Flaubert: A Biography*. New York: Fromm, 1990.
Sartre, Jean-Paul. *L'Idiot de la famille*. 3 vols. Paris: Gallimard, 1971–72. Rev. ed. 1988. Trans. as *The Family Idiot*. Trans. Carol Cosman. 5 vols. Chicago: University of Chicago Press, 1981–93.
Starkie, Enid. *Flaubert: The Making of the Master*. New York: Atheneum, 1967.
———. *Flaubert, the Master*. New York: Atheneum, 1971.
Steegmuller, Francis. *Flaubert and* Madame Bovary: *A Double Portrait*. 1939. Rev. ed. New York: Farrar, Straus and Giroux, 1968.

CORRESPONDENCE

Bollème, Geneviève, ed. *Extraits de la correspondance; ou, Préface à la vie d'écrivain*. Paris: Seuil, 1963.
Bruneau, Jean, ed. *Gustave Flaubert. Correspondance*. 5 vols. Paris, Gallimard, 1973–98.
Carlut, Charles. *La correspondance de Flaubert: Etude et répertoire critique*. Columbus: Ohio State University Press, 1968.
Flaubert, Gustave. *Correspondance*. Enl. ed. 9 vols. Paris: Conard, 1926–33; *Correspondance: Supplément*. 4 vols. Paris: Conard, 1954.
Steegmuller, Francis, ed. and trans. *The Letters of Gustave Flaubert*. 2 vols. Cambridge, MA: Harvard University Press, 1980–82.

CRITICAL STUDIES: GENERAL INTRODUCTIONS AND COLLECTIONS OF ESSAYS

Brombert, Victor. *The Novels of Flaubert: A Study of Themes and Techniques*. Princeton: Princeton University Press, 1966.
Debray-Genette, Raymonde, ed. *Flaubert*. Paris: Didot, 1970.
Flaubert, Gustave. *Madame Bovary: Backgrounds and Sources: Essays in Criticism*. Ed. Paul de Man. New York: Norton, 1965.
Gans, Eric. Madame Bovary: *The End of Romance*. Boston: Twayne, 1989.
Ginsburg, Michal Peled. *Flaubert Writing: A Study in Narrative Strategies*. Stanford: Stanford University Press, 1986.
Girard, René. *Deceit, Desire, and the Novel: Self and Other in Literary Structure*. Trans. Yvonne Freccero. Baltimore: Johns Hopkins University Press, 1965. Trans. of *Mensonge romantique et vérité romanesque*. Paris: Grasset, 1961.
Hinton, Laura. *The Perverse Gaze of Sympathy: Sadomasochistic Sentiments from* Clarissa *to* Rescue 911. Albany: State University of New York Press, 1999.

Lloyd, Rosemary. *Madame Bovary*. London: Unwin Hyman, 1990.

Nadeau, Maurice. *Gustave Flaubert écrivain*. Paris: Lettres Nouvelles, 1969. Trans. Barbara Bray, as *The Greatness of Flaubert*. New York: Library Press, 1972.

Porter, Laurence M., ed. *Critical Essays on Gustave Flaubert*. Boston: Hall, 1986.

Porter, Laurence M., and Eugene F. Gray, eds. *Approaches to Teaching Flaubert's* Madame Bovary. New York: Modern Language Association, 1995.

Sainte-Beuve, Charles-Augustin. "*Madame Bovary* de Gustave Flaubert." In Charles-Augustin Sainte-Beuve, *Causeries du Lundi*. Vol. 13. Paris: Garnier, [1858]. 346–63. Trans. in Gustave Flaubert, *Madame Bovary*, ed. Paul de Man. New York: Norton, 1965. 325–36.

Schor, Naomi, and Henry F. Majewski, eds. *Flaubert and Postmodernism*. Lincoln: University of Nebraska Press, 1984.

Thibaudet, Albert. *Gustave Flaubert*. Paris: Plon-Nourrit, 1922; Gallimard, 1935, rev. ed., 1963. Saint-Armand (Cher): S.E.P.C., 1992. Extracts trans. in Gustave Flaubert, *Madame Bovary*, ed. Paul de Man. New York: Norton, 1965. 371–83.

Thorlby, Anthony. *Gustave Flaubert and the Art of Realism*. New Haven: Yale University Press, 1957.

Williams, Tony, and Mary Orr, eds. *New Approaches in Flaubert Studies*. Lewiston, NY: Mellen, 1999.

CRITICAL STUDIES, SPECIFIC TOPICS

Auerbach, Erich. *Mimesis: The Representation of Reality in Western Literature*. Trans. Willard R. Trask. Princeton: Princeton University Press, 1953.

Bart, Benjamin F. "Male Hysteria in *Salammbô*." *Nineteenth-Century French Studies* 12.3 (1984): 313–21.

Bart, Benjamin F., and Robert Francis Cook. *The Legendary Sources of Flaubert's* Saint Julien. Toronto: University of Toronto Press, 1977.

Barthes, Roland. "L'Artisanat du style." In Roland Barthes, *Le Degré zéro de l'écriture*. Paris: Seuil, 1953. Trans. Annette Lavers and Jonathan Cape, as *Writing Degree Zero*. London: Cape, 1967. 68–72.

———. "The Reality Effect." In Tzvetan Todorov, ed. *French Literary Theory Today: A Reader*. Cambridge: Cambridge University Press; Paris: Editions de la Maison des Sciences de l'Homme, 1982. 11–17.

Baudelaire, Charles. "*Madame Bovary*." In Charles Baudelaire, *Œuvres complètes*. Paris: Seuil, 1968. 449–53.

Bem, Jeanne. "*Désir et savoir dans l'œuvre de Flaubert: Etude de* La Tentation de saint Antoine." Neuchâtel: La Baconnière, 1979.

Bersani, Leo. "Flaubert and the Threats of Imagination." In Leo Bersani, *Balzac to Beckett: Center and Circumference in French Fiction*. New York: Oxford University Press, 1970. 140–91.

Bruneau, Jean. *Les Débuts littéraires de Gustave Flaubert, 1831–1845*. Paris: Colin, 1962.

Culler, Jonathan. *Flaubert: The Uses of Uncertainty*. 1974. Rev. ed. Ithaca: Cornell University Press, 1985.

Donato, Eugenio. *The Script of Decadence*. New York: Oxford University Press, 1993.

Dottin-Orsini, Mireille. *Cette femme qu'ils disent fatale*. Paris: Grasset, 1993.

Felman, Shoshana. *La folie et la chose littéraire*. Paris: Seuil, 1978. Trans. Martha Noel Evans and Shoshana Felman, as *Writing and Madness*. Ithaca: Cornell University Press, 1985.

Green, Anne. *Flaubert and the Historical Novel*: Salammbô *Reassessed*. Cambridge: Cambridge University Press, 1982.

Haig, Stirling. *Flaubert and the Gift of Speech: Dialogue and Discourse in Four Modern Novels*. Cambridge: Cambridge University Press, 1986.

Israel-Pelletier, Aimée. *Flaubert's Straight and Suspect Saints: The Unity of* Trois Contes. Amsterdam: Benjamins, 1991.

Issacharoff, Michael. "*Trois Contes* et le problème de la non-linéarité." *Littérature* 15 (1974): 27–40.

Kaplan, Louise J. *Female Perversions: The Temptations of Emma Bovary*. New York: Doubleday, 1991.

Kempf, Roger. "Flaubert: Le double pupitre." In Roger Kempf, *Mœurs: Éthnologie et fiction*. Paris: Seuil, 1976. 69–95.

Le Calvez, Eric. *Flaubert topographe*: L'Education sentimentale: *Essai de poétique génétique*. Amsterdam: Rodopi, 1997.

Lukács, Georg. *The Historical Novel*. Trans. Hannah Mitchell and Stanley Mitchell. London: Merlin, 1962.

Mrosovsky, Kitty, ed. "Introduction." In Gustave Flaubert, *The Temptation of Saint Anthony*. Ithaca: Cornell University Press, 1981. 3–56.

Mullen Hohl, Anne. *Exoticism in* Salammbô: *The Languages of Myth, Religion, and War*. Birmingham, AL: Summa, 1995.

Paulson, William. *Sentimental Education: The Complexity of Disenchantment*. New York: Twayne, 1992.

Porter, Laurence M. "Emma Bovary's Narcissism Revisited." In Graham Falconer and Mary Donaldson-Evans, eds. *Kaleidoscope: Essays on Nineteenth-Century French Literature in Honor of Thomas H. Goetz*. Toronto: Centre d'Etudes Romantiques, Joseph Sablé, 1996. 85–97.

———. *The Literary Dream in French Romanticism: A Psychoanalytic Interpretation*. Detroit: Wayne State University Press, 1979. 47–67.

———. "The Rhetoric of Deconstruction: Donato and Flaubert." *Nineteenth-Century French Studies* 20. 1–2 (1991–92): 128–36.

Poulet, Georges. "Flaubert." *Studies in Human Time*. Trans. Elliott Coleman. Baltimore: Johns Hopkins University Press, 1956. 248–62.

Richard, Jean-Pierre. "La Création de la forme chez Flaubert." In Jean-Pierre Richard, *Littérature et sensation*. Paris: Seuil, 1954. 119–219.

Seznec, Jean. *Nouvelles études sur* La Tentation de saint Antoine. London: Warburg Institute, University of London, 1949.

———. *Les Sources de l'épisode des dieux dans* La Tentation de saint Antoine *(Première version, 1849)*. Paris: Vrin, 1940.

Tanner, Tony. *Adultery in the Novel: Contract and Transgression*. Baltimore: Johns Hopkins University Press, 1979.

Trilling, Lionel. "Introduction." In Gustave Flaubert, *Bouvard and Pécuchet*, trans. T. W. Earp and G. W. Stonier. New York: New Directions, 1954. v–xxxvii.

Unwin, Timothy. *Art et infini: L'Œuvre de jeunesse de Gustave Flaubert*. Amsterdam: Rodopi, 1991.

Vargas Llosa, Mario. *L'Orgie perpétuelle* (*Flaubert et* Madame Bovary), trans. Albert

Bensoussan. Paris: Gallimard, 1978. Trans. as *The Perpetual Orgy: Flaubert and* Madame Bovary, trans. Helen Lane. New York: Farrar, 1986.

Williams, David Anthony. "Gustave Flaubert: *Sentimental Education* (1869)." In David Anthony Williams ed., *The Monster in the Mirror*. Oxford: Oxford University Press, 1978. 75–101.

EDITIONS: FRENCH

Flaubert, Gustave. *Bouvard et Pécuchet*. Ed. Alberto Cento. Naples: Istituto universitario orientale, 1964.

———. *Bouvard et Pécuchet*. Ed. Claudine Gothot-Mersch. Paris: Gallimard, 1979.

———. *Dictionnaire des idées reçues*. Ed. Lea Caminiti. Diplomatic edition of the Rouen mss. Paris: Nizet, 1966.

———. *L'Education sentimentale*. Ed. Alan Raitt. 2 vols. Paris: Imprimerie Nationale, 1979.

———. *L'Education sentimentale*. Ed. Peter M. Wetherill. Paris: Garnier, 1984.

———. *Madame Bovary*. Ed. Claudine Gothot-Mersch. Classiques Garnier. Paris: Garnier, 1971.

———. *Les Œuvres*. ed. Maurice Nadeau. 18 vols. Lausanne: Rencontre, 1964–65 (small format, contains all essentials).

———. *Œuvres complètes*. Ed. Maurice Bardèche. 16 vols. Paris: Club de l'Honnête Homme, 1971–76 (unusually complete, textually unreliable).

———. *Œuvres complètes*. Ed. Bernard Masson. 2 vols. Paris: Seuil, 1964 (convenient compact format).

———. *Le second volume de* Bouvard et Pécuchet. Ed. Alberto Cento and Lea Caminiti Pennarola. Naples: Liguori, 1981.

———. *Trois Contes*. Ed. Colin Duckworth. London: Harrap, 1959.

———. *Voyages*. Ed. René Dumesnil. 2 vols. Paris: Les Belles Lettres, 1948.

EDITIONS: ENGLISH TRANSLATIONS

Flaubert, Gustave. *Bouvard and Pécuchet*. Trans. T. W. Earp and G. W. Stonier. New York: New Directions, 1954.

———. *Bouvard and Pécuchet*. Trans. Allen J. Krailsheimer. New York: Viking, 1978.

———. *Candidate: A Humorous Political Drama in Four Acts*. New York: Fertig, 1978.

———. *The Dictionary of Accepted Ideas*. Trans. and ed. Jacques Barzun. Norfolk, CT: New Directions, 1954; New York: New Directions, 1968.

———. *Early Writings*. Trans. and ed. Robert Griffin. Lincoln: University of Nebraska Press, 1991.

———. *Flaubert in Egypt: A Sensibility on Tour: A Narrative Drawn from Gustave Flaubert's Travel Notes and Letters*. Trans. and ed. Francis Steegmuller. Baltimore: Penguin, 1996.

———. *Flaubert-Sand: The Correspondence of Gustave Flaubert and George Sand*. Ed. Alphonse Jacob, trans. Francis Steegmuller and Barbara Bray. London: Harvill. 1993.

———. *Madame Bovary*. trans. Eleanor Marx Aveling and Paul de Man, ed. Paul de Man. New York: Norton, 1965.

———. *Madame Bovary*. Trans. Lowell Bair. New York: Bantam, 1987.

———. *Madame Bovary: Life in a Country Town*. Trans. Gerald Manley Hopkins. Ed. Terence Cave. World's Classics. New York: Oxford University Press, 1998.

———. *Madame Bovary*. Trans. and introd. Francis Steegmuller. New York: Random House, 1981.

———. *November*, Trans. Frank Jellinek. New York: Carroll & Graf, 1987.

———. *Salammbô*. Trans. A. J. Krailsheimer. New York: Penguin, 1977.

———. *Selected Letters*. Trans. Geoffrey Wall. Baltimore: Penguin, 1997.

———. *Sentimental Education*. Trans. Robert Baldick. New York: Penguin, 1991.

———. *A Simple Heart*. Trans. Arthur McDowall. New York: New Directions, 1996.

———. *The Temptation of Saint Anthony*. New York: Penguin, 1983.

———. *Three Tales*. Trans. Allen J. Krailsheimer. New York: Oxford University Press, 1999.

———. *Traveling through Brittany*. Trans. Walter Dunne. Green Integer, 2000. Trans. of *Par les champs et par les grèves*.

STYLISTIC STUDIES

Bally, Charles. "Le style indirect libre en français moderne." *Germanisch-Romanische Monatsschrift* 4 (1912): 549–56, 597–606.

Bruneau, Charles. *L'Epoque réaliste*. Part 2, vol. 13 of *Histoire de la langue française: Des origines à 1900*. Ed. Ferdinand Brunot. Paris: Colin, 1972.

Brunetière, Ferdinand. "Le naturalisme française: Etude sur Gustave Flaubert." In Ferdinand Brunetière, *Le Roman naturaliste*. 1883. Paris: Calmann-Lévy, 1896. 149–203.

Carlut, Charles, Pierre Dubé, and J. Raymond Dugan, comps. *A Concordance to Flaubert's* Madame Bovary. 2 vols. New York: Garland, 1978.

Goldin, Jeanne, ed. *Les Comices agricoles de* Madame Bovary *de Flaubert*. 2 vols. Geneva: Droz, 1984.

Gothot-Mersch, Claudine. *La Genèse de* Madame Bovary. Paris: Corti, 1966.

Houston, John Porter. "Flaubert." In John Porter Houston, *The Traditions of French Prose Style: A Rhetorical Study*. Baton Rouge: Louisiana State University Press, 1981. 204–31.

Lanson, Gustave. *L'Art de la prose*. 1909. Paris: Nizet, 1968.

Lombard, Alf. *Les Constructions nominales dans le français moderne*. Uppsala: Almqvist, 1930.

Strauch, Gérard. "De quelques interprétations récentes du style indirect libre." *Recherches anglaises et américaines* 7 (1974): 40–73.

Ullmann, Stephen. "Reported Speech and Internal Monologue in Flaubert." In Stephen Ullmann, *Style in the French Novel*. 1957. New York: Barnes, 1964. 94–120.

INDEX

Page numbers in **bold type** refer to main entries in the encyclopedia. Abbreviations: F. = Flaubert; works by Flaubert are abbreviated and placed in parentheses as indicated in the Preface.

CONTRIBUTORS

Ehsan Ahmed, Michigan State University (EA)
Anita Alkhas, University of Wisconsin at Milwaukee (AA)
Julie Wegner Arnold, Alma College (JWA)
Yvonne Bargues-Rollins, North Carolina State University (YBR)
Geoffrey Barto, Michigan State University (GB)
Carole Borne, Clemson University (CB)
Carine Bourget-Krunz, Pima Community College, Tucson, Arizona (CBK)
Scott D. Carpenter, Carleton College (SDC)
William Cloonan, Florida State University (WC)
Isabelle Cassagne De Marte, University of North Texas (IC)
Mary Donaldson-Evans, University of Delaware (MDE)
Lucia Flórido, Michigan State University (LF)
Dina Foster, Georgia Perimeter College, Clarkston (DF)
Chantelle Gonthier, University of New Mexico (CG)
Eugene F. Gray, Michigan State University (EFG)
Deborah Harter, Rice University (DH)
Deborah Jenson, University of New Mexico (DJ)
Dorothy Jean Kelly, Boston University (DJK)
Larry Kuiper, University of Wisconsin at Milwaukee (LK)
Eric J. Le Calvez, Georgia State University (ELC)
Rosemary Lloyd, Indiana University (RL)
Mary McCullough, Baylor University (MMC)
E. Nicole Meyer, University of Wisconsin, Green Bay (ENM)
Jean Morris, Muskingum College (JM)

Shawn Morrison, College of Charleston (SM)

Anne Mullen Hohl, Seton Hall University (AMH)

Marshall C. Olds, University of Nebraska (MCO)

Adrianna Paliyenko, Colby College (AP)

Allan H. Pasco, University of Kansas (AHP)

Agnès Peysson-Zeiss, Penn Charter School, Philadelphia (APZ)

Luciano Campos Picanço, Davidson College (LCP)

Laurence M. Porter, Michigan State University (LMP)

Carol Rifelj, Middlebury College (CR)

Lawrence R. Schehr, University of Illinois (LRS)

Catherine Tamareille, Michigan State University (CT)

Sheila Teahan, Michigan State University (ST)

About the Editor

LAURENCE M. PORTER is Professor of French, Comparative Literature, and African Studies at Michigan State University. His previous books include *Critical Essays on Gustave Flaubert* (1986), *The Crisis of French Symbolism* (1990), and *Approaches to Teaching Flaubert's "Madame Bovary"* (1995). His articles have appeared in numerous journals, such as *Nineteenth-Century French Studies, Studies in Romanticism, Comparative Literature Studies*, and *French Review*.